# Scotland

## The Complete International
## Football Record

# Scotland

## The Complete International Football Record

*Richard Keir*

breedon **books**
PUBLISHING

First published in Great Britain in 2001 by
The Breedon Books Publishing Company Limited
Breedon House, 3 The Parker Centre, Derby, DE21 4SZ.

## About the Author

Richard Keir, 32, was educated at Uddingston Grammar School and is employed
as a travel consultant based in Glasgow.
He has been a follower of the Scottish national team for the last decade and
a keen football fan from an early age.
He enjoys travelling (especially to Africa) and is also a keen hillwalker.

ISBN 1 85983 232 6

Printed and bound by Butler & Tanner, Frome, Somerset, England.
Jacket printing by GreenShires, Leicester, England.

# Contents

# Foreword

I have been priveleged to be involved with the Scotland International Squad for the last 15 years and have experienced many moments of great joy and, equally, extreme sadness. This is the nature of the business.

However, it's only when a resource such as Richard Keir has produced is available that many forgotten memories come flooding back into focus. The superb statistical analysis, grouped under three headings, matches, players and general statistics serve to remind me of the great experiences I have encountered with Scotland. Every conceivable piece of information is available – a great credit to the meticulous, painstaking work of the author.

If vivid memories come flooding back from my years on the bench, there are many more as a member of the Tartan Army prior to my involvement with the team. It is to the author's credit that he can make every match played since 1872 a clearly defined entity of indisputable accuracy. The book makes essential reading for every fan, media representative, manager, official and player.

Let's hope there are more and more positive facts to record in the years ahead.

Craig Brown
National Coach & Director of Football Development
Scottish Football Association

# Introduction

This is the statistical history of the Scottish national team which covers every official match played from 30 November 1872 until 25 April 2001 – 614 matches in total.

The book is split into three chapters:

The first chapter contains information for each match (team line-ups, venue, attendance, goalscorers, etc.).

The second chapter contains information for each player (list of appearances and goals scored, date and place of birth, etc.).

The third chapter contains general statistical information all-time lists (appearances, goalscorers, captains, managers, etc.) and records (largest win/defeat, highest/lowest attendance, etc.).

I am indebted to all of the associations, clubs, newspapers and individuals (listed in the Acknowledgements) for providing the information that was missing from my records and also to Craig Brown for kindly agreeing to contribute the foreword.

Richard Keir
May 2001.

# Acknowledgements

## Associations

| | | |
|---|---|---|
| Argentina | Australia | Austria |
| Belgium | Brazil | Bulgaria |
| Canada | Chile | Cyprus |
| Czech Republic | Denmark | Finland |
| Germany | Hungary | Iceland |
| Ireland (Republic of) | Israel | Latvia |
| Lithuania | Luxembourg | Malta |
| Netherlands | Norway | Poland |
| Portugal | Romania | Russia |
| Spain | Sweden | Switzerland |
| Uruguay | Wales | |

## Clubs

| | | |
|---|---|---|
| Bohemians, Dublin | Brighton & Hove Albion | Glenavon, Lurgan |
| Glentoran, Belfast | Leicester City | Middlesbrough |
| Portsmouth | Southampton | |

## Newspapers

| | | |
|---|---|---|
| Argentina | — | *La Nación*, Buenos Aires |
| | | *La Prensa*, Buenos Aires |
| Austria | — | *Wiener Zeitung*, Vienna |
| Brazil | — | *Jornal do Brasil*, Rio de Janeiro |
| Chile | — | *El Mercurio*, Santiago |
| Ireland (Northern) | — | *The Telegraph*, Belfast |
| Luxembourg | — | *Luxemburger Wort*, Luxembourg-Ville |
| Netherlands | — | *Nieuwe Algemeen Handelsblad*, Amsterdam |
| Norway | — | *Idrettslev*, Oslo |
| Peru | — | *La Prensa*, Lima |
| Scotland | — | *Daily Record*, Glasgow |
| | | *The Herald*, Glasgow |
| | | *The Scotsman*, Edinburgh |
| Switzerland | — | *Neue Zürcher Zeitung*, Zurich |
| Yugoslavia | — | *Vjesnik*, Zagreb |

## Individuals

| | | |
|---|---|---|
| Mr John Duffy | — | c/o Northern Ireland FA |
| Mr Richard Carpenter | — | c/o Cardiff City |
| Mr Ray Simpson | — | c/o Burnley |
| Mr John McClelland | — | c/o Leeds United |
| Mr Dawson Simpson | — | c/o Distillery, Belfast |
| Mr Steve Carter | — | c/o *The Huddersfield Examiner* |

Photographs supplied by the SNS Agency of Glasgow and Empics.

# Abbreviations

P — Matches played  
W — Matches won  
D — Matches drawn  
L — Matches lost  
F — Goals for  
A — Goals against  

Att — Attendance  
(s) — Substitute  
pen — Penalty  
a.e.t. — After extra-time  
o.g. — Own-goal  

# Text Notes

## Chapter 1

**1**—583  
(World Cup — Qualifier)  
11 October 1997  

Referee: Pillar (Hungary)  
Celtic Park, Glasgow (Att: 47,613)  

| SCOTLAND 2-0 LATVIA | Half-time 1-0 |
|---|---|

**2**—(83) James LEIGHTON (Aberdeen) — Olegs KARAVAJEVS  
(22) Craig BURLEY (Celtic) — Valentins LOBANOVS  
(50) Thomas BOYD (Celtic) — Mihails ZEMLINSKIS  
(23) Colin CALDERWOOD (Tottenham Hotspur) — Igors STEPANOVS  
(28) Colin HENDRY (Blackburn Rovers) — Iurijs SEVLAKOVS  
(5) Christian DAILLY (Derby County) — Imants BLEIDELIS  
(55) Gary McALLISTER (Coventry City) captain — Valerijs IVANOVS  
(9) Paul LAMBERT (Borussia Dortmund) — Olegs BLAGONADEZDINS  
(45) John COLLINS (Monaco) — Aleksandrs JELISEJEVS  
(37) Gordon DURIE (Rangers) — Vladimirs BABICEVS  
(33) Kevin GALLACHER (Blackburn Rovers) — Marians PAHARS  

### Substitutions

(18) Thomas McKINLAY (Celtic)  
    for Boyd 81 mins —**3**  
(3) Simon DONNELLY (Celtic)  
    for Durie 84 mins  
(31) William McKINLAY (Blackburn Rovers)  
    for Burley 89 mins  

Andrejs STOLCERS  
    for Blagonadezdins 61 mins  
Vits RIMKUS  
    for Jelisejevs 68 mins  

### Goals

Gallacher (43 mins) —**4**    1-0  
Durie (80 mins)    2-0  

1. Match number
2. Appearance number
3. Substitution time
4. Goal time

## Chapter 2

**1**—900   Arthur Graham (11/2)—**2**   — (with Leeds United)  
     26 October 1952, Glasgow—**3**   1977 v East Germany (s)—**4**.  
         1978 v Austria (s), Norway  
         1979 v Wales, Northern Ireland (1),  
             England, Argentina (1),—**5**  
             Norway, Peru (s), Austria  
         1981 v Wales  

1. Player number
2. Appearances/goals
3. Birthdate/birthplace
4. Substitute appearance
5. Number of goals scored

# 1872

| P | W | D | L | F | A |
|---|---|---|---|---|---|
| 1 | 0 | 1 | 0 | 0 | 0 |

**1**
(Friendly)                                                    Referee: Keay (Scotland)
30 November 1872        West of Scotland Cricket Ground, Glasgow (Att: 3,000)

### SCOTLAND 0-0 ENGLAND

| (1) | Robert GARDNER (Queen's Park) captain | Robert BARKER |
|---|---|---|
| (1) | Joseph TAYLOR (Queen's Park) | Ernest GREENHALGH |
| (1) | William KER (Queen's Park) | Reginald WELCH |
| (1) | James THOMSON (Queen's Park) | Frederick CHAPPEL |
| (1) | James SMITH (Queen's Park) | William MAYNARD |
| (1) | William MacKINNON (Queen's Park) | John BROCKBANK |
| (1) | James WEIR (Queen's Park) | John CLEGG |
| (1) | Robert LECKIE (Queen's Park) | Arnold SMITH |
| (1) | David WOTHERSPOON (Queen's Park) | Cuthbert OTTAWAY |
| (1) | Robert SMITH (Queen's Park) | Charles CHENERY |
| (1) | Alexander RHIND (Queen's Park) | Charles MORICE |

# 1873

| P | W | D | L | F | A |
|---|---|---|---|---|---|
| 1 | 0 | 0 | 1 | 2 | 4 |

**2**
(Friendly)                                                    Referee: Lloyd (England)
8 March 1873                     Kennington Oval, London (Att: 3,000)

### ENGLAND 4-2 SCOTLAND                          Half-time 2-0

| (2) | Robert GARDNER (Queen's Park) captain | Alexander MORTEN |
|---|---|---|
| (2) | Joseph TAYLOR (Queen's Park) | Ernest GREENHALGH |
| (2) | William KER (Queen's Park) | Leonard HOWELL |
| (2) | James THOMSON (Queen's Park) | Alfred GOODWYN |
| (2) | Robert SMITH (Queen's Park) | Pelham VON DONOP |
| (2) | William MacKINNON (Queen's Park) | Alexander BONSOR |
| (1) | Henry RENNY-TAILYOUR (Royal Engineers) | William CLEGG |
| (1) | Arthur KINNAIRD (The Wanderers) | Robert VIDAL |
| (1) | John BLACKBURN (Royal Engineers) | George HERON |
| (1) | William GIBB (Clydesdale) | Charles CHENERY |
| (2) | David WOTHERSPOON (Queen's Park) | William KENYON-SLANEY |

|  |  | Goals |  |
|---|---|---|---|
|  |  | 0-1 | Kenyon-Slaney (1 mins) |
|  |  | 0-2 | Bonsor (10 mins) |
| Renny-Tailyour |  | 1-2 |  |
| Gibb (70 mins) |  | 2-2 |  |
|  |  | 2-3 | Kenyon-Slaney (75 mins) |
|  |  | 2-4 | Chenery (85 mins) |

# 1874

| P | W | D | L | F | A |
|---|---|---|---|---|---|
| 1 | 1 | 0 | 0 | 2 | 1 |

**3**
(Friendly)                                                    Referee: Rae (Scotland)
7 March 1874            West of Scotland Cricket Ground, Glasgow (Att: 7,000)

### SCOTLAND 2-1 ENGLAND                          Half-time 1-1

| (3) | Robert GARDNER (Clydesdale) | Reginald WELCH |
|---|---|---|
| (1) | John HUNTER (Third Lanark) | Robert OGILVIE |
| (3) | Joseph TAYLOR (Queen's Park) | Alfred STRATFORD |
| (1) | Charles CAMPBELL (Queen's Park) | Francis BIRLEY |
| (3) | James THOMSON (Queen's Park) captain | Cuthbert OTTAWAY |
| (2) | James WEIR (Queen's Park) | John OWEN |
| (1) | John FERGUSON (Vale of Leven) | Charles WOLLASTON |
| (1) | Henry McNEIL (Queen's Park) | George HERON |
| (3) | William MacKINNON (Queen's Park) | John EDWARDS |
| (1) | Angus McKINNON (Queen's Park) | Robert KINGSFORD |
| (1) | Frederick ANDERSON (Clydesdale) | Charles CHENERY |

|  |  | Goals |  |
|---|---|---|---|
|  |  | 0-1 | Kingsford (28 mins) |
| Anderson (42 mins) |  | 1-1 |  |
| McKinnon (47 mins) |  | 2-1 |  |

# 1875

| P | W | D | L | F | A |
|---|---|---|---|---|---|
| 1 | 0 | 1 | 0 | 2 | 2 |

**4**
(Friendly)                                                    Referee: Marindin (England)
6 March 1875                     Kennington Oval, London (Att: 2,000)

### ENGLAND 2-2 SCOTLAND                          Half-time 1-1

| (4) | Robert GARDNER (Clydesdale) | William CARR |
|---|---|---|
| (2) | John HUNTER (Eastern) | Edward HAYGARTH |
| (4) | Joseph TAYLOR (Queen's Park) captain | William RAWSON |
| (1) | Alexander KENNEDY (Eastern) | Francis BIRLEY |
| (1) | Alexander McLINTOCK (Vale of Leven) | Pelham VON DONOP |
| (3) | James WEIR (Queen's Park) | Charles WOLLASTON |
| (4) | William MacKINNON (Queen's Park) | Charles ALCOCK |
| (2) | Henry McNEIL (Queen's Park) | Herbert RAWSON |
| (1) | Thomas HIGHET (Queen's Park) | Alexander BONSOR |
| (1) | Peter ANDREWS (Eastern) | George HERON |
| (1) | John McPHERSON (Clydesdale) | Richard GEAVES |

|  |  | Goals |  |
|---|---|---|---|
|  |  | 0-1 | Wollaston (5 mins) |
| McNeil |  | 1-1 |  |
|  |  | 1-2 | Alcock (70 mins) |
| Andrews (75 mins) |  | 2-2 |  |

# 1876

| P | W | D | L | F | A |
|---|---|---|---|---|---|
| 2 | 2 | 0 | 0 | 7 | 0 |

**5**
(Friendly)                                                    Referee: Mitchell (Scotland)
4 March 1876            West of Scotland Cricket Ground, Glasgow (Att: 15,000)

### SCOTLAND 3-0 ENGLAND                          Half-time 3-0

| (1) | Alexander McGEOCH (Dumbreck) | Arthur SAVAGE |
|---|---|---|
| (5) | Joseph TAYLOR (Queen's Park) captain | Edgar FIELD |
| (3) | John HUNTER (Third Lanark) | Frederick GREEN |
| (2) | Alexander McLINTOCK (Vale of Leven) | Beaumont JARRETT |
| (2) | Alexander KENNEDY (Eastern) | Ernest BAMBRIDGE |
| (3) | Henry McNEIL (Queen's Park) | Walter BUCHANAN |
| (5) | William MacKINNON (Queen's Park) | George HERON |
| (2) | Thomas HIGHET (Queen's Park) | Charles SMITH |
| (1) | William MILLER (Third Lanark) | William MAYNARD |
| (2) | John FERGUSON (Vale of Leven) | Charles HERON |
| (1) | John BAIRD (Vale of Leven) | Arthur CURSHAM |

|  | Goals |  |
|---|---|---|
| MacKinnon (8 mins) | 1-0 |  |
| McNeil (12 mins) | 2-0 |  |
| Highet (16 mins) | 3-0 |  |

**6**
(Friendly)                                                    Referee: Gardner (Scotland)
25 March 1876          West of Scotland Cricket Ground, Glasgow (Att: 17,000)

### SCOTLAND 4-0 WALES                          Half-time 1-0

| (2) | Alexander McGEOCH (Dumbreck) | David THOMSON |
|---|---|---|
| (6) | Joseph TAYLOR (Queen's Park) | William EVANS |
| (1) | Robert NEILL (Queen's Park) | Samuel KENRICK |
| (3) | Alexander KENNEDY (Eastern) | Edwin CROSS |
| (2) | Charles CAMPBELL (Queen's Park) captain | William WILLIAMS |
| (3) | Thomas HIGHET (Queen's Park) | Daniel GREY |
| (3) | John FERGUSON (Vale of Leven) | William DAVIES |
| (1) | James LANG (Clydesdale) | George THOMSON |
| (6) | William MacKINNON (Queen's Park) | John EDWARDS |
| (1) | Moses McNEIL (Rangers) | John JONES |
| (4) | Henry McNEIL (Queen's Park) | Alfred DAVIES |

|  | Goals |  |
|---|---|---|
| Ferguson (40 mins) | 1-0 |  |
| Lang (48 mins) | 2-0 |  |
| MacKinnon (53 mins) | 3-0 |  |
| H.McNeil | 4-0 |  |

# 1877

| P | W | D | L | F | A |
|---|---|---|---|---|---|
| 2 | 2 | 0 | 0 | 5 | 1 |

(Friendly)  
March 1877  
**ENGLAND 1-3 SCOTLAND**  
Referee: Ogilvie (England)  
Kennington Oval, London (Att: 2,000)  
Half-time 0-1

| | | |
|---|---|---|
| ) | Alexander McGEOCH (Dumbreck) | Morton BETTS |
| ) | Robert NEILL (Queen's Park) | William LINDSAY |
| ) | Thomas VALLANCE (Rangers) | Lindsay BURY |
| ) | Charles CAMPBELL (Queen's Park) captain | Beaumont JARRETT |
| ) | James PHILLIPS (Queen's Park) | William RAWSON |
| ) | James RICHMOND (Clydesdale) | Charles WOLLASTON |
| ) | William MacKINNON (Queen's Park) | Alfred LYTTLETON |
| ) | John McGREGOR (Vale of Leven) | William MOSFORTH |
| ) | John McDOUGALL (Vale of Leven) | Arthur CURSHAM |
| ) | John SMITH (Mauchline) | John BAIN |
| ) | John FERGUSON (Vale of Leven) | Cecil WINGFIELD-STRATFORD |

| | Goals | |
|---|---|---|
| erguson | 1-0 | |
| chmond (48 mins) | 2-0 | |
| | 2-1 | Lyttleton (55 mins) |
| erguson (86 mins) | 3-1 | |

(Friendly)  
March 1877  
**WALES 0-2 SCOTLAND**  
Referee: Dick (Scotland)  
The Racecourse, Wrexham (Att: 4,000)  
Half-time 0-0

| | | |
|---|---|---|
| ) | Alexander McGEOCH (Dumbreck) | Thomas BURNETT |
| ) | Robert NEILL (Queen's Park) | William EVANS |
| ) | Thomas VALLANCE (Rangers) | Samuel KENRICK |
| ) | James PHILLIPS (Queen's Park) | John MORGAN |
| ) | Charles CAMPBELL (Queen's Park) captain | Edwin CROSS |
| ) | John SMITH (Mauchline) | William DAVIES |
| ) | John McGREGOR (Vale of Leven) | Alfred DAVIES |
| ) | John FERGUSON (Vale of Leven) | John PRICE |
| ) | John McDOUGALL (Vale of Leven) | Alexander JONES |
| ) | Henry McNEIL (Queen's Park) | John HUGHES |
| ) | John HUNTER (Third Lanark) | George THOMSON |

| | Goals | |
|---|---|---|
| ampbell | 1-0 | |
| vans o.g | 2-0 | |

# 1878

| P | W | D | L | F | A |
|---|---|---|---|---|---|
| 2 | 2 | 0 | 0 | 16 | 2 |

(Friendly)  
March 1878  
**SCOTLAND 7-2 ENGLAND**  
Referee: Dick (Scotland)  
First Hampden Park, Glasgow (Att: 10,000)  
Half-time 4-0

| | | |
|---|---|---|
| 5) | Robert GARDNER (Clydesdale) | Conrad WARNER |
| 1) | Andrew McINTYRE (Vale of Leven) | John HUNTER |
| 5) | Thomas VALLANCE (Rangers) | Edward LYTTLETON |
| 5) | Charles CAMPBELL (Queen's Park) captain | Beaumont JARRETT |
| 4) | Alexander KENNEDY (Third Lanark) | Norman BAILEY |
| 2) | James RICHMOND (Queen's Park) | Arthur CURSHAM |
| 3) | John McGREGOR (Vale of Leven) | Percy FAIRCLOUGH |
| 3) | John McDOUGALL (Vale of Leven) | John WYLIE |
| 4) | Thomas HIGHET (Queen's Park) | Henry WACE |
| 3) | William MacKINNON (Queen's Park) | George HERON |
| 5) | Henry McNEIL (Queen's Park) | William MOSFORTH |

| | Goals | |
|---|---|---|
| McDougall (7 mins) | 1-0 | |
| McGregor (32 mins) | 2-0 | |
| McNeil (39 mins) | 3-0 | |
| McDougall (41 mins) | 4-0 | |
| McDougall (46 mins) | 5-0 | |
| MacKinnon (62 mins) | 6-0 | |
| | 6-1 | Wylie (65 mins) |
| McNeil (70 mins) | 7-1 | |
| | 7-2 | Cursham (75 mins) |

10  
(Friendly)  
23 March 1878  
**SCOTLAND 9-0 WALES**  
Referee: Gardner (Scotland)  
First Hampden Park, Glasgow (Att: 6,000)  
Half-time 6-0

| | | |
|---|---|---|
| (1) | Robert PARLANE (Vale of Leven) | Edward PHENNAH |
| (1) | James DUNCAN (Alexandra Athletic) | George HIGHAM |
| (4) | Robert NEILL (Queen's Park) captain | John POWELL |
| (3) | James PHILLIPS (Queen's Park) | Henry EDWARDS |
| (1) | David DAVIDSON (Queen's Park) | William WILLIAMS |
| (6) | John FERGUSON (Vale of Leven) | George SAVIN |
| (2) | John BAIRD (Vale of Leven) | James DAVIES |
| (2) | James LANG (Third Lanark) | Daniel GREY |
| (4) | James WEIR (Queen's Park) | Thomas BRITTEN |
| (1) | James WATSON (Rangers) | John PRICE |
| (1) | Peter CAMPBELL (Rangers) | Charles EDWARDS |

| | Goals | |
|---|---|---|
| Campbell (4 mins) | 1-0 | |
| Weir (15 mins) | 2-0 | |
| Campbell (18 mins) | 3-0 | |
| Baird (37 mins) | 4-0 | |
| Ferguson (38 mins) | 5-0 | |
| Weir (42 mins) | 6-0 | |
| Ferguson (50 mins) | 7-0 | |
| Watson | 8-0 | |
| Lang | 9-0 | |

# 1879

| P | W | D | L | F | A |
|---|---|---|---|---|---|
| 2 | 1 | 0 | 1 | 7 | 5 |

11  
(Friendly)  
5 April 1879  
**ENGLAND 5-4 SCOTLAND**  
Referee: Wollaston (England)  
Kennington Oval, London (Att: 4,500)  
Half-time 1-4

| | | |
|---|---|---|
| (2) | Robert PARLANE (Vale of Leven) | Reginald BIRKETT |
| (1) | William SOMERS (Third Lanark) | Edward CHRISTIAN |
| (7) | Henry McNEIL (Queen's Park) | Harold MORSE |
| (4) | Thomas VALLANCE (Rangers) | James PRINSEP |
| (6) | Charles CAMPBELL (Queen's Park) captain | Norman BAILEY |
| (1) | John McPHERSON (Vale of Leven) | Arnold HILLS |
| (1) | William BEVERIDGE (Ayr Academy) | Arthur GOODYER |
| (3) | John SMITH (Mauchline) | Henry WACE |
| (4) | John McDOUGALL (Vale of Leven) | Francis SPARKS |
| (1) | Robert PATON (Vale of Leven) | William MOSFORTH |
| (9) | William MacKINNON (Queen's Park) | Edward BAMBRIDGE |

| | Goals | |
|---|---|---|
| | 0-1 | Mosforth (5 mins) |
| MacKinnon (15 mins) | 1-1 | |
| McDougall (23 mins) | 2-1 | |
| Smith (26 mins) | 3-1 | |
| MacKinnon (41 mins) | 4-1 | |
| | 4-2 | Bambridge (48 mins) |
| | 4-3 | Goodyer (60 mins) |
| | 4-4 | Bailey (75 mins) |
| | 4-5 | Bambridge (83 mins) |

12  
(Friendly)  
7 April 1879  
**WALES 0-3 SCOTLAND**  
Referee: Cooper (Wales)  
The Racecourse, Wrexham (Att: 2,000)  
Half-time 0-1

| | | |
|---|---|---|
| (3) | Robert PARLANE (Vale of Leven) | John DAVIES |
| (5) | Thomas VALLANCE (Rangers) | Samuel KENRICK |
| (2) | William SOMERS (Third Lanark) | John MORGAN |
| (2) | John McPHERSON (Vale of Leven) | Knyvett CROSSE |
| (2) | David DAVIDSON (Queen's Park) | William WILLIAMS |
| (8) | Henry McNEIL (Queen's Park) | James LLOYD |
| (5) | John McDOUGALL (Vale of Leven) captain | George WOOSNAM |
| (2) | Peter CAMPBELL (Rangers) | John HUGHES |
| (2) | Robert PATON (Vale of Leven) | John ROBERTS |
| (2) | William BEVERIDGE (Ayr Academy) | William ROBERTS |
| (4) | John SMITH (Mauchline) | John VAUGHAN |

| | Goals | |
|---|---|---|
| Campbell (34 mins) | 1-0 | |
| Smith | 2-0 | |
| Smith | 3-0 | |

# 1880

| | P | W | D | L | F | A |
|---|---|---|---|---|---|---|
| | 2 | 2 | 0 | 0 | 10 | 5 |

**13**
(Friendly) — Referee: Hamilton (Scotland)
13 March 1880 — First Hampden Park, Glasgow (Att: 12,000)

**SCOTLAND 5-4 ENGLAND** — **Half-time 3-2**

| (1) | Archibald ROWAN (Caledonian) | Harold SWEPSTONE |
|---|---|---|
| (3) | Alexander McLINTOCK (Vale of Leven) | Edwin LUNTLEY |
| (5) | Robert NEILL (Queen's Park) captain | Thomas BRINDLE |
| (7) | Charles CAMPBELL (Queen's Park) | Norman BAILEY |
| (3) | John McPHERSON (Vale of Leven) | John HUNTER |
| (5) | John SMITH (Edinburgh University) | Segar BASTARD |
| (2) | Moses McNEIL (Rangers) | Charles WOLLASTON |
| (1) | George KER (Queen's Park) | Samuel WIDDOWSON |
| (4) | John McGREGOR (Vale of Leven) | Francis SPARKS |
| (3) | John BAIRD (Vale of Leven) | William MOSFORTH |
| (1) | John KAY (Queen's Park) | Edward BAMBRIDGE |

| | Goals | |
|---|---|---|
| Ker (5 mins) | 1-0 | |
| | 1-1 | Mosforth (8 mins) |
| Baird (39 mins) | 2-1 | |
| | 2-2 | Bambridge (42 mins) |
| Ker (44 mins) | 3-2 | |
| Ker (48 mins) | 4-2 | |
| Kay (67 mins) | 5-2 | |
| | 5-3 | Bambridge (87 mins) |
| | 5-4 | Sparks (89 mins) |

**14**
(Friendly) — Referee: Stuart (Scotland)
27 March 1880 — First Hampden Park, Glasgow (Att: 2,000)

**SCOTLAND 5-1 WALES** — **Half-time 2-0**

| (1) | George GILLESPIE (Rangers) | Harold HIBBOTT |
|---|---|---|
| (3) | William SOMERS (Queen's Park) | John MORGAN |
| (1) | Archibald LANG (Dumbarton) | John POWELL |
| (3) | David DAVIDSON (Queen's Park) captain | Edward BOWEN |
| (1) | Hugh McINTYRE (Rangers) | Henry EDWARDS |
| (1) | James DOUGLAS (Renfrew) | William OWEN |
| (1) | J McADAM (Third Lanark) | William ROBERTS |
| (1) | Malcolm FRASER (Queen's Park) | John ROBERTS |
| (1) | Joseph LINDSAY (Dumbarton) | John PRICE |
| (1) | John CAMPBELL (South Western) | Thomas BRITTEN |
| (3) | William BEVERIDGE (Edinburgh University) | John VAUGHAN |

| | Goals | |
|---|---|---|
| Davidson (38 mins) | 1-0 | |
| Beveridge (40 mins) | 2-0 | |
| Lindsay | 3-0 | |
| McAdam | 4-0 | |
| Campbell | 5-0 | |
| | 5-1 | W.Roberts |

# 1881

| | P | W | D | L | F | A |
|---|---|---|---|---|---|---|
| | 2 | 2 | 0 | 0 | 11 | 2 |

**15**
(Friendly) — Referee: Marindin (England)
12 March 1881 — Kennington Oval, London (Att: 8,500)

**ENGLAND 1-6 SCOTLAND** — **Half-time 0-1**

| (2) | George GILLESPIE (Rangers) | John HAWTREY |
|---|---|---|
| (1) | Andrew WATSON (Queen's Park) | Edgar FIELD |
| (6) | Thomas VALLANCE (Rangers) | Claude WILSON |
| (8) | Charles CAMPBELL (Queen's Park) captain | Norman BAILEY |
| (4) | David DAVIDSON (Queen's Park) | John HUNTER |
| (1) | David HILL (Rangers) | George HOLDEN |
| (1) | William McGUIRE (Beith) | Thurston ROSTRON |
| (2) | George KER (Queen's Park) | Reginald MacAULEY |
| (2) | Joseph LINDSAY (Dumbarton) | Clement MITCHELL |
| (9) | Henry McNEIL (Queen's Park) | John HARGREAVES |
| (6) | John SMITH (Edinburgh University) | Edward BAMBRIDGE |

| | Goals | |
|---|---|---|
| Smith (10 mins) | 1-0 | |
| Hill (53 mins) | 2-0 | |
| | 2-1 | Bambridge (64 mins) |
| Smith (69 mins) | 3-1 | |
| Ker (74 mins) | 4-1 | |
| Smith (79 mins) | 5-1 | |
| Ker (89 mins) | 6-1 | |

**16**
(Friendly) — Referee: Kenrick (Wales)
14 March 1881 — The Racecourse, Wrexham (Att: 1,500)

**WALES 1-5 SCOTLAND** — **Half-time 1-4**

| (3) | George GILLESPIE (Rangers) | Robert McMILLAN |
|---|---|---|
| (2) | Andrew WATSON (Queen's Park) | John MORGAN |
| (7) | Thomas VALLANCE (Rangers) | John ROBERTS |
| (4) | John McPHERSON (Vale of Leven) | William WILLIAMS |
| (5) | David DAVIDSON (Queen's Park) captain | William BELL |
| (2) | William McGUIRE (Beith) | William OWEN |
| (2) | David HILL (Rangers) | Thomas LEWIS |
| (3) | George KER (Queen's Park) | John PRICE |
| (3) | Joseph LINDSAY (Dumbarton) | Knyvett CROSSE |
| (10) | Henry McNEIL (Queen's Park) | William ROBERTS |
| (7) | John SMITH (Edinburgh University) | John VAUGHAN |

| | Goals | |
|---|---|---|
| | 0-1 | Crosse (5 mins) |
| Ker (7 mins) | 1-1 | |
| McNeil (9 mins) | 2-1 | |
| Bell (10 mins o.g.) | 3-1 | |
| Ker (44 mins) | 4-1 | |
| Morgan (52 mins o.g.) | 5-1 | |

# 1882

| | P | W | D | L | F | A |
|---|---|---|---|---|---|---|
| | 2 | 2 | 0 | 0 | 10 | 1 |

**17**
(Friendly) — Referee: Wallace (Scotland)
11 March 1882 — First Hampden Park, Glasgow (Att: 10,000)

**SCOTLAND 5-1 ENGLAND** — **Half-time 2-1**

| (4) | George GILLESPIE (Rangers) | Harold SWEPSTONE |
|---|---|---|
| (3) | Andrew WATSON (Queen's Park) | Haydock GREENWOOD |
| (2) | Andrew McINTYRE (Vale of Leven) | Alfred JONES |
| (9) | Charles CAMPBELL (Queen's Park) captain | Norman BAILEY |
| (1) | Peter MILLER (Dumbarton) | John HUNTER |
| (2) | Malcolm FRASER (Queen's Park) | Henry CURSHAM |
| (1) | William ANDERSON (Queen's Park) | Edward PARRY |
| (4) | George KER (Queen's Park) | Oliver VAUGHTON |
| (1) | William HARROWER (Queen's Park) | Arthur BROWN |
| (2) | John KAY (Queen's Park) | William MOSFORTH |
| (1) | Robert McPHERSON (Arthurlie) | Edward BAMBRIDGE |

| | Goals | |
|---|---|---|
| Harrower (15 mins) | 1-0 | |
| | 1-1 | Vaughton (35 mins) |
| Ker (43 mins) | 2-1 | |
| McPherson (46 mins) | 3-1 | |
| Ker (70 mins) | 4-1 | |
| Kay (85 mins) | 5-1 | |

**18**
(Friendly) — Referee: Hamilton (Scotland)
25 March 1882 — First Hampden Park, Glasgow (Att: 5,000)

**SCOTLAND 5-0 WALES** — **Half-time 1-0**

| (2) | Archibald ROWAN (Queen's Park) captain | Henry PHOENIX |
|---|---|---|
| (1) | Andrew HOLM (Queen's Park) | John MORGAN |
| (2) | James DUNCAN (Alexandra Athletic) | John POWELL |
| (10) | Charles CAMPBELL (Queen's Park) | Henry EDWARDS |
| (5) | Alexander KENNEDY (Third Lanark) | William WILLIAMS |
| (3) | Malcolm FRASER (Queen's Park) | John ROBERTS |
| (3) | David HILL (Rangers) | William OWEN |
| (5) | George KER (Queen's Park) | Walter ROBERTS |
| (1) | James McAULAY (Dumbarton) | John PRICE |
| (3) | John KAY (Queen's Park) | John ROBERTS |
| (3) | James RICHMOND (Queen's Park) | John VAUGHAN |

| | Goals | |
|---|---|---|
| Kay (25 mins) | 1-0 | |
| Ker | 2-0 | |
| Fraser | 3-0 | |
| Fraser | 4-0 | |
| McAulay (88 mins) | 5-0 | |

# 1883

| P | W | D | L | F | A |
|---|---|---|---|---|---|
| 2 | 2 | 0 | 0 | 6 | 2 |

## 19
(Friendly)  
10 March 1883  

Referee: Sinclair (Ireland)  
Bramall Lane, Sheffield (Att: 7,000)

### ENGLAND 2-3 SCOTLAND — Half-time 2-2

| | | | |
|---|---|---|---|
| (2) | James McAULAY (Dumbarton) | | Harold SWEPSTONE |
| (2) | Andrew HOLM (Queen's Park) captain | | Percy DE PARAVINCINI |
| (1) | Michael PATON (Dumbarton) | | Alfred JONES |
| (2) | Peter MILLER (Dumbarton) | | Norman BAILEY |
| (5) | John McPHERSON (Vale of Leven) | | Stuart MACRAE |
| (4) | Malcolm FRASER (Queen's Park) | | Oliver WHATELEY |
| (2) | William ANDERSON (Queen's Park) | | Arthur CURSHAM |
| (8) | John SMITH (Queen's Park) | | Harold GOODHART |
| (1) | John INGLIS (Rangers) | | Clement MITCHELL |
| (4) | John KAY (Queen's Park) | | Henry CURSHAM |
| (1) | William McKINNON (Dumbarton) | | William COBBOLD |

| | Goals | |
|---|---|---|
| Smith (22 mins) | 1-0 | |
| | 1-1 | Mitchell (24 mins) |
| Smith (39 mins) | 2-1 | |
| | 2-2 | Cobbold (43 mins) |
| Fraser (86 mins) | 3-2 | |

## 20
(Friendly)  
12 March 1883  

Referee: Lythgoe (England)  
The Racecourse, Wrexham (Att: 2,000)

### WALES 0-3 SCOTLAND — Half-time 0-2

| | | | |
|---|---|---|---|
| (3) | James McAULAY (Dumbarton) | | Richard GOUGH |
| (3) | Andrew HOLM (Queen's Park) captain | | Frederick HUGHES |
| (1) | Walter ARNOTT (Queen's Park) | | John POWELL |
| (3) | Peter MILLER (Dumbarton) | | Edward BOWEN |
| (6) | John McPHERSON (Vale of Leven) | | Henry EDWARDS |
| (5) | Malcolm FRASER (Queen's Park) | | John JONES |
| (3) | William ANDERSON (Queen's Park) | | William OWEN |
| (9) | John SMITH (Queen's Park) | | Walter ROBERTS |
| (2) | John INGLIS (Rangers) | | John PRICE |
| (5) | John KAY (Queen's Park) | | William ROBERTS |
| (2) | William McKINNON (Dumbarton) | | John VAUGHAN |

| | Goals | |
|---|---|---|
| Smith (35 mins) | 1-0 | |
| Fraser (38 mins) | 2-0 | |
| Anderson | 3-0 | |

# 1884

| P | W | D | L | F | A |
|---|---|---|---|---|---|
| 3 | 3 | 0 | 0 | 10 | 1 |

## 21
(Home International Championship)  
26 January 1884  

Referee: Hindle (England)  
Ballynafeigh Park, Belfast (Att: 2,000)

### IRELAND 0-5 SCOTLAND — Half-time 0-2

| | | | |
|---|---|---|---|
| (1) | John INGLIS (Kilmarnock Athletic) | | R HUNTER |
| (1) | John FORBES (Vale of Leven) | | Robert WILSON |
| (2) | Walter ARNOTT (Queen's Park) captain | | William CRONE |
| (1) | John GRAHAM (Annbank) | | John HASTINGS |
| (1) | William FULTON (Abercorn) | | Thomas MOLYNEUX |
| (1) | Robert BROWN (Dumbarton) | | A. DILL |
| (1) | Samuel THOMSON (Boswell) | | Arthur SPILLER |
| (1) | James GOSSLAND (Rangers) | | John GIBB |
| (1) | John GOUDIE (Abercorn) | | William MORROW |
| (2) | William HARROWER (Queen's Park) | | John DAVISON |
| (1) | J. McAULAY (Arthurlie) | | Arthur GAUSSEN |

| | Goals | |
|---|---|---|
| Harrower (12 mins) | 1-0 | |
| Gossland | 2-0 | |
| Goudie (60 mins) | 3-0 | |
| Gossland | 4-0 | |
| Harrower (86 mins) | 5-0 | |

## 22
(Home International Championship)  
15 March 1884  

Referee: Sinclair (Ireland)  
Cathkin Park, Glasgow (Att: 10,000)

### SCOTLAND 1-0 ENGLAND — Half-time 1-0

| | | | |
|---|---|---|---|
| (4) | James McAULAY (Dumbarton) | | William ROSE |
| (3) | Walter ARNOTT (Queen's Park) | | Joseph BEVERLEY |
| (2) | John FORBES (Vale of Leven) | | Alfred DOBSON |
| (11) | Charles CAMPBELL (Queen's Park) captain | | Stuart MACRAE |
| (7) | John McPHERSON (Vale of Leven) | | Norman BAILEY |
| (4) | William ANDERSON (Queen's Park) | | Charles WILSON |
| (1) | Francis SHAW (Pollokshields Athletic) | | George HOLDEN |
| (10) | John SMITH (Queen's Park) | | Oliver VAUGHTON |
| (4) | Joseph LINDSAY (Dumbarton) | | William BROMLEY-DAVENPORT |
| (1) | Robert CHRISTIE (Queen's Park) | | Edward BAMBRIDGE |
| (3) | William McKINNON (Dumbarton) | | William GUNN |

| | Goals |
|---|---|
| Smith (7 mins) | 1-0 |

## 23
(Home International Championship)  
29 March 1884  

Referee: Sloane (England)  
Cathkin Park, Glasgow (Att: 5,000)

### SCOTLAND 4-1 WALES — Half-time 1-1

| | | | |
|---|---|---|---|
| (1) | Thomas TURNER (Arthurlie) | | Elias OWEN |
| (2) | Michael PATON (Dumbarton) captain | | Robert ROBERTS |
| (3) | John FORBES (Vale of Leven) | | Charles CONDE |
| (6) | Alexander KENNEDY (Third Lanark) | | Frederick HUGHES |
| (1) | James McINTYRE (Rangers) | | Thomas BURKE |
| (2) | Robert BROWN (Dumbarton) | | John JONES |
| (2) | Francis SHAW (Pollokshields Athletic) | | William OWEN |
| (2) | Samuel THOMSON (Boswell) | | Walter ROBERTS |
| (5) | Joseph LINDSAY (Dumbarton) | | Edward SHAW |
| (6) | John KAY (Queen's Park) | | John EYTON-JONES |
| (4) | William McKINNON (Dumbarton) | | Robert JONES |

| | Goals | |
|---|---|---|
| | 0-1 | R.Roberts (7 mins) |
| Lindsay (22 mins) | 1-1 | |
| Shaw (49 mins) | 2-1 | |
| Kay | 3-1 | |
| Kay (87 mins) | 4-1 | |

# 1885

| P | W | D | L | F | A |
|---|---|---|---|---|---|
| 3 | 2 | 1 | 0 | 17 | 4 |

## 24
(Home International Championship)  
14 March 1885  

Referee: Dix (England)  
First Hampden Park, Glasgow (Att: 6,000)

### SCOTLAND 8-2 IRELAND — Half-time 4-0

| | | | |
|---|---|---|---|
| (1) | William CHALMERS (Rangers) | | Anthony HENDERSON |
| (1) | Hugh McHARDY (Rangers) | | George HEWISON |
| (1) | James NIVEN (Moffat) | | R. JOHNSTON |
| (1) | Robert KELSO (Renton) | | Robert MUIR |
| (8) | John McPHERSON (Vale of Leven) captain | | William HOUSTON |
| (1) | Alexander BARBOUR (Renton) | | William EAMES |
| (1) | John MARSHALL (Third Lanark) | | T. McLEAN |
| (1) | William TURNER (Pollokshields Athletic) | | Joseph SHERRARD |
| (1) | Alexander HIGGINS (Kilmarnock) | | John GIBB |
| (1) | Robert CALDERWOOD (Cartvale) | | George McGEE |
| (1) | W. LAMONT (Pilgrims) | | A. DILL |

| | Goals | |
|---|---|---|
| Lamont (10 mins) | 1-0 | |
| Turner (12 mins) | 2-0 | |
| Calderwood (15 mins) | 3-0 | |
| Marshall (35 mins) | 4-0 | |
| Higgins (51 mins) | 5-0 | |
| Barbour (53 mins) | 6-0 | |
| Higgins | 7-0 | |
| Higgins | 8-0 | |
| | 8-1 | Gibb (81 mins) |
| | 8-2 | Gibb (89 mins) |

## 25

(Home International Championship)
21 March 1885
Referee: Sinclair (Ireland)
Kennington Oval, London (Att: 8,000)

**ENGLAND 1-1 SCOTLAND** — Half-time 0-1

| | | |
|---|---|---|
| (5) | James McAULAY (Dumbarton) | William ARTHUR |
| (4) | Walter ARNOTT (Queen's Park) | Arthur WALTERS |
| (3) | Michael PATON (Dumbarton) | Percy WALTERS |
| (12) | Charles CAMPBELL (Queen's Park) captain | Andrew AMOS |
| (1) | John GOW (Queen's Park) | Norman BAILEY |
| (5) | William ANDERSON (Queen's Park) | James FORREST |
| (1) | Alexander HAMILTON (Queen's Park) | Joseph LOFTHOUSE |
| (1) | William SELLAR (Battlefield) | Thomas DANKS |
| (6) | Joseph LINDSAY (Dumbarton) | James BROWN |
| (1) | David ALLAN (Queen's Park) | William COBBOLD |
| (2) | Robert CALDERWOOD (Cartvale) | Edward BAMBRIDGE |

| | Goals | |
|---|---|---|
| Lindsay (20 mins) | 1-0 | |
| | 1-1 | Bambridge (57 mins) |

## 26

(Home International Championship)
23 March 1885
Referee: Sloane (England)
The Racecourse, Wrexham (Att: 2,000)

**WALES 1-8 SCOTLAND** — Half-time 0-3

| | | |
|---|---|---|
| (6) | James McAULAY (Dumbarton) | Robert MILLS-ROBERTS |
| (5) | Walter ARNOTT (Queen's Park) | George THOMAS |
| (4) | Michael PATON (Dumbarton) captain | Seth POWELL |
| (2) | Robert KELSO (Renton) | Thomas BURKE |
| (1) | Leitch KEIR (Renton) | William FOULKES |
| (2) | Alexander HAMILTON (Queen's Park) | Humphrey JONES |
| (6) | William ANDERSON (Queen's Park) | James LLOYD |
| (7) | Joseph LINDSAY (Dumbarton) | Job WILDING |
| (3) | Robert CALDERWOOD (Cartvale) | Harold HIBBOTT |
| (1) | Robert BROWN (Dumbarton) | George FARMER |
| (2) | David ALLAN (Queen's Park) | Robert JONES |

| | Goals | |
|---|---|---|
| Calderwood (8 mins) | 1-0 | |
| Anderson | 2-0 | |
| Allan | 3-0 | |
| | 3-1 | R.Jones (54 mins) |
| Lindsay (56 mins) | 4-1 | |
| Anderson (76 mins) | 5-1 | |
| Calderwood | 6-1 | |
| Lindsay | 7-1 | |
| Lindsay | 8-1 | |

## 1886

| P | W | D | L | F | A |
|---|---|---|---|---|---|
| 3 | 2 | 1 | 0 | 12 | 4 |

## 27

(Home International Championship)
20 March 1886
Referee: Wolstenholme (Ireland)
Ballynafeigh Park, Belfast (Att: 3,000)

**IRELAND 2-7 SCOTLAND** — Half-time 2-5

| | | |
|---|---|---|
| (1) | James CONNOR (Airdrie) | Shaw GILLESPIE |
| (1) | Andrew THOMSON (Arthurlie) | James WATSON |
| (1) | William McLEOD (Queen's Park) | William CRONE |
| (1) | John CAMERON (Rangers) | Thomas MOLYNEUX |
| (2) | Leitch KEIR (Dumbarton) | W. DEVINE |
| (1) | Robert FLEMING (Morton) | John HASTINGS |
| (1) | John LAMBIE (Queen's Park) captain | John McCLATCHEY |
| (1) | Charles HEGGIE (Rangers) | Samuel JOHNSTON |
| (2) | William TURNER (Pollokshields Athletic) | John GIBB |
| (1) | James GOURLAY (Cambuslang) | J. CONDY |
| (1) | Michael DUNBAR (Cartvale) | William TURNER |

| | Goals | |
|---|---|---|
| Heggie (15 mins) | 1-0 | |
| Heggie (18 mins) | 2-0 | |
| | 2-1 | Condy |
| Heggie | 3-1 | |
| Lambie | 4-1 | |
| Dunbar | 5-1 | |
| | 5-2 | Johnston (44 mins) |
| Heggie | 6-2 | |
| Gourlay | 7-2 | |

## 28

(Home International Championship)
27 March 1886
Referee: Hunter (Wales)
First Hampden Park, Glasgow (Att: 11,000)

**SCOTLAND 1-1 ENGLAND** — Half-time 0-1

| | | |
|---|---|---|
| (7) | James McAULAY (Dumbarton) | William ARTHUR |
| (6) | Walter ARNOTT (Queen's Park) captain | Arthur WALTERS |
| (5) | Michael PATON (Dumbarton) | Percy WALTERS |
| (13) | Charles CAMPBELL (Queen's Park) | Norman BAILEY |
| (1) | John MacDONALD (Edinburgh University) | Ralph SQUIRE |
| (3) | Alexander HAMILTON (Queen's Park) | James FORREST |
| (2) | William SELLAR (Battlefield) | Benjamin SPILSBURY |
| (1) | George SOMERVILLE (Queen's Park) | George BRANN |
| (8) | Joseph LINDSAY (Dumbarton) | Tinsley LINDLEY |
| (1) | Woodville GRAY (Pollokshields Athletic) | William COBBOLD |
| (1) | Ralph AITKEN (Dumbarton) | Edward BAMBRIDGE |

| | Goals | |
|---|---|---|
| | 0-1 | Lindley (35 mins) |
| Somerville (80 mins) | 1-1 | |

## 29

(Home International Championship)
10 April 1886
Referee: Sinclair (Ireland)
First Hampden Park, Glasgow (Att: 5,500)

**SCOTLAND 4-1 WALES** — Half-time 1-0

| | | |
|---|---|---|
| (5) | George GILLESPIE (Queen's Park) | Albert HERSEE |
| (1) | James LUNDIE (Hibernian) | Alfred DAVIES |
| (1) | William SEMPLE (Cambuslang) captain | Frederick JONES |
| (3) | Robert KELSO (Renton) | John VAUGHAN |
| (1) | Andrew JACKSON (Cambuslang) | William BELL |
| (2) | John MARSHALL (Third Lanark) | Humphrey JONES |
| (1) | Robert McCORMICK (Abercorn) | Richard WILLIAMS |
| (1) | James McGHEE (Hibernian) | William ROBERTS |
| (3) | William HARROWER (Queen's Park) | John DOUGHTY |
| (3) | David ALLAN (Queen's Park) | Herbert SISSON |
| (1) | James McCALL (Renton) | William LEWIS |

| | Goals | |
|---|---|---|
| McCormick (30 mins) | 1-0 | |
| McCall (47 mins) | 2-0 | |
| Allan (53 mins) | 3-0 | |
| Harrower (56 mins) | 4-0 | |
| | 4-1 | Vaughan (88 mins) |

## 1887

| P | W | D | L | F | A |
|---|---|---|---|---|---|
| 3 | 3 | 0 | 0 | 9 | 3 |

## 30

(Home International Championship)
19 February 1887
Referee: Hunter (Wales)
First Hampden Park, Glasgow (Att: 1,000)

**SCOTLAND 4-1 IRELAND** — Half-time 2-1

| | | |
|---|---|---|
| (1) | John DOIG (Arbroath) | Shaw GILLESPIE |
| (1) | Andrew WHITELAW (Vale of Leven) | W. FOX |
| (1) | Robert SMELLIE (Queen's Park) | John WATSON |
| (1) | John WEIR (Third Lanark) | T. MOORE |
| (1) | Thomas McMILLAN (Dumbarton) | Archibald ROSBOTHAM |
| (1) | J. HUTTON (St Bernard's) | Robert BAXTER |
| (1) | Thomas JENKINSON (Hearts) | John REID |
| (2) | John LAMBIE (Queen's Park) captain | Olphert STANFIELD |
| (1) | William WATT (Queen's Park) | Frederick BROWNE |
| (1) | James LOWE (St Bernard's) | John PEDEN |
| (1) | William JOHNSTONE (Third Lanark) | John GIBB |

| | Goals | |
|---|---|---|
| Watt (5 mins) | 1-0 | |
| | 1-1 | Browne (41 mins) |
| Jenkinson (43 mins) | 2-1 | |
| Johnstone (55 mins) | 3-1 | |
| Lowe (75 mins) | 4-1 | |

## 31

(Home International Championship)     Referee: Sinclair (Ireland)
19 March 1887     Leamington Road, Blackburn (Att: 12,000)

### ENGLAND 2-3 SCOTLAND     Half-time 1-1

| | | |
|---|---|---|
| (8) | James McAULAY (Dumbarton) captain | Robert ROBERTS |
| (7) | Walter ARNOTT (Queen's Park) | Percy WALTERS |
| (4) | John FORBES (Vale of Leven) | Arthur WALTERS |
| (4) | Robert KELSO (Renton) | Norman BAILEY |
| (1) | John AULD (Third Lanark) | George HAWORTH |
| (3) | Leitch KEIR (Dumbarton) | James FORREST |
| (3) | John MARSHALL (Third Lanark) | Edward BAMBRIDGE |
| (1) | William ROBERTSON (Dumbarton) | William COBBOLD |
| (3) | William SELLAR (Battlefield) | Joseph LOFTHOUSE |
| (2) | James McCALL (Renton) | Frederick DEWHURST |
| (1) | James ALLAN (Queen's Park) | Tinsley LINDLEY |

| | Goals | |
|---|---|---|
| McCall (30 mins) | 1-0 | |
| | 1-1 | Lindley (32 mins) |
| Keir (68 mins) | 2-1 | |
| | 2-2 | Dewhurst (69 mins) |
| Allan (70 mins) | 3-2 | |

## 32

(Home International Championship)     Referee: Hall (England)
21 March 1887     The Racecourse, Wrexham (Att: 2,000)

### WALES 0-2 SCOTLAND     Half-time 0-1

| | | |
|---|---|---|
| (9) | James McAULAY (Dumbarton) captain | James TRAINER |
| (8) | Walter ARNOTT (Queen's Park) | Alfred DAVIES |
| (5) | John FORBES (Vale of Leven) | John POWELL |
| (5) | Robert KELSO (Renton) | Robert ROBERTS |
| (2) | John AULD (Third Lanark) | James MORRIS |
| (4) | Leitch KEIR (Dumbarton) | Thomas BURKE |
| (4) | John MARSHALL (Third Lanark) | John CHALLEN |
| (2) | William ROBERTSON (Dumbarton) | Richard JONES |
| (4) | William SELLAR (Battlefield) | William PRYCE-JONES |
| (3) | James McCALL (Renton) | William LEWIS |
| (2) | James ALLAN (Queen's Park) | John DOUGHTY |

| | Goals | |
|---|---|---|
| Robertson (40 mins) | 1-0 | |
| Allan (80 mins) | 2-0 | |

## 1888

| P | W | D | L | F | A |
|---|---|---|---|---|---|
| 3 | 2 | 0 | 1 | 15 | 8 |

## 33

(Home International Championship)     Referee: Clegg (England)
10 March 1888     Easter Road, Edinburgh (Att: 8,000)

### SCOTLAND 5-1 WALES     Half-time 3-1

| | | |
|---|---|---|
| (1) | James WILSON (Vale of Leven) | James TRAINER |
| (1) | Andrew HANNAH (Renton) | David JONES |
| (2) | Robert SMELLIE (Queen's Park) captain | John POWELL |
| (1) | James JOHNSTONE (Abercorn) | Thomas BURKE |
| (2) | James GOURLAY (Cambuslang) | Joseph DAVIES |
| (1) | James McLAREN (Hibernian) | Robert ROBERTS |
| (1) | Alexander LATTA (Dumbarton Athletic) | William PRYCE-JONES |
| (1) | William GROVES (Hibernian) | Job WILDING |
| (1) | William PAUL (Partick Thistle) | John DOUGHTY |
| (1) | John McPHERSON (Kilmarnock) | George OWEN |
| (1) | Neil MUNRO (Abercorn) | Roger DOUGHTY |

| | Goals | |
|---|---|---|
| Paul (6 mins) | 1-0 | |
| Munro (30 mins) | 2-0 | |
| Latta (33 mins) | 3-0 | |
| | 3-1 | J. Doughty (41 mins) |
| Groves (65 mins) | 4-1 | |
| Latta (75 mins) | 5-1 | |

## 34

(Home International Championship)     Referee: Sinclair (Ireland)
17 March 1888     First Hampden Park, Glasgow (Att: 10,000)

### SCOTLAND 0-5 ENGLAND     Half-time 0-4

| | | |
|---|---|---|
| (1) | John LINDSAY (Renton) | William MOON |
| (9) | Walter ARNOTT (Queen's Park) | Robert HOWARTH |
| (1) | Donald GOW (Rangers) captain | Percy WALTERS |
| (1) | James KELLY (Renton) | Henry ALLEN |
| (5) | Leitch KEIR (Dumbarton) | George HAWORTH |
| (6) | Robert KELSO (Renton) | Cecil HOLDEN-WHITE |
| (4) | Alexander HAMILTON (Queen's Park) | George WOODHALL |
| (1) | William BERRY (Queen's Park) | John GOODALL |
| (5) | William SELLAR (Battlefield) | Tinsley LINDLEY |
| (4) | James McCALL (Renton) | Dennis HODGETTS |
| (3) | John LAMBIE (Queen's Park) | Frederick DEWHURST |

| | Goals | |
|---|---|---|
| | 0-1 | Lindley (32 mins) |
| | 0-2 | Hodgetts (34 mins) |
| | 0-3 | Dewhurst (40 mins) |
| | 0-4 | Goodall (43 mins) |
| | 0-5 | Dewhurst (49 mins) |

## 35

(Home International Championship)     Referee: Parlane (Scotland)
24 March 1888     Solitude, Belfast (Att: 5,000)

### IRELAND 2-10 SCOTLAND     Half-time 2-7

| | | |
|---|---|---|
| (1) | John McLEOD (Dumbarton) | Ralph LAWTHER |
| (1) | Duncan STEWART (Dumbarton) captain | Robert WILSON |
| (1) | Archibald McCALL (Renton) | Frederick BROWNE |
| (1) | Allan STEWART (Queen's Park) | James FORSYTHE |
| (1) | George DEWAR (Dumbarton) | Archibald ROSBOTHAM |
| (2) | Andrew JACKSON (Cambuslang) | Thomas MOLYNEUX |
| (1) | Neil McCALLUM (Renton) | William DALTON |
| (1) | John GOW (Rangers) | Olphert STANFIELD |
| (1) | William DICKSON (Strathmore) | John BARRY |
| (1) | Thomas BRECKENRIDGE (Hearts) | John LEMON |
| (2) | Ralph AITKEN (Dumbarton) | William TURNER |

| | Goals | |
|---|---|---|
| Dewar (5 mins) | 1-0 | |
| Dickson (8 mins) | 2-0 | |
| Breckenridge (15 mins) | 3-0 | |
| | 3-1 | Dalton |
| | 3-2 | Dalton |
| Aitken | 4-2 | |
| Dickson (33 mins) | 5-2 | |
| Dickson (40 mins) | 6-2 | |
| Dickson (45 mins) | 7-2 | |
| McCallum (53 mins) | 8-2 | |
| Wilson (77 mins o.g.) | 9-2 | |
| A.Stewart (83 mins) | 10-2 | |

## 1889

| P | W | D | L | F | A |
|---|---|---|---|---|---|
| 3 | 2 | 1 | 0 | 10 | 2 |

## 36

(Home International Championship)     Referee: Stacey (England)
9 March 1889     Ibrox Park, Glasgow (Att: 6,000)

### SCOTLAND 7-0 IRELAND     Half-time 4-0

| | | |
|---|---|---|
| (2) | John DOIG (Arbroath) | John CLUGSTON |
| (1) | James ADAMS (Hearts) | John McVICKER |
| (1) | Thomas McKEOWN (Celtic) | Robert CRONE |
| (1) | Thomas ROBERTSON (Queen's Park) captain | John THOMPSON |
| (1) | David CALDERHEAD (Queen of the South Wand) | James CHRISTIAN |
| (1) | John BUCHANAN (Cambuslang) | William CRONE |
| (1) | Francis WATT (Kilbirnie) | Samuel TORRANS |
| (1) | Thomas McINNES (Cowlairs) | Olphert STANFIELD |
| (2) | William GROVES (Celtic) | John GIBB |
| (1) | R. BOYD (Mossend Swifts) | James WILTON |
| (1) | David BLACK (Hurlford) | John PEDEN |

| | Goals | |
|---|---|---|
| Watt (7 mins) | 1-0 | |
| Watt (10 mins) | 2-0 | |
| Black (25 mins) | 3-0 | |
| Groves (32 mins) | 4-0 | |
| Groves (50 mins) | 5-0 | |
| Groves | 6-0 | |
| McInnes (88 mins) | 7-0 | |

**37**

(Home International Championship)  
13 April 1889  
Referee: Sinclair (Ireland)  
Kennington Oval, London (Att: 10,000)

### ENGLAND 2-3 SCOTLAND — Half-time 2-0

| | | |
|---|---|---|
| (2) | James WILSON (Vale of Leven) | William MOON |
| (3) | Robert SMELLIE (Queen's Park) captain | Arthur WALTERS |
| (10) | Walter ARNOTT (Queen's Park) | Percy WALTERS |
| (2) | James KELLY (Celtic) | Henry HAMMOND |
| (2) | George DEWAR (Dumbarton) | Henry ALLEN |
| (2) | James McLAREN (Celtic) | James FORREST |
| (1) | James OSWALD (Third Lanark) | William BASSETT |
| (2) | William BERRY (Queen's Park) | John GOODALL |
| (2) | Alexander LATTA (Dumbarton Athletic) | John BRODIE |
| (2) | John McPHERSON (Cowlairs) | David WEIR |
| (2) | Neil MUNRO (Abercorn) | Tinsley LINDLEY |

| | Goals | |
|---|---|---|
| | 0-1 | Bassett (15 mins) |
| | 0-2 | Weir (17 mins) |
| Munro (55 mins) | 1-2 | |
| Oswald (82 mins) | 2-2 | |
| McPherson (90 mins) | 3-2 | |

**38**

(Home International Championship)  
15 April 1889  
Referee: Sinclair (Ireland)  
The Racecourse, Wrexham (Att: 6,000)

### WALES 0-0 SCOTLAND

| | | |
|---|---|---|
| (2) | John McLEOD (Dumbarton) | Allen PUGH |
| (1) | Andrew THOMSON (Third Lanark) captain | Alfred DAVIES |
| (1) | James RAE (Third Lanark) | David JONES |
| (2) | Allan STEWART (Queen's Park) | Robert ROBERTS |
| (1) | Alexander LOCHHEAD (Third Lanark) | Joseph DAVIES |
| (3) | John AULD (Third Lanark) | Humphrey JONES |
| (2) | Francis WATT (Kilbirnie) | Joseph DAVIES |
| (1) | Henry CAMPBELL (Renton) | William OWEN |
| (2) | William PAUL (Partick Thistle) | John DOUGHTY |
| (2) | William JOHNSTONE (Third Lanark) | George OWEN |
| (1) | James HANNAH (Third Lanark) | William LEWIS |

**Substitutions**

| | |
|---|---|
| | Samuel GILLAM |
| | for Pugh 30 mins |

# 1890

| P | W | D | L | F | A |
|---|---|---|---|---|---|
| 3 | 2 | 1 | 0 | 10 | 2 |

**39**

(Home International Championship)  
22 March 1890  
Referee: Finlay (Ireland)  
Underwood Park, Paisley (Att: 7,500)

### SCOTLAND 5-0 WALES — Half-time 3-0

| | | |
|---|---|---|
| (6) | George GILLESPIE (Rangers) captain | James TRAINER |
| (2) | Andrew WHITELAW (Vale of Leven) | William JONES |
| (1) | John MURRAY (Vale of Leven) | Samuel JONES |
| (1) | Matthew McQUEEN (Leith Athletic) | Peter GRIFFITHS |
| (1) | Andrew BROWN (St Mirren) | Humphrey JONES |
| (1) | Hugh WILSON (Newmilns) | Robert ROBERTS |
| (1) | J BROWN (Cambuslang) | David LEWIS |
| (3) | Francis WATT (Kilbirnie) | Oswald DAVIES |
| (3) | William PAUL (Partick Thistle) | William OWEN |
| (1) | James DUNLOP (St Mirren) | Richard JARRETT |
| (1) | Daniel BRUCE (Vale of Leven) | William TURNER |

| | Goals | |
|---|---|---|
| Wilson | 1-0 | |
| Paul (36 mins) | 2-0 | |
| Paul (43 mins) | 3-0 | |
| Paul | 4-0 | |
| Paul (70 mins) | 5-0 | |

**40**

(Home International Championship)  
29 March 1890  
Referee: Stacey (England)  
Ballynafeigh Park, Belfast (Att: 5,000)

### IRELAND 1-4 SCOTLAND — Half-time 1-1

| | | |
|---|---|---|
| (3) | John McLEOD (Dumbarton) captain | John CLUGSTON |
| (1) | R. HUNTER (St Mirren) | Robert STEWART |
| (2) | James RAE (Third Lanark) | Robert CRONE |
| (1) | J RUSSELL (Cambuslang) | John REID |
| (1) | Isaac BEGBIE (Hearts) | Samuel SPENCER |
| (1) | David MITCHELL (Rangers) | Samuel COOKE |
| (1) | Thomas WYLIE (Rangers) | William DALTON |
| (1) | Gilbert RANKIN (Vale of Leven) | George GAFFIKIN |
| (3) | John McPHERSON (Cowlairs) | Olphert STANFIELD |
| (1) | John BELL (Dumbarton) | Samuel TORRANS |
| (1) | David BAIRD (Hearts) | John PEDEN |

| | Goals | |
|---|---|---|
| Rankin (10 mins) | 1-0 | |
| | 1-1 | Peden |
| Wylie (50 mins) | 2-1 | |
| McPherson | 3-1 | |
| Rankin | 4-1 | |

**41**

(Home International Championship)  
5 April 1890  
Referee: Reid (Ireland)  
Second Hampden Park, Glasgow (Att: 26,379)

### SCOTLAND 1-1 ENGLAND — Half-time 1-1

| | | |
|---|---|---|
| (3) | James WILSON (Vale of Leven) | William MOON |
| (11) | Walter ARNOTT (Queen's Park) | Arthur WALTERS |
| (2) | Thomas McKEOWN (Celtic) | Percy WALTERS |
| (2) | Thomas ROBERTSON (Queen's Park) | George HAWORTH |
| (3) | James KELLY (Celtic) | Henry ALLEN |
| (3) | James McLAREN (Celtic) captain | Alfred SHELTON |
| (3) | William GROVES (Celtic) | William BASSETT |
| (3) | William BERRY (Queen's Park) | Edward CURREY |
| (3) | William JOHNSTONE (Third Lanark) | Tinsley LINDLEY |
| (4) | John McPHERSON (Cowlairs) | Harold WOOD |
| (5) | James McCALL (Renton) | Harold DAFT |

| | Goals | |
|---|---|---|
| | 0-1 | Wood (17 mins) |
| McPherson (37 mins) | 1-1 | |

# 1891

| P | W | D | L | F | A |
|---|---|---|---|---|---|
| 3 | 2 | 0 | 1 | 7 | 6 |

**42**

(Home International Championship)  
21 March 1891  
Referee: Crump (England)  
The Racecourse, Wrexham (Att: 4,000)

### WALES 3-4 SCOTLAND — Half-time 2-1

| | | |
|---|---|---|
| (1) | J McCORKINDALE (Partick Thistle) | James TRAINER |
| (1) | Archibald RITCHIE (East Stirlingshire) | Seth POWELL |
| (1) | James HEPBURN (Alloa Athletic) | David JONES |
| (2) | Matthew McQUEEN (Leith Athletic) | Arthur LEA |
| (2) | Andrew BROWN (St Mirren) | Humphrey JONES |
| (3) | Thomas ROBERTSON (Queen's Park) captain | Charles PARRY |
| (1) | William GULLILAND (Queen's Park) | Joseph DAVIES |
| (1) | Robert BUCHANAN (Abercorn) | William OWEN |
| (1) | James LOGAN (Ayr United) | William TURNER |
| (2) | R. BOYD (Mossend Swifts) | John BOWDLER |
| (1) | Alexander KEILLOR (Montrose) | William LEWIS |

| | Goals | |
|---|---|---|
| Logan | 1-0 | |
| | 1-1 | Bowdler |
| | 1-2 | Owen |
| Buchanan | 2-2 | |
| Boyd | 3-2 | |
| | 3-3 | Bowdler |
| Boyd | 4-3 | |

## 43

(Home International Championship)
28 March 1891
Referee: Stacey (England)
Celtic Park, Glasgow (Att: 8,000)

### SCOTLAND 2-1 IRELAND — Half-time 1-0

| | | |
|---|---|---|
| (7) | George GILLESPIE (Queen's Park) captain | Joseph LOYAL |
| (1) | Donald SILLARS (Queen's Park) | William GORDON |
| (1) | William PAUL (Dykebar) | George FORBES |
| (1) | T. HAMILTON (Hurlford) | Alexander CRAWFORD |
| (1) | James CLELAND (Royal Albert) | John REYNOLDS |
| (1) | James CAMPBELL (Kilmarnock) | Richard MOORE |
| (1) | James LOW (Cambuslang) | William DALTON |
| (1) | Robert CLEMENTS (Leith Athletic) | George GAFFIKIN |
| (1) | William BOWIE (Linthouse) | Olphert STANFIELD |
| (1) | Thomas WADDELL (Queen's Park) | David BRISBY |
| (1) | J. FRASER (Moffat) | Samuel TORRANS |

**Goals**

| | | |
|---|---|---|
| Low (6 mins) | 1-0 | |
| Waddell (60 mins) | 2-0 | |
| | 2-1 | Stanfield (85 mins) |

## 44

(Home International Championship)
4 April 1891
Referee: Morrow (Ireland)
Ewood Park, Blackburn (Att: 31,000)

### ENGLAND 2-1 SCOTLAND — Half-time 2-0

| | | |
|---|---|---|
| (4) | James WILSON (Vale of Leven) | William MOON |
| (12) | Walter ARNOTT (Queen's Park) captain | Robert HOWARTH |
| (4) | Robert SMELLIE (Queen's Park) | Robert HOLMES |
| (2) | Isaac BEGBIE (Hearts) | Albert SMITH |
| (1) | John McPHERSON (Hearts) | John HOLT |
| (1) | John HILL (Hearts) | Alfred SHELTON |
| (2) | Gilbert RANKIN (Vale of Leven) | William BASSETT |
| (4) | Francis WATT (Kilbirnie) | John GOODALL |
| (6) | William SELLAR (Queen's Park) | Frederick GEARY |
| (4) | William BERRY (Queen's Park) | Edgar CHADWICK |
| (2) | David BAIRD (Hearts) | Alfred MILWARD |

**Goals**

| | | |
|---|---|---|
| | 0-1 | Goodall (20 mins) |
| | 0-2 | Chadwick (30 mins) |
| Watt (85 mins) | 1-2 | |

---

# 1892

| P | W | D | L | F | A |
|---|---|---|---|---|---|
| 3 | 2 | 0 | 1 | 10 | 7 |

## 45

(Home International Championship)
19 March 1892
Referee: Taylor (Wales)
Solitude, Belfast (Att: 10,500)

### IRELAND 2-3 SCOTLAND — Half-time 1-2

| | | |
|---|---|---|
| (1) | Andrew BAIRD (Queen's Park) | John CLUGSTON |
| (1) | George BOWMAN (Montrose) | William GORDON |
| (1) | John DRUMMOND (Falkirk) | Robert STEWART |
| (1) | Robert MARSHALL (Rangers) | Nathaniel McKEOWN |
| (4) | Thomas ROBERTSON (Queen's Park) captain | Samuel SPENCER |
| (1) | Peter DOWDS (Celtic) | William CUNNINGHAM |
| (2) | William GULLILAND (Queen's Park) | William DALTON |
| (1) | David McPHERSON (Kilmarnock) | George GAFFIKIN |
| (1) | James ELLIS (Mossend Swifts) | James WILLIAMSON |
| (1) | William LAMBIE (Queen's Park) | Olphert STANFIELD |
| (2) | Alexander KEILLOR (Montrose) | Samuel TORRANS |

**Goals**

| | | |
|---|---|---|
| Keillor (17 mins) | 1-0 | |
| Lambie (28 mins) | 2-0 | |
| | 2-1 | Williamson (42 mins) |
| Ellis | 3-1 | |
| | 3-2 | Gaffikin (86 mins) |

## 46

(Home International Championship)
26 March 1892
Referee: Reid (Ireland)
Tynecastle Park, Edinburgh (Att: 600)

### SCOTLAND 6-1 WALES — Half-time 4-0

| | | |
|---|---|---|
| (1) | Robert DOWNIE (Third Lanark) | James TRAINER |
| (2) | James ADAMS (Hearts) | Smart ARRIDGE |
| (1) | James ORR (Kilmarnock) | Seth POWELL |
| (3) | Isaac BEGBIE (Hearts) | William HUGHES |
| (2) | James CAMPBELL (Kilmarnock) | Caesar JENKYNS |
| (2) | John HILL (Hearts) captain | Robert ROBERTS |
| (1) | John TAYLOR (Dumbarton) | Job WILDING |
| (1) | William THOMSON (Dumbarton) | William OWEN |
| (1) | James HAMILTON (Queen's Park) | William LEWIS |
| (5) | John McPHERSON (Rangers) | Thomas EGAN |
| (3) | David BAIRD (Hearts) | Benjamin LEWIS |

**Goals**

| | | |
|---|---|---|
| Thomson (1 mins) | 1-0 | |
| Hamilton | 2-0 | |
| McPherson (15 mins) | 3-0 | |
| McPherson (44 mins) | 4-0 | |
| Baird | 5-0 | |
| Hamilton | 6-0 | |
| | 6-1 | B. Lewis (87 mins) |

## 47

(Home International Championship)
2 April 1892
Referee: Smith (Scotland)
Ibrox Park, Glasgow (Att: 20,000)

### SCOTLAND 1-4 ENGLAND — Half-time 0-4

| | | |
|---|---|---|
| (4) | John McLEOD (Dumbarton) | George TOONE |
| (1) | Daniel DOYLE (Celtic) | Arthur DUNN |
| (13) | Walter ARNOTT (Queen's Park) | Robert HOLMES |
| (4) | James KELLY (Celtic) | John REYNOLDS |
| (7) | William SELLAR (Queen's Park) captain | John HOLT |
| (2) | David MITCHELL (Rangers) | Alfred SHELTON |
| (2) | Donald SILLARS (Queen's Park) | William BASSETT |
| (1) | William TAYLOR (Hearts) | John GOODALL |
| (2) | Thomas WADDELL (Queen's Park) | John SOUTHWORTH |
| (1) | Alexander McMAHON (Celtic) | Edgar CHADWICK |
| (2) | John BELL (Dumbarton) | Dennis HODGETTS |

**Goals**

| | | |
|---|---|---|
| | 0-1 | Chadwick (1 min) |
| | 0-2 | Goodall (20 mins) |
| | 0-3 | Southworth (25 mins) |
| | 0-4 | Goodall (26 mins) |
| Bell (80 mins) | 1-4 | |

---

# 1893

| P | W | D | L | F | A |
|---|---|---|---|---|---|
| 3 | 2 | 0 | 1 | 16 | 6 |

## 48

(Home International Championship)
18 March 1893
Referee: Stacey (England)
The Racecourse, Wrexham (Att: 4,500)

### WALES 0-8 SCOTLAND — Half-time 0-5

| | | |
|---|---|---|
| (5) | John McLEOD (Dumbarton) | Samuel JONES |
| (2) | Daniel DOYLE (Celtic) | Oliver TAYLOR |
| (1) | Robert FOYERS (St Bernard's) | Frederick JONES |
| (3) | Donald SILLARS (Queen's Park) captain | George WILLIAMS |
| (1) | Andrew McCREADIE (Rangers) | Edwin WILLIAMS |
| (1) | David STEWART (Queen's Park) | Edward MORRIS |
| (1) | John TAYLOR (Dumbarton) | William OWEN |
| (2) | William THOMSON (Dumbarton) | James VAUGHAN |
| (1) | John MADDEN (Celtic) | John BUTLER |
| (1) | John BARKER (Rangers) | Benjamin LEWIS |
| (2) | William LAMBIE (Queen's Park) | Harold BOWDLER |

**Goals**

| | | |
|---|---|---|
| Madden (4 mins) | 1-0 | |
| Madden (20 mins) | 2-0 | |
| Barker | 3-0 | |
| Barker | 4-0 | |
| Barker | 5-0 | |
| Madden (47 mins) | 6-0 | |
| Lambie | 7-0 | |
| Madden (89 mins) | 8-0 | |

## 49

(Home International Championship)
25 March 1893

Referee: Taylor (Wales)
Celtic Park, Glasgow (Att: 12,000)

### SCOTLAND 6-1 IRELAND — Half-time 4-1

| | | | |
|---|---|---|---|
| (2) | John LINDSAY (Renton) | John CLUGSTON | |
| (3) | James ADAMS (Hearts) | William GORDON | |
| (5) | Robert SMELLIE (Queen's Park) | Robert TORRANS | |
| (1) | William MALEY (Celtic) | Nathaniel McKEOWN | |
| (5) | James KELLY (Celtic) captain | Samuel JOHNSTON | |
| (3) | David MITCHELL (Rangers) | Samuel TORRANS | |
| (8) | William SELLAR (Queen's Park) | James SMALL | |
| (3) | Thomas WADDELL (Queen's Park) | George GAFFIKIN | |
| (2) | James HAMILTON (Queen's Park) | James WILLIAMSON | |
| (2) | Alexander McMAHON (Celtic) | James WILTON | |
| (1) | John CAMPBELL (Celtic) | John PEDEN | |

| | Goals | |
|---|---|---|
| Sellar (10 mins) | 1-0 | |
| S.Torrans (20 mins o.g.) | 2-0 | |
| Sellar (27 mins) | 3-0 | |
| McMahon (28 mins) | 4-0 | |
| | 4-1 | Gaffikin (44 mins) |
| Kelly | 5-1 | |
| Hamilton | 6-1 | |

## 50

(Home International Championship)
1 April 1893

Referee: Clegg (England)
Richmond Athletic Ground, London (Att: 16,000)

### ENGLAND 5-2 SCOTLAND — Half-time 1-1

| | | |
|---|---|---|
| (3) | John LINDSAY (Renton) | Leslie GAY |
| (14) | Walter ARNOTT (Queen's Park) | Alban HARRISON |
| (6) | Robert SMELLIE (Queen's Park) | Robert HOLMES |
| (2) | William MALEY (Celtic) | John REYNOLDS |
| (6) | James KELLY (Celtic) captain | John HOLT |
| (4) | David MITCHELL (Rangers) | George KINSEY |
| (9) | William SELLAR (Queen's Park) | William BASSETT |
| (4) | Thomas WADDELL (Queen's Park) | Robert GOSLING |
| (3) | James HAMILTON (Queen's Park) | George COTTERILL |
| (3) | Alexander McMAHON (Celtic) | Edgar CHADWICK |
| (2) | John CAMPBELL (Celtic) | Frederick SPIKSLEY |

| | Goals | |
|---|---|---|
| | 0-1 | Gosling (15 mins) |
| Sellar (20 mins) | 1-1 | |
| Sellar (47 mins) | 2-1 | |
| | 2-2 | Cotterill (65 mins) |
| | 2-3 | Spiksley (75 mins) |
| | 2-4 | Spiksley (80 mins) |
| | 2-5 | Reynolds (86 mins) |

# 1894

| P | W | D | L | F | A |
|---|---|---|---|---|---|
| 3 | 2 | 1 | 0 | 9 | 5 |

## 51

(Home International Championship)
24 March 1894

Referee: McBride (Ireland)
Rugby Park, Kilmarnock (Att: 10,000)

### SCOTLAND 5-2 WALES — Half-time 2-2

| | | |
|---|---|---|
| (2) | Andrew BAIRD (Queen's Park) | Samuel GILLAM |
| (1) | David CRAWFORD (St Mirren) | Oliver TAYLOR |
| (2) | Robert FOYERS (St Bernard's) | Abel HUGHES |
| (1) | Edward McBAIN (St Mirren) | George WILLIAMS |
| (7) | James KELLY (Celtic) captain | Thomas CHAPMAN |
| (1) | John JOHNSTONE (Kilmarnock) | Thomas WORTHINGTON |
| (1) | Andrew STEWART (Third Lanark) | Hugh MORRIS |
| (1) | Thomas CHAMBERS (Hearts) | Benjamin LEWIS |
| (1) | David ALEXANDER (East Stirlingshire) | William LEWIS |
| (1) | Davidson BERRY (Queen's Park) | John REA |
| (2) | John BARKER (Rangers) | Edwin JAMES |

| | Goals | |
|---|---|---|
| | 0-1 | Morris |
| | 0-2 | Morris |
| Berry (42 mins) | 1-2 | |
| Barker (44 mins) | 2-2 | |
| Chambers (70 mins) | 3-2 | |
| Alexander | 4-2 | |
| Johnstone | 5-2 | |

## 52

(Home International Championship)
31 March 1894

Referee: Phennah (Wales)
Solitude, Belfast (Att: 6,000)

### IRELAND 1-2 SCOTLAND — Half-time 0-2

| | | |
|---|---|---|
| (1) | Francis BARRETT (Dundee) | Thomas SCOTT |
| (2) | David CRAWFORD (St Mirren) | Robert STEWART |
| (2) | John DRUMMOND (Rangers) | Samuel TORRANS |
| (2) | Robert MARSHALL (Rangers) captain | Nathaniel McKEOWN |
| (1) | William LONGAIR (Dundee) | John BURNETT |
| (2) | David STEWART (Queen's Park) | Robert MILNE |
| (3) | John TAYLOR (Dumbarton) | William DALTON |
| (1) | James BLESSINGTON (Celtic) | George GAFFIKIN |
| (2) | David ALEXANDER (East Stirlingshire) | Olphert STANFIELD |
| (1) | Robert SCOTT (Airdrie) | William GIBSON |
| (3) | Alexander KEILLOR (Dundee) | James BARRON |

| | Goals | |
|---|---|---|
| Torrans (25 mins o.g.) | 1-0 | |
| Taylor (28 mins) | 2-0 | |
| | 2-1 | Stanfield |

## 53

(Home International Championship)
7 April 1894

Referee: Reid (Ireland)
Celtic Park, Glasgow (Att: 45,017)

### SCOTLAND 2-2 ENGLAND — Half-time 1-1

| | | |
|---|---|---|
| (1) | David HADDOW (Rangers) | Leslie GAY |
| (4) | Donald SILLARS (Queen's Park) | Thomas CLARE |
| (3) | Daniel DOYLE (Celtic) captain | Frederick PELLY |
| (4) | Isaac BEGBIE (Hearts) | John REYNOLDS |
| (2) | Andrew McCREADIE (Rangers) | John HOLT |
| (5) | David MITCHELL (Rangers) | Ernest NEEDHAM |
| (3) | William GULLILAND (Queen's Park) | William BASSETT |
| (2) | James BLESSINGTON (Celtic) | John GOODALL |
| (4) | Alexander McMAHON (Celtic) | Gilbert SMITH |
| (6) | John McPHERSON (Rangers) | Edgar CHADWICK |
| (3) | William LAMBIE (Queen's Park) | Frederick SPIKSLEY |

| | Goals | |
|---|---|---|
| Lambie (7 mins) | 1-0 | |
| | 1-1 | Goodall (35 mins) |
| McMahon (75 mins) | 2-1 | |
| | 2-2 | Reynolds (85 mins) |

# 1895

| P | W | D | L | F | A |
|---|---|---|---|---|---|
| 3 | 1 | 1 | 1 | 5 | 6 |

## 54

(Home International Championship)
23 March 1895

Referee: Jope (England)
The Racecourse, Wrexham (Att: 4,000)

### WALES 2-2 SCOTLAND — Half-time 1-2

| | | |
|---|---|---|
| (2) | Francis BARRETT (Dundee) | Samuel JONES |
| (5) | Donald SILLARS (Queen's Park) captain | Robert LLOYD |
| (1) | Robert GLEN (Renton) | Charles PARRY |
| (1) | James SIMPSON (Third Lanark) | George WILLIAMS |
| (1) | William McCOLL (Renton) | Thomas CHAPMAN |
| (4) | Alexander KEILLOR (Dundee) | John JONES |
| (1) | John FYFE (Third Lanark) | Joseph DAVIES |
| (1) | John MURRAY (Renton) | Benjamin LEWIS |
| (2) | John MADDEN (Celtic) | Harold TRAINER |
| (1) | William SAWERS (Dundee) | William LEWIS |
| (1) | John DIVERS (Celtic) | John REA |

| | Goals | |
|---|---|---|
| | 0-1 | W. Lewis |
| Madden | 1-1 | |
| Divers (39 mins) | 2-1 | |
| | 2-2 | Chapman |

## 55

(Home International Championship)
30 March 1895
Referee: Mitchell (England)
Celtic Park, Glasgow (Att: 15,000)

### SCOTLAND 3-1 IRELAND — Half-time 1-1

| | | |
|---|---|---|
| (1) | Daniel McARTHUR (Celtic) | Thomas SCOTT |
| (3) | John DRUMMOND (Rangers) captain | John PONSONBY |
| (4) | Daniel DOYLE (Celtic) | Lewis SCOTT |
| (2) | James SIMPSON (Third Lanark) | Hymie McKEE |
| (1) | David RUSSELL (Hearts) | Thomas ALEXANDER |
| (1) | Neil GIBSON (Rangers) | Thomas McCLATCHEY |
| (4) | John TAYLOR (St Mirren) | Thomas MORRISON |
| (5) | Thomas WADDELL (Queen's Park) | William SHERRARD |
| (7) | John McPHERSON (Rangers) | Olphert STANFIELD |
| (1) | John WALKER (Hearts) | William GIBSON |
| (4) | William LAMBIE (Queen's Park) | James BARRON |

**Goals**

| | | |
|---|---|---|
| Lambie (1 min) | 1-0 | |
| | 1-1 | Sherrard |
| Walker | 2-1 | |
| Walker | 3-1 | |

## 56

(Home International Championship)
6 April 1895
Referee: Reid (Ireland)
Goodison Park, Liverpool (Att: 42,500)

### ENGLAND 3-0 SCOTLAND — Half-time 3-0

| | | |
|---|---|---|
| (2) | Daniel McARTHUR (Celtic) | John SUTCLIFFE |
| (4) | John DRUMMOND (Rangers) | Lewis LODGE |
| (5) | Daniel DOYLE (Celtic) | James CRABTREE |
| (2) | David RUSSELL (Hearts) | John REYNOLDS |
| (3) | James SIMPSON (Third Lanark) | John HOLT |
| (2) | Neil GIBSON (Rangers) | Ernest NEEDHAM |
| (5) | William LAMBIE (Queen's Park) | William BASSETT |
| (8) | John McPHERSON (Rangers) | Stephen BLOOMER |
| (2) | James OSWALD (St Bernard's) captain | John GOODALL |
| (6) | Thomas WADDELL (Queen's Park) | Robert GOSLING |
| (4) | William GULLILAND (Queen's Park) | Stephen SMITH |

**Goals**

| | | |
|---|---|---|
| | 0-1 | Bloomer (30 mins) |
| | 0-2 | Gibson (35 mins o.g.) |
| | 0-3 | Smith (44 mins) |

## 1896

| P | W | D | L | F | A |
|---|---|---|---|---|---|
| 3 | 2 | 1 | 0 | 9 | 4 |

## 57

(Home International Championship)
21 March 1896
Referee: McBride (Ireland)
Carolina Port, Dundee (Att: 11,700)

### SCOTLAND 4-0 WALES — Half-time 2-0

| | | |
|---|---|---|
| (1) | Robert MacFARLANE (Morton) | James TRAINER |
| (1) | Duncan McLEAN (St Bernard's) | Charles PARRY |
| (2) | Robert GLEN (Renton) | John MATTHIAS |
| (1) | John GILLESPIE (Queen's Park) captain | Joseph ROGERS |
| (1) | Robert NEIL (Hibernian) | Caesar JENKYNS |
| (1) | William BLAIR (Third Lanark) | John JONES |
| (1) | William THOMSON (Dundee) | David PUGH |
| (1) | Daniel PATON (St Bernard's) | John GARNER |
| (1) | Robert McCOLL (Queen's Park) | Arthur MORRIS |
| (1) | Alexander KING (Hearts) | John REA |
| (5) | Alexander KEILLOR (Dundee) | William LEWIS |

**Goals**

| | | |
|---|---|---|
| Neil | 1-0 | |
| Keillor | 2-0 | |
| Paton | 3-0 | |
| Neil | 4-0 | |

## 58

(Home International Championship)
28 March 1896
Referee: Cooper (England)
Solitude, Belfast (Att: 8,000)

### IRELAND 3-3 SCOTLAND — Half-time 3-2

| | | |
|---|---|---|
| (1) | Kenneth ANDERSON (Queen's Park) | Thomas SCOTT |
| (1) | Peter MEECHAN (Celtic) | John PONSONBY |
| (5) | John DRUMMOND (Rangers) | Samuel TORRANS |
| (3) | Neil GIBSON (Rangers) | Hugh GORDON |
| (8) | James KELLY (Celtic) captain | Robert MILNE |
| (1) | George HOGG (Hearts) | James FITZPATRICK |
| (1) | Patrick MURRAY (Hibernian) | Giddy BAIRD |
| (3) | James BLESSINGTON (Celtic) | E. MORROGH |
| (2) | Robert McCOLL (Queen's Park) | Olphert STANFIELD |
| (1) | John CAMERON (Queen's Park) | James BARRON |
| (6) | William LAMBIE (Queen's Park) | John PEDEN |

**Goals**

| | | |
|---|---|---|
| McColl (7 mins) | 1-0 | |
| | 1-1 | Barron |
| McColl | 2-1 | |
| | 2-2 | Barron |
| | 2-3 | Milne (43 mins pen) |
| Murray (78 mins) | 3-3 | |

## 59

(Home International Championship)
4 April 1896
Referee: Jones (Wales)
Celtic Park, Glasgow (Att: 56,500)

### SCOTLAND 2-1 ENGLAND — Half-time 2-0

| | | |
|---|---|---|
| (3) | John DOIG (Sunderland) | George RAIKES |
| (6) | John DRUMMOND (Rangers) captain | Lewis LODGE |
| (1) | Thomas BRANDON (Blackburn Rovers) | William OAKLEY |
| (2) | George HOGG (Hearts) | Arthur HENFREY |
| (1) | James COWAN (Aston Villa) | Thomas CRAWSHAW |
| (4) | Neil GIBSON (Rangers) | James CRABTREE |
| (2) | Alexander KING (Hearts) | William BASSETT |
| (7) | William LAMBIE (Queen's Park) | John GOODALL |
| (1) | Thomas HYSLOP (Stoke City) | Gilbert SMITH |
| (4) | James BLESSINGTON (Celtic) | Harold WOOD |
| (3) | John BELL (Everton) | Cuthbert BURNUP |

**Goals**

| | | |
|---|---|---|
| Lambie (22 mins) | 1-0 | |
| Bell (33 mins) | 2-0 | |
| | 2-1 | Bassett (80 mins) |

## 1897

| P | W | D | L | F | A |
|---|---|---|---|---|---|
| 3 | 2 | 1 | 0 | 9 | 4 |

## 60

(Home International Championship)
20 March 1897
Referee: Armitt (England)
The Racecourse, Wrexham (Att: 5,000)

### WALES 2-2 SCOTLAND — Half-time 1-1

| | | |
|---|---|---|
| (1) | John PATRICK (St Mirren) | James TRAINER |
| (1) | John RITCHIE (Queen's Park) captain | William JONES |
| (1) | David GARDNER (Third Lanark) | John MATTHIAS |
| (1) | Bernard BRESLIN (Hibernian) | Sydney DARVELL |
| (3) | David RUSSELL (Celtic) | John MATES |
| (6) | Alexander KEILLOR (Dundee) | John JONES |
| (1) | John KENNEDY (Hibernian) | William MEREDITH |
| (1) | Patrick MURRAY (Hibernian) | David PUGH |
| (3) | James OSWALD (Rangers) | Morgan MORGAN-OWEN |
| (1) | J McMILLAN (St Bernard's) | John REA |
| (2) | John WALKER (Hearts) | William LEWIS |

**Goals**

| | | |
|---|---|---|
| Ritchie (11 mins pen) | 1-0 | |
| | 1-1 | Morgan-Owen (40 mins) |
| Walker | 2-1 | |
| | 2-2 | Pugh |

19

**61**
(Home International Championship)
27 March 1897

Referee: Cooper (England)
Ibrox Park, Glasgow (Att: 15,000)

### SCOTLAND 5-1 IRELAND | Half-time 4-0

| (1) | Matthew DICKIE (Rangers) | | James THOMPSON |
|---|---|---|---|
| (2) | Duncan McLEAN (St Bernard's) | | John PONSONBY |
| (7) | John DRUMMOND (Rangers) captain | | Samuel TORRANS |
| (5) | Neil GIBSON (Rangers) | | John PYPER |
| (1) | William BAIRD (St Bernard's) | | Robert MILNE |
| (3) | David STEWART (Queen's Park) | | George McMASTER |
| (1) | Thomas LOW (Rangers) | | James CAMPBELL |
| (9) | John McPHERSON (Rangers) | | Olphert STANFIELD |
| (3) | Robert McCOLL (Queen's Park) | | James PYPER |
| (3) | Alexander KING (Celtic) | | John DARLING |
| (8) | William LAMBIE (Queen's Park) | | John PEDEN |

| | Goals | |
|---|---|---|
| McPherson | 1-0 | |
| Gibson | 2-0 | |
| McColl | 3-0 | |
| King | 4-0 | |
| | 4-1 | James Pyper |
| McPherson | 5-1 | |

**62**
(Home International Championship)
3 April 1897

Referee: Gough (Wales)
Crystal Palace, London (Att: 35,000)

### ENGLAND 1-2 SCOTLAND | Half-time 1-1

| (2) | John PATRICK (St Mirren) | | John ROBINSON |
|---|---|---|---|
| (1) | Nicol SMITH (Rangers) | | Howard SPENCER |
| (6) | Daniel DOYLE (Celtic) | | William OAKLEY |
| (6) | Neil GIBSON (Rangers) | | John REYNOLDS |
| (2) | James COWAN (Aston Villa) | | Thomas CRAWSHAW |
| (2) | Hugh WILSON (Sunderland) | | Ernest NEEDHAM |
| (4) | John BELL (Everton) | | William ATHERSMITH |
| (1) | James MILLAR (Rangers) | | Stephen BLOOMER |
| (1) | George ALLAN (Liverpool) | | Gilbert SMITH |
| (2) | Thomas HYSLOP (Rangers) | | Edgar CHADWICK |
| (9) | William LAMBIE (Queen's Park) captain | | Alfred MILWARD |

| | Goals | |
|---|---|---|
| | 0-1 | Bloomer (19 mins) |
| Hyslop (27 mins) | 1-1 | |
| Millar (83 mins) | 2-1 | |

# 1898

| P | W | D | L | F | A |
|---|---|---|---|---|---|
| 3 | 2 | 0 | 1 | 9 | 5 |

**63**
(Home International Championship)
19 March 1898

Referee: Stacey (England)
Fir Park, Motherwell (Att: 3,500)

### SCOTLAND 5-2 WALES | Half-time 4-1

| (1) | W WATSON (Falkirk) | | James TRAINER |
|---|---|---|---|
| (2) | Nicol SMITH (Rangers) | | Charles PARRY |
| (1) | Matthew SCOTT (Airdrie) captain | | David JONES |
| (3) | William THOMSON (Dumbarton) | | Richard JONES |
| (1) | Alexander CHRISTIE (Queen's Park) | | Caesar JENKYNS |
| (1) | Peter CAMPBELL (Morton) | | John JONES |
| (1) | James GILLESPIE (Third Lanark) | | Edwin JAMES |
| (2) | James MILLAR (Rangers) | | Thomas THOMAS |
| (1) | James McKIE (East Stirlingshire) | | Morgan MORGAN-OWEN |
| (1) | Hugh MORGAN (St Mirren) | | Arthur MORRIS |
| (1) | Robert FINDLAY (Kilmarnock) | | Alfred WATKINS |

| | Goals | |
|---|---|---|
| Gillespie (12 mins) | 1-0 | |
| Gillespie | 2-0 | |
| McKie | 3-0 | |
| McKie (40 mins) | 4-0 | |
| | 4-1 | Thomas (44 mins) |
| Gillespie | 5-1 | |
| | 5-2 | Morgan-Owen |

The Scotland team pictured before the game against England in April 1897. Back row (left to right): N. Smith, J. Patrick, J. Aitken (trainer), J. Bell, T. Hyslop, J.K. McDowall (SFA secretary), G. Allan, H. Wilson. Front row: W. Crichton (SFA president), J. Cowan, J. Millar, W.A. Lambie, D. Doyle, N. Gibson, D. McKenzie (SFA vice-president).

**64**

(Home International Championship)
26 March 1898

Referee: Lewis (England)
Solitude, Belfast (Att: 5,000)

**IRELAND 0-3 SCOTLAND**                    Half-time 0-2

| | | |
|---|---|---|
| (2) | Kenneth ANDERSON (Queen's Park) | Thomas SCOTT |
| (7) | Robert KELSO (Dundee) captain | William GIBSON |
| (7) | Daniel DOYLE (Celtic) | Samuel TORRANS |
| (4) | William THOMSON (Dumbarton) | William ANDERSON |
| (4) | David RUSSELL (Celtic) | Robert MILNE |
| (4) | Alexander KING (Celtic) | Michael COCHRANE |
| (1) | William STEWART (Queen's Park) | James CAMPBELL |
| (3) | John CAMPBELL (Celtic) | John MERCER |
| (4) | Robert McCOLL (Queen's Park) | James PYPER |
| (3) | John WALKER (Hearts) | James McCASHIN |
| (1) | Thomas ROBERTSON (Hearts) | John PEDEN |

| | Goals | |
|---|---|---|
| Robertson (30 mins) | 1-0 | |
| McColl (42 mins) | 2-0 | |
| Stewart (70 mins) | 3-0 | |

---

**65**

(Home International Championship)
2 April 1898

Referee: Robertson (Scotland)
Celtic Park, Glasgow (Att: 40,000)

**SCOTLAND 1-3 ENGLAND**                    Half-time 0-2

| | | |
|---|---|---|
| (3) | Kenneth ANDERSON (Queen's Park) | John ROBINSON |
| (8) | John DRUMMOND (Rangers) | William OAKLEY |
| (8) | Daniel DOYLE (Celtic) | William WILLIAMS |
| (7) | Neil GIBSON (Rangers) | Frank FORMAN |
| (3) | James COWAN (Aston Villa) captain | Charles WREFORD-BROWN |
| (1) | John ROBERTSON (Everton) | Ernest NEEDHAM |
| (5) | John BELL (Everton) | William ATHERSMITH |
| (4) | John CAMPBELL (Celtic) | Stephen BLOOMER |
| (1) | William MAXWELL (Stoke City) | Gilbert SMITH |
| (3) | James MILLAR (Rangers) | George WHELDON |
| (1) | Alexander SMITH (Rangers) | Frederick SPIKSLEY |

| | Goals | |
|---|---|---|
| | 0-1 | Wheldon (3 mins) |
| | 0-2 | Bloomer (23 mins) |
| Millar (48 mins) | 1-2 | |
| | 1-3 | Bloomer (72 mins) |

---

# 1899

| P | W | D | L | F | A |
|---|---|---|---|---|---|
| 3 | 2 | 0 | 1 | 16 | 3 |

**66**

(Home International Championship)
18 March 1899

Referee: Sutcliffe (England)
The Racecourse, Wrexham (Att: 12,000)

**WALES 0-6 SCOTLAND**                    Half-time 0-1

| | | |
|---|---|---|
| (3) | Daniel McARTHUR (Celtic) | James TRAINER |
| (3) | Nicol SMITH (Rangers) captain | John MATTHIAS |
| (1) | David STORRIER (Celtic) | Horace BLEW |
| (8) | Neil GIBSON (Rangers) | George RICHARDS |
| (1) | Harold MARSHALL (Celtic) | John JONES |
| (5) | Alexander KING (Celtic) | Edward HUGHES |
| (1) | John CAMPBELL (Rangers) | Frederick KELLY |
| (1) | Robert HAMILTON (Rangers) | Trevor OWEN |
| (5) | Robert McCOLL (Queen's Park) | Morgan MORGAN-OWEN |
| (6) | John BELL (Celtic) | Ralph JONES |
| (2) | Davidson BERRY (Queen's Park) | Arthur MORRIS |

| | Goals | |
|---|---|---|
| Campbell (22 mins) | 1-0 | |
| McColl (50 mins) | 2-0 | |
| Campbell | 3-0 | |
| Marshall | 4-0 | |
| McColl | 5-0 | |
| McColl | 6-0 | |

---

**67**

(Home International Championship)
25 March 1899

Referee: Sutcliffe (England)
Celtic Park, Glasgow (Att: 12,000)

**SCOTLAND 9-1 IRELAND**                    Half-time 5-0

| | | |
|---|---|---|
| (2) | Matthew DICKIE (Rangers) | James LEWIS |
| (4) | Nicol SMITH (Rangers) | Samuel SWAN |
| (2) | David STORRIER (Celtic) captain | Thomas FOREMAN |
| (9) | Neil GIBSON (Rangers) | William ANDERSON |
| (2) | Alexander CHRISTIE (Queen's Park) | Archibald GOODALL |
| (6) | Alexander KING (Celtic) | John McSHANE |
| (2) | John CAMPBELL (Rangers) | George SHEEHAN |
| (2) | Robert HAMILTON (Rangers) | James MELDON |
| (6) | Robert McCOLL (Queen's Park) | James PYPER |
| (3) | Davidson BERRY (Queen's Park) | James McCASHIN |
| (7) | John BELL (Celtic) | Joseph McALLEN |

| | Goals | |
|---|---|---|
| McColl (5 mins) | 1-0 | |
| Christie | 2-0 | |
| Hamilton | 3-0 | |
| McColl | 4-0 | |
| Bell | 5-0 | |
| McColl (47 mins) | 6-0 | |
| | 6-1 | Goodall |
| Hamilton | 7-1 | |
| Campbell | 8-1 | |
| Campbell | 9-1 | |

---

**68**

(Home International Championship)
8 April 1899

Referee: Torrans (Ireland)
Villa Park, Birmingham (Att: 25,590)

**ENGLAND 2-1 SCOTLAND**                    Half-time 2-0

| | | |
|---|---|---|
| (4) | John DOIG (Sunderland) | John ROBINSON |
| (5) | Nicol SMITH (Rangers) captain | Henry THICKETT |
| (3) | David STORRIER (Celtic) | James CRABTREE |
| (10) | Neil GIBSON (Rangers) | Raby HOWELL |
| (3) | Alexander CHRISTIE (Queen's Park) | Frank FORMAN |
| (2) | John ROBERTSON (Southampton) | Ernest NEEDHAM |
| (3) | John CAMPBELL (Rangers) | William ATHERSMITH |
| (3) | Robert HAMILTON (Rangers) | Stephen BLOOMER |
| (7) | Robert McCOLL (Queen's Park) | Gilbert SMITH |
| (2) | Hugh MORGAN (Liverpool) | James SETTLE |
| (8) | John BELL (Celtic) | Frederick FORMAN |

| | Goals | |
|---|---|---|
| | 0-1 | Smith (25 mins) |
| | 0-2 | Settle (40 mins) |
| Hamilton (52 mins) | 1-2 | |

---

# 1900

| P | W | D | L | F | A |
|---|---|---|---|---|---|
| 3 | 3 | 0 | 0 | 12 | 3 |

**69**

(Home International Championship)
3 February 1900

Referee: Sutcliffe (England)
Pittodrie Park, Aberdeen (Att: 12,500)

**SCOTLAND 5-2 WALES**                    Half-time 4-1

| | | |
|---|---|---|
| (3) | Matthew DICKIE (Rangers) | Frederick GRIFFITHS |
| (6) | Nicol SMITH (Rangers) | Charles THOMAS |
| (3) | David CRAWFORD (Rangers) | Charles MORRIS |
| (1) | James IRONS (Queen's Park) | Samuel MEREDITH |
| (2) | Robert NEIL (Rangers) | John JONES |
| (3) | John ROBERTSON (Rangers) | William HARRISON |
| (9) | John BELL (Celtic) | David PUGH |
| (1) | David WILSON (Queen's Park) | William BUTLER |
| (8) | Robert McCOLL (Queen's Park) | Richard JONES |
| (4) | Robert HAMILTON (Rangers) captain | Thomas PARRY |
| (2) | Alexander SMITH (Rangers) | Alfred WATKINS |

| | Goals | |
|---|---|---|
| Bell (2 mins) | 1-0 | |
| Wilson (7 mins) | 2-0 | |
| Wilson (35 mins) | 3-0 | |
| Hamilton (37 mins) | 4-0 | |
| | 4-1 | Parry (44 mins) |
| | 4-2 | Butler (52 mins) |
| A.Smith (60 mins) | 5-2 | |

## 70

(Home International Championship)
3 March 1900

Referee: Sutcliffe (England)
Solitude, Belfast (Att: 6,000)

### IRELAND 0-3 SCOTLAND — Half-time 0-2

| | | |
|---|---|---|
| (1) | Henry RENNIE (Hearts) | James LEWIS |
| (7) | Nicol SMITH (Rangers) | John PYPER |
| (3) | Robert GLEN (Hibernian) | Michael COCHRANE |
| (11) | Neil GIBSON (Rangers) | John McSHANE |
| (2) | Harold MARSHALL (Celtic) captain | John BARRY |
| (1) | William ORR (Celtic) | Hugh MAGINNIS |
| (2) | William STEWART (Queen's Park) | James CAMPBELL |
| (1) | Robert WALKER (Hearts) | John DARLING |
| (5) | John CAMPBELL (Celtic) | Patrick McAULEY |
| (1) | Patrick CALLAGHAN (Hibernian) | Alfred KEARNS |
| (3) | Alexander SMITH (Rangers) | Joseph McALLEN |

Goals

| | |
|---|---|
| Campbell (8 mins) | 1-0 |
| A. Smith (23 mins) | 2-0 |
| Campbell (83 mins) | 3-0 |

## 71

(Home International Championship)
7 April 1900

Referee: Torrans (Ireland)
Celtic Park, Glasgow (Att: 63,000)

### SCOTLAND 4-1 ENGLAND — Half-time 4-1

| | | |
|---|---|---|
| (2) | Henry RENNIE (Hearts) | John ROBINSON |
| (8) | Nicol SMITH (Rangers) | William OAKLEY |
| (9) | John DRUMMOND (Rangers) | James CRABTREE |
| (12) | Neil GIBSON (Rangers) | William JOHNSON |
| (1) | Alexander RAISBECK (Liverpool) | Arthur CHADWICK |
| (4) | John ROBERTSON (Rangers) captain | Ernest NEEDHAM |
| (10) | John BELL (Celtic) | William ATHERSMITH |
| (2) | Robert WALKER (Hearts) | Stephen BLOOMER |
| (9) | Robert McCOLL (Queen's Park) | Gilbert SMITH |
| (6) | John CAMPBELL (Celtic) | George WILSON |
| (4) | Alexander SMITH (Rangers) | John PLANT |

Goals

| | | |
|---|---|---|
| McColl (1 min) | 1-0 | |
| Bell (6 mins) | 2-0 | |
| McColl (25 mins) | 3-0 | |
| | 3-1 | Bloomer (35 mins) |
| McColl (44 mins) | 4-1 | |

# 1901

| P | W | D | L | F | A |
|---|---|---|---|---|---|
| 3 | 1 | 2 | 0 | 14 | 3 |

## 72

(Home International Championship)
23 February 1901

Referee: Gough (Wales)
Celtic Park, Glasgow (Att: 15,000)

### SCOTLAND 11-0 IRELAND — Half-time 5-0

| | | |
|---|---|---|
| (1) | George McWATTIE (Queen's Park) | Samuel McALPINE |
| (9) | Nicol SMITH (Rangers) | William GIBSON |
| (1) | Bernard BATTLES (Celtic) | Samuel TORRANS |
| (5) | David RUSSELL (Celtic) | Patrick FARRELL |
| (1) | George ANDERSON (Kilmarnock) | James CONNOR |
| (5) | John ROBERTSON (Rangers) | Michael COCHRANE |
| (7) | John CAMPBELL (Celtic) | James SCOTT |
| (4) | John CAMPBELL (Rangers) | James SMITH |
| (5) | Robert HAMILTON (Rangers) captain | James CAMPBELL |
| (5) | Alexander McMAHON (Celtic) | Harold O'REILLY |
| (5) | Alexander SMITH (Rangers) | Robert CLARKE |

Goals

| | |
|---|---|
| McMahon (6 mins) | 1-0 |
| McMahon | 2-0 |
| Russell | 3-0 |
| Campbell (Celtic) (30 mins) | 4-0 |
| McMahon | 5-0 |
| McMahon | 6-0 |
| Hamilton | 7-0 |
| Hamilton | 8-0 |
| Campbell (Celtic) | 9-0 |
| Hamilton | 10-0 |
| Hamilton | 11-0 |

## 73

(Home International Championship)
2 March 1901

Referee: Sutcliffe (England)
The Racecourse, Wrexham (Att: 5,000)

### WALES 1-1 SCOTLAND — Half-time 0-0

| | | |
|---|---|---|
| (2) | George McWATTIE (Queen's Park) | Leigh ROOSE |
| (10) | Nicol SMITH (Rangers) | Samuel MEREDITH |
| (2) | Bernard BATTLES (Celtic) | Charles MORRIS |
| (13) | Neil GIBSON (Rangers) | Maurice PARRY |
| (6) | David RUSSELL (Celtic) | William JONES |
| (6) | John ROBERTSON (Rangers) captain | Edward HUGHES |
| (1) | Mark BELL (Hearts) | David PUGH |
| (3) | Robert WALKER (Hearts) | John JONES |
| (10) | Robert McCOLL (Queen's Park) | Morgan MORGAN-OWEN |
| (8) | John CAMPBELL (Celtic) | Thomas PARRY |
| (6) | Alexander SMITH (Rangers) | Ephraim WILLIAMS |

Goals

| | | |
|---|---|---|
| Robertson (74 mins) | 1-0 | |
| | 1-1 | T.Parry (78 mins) |

## 74

(Home International Championship)
30 March 1901

Referee: Torrans (Ireland)
Crystal Palace, London (Att: 18,520)

### ENGLAND 2-2 SCOTLAND — Half-time 1-0

| | | |
|---|---|---|
| (3) | Henry RENNIE (Hibernian) | John SUTCLIFFE |
| (3) | Bernard BATTLES (Celtic) | James IREMONGER |
| (10) | John DRUMMOND (Rangers) | William OAKLEY |
| (1) | Andrew AITKEN (Newcastle United) | Albert WILKES |
| (2) | Alexander RAISBECK (Liverpool) | Frank FORMAN |
| (7) | John ROBERTSON (Rangers) captain | Ernest NEEDHAM |
| (4) | Robert WALKER (Hearts) | Walter BENNETT |
| (9) | John CAMPBELL (Celtic) | Stephen BLOOMER |
| (11) | Robert McCOLL (Queen's Park) | Gilbert SMITH |
| (6) | Robert HAMILTON (Rangers) | Reginald FOSTER |
| (7) | Alexander SMITH (Rangers) | Frederick BLACKBURN |

Goals

| | | |
|---|---|---|
| | 0-1 | Blackburn (36 mins) |
| Campbell (48 mins) | 1-1 | |
| Hamilton (75 mins) | 2-1 | |
| | 2-2 | Bloomer (80 mins) |

# 1902

| P | W | D | L | F | A |
|---|---|---|---|---|---|
| 3 | 2 | 1 | 0 | 12 | 4 |

## 75

(Home International Championship)
1 March 1902

Referee: Bye (England)
Grosvenor Park, Belfast (Att: 15,000)

### IRELAND 1-5 SCOTLAND — Half-time 0-1

| | | |
|---|---|---|
| (4) | Henry RENNIE (Hibernian) | James NOLAN-WHELAN |
| (11) | Nicol SMITH (Rangers) | William GIBSON |
| (11) | John DRUMMOND (Rangers) | John PYPER |
| (1) | George KEY (Hearts) | John DARLING |
| (1) | Albert BUICK (Hearts) captain | Archibald GOODALL |
| (8) | John ROBERTSON (Rangers) | Robert MILNE |
| (1) | William McCARTNEY (Hibernian) | James CAMPBELL |
| (5) | Robert WALKER (Hearts) | Thomas MORRISON |
| (7) | Robert HAMILTON (Rangers) | Andrew GARA |
| (10) | John CAMPBELL (Celtic) | Alfred KEARNS |
| (8) | Alexander SMITH (Rangers) | Joseph McALLEN |

Goals

| | | |
|---|---|---|
| Hamilton (43 mins) | 1-0 | |
| Walker (49 mins) | 2-0 | |
| Hamilton (70 mins) | 3-0 | |
| Hamilton (74 mins) | 4-0 | |
| Buick (76 mins) | 5-0 | |
| | 5-1 | Milne (89 mins) |

The wreck of the terrace after the Ibrox disaster of 1902 when 26 people fell to their deaths at the Scotland-England game which was abandoned and replayed at Villa Park a month later.

## 76

(Home International Championship)
15 March 1902

Referee: McBride (Ireland)
Cappielow Park, Greenock (Att: 5,284)

### SCOTLAND 5-1 WALES — Half-time 1-0

| | | |
|---|---|---|
| (5) | Henry RENNIE (Hibernian) | Leigh ROOSE |
| (1) | Henry ALLAN (Hearts) | Horace BLEW |
| (12) | John DRUMMOND (Rangers) | Robert MORRIS |
| (3) | Hugh WILSON (Third Lanark) | Maurice PARRY |
| (2) | Albert BUICK (Hearts) | John JONES |
| (9) | John ROBERTSON (Rangers) | William JONES |
| (11) | John CAMPBELL (Celtic) captain | William MEREDITH |
| (6) | Robert WALKER (Hearts) | Llewelyn GRIFFITHS |
| (8) | Robert HAMILTON (Rangers) | Hugh MORGAN-OWEN |
| (6) | Alexander McMAHON (Celtic) | Richard MORRIS |
| (9) | Alexander SMITH (Rangers) | Joseph OWENS |

| | Goals | |
|---|---|---|
| Smith | 1-0 | |
| Buick | 2-0 | |
| Smith | 3-0 | |
| Drummond | 4-0 | |
| | 4-1 | Morgan-Owen |
| Smith (88 mins) | 5-1 | |

## 77

(Home International Championship)
3 May 1902

Referee: Torrans (Ireland)
Villa Park, Birmingham (Att: 15,000)

### ENGLAND 2-2 SCOTLAND — Half-time 0-2

| | | |
|---|---|---|
| (6) | Henry RENNIE (Hibernian) | William GEORGE |
| (12) | Nicol SMITH (Rangers) | Robert CROMPTON |
| (13) | John DRUMMOND (Rangers) | George MOLYNEUX |
| (2) | Andrew AITKEN (Newcastle United) captain | Albert WILKES |
| (3) | Alexander RAISBECK (Liverpool) | Frank FORMAN |
| (10) | John ROBERTSON (Rangers) | Albert HOULKER |
| (1) | Robert TEMPLETON (Aston Villa) | William HOGG |
| (7) | Robert WALKER (Hearts) | Stephen BLOOMER |
| (12) | Robert McCOLL (Newcastle United) | William BEATS |
| (1) | Ronald ORR (Newcastle United) | James SETTLE |
| (10) | Alexander SMITH (Rangers) | John COX |

| | Goals | |
|---|---|---|
| Templeton (3 mins) | 1-0 | |
| Orr (28 mins) | 2-0 | |
| | 2-1 | Settle (65 mins) |
| | 2-2 | Wilkes (67 mins) |

# 1903

| P | W | D | L | F | A |
|---|---|---|---|---|---|
| 3 | 2 | 0 | 1 | 3 | 3 |

## 78

(Home International Championship)
9 March 1903

Referee: Kirkham (England)
The Arms Park, Cardiff (Att: 11,000)

### WALES 0-1 SCOTLAND — Half-time 0-1

| | | |
|---|---|---|
| (7) | Henry RENNIE (Hibernian) | Robert EVANS |
| (1) | Andrew McCOMBIE (Sunderland) | Horace BLEW |
| (1) | James WATSON (Sunderland) | Charles MORRIS |
| (3) | Andrew AITKEN (Newcastle United) | Maurice PARRY |
| (4) | Alexander RAISBECK (Liverpool) captain | Morgan MORGAN-OWEN |
| (11) | John ROBERTSON (Rangers) | Thomas DAVIES |
| (2) | Robert TEMPLETON (Newcastle United) | William MEREDITH |
| (8) | Robert WALKER (Hearts) | Walter WATKINS |
| (12) | John CAMPBELL (Celtic) | Arthur MORRIS |
| (1) | Finlay SPEEDIE (Rangers) | Richard MORRIS |
| (11) | Alexander SMITH (Rangers) | Robert ATHERTON |

| | Goals | |
|---|---|---|
| Speedie (25 mins) | 1-0 | |

## 79

(Home International Championship)
21 March 1903

Referee: Kirkham (England)
Celtic Park, Glasgow (Att: 17,000)

### SCOTLAND 0-2 IRELAND — Half-time 0-1

| | | |
|---|---|---|
| (8) | Henry RENNIE (Hibernian) | William SCOTT |
| (1) | Archibald GRAY (Hibernian) | Alexander McCARTNEY |
| (14) | John DRUMMOND (Rangers) captain | Peter BOYLE |
| (1) | John CROSS (Third Lanark) | John DARLING |
| (1) | Peter ROBERTSON (Dundee) | Robert MILNE |
| (2) | William ORR (Celtic) | Hugh MAGINNIS |
| (1) | David LINDSAY (St Mirren) | John MERCER |
| (9) | Robert WALKER (Hearts) | James SHERIDAN |
| (1) | William PORTEOUS (Hearts) | Maurice CONNOR |
| (2) | Finlay SPEEDIE (Rangers) | Thomas SHANKS |
| (12) | Alexander SMITH (Rangers) | John KIRWAN |

| | Goals | |
|---|---|---|
| | 0-1 | Connor (9 mins) |
| | 0-2 | Kirwan (83 mins) |

Scotland put England goalkeeper Baddeley under pressure at Sheffield in 1903.

## 80

(Home International Championship)
4 April 1903

Referee: Nunnerley (Wales)
Bramall Lane, Sheffield (Att: 32,000)

### ENGLAND 1-2 SCOTLAND — Half-time 1-0

| | | | |
|---|---|---|---|
| (5) | John DOIG (Sunderland) | Thomas BADDELEY | |
| (2) | Andrew McCOMBIE (Sunderland) | Robert CROMPTON | |
| (2) | James WATSON (Sunderland) | George MOLYNEUX | |
| (4) | Andrew AITKEN (Newcastle United) | William JOHNSON | |
| (5) | Alexander RAISBECK (Liverpool) captain | Thomas BOOTH | |
| (12) | John ROBERTSON (Rangers) | Albert HOULKER | |
| (3) | Robert TEMPLETON (Newcastle United) | Henry DAVIS | |
| (10) | Robert WALKER (Hearts) | Percival HUMPHREYS | |
| (9) | Robert HAMILTON (Rangers) | Vivian WOODWARD | |
| (3) | Finlay SPEEDIE (Rangers) | Arthur CAPES | |
| (13) | Alexander SMITH (Rangers) | John COX | |

| | Goals | |
|---|---|---|
| | 0-1 | Woodward (10 mins) |
| Speedie (57 mins) | 1-1 | |
| Walker (59 mins) | 2-1 | |

Goalkeeper Ted Doig punches clear from an England attack at Sheffield in April 1903. Doig performed brilliantly in restricting England to only one goal as the Scots won 2-1.

# 1904

| P | W | D | L | F | A |
|---|---|---|---|---|---|
| 3 | 0 | 2 | 1 | 2 | 3 |

## 81

(Home International Championship)
12 March 1904

Referee: Kirkham (England)
Dens Park, Dundee (Att: 12,000)

### SCOTLAND 1-1 WALES — Half-time 1-0

| | | | |
|---|---|---|---|
| (1) | Leslie SKENE (Queen's Park) | David DAVIES | |
| (1) | Thomas JACKSON (St Mirren) | Horace BLEW | |
| (1) | James SHARP (Dundee) captain | Thomas DAVIES | |
| (3) | William ORR (Celtic) | George RICHARDS | |
| (1) | Thomas SLOAN (Third Lanark) | Edward HUGHES | |
| (13) | John ROBERTSON (Rangers) | John JONES | |
| (4) | John WALKER (Rangers) | Arthur DAVIES | |
| (11) | Robert WALKER (Hearts) | Walter WATKINS | |
| (1) | Alexander BENNETT (Celtic) | Arthur GREEN | |
| (1) | Alexander MacFARLANE (Dundee) | Richard MORRIS | |
| (1) | George WILSON (Hearts) | Robert ATHERTON | |

| | Goals | |
|---|---|---|
| R.Walker (5 mins) | 1-0 | |
| | 1-1 | Atherton (65 mins) |

## 82

(Home International Championship)
26 March 1904

Referee: Kirkham (England)
Dalymount Park, Dublin (Att: 1,000)

### IRELAND 1-1 SCOTLAND — Half-time 0-1

| | | | |
|---|---|---|---|
| (9) | Henry RENNIE (Hibernian) | William SCOTT | |
| (2) | Thomas JACKSON (St Mirren) | William McCRACKEN | |
| (1) | John CAMERON (St Mirren) | Alexander McCARTNEY | |
| (1) | George HENDERSON (Rangers) | English McCONNELL | |
| (1) | Charles THOMSON (Hearts) | Robert MILNE | |
| (14) | John ROBERTSON (Rangers) captain | Hugh MAGINNIS | |
| (5) | John WALKER (Rangers) | James CAMPBELL | |
| (12) | Robert WALKER (Hearts) | James SHERIDAN | |
| (10) | Robert HAMILTON (Rangers) | Harold O'REILLY | |
| (4) | Hugh WILSON (Third Lanark) | Harold SLOAN | |
| (14) | Alexander SMITH (Rangers) | John KIRWAN | |

| | Goals | |
|---|---|---|
| Hamilton (22 mins) | 1-0 | |
| | 1-1 | Sheridan (74 mins) |

## 83

(Home International Championship)
9 April 1904

Referee: Nunnerley (Wales)
Celtic Park, Glasgow (Att: 45,000)

### SCOTLAND 0-1 ENGLAND — Half-time 0-0

| | | | |
|---|---|---|---|
| (1) | Peter McBRIDE (Preston North End) | Thomas BADDELEY | |
| (3) | Thomas JACKSON (St Mirren) | Robert CROMPTON | |
| (3) | James WATSON (Sunderland) | Herbert BURGESS | |
| (5) | Andrew AITKEN (Newcastle United) | Samuel WOLSTENHOLME | |
| (6) | Alexander RAISBECK (Liverpool) | Bernard WILKINSON | |
| (15) | John ROBERTSON (Rangers) captain | Alexander LEAKE | |
| (1) | Thomas NIBLO (Aston Villa) | John RUTHERFORD | |
| (13) | Robert WALKER (Hearts) | Stephen BLOOMER | |
| (1) | Alexander BROWN (Middlesbrough) | Vivian WOODWARD | |
| (2) | Ronald ORR (Newcastle United) | Stanley HARRIS | |
| (4) | Robert TEMPLETON (Newcastle United) | Frederick BLACKBURN | |

| Goals | |
|---|---|
| 0-1 | Bloomer (64 mins) |

# 1905

| P | W | D | L | F | A |
|---|---|---|---|---|---|
| 3 | 1 | 0 | 2 | 5 | 4 |

## 84

(Home International Championship)
6 March 1905

Referee: Kirkham (England)
The Racecourse, Wrexham (Att: 6,000)

### WALES 3-1 SCOTLAND — Half-time 1-0

| | | | |
|---|---|---|---|
| (10) | Henry RENNIE (Hibernian) | Leigh ROOSE | |
| (3) | Andrew McCOMBIE (Newcastle United) | Horace BLEW | |
| (4) | Thomas JACKSON (St Mirren) captain | Charles MORRIS | |
| (6) | Andrew AITKEN (Newcastle United) | George LATHAM | |
| (2) | Charles THOMSON (Hearts) | Edward HUGHES | |
| (16) | John ROBERTSON (Rangers) | John HUGHES | |
| (5) | Robert TEMPLETON (Woolwich Arsenal) | William MEREDITH | |
| (14) | Robert WALKER (Hearts) | Arthur DAVIES | |
| (1) | Samuel KENNEDY (Partick Thistle) | Walter WATKINS | |
| (1) | Thomas FITCHIE (Woolwich Arsenal) | Arthur MORRIS | |
| (15) | Alexander SMITH (Rangers) | Alfred OLIVER | |

| | Goals | |
|---|---|---|
| | 0-1 | Watkins (30 mins) |
| | 0-2 | A.Morris (47 mins) |
| | 0-3 | Meredith (76 mins) |
| Robertson (86 mins) | 1-3 | |

**85**

(Home International Championship)
18 March 1905

Referee: Kirkham (England)
Celtic Park, Glasgow (Att: 35,000)

## SCOTLAND 4-0 IRELAND | Half-time 2-0

| | | |
|---|---|---|
| (1) | William HOWDEN (Partick Thistle) | William SCOTT |
| (1) | Donald McLEOD (Celtic) | William McCRACKEN |
| (1) | William McINTOSH (Third Lanark) | Alexander McCARTNEY |
| (14) | Neil GIBSON (Partick Thistle) captain | John DARLING |
| (3) | Charles THOMSON (Hearts) | James CONNOR |
| (1) | James HAY (Celtic) | English McCONNELL |
| (1) | James McMENEMY (Celtic) | John MERCER |
| (15) | Robert WALKER (Hearts) | James MAXWELL |
| (1) | James QUINN (Celtic) | Neill MURPHY |
| (1) | Peter SOMERS (Celtic) | Charles O'HAGAN |
| (2) | George WILSON (Hearts) | John KIRWAN |

Goals

| | |
|---|---|
| Thomson (14 mins pen) | 1-0 |
| Walker (35 mins) | 2-0 |
| Quinn (50 mins) | 3-0 |
| Thomson (61 mins pen) | 4-0 |

**86**

(Home International Championship)
1 April 1905

Referee: Nunnerley (Wales)
Crystal Palace, London (Att: 32,000)

## ENGLAND 1-0 SCOTLAND | Half-time 0-0

| | | |
|---|---|---|
| (1) | John LYALL (Sheffield Wednesday) | James LINACRE |
| (4) | Andrew McCOMBIE (Newcastle United) | Howard SPENCER |
| (4) | James WATSON (Sunderland) | Herbert SMITH |
| (7) | Andrew AITKEN (Newcastle United) | Herod RUDDLESDIN |
| (4) | Charles THOMSON (Hearts) captain | Charles ROBERTS |
| (1) | Peter McWILLIAM (Newcastle United) | Alexander LEAKE |
| (16) | Robert WALKER (Hearts) | John SHARP |
| (1) | James HOWIE (Newcastle United) | Stephen BLOOMER |
| (1) | Alexander YOUNG (Everton) | Vivian WOODWARD |
| (2) | Peter SOMERS (Celtic) | Joseph BACHE |
| (3) | George WILSON (Hearts) | George BRIDGETT |

Goals

| | | |
|---|---|---|
| | 0-1 | Bache (80 mins) |

# 1906

| P | W | D | L | F | A |
|---|---|---|---|---|---|
| 3 | 2 | 0 | 1 | 3 | 3 |

**87**

(Home International Championship)
3 March 1906

Referee: Lewis (England)
Tynecastle Park, Edinburgh (Att: 25,000)

## SCOTLAND 0-2 WALES | Half-time 0-0

| | | |
|---|---|---|
| (1) | James RAESIDE (Third Lanark) | Leigh ROOSE |
| (2) | Donald McLEOD (Celtic) | Horace BLEW |
| (1) | Andrew RICHMOND (Queen's Park) | Charles MORRIS |
| (1) | Alexander McNAIR (Celtic) | Edwin HUGHES |
| (5) | Charles THOMSON (Hearts) captain | Morgan MORGAN-OWEN |
| (1) | John MAY (Rangers) | George LATHAM |
| (1) | George STEWART (Hibernian) | William JONES |
| (2) | Alexander MacFARLANE (Dundee) | Richard MORRIS |
| (2) | James QUINN (Celtic) | John JONES |
| (2) | Thomas FITCHIE (Woolwich Arsenal) | Richard JONES |
| (4) | George WILSON (Hearts) | Robert EVANS |

Goals

| | | |
|---|---|---|
| 0-1 | W.Jones (50 mins) | |
| 0-2 | J.Jones (65 mins) | |

**88**

(Home International Championship)
17 March 1906

Referee: Bye (England)
Dalymount Park, Dublin (Att: 8,000)

## IRELAND 0-1 SCOTLAND | Half-time 0-0

| | | |
|---|---|---|
| (11) | Henry RENNIE (Hibernian) | Frederick McKEE |
| (3) | Donald McLEOD (Celtic) | George WILLIS |
| (1) | David HILL (Third Lanark) | John DARLING |
| (1) | James YOUNG (Celtic) | John WRIGHT |
| (6) | Charles THOMSON (Hearts) captain | Robert MILNE |
| (2) | John MAY (Rangers) | Joseph LEDWIDGE |
| (1) | Gladstone HAMILTON (Port Glasgow Athletic) | Andrew HUNTER |
| (17) | Robert WALKER (Hearts) | Thomas MULHOLLAND |
| (3) | James QUINN (Celtic) | Thomas WADDELL |
| (3) | Thomas FITCHIE (Woolwich Arsenal) | Charles O'HAGAN |
| (16) | Alexander SMITH (Rangers) | John KIRWAN |

Goals

| | |
|---|---|
| Fitchie (52 mins) | 1-0 |

Scotland against England at the Crystal Palace in April 1905. England were outplayed but won the match thanks to a brilliant individual goal from Joe Bache 10 minutes from time.

# SCŌTLAND'S NEW INTERNATIONALS

Crawford.]
**G. WILSON**
(*Heart of Midlothian*).

R. Thiele.]
**CHAS. THOMSON**
(*Heart of Midlothian*).

Maclure MacDonald.]
**J. HAY**
(*Celtic*).

Maclure MacDonald.]
**P. SOMERS**
(*Celtic*).

Elbourne.]
**T. T. FITCHIE**
(*Woolwich Arsenal*)

Stuart and Winfield.]
**P. MacWILLIAM**
(*Newcastle United*)

Furniss.]
**J. LYALL**
(*Sheffield Wednesday*).

Starfield.]
**A. YOUNG**
(*Everton*).

C. FOLKARD.

J. H. Thompson.]
**J. HOWIE**
(*Newcastle United*).

How the 1905 *The Book of Football* showed 'Scotland's new internationals'.

**89**

(Home International Championship)
7 April 1906

Referee: Nunnerley (Wales)
Hampden Park, Glasgow (Att: 102,741)

### SCOTLAND 2-1 ENGLAND — Half-time 1-0

| | | | |
|---|---|---|---|
| (2) | Peter McBRIDE (Preston North End) | | James ASHCROFT |
| (4) | Donald McLEOD (Celtic) | | Robert CROMPTON |
| (1) | William DUNLOP (Liverpool) | | Herbert BURGESS |
| (8) | Andrew AITKEN (Newcastle United) | | Benjamin WARREN |
| (7) | Alexander RAISBECK (Liverpool) captain | | Colin VEITCH |
| (2) | Peter McWILLIAM (Newcastle United) | | Joseph MAKEPEACE |
| (2) | George STEWART (Hibernian) | | Richard BOND |
| (1) | James HOWIE (Newcastle United) | | Samuel DAY |
| (1) | Alexander MENZIES (Hearts) | | Albert SHEPHERD |
| (1) | George LIVINGSTON (Manchester City) | | Stanley HARRIS |
| (17) | Alexander SMITH (Rangers) | | James CONLIN |

| | Goals | |
|---|---|---|
| Howie (40 mins) | 1-0 | |
| Howie (55 mins) | 2-0 | |
| | 2-1 | Shepherd (81 mins) |

# 1907

| P | W | D | L | F | A |
|---|---|---|---|---|---|
| 3 | 1 | 1 | 1 | 4 | 2 |

**90**

(Home International Championship)
4 March 1907

Referee: Mason (England)
The Racecourse, Wrexham (Att: 7,715)

### WALES 1-0 SCOTLAND — Half-time 0-0

| | | | |
|---|---|---|---|
| (3) | Peter McBRIDE (Preston North End) | | Leigh ROOSE |
| (5) | Thomas JACKSON (St Mirren) | | Horace BLEW |
| (2) | James SHARP (Woolwich Arsenal) | | Charles MORRIS |
| (9) | Andrew AITKEN (Middlesbrough) | | George LATHAM |
| (7) | Charles THOMSON (Hearts) captain | | Lloyd DAVIES |
| (2) | Peter McWILLIAM (Newcastle United) | | Ioan PRICE |
| (3) | George STEWART (Manchester City) | | William MEREDITH |
| (2) | George LIVINGSTON (Rangers) | | William JONES |
| (2) | Alexander YOUNG (Everton) | | Hugh MORGAN-OWEN |
| (4) | Thomas FITCHIE (Queen's Park) | | Arthur MORRIS |
| (18) | Alexander SMITH (Rangers) | | Gordon JONES |

| | Goals | |
|---|---|---|
| | 0-1 | A. Morris (50 mins) |

**91**

(Home International Championship)
16 March 1907

Referee: Lewis (England)
Celtic Park, Glasgow (Att: 26,000)

### SCOTLAND 3-0 IRELAND — Half-time 1-0

| | | | |
|---|---|---|---|
| (1) | William MUIR (Dundee) | | William SCOTT |
| (6) | Thomas JACKSON (St Mirren) | | George WILLIS |
| (1) | William AGNEW (Kilmarnock) | | Alexander McCARTNEY |
| (1) | William KEY (Queen's Park) | | John WRIGHT |
| (8) | Charles THOMSON (Hearts) captain | | James CONNOR |
| (2) | Alexander McNAIR (Celtic) | | George McCLURE |
| (2) | Alexander BENNETT (Celtic) | | John BLAIR |
| (18) | Robert WALKER (Hearts) | | James MAXWELL |
| (1) | Frank O'ROURKE (Airdrie) | | Edward McGUIRE |
| (3) | Peter SOMERS (Celtic) | | Charles O'HAGAN |
| (1) | John FRASER (Dundee) | | Samuel YOUNG |

| | Goals | |
|---|---|---|
| O'Rourke (40 mins) | 1-0 | |
| Walker (48 mins) | 2-0 | |
| Thomson (82 mins pen) | 3-0 | |

**92**

(Home International Championship)
6 April 1907

Referee: Robertson (Scotland)
St James' Park, Newcastle (Att: 35,829)

### ENGLAND 1-1 SCOTLAND — Half-time 1-1

| | | | |
|---|---|---|---|
| (4) | Peter McBRIDE (Preston North End) | | Samuel HARDY |
| (9) | Charles THOMSON (Hearts) | | Robert CROMPTON |
| (3) | James SHARP (Woolwich Arsenal) | | Jesse PENNINGTON |
| (10) | Andrew AITKEN (Middlesbrough) | | Benjamin WARREN |
| (8) | Alexander RAISBECK (Liverpool) captain | | William WEDLOCK |
| (4) | Peter McWILLIAM (Newcastle United) | | Colin VEITCH |
| (4) | George STEWART (Manchester City) | | John RUTHERFORD |
| (19) | Robert WALKER (Hearts) | | Stephen BLOOMER |
| (1) | Andrew WILSON (Sheffield Wednesday) | | Vivian WOODWARD |
| (1) | Walter WHITE (Bolton Wanderers) | | James STEWART |
| (5) | George WILSON (Everton) | | Harold HARDMAN |

| | Goals | |
|---|---|---|
| Crompton (2 mins o.g.) | 1-0 | |
| | 1-1 | Bloomer (42 mins) |

# 1908

| P | W | D | L | F | A |
|---|---|---|---|---|---|
| 3 | 2 | 1 | 0 | 8 | 2 |

**93**

(Home International Championship)
7 March 1908

Referee: Mason (England)
Dens Park, Dundee (Att: 18,000)

### SCOTLAND 2-1 WALES — Half-time 0-1

| | | | |
|---|---|---|---|
| (12) | Henry RENNIE (Hibernian) | | Leigh ROOSE |
| (2) | William AGNEW (Kilmarnock) | | Horace BLEW |
| (1) | George CHAPLIN (Dundee) | | Charles MORRIS |
| (3) | Alexander McNAIR (Celtic) | | Edwin HUGHES |
| (10) | Charles THOMSON (Hearts) captain | | Maurice PARRY |
| (1) | James GALT (Rangers) | | Lloyd DAVIES |
| (3) | Alexander BENNETT (Celtic) | | William DAVIES |
| (20) | Robert WALKER (Hearts) | | William JONES |
| (1) | James SPEIRS (Rangers) | | William DAVIES |
| (3) | Alexander MacFARLANE (Dundee) | | Arthur GREEN |
| (1) | William LENNIE (Aberdeen) | | Robert EVANS |

| | Goals | |
|---|---|---|
| | 0-1 | Jones (30 mins) |
| Bennett (60 mins) | 1-1 | |
| Lennie (87 mins) | 2-1 | |

**94**

(Home International Championship)
14 March 1908

Referee: Ibbotson (England)
Dalymount Park, Dublin (Att: 10,000)

### IRELAND 0-5 SCOTLAND — Half-time 0-2

| | | | |
|---|---|---|---|
| (13) | Henry RENNIE (Hibernian) | | William SCOTT |
| (1) | James MITCHELL (Kilmarnock) | | Alexander CRAIG |
| (3) | William AGNEW (Kilmarnock) | | Alexander McCARTNEY |
| (3) | John MAY (Rangers) | | Valentine HARRIS |
| (11) | Charles THOMSON (Hearts) captain | | James CONNOR |
| (2) | James GALT (Rangers) | | English McCONNELL |
| (6) | Robert TEMPLETON (Kilmarnock) | | John BLAIR |
| (21) | Robert WALKER (Hearts) | | Denis HANNON |
| (4) | James QUINN (Celtic) | | William ANDREWS |
| (13) | Robert McCOLL (Queen's Park) | | Charles O'HAGAN |
| (2) | William LENNIE (Aberdeen) | | Samuel YOUNG |

| | Goals | |
|---|---|---|
| Quinn (3 mins) | 1-0 | |
| Galt (23 mins) | 2-0 | |
| Quinn | 3-0 | |
| Quinn (70 mins) | 4-0 | |
| Quinn (75 mins) | 5-0 | |

**95**

(Home International Championship)
4 April 1908

Referee: Mason (England)
Hampden Park, Glasgow (Att: 121,452)

### SCOTLAND 1-1 ENGLAND — Half-time 1-0

| | | | |
|---|---|---|---|
| (5) | Peter McBRIDE (Preston North End) | | Samuel HARDY |
| (4) | Alexander McNAIR (Celtic) | | Robert CROMPTON |
| (4) | James SHARP (Woolwich Arsenal) | | Jesse PENNINGTON |
| (11) | Andrew AITKEN (Middlesbrough) | | Benjamin WARREN |
| (12) | Charles THOMSON (Hearts) captain | | William WEDLOCK |
| (4) | John MAY (Rangers) | | Evelyn LINTOTT |
| (3) | James HOWIE (Newcastle United) | | John RUTHERFORD |
| (22) | Robert WALKER (Hearts) | | Vivian WOODWARD |
| (2) | Andrew WILSON (Sheffield Wednesday) | | George HILSDON |
| (2) | Walter WHITE (Bolton Wanderers) | | James WINDRIDGE |
| (5) | James QUINN (Celtic) | | George BRIDGETT |

| | Goals | |
|---|---|---|
| Wilson (27 mins) | 1-0 | |
| | 1-1 | Windridge (75 mins) |

# 1909

| | P | W | D | L | F | A |
|---|---|---|---|---|---|---|
| | 3 | 1 | 0 | 2 | 7 | 5 |

## 96

(Home International Championship)
1 March 1909

Referee: Campbell (England)
The Racecourse, Wrexham (Att: 6,000)

### WALES 3-2 SCOTLAND — Half-time 3-0

| | | |
|---|---|---|
| (6) | Peter McBRIDE (Preston North End) | Leigh ROOSE |
| (1) | Thomas COLLINS (Hearts) | Horace BLEW |
| (5) | James SHARP (Fulham) | Charles MORRIS |
| (5) | John MAY (Rangers) | Maurice PARRY |
| (13) | Charles THOMSON (Sunderland) captain | Ernest PEAKE |
| (5) | Peter McWILLIAM (Newcastle United) | Ioan PRICE |
| (4) | Alexander BENNETT (Rangers) | William MEREDITH |
| (1) | John HUNTER (Dundee) | George WYNN |
| (23) | Robert WALKER (Hearts) | William DAVIES |
| (4) | Peter SOMERS (Celtic) | William JONES |
| (1) | Harold PAUL (Queen's Park) | Robert EVANS |

Goals

| | | |
|---|---|---|
| | 0-1 | Davies (25 mins) |
| | 0-2 | Jones (29 mins) |
| | 0-3 | Davies (39 mins) |
| Walker (70 mins) | 1-3 | |
| Paul (73 mins) | 2-3 | |

## 97

(Home International Championship)
15 March 1909

Referee: Mason (England)
Ibrox Park, Glasgow (Att: 24,000)

### SCOTLAND 5-0 IRELAND — Half-time 2-0

| | | |
|---|---|---|
| (1) | James BROWNLIE (Third Lanark) | William SCOTT |
| (1) | James MAIN (Hibernian) | Alexander CRAIG |
| (5) | James WATSON (Middlesbrough) | Alexander McCARTNEY |
| (1) | William WALKER (Clyde) | Valentine HARRIS |
| (1) | James STARK (Rangers) captain | English McCONNELL |
| (2) | James HAY (Celtic) | Harold SLOAN |
| (5) | Alexander BENNETT (Rangers) | Andrew HUNTER |
| (2) | James McMENEMY (Celtic) | William LACEY |
| (1) | Alexander THOMSON (Airdrie) | William GREER |
| (4) | Alexander MacFARLANE (Dundee) | Charles WEBB |
| (2) | Harold PAUL (Queen's Park) | John KIRWAN |

Goals

| | |
|---|---|
| McMenemy (15 mins) | 1-0 |
| MacFarlane (20 mins) | 2-0 |
| Thomson (48 mins) | 3-0 |
| McMenemy (77 mins) | 4-0 |
| Paul (84 mins) | 5-0 |

## 98

(Home International Championship)
3 April 1909

Referee: Stark (Scotland)
Crystal Palace, London (Att: 27,000)

### ENGLAND 2-0 SCOTLAND — Half-time 2-0

| | | |
|---|---|---|
| (2) | James BROWNLIE (Third Lanark) | Samuel HARDY |
| (2) | John CAMERON (Chelsea) | Robert CROMPTON |
| (6) | James WATSON (Middlesbrough) | Jesse PENNINGTON |
| (5) | Alexander McNAIR (Celtic) | Benjamin WARREN |
| (2) | James STARK (Rangers) captain | William WEDLOCK |
| (6) | Peter McWILLIAM (Newcastle United) | Evelyn LINTOTT |
| (6) | Alexander BENNETT (Rangers) | Frederick PENTLAND |
| (24) | Robert WALKER (Hearts) | Harold FLEMING |
| (6) | James QUINN (Celtic) | Bertram FREEMAN |
| (6) | George WILSON (Newcastle United) | George HOLLEY |
| (3) | Harold PAUL (Queen's Park) | George WALL |

Goals

| | | |
|---|---|---|
| | 0-1 | Wall (3 mins) |
| | 0-2 | Wall (10 mins) |

# 1910

| | P | W | D | L | F | A |
|---|---|---|---|---|---|---|
| | 3 | 2 | 0 | 1 | 3 | 1 |

## 99

(Home International Championship)
5 March 1910

Referee: Bamlett (England)
Rugby Park, Kilmarnock (Att: 22,000)

### SCOTLAND 1-0 WALES — Half-time 0-0

| | | |
|---|---|---|
| (3) | James BROWNLIE (Third Lanark) | Leigh ROOSE |
| (1) | George LAW (Rangers) | Jeffrey JONES |
| (2) | James MITCHELL (Kilmarnock) | Charles MORRIS |
| (6) | Alexander McNAIR (Celtic) | Edwin HUGHES |
| (1) | William LONEY (Celtic) | Ernest PEAKE |
| (3) | James HAY (Celtic) captain | Llewelyn DAVIES |
| (7) | Alexander BENNETT (Rangers) | William MEREDITH |
| (3) | James McMENEMY (Celtic) | William DAVIES |
| (7) | James QUINN (Celtic) | Evan JONES |
| (1) | Andrew DEVINE (Falkirk) | Arthur MORRIS |
| (1) | George ROBERTSON (Motherwell) | Robert EVANS |

Goals

| | |
|---|---|
| Devine (86 mins) | 1-0 |

## 100

(Home International Championship)
19 March 1910

Referee: Howcroft (England)
Windsor Park, Belfast (Att: 17,000)

### IRELAND 1-0 SCOTLAND — Half-time 0-0

| | | |
|---|---|---|
| (4) | James BROWNLIE (Third Lanark) | William SCOTT |
| (2) | George LAW (Rangers) | Samuel BURNISON |
| (3) | James MITCHELL (Kilmarnock) | Patrick McCANN |
| (2) | William WALKER (Clyde) | Valentine HARRIS |
| (2) | William LONEY (Celtic) | English McCONNELL |
| (4) | James HAY (Celtic) captain | John DARLING |
| (1) | George SINCLAIR (Hearts) | Walter RENNEVILLE |
| (1) | John McTAVISH (Falkirk) | William LACEY |
| (8) | James QUINN (Celtic) | John MURRAY |
| (1) | Alexander HIGGINS (Newcastle United) | John MURPHY |
| (7) | Robert TEMPLETON (Kilmarnock) | Frank THOMPSON |

Goals

| | | |
|---|---|---|
| | 0-1 | Thompson (65 mins) |

## 101

(Home International Championship)
2 April 1910

Referee: Mason (England)
Hampden Park, Glasgow (Att: 106,205)

### SCOTLAND 2-0 ENGLAND — Half-time 2-0

| | | |
|---|---|---|
| (5) | James BROWNLIE (Third Lanark) | Samuel HARDY |
| (3) | George LAW (Rangers) | Robert CROMPTON |
| (5) | James HAY (Celtic) | Jesse PENNINGTON |
| (12) | Andrew AITKEN (Leicester Fosse) | Andrew DUCAT |
| (14) | Charles THOMSON (Sunderland) captain | William WEDLOCK |
| (7) | Peter McWILLIAM (Newcastle United) | Joseph MAKEPEACE |
| (8) | Alexander BENNETT (Rangers) | Richard BOND |
| (4) | James McMENEMY (Celtic) | William HIBBERT |
| (9) | James QUINN (Celtic) | John PARKINSON |
| (2) | Alexander HIGGINS (Newcastle United) | Harold HARDINGE |
| (8) | Robert TEMPLETON (Kilmarnock) | George WALL |

Goals

| | |
|---|---|
| McMenemy (20 mins) | 1-0 |
| Quinn (32 mins) | 2-0 |

# 1911

| P | W | D | L | F | A |
|---|---|---|---|---|---|
| 3 | 1 | 2 | 0 | 5 | 3 |

## 102
(Home International Championship)
6 March 1911

Referee: Mason (England)
Ninian Park, Cardiff (Att: 14,000)

### WALES 2-2 SCOTLAND — Half-time 1-1

| | | |
|---|---|---|
| (6) | James BROWNLIE (Third Lanark) | Leigh ROOSE |
| (1) | Donald COLMAN (Aberdeen) | Charles MORRIS |
| (1) | John WALKER (Swindon Town) | Thomas HEWITT |
| (1) | Thomas TAIT (Sunderland) | Edwin HUGHES |
| (1) | Wilfrid LOW (Newcastle United) | Lloyd DAVIES |
| (8) | Peter McWILLIAM (Newcastle United) captain | Llewelyn DAVIES |
| (9) | Alexander BENNETT (Rangers) | William MEREDITH |
| (5) | James McMENEMY (Celtic) | Evan JONES |
| (1) | William REID (Rangers) | William DAVIES |
| (5) | Alexander MacFARLANE (Dundee) | Arthur MORRIS |
| (11) | Robert HAMILTON (Dundee) | Edward VIZARD |

Goals

| | | |
|---|---|---|
| | 0-1 | A.Morris (20 mins) |
| Hamilton | 1-1 | |
| | 1-2 | A.Morris (67 mins) |
| Hamilton (89 mins) | 2-2 | |

## 103
(Home International Championship)
18 March 1911

Referee: Bamlett (England)
Celtic Park, Glasgow (Att: 32,000)

### SCOTLAND 2-0 IRELAND — Half-time 1-0

| | | |
|---|---|---|
| (7) | James BROWNLIE (Third Lanark) | William SCOTT |
| (2) | Donald COLMAN (Aberdeen) | Samuel BURNISON |
| (2) | John WALKER (Swindon Town) | Patrick McCANN |
| (13) | Andrew AITKEN (Leicester Fosse) captain | Valentine HARRIS |
| (15) | Charles THOMSON (Sunderland) | James CONNOR |
| (6) | James HAY (Celtic) | Harold HAMPTON |
| (1) | Angus DOUGLAS (Chelsea) | William LACEY |
| (6) | James McMENEMY (Celtic) | Denis HANNON |
| (2) | William REID (Rangers) | John McDONNELL |
| (3) | Alexander HIGGINS (Newcastle United) | Charles WEBB |
| (19) | Alexander SMITH (Rangers) | Thomas WALKER |

Goals

| | | |
|---|---|---|
| Reid (23 mins) | 1-0 | |
| McMenemy (53 mins) | 2-0 | |

## 104
(Home International Championship)
1 April 1911

Referee: Nunnerley (Wales)
Goodison Park, Liverpool (Att: 38,000)

### ENGLAND 1-1 SCOTLAND — Half-time 1-0

| | | |
|---|---|---|
| (1) | James LAWRENCE (Newcastle United) | Reginald WILLIAMSON |
| (3) | Donald COLMAN (Aberdeen) | Robert CROMPTON |
| (3) | John WALKER (Swindon Town) | Jesse PENNINGTON |
| (14) | Andrew AITKEN (Leicester Fosse) | Benjamin WARREN |
| (2) | Wilfrid LOW (Newcastle United) | William WEDLOCK |
| (7) | James HAY (Celtic) captain | Kenneth HUNT |
| (10) | Alexander BENNETT (Rangers) | John SIMPSON |
| (7) | James McMENEMY (Celtic) | James STEWART |
| (3) | William REID (Rangers) | George WEBB |
| (4) | Alexander HIGGINS (Newcastle United) | Joseph BACHE |
| (20) | Alexander SMITH (Rangers) | Robert EVANS |

Goals

| | | |
|---|---|---|
| | 0-1 | Stewart (20 mins) |
| Higgins (88 mins) | 1-1 | |

# 1912

| P | W | D | L | F | A |
|---|---|---|---|---|---|
| 3 | 2 | 1 | 0 | 6 | 2 |

## 105
(Home International Championship)
2 March 1912

Referee: Mason (England)
Tynecastle Park, Edinburgh (Att: 32,000)

### SCOTLAND 1-0 WALES — Half-time 0-0

| | | |
|---|---|---|
| (8) | James BROWNLIE (Third Lanark) | Robert EVANS |
| (7) | Alexander McNAIR (Celtic) | Llewelyn DAVIES |
| (4) | John WALKER (Swindon Town) | Lloyd DAVIES |
| (1) | Robert MERCER (Hearts) | Joseph JONES |
| (16) | Charles THOMSON (Sunderland) captain | Edwin HUGHES |
| (8) | James HAY (Newcastle United) | Moses RUSSELL |
| (2) | George SINCLAIR (Hearts) | William MEREDITH |
| (8) | James McMENEMY (Celtic) | George WYNN |
| (10) | James QUINN (Celtic) | Evan JONES |
| (25) | Robert WALKER (Hearts) | James WILLIAMS |
| (2) | George ROBERTSON (Sheffield Wednesday) | Edward VIZARD |

Goals

| | | |
|---|---|---|
| Quinn (87 mins) | 1-0 | |

## 106
(Home International Championship)
16 March 1912

Referee: Bamlett (England)
Windsor Park, Belfast (Att: 12,000)

### IRELAND 1-4 SCOTLAND — Half-time 1-2

| | | |
|---|---|---|
| (9) | James BROWNLIE (Third Lanark) | James HANNA |
| (8) | Alexander McNAIR (Celtic) captain | George WILLIS |
| (5) | John WALKER (Swindon Town) | Alexander CRAIG |
| (1) | James GORDON (Rangers) | John DARLING |
| (3) | Wilfrid LOW (Newcastle United) | Patrick O'CONNELL |
| (1) | Alexander BELL (Manchester United) | Joseph MORAN |
| (3) | George SINCLAIR (Hearts) | John HOUSTON |
| (26) | Robert WALKER (Hearts) | James McKNIGHT |
| (4) | William REID (Rangers) | James McAULEY |
| (1) | Walter AITKENHEAD (Blackburn Rovers) | Joseph ENRIGHT |
| (9) | Robert TEMPLETON (Kilmarnock) | Samuel YOUNG |

Goals

| | | |
|---|---|---|
| Aitkenhead (8 mins) | 1-0 | |
| Aitkenhead (23 mins) | 2-0 | |
| | 2-1 | McKnight (42 mins pen) |
| Reid | 3-1 | |
| R.Walker | 4-1 | |

## 107
(Home International Championship)
23 March 1912

Referee: Mason (England)
Hampden Park, Glasgow (Att: 127,307)

### SCOTLAND 1-1 ENGLAND — Half-time 1-1

| | | |
|---|---|---|
| (10) | James BROWNLIE (Third Lanark) | Reginald WILLIAMSON |
| (9) | Alexander McNAIR (Celtic) captain | Robert CROMPTON |
| (6) | John WALKER (Swindon Town) | Jesse PENNINGTON |
| (2) | James GORDON (Rangers) | John BRITTLETON |
| (17) | Charles THOMSON (Sunderland) | William WEDLOCK |
| (9) | James HAY (Newcastle United) | Joseph MAKEPEACE |
| (10) | Robert TEMPLETON (Kilmarnock) | John SIMPSON |
| (27) | Robert WALKER (Hearts) | Frank JEFFERIS |
| (1) | David McLEAN (Sheffield Wednesday) | Bertram FREEMAN |
| (3) | Andrew WILSON (Sheffield Wednesday) | George HOLLEY |
| (11) | James QUINN (Celtic) | George WALL |

Goals

| | | |
|---|---|---|
| Wilson (7 mins) | 1-0 | |
| | 1-1 | Holley (13 mins) |

# 1913

| P | W | D | L | F | A |
|---|---|---|---|---|---|
| 3 | 1 | 1 | 1 | 2 | 2 |

## 108
(Home International Championship)
3 March 1913

Referee: Baker (England)
The Racecourse, Wrexham (Att: 8,000)

### WALES 0-0 SCOTLAND

| (11) | James BROWNLIE (Third Lanark) | William BAILIFF |
|---|---|---|
| (1) | Robert ORROCK (Falkirk) | Thomas HEWITT |
| (7) | John WALKER (Swindon Town) | Llewelyn DAVIES |
| (3) | James GORDON (Rangers) | Edwin HUGHES |
| (18) | Charles THOMSON (Sunderland) captain | Lloyd DAVIES |
| (1) | James CAMPBELL (Sheffield Wednesday) | William JONES |
| (1) | Andrew McATEE (Celtic) | William MEREDITH |
| (28) | Robert WALKER (Hearts) | George WYNN |
| (5) | William REID (Rangers) | Walter DAVIS |
| (4) | Andrew WILSON (Sheffield Wednesday) | James ROBERTS |
| (11) | Robert TEMPLETON (Kilmarnock) | Edward VIZARD |

## 109
(Home International Championship)
15 March 1913

Referee: Adams (England)
Dalymount Park, Dublin (Att: 12,000)

### IRELAND 1-2 SCOTLAND          Half-time 1-2

| (12) | James BROWNLIE (Third Lanark) | William SCOTT |
|---|---|---|
| (4) | Donald COLMAN (Aberdeen) captain | William McCONNELL |
| (8) | John WALKER (Swindon Town) | Peter WARREN |
| (2) | Robert MERCER (Hearts) | William ANDREWS |
| (1) | Thomas LOGAN (Falkirk) | Valentine HARRIS |
| (1) | Peter NELLIES (Hearts) | Harold HAMPTON |
| (11) | Alexander BENNETT (Rangers) | John HOUSTON |
| (4) | James GORDON (Rangers) | James McKNIGHT |
| (6) | William REID (Rangers) | William GILLESPIE |
| (1) | James CROAL (Falkirk) | James McAULEY |
| (3) | George ROBERTSON (Sheffield Wednesday) | Frank THOMPSON |

| | Goals | |
|---|---|---|
| Reid (16 mins) | 1-0 | |
| Bennett (32 mins) | 2-0 | |
| | 2-1 | McKnight (42 mins) |

## 110
(Home International Championship)
5 April 1913

Referee: Jackson (Scotland)
Stamford Bridge, London (Att: 52,500)

### ENGLAND 1-0 SCOTLAND          Half-time 1-0

| (13) | James BROWNLIE (Third Lanark) | Samuel HARDY |
|---|---|---|
| (10) | Alexander McNAIR (Celtic) | Robert CROMPTON |
| (9) | John WALKER (Swindon Town) | Jesse PENNINGTON |
| (5) | James GORDON (Rangers) | John BRITTLETON |
| (19) | Charles THOMSON (Sunderland) captain | Joseph McCALL |
| (1) | David WILSON (Oldham Athletic) | William WATSON |
| (1) | Joseph DONNACHIE (Oldham Athletic) | John SIMPSON |
| (29) | Robert WALKER (Hearts) | Harold FLEMING |
| (7) | William REID (Rangers) | Joseph HAMPTON |
| (5) | Andrew WILSON (Sheffield Wednesday) | George HOLLEY |
| (4) | George ROBERTSON (Sheffield Wednesday) | Joseph HODKINSON |

| | Goals | |
|---|---|---|
| | 0-1 | Hampton (37 mins) |

# 1914

| P | W | D | L | F | A |
|---|---|---|---|---|---|
| 3 | 1 | 2 | 0 | 4 | 2 |

## 111
(Home International Championship)
28 February 1914

Referee: Taylor (England)
Celtic Park, Glasgow (Att: 10,000)

### SCOTLAND 0-0 WALES

| (14) | James BROWNLIE (Third Lanark) | Edward PEERS |
|---|---|---|
| (1) | Thomas KELSO (Dundee) | Thomas HEWITT |
| (1) | Joseph DODDS (Celtic) | William JENNINGS |
| (2) | Peter NELLIES (Hearts) captain | Thomas MATTHIAS |
| (1) | Peter PURSELL (Queen's Park) | Lloyd DAVIES |
| (1) | Harold ANDERSON (Raith Rovers) | Joseph JONES |
| (1) | Alexander DONALDSON (Bolton Wanderers) | William MEREDITH |
| (9) | James McMENEMY (Celtic) | George WYNN |
| (1) | James REID (Airdrie) | Walter DAVIS |
| (2) | James CROAL (Falkirk) | William JONES |
| (1) | John BROWNING (Celtic) | John EVANS |

## 112
(Home International Championship)
14 March 1914

Referee: Bamlett (England)
Windsor Park, Belfast (Att: 31,000)

### IRELAND 1-1 SCOTLAND          Half-time 0-0

| (15) | James BROWNLIE (Third Lanark) | Frederick McKEE |
|---|---|---|
| (2) | Joseph DODDS (Celtic) | William McCONNELL |
| (11) | Alexander McNAIR (Celtic) captain | Alexander CRAIG |
| (6) | James GORDON (Rangers) | Valentine HARRIS |
| (20) | Charles THOMSON (Sunderland) | Patrick O'CONNELL |
| (10) | James HAY (Newcastle United) | Michael HAMILL |
| (2) | Alexander DONALDSON (Bolton Wanderers) | John HOUSTON |
| (10) | James McMENEMY (Celtic) | Robert NIXON |
| (8) | William REID (Rangers) | Samuel YOUNG |
| (6) | Andrew WILSON (Sheffield Wednesday) | William LACEY |
| (2) | Joseph DONNACHIE (Oldham Athletic) | Frank THOMPSON |

| | Goals | |
|---|---|---|
| Donnachie (70 mins) | 1-0 | |
| | 1-1 | Young (89 mins) |

## 113
(Home International Championship)
4 April 1914

Referee: Bamlett (England)
Hampden Park, Glasgow (Att: 105,000)

### SCOTLAND 3-1 ENGLAND          Half-time 1-1

| (16) | James BROWNLIE (Third Lanark) | Samuel HARDY |
|---|---|---|
| (12) | Alexander McNAIR (Celtic) | Robert CROMPTON |
| (3) | Joseph DODDS (Celtic) | Jesse PENNINGTON |
| (7) | James GORDON (Rangers) captain | Albert STURGESS |
| (21) | Charles THOMSON (Sunderland) | Joseph McCALL |
| (11) | James HAY (Newcastle United) | Robert McNEAL |
| (3) | Alexander DONALDSON (Bolton Wanderers) | Frederick WALDEN |
| (11) | James McMENEMY (Celtic) | Harold FLEMING |
| (9) | William REID (Rangers) | Joseph HAMPTON |
| (3) | James CROAL (Falkirk) | Joseph SMITH |
| (3) | Joseph DONNACHIE (Oldham Athletic) | Edwin MOSSCROP |

| | Goals | |
|---|---|---|
| Thomson (2 mins) | 1-0 | |
| | 1-1 | Fleming (15 mins) |
| McMenemy (50 mins) | 2-1 | |
| Reid (67 mins) | 3-1 | |

# 1920

| P | W | D | L | F | A |
|---|---|---|---|---|---|
| 3 | 1 | 1 | 1 | 8 | 6 |

## 114

**(Home International Championship)**
26 February 1920

Referee: Mason (England)
Ninian Park, Cardiff (Att: 16,000)

### WALES 1-1 SCOTLAND — Half-time 1-0

| (1) | Kenneth CAMPBELL (Liverpool) | Edward PEERS |
|---|---|---|
| (13) | Alexander McNAIR (Celtic) | Harold MILLERSHIP |
| (1) | David THOMSON (Dundee) | Moses RUSSELL |
| (8) | James GORDON (Rangers) | Thomas MATTHIAS |
| (1) | William CRINGAN (Celtic) captain | Joseph JONES |
| (1) | James McMULLAN (Partick Thistle) | William JENNINGS |
| (2) | James REID (Airdrie) | William MEREDITH |
| (1) | John CROSBIE (Ayr United) | Ivor JONES |
| (1) | Andrew WILSON (Dunfermline Athletic) | Stanley DAVIES |
| (1) | Thomas CAIRNS (Rangers) | Richard RICHARDS |
| (1) | Alan MORTON (Queen's Park) | John EVANS |

Goals

| | |
|---|---|
| 0-1 | Evans (5 mins) |
| Cairns (78 mins) 1-1 | |

## 115

**(Home International Championship)**
13 March 1920

Referee: Mason (England)
Celtic Park, Glasgow (Att: 39,757)

### SCOTLAND 3-0 IRELAND — Half-time 2-0

| (2) | Kenneth CAMPBELL (Liverpool) | Elisha SCOTT |
|---|---|---|
| (14) | Alexander McNAIR (Celtic) captain | Robert MANDERSON |
| (1) | James BLAIR (Sheffield Wednesday) | David ROLLO |
| (1) | James BOWIE (Rangers) | Michael HAMILL |
| (4) | Wilfrid LOW (Newcastle United) | William LACEY |
| (9) | James GORDON (Rangers) | William EMERSON |
| (4) | Alexander DONALDSON (Bolton Wanderers) | Patrick ROBINSON |
| (12) | James McMENEMY (Celtic) | Patrick GALLAGHER |
| (2) | Andrew WILSON (Dunfermline Athletic) | Edward BROOKS |
| (1) | Andrew CUNNINGHAM (Rangers) | William GILLESPIE |
| (2) | Alan MORTON (Queen's Park) | James McCANDLESS |

Goals

| | |
|---|---|
| Wilson (8 mins) | 1-0 |
| Morton (42 mins) | 2-0 |
| Cunningham (55 mins) | 3-0 |

## 116

**(Home International Championship)**
10 April 1920

Referee: Dougray (Scotland)
Hillsborough, Sheffield (Att: 35,000)

### ENGLAND 5-4 SCOTLAND — Half-time 2-4

| (3) | Kenneth CAMPBELL (Partick Thistle) | Samuel HARDY |
|---|---|---|
| (15) | Alexander McNAIR (Celtic) captain | Ephraim LONGWORTH |
| (2) | James BLAIR (Sheffield Wednesday) | Jesse PENNINGTON |
| (2) | James BOWIE (Rangers) | Andrew DUCAT |
| (5) | Wilfrid LOW (Newcastle United) | Joseph McCALL |
| (10) | James GORDON (Rangers) | Arthur GRIMSDELL |
| (5) | Alexander DONALDSON (Bolton Wanderers) | Charles WALLACE |
| (1) | Thomas MILLER (Liverpool) | Robert KELLY |
| (1) | Andrew WILSON (Dunfermline Athletic) | John COCK |
| (1) | John PATERSON (Leicester City) | Frederick MORRIS |
| (1) | Alexander TROUP (Dundee) | Alfred QUANTRILL |

Goals

| | | |
|---|---|---|
| | 0-1 | Cock (9 mins) |
| Miller (13 mins) | 1-1 | |
| | 1-2 | Quantrill (15 mins) |
| Wilson (21 mins) | 2-2 | |
| Donaldson (31 mins) | 3-2 | |
| Miller (40 mins) | 4-2 | |
| | 4-3 | Kelly (57 mins) |
| | 4-4 | Morris (67 mins) |
| | 4-5 | Kelly (73 mins) |

# 1921

| P | W | D | L | F | A |
|---|---|---|---|---|---|
| 3 | 3 | 0 | 0 | 7 | 1 |

## 117

**(Home International Championship)**
12 February 1921

Referee: Mason (England)
Pittodrie Park, Aberdeen (Att: 20,824)

### SCOTLAND 2-1 WALES — Half-time 1-1

| (4) | Kenneth CAMPBELL (Partick Thistle) captain | Edward PEERS |
|---|---|---|
| (1) | John MARSHALL (Middlesbrough) | Harold MILLERSHIP |
| (1) | William McSTAY (Celtic) | Moses RUSSELL |
| (1) | Joseph HARRIS (Partick Thistle) | Frederick KEENOR |
| (1) | Charles PRINGLE (St Mirren) | Joseph JONES |
| (2) | James McMULLAN (Partick Thistle) | Thomas MATTHIAS |
| (1) | Alexander ARCHIBALD (Rangers) | David WILLIAMS |
| (2) | Andrew CUNNINGHAM (Rangers) | David COLLIER |
| (4) | Andrew WILSON (Dunfermline Athletic) | Francis HODDINOTT |
| (1) | Joseph CASSIDY (Celtic) | Stanley DAVIES |
| (2) | Alexander TROUP (Dundee) | Edward VIZARD |

Goals

| | | |
|---|---|---|
| Wilson (10 mins) | 1-0 | |
| | 1-1 | Collier (30 mins) |
| Wilson (46 mins) | 2-1 | |

## 118

**(Home International Championship)**
26 February 1921

Referee: Ward (England)
Windsor Park, Belfast (Att: 30,000)

### IRELAND 0-2 SCOTLAND — Half-time 0-1

| (5) | Kenneth CAMPBELL (Partick Thistle) | Elisha SCOTT |
|---|---|---|
| (2) | John MARSHALL (Middlesbrough) | James MULLIGAN |
| (2) | William McSTAY (Celtic) | David ROLLO |
| (2) | Joseph HARRIS (Partick Thistle) | William LACEY |
| (1) | John GRAHAM (Arsenal) | Ernest SMITH |
| (3) | James McMULLAN (Partick Thistle) | Michael O'BRIEN |
| (1) | Alexander McNAB (Morton) | Samuel McGREGOR |
| (2) | Thomas MILLER (Manchester United) | James FERRIS |
| (5) | Andrew WILSON (Dunfermline Athletic) captain | Daniel McKINNEY |
| (2) | Joseph CASSIDY (Celtic) | Michael HAMILL |
| (3) | Alexander TROUP (Dundee) | Louis BOOKMAN |

Goals

| | |
|---|---|
| Wilson (11 mins pen) | 1-0 |
| Cassidy (89 mins) | 2-0 |

## 119

**(Home International Championship)**
9 April 1921

Referee: Ward (England)
Hampden Park, Glasgow (Att: 85,000)

### SCOTLAND 3-0 ENGLAND — Half-time 1-0

| (1) | John EWART (Bradford City) | Harold GOUGH |
|---|---|---|
| (3) | John MARSHALL (Middlesbrough) captain | Thomas SMART |
| (3) | James BLAIR (Cardiff City) | John SILCOCK |
| (1) | Stewart DAVIDSON (Middlesbrough) | Bertram SMITH |
| (1) | George BREWSTER (Everton) | George WILSON |
| (4) | James McMULLAN (Partick Thistle) | Arthur GRIMSDELL |
| (2) | Alexander McNAB (Morton) | Samuel CHEDGZOY |
| (3) | Thomas MILLER (Manchester United) | Robert KELLY |
| (6) | Andrew WILSON (Dunfermline Athletic) | Henry CHAMBERS |
| (3) | Andrew CUNNINGHAM (Rangers) | Herbert BLISS |
| (3) | Alan MORTON (Rangers) | James DIMMOCK |

Goals

| | |
|---|---|
| Wilson (20 mins) | 1-0 |
| Morton (46 mins) | 2-0 |
| Cunningham (57 mins) | 3-0 |

# 1922

| P | W | D | L | F | A |
|---|---|---|---|---|---|
| 3 | 2 | 0 | 1 | 4 | 3 |

## 120

(Home International Championship)                    Referee: Ward (England)
4 February 1922                    The Racecourse, Wrexham (Att: 8,000)

### WALES 2-1 SCOTLAND                    Half-time 2-0

| (6) | Kenneth CAMPBELL (Partick Thistle) | Edward PEERS |
| (4) | John MARSHALL (Middlesbrough) captain | Edward PARRY |
| (1) | Donald McKINLAY (Liverpool) | James EVANS |
| (1) | David MEIKLEJOHN (Rangers) | Herbert EVANS |
| (1) | Michael GILHOOLEY (Hull City) | Joseph JONES |
| (1) | William COLLIER (Raith Rovers) | Thomas MATTHIAS |
| (2) | Alexander ARCHIBALD (Rangers) | Stanley DAVIES |
| (1) | John WHITE (Albion Rovers) | Leonard DAVIES |
| (7) | Andrew WILSON (Middlesbrough) | Richard RICHARDS |
| (1) | Frank WALKER (Third Lanark) | Edward VIZARD |
| (4) | Alan MORTON (Rangers) | Ivor JONES |

| | | Goals | |
| | | 0-1 | L. Davies (7 mins) |
| | | 0-2 | S. Davies (25 mins) |
| Archibald (65 mins) | | 1-2 | |

## 121

(Home International Championship)                    Referee: Ward (England)
4 March 1922                    Celtic Park, Glasgow (Att: 36,000)

### SCOTLAND 2-1 IRELAND                    Half-time 0-1

| (7) | Kenneth CAMPBELL (Partick Thistle) | Francis COLLINS |
| (5) | John MARSHALL (Middlesbrough) | William McCRACKEN |
| (2) | Donald McKINLAY (Liverpool) | William McCANDLESS |
| (1) | James HOGG (Ayr United) | Robert McCRACKEN |
| (2) | William CRINGAN (Celtic) | Michael O'BRIEN |
| (1) | Thomas MUIRHEAD (Rangers) | William EMERSON |
| (6) | Alexander DONALDSON (Bolton Wanderers) | William LACEY |
| (1) | James KINLOCH (Partick Thistle) | Patrick GALLAGHER |
| (8) | Andrew WILSON (Middlesbrough) | Robert IRVINE |
| (4) | Andrew CUNNINGHAM (Rangers) captain | William GILLESPIE |
| (4) | Alexander TROUP (Dundee) | David LYNER |

| | | Goals | |
| | | 0-1 | Gillespie (42 mins) |
| Wilson (60 mins) | | 1-1 | |
| Wilson (83 mins) | | 2-1 | |

## 122

(Home International Championship)                    Referee: Dougray (Scotland)
8 April 1922                    Villa Park, Birmingham (Att: 33,646)

### ENGLAND 0-1 SCOTLAND                    Half-time 0-0

| (8) | Kenneth CAMPBELL (Partick Thistle) | Jeremiah DAWSON |
| (6) | John MARSHALL (Middlesbrough) | Thomas CLAY |
| (4) | James BLAIR (Cardiff City) captain | Samuel WADSWORTH |
| (1) | John GILCHRIST (Celtic) | Frank MOSS |
| (3) | William CRINGAN (Celtic) | George WILSON |
| (1) | Neil McBAIN (Manchester United) | Thomas BROMILOW |
| (3) | Alexander ARCHIBALD (Rangers) | Richard YORK |
| (2) | John CROSBIE (Birmingham) | Robert KELLY |
| (9) | Andrew WILSON (Middlesbrough) | William RAWLINGS |
| (2) | Thomas CAIRNS (Rangers) | William WALKER |
| (5) | Alan MORTON (Rangers) | William SMITH |

| | | Goals | |
| Wilson (63 mins) | | 1-0 | |

# 1923

| P | W | D | L | F | A |
|---|---|---|---|---|---|
| 3 | 2 | 1 | 0 | 5 | 2 |

## 123

(Home International Championship)                    Referee: Ward (England)
3 March 1923                    Windsor Park, Belfast (Att: 31,000)

### IRELAND 0-1 SCOTLAND                    Half-time 0-0

| (1) | William HARPER (Hibernian) | Thomas FARQUHARSON |
| (1) | John HUTTON (Aberdeen) | William McCRACKEN |
| (5) | James BLAIR (Cardiff City) captain | John CURRAN |
| (1) | David STEELE (Huddersfield Town) | Samuel IRVING |
| (1) | David MORRIS (Raith Rovers) | George MOORHEAD |
| (2) | Neil McBAIN (Everton) | William EMERSON |
| (4) | Alexander ARCHIBALD (Rangers) | Hamilton McKENZIE |
| (2) | John WHITE (Hearts) | Patrick GALLAGHER |
| (10) | Andrew WILSON (Middlesbrough) | George REID |
| (3) | Joseph CASSIDY (Celtic) | William GILLESPIE |
| (6) | Alan MORTON (Rangers) | William MOORE |

| | | Goals | |
| Wilson (69 mins) | | 1-0 | |

## 124

(Home International Championship)                    Referee: Baker (England)
17 March 1923                    Love Street, Paisley (Att: 25,000)

### SCOTLAND 2-0 WALES                    Half-time 1-0

| (2) | William HARPER (Hibernian) | George GODDING |
| (2) | John HUTTON (Aberdeen) | Moses RUSSELL |
| (6) | James BLAIR (Cardiff City) | James EVANS |
| (1) | John McNAB (Liverpool) | Thomas MATTHIAS |
| (4) | William CRINGAN (Celtic) captain | Frederick KEENOR |
| (2) | David STEELE (Huddersfield Town) | Robert JOHN |
| (1) | Henry RITCHIE (Hibernian) | David WILLIAMS |
| (5) | Andrew CUNNINGHAM (Rangers) | Robert DAVIES |
| (11) | Andrew WILSON (Middlesbrough) | Stanley DAVIES |
| (3) | Thomas CAIRNS (Rangers) | Leonard DAVIES |
| (7) | Alan MORTON (Rangers) | David NICHOLAS |

| | | Goals | |
| Wilson (7 mins) | | 1-0 | |
| Wilson (55 mins) | | 2-0 | |

## 125

(Home International Championship)                    Referee: Ward (England)
14 April 1923                    Hampden Park, Glasgow (Att: 71,000)

### SCOTLAND 2-2 ENGLAND                    Half-time 1-2

| (3) | William HARPER (Hibernian) | Edward TAYLOR |
| (3) | John HUTTON (Aberdeen) | Ephraim LONGWORTH |
| (7) | James BLAIR (Cardiff City) | Samuel WADSWORTH |
| (3) | David STEELE (Huddersfield Town) | Frederick KEAN |
| (5) | William CRINGAN (Celtic) captain | George WILSON |
| (2) | Thomas MUIRHEAD (Rangers) | John TRESADERN |
| (1) | Denis LAWSON (St Mirren) | Samuel CHEDGZOY |
| (6) | Andrew CUNNINGHAM (Rangers) | Robert KELLY |
| (12) | Andrew WILSON (Middlesbrough) | Victor WATSON |
| (4) | Thomas CAIRNS (Rangers) | Henry CHAMBERS |
| (8) | Alan MORTON (Rangers) | Frederick TUNSTALL |

| | | Goals | |
| Cunningham (28 mins) | | 1-0 | |
| | | 1-1 | Kelly (31 mins) |
| | | 1-2 | Watson (42 mins) |
| Wilson (55 mins) | | 2-2 | |

## 1924

| P | W | D | L | F | A |
|---|---|---|---|---|---|
| 3 | 1 | 1 | 1 | 3 | 3 |

### 126
(Home International Championship)
16 February 1924
Referee: Andrews (England)
Ninian Park, Cardiff (Att: 26,000)

**WALES 2-0 SCOTLAND**   Half-time 0-0

| | | |
|---|---|---|
| (4) | William HARPER (Hibernian) | Albert GRAY |
| (7) | John MARSHALL (Llanelli) | Moses RUSSELL |
| (8) | James BLAIR (Cardiff City) captain | John JENKINS |
| (2) | David MEIKLEJOHN (Rangers) | Herbert EVANS |
| (3) | Neil McBAIN (Everton) | Frederick KEENOR |
| (3) | Thomas MUIRHEAD (Rangers) | William JENNINGS |
| (5) | Alexander ARCHIBALD (Rangers) | William DAVIES |
| (1) | William RUSSELL (Airdrie) | Ivor JONES |
| (4) | Joseph CASSIDY (Celtic) | Leonard DAVIES |
| (1) | John McKAY (Blackburn Rovers) | Richard RICHARDS |
| (9) | Alan MORTON (Rangers) | Edward VIZARD |

| | Goals | |
|---|---|---|
| | 0-1 | W.Davies (61 mins) |
| | 0-2 | L.Davies (72 mins) |

### 127
(Home International Championship)
1 March 1924
Referee: Watson (England)
Celtic Park, Glasgow (Att: 30,000)

**SCOTLAND 2-0 IRELAND**   Half-time 0-0

| | | |
|---|---|---|
| (5) | William HARPER (Hibernian) | Thomas FARQUHARSON |
| (4) | John HUTTON (Aberdeen) captain | David ROLLO |
| (1) | James HAMILTON (St Mirren) | William McCANDLESS |
| (1) | Peter KERR (Hibernian) | Samuel IRVING |
| (2) | David MORRIS (Raith Rovers) | Michael O'BRIEN |
| (5) | James McMULLAN (Partick Thistle) | Gerald MORGAN |
| (3) | James REID (Airdrie) | Daniel McKINNEY |
| (7) | Andrew CUNNINGHAM (Rangers) | Patrick GALLAGHER |
| (1) | Hugh GALLACHER (Airdrie) | Robert IRVINE |
| (5) | Thomas CAIRNS (Rangers) | William GILLESPIE |
| (10) | Alan MORTON (Rangers) | John McGRILLEN |

| | Goals | |
|---|---|---|
| Cunningham (86 mins) | 1-0 | |
| Morris (88 mins) | 2-0 | |

### 128
(Home International Championship)
12 April 1924
Referee: Dougray (Scotland)
Wembley Stadium, London (Att: 37,250)

**ENGLAND 1-1 SCOTLAND**   Half-time 0-1

| | | |
|---|---|---|
| (6) | William HARPER (Hibernian) | Edward TAYLOR |
| (1) | John SMITH (Ayr United) | Thomas SMART |
| (1) | Philip McCLOY (Ayr United) | Samuel WADSWORTH |
| (1) | William CLUNAS (Sunderland) | Frank MOSS |
| (3) | David MORRIS (Raith Rovers) | Charles SPENCER |
| (6) | James McMULLAN (Partick Thistle) captain | Percival BARTON |
| (6) | Alexander ARCHIBALD (Rangers) | William BUTLER |
| (1) | William COWAN (Newcastle United) | David JACK |
| (1) | Neil HARRIS (Newcastle United) | Charles BUCHAN |
| (8) | Andrew CUNNINGHAM (Rangers) | William WALKER |
| (11) | Alan MORTON (Rangers) | Frederick TUNSTALL |

| | Goals | |
|---|---|---|
| Cowan (40 mins) | 1-0 | |
| | 1-1 | Walker (60 mins) |

## 1925

| P | W | D | L | F | A |
|---|---|---|---|---|---|
| 4 | 4 | 0 | 0 | 11 | 1 |

### 129
(Home International Championship)
14 February 1925
Referee: Ward (England)
Tynecastle Park, Edinburgh (Att: 25,000)

**SCOTLAND 3-1 WALES**   Half-time 2-1

| | | |
|---|---|---|
| (7) | William HARPER (Hibernian) | Albert GRAY |
| (1) | James NELSON (Cardiff City) | John JENKINS |
| (3) | William McSTAY (Celtic) | Moses RUSSELL |
| (3) | David MEIKLEJOHN (Rangers) | Stanley DAVIES |
| (4) | David MORRIS (Raith Rovers) captain | Frederick KEENOR |
| (1) | Robert BENNIE (Airdrie) | William WILLIAMS |
| (1) | Alexander JACKSON (Aberdeen) | William DAVIES |
| (1) | James DUNN (Hibernian) | John NICHOLLS |
| (2) | Hugh GALLACHER (Airdrie) | Leonard DAVIES |
| (6) | Thomas CAIRNS (Rangers) | George BEADLES |
| (12) | Alan MORTON (Rangers) | Frederick COOK |

| | Goals | |
|---|---|---|
| Meiklejohn (9 mins) | 1-0 | |
| Gallacher (20 mins) | 2-0 | |
| | 2-1 | Williams (43 mins) |
| Gallacher (61 mins) | 3-1 | |

### 130
(Home International Championship)
28 February 1925
Referee: Watson (England)
Windsor Park, Belfast (Att: 41,000)

**IRELAND 0-3 SCOTLAND**   Half-time 0-3

| | | |
|---|---|---|
| (8) | William HARPER (Hibernian) | Thomas FARQUHARSON |
| (2) | James NELSON (Cardiff City) | Robert MANDERSON |
| (4) | William McSTAY (Celtic) | William McCANDLESS |
| (4) | David MEIKLEJOHN (Rangers) | James CHATTON |
| (5) | David MORRIS (Raith Rovers) captain | Michael O'BRIEN |
| (2) | Robert BENNIE (Airdrie) | Samuel IRVING |
| (2) | Alexander JACKSON (Aberdeen) | David MARTIN |
| (2) | James DUNN (Hibernian) | Patrick GALLAGHER |
| (3) | Hugh GALLACHER (Airdrie) | Edward CARROLL |
| (7) | Thomas CAIRNS (Rangers) | William GILLESPIE |
| (13) | Alan MORTON (Rangers) | Joseph TONER |

| | Goals | |
|---|---|---|
| Meiklejohn (4 mins) | 1-0 | |
| Gallacher (25 mins) | 2-0 | |
| Dunn (35 mins) | 3-0 | |

### 131
(Home International Championship)
4 April 1925
Referee: Ward (England)
Hampden Park, Glasgow (Att: 92,000)

**SCOTLAND 2-0 ENGLAND**   Half-time 1-0

| | | |
|---|---|---|
| (9) | William HARPER (Hibernian) | Richard PYM |
| (5) | William McSTAY (Celtic) | William ASHURST |
| (2) | Philip McCLOY (Ayr United) | Samuel WADSWORTH |
| (5) | David MEIKLEJOHN (Rangers) | Thomas MAGEE |
| (6) | David MORRIS (Raith Rovers) captain | John TOWNROW |
| (7) | James McMULLAN (Partick Thistle) | Leonard GRAHAM |
| (3) | Alexander JACKSON (Aberdeen) | Robert KELLY |
| (2) | William RUSSELL (Airdrie) | James SEED |
| (4) | Hugh GALLACHER (Airdrie) | Frank ROBERTS |
| (8) | Thomas CAIRNS (Rangers) | William WALKER |
| (14) | Alan MORTON (Rangers) | Frederick TUNSTALL |

| | Goals | |
|---|---|---|
| Gallacher (36 mins) | 1-0 | |
| Gallacher (86 mins) | 2-0 | |

### 132
(Home International Championship)
31 October 1925
Referee: Pinkstone (England)
Ninian Park, Cardiff (Att: 18,000)

**WALES 0-3 SCOTLAND**   Half-time 0-0

| | | |
|---|---|---|
| (1) | William ROBB (Rangers) | Albert GRAY |
| (5) | John HUTTON (Aberdeen) | Moses RUSSELL |
| (6) | William McSTAY (Celtic) | John JENKINS |
| (2) | William CLUNAS (Sunderland) | Samuel BENNION |
| (1) | Thomas TOWNSLEY (Falkirk) captain | Frederick KEENOR |
| (8) | James McMULLAN (Partick Thistle) | James LEWIS |
| (4) | Alexander JACKSON (Huddersfield Town) | David WILLIAMS |
| (1) | John DUNCAN (Leicester City) | William DAVIES |
| (5) | Hugh GALLACHER (Airdrie) | Stanley DAVIES |
| (1) | Alexander JAMES (Preston North End) | Richard RICHARDS |
| (1) | Adam McLEAN (Celtic) | Edward VIZARD |

| | Goals | |
|---|---|---|
| Duncan (70 mins) | 1-0 | |
| McLean (80 mins) | 2-0 | |
| Clunas (82 mins) | 3-0 | |

# 1926

| P | W | D | L | F | A |
|---|---|---|---|---|---|
| 3 | 3 | 0 | 0 | 8 | 0 |

## 133
(Home International Championship)
27 February 1926

Referee: Watson (England)
Ibrox Park, Glasgow (Att: 30,000)

### SCOTLAND 4-0 IRELAND      Half-time 2-0

| (10) | William HARPER (Arsenal) | Elisha SCOTT |
| (6) | John HUTTON (Aberdeen) | Robert MANDERSON |
| (7) | William McSTAY (Celtic) captain | Thomas WATSON |
| (1) | Peter WILSON (Celtic) | Samuel IRVING |
| (1) | John McDOUGALL (Airdrie) | Joseph GOWDY |
| (3) | Robert BENNIE (Airdrie) | Thomas SLOAN |
| (5) | Alexander JACKSON (Huddersfield Town) | Andrew BOTHWELL |
| (9) | Andrew CUNNINGHAM (Rangers) | Alexander STEELE |
| (6) | Hugh GALLACHER (Newcastle United) | Samuel CURRAN |
| (1) | Thomas McINALLY (Celtic) | William GILLESPIE |
| (2) | Adam McLEAN (Celtic) | John MAHOOD |

| | Goals |
|---|---|
| Gallacher (13 mins) | 1-0 |
| Cunningham (40 mins) | 2-0 |
| Gallacher (60 mins) | 3-0 |
| Gallacher (66 mins) | 4-0 |

Action around Ireland's goal at Ibrox in February 1926. Below: Hughie Gallacher scores one of his three goals in the 4-0 win over the Irish.

## 134
(Home International Championship)
17 April 1926

Referee: Dougray (Scotland)
Old Trafford, Manchester (Att: 49,000)

### ENGLAND 0-1 SCOTLAND      Half-time 0-1

| (11) | William HARPER (Arsenal) | Edward TAYLOR |
| (7) | John HUTTON (Aberdeen) | Frederick GOODALL |
| (8) | William McSTAY (Celtic) captain | Thomas MORT |
| (1) | James GIBSON (Partick Thistle) | Willis EDWARDS |
| (1) | William SUMMERS (St Mirren) | John HILL |
| (9) | James McMULLAN (Manchester City) | George GREEN |
| (6) | Alexander JACKSON (Huddersfield Town) | Richard YORK |
| (1) | Alexander THOMSON (Celtic) | Sydney PUDDEFOOT |
| (7) | Hugh GALLACHER (Newcastle United) | Edward HARPER |
| (10) | Andrew CUNNINGHAM (Rangers) | William WALKER |
| (5) | Alexander TROUP (Everton) | James RUFFELL |

| | Goals |
|---|---|
| Jackson (37 mins) | 1-0 |

## 135
(Home International Championship)
30 October 1926

Referee: Forshaw (England)
Ibrox Park, Glasgow (Att: 41,000)

### SCOTLAND 3-0 WALES      Half-time 2-0

| (1) | Allan McCLORY (Motherwell) | Albert GRAY |
| (9) | William McSTAY (Celtic) captain | Thomas EVANS |
| (1) | William WISEMAN (Queen's Park) | John JENKINS |
| (2) | James GIBSON (Partick Thistle) | Samuel BENNION |
| (1) | Robert GILLESPIE (Queen's Park) | Frederick KEENOR |
| (10) | James McMULLAN (Manchester City) | William JENNINGS |
| (7) | Alexander JACKSON (Huddersfield Town) | William DAVIES |
| (11) | Andrew CUNNINGHAM (Rangers) | Stanley DAVIES |
| (8) | Hugh GALLACHER (Newcastle United) | John FOWLER |
| (2) | Thomas McINALLY (Celtic) | Charles JONES |
| (3) | Adam McLEAN (Celtic) | Edward VIZARD |

| | Goals |
|---|---|
| Gallacher (20 mins) | 1-0 |
| Jackson (33 mins) | 2-0 |
| Jackson (73 mins) | 3-0 |

# 1927

| P | W | D | L | F | A |
|---|---|---|---|---|---|
| 3 | 1 | 1 | 1 | 5 | 4 |

## 136
(Home International Championship)
26 February 1927

Referee: Watson (England)
Windsor Park, Belfast (Att: 40,000)

### IRELAND 0-2 SCOTLAND      Half-time 0-1

| (1) | John HARKNESS (Queen's Park) | Elisha SCOTT |
| (8) | John HUTTON (Blackburn Rovers) | Andrew McCLUGGAGE |
| (10) | William McSTAY (Celtic) captain | William McCONNELL |
| (4) | Thomas MUIRHEAD (Rangers) | Joseph GOWDY |
| (3) | James GIBSON (Partick Thistle) | Thomas SLOAN |
| (1) | Thomas CRAIG (Rangers) | David McMULLAN |
| (8) | Alexander JACKSON (Huddersfield Town) | John McGRILLEN |
| (3) | James DUNN (Hibernian) | Patrick GALLAGHER |
| (9) | Hugh GALLACHER (Newcastle United) | Hugh DAVEY |
| (1) | James HOWIESON (St Mirren) | Samuel IRVING |
| (15) | Alan MORTON (Rangers) | Joseph TONER |

| | Goals |
|---|---|
| Morton (44 mins) | 1-0 |
| Morton (88 mins) | 2-0 |

Alex Jackson scores the only goal of the game at Old Trafford in April 1926, consigning England to the wooden spoon in that season's Home International Championship.

**137**
(Home International Championship)
2 April 1927

Referee: Ward (England)
Hampden Park, Glasgow (Att: 111,214)

### SCOTLAND 1-2 ENGLAND — Half-time 0-0

| | | |
|---|---|---|
| (2) | John HARKNESS (Queen's Park) | John BROWN |
| (11) | William McSTAY (Celtic) captain | Frederick GOODALL |
| (1) | Robert THOMSON (Falkirk) | Herbert JONES |
| (1) | Thomas MORRISON (St Mirren) | Willis EDWARDS |
| (4) | James GIBSON (Partick Thistle) | John HILL |
| (11) | James McMULLAN (Manchester City) | Sidney BISHOP |
| (4) | Adam McLEAN (Celtic) | Joseph HULME |
| (12) | Andrew CUNNINGHAM (Rangers) | William DEAN |
| (10) | Hugh GALLACHER (Newcastle United) | Arthur RIGBY |
| (1) | Robert McPHAIL (Airdrie) | George BROWN |
| (16) | Alan MORTON (Rangers) | Louis PAGE |

**Goals**

| | | |
|---|---|---|
| Morton (53 mins) | 1-0 | |
| | 1-1 | Dean (69 mins) |
| | 1-2 | Dean (88 mins) |

**138**
(Home International Championship)
29 October 1927

Referee: Kingscott (England)
The Racecourse, Wrexham (Att: 16,000)

### WALES 2-2 SCOTLAND — Half-time 1-2

| | | |
|---|---|---|
| (2) | William ROBB (Hibernian) | Albert GRAY |
| (9) | John HUTTON (Blackburn Rovers) | Moses RUSSELL |
| (12) | William McSTAY (Celtic) | Thomas EVANS |
| (6) | David MEIKLEJOHN (Rangers) | Samuel BENNION |
| (5) | James GIBSON (Aston Villa) | Frederick KEENOR |
| (12) | James McMULLAN (Manchester City) captain | Stanley DAVIES |
| (9) | Alexander JACKSON (Huddersfield Town) | William HOLE |
| (1) | Robert McKAY (Newcastle United) | Leonard DAVIES |
| (11) | Hugh GALLACHER (Newcastle United) | John FOWLER |
| (1) | George STEVENSON (Motherwell) | Ernest CURTIS |
| (17) | Alan MORTON (Rangers) | Frederick COOK |

**Goals**

| | | |
|---|---|---|
| Gallacher (14 mins) | 1-0 | |
| Hutton (16 mins pen) | 2-0 | |
| | 2-1 | Curtis (44 mins) |
| | 2-2 | Gibson (76 mins o.g.) |

# 1928

| P | W | D | L | F | A |
|---|---|---|---|---|---|
| 3 | 2 | 0 | 1 | 9 | 4 |

**139**
(Home International Championship)
25 February 1928

Referee: Ward (England)
Firhill Park, Glasgow (Att: 55,000)

### SCOTLAND 0-1 IRELAND — Half-time 0-1

| | | |
|---|---|---|
| (2) | Allan McCLORY (Motherwell) | Elisha SCOTT |
| (10) | John HUTTON (Blackburn Rovers) | Andrew McCLUGGAGE |
| (13) | William McSTAY (Celtic) | Robert HAMILTON |
| (5) | Thomas MUIRHEAD (Rangers) captain | Samuel IRVING |
| (7) | David MEIKLEJOHN (Rangers) | George MOORHEAD |
| (2) | Thomas CRAIG (Rangers) | Gerald MORGAN |
| (2) | Henry RITCHIE (Hibernian) | James CHAMBERS |
| (4) | James DUNN (Hibernian) | Robert IRVINE |
| (1) | James McGRORY (Celtic) | Samuel CURRAN |
| (2) | George STEVENSON (Motherwell) | James FERRIS |
| (18) | Alan MORTON (Rangers) | John MAHOOD |

**Goals**

| | | |
|---|---|---|
| | 0-1 | Chambers (10 mins) |

**140**
(Home International Championship)
31 March 1928

Referee: Bell (Scotland)
Wembley Stadium, London (Att: 80,868)

### ENGLAND 1-5 SCOTLAND — Half-time 0-2

| | | |
|---|---|---|
| (3) | John HARKNESS (Queen's Park) | Arthur HUFTON |
| (3) | James NELSON (Cardiff City) | Frederick GOODALL |
| (1) | Thomas LAW (Chelsea) | Herbert JONES |
| (6) | James GIBSON (Aston Villa) | Willis EDWARDS |
| (1) | Thomas BRADSHAW (Bury) | Thomas WILSON |
| (13) | James McMULLAN (Manchester City) captain | Henry HEALLESS |
| (10) | Alexander JACKSON (Huddersfield Town) | Joseph HULME |
| (5) | James DUNN (Hibernian) | Robert KELLY |
| (12) | Hugh GALLACHER (Newcastle United) | William DEAN |
| (2) | Alexander JAMES (Preston North End) | Joseph BRADFORD |
| (19) | Alan MORTON (Rangers) | William SMITH |

**Goals**

| | | |
|---|---|---|
| Jackson (3 mins) | 1-0 | |
| James (44 mins) | 2-0 | |
| Jackson (65 mins) | 3-0 | |
| James (66 mins) | 4-0 | |
| Jackson (85 mins) | 5-0 | |
| | 5-1 | Kelly (89 mins) |

Hughie Gallacher narrowly misses scoring against England at Wembley in 1928 in what was arguably Scotland's most famous victory.

The Scotland team meet the Duke of York – later King George VI – before the match at Wembley in March 1928.

## 141

(Home International Championship)
27 October 1928

Referee: Kingscott (England)
Ibrox Park, Glasgow (Att: 55,000)

### SCOTLAND 4-2 WALES — Half-time 2-1

| | | |
|---|---|---|
| (4) | John HARKNESS (Hearts) | Albert GRAY |
| (1) | Douglas GRAY (Rangers) | Ernest MORLEY |
| (1) | Daniel BLAIR (Clyde) | William JENNINGS |
| (6) | Thomas MUIRHEAD (Rangers) | Samuel BENNION |
| (1) | William KING (Queen's Park) | Frederick KEENOR |
| (14) | James McMULLAN (Manchester City) captain | David EVANS |
| (11) | Alexander JACKSON (Huddersfield Town) | William HOLE |
| (6) | James DUNN (Everton) | William DAVIES |
| (13) | Hugh GALLACHER (Newcastle United) | Wilfred LEWIS |
| (2) | Robert McPHAIL (Rangers) | Leonard DAVIES |
| (20) | Alan MORTON (Rangers) | David WILLIAMS |

| Goals | | |
|---|---|---|
| | 0-1 | W. Davies (12 mins) |
| Gallacher (25 mins) | 1-1 | |
| Gallacher (42 mins) | 2-1 | |
| Gallacher (49 mins) | 3-1 | |
| Dunn (56 mins) | 4-1 | |
| | 4-2 | W. Davies (75 mins) |

# 1929

| P | W | D | L | F | A |
|---|---|---|---|---|---|
| 6 | 5 | 1 | 0 | 22 | 9 |

## 142

(Home International Championship)
23 February 1929

Referee: Fogg (England)
Windsor Park, Belfast (Att: 35,000)

### IRELAND 3-7 SCOTLAND — Half-time 2-4

| | | |
|---|---|---|
| (5) | John HARKNESS (Hearts) | Elisha SCOTT |
| (2) | Douglas GRAY (Rangers) | Andrew McCLUGGAGE |
| (2) | Daniel BLAIR (Clyde) | Hugh FLACK |
| (7) | Thomas MUIRHEAD (Rangers) | Joseph MILLER |
| (8) | David MEIKLEJOHN (Rangers) | George MOORHEAD |
| (15) | James McMULLAN (Manchester City) captain | Alexander STEELE |
| (12) | Alexander JACKSON (Huddersfield Town) | James CHAMBERS |
| (1) | William CHALMERS (Queen's Park) | Richard ROWLEY |
| (14) | Hugh GALLACHER (Newcastle United) | Joseph BAMBRICK |
| (3) | Alexander JAMES (Preston North End) | Lawrence CUMMING |
| (21) | Alan MORTON (Rangers) | John MAHOOD |

| Goals | | |
|---|---|---|
| Gallacher (3 mins) | 1-0 | |
| Gallacher (9 mins) | 2-0 | |
| Gallacher (14 mins) | 3-0 | |
| | 3-1 | Rowley (16 mins) |
| Jackson (36 mins) | 4-1 | |
| | 4-2 | Rowley (42 mins) |
| Gallacher (51 mins) | 5-2 | |
| | 5-3 | Bambrick (58 mins) |
| Gallacher (76 mins) | 6-3 | |
| Jackson (82 mins) | 7-3 | |

## 143

(Home International Championship)
13 April 1929

Referee: Josephs (England)
Hampden Park, Glasgow (Att: 110,512)

### SCOTLAND 1-0 ENGLAND — Half-time 0-0

| | | |
|---|---|---|
| (6) | John HARKNESS (Hearts) | John HACKING |
| (1) | James CRAPNELL (Airdrie) | Thomas COOPER |
| (1) | Joseph NIBLOE (Kilmarnock) | Ernest BLENKINSOP |
| (1) | John BUCHANAN (Rangers) | Willis EDWARDS |
| (9) | David MEIKLEJOHN (Rangers) | James SEDDON |
| (16) | James McMULLAN (Manchester City) captain | Henry NUTTALL |
| (13) | Alexander JACKSON (Huddersfield Town) | John BRUTON |
| (1) | Alexander CHEYNE (Aberdeen) | George BROWN |
| (15) | Hugh GALLACHER (Newcastle United) | William DEAN |
| (4) | Alexander JAMES (Preston North End) | William WAINSCOAT |
| (22) | Alan MORTON (Rangers) | James RUFFELL |

| | Goals | |
|---|---|---|
| Cheyne (90 mins) | 1-0 | |

## 144

(Friendly)
26 May 1929

Referee: Schielderop (Norway)
Brann Stadion, Bergen (Att: 4,000)

### NORWAY 3-7 SCOTLAND — Half-time 2-3

| | | |
|---|---|---|
| (1) | Alexander McLAREN (St Johnstone) | Hugo HOFSTAD |
| (2) | James CRAPNELL (Airdrie) | Haakon WALDE |
| (2) | Joseph NIBLOE (Kilmarnock) | Egil-Brenna LUND |
| (1) | William IMRIE (St Johnstone) | Ravn TOLLEFSEN |
| (1) | Allan CRAIG (Motherwell) | Alexander OLSEN |
| (3) | Thomas CRAIG (Rangers) captain | Kjeld KJOS |
| (1) | James NISBET (Ayr United) | Kaare KONGSVIK |
| (2) | Alexander CHEYNE (Aberdeen) | Oscar THORSTENSEN |
| (1) | David McCRAE (St Mirren) | Robert DANIELSEN |
| (1) | Robert RANKIN (St Mirren) | Kaare LIE |
| (1) | Robert HOWE (Hamilton Academical) | Sverre BERG-JOHANNESEN |

| Goals | | |
|---|---|---|
| | 0-1 | Kongsvik (4 mins) |
| Rankin (6 mins) | 1-1 | |
| T. Craig (27 mins) | 2-1 | |
| Cheyne (30 mins) | 3-1 | |
| | 3-2 | Berg-Johannesen (37 mins) |
| Nisbet (47 mins) | 4-2 | |
| Nisbet (52 mins) | 5-2 | |
| Cheyne (64 mins) | 6-2 | |
| Cheyne (68 mins) | 7-2 | |
| | 7-3 | Kongsvik (76 mins) |

## 145

(Friendly)
1 June 1929

Referee: Ohlsson (Sweden)
Deutsches Stadion, Berlin (Att: 40,000)

### GERMANY 1-1 SCOTLAND — Half-time 0-0

| | | |
|---|---|---|
| (2) | Alexander McLAREN (St Johnstone) | Heinrich STUHLFAUTH |
| (3) | Douglas GRAY (Rangers) | Franz SCHÜTZ |
| (3) | James CRAPNELL (Airdrie) | Hans BRUNKE |
| (1) | Hugh MORTON (Kilmarnock) | Hans GEIGER |
| (2) | William IMRIE (St Johnstone) | Hans GRUBER |
| (4) | Thomas CRAIG (Rangers) captain | Conrad HEIDKAMP |
| (2) | James NISBET (Ayr United) | Hans RUCH |
| (3) | Alexander CHEYNE (Aberdeen) | Johannes SOBECK |
| (2) | David McCRAE (St Mirren) | Josef PÖTTINGER |
| (2) | Robert RANKIN (St Mirren) | Richard HOFMANN |
| (1) | James FLEMING (Rangers) | Ludwig HOFMANN |

| Goals | | |
|---|---|---|
| | 0-1 | Ruch (49 mins) |
| Imrie (87 mins) | 1-1 | |

## 146

(Friendly)
4 June 1929

Referee: Langenus (Belgium)
Olympisch Stadion, Amsterdam (Att: 24,000)

### NETHERLANDS 0-2 SCOTLAND — Half-time 0-2

| | | |
|---|---|---|
| (3) | Alexander McLAREN (St Johnstone) | Gejus VAN DER MEULEN |
| (4) | Douglas GRAY (Rangers) | Sjaak DE BRUIJN |
| (3) | Joseph NIBLOE (Kilmarnock) | Dolf VAN KOL |
| (4) | Hugh MORTON (Kilmarnock) | Huib DE LEEUW |
| (2) | Allan CRAIG (Motherwell) | Maarten GROBBE |
| (5) | Thomas CRAIG (Rangers) captain | Koos VAN DER WILDT |
| (3) | James NISBET (Ayr United) | Gep LANDAAL |
| (4) | Alexander CHEYNE (Aberdeen) | Felix SMEETS |
| (2) | James FLEMING (Rangers) | Wim TAP |
| (3) | Robert RANKIN (St Mirren) | Cor KOOLS |
| (2) | Robert HOWE (Hamilton Academical) | Frans HOMBÖRG |

| Goals | | |
|---|---|---|
| Fleming (31 mins) | 1-0 | |
| Rankin (44 mins pen) | 2-0 | |

**147**

(Home International Championship)
26 October 1929

Referee: McLean (Northern Ireland)
Ninian Park, Cardiff (Att: 25,000)

## WALES 2-4 SCOTLAND — Half-time 0-2

| | | |
|---|---|---|
| (7) | John HARKNESS (Hearts) | Albert GRAY |
| (5) | Douglas GRAY (Rangers) | Benjamin WILLIAMS |
| (4) | Joseph NIBLOE (Kilmarnock) | Arthur LUMBERG |
| (7) | James GIBSON (Aston Villa) | Samuel BENNION |
| (1) | John JOHNSTONE (Hearts) | Frederick KEENOR |
| (6) | Thomas CRAIG (Rangers) | Robert JOHN |
| (14) | Alexander JACKSON (Huddersfield Town) | William DAVIES |
| (8) | Thomas MUIRHEAD (Rangers) captain | Eugene O'CALLAGHAN |
| (16) | Hugh GALLACHER (Newcastle United) | Leonard DAVIES |
| (5) | Alexander JAMES (Arsenal) | Charles JONES |
| (23) | Alan MORTON (Rangers) | Frederick COOK |

| | Goals | |
|---|---|---|
| Gallacher (7 mins) | 1-0 | |
| Gallacher (20 mins) | 2-0 | |
| | 2-1 | O'Callaghan (55 mins) |
| | 2-2 | L.Davies (63 mins) |
| James (74 mins) | 3-2 | |
| Gibson (77 mins) | 4-2 | |

# 1930

| P | W | D | L | F | A |
|---|---|---|---|---|---|
| 4 | 2 | 1 | 1 | 8 | 7 |

**148**

(Home International Championship)
22 February 1930

Referee: Josephs (England)
Celtic Park, Glasgow (Att: 30,000)

## SCOTLAND 3-1 IRELAND — Half-time 1-1

| | | |
|---|---|---|
| (1) | Robert MIDDLETON (Cowdenbeath) | Alfred GARDINER |
| (6) | Douglas GRAY (Rangers) | Samuel RUSSELL |
| (2) | William WISEMAN (Queen's Park) | Robert HAMILTON |
| (8) | James GIBSON (Aston Villa) | Robert McDONALD |
| (10) | David MEIKLEJOHN (Rangers) captain | John JONES |
| (7) | Thomas CRAIG (Rangers) | Thomas SLOAN |
| (15) | Alexander JACKSON (Huddersfield Town) | James CHAMBERS |
| (3) | George STEVENSON (Motherwell) | Robert IRVINE |
| (17) | Hugh GALLACHER (Newcastle United) | Joseph BAMBRICK |
| (6) | Alexander JAMES (Arsenal) | James McCAMBRIDGE |
| (24) | Alan MORTON (Rangers) | Harold McCAW |

| | Goals | |
|---|---|---|
| Gallacher (32 mins) | 1-0 | |
| | 1-1 | McCaw (40 mins) |
| Gallacher (61 mins) | 2-1 | |
| Stevenson (70 mins) | 3-1 | |

**149**

(Home International Championship)
5 April 1930

Referee: McLean (Northern Ireland)
Wembley Stadium, London (Att: 87,375)

## ENGLAND 5-2 SCOTLAND — Half-time 4-0

| | | |
|---|---|---|
| (8) | John HARKNESS (Hearts) | Henry HIBBS |
| (7) | Douglas GRAY (Rangers) | Frederick GOODALL |
| (2) | Thomas LAW (Chelsea) | Ernest BLENKINSOP |
| (2) | John BUCHANAN (Rangers) | Alfred STRANGE |
| (11) | David MEIKLEJOHN (Rangers) captain | Maurice WEBSTER |
| (8) | Thomas CRAIG (Rangers) | William MARSDEN |
| (16) | Alexander JACKSON (Huddersfield Town) | Samuel CROOKS |
| (7) | Alexander JAMES (Arsenal) | David JACK |
| (3) | James FLEMING (Rangers) | Victor WATSON |
| (4) | George STEVENSON (Motherwell) | Joseph BRADFORD |
| (25) | Alan MORTON (Rangers) | Ellis RIMMER |

| | Goals | |
|---|---|---|
| | 0-1 | Watson (12 mins) |
| | 0-2 | Watson (28 mins) |
| | 0-3 | Rimmer (30 mins) |
| | 0-4 | Jack (33 mins) |
| Fleming (48 mins) | 1-4 | |
| | 1-5 | Rimmer (54 mins) |
| Fleming (62 mins) | 2-5 | |

**150**

(Friendly)
18 May 1930

Referee: Van Praag (Belgium)
Stade Olympique du Colombes, Paris (Att: 25,000)

## FRANCE 0-2 SCOTLAND — Half-time 0-1

| | | |
|---|---|---|
| (1) | John THOMSON (Celtic) | Alexis THÉPOT |
| (4) | James NELSON (Cardiff City) | Manuel ANATOL |
| (4) | James CRAPNELL (Airdrie) captain | Marcel CAPELLE |
| (2) | Peter WILSON (Celtic) | Jean LAURENT |
| (1) | George WALKER (St Mirren) | Maurice BANIDE |
| (1) | Frank HILL (Aberdeen) | Augustin CHANTREL |
| (17) | Alexander JACKSON (Huddersfield Town) | Marcel KAUFFMANN |
| (5) | Alexander CHEYNE (Aberdeen) | Henri PAVILLARD |
| (18) | Hugh GALLACHER (Newcastle United) | Marcel PINEL |
| (5) | George STEVENSON (Motherwell) | Edmond DELFOUR |
| (1) | James CONNOR (Sunderland) | Pierre KORB |

| | Goals | |
|---|---|---|
| Gallacher (42 mins) | 1-0 | |
| Gallacher (85 mins) | 2-0 | |

**151**

(Home International Championship)
25 October 1930

Referee: Lines (England)
Ibrox Park, Glasgow (Att: 23,106)

## SCOTLAND 1-1 WALES — Half-time 1-1

| | | |
|---|---|---|
| (2) | John THOMSON (Celtic) | Leonard EVANS |
| (8) | Douglas GRAY (Rangers) | Frederick DEWEY |
| (1) | John GILMOUR (Dundee) | Wynne CROMPTON |
| (1) | Colin McNAB (Dundee) | William ROGERS |
| (2) | Robert GILLESPIE (Queen's Park) captain | Frederick KEENOR |
| (2) | Frank HILL (Aberdeen) | Emrys ELLIS |
| (1) | Daniel McRORIE (Morton) | William COLLINS |
| (1) | George BROWN (Rangers) | John NEAL |
| (1) | Bernard BATTLES (Hearts) | Thomas BAMFORD |
| (6) | George STEVENSON (Motherwell) | Walter ROBBINS |
| (26) | Alan MORTON (Rangers) | William THOMAS |

| | Goals | |
|---|---|---|
| | 0-1 | Bamford (6 mins) |
| Battles (37 mins) | 1-1 | |

# 1931

| P | W | D | L | F | A |
|---|---|---|---|---|---|
| 7 | 4 | 1 | 2 | 11 | 13 |

**152**

(Home International Championship)
21 February 1931

Referee: Hull (England)
Windsor Park, Belfast (Att: 20,000)

## IRELAND 0-0 SCOTLAND

| | | |
|---|---|---|
| (3) | John THOMSON (Celtic) | Alfred GARDINER |
| (5) | James CRAPNELL (Airdrie) | John McNINCH |
| (5) | Joseph NIBLOE (Kilmarnock) | Robert FULTON |
| (3) | Peter WILSON (Celtic) | William McCLEERY |
| (2) | George WALKER (St Mirren) | John JONES |
| (3) | Frank HILL (Aberdeen) | Thomas SLOAN |
| (1) | John MURDOCH (Motherwell) | Hugh BLAIR |
| (1) | Peter SCARFF (Celtic) | Edward FALLOON |
| (1) | Benjamin YORSTON (Aberdeen) | Frederick ROBERTS |
| (3) | Robert McPHAIL (Rangers) | John GEARY |
| (27) | Alan MORTON (Rangers) captain | Harold McCAW |

**153**

(Home International Championship)
28 March 1931

Referee: Atwood (Wales)
Hampden Park, Glasgow (Att: 129,810)

## SCOTLAND 2-0 ENGLAND — Half-time 0-0

| | | |
|---|---|---|
| (4) | John THOMSON (Celtic) | Henry HIBBS |
| (3) | Daniel BLAIR (Clyde) | Frederick GOODALL |
| (6) | Joseph NIBLOE (Kilmarnock) | Ernest BLENKINSOP |
| (2) | Colin McNAB (Dundee) | Alfred STRANGE |
| (12) | David MEIKLEJOHN (Rangers) captain | Herbert ROBERTS |
| (1) | John MILLER (St Mirren) | Austin CAMPBELL |
| (7) | Alexander ARCHIBALD (Rangers) | Samuel CROOKS |
| (7) | George STEVENSON (Motherwell) | Gordon HODGSON |
| (2) | James McGRORY (Celtic) | William DEAN |
| (4) | Robert McPHAIL (Rangers) | Harold BURGESS |
| (28) | Alan MORTON (Rangers) | John CRAWFORD |

| | Goals | |
|---|---|---|
| Stevenson (60 mins) | 1-0 | |
| McGrory (62 mins) | 2-0 | |

Welsh goalkeeper Len Evans and his fellow defenders are in a tangle at Ibrox in October 1930.

## 154

(Friendly)
16 May 1931

Referee: Ruoff (Switzerland)
Hohe Warte Stadion, Vienna (Att: 45,000)

### AUSTRIA 5-0 SCOTLAND — Half-time 2-0

| | | |
|---|---|---|
| (1) | John JACKSON (Partick Thistle) | Rudolf HIDEN |
| (4) | Daniel BLAIR (Clyde) captain | Roman SCHRAMSEIS |
| (7) | Joseph NIBLOE (Kilmarnock) | Josef BLUM |
| (3) | Colin McNAB (Dundee) | Georg BRAUN |
| (1) | James McDOUGALL (Liverpool) | Josef SMISTIK |
| (3) | George WALKER (St Mirren) | Karl GALL |
| (1) | Andrew LOVE (Aberdeen) | Karl ZISCHEK |
| (1) | James PATERSON (Cowdenbeath) | Friedrich GSCHWEIDL |
| (1) | James EASSON (Portsmouth) | Matthias SINDELAR |
| (1) | James ROBERTSON (Dundee) | Anton SCHALL |
| (1) | Daniel LIDDLE (East Fife) | Adolf VOGEL |

Goals
| | | |
|---|---|---|
| | 0-1 | Schall (8 mins) |
| | 0-2 | Zischek (13 mins) |
| | 0-3 | Vogel (49 mins) |
| | 0-4 | Zischek (69 mins) |
| | 0-5 | Sindelar (77 mins) |

## 155

(Friendly)
20 May 1931

Referee: Bauwens (Germany)
Stadio Nazionale del PNF, Rome (Att: 25,000)

### ITALY 3-0 SCOTLAND — Half-time 2-0

| | | |
|---|---|---|
| (2) | John JACKSON (Partick Thistle) | Giampiero COMBI |
| (5) | Daniel BLAIR (Clyde) | Eraldo MONZEGLIO |
| (8) | Joseph NIBLOE (Kilmarnock) | Umberto CALIGARIS |
| (4) | Colin McNAB (Dundee) | Attilio FERRARIS |
| (2) | James McDOUGALL (Liverpool) captain | Fulvio BERNARDINI |
| (2) | John MILLER (St Mirren) | Luigi BERTOLINI |
| (2) | Andrew LOVE (Aberdeen) | Raffaele COSTANTINO |
| (2) | James PATERSON (Cowdenbeath) | Renato CESARINI |
| (1) | William BOYD (Clyde) | Giuseppe MEAZZA |
| (2) | James ROBERTSON (Dundee) | Giovanni FERRARI |
| (2) | Daniel LIDDLE (East Fife) | Raimondo ORSI |

Goals
| | | |
|---|---|---|
| | 0-1 | Costantino (6 mins) |
| | 0-2 | Meazza (42 mins) |
| | 0-3 | Orsi (87 mins) |

## 156

(Friendly)
24 May 1931

Referee: Carraro (Italy)
Parc des Charmilles, Geneva (Att: 10,000)

### SWITZERLAND 2-3 SCOTLAND — Half-time 1-2

| | | |
|---|---|---|
| (3) | John JACKSON (Partick Thistle) | Charles PASCHE |
| (6) | James CRAPNELL (Airdrie) captain | Severino MINELLI |
| (9) | Joseph NIBLOE (Kilmarnock) | Rudolf RAMSEYER |
| (5) | Colin McNAB (Dundee) | Edmond LOICHOT |
| (4) | George WALKER (St Mirren) | Otto IMHOF |
| (3) | John MILLER (St Mirren) | Gabriele GILARDONI |
| (3) | Andrew LOVE (Aberdeen) | Edmond KRAMER |
| (3) | James PATERSON (Cowdenbeath) | André SYRVET |
| (2) | William BOYD (Clyde) | Albert BUCHE |
| (2) | James EASSON (Portsmouth) | André ABEGGLEN |
| (3) | Daniel LIDDLE (East Fife) | Max FAUGUEL |

Goals
| | | |
|---|---|---|
| Easson (22 mins) | 1-0 | |
| Boyd (24 mins) | 2-0 | |
| | 2-1 | Buche (31 mins) |
| | 2-2 | Fauguel (66 mins) |
| Love (89 mins) | 3-2 | |

## 157

(Home International Championship)
19 September 1931

Referee: Caswell (England)
Ibrox Park, Glasgow (Att: 40,000)

### SCOTLAND 3-1 IRELAND — Half-time 2-1

| | | |
|---|---|---|
| (1) | Robert HEPBURN (Ayr United) | Alfred GARDINER |
| (6) | Daniel BLAIR (Clyde) | John McNINCH |
| (1) | Robert McAULAY (Rangers) | Robert HAMILTON |
| (1) | Alexander MASSIE (Hearts) | William McCLEERY |
| (13) | David MEIKLEJOHN (Rangers) captain | John JONES |
| (2) | George BROWN (Rangers) | William GOWDY |
| (1) | James CRAWFORD (Queen's Park) | Hugh BLAIR |
| (8) | George STEVENSON (Motherwell) | Richard ROWLEY |
| (3) | James McGRORY (Celtic) | James DUNNE |
| (5) | Robert McPHAIL (Rangers) | John GEARY |
| (2) | James CONNOR (Sunderland) | James CHAMBERS |

Goals
| | | |
|---|---|---|
| Stevenson (5 mins) | 1-0 | |
| | 1-1 | Dunne (20 mins) |
| McGrory (34 mins) | 2-1 | |
| McPhail (72 mins) | 3-1 | |

## 158

(Home International Championship)
31 October 1931

Referee: Caswell (England)
The Racecourse, Wrexham (Att: 10,860)

### WALES 2-3 SCOTLAND — Half-time 1-2

| | | |
|---|---|---|
| (9) | John HARKNESS (Hearts) | Albert GRAY |
| (7) | Daniel BLAIR (Clyde) | Aneurin RICHARDS |
| (2) | Robert McAULAY (Rangers) | Arthur LUMBERG |
| (2) | Alexander MASSIE (Hearts) | Thomas EDWARDS |
| (14) | David MEIKLEJOHN (Rangers) captain | Thomas GRIFFITHS |
| (3) | George BROWN (Rangers) | Edward LAWRENCE |
| (1) | Robert THOMSON (Celtic) | Philip GRIFFITHS |
| (9) | George STEVENSON (Motherwell) | Eugene O'CALLAGHAN |
| (4) | James McGRORY (Celtic) | Ernest GLOVER |
| (6) | Robert McPHAIL (Rangers) | Walter ROBBINS |
| (29) | Alan MORTON (Rangers) | Ernest CURTIS |

Goals
| | | |
|---|---|---|
| | 0-1 | Curtis (15 mins pen) |
| Stevenson (25 mins) | 1-1 | |
| Thomson (31 mins) | 2-1 | |
| McGrory (55 mins) | 3-1 | |
| | 3-2 | O'Callaghan (78 mins) |

# 1932

| P | W | D | L | F | A |
|---|---|---|---|---|---|
| 4 | 2 | 0 | 2 | 9 | 9 |

## 159

(Home International Championship)
9 April 1932

Referee: Thompson (Northern Ireland)
Wembley Stadium, London (Att: 92,180)

### ENGLAND 3-0 SCOTLAND — Half-time 1-0

| | | |
|---|---|---|
| (1) | Thomas HAMILTON (Rangers) | Harold PEARSON |
| (7) | James CRAPNELL (Airdrie) captain | George SHAW |
| (10) | Joseph NIBLOE (Kilmarnock) | Ernest BLENKINSOP |
| (6) | Colin McNAB (Dundee) | Alfred STRANGE |
| (3) | Allan CRAIG (Motherwell) | James O'DOWD |
| (4) | George BROWN (Rangers) | Samuel WEAVER |
| (8) | Alexander ARCHIBALD (Rangers) | Samuel CROOKS |
| (1) | James MARSHALL (Rangers) | Robert BARCLAY |
| (1) | Neil DEWAR (Third Lanark) | Thomas WARING |
| (1) | Charles NAPIER (Celtic) | Thomas JOHNSON |
| (30) | Alan MORTON (Rangers) | William HOUGHTON |

Goals
| | | |
|---|---|---|
| | 0-1 | Waring (36 mins) |
| | 0-2 | Barclay (79 mins) |
| | 0-3 | Crooks (88 mins) |

## 160

(Friendly)
8 May 1932

Referee: Carraro (Italy)
Stade Olympique du Colombes, Paris (Att: 8,000)

### FRANCE 1-3 SCOTLAND — Half-time 1-3

| | | |
|---|---|---|
| (10) | John HARKNESS (Hearts) | Alexis THÉPOT |
| (8) | James CRAPNELL (Airdrie) | Manuel ANATOL |
| (11) | Joseph NIBLOE (Kilmarnock) | André CHARDAR |
| (3) | Alexander MASSIE (Hearts) | Emile SCHARWATH |
| (3) | Robert GILLESPIE (Queen's Park) captain | Joseph KAUCSAR |
| (4) | John MILLER (St Mirren) | Jean LAURENT |
| (2) | James CRAWFORD (Queen's Park) | Ernest LIBERATI |
| (2) | Alexander THOMSON (Celtic) | Joseph ALCAZAR |
| (2) | Neil DEWAR (Third Lanark) | Robert MERCIER |
| (7) | Robert McPHAIL (Rangers) | René GÉRARD |
| (31) | Alan MORTON (Rangers) | Marcel LANGILLER |

Goals
| | | |
|---|---|---|
| Dewar (14 mins) | 1-0 | |
| Dewar (27 mins) | 2-0 | |
| Dewar (40 mins) | 3-0 | |
| | 3-1 | Langiller (43 mins pen) |

France's goalkeeper Alex Thépot collects the ball from a Scotland forward in Paris in May 1932.

# 1933

| P | W | D | L | F | A |
|---|---|---|---|---|---|
| 4 | 1 | 1 | 2 | 7 | 8 |

## 161

(Home International Championship)
17 September 1932

Referee: Harper (England)
Windsor Park, Belfast (Att: 40,000)

### IRELAND 0-4 SCOTLAND — Half-time 0-2

| | | |
|---|---|---|
| (4) | Alexander McLAREN (St Johnstone) | Elisha SCOTT |
| (9) | Douglas GRAY (Rangers) | William COOK |
| (9) | James CRAPNELL (Airdrie) captain | Robert FULTON |
| (4) | Alexander MASSIE (Hearts) | Edward FALLOON |
| (2) | John JOHNSTONE (Hearts) | John JONES |
| (1) | William TELFER (Motherwell) | William GOWDY |
| (3) | James CRAWFORD (Queen's Park) | Edward MITCHELL |
| (10) | George STEVENSON (Motherwell) | Thomas PRIESTLEY |
| (5) | James McGRORY (Celtic) | William MILLAR |
| (8) | Robert McPHAIL (Rangers) | Samuel ENGLISH |
| (1) | James KING (Hamilton Academical) | James KELLY |

| | Goals | |
|---|---|---|
| King (3 mins) | 1-0 | |
| McPhail (35 mins) | 2-0 | |
| McPhail (67 mins) | 3-0 | |
| McGrory (75 mins) | 4-0 | |

## 162

(Home International Championship)
26 October 1932

Referee: Harper (England)
Tynecastle Park, Edinburgh (Att: 31,000)

### SCOTLAND 2-5 WALES — Half-time 0-4

| | | |
|---|---|---|
| (5) | Alexander McLAREN (St Johnstone) | William JOHN |
| (10) | Douglas GRAY (Rangers) | Benjamin WILLIAMS |
| (8) | Daniel BLAIR (Aston Villa) | Benjamin ELLIS |
| (1) | Hugh WALES (Motherwell) | Frederick KEENOR |
| (3) | John JOHNSTONE (Hearts) captain | Thomas GRIFFITHS |
| (1) | John THOMSON (Everton) | David RICHARDS |
| (4) | James CRAWFORD (Queen's Park) | Cuthbert PHILLIPS |
| (3) | Alexander THOMSON (Celtic) | Eugene O'CALLAGHAN |
| (3) | Neil DEWAR (Third Lanark) | David ASTLEY |
| (8) | Alexander JAMES (Arsenal) | Walter ROBBINS |
| (1) | Douglas DUNCAN (Derby County) | David LEWIS |

| | Goals | |
|---|---|---|
| | 0-1 | J. Thomson (9 mins o.g.) |
| | 0-2 | Griffiths (20 mins) |
| | 0-3 | O'Callaghan (25 mins) |
| | 0-4 | Astley (43 mins) |
| | 0-5 | O'Callaghan (46 mins) |
| Dewar (63 mins) | 1-5 | |
| Duncan (70 mins) | 2-5 | |

## 163

(Home International Championship)
1 April 1933

Referee: Thompson (Northern Ireland)
Hampden Park, Glasgow (Att: 134,170)

### SCOTLAND 2-1 ENGLAND — Half-time 1-1

| | | |
|---|---|---|
| (4) | John JACKSON (Partick Thistle) | Henry HIBBS |
| (1) | Andrew ANDERSON (Hearts) | Thomas COOPER |
| (1) | Peter McGONAGLE (Celtic) | Ernest BLENKINSOP |
| (4) | Peter WILSON (Celtic) | Alfred STRANGE |
| (4) | Robert GILLESPIE (Queen's Park) captain | Ernest HART |
| (5) | George BROWN (Rangers) | Samuel WEAVER |
| (5) | James CRAWFORD (Queen's Park) | Joseph HULME |
| (2) | James MARSHALL (Rangers) | Ronald STARLING |
| (6) | James McGRORY (Celtic) | George HUNT |
| (9) | Robert McPHAIL (Rangers) | John PICKERING |
| (2) | Douglas DUNCAN (Derby County) | John ARNOLD |

| | Goals | |
|---|---|---|
| McGrory (4 mins) | 1-0 | |
| | 1-1 | Hunt (30 mins) |
| McGrory (81 mins) | 2-1 | |

## 164

(Home International Championship)
16 September 1933

Referee: Wood (England)
Celtic Park, Glasgow (Att: 27,131)

### SCOTLAND 1-2 IRELAND — Half-time 0-2

| | | |
|---|---|---|
| (11) | John HARKNESS (Hearts) | Elisha SCOTT |
| (2) | Andrew ANDERSON (Hearts) | Thomas WILLIGHAN |
| (2) | Peter McGONAGLE (Celtic) captain | Robert FULTON |
| (5) | Alexander MASSIE (Hearts) | John McMAHON |
| (1) | Alexander LOW (Falkirk) | John JONES |
| (2) | William TELFER (Motherwell) | William MITCHELL |
| (1) | James BOYD (Newcastle United) | Hugh BLAIR |
| (1) | Alexander VENTERS (Cowdenbeath) | Alexander STEVENSON |
| (7) | James McGRORY (Celtic) | David MARTIN |
| (10) | Robert McPHAIL (Rangers) | John COULTER |
| (2) | James KING (Hamilton Academical) | John MAHOOD |

| | Goals | |
|---|---|---|
| | 0-1 | Martin (8 mins) |
| | 0-2 | Martin (13 mins) |
| McPhail (60 mins) | 1-2 | |

## 165

(Home International Championship)
4 October 1933

Referee: Wood (England)
Ninian Park, Cardiff (Att: 40,000)

### WALES 3-2 SCOTLAND — Half-time 2-0

| | | |
|---|---|---|
| (12) | John HARKNESS (Hearts) | William JOHN |
| (3) | Andrew ANDERSON (Hearts) captain | Sidney LAWRENCE |
| (1) | Duncan URQUHART (Hibernian) | Benjamin ELLIS |
| (1) | Matthew BUSBY (Manchester City) | James MURPHY |
| (1) | John BLAIR (Motherwell) | Thomas GRIFFITHS |
| (1) | James McLUCKIE (Manchester City) | David RICHARDS |
| (1) | Francis McGURK (Birmingham) | Cuthbert PHILLIPS |
| (1) | John McMENEMY (Motherwell) | Eugene O'CALLAGHAN |
| (1) | William McFADYEN (Motherwell) | David ASTLEY |
| (3) | James EASSON (Portsmouth) | Walter ROBBINS |
| (3) | Douglas DUNCAN (Derby County) | William EVANS |

| | Goals | |
|---|---|---|
| | 0-1 | Evans (25 mins) |
| | 0-2 | Robbins (35 mins) |
| | 0-3 | Astley (56 mins) |
| McFadyen (76 mins) | 1-3 | |
| Duncan (81 mins) | 2-3 | |

**66**

(Friendly)
29 November 1933

Referee: Langenus (Belgium)
Hampden Park, Glasgow (Att: 62,000)

### SCOTLAND 2-2 AUSTRIA — Half-time 1-1

| | | |
|---|---|---|
| 1) | James KENNAWAY (Celtic) | Peter PLATZER |
| 4) | Andrew ANDERSON (Hearts) | Anton JANDA |
| 3) | Peter McGONAGLE (Celtic) | Karl SESTA |
| 15) | David MEIKLEJOHN (Rangers) captain | Franz WAGNER |
| 1) | Philip WATSON (Blackpool) | Josef SMISTIK |
| 5) | George BROWN (Rangers) | Walter NAUSCH |
| 1) | Duncan OGILVIE (Motherwell) | Karl ZISCHEK |
| 1) | Robert BRUCE (Middlesbrough) | Josef BICAN |
| 2) | William McFADYEN (Motherwell) | Matthias SINDELAR |
| 11) | Robert McPHAIL (Rangers) | Anton SCHALL |
| 4) | Douglas DUNCAN (Derby County) | Ralf VIERTEL |

| | Goals | |
|---|---|---|
| Meiklejohn (7 mins) | 1-0 | |
| | 1-1 | Zischek (41 mins) |
| McFadyen (49 mins) | 2-1 | |
| | 2-2 | Schall (53 mins) |

## 1934

| P | W | D | L | F | A |
|---|---|---|---|---|---|
| 3 | 1 | 0 | 2 | 4 | 7 |

**67**

(Home International Championship)
14 April 1934

Referee: Thompson (Northern Ireland)
Wembley Stadium, London (Att: 92,363)

### ENGLAND 3-0 SCOTLAND — Half-time 1-0

| | | |
|---|---|---|
| 5) | John JACKSON (Chelsea) | Frank MOSS |
| 5) | Andrew ANDERSON (Hearts) | Thomas COOPER |
| 4) | Peter McGONAGLE (Celtic) | Edris HAPGOOD |
| 5) | Alexander MASSIE (Hearts) captain | Lewis STOKER |
| 1) | Thomas SMITH (Kilmarnock) | Ernest HART |
| 5) | John MILLER (St Mirren) | Wilfred COPPING |
| 1) | William COOK (Bolton Wanderers) | Samuel CROOKS |
| 3) | James MARSHALL (Rangers) | Horatio CARTER |
| 19) | Hugh GALLACHER (Chelsea) | John BOWERS |
| 1) | George STEVENSON (Motherwell) | Clifford BASTIN |
| 3) | James CONNOR (Sunderland) | Eric BROOK |

| | Goals | |
|---|---|---|
| | 0-1 | Bastin (43 mins) |
| | 0-2 | Brook (80 mins) |
| | 0-3 | Bowers (88 mins) |

**68**

(Home International Championship)
20 October 1934

Referee: Mee (England)
Windsor Park, Belfast (Att: 39,752)

### IRELAND 2-1 SCOTLAND — Half-time 0-1

| | | |
|---|---|---|
| 1) | James DAWSON (Rangers) | Elisha SCOTT |
| 5) | Andrew ANDERSON (Hearts) | James MACKIE |
| 5) | Peter McGONAGLE (Celtic) | Robert FULTON |
| 7) | Alexander MASSIE (Hearts) captain | Walter McMILLEN |
| 1) | James SIMPSON (Rangers) | John JONES |
| 1) | Andrew HERD (Hearts) | William MITCHELL |
| 2) | William COOK (Bolton Wanderers) | Harold DUGGAN |
| 12) | George STEVENSON (Motherwell) | William GOWDY |
| 1) | James SMITH (Rangers) | David MARTIN |
| 1) | Patrick GALLACHER (Sunderland) | Alexander STEVENSON |
| 1) | James CONNOR (Sunderland) | John COULTER |

| | Goals | |
|---|---|---|
| Gallacher (43 mins) | 1-0 | |
| | 1-1 | Martin (76 mins) |
| | 1-2 | Coulter (89 mins) |

## Right column

**169**

(Home International Championship)
21 November 1934

Referee: Thompson (Northern Ireland)
Pittodrie Park, Aberdeen (Att: 26,334)

### SCOTLAND 3-2 WALES — Half-time 1-0

| | | |
|---|---|---|
| (3) | Allan McCLORY (Motherwell) | William JOHN |
| (7) | Andrew ANDERSON (Hearts) | Sidney LAWRENCE |
| (6) | Peter McGONAGLE (Celtic) | David JONES |
| (8) | Alexander MASSIE (Hearts) | James MURPHY |
| (2) | James SIMPSON (Rangers) captain | Harold HANFORD |
| (7) | George BROWN (Rangers) | David RICHARDS |
| (3) | William COOK (Bolton Wanderers) | Idris HOPKINS |
| (1) | Thomas WALKER (Hearts) | Ronald WILLIAMS |
| (1) | David McCULLOCH (Hearts) | David ASTLEY |
| (2) | Charles NAPIER (Celtic) | Thomas MILLS |
| (5) | Douglas DUNCAN (Derby County) | Cuthbert PHILLIPS |

| | Goals | |
|---|---|---|
| Duncan (23 mins) | 1-0 | |
| Napier (46 mins) | 2-0 | |
| | 2-1 | Phillips (73 mins) |
| Napier (85 mins) | 3-1 | |
| | 3-2 | Astley (88 mins) |

## 1935

| P | W | D | L | F | A |
|---|---|---|---|---|---|
| 3 | 2 | 1 | 0 | 5 | 2 |

**170**

(Home International Championship)
6 April 1935

Referee: Thompson (Northern Ireland)
Hampden Park, Glasgow (Att: 129,693)

### SCOTLAND 2-0 ENGLAND — Half-time 1-0

| | | |
|---|---|---|
| (6) | John JACKSON (Chelsea) | Henry HIBBS |
| (8) | Andrew ANDERSON (Hearts) | Charles MALE |
| (1) | George CUMMINGS (Partick Thistle) | Edris HAPGOOD |
| (9) | Alexander MASSIE (Hearts) | Clifford BRITTON |
| (3) | James SIMPSON (Rangers) captain | John BARKER |
| (8) | George BROWN (Rangers) | Walter ALSFORD |
| (3) | Charles NAPIER (Celtic) | Albert GELDARD |
| (2) | Thomas WALKER (Hearts) | Clifford BASTIN |
| (20) | Hugh GALLACHER (Derby County) | Robert GURNEY |
| (12) | Robert McPHAIL (Rangers) | Raymond WESTWOOD |
| (6) | Douglas DUNCAN (Derby County) | Eric BROOK |

| | Goals | |
|---|---|---|
| Duncan (43 mins) | 1-0 | |
| Duncan (50 mins) | 2-0 | |

**171**

(Home International Championship)
5 October 1935

Referee: Caswell (England)
Ninian Park, Cardiff (Att: 35,004)

### WALES 1-1 SCOTLAND — Half-time 1-1

| | | |
|---|---|---|
| (7) | John JACKSON (Chelsea) | William JOHN |
| (9) | Andrew ANDERSON (Hearts) | Sidney LAWRENCE |
| (2) | George CUMMINGS (Partick Thistle) | Robert JOHN |
| (10) | Alexander MASSIE (Hearts) | James MURPHY |
| (4) | James SIMPSON (Rangers) captain | Thomas GRIFFITHS |
| (9) | George BROWN (Rangers) | David RICHARDS |
| (1) | James DELANEY (Celtic) | Cuthbert PHILLIPS |
| (3) | Thomas WALKER (Hearts) | Brynmor JONES |
| (1) | Matthew ARMSTRONG (Aberdeen) | Ernest GLOVER |
| (1) | William MILLS (Aberdeen) | Leslie JONES |
| (7) | Douglas DUNCAN (Derby County) | Walter ROBBINS |

| | Goals | |
|---|---|---|
| Duncan (35 mins) | 1-0 | |
| | 1-1 | Phillips (42 mins) |

**172**

(Home International Championship)　　　　Referee: Nattrass (England)
13 November 1935　　　　Tynecastle Park, Edinburgh (Att: 30,000)

### SCOTLAND 2-1 IRELAND　　　　Half-time 0-0

| | | |
|---|---|---|
| (8) | John JACKSON (Chelsea) | Elisha SCOTT |
| (10) | Andrew ANDERSON (Hearts) | William COOK |
| (3) | George CUMMINGS (Partick Thistle) | Robert FULTON |
| (11) | Alexander MASSIE (Hearts) | Keiller McCULLOUGH |
| (5) | James SIMPSON (Rangers) captain | John JONES |
| (1) | Alexander HASTINGS (Sunderland) | William MITCHELL |
| (2) | James DELANEY (Celtic) | Harold DUGGAN |
| (4) | Thomas WALKER (Hearts) | Alexander STEVENSON |
| (2) | Matthew ARMSTRONG (Aberdeen) | Joseph BAMBRICK |
| (2) | William MILLS (Aberdeen) | Peter DOHERTY |
| (8) | Douglas DUNCAN (Derby County) | James KELLY |

Goals

| | | |
|---|---|---|
| | 0-1 | Kelly (49 mins) |
| Walker (58 mins) | 1-1 | |
| Duncan (89 mins) | 2-1 | |

## 1936

| P | W | D | L | F | A |
|---|---|---|---|---|---|
| 4 | 2 | 1 | 1 | 7 | 4 |

**173**

(Home International Championship)　　　　Referee: Hamilton (Northern Ireland)
4 April 1936　　　　Wembley Stadium, London (Att: 93,267)

### ENGLAND 1-1 SCOTLAND　　　　Half-time 1-0

| | | |
|---|---|---|
| (2) | James DAWSON (Rangers) | Edward SAGAR |
| (11) | Andrew ANDERSON (Hearts) | Charles MALE |
| (4) | George CUMMINGS (Aston Villa) | Edris HAPGOOD |
| (12) | Alexander MASSIE (Aston Villa) | William CRAYSTON |
| (6) | James SIMPSON (Rangers) captain | John BARKER |
| (10) | George BROWN (Rangers) | John BRAY |
| (1) | John CRUM (Celtic) | Samuel CROOKS |
| (5) | Thomas WALKER (Hearts) | Robert BARCLAY |
| (2) | David McCULLOCH (Brentford) | George CAMSELL |
| (2) | Alexander VENTERS (Rangers) | Clifford BASTIN |
| (9) | Douglas DUNCAN (Derby County) | Eric BROOK |

Goals

| | | |
|---|---|---|
| | 0-1 | Camsell (30 mins) |
| Walker (77 mins pen) | 1-1 | |

**174**

(Friendly)　　　　Referee: Nattrass (England)
14 October 1936　　　　Ibrox Park, Glasgow (Att: 50,000)

### SCOTLAND 2-0 GERMANY　　　　Half-time 0-0

| | | |
|---|---|---|
| (3) | James DAWSON (Rangers) | Hans JAKOB |
| (12) | Andrew ANDERSON (Hearts) | Reinhold MÜNZENBERG |
| (5) | George CUMMINGS (Aston Villa) | Andreas MUNKERT |
| (13) | Alexander MASSIE (Aston Villa) | Paul JANES |
| (7) | James SIMPSON (Rangers) captain | Ludwig GOLDBRUNNER |
| (11) | George BROWN (Rangers) | Albin KITZINGER |
| (3) | James DELANEY (Celtic) | Franz ELBERN |
| (6) | Thomas WALKER (Hearts) | Rudolf GELLESCH |
| (3) | Matthew ARMSTRONG (Aberdeen) | Otto SIFFLING |
| (13) | Robert McPHAIL (Rangers) | Fritz SZEPAN |
| (10) | Douglas DUNCAN (Derby County) | Adolf URBAN |

Goals

| | | |
|---|---|---|
| Delaney (67 mins) | 1-0 | |
| Delaney (83 mins) | 2-0 | |

**175**

(Home International Championship)　　　　Referee: Thompson (England)
31 October 1936　　　　Windsor Park, Belfast (Att: 45,000)

### IRELAND 1-3 SCOTLAND　　　　Half-time 1-1

| | | |
|---|---|---|
| (4) | James DAWSON (Rangers) | Thomas BREEN |
| (13) | Andrew ANDERSON (Hearts) | William COOK |
| (1) | Robert ANCELL (Newcastle United) | Robert FULTON |
| (14) | Alexander MASSIE (Aston Villa) | Walter McMILLEN |
| (8) | James SIMPSON (Rangers) captain | John JONES |
| (12) | George BROWN (Rangers) | William MITCHELL |
| (1) | Alexander MUNRO (Hearts) | Noel KERNAGHAN |
| (7) | Thomas WALKER (Hearts) | Keiller McCULLOUGH |
| (3) | David McCULLOCH (Brentford) | David MARTIN |
| (4) | Charles NAPIER (Derby County) | John COULTER |
| (11) | Douglas DUNCAN (Derby County) | James KELLY |

Goals

| | | |
|---|---|---|
| | 0-1 | Kernaghan (25 mins) |
| Napier (27 mins) | 1-1 | |
| Munro (47 mins) | 2-1 | |
| McCulloch (63 mins) | 3-1 | |

**176**

(Home International Championship)　　　　Referee: Barton (England)
2 December 1936　　　　Dens Park, Dundee (Att: 23,858)

### SCOTLAND 1-2 WALES　　　　Half-time 0-1

| | | |
|---|---|---|
| (5) | James DAWSON (Rangers) | Albert GRAY |
| (14) | Andrew ANDERSON (Hearts) | Herbert TURNER |
| (2) | Robert ANCELL (Newcastle United) | Benjamin ELLIS |
| (15) | Alexander MASSIE (Aston Villa) | James MURPHY |
| (9) | James SIMPSON (Rangers) captain | Thomas GRIFFITHS |
| (13) | George BROWN (Rangers) | David RICHARDS |
| (2) | Alexander MUNRO (Hearts) | Idris HOPKINS |
| (8) | Thomas WALKER (Hearts) | Brynmor JONES |
| (4) | David McCULLOCH (Brentford) | Ernest GLOVER |
| (3) | William MILLS (Aberdeen) | Leslie JONES |
| (12) | Douglas DUNCAN (Derby County) | Seymour MORRIS |

Goals

| | | |
|---|---|---|
| | 0-1 | Glover (22 mins) |
| Walker (59 mins) | 1-1 | |
| | 1-2 | Glover (77 mins) |

## 1937

| P | W | D | L | F | A |
|---|---|---|---|---|---|
| 6 | 3 | 2 | 1 | 14 | 6 |

**177**

(Home International Championship)　　　　Referee: McLean (Northern Ireland)
17 April 1937　　　　Hampden Park, Glasgow (Att: 149,547)

### SCOTLAND 3-1 ENGLAND　　　　Half-time 0-1

| | | |
|---|---|---|
| (6) | James DAWSON (Rangers) | Victor WOODLEY |
| (15) | Andrew ANDERSON (Hearts) | Charles MALE |
| (1) | Andrew BEATTIE (Preston North End) | Samuel BARKAS |
| (16) | Alexander MASSIE (Aston Villa) | Clifford BRITTON |
| (10) | James SIMPSON (Rangers) captain | Alfred YOUNG |
| (14) | George BROWN (Rangers) | John BRAY |
| (4) | James DELANEY (Celtic) | Stanley MATTHEWS |
| (9) | Thomas WALKER (Hearts) | Horatio CARTER |
| (1) | Frank O'DONNELL (Preston North End) | Frederick STEELE |
| (14) | Robert McPHAIL (Rangers) | Ronald STARLING |
| (13) | Douglas DUNCAN (Derby County) | Joseph JOHNSON |

Goals

| | | |
|---|---|---|
| | 0-1 | Steele (40 mins) |
| O'Donnell (47 mins) | 1-1 | |
| McPhail (80 mins) | 2-1 | |
| McPhail (88 mins) | 3-1 | |

**178**

(Friendly)　　　　Referee: Langenus (Belgium)
9 May 1937　　　　Prater Stadium, Vienna (Att: 63,000)

### AUSTRIA 1-1 SCOTLAND　　　　Half-time 0-0

| | | |
|---|---|---|
| (7) | James DAWSON (Rangers) | Peter PLATZER |
| (16) | Andrew ANDERSON (Hearts) | Karl SESTA |
| (2) | Andrew BEATTIE (Preston North End) | Willibald SCHMAUS |
| (17) | Alexander MASSIE (Aston Villa) | Karl ADAMEK |
| (11) | James SIMPSON (Rangers) captain | Josef PEKAREK |
| (1) | Alexander McNAB (Sunderland) | Walter NAUSCH |
| (5) | James DELANEY (Celtic) | Rudolf GEITER |
| (10) | Thomas WALKER (Hearts) | Josef STROH |
| (2) | Frank O'DONNELL (Preston North End) | Matthias SINDELAR |
| (5) | Charles NAPIER (Derby County) | Camillo JERUSALEM |
| (1) | Torrance GILLICK (Everton) | Johann PESSER |

Goals

| | | |
|---|---|---|
| | 0-1 | Jerusalem (78 mins) |
| O'Donnell (80 mins) | 1-1 | |

**179**
(Friendly)
15 May 1937

Referee: Bauwens (Germany)
Sparta Stadion, Prague (Att: 35,000)

## CZECHOSLOVAKIA 1-3 SCOTLAND — Half-time 1-2

| (8) | James DAWSON (Rangers) | Frantisek PLÁNICKA |
|---|---|---|
| (1) | Robert HOGG (Celtic) | Jaroslav BURGR |
| (3) | Andrew BEATTIE (Preston North End) | Josef CTYROKY |
| (1) | Charles THOMSON (Sunderland) | Josef KOSTALEK |
| (12) | James SIMPSON (Rangers) captain | Jaroslav BOUCEK |
| (15) | George BROWN (Rangers) | Karel KOLSKY |
| (6) | James DELANEY (Celtic) | Vilém ZLATNÍK |
| (11) | Thomas WALKER (Hearts) | Frantisek SVOBODA |
| (3) | Frank O'DONNELL (Preston North End) | Jiří SOBOTKA |
| (15) | Robert McPHAIL (Rangers) | Vlastimil KOPECKY |
| (2) | Torrance GILLICK (Everton) | Antonín PUC |

Goals

| | | |
|---|---|---|
| Simpson (14 mins) | 1-0 | |
| | 1-1 | Puc (31 mins) |
| McPhail (32 mins) | 2-1 | |
| Gillick (69 mins) | 3-1 | |

**180**
(Home International Championship)
30 October 1937

Referee: Argent (England)
Ninian Park, Cardiff (Att: 41,800)

## WALES 2-1 SCOTLAND — Half-time 1-0

| (9) | James DAWSON (Rangers) | Albert GRAY |
|---|---|---|
| (17) | Andrew ANDERSON (Hearts) | Herbert TURNER |
| (6) | George CUMMINGS (Aston Villa) | William HUGHES |
| (18) | Alexander MASSIE (Aston Villa) | James MURPHY |
| (13) | James SIMPSON (Rangers) captain | Harold HANFORD |
| (16) | George BROWN (Rangers) | David RICHARDS |
| (1) | Robert MAIN (Rangers) | Cuthbert PHILLIPS |
| (12) | Thomas WALKER (Hearts) | Leslie JONES |
| (4) | Frank O'DONNELL (Preston North End) | Edwin PERRY |
| (16) | Robert McPHAIL (Rangers) | Brynmor JONES |
| (14) | Douglas DUNCAN (Derby County) | Seymour MORRIS |

Goals

| | | |
|---|---|---|
| | 0-1 | B.Jones (26 mins) |
| | 0-2 | Morris (51 mins) |
| Massie (72 mins) | 1-2 | |

**181**
(Home International Championship)
10 November 1937

Referee: Jewell (England)
Pittodrie Park, Aberdeen (Att: 21,878)

## SCOTLAND 1-1 IRELAND — Half-time 0-1

| (10) | James DAWSON (Rangers) | Thomas BREEN |
|---|---|---|
| (18) | Andrew ANDERSON (Hearts) | William HAYES |
| (7) | George CUMMINGS (Aston Villa) | William COOK |
| (1) | Duncan McKENZIE (Brentford) | Matthew DOHERTY |
| (14) | James SIMPSON (Rangers) captain | Walter McMILLEN |
| (2) | Alexander HASTINGS (Sunderland) | William MITCHELL |
| (7) | James DELANEY (Celtic) | John BROWN |
| (13) | Thomas WALKER (Hearts) | James McALINDEN |
| (2) | James SMITH (Rangers) | David MARTIN |
| (17) | Robert McPHAIL (Rangers) | Peter DOHERTY |
| (1) | Robert REID (Brentford) | John COULTER |

Goals

| | | |
|---|---|---|
| | 0-1 | P.Doherty (14 mins) |
| Smith (49 mins) | 1-1 | |

**182**
(Friendly)
8 December 1937

Referee: Thompson (England)
Hampden Park, Glasgow (Att: 41,000)

## SCOTLAND 5-0 CZECHOSLOVAKIA — Half-time 3-0

| (1) | William WAUGH (Hearts) | Frantisek PLÁNICKA |
|---|---|---|
| (19) | Andrew ANDERSON (Hearts) captain | Josef KOSTALEK |
| (8) | George CUMMINGS (Aston Villa) | Ferdinand DAUCIK |
| (1) | George ROBERTSON (Kilmarnock) | Antonin VODICKA |
| (1) | Robert JOHNSTON (Sunderland) | Jaroslav BOUCEK |
| (17) | George BROWN (Rangers) | Karel KOLSKY |
| (1) | Peter BUCHANAN (Chelsea) | Ján RIHA |
| (14) | Thomas WALKER (Hearts) | Jiří SOBOTKA |
| (5) | David McCULLOCH (Brentford) | Josef ZEMAN |
| (1) | Andrew BLACK (Hearts) | Oldrich NEJEDLY |
| (1) | David KINNEAR (Rangers) | Antonín PUC |

Goals

| | |
|---|---|
| Black (1 min) | 1-0 |
| McCulloch (30 mins) | 2-0 |
| Buchanan (38 mins) | 3-0 |
| McCulloch (62 mins) | 4-0 |
| Kinnear (70 mins) | 5-0 |

# 1938

| P | W | D | L | F | A |
|---|---|---|---|---|---|
| 5 | 5 | 0 | 0 | 12 | 4 |

**183**
(Home International Championship)
9 April 1938

Referee: Hamilton (Northern Ireland)
Wembley Stadium, London (Att: 93,267)

## ENGLAND 0-1 SCOTLAND — Half-time 0-1

| (1) | David CUMMING (Middlesbrough) | Victor WOODLEY |
|---|---|---|
| (20) | Andrew ANDERSON (Hearts) | Bert SPROSTON |
| (4) | Andrew BEATTIE (Preston North End) | Edris HAPGOOD |
| (1) | William SHANKLY (Preston North End) | Charles WILLINGHAM |
| (2) | Thomas SMITH (Preston North End) | Stanley CULLIS |
| (18) | George BROWN (Rangers) captain | Wilfred COPPING |
| (1) | John MILNE (Middlesbrough) | Stanley MATTHEWS |
| (15) | Thomas WALKER (Hearts) | George HALL |
| (5) | Frank O'DONNELL (Blackpool) | Michael FENTON |
| (1) | George MUTCH (Preston North End) | Joseph STEPHENSON |
| (2) | Robert REID (Brentford) | Clifford BASTIN |

Goals

| | |
|---|---|
| Walker (6 mins) | 1-0 |

Action around the Scottish goal at Wembley in April 1938. Hearts' Tommy Walker scored the only goal of the game after six minutes.

(Friendly)
21 May 1938

Referee: Argent (England)
Olympisch Stadion, Amsterdam (Att: 50,000)

### NETHERLANDS 1-3 SCOTLAND — Half-time 0-0

| | | | |
|---|---|---|---|
| (11) | James DAWSON (Rangers) | | Adrianus VAN MALE |
| (21) | Andrew ANDERSON (Hearts) | | Bartholomeus WEBER |
| (1) | James CARABINE (Third Lanark) | | Hubertus CALDENHOVE |
| (1) | Thomas McKILLOP (Rangers) | | Jacob PAAUWE |
| (1) | James DYKES (Hearts) | | Willem ANDERIESEN |
| (19) | George BROWN (Rangers) captain | | Gerardus VAN HEEL |
| (3) | Alexander MUNRO (Blackpool) | | Frank WELS |
| (16) | Thomas WALKER (Hearts) | | Hendrik VAN SPAANDONCK |
| (6) | Frank O'DONNELL (Blackpool) | | Leendert VENTE |
| (2) | Andrew BLACK (Hearts) | | Frederik VAN DER VEEN |
| (1) | Francis MURPHY (Celtic) | | Hubertus DE HARDER |

| | Goals | |
|---|---|---|
| Black (52 mins) | 1-0 | |
| Murphy (56 mins) | 2-0 | |
| Walker (70 mins) | 3-0 | |
| | 3-1 | Vente (85 mins) |

---

185

(Home International Championship)
8 October 1938

Referee: Mortimer (England)
Windsor Park, Belfast (Att: 40,000)

### IRELAND 0-2 SCOTLAND — Half-time 0-1

| | | | |
|---|---|---|---|
| (12) | James DAWSON (Rangers) | | Thomas BREEN |
| (2) | James CARABINE (Third Lanark) captain | | William HAYES |
| (5) | Andrew BEATTIE (Preston North End) | | William COOK |
| (2) | William SHANKLY (Preston North End) | | Walter McMILLEN |
| (2) | James DYKES (Hearts) | | Matthew O'MAHONEY |
| (1) | George PATERSON (Celtic) | | Robert BROWNE |
| (8) | James DELANEY (Celtic) | | John BROWN |
| (17) | Thomas WALKER (Hearts) | | James McALINDEN |
| (2) | John CRUM (Celtic) | | David MARTIN |
| (1) | John DIVERS (Celtic) | | Alexander STEVENSON |
| (3) | Torrance GILLICK (Everton) | | John COULTER |

| | Goals | |
|---|---|---|
| Delaney (33 mins) | 1-0 | |
| Walker (48 mins) | 2-0 | |

---

186

(Home International Championship)
9 November 1938

Referee: Thompson (England)
Tynecastle Park, Edinburgh (Att: 34,810)

### SCOTLAND 3-2 WALES — Half-time 1-1

| | | | |
|---|---|---|---|
| (1) | John BROWN (Clyde) | | William JOHN |
| (22) | Andrew ANDERSON (Hearts) captain | | William WHATLEY |
| (6) | Andrew BEATTIE (Preston North End) | | William HUGHES |
| (3) | William SHANKLY (Preston North End) | | Donald DEARSON |
| (1) | Robert BAXTER (Middlesbrough) | | Thomas JONES |
| (1) | Archibald MILLER (Hearts) | | David RICHARDS |
| (9) | James DELANEY (Celtic) | | Idris HOPKINS |
| (18) | Thomas WALKER (Hearts) | | Leslie JONES |
| (6) | David McCULLOCH (Derby County) | | David ASTLEY |
| (1) | Robert BEATTIE (Preston North End) | | Brynmor JONES |
| (4) | Torrance GILLICK (Everton) | | Reginald CUMNER |

| | Goals | |
|---|---|---|
| | 0-1 | Astley (20 mins) |
| Gillick (38 mins) | 1-1 | |
| Walker (83 mins) | 2-1 | |
| Walker (84 mins) | 3-1 | |
| | 3-2 | L.Jones (86 mins) |

---

187

(Friendly)
7 December 1938

Referee: Nattrass (England)
Ibrox Park, Glasgow (Att: 23,000)

### SCOTLAND 3-1 HUNGARY — Half-time 3-0

| | | | |
|---|---|---|---|
| (13) | James DAWSON (Rangers) | | Antal SZABÓ |
| (23) | Andrew ANDERSON (Hearts) captain | | Lajos KORÁNYI |
| (7) | Andrew BEATTIE (Preston North End) | | Sándor BIRÓ |
| (4) | William SHANKLY (Preston North End) | | Gyula POLGÁR |
| (2) | Robert BAXTER (Middlesbrough) | | József TURAY |
| (1) | James SYMON (Rangers) | | Gyula DUDAS |
| (1) | Alexander McSPADYEN (Partick Thistle) | | Pál TITKOS |
| (19) | Thomas WALKER (Hearts) | | László CSEH |
| (7) | David McCULLOCH (Derby County) | | György SÁROSI |
| (3) | Andrew BLACK (Hearts) | | Géza TOLDI |
| (5) | Torrance GILLICK (Everton) | | László GYETVAI |

| | Goals | |
|---|---|---|
| Walker (19 mins pen) | 1-0 | |
| Black (27 mins) | 2-0 | |
| Gillick (28 mins) | 3-0 | |
| | 3-1 | Sárosi (72 mins pen) |

---

# 1939

| P | W | D | L | F | A |
|---|---|---|---|---|---|
| 1 | 0 | 0 | 1 | 1 | 2 |

188

(Home International Championship)
15 April 1939

Referee: Hamilton (Northern Ireland)
Hampden Park, Glasgow (Att: 149,269)

### SCOTLAND 1-2 ENGLAND — Half-time 1-0

| | | | |
|---|---|---|---|
| (14) | James DAWSON (Rangers) | | Victor WOODLEY |
| (3) | James CARABINE (Third Lanark) | | William MORRIS |
| (9) | George CUMMINGS (Aston Villa) | | Edris HAPGOOD |
| (5) | William SHANKLY (Preston North End) | | Charles WILLINGHAM |
| (3) | Robert BAXTER (Middlesbrough) | | Stanley CULLIS |
| (2) | Alexander McNAB (West Bromwich Albion) | | Joseph MERCER |
| (2) | Alexander McSPADYEN (Partick Thistle) | | Stanley MATTHEWS |
| (20) | Thomas WALKER (Hearts) | | George HALL |
| (1) | James DOUGALL (Preston North End) captain | | Thomas LAWTON |
| (3) | Alexander VENTERS (Rangers) | | Leonard GOULDEN |
| (2) | John MILNE (Middlesbrough) | | Albert BEASLEY |

| | Goals | |
|---|---|---|
| Dougall (21 mins) | 1-0 | |
| | 1-1 | Beasley (66 mins) |
| | 1-2 | Lawton (88 mins) |

---

# 1946

| P | W | D | L | F | A |
|---|---|---|---|---|---|
| 2 | 0 | 1 | 1 | 1 | 3 |

189

(Home International Championship)
19 October 1946

Referee: Evans (England)
The Racecourse, Wrexham (Att: 29,568)

### WALES 3-1 SCOTLAND — Half-time 0-0

| | | | |
|---|---|---|---|
| (1) | William MILLER (Celtic) | | Cyril SIDLOW |
| (1) | James STEPHEN (Bradford) captain | | Raymond LAMBERT |
| (1) | David SHAW (Hibernian) | | William HUGHES |
| (1) | Hugh BROWN (Partick Thistle) | | Douglas WITCOMB |
| (1) | Frank BRENNAN (Newcastle United) | | Thomas JONES |
| (1) | John HUSBAND (Partick Thistle) | | William BURGESS |
| (1) | William WADDELL (Rangers) | | William JONES |
| (1) | Cornelius DOUGALL (Birmingham City) | | Aubrey POWELL |
| (1) | William THORNTON (Rangers) | | Trevor FORD |
| (1) | James BLAIR (Blackpool) | | Brynmor JONES |
| (1) | William LIDDELL (Liverpool) | | George EDWARDS |

| | Goals | |
|---|---|---|
| Waddell (49 mins pen) | 1-0 | |
| | 1-1 | B.Jones (52 mins) |
| | 1-2 | Ford (78 mins) |
| | 1-3 | Stephen (87 mins o.g.) |

---

190

(Home International Championship)
27 November 1946

Referee: Reader (England)
Hampden Park, Glasgow (Att: 98,776)

### SCOTLAND 0-0 IRELAND

| | | | |
|---|---|---|---|
| (1) | Robert BROWN (Rangers) | | Edward HINTON |
| (1) | George YOUNG (Rangers) | | William GORMAN |
| (2) | David SHAW (Hibernian) captain | | James FEENEY |
| (1) | William CAMPBELL (Morton) | | Cornelius MARTIN |
| (2) | Frank BRENNAN (Newcastle United) | | John VERNON |
| (1) | Hugh LONG (Clyde) | | Peter FARRELL |
| (1) | Gordon SMITH (Hibernian) | | David COCHRANE |
| (1) | George HAMILTON (Aberdeen) | | John CAREY |
| (2) | William THORNTON (Rangers) | | David WALSH |
| (1) | James DUNCANSON (Rangers) | | Alexander STEVENSON |
| (2) | William LIDDELL (Liverpool) | | Thomas EGLINGTON |

# 1947

| | P | W | D | L | F | A |
|---|---|---|---|---|---|---|
| | 5 | 1 | 1 | 3 | 9 | 7 |

## 191
(Home International Championship)
12 April 1947
Referee: De La Salle (France)
Wembley Stadium, London (Att: 98,200)

### ENGLAND 1-1 SCOTLAND — Half-time 0-1

| | | | |
|---|---|---|---|
| (2) | William MILLER (Celtic) | | Frank SWIFT |
| (2) | George YOUNG (Rangers) | | Lawrence SCOTT |
| (4) | John SHAW (Rangers) captain | | George HARDWICK |
| (1) | Archibald MacAULEY (Brentford) | | William WRIGHT |
| (1) | William WOODBURN (Rangers) | | Cornelius FRANKLIN |
| (1) | Alexander FORBES (Sheffield United) | | Harold JOHNSTON |
| (2) | Gordon SMITH (Hibernian) | | Stanley MATTHEWS |
| (1) | Andrew McLAREN (Preston North End) | | Horatio CARTER |
| (10) | James DELANEY (Manchester United) | | Thomas LAWTON |
| (1) | William STEEL (Morton) | | Wilfred MANNION |
| (1) | Thomas PEARSON (Newcastle United) | | James MULLEN |

Goals
McLaren (16 mins) — 1-0
1-1 — Carter (56 mins)

## 192
(Friendly)
18 May 1947
Referee: Laursen (Denmark)
Heysel Stadion, Brussels (Att: 51,161)

### BELGIUM 2-1 SCOTLAND — Half-time 1-0

| | | | |
|---|---|---|---|
| (3) | William MILLER (Celtic) | | François DAENEN |
| (3) | George YOUNG (Rangers) | | Léon AERNAUDTS |
| (2) | John SHAW (Rangers) captain | | Joseph PANNAYE |
| (2) | Hugh BROWN (Partick Thistle) | | Alfons DE BUCK |
| (2) | William WOODBURN (Rangers) | | Jules HENRIET |
| (2) | Alexander FORBES (Sheffield United) | | Fernand MASSAY |
| (1) | Robert CAMPBELL (Falkirk) | | Victor LEMBERECHTS |
| (1) | Andrew McLAREN (Preston North End) | | Henri COPPENS |
| (1) | Robert FLAVELL (Airdrie) | | Albert DE CLEYN |
| (2) | William STEEL (Morton) | | Léopold ANOUL |
| (2) | Thomas PEARSON (Newcastle United) | | René THIRIFAYS |

Goals
0-1 — Anoul (28 mins)
Steel (64 mins) — 1-1
1-2 — Anoul (77 mins)

## 193
(Friendly)
24 May 1947
Referee: Wauters (Belgium)
Stade Municipal, Luxembourg-Ville (Att: 4,000)

### LUXEMBOURG 0-6 SCOTLAND — Half-time 0-2

| | | | |
|---|---|---|---|
| (4) | William MILLER (Celtic) | | Bernard MICHAUX |
| (4) | George YOUNG (Rangers) | | René MARCHETTI |
| (3) | John SHAW (Rangers) captain | | François DUMONT |
| (3) | Hugh BROWN (Partick Thistle) | | Alphonse FEYDER |
| (3) | William WOODBURN (Rangers) | | Arnold KIEFFER |
| (3) | Alexander FORBES (Sheffield United) | | Rémy WAGNER |
| (1) | William MacFARLANE (Hearts) | | Paul FELLER |
| (3) | Andrew McLAREN (Preston North End) | | Camille LIBAR |
| (2) | Robert FLAVELL (Airdrie) | | Nicolas KETTEL |
| (3) | William STEEL (Morton) | | Marcel REWENIG |
| (2) | Robert CAMPBELL (Falkirk) | | Léon LETSCH |

Substitutions
Fernand GUTH
for Letsch 82 mins

Goals
Flavell (6 mins) — 1-0
Steel (13 mins) — 2-0
Steel (48 mins) — 3-0
McLaren (60 mins) — 4-0
Flavell (69 mins) — 5-0
Forbes (86 mins) — 6-0

## 194
(Home International Championship)
4 October 1947
Referee: Smith (England)
Windsor Park, Belfast (Att: 52,000)

### IRELAND 2-0 SCOTLAND — Half-time 1-0

| | | | |
|---|---|---|---|
| (5) | William MILLER (Celtic) | | Edward HINTON |
| (5) | George YOUNG (Rangers) | | Cornelius MARTIN |
| (4) | John SHAW (Rangers) captain | | Thomas AHERNE |
| (2) | Archibald MacAULEY (Arsenal) | | William WALSH |
| (4) | William WOODBURN (Rangers) | | John VERNON |
| (4) | Alexander FORBES (Sheffield United) | | Peter FARRELL |
| (11) | James DELANEY (Manchester United) | | David COCHRANE |
| (1) | James WATSON (Motherwell) | | Samuel SMYTH |
| (3) | William THORNTON (Rangers) | | David WALSH |
| (4) | William STEEL (Derby County) | | Alexander STEVENSON |
| (3) | William LIDDELL (Liverpool) | | Thomas EGLINGTON |

Goals
0-1 — Smyth (35 mins)
0-2 — Smyth (54 mins)

## 195
(Home International Championship)
12 November 1947
Referee: Ellis (England)
Hampden Park, Glasgow (Att: 88,000)

### SCOTLAND 1-2 WALES — Half-time 1-2

| | | | |
|---|---|---|---|
| (6) | William MILLER (Celtic) | | Cyril SIDLOW |
| (1) | John GOVAN (Hibernian) | | Alfred SHERWOOD |
| (2) | James STEPHEN (Bradford) | | Walley BARNES |
| (3) | Archibald MacAULEY (Arsenal) | | Ivor POWELL |
| (5) | William WOODBURN (Rangers) captain | | Thomas JONES |
| (5) | Alexander FORBES (Sheffield United) | | William BURGESS |
| (3) | Gordon SMITH (Hibernian) | | Sidney THOMAS |
| (4) | Andrew McLAREN (Preston North End) | | Aubrey POWELL |
| (12) | James DELANEY (Manchester United) | | Trevor FORD |
| (5) | William STEEL (Derby County) | | George LOWRIE |
| (4) | William LIDDELL (Liverpool) | | George EDWARDS |

Goals
McLaren (10 mins) — 1-0
1-1 — Ford (35 mins)
1-2 — Lowrie (42 mins)

# 1948

| | P | W | D | L | F | A |
|---|---|---|---|---|---|---|
| | 6 | 3 | 0 | 3 | 9 | 10 |

## 196
(Home International Championship)
10 April 1948
Referee: Maxwell (Northern Ireland)
Hampden Park, Glasgow (Att: 135,376)

### SCOTLAND 0-2 ENGLAND — Half-time 0-1

| | | | |
|---|---|---|---|
| (1) | Ian BLACK (Southampton) | | Frank SWIFT |
| (2) | John GOVAN (Hibernian) | | Lawrence SCOTT |
| (3) | David SHAW (Hibernian) | | George HARDWICK |
| (2) | William CAMPBELL (Morton) | | William WRIGHT |
| (6) | George YOUNG (Rangers) captain | | Cornelius FRANKLIN |
| (4) | Archibald MacAULEY (Arsenal) | | Henry COCKBURN |
| (13) | James DELANEY (Manchester United) | | Stanley MATTHEWS |
| (1) | James COMBE (Hibernian) | | Stanley MORTENSEN |
| (4) | William THORNTON (Rangers) | | Thomas LAWTON |
| (6) | William STEEL (Derby County) | | Stanley PEARSON |
| (5) | William LIDDELL (Liverpool) | | Thomas FINNEY |

Goals
0-1 — Finney (44 mins)
0-2 — Mortensen (62 mins)

## 197
(Friendly)
28 April 1948
Referee: Ling (England)
Hampden Park, Glasgow (Att: 70,000)

### SCOTLAND 2:0 BELGIUM — Half-time 1-0

| | | | |
|---|---|---|---|
| (1) | James COWAN (Morton) | | François DAENEN |
| (3) | John GOVAN (Hibernian) | | Léon AERNAUDTS |
| (4) | David SHAW (Hibernian) | | Léopold ANOUL |
| (3) | William CAMPBELL (Morton) | | Alfons DE BUCK |
| (7) | George YOUNG (Rangers) (captain) | | Victor ERROELEN |
| (5) | Archibald MacAULEY (Arsenal) | | Jules HENRIET |
| (4) | Gordon SMITH (Hibernian) | | Victor LEMBERECHTS |
| (2) | James COMBE (Hibernian) | | Henri GOVARD |
| (1) | Leslie JOHNSTON (Clyde) | | Jozef MERMANS |
| (1) | Edward TURNBULL (Hibernian) | | August VAN STEENLANT |
| (1) | David DUNCAN (East Fife) | | Albert DE CLEYN |

Goals
Combe (25 mins) — 1-0
Duncan (59 mins) — 2-0

**198**

(Friendly)

17 May 1948

Referee: Beranech (Austria)

Wankdorf Stadion, Berne (Att: 30,000)

### SWITZERLAND 2:1 SCOTLAND — Half-time 1-1

| | | | |
|---|---|---|---|
| (2) | James COWAN (Morton) | | Eugenio CORRODI |
| (4) | John GOVAN (Hibernian) | | André BELLI |
| (5) | David SHAW (Hibernian) | | Willy STEFFEN |
| (4) | William CAMPBELL (Morton) | | Gerhard LUSENTI |
| (8) | George YOUNG (Rangers) captain | | Olivier EGGIMANN |
| (6) | Archibald MacAULEY (Arsenal) | | Roger BOCQUET |
| (5) | Gordon SMITH (Hibernian) | | Alfred BICKEL |
| (3) | James COMBE (Hibernian) | | Hans-Peter FRIEDLÄNDER |
| (2) | Leslie JOHNSTON (Clyde) | | Lauro AMADO |
| (2) | Edward TURNBULL (Hibernian) | | René MAILLARD |
| (2) | David DUNCAN (East Fife) | | Jacques FATTON |

Substitutions

Jean TAMINI for Bickel 46 mins

Goals

| | | |
|---|---|---|
| Johnston (19 mins) | 1-0 | |
| | 1-1 | Maillard (45 mins) |
| | 1-2 | Fatton (78 mins) |

---

**199**

(Friendly)

23 May 1948

Referee: Van der Meer (Netherlands)

Stade Olympique du Colombes, Paris (Att: 46,032)

### FRANCE 3-0 SCOTLAND — Half-time 0-0

| | | | |
|---|---|---|---|
| (3) | James COWAN (Morton) | | Julien DARUI |
| (5) | John GOVAN (Hibernian) | | Guy HUGUET |
| (6) | David SHAW (Hibernian) | | Roger MARCHE |
| (5) | William CAMPBELL (Morton) | | Antoine CUISSARD |
| (9) | George YOUNG (Rangers) captain | | Jean GRÉGOIRE |
| (7) | Archibald MacAULEY (Arsenal) | | Jean PROUFF |
| (1) | Edward RUTHERFORD (Rangers) | | Georges SESIA |
| (7) | William STEEL (Derby County) | | Jean BARATTE |
| (6) | Gordon SMITH (Hibernian) | | Emile BONGIORNI |
| (1) | Charles COX (Hearts) | | Larbi BEN BAREK |
| (3) | David DUNCAN (East Fife) | | Pierre FLAMION |

Goals

| | | |
|---|---|---|
| | 0-1 | Bongiorni (55 mins) |
| | 0-2 | Flamion (60 mins) |
| | 0-3 | Baratte (79 mins) |

---

**200**

(Home International Championship)

23 October 1948

Referee: Maxwell (Northern Ireland)

Ninian Park, Cardiff (Att: 59,911)

### WALES 1-3 SCOTLAND — Half-time 1-3

| | | | |
|---|---|---|---|
| (4) | James COWAN (Morton) | | Cyril SIDLOW |
| (1) | Hugh HOWIE (Hibernian) | | Alfred SHERWOOD |
| (7) | David SHAW (Hibernian) | | Walley BARNES |
| (1) | Robert EVANS (Celtic) | | Roy PAUL |
| (10) | George YOUNG (Rangers) captain | | Frederick STANSFIELD |
| (1) | William REDPATH (Motherwell) | | William BURGESS |
| (2) | William WADDELL (Rangers) | | Sidney THOMAS |
| (1) | James MASON (Third Lanark) | | William LUCAS |
| (1) | Lawrence REILLY (Hibernian) | | Trevor FORD |
| (8) | William STEEL (Derby County) | | Brynmor JONES |
| (1) | John KELLY (Barnsley) | | William JONES |

Goals

| | | |
|---|---|---|
| Howie (15 mins) | 1-0 | |
| Waddell (20 mins) | 2-0 | |
| | 2-1 | B.Jones (22 mins) |
| Waddell (30 mins) | 3-1 | |

---

**201**

(Home International Championship)

17 November 1948

Referee: Evans (England)

Hampden Park, Glasgow (Att: 93,182)

### SCOTLAND 3-2 IRELAND — Half-time 1-2

| | | | |
|---|---|---|---|
| (2) | Robert BROWN (Rangers) | | William SMYTH |
| (6) | John GOVAN (Hibernian) | | John CAREY |
| (8) | David SHAW (Hibernian) | | Rory KEANE |
| (2) | Robert EVANS (Celtic) | | James McCABE |
| (11) | George YOUNG (Rangers) captain | | John VERNON |
| (2) | William REDPATH (Motherwell) | | William WALSH |
| (3) | William WADDELL (Rangers) | | David COCHRANE |
| (2) | James MASON (Third Lanark) | | Samuel SMYTH |
| (1) | William HOULISTON (Queen of the South) | | David WALSH |
| (9) | William STEEL (Derby County) | | Peter DOHERTY |
| (2) | John KELLY (Barnsley) | | John O'DRISCOLL |

Goals

| | | |
|---|---|---|
| | 0-1 | D. Walsh (1 min) |
| | 0-2 | D. Walsh (4 mins) |
| Houliston (27 mins) | 1-2 | |
| Mason (72 mins) | 2-2 | |
| Houliston (89 mins) | 3-2 | |

---

# 1949

| P | W | D | L | F | A |
|---|---|---|---|---|---|
| 4 | 4 | 0 | 0 | 15 | 3 |

**202**

(Home International Championship)

9 April 1949

Referee: Griffiths (Wales)

Wembley Stadium, London (Att: 98,188)

### ENGLAND 1-3 SCOTLAND — Half-time 0-1

| | | | |
|---|---|---|---|
| (5) | James COWAN (Morton) | | Frank SWIFT |
| (12) | George YOUNG (Rangers) captain | | John ASTON |
| (1) | Samuel COX (Rangers) | | John HOWE |
| (3) | Robert EVANS (Celtic) | | William WRIGHT |
| (6) | William WOODBURN (Rangers) | | Cornelius FRANKLIN |
| (1) | George AITKEN (East Fife) | | Henry COCKBURN |
| (4) | William WADDELL (Rangers) | | Stanley MATTHEWS |
| (3) | James MASON (Third Lanark) | | Stanley MORTENSEN |
| (2) | William HOULISTON (Queen of the South) | | John MILBURN |
| (10) | William STEEL (Derby County) | | Stanley PEARSON |
| (2) | Lawrence REILLY (Hibernian) | | Thomas FINNEY |

Goals

| | | |
|---|---|---|
| Mason (28 mins) | 1-0 | |
| Steel (52 mins) | 2-0 | |
| Reilly (61 mins) | 3-0 | |
| | 3-1 | Milburn (75 mins) |

---

**203**

(Friendly)

27 April 1949

Referee: Ling (England)

Hampden Park, Glasgow (Att: 125,683)

### SCOTLAND 2-0 FRANCE — Half-time 1-0

| | | | |
|---|---|---|---|
| (6) | James COWAN (Morton) | | René VIGNAL |
| (13) | George YOUNG (Rangers) captain | | Marcel SALVA |
| (2) | Samuel COX (Rangers) | | Roger MARCHE |
| (4) | Robert EVANS (Celtic) | | Robert JONQUET |
| (7) | William WOODBURN (Rangers) | | Roger MINDONNET |
| (2) | George AITKEN (East Fife) | | Louis HON |
| (5) | William WADDELL (Rangers) | | Roger GABET |
| (5) | William THORNTON (Rangers) | | Antoine CUISSARD |
| (3) | William HOULISTON (Queen of the South) | | Jean BARATTE |
| (11) | William STEEL (Derby County) | | Albert BATTEUX |
| (3) | Lawrence REILLY (Hibernian) | | Pierre FLAMION |

Goals

| | | |
|---|---|---|
| Steel (37 mins) | 1-0 | |
| Steel (80 mins) | 2-0 | |

---

**204**

(Home International Championship/World Cup - Qualifier)

1 October 1949

Referee: Mortimer (England)

Windsor Park, Belfast (Att: 55,000)

### IRELAND 2-8 SCOTLAND — Half-time 0-5

| | | | |
|---|---|---|---|
| (7) | James COWAN (Morton) | | Patrick KELLY |
| (14) | George YOUNG (Rangers) captain | | Gerard BOWLER |
| (3) | Samuel COX (Rangers) | | Alfred McMICHAEL |
| (5) | Robert EVANS (Celtic) | | Daniel BLANCHFLOWER |
| (8) | William WOODBURN (Rangers) | | John VERNON |
| (3) | George AITKEN (East Fife) | | Roy FERRIS |
| (6) | William WADDELL (Rangers) | | David COCHRANE |
| (4) | James MASON (Third Lanark) | | Samuel SMYTH |
| (1) | Henry MORRIS (East Fife) | | Robert BRENNAN |
| (12) | William STEEL (Derby County) | | Edward CROSSAN |
| (4) | Lawrence REILLY (Hibernian) | | John McKENNA |

Goals

| | | |
|---|---|---|
| Morris (2 mins) | 1-0 | |
| Waddell (5 mins) | 2-0 | |
| Steel (25 mins) | 3-0 | |
| Reilly (26 mins) | 4-0 | |
| Waddell (42 mins pen) | 5-0 | |
| | 5-1 | Smyth (50 mins) |
| | 5-2 | Smyth (59 mins) |
| Morris (70 mins) | 6-2 | |
| Mason (80 mins) | 7-2 | |
| Morris (89 mins) | 8-2 | |

## 205

(Home International Championship/World Cup — Qualifier)

9 November 1949

Referee: Law (England)
Hampden Park, Glasgow (Att: 73,781)

### SCOTLAND 2-0 WALES — Half-time 1-0

| | | |
|---|---|---|
| (8) | James COWAN (Morton) | Keith JONES |
| (15) | George YOUNG (Rangers) captain | Walley BARNES |
| (4) | Samuel COX (Rangers) | Alfred SHERWOOD |
| (6) | Robert EVANS (Celtic) | Ivor POWELL |
| (9) | William WOODBURN (Rangers) | Thomas JONES |
| (4) | George AITKEN (East Fife) | William BURGESS |
| (6) | William LIDDELL (Liverpool) | Maldwyn GRIFFITHS |
| (1) | John McPHAIL (Celtic) | Roy PAUL |
| (1) | Alexander LINWOOD (Clyde) | Trevor FORD |
| (13) | William STEEL (Derby County) | Royston CLARKE |
| (5) | Lawrence REILLY (Hibernian) | George EDWARDS |

Goals

| | |
|---|---|
| McPhail (25 mins) | 1-0 |
| Linwood (78 mins) | 2-0 |

---

# 1950

| P | W | D | L | F | A |
|---|---|---|---|---|---|
| 7 | 4 | 1 | 2 | 15 | 7 |

## 206

(Home International Championship/World Cup — Qualifier)

15 April 1950

Referee: Leafe (England)
Hampden Park, Glasgow (Att: 133,300)

### SCOTLAND 0-1 ENGLAND — Half-time 0-0

| | | |
|---|---|---|
| (9) | James COWAN (Morton) | Frederick WILLIAMS |
| (16) | George YOUNG (Rangers) captain | Alfred RAMSEY |
| (5) | Samuel COX (Rangers) | John ASTON |
| (1) | John McCOLL (Rangers) | William WRIGHT |
| (10) | William WOODBURN (Rangers) | Cornelius FRANKLIN |
| (6) | Alexander FORBES (Arsenal) | James DICKINSON |
| (7) | William WADDELL (Rangers) | Thomas FINNEY |
| (1) | William MOIR (Bolton Wanderers) | Wilfred MANNION |
| (1) | William BAULD (Hearts) | Stanley MORTENSEN |
| (14) | William STEEL (Derby County) | Roy BENTLEY |
| (7) | William LIDDELL (Liverpool) | Robert LANGTON |

Goals

| | | |
|---|---|---|
| | 0-1 | Bentley (64 mins) |

## 207

(Friendly)

26 April 1950

Referee: Reader (England)
Hampden Park, Glasgow (Att: 123,751)

### SCOTLAND 3-1 SWITZERLAND — Half-time 3-1

| | | |
|---|---|---|
| (10) | James COWAN (Morton) | Georges STUBER |
| (17) | George YOUNG (Rangers) captain | Rudolf GYGER |
| (6) | Samuel COX (Rangers) | Willy STEFFEN |
| (7) | Robert EVANS (Celtic) | André NEURY |
| (1) | Robert DOUGAN (Hearts) | Olivier EGGIMANN |
| (5) | George AITKEN (East Fife) | Roger BOCQUET |
| (3) | Robert CAMPBELL (Chelsea) | Alfred BICKEL |
| (1) | Allan BROWN (East Fife) | Charles ANTENEN |
| (2) | William BAULD (Hearts) | Jean TAMINI |
| (15) | William STEEL (Derby County) | René BADER |
| (6) | Lawrence REILLY (Hibernian) | Jacques FATTON |

Goals

| | | |
|---|---|---|
| Bauld (9 mins) | 1-0 | |
| | 1-1 | Antenen (20 mins) |
| Campbell (38 mins) | 2-1 | |
| Brown (44 mins) | 3-1 | |

## 208

(Friendly)

21 May 1950

Referee: Anzano (Spain)
Estadio Nacional, Lisbon (Att: 68,000)

### PORTUGAL 2-2 SCOTLAND — Half-time 2-2

| | | |
|---|---|---|
| (11) | James COWAN (Morton) | ERNESTO Oliveira |
| (18) | George YOUNG (Rangers) captain | Octávio BARROSA |
| (7) | Samuel COX (Rangers) | Angelo CARVALHO |
| (8) | Robert EVANS (Celtic) | Carlos CANÁRIO |
| (11) | William WOODBURN (Rangers) | FÉLIX Antunes |
| (7) | Alexander FORBES (Arsenal) | SERAFIM Batista |
| (4) | Robert CAMPBELL (Chelsea) | Mário NOBRE |
| (2) | Allan BROWN (East Fife) | Manuel VASQUES |
| (3) | William BAULD (Hearts) | Henrique BEN DAVID |
| (16) | William STEEL (Derby County) | José TRAVAÇOS |
| (8) | William LIDDELL (Liverpool) | ALBANO Pereira |

Goals

| | | |
|---|---|---|
| | 0-1 | Travaços (9 mins) |
| Bauld (20 mins) | 1-1 | |
| Brown (23 mins) | 2-1 | |
| | 2-2 | Albano (29 mins) |

## 209

(Friendly)

27 May 1950

Referee: Arque (Spain)
Stade Olympique du Colombes, Paris (Att: 35,568)

### FRANCE 0-1 SCOTLAND — Half-time 0-0

| | | |
|---|---|---|
| (12) | James COWAN (Morton) | Abderrahman IBRIR |
| (19) | George YOUNG (Rangers) captain | Guy HUGUET |
| (8) | Samuel COX (Rangers) | Roger MARCHE |
| (2) | John McCOLL (Rangers) | Jean GRÉGOIRE |
| (12) | William WOODBURN (Rangers) | Roger LAMY |
| (8) | Alexander FORBES (Arsenal) | Antoine CUISSARD |
| (5) | Robert CAMPBELL (Chelsea) | Henri BAILLOT |
| (3) | Allan BROWN (East Fife) | André STRAPPE |
| (7) | Lawrence REILLY (Hibernian) | Jean BARATTE |
| (17) | William STEEL (Derby County) | Jean GRUMELLON |
| (9) | William LIDDELL (Liverpool) | Georges DARD |

Goals

| | |
|---|---|
| Brown (69 mins) | 1-0 |

## 210

(Home International Championship)

21 October 1950

Referee: Ellis (England)
Ninian Park, Cardiff (Att: 50,000)

### WALES 1-3 SCOTLAND — Half-time 0-1

| | | |
|---|---|---|
| (13) | James COWAN (Morton) | Brynley PARRY |
| (20) | George YOUNG (Rangers) captain | Walley BARNES |
| (1) | William McNAUGHT (Raith Rovers) | Alfred SHERWOOD |
| (3) | John McCOLL (Rangers) | Ivor POWELL |
| (13) | William WOODBURN (Rangers) | Roy PAUL |
| (9) | Alexander FORBES (Arsenal) | William BURGESS |
| (1) | Robert COLLINS (Celtic) | Harold WILLIAMS |
| (2) | John McPHAIL (Celtic) | Brynley ALLEN |
| (8) | Lawrence REILLY (Hibernian) | Trevor FORD |
| (18) | William STEEL (Dundee) | Aubrey POWELL |
| (10) | William LIDDELL (Liverpool) | Royston CLARKE |

Goals

| | | |
|---|---|---|
| Reilly (23 mins) | 1-0 | |
| Reilly (65 mins) | 2-0 | |
| | 2-1 | A.Powell (68 mins) |
| Liddell (72 mins) | 3-1 | |

## 211

(Home International Championship)

1 November 1950

Referee: Griffiths (Wales)
Hampden Park, Glasgow (Att: 83,142)

### SCOTLAND 6-1 IRELAND — Half-time 2-1

| | | |
|---|---|---|
| (14) | James COWAN (Morton) | Hugh KELLY |
| (21) | George YOUNG (Rangers) captain | Charles GALLOGLY |
| (2) | William McNAUGHT (Raith Rovers) | Alfred McMICHAEL |
| (4) | John McCOLL (Rangers) | Daniel BLANCHFLOWER |
| (14) | William WOODBURN (Rangers) | John VERNON |
| (10) | Alexander FORBES (Arsenal) | Wilbur CUSH |
| (2) | Robert COLLINS (Celtic) | John CAMPBELL |
| (5) | James MASON (Third Lanark) | Kevin McGARRY |
| (3) | John McPHAIL (Celtic) | Edward McMORRAN |
| (19) | William STEEL (Dundee) | Peter DOHERTY |
| (11) | William LIDDELL (Liverpool) | John McKENNA |

Goals

| | | |
|---|---|---|
| McPhail (8 mins) | 1-0 | |
| McPhail (13 mins) | 2-0 | |
| | 2-1 | McGarry (43 mins) |
| Steel (53 mins) | 3-1 | |
| Steel (57 mins) | 4-1 | |
| Steel (66 mins) | 5-1 | |
| Steel (79 mins) | 6-1 | |

## 212

(Friendly)
13 December 1950

Referee: Ling (England)
Hampden Park, Glasgow (Att: 68,000)

### SCOTLAND 0-1 AUSTRIA — Half-time 0-1

| | | | |
|---|---|---|---|
| (15) | James COWAN (Morton) | | Walter ZEMAN |
| (22) | George YOUNG (Rangers) captain | | Rudolf ROCKL |
| (3) | William McNAUGHT (Raith Rovers) | | Ernst HAPPEL |
| (9) | Robert EVANS (Celtic) | | Gerhard HANAPPI |
| (15) | William WOODBURN (Rangers) | | Ernst OCWIRK |
| (11) | Alexander FORBES (Arsenal) | | Leopold GERNHARDT |
| (3) | Robert COLLINS (Celtic) | | Ernst MELCHIOR |
| (3) | Edward TURNBULL (Hibernian) | | Karl DECKER |
| (4) | John McPHAIL (Celtic) | | Theodor WAGNER |
| (20) | William STEEL (Dundee) | | Ernst STOJASPAL |
| (12) | William LIDDELL (Liverpool) | | Lukas AUREDNIK |

| | Goals | |
|---|---|---|
| | 0-1 | Melchior (26 mins) |

# 1951

| P | W | D | L | F | A |
|---|---|---|---|---|---|
| 7 | 5 | 0 | 2 | 15 | 8 |

## 213

(Home International Championship)
14 April 1951

Referee: Mitchell (Scotland)
Wembley Stadium, London (Att: 98,000)

### ENGLAND 2-3 SCOTLAND — Half-time 1-1

| | | | |
|---|---|---|---|
| (16) | James COWAN (Morton) | | Frederick WILLIAMS |
| (23) | George YOUNG (Rangers) captain | | Alfred RAMSEY |
| (9) | Samuel COX (Rangers) | | William ECKERSLEY |
| (10) | Robert EVANS (Celtic) | | Harold JOHNSTON |
| (16) | William WOODBURN (Rangers) | | John FROGGATT |
| (3) | William REDPATH (Motherwell) | | William WRIGHT |
| (8) | William WADDELL (Rangers) | | Stanley MATTHEWS |
| (1) | Robert JOHNSTONE (Hibernian) | | Wilfred MANNION |
| (9) | Lawrence REILLY (Hibernian) | | Stanley MORTENSEN |
| (21) | William STEEL (Dundee) | | Harold HASSALL |
| (13) | William LIDDELL (Liverpool) | | Thomas FINNEY |

| | Goals | |
|---|---|---|
| | 0-1 | Hassall (26 mins) |
| Johnstone (33 mins) | 1-1 | |
| Reilly (47 mins) | 2-1 | |
| Liddell (53 mins) | 3-1 | |
| | 3-2 | Finney (63 mins) |

## 214

(Friendly)
12 May 1951

Referee: Evans (England)
Hampden Park, Glasgow (Att: 75,000)

### SCOTLAND 3-1 DENMARK — Half-time 1-1

| | | | |
|---|---|---|---|
| (17) | James COWAN (Morton) | | Eigil NIELSEN |
| (24) | George YOUNG (Rangers) captain | | Dan OHLAND-ANDERSEN |
| (10) | Samuel COX (Rangers) | | Poul PETERSEN |
| (1) | James SCOULAR (Portsmouth) | | Erik HANSEN |
| (17) | William WOODBURN (Rangers) | | Edvin HANSEN |
| (4) | William REDPATH (Motherwell) | | Steen BLICHER |
| (9) | William WADDELL (Rangers) | | James RONVANG |
| (2) | Robert JOHNSTONE (Hibernian) | | Jorgen HANSEN |
| (10) | Lawrence REILLY (Hibernian) | | Jens TORSTENSEN |
| (22) | William STEEL (Dundee) | | Knud LUNDBERG |
| (1) | Robert MITCHELL (Newcastle United) | | Jens HANSEN |

| | Goals | |
|---|---|---|
| | 0-1 | Jorgen Hansen (6 mins) |
| Steel (33 mins) | 1-1 | |
| Reilly (59 mins) | 2-1 | |
| Mitchell (86 mins) | 3-1 | |

## 215

(Friendly)
16 May 1951

Referee: Mortimer (England)
Hampden Park, Glasgow (Att: 75,394)

### SCOTLAND 1-0 FRANCE — Half-time 0-0

| | | | |
|---|---|---|---|
| (18) | James COWAN (Morton) | | Stéphane DAKOSKI |
| (25) | George YOUNG (Rangers) captain | | Guy HUGUET |
| (11) | Samuel COX (Rangers) | | Roger MARCHE |
| (2) | James SCOULAR (Portsmouth) | | Antoine BONIFACI |
| (18) | William WOODBURN (Rangers) | | Robert JONQUET |
| (5) | William REDPATH (Motherwell) | | Antoine CUISSARD |
| (10) | William WADDELL (Rangers) | | René ALPSTEG |
| (3) | Robert JOHNSTONE (Hibernian) | | André STRAPPE |
| (11) | Lawrence REILLY (Hibernian) | | Jean BARATTE |
| (23) | William STEEL (Dundee) | | Edouard KARGU |
| (2) | Robert MITCHELL (Newcastle United) | | Edmond HAAN |

| | Goals | |
|---|---|---|
| Reilly (78 mins) | 1-0 | |

## 216

(Friendly)
20 May 1951

Referee: Fauquemberge (France)
Heysel Stadium, Brussels (Att: 55,135)

### BELGIUM 0-5 SCOTLAND — Half-time 0-2

| | | | |
|---|---|---|---|
| (19) | James COWAN (Morton) | | Henri MEERT |
| (26) | George YOUNG (Rangers) captain | | Arsène VAILLANT |
| (12) | Samuel COX (Rangers) | | Léopold ANOUL |
| (5) | John McCOLL (Rangers) | | Jan VAN DER AUWERA |
| (19) | William WOODBURN (Rangers) | | Louis CARRÉ |
| (6) | William REDPATH (Motherwell) | | Victor MEES |
| (11) | William WADDELL (Rangers) | | Victor LEMBERECHTS |
| (6) | James MASON (Third Lanark) | | Freddy CHAVES |
| (2) | George HAMILTON (Aberdeen) | | Henri COPPENS |
| (24) | William STEEL (Dundee) | | Jozef MERMANS |
| (12) | Lawrence REILLY (Hibernian) | | François SERMON |

| | Goals | |
|---|---|---|
| Hamilton (8 mins) | 1-0 | |
| Mason (17 mins) | 2-0 | |
| Hamilton (58 mins) | 3-0 | |
| Hamilton (65 mins) | 4-0 | |
| Waddell (81 mins) | 5-0 | |

## 217

(Friendly)
27 May 1951

Referee: Lutz (Switzerland)
Prater Stadion, Vienna (Att: 65,000)

### AUSTRIA 4-0 SCOTLAND — Half-time 1-0

| | | | |
|---|---|---|---|
| (20) | James COWAN (Morton) | | Walter ZEMAN |
| (27) | George YOUNG (Rangers) captain | | Rudolf ROCKL |
| (13) | Samuel COX (Rangers) | | Ernst HAPPEL |
| (3) | James SCOULAR (Portsmouth) | | Gerhard HANAPPI |
| (20) | William WOODBURN (Rangers) | | Ernst OCWIRK |
| (7) | William REDPATH (Motherwell) | | Leopold GERNHARDT |
| (12) | William WADDELL (Rangers) | | Ernst MELCHIOR |
| (7) | James MASON (Third Lanark) | | Johann RIEGLER |
| (3) | George HAMILTON (Aberdeen) | | Theodor WAGNER |
| (25) | William STEEL (Dundee) | | Erich PROBST |
| (13) | Lawrence REILLY (Hibernian) | | Alfred KORNER |

| | Goals | |
|---|---|---|
| | 0-1 | Hanappi (42 mins) |
| | 0-2 | Hanappi (56 mins) |
| | 0-3 | Wagner (69 mins pen) |
| | 0-4 | Wagner (88 mins) |

## 218

(Home International Championship)
6 October 1951

Referee: Evans (England)
Windsor Park, Belfast (Att: 56,946)

### IRELAND 0-3 SCOTLAND — Half-time 0-2

| | | | |
|---|---|---|---|
| (21) | James COWAN (Morton) | | Norman UPRICHARD |
| (28) | George YOUNG (Rangers) captain | | Leonard GRAHAM |
| (14) | Samuel COX (Rangers) | | Alfred McMICHAEL |
| (11) | Robert EVANS (Celtic) | | William DICKSON |
| (21) | William WOODBURN (Rangers) | | John VERNON |
| (8) | William REDPATH (Motherwell) | | Roy FERRIS |
| (13) | William WADDELL (Rangers) | | William BINGHAM |
| (4) | Robert JOHNSTONE (Hibernian) | | James McILROY |
| (14) | Lawrence REILLY (Hibernian) | | Edward McMORRAN |
| (1) | Thomas ORR (Morton) | | Robert PEACOCK |
| (14) | William LIDDELL (Liverpool) | | Charles TULLY |

| | Goals | |
|---|---|---|
| Orr (32 mins) | 1-0 | |
| Johnstone (44 mins) | 2-0 | |
| Johnstone (62 mins) | 3-0 | |

## 219

(Home International Championship)
14 November 1951

Referee: Morris (Northern Ireland)
Hampden Park, Glasgow (Att: 71,272)

### SCOTLAND 0-1 WALES — Half-time 0-0

| | | | |
|---|---|---|---|
| (22) | James COWAN (Morton) | | William SHORTT |
| (29) | George YOUNG (Rangers) captain | | Walley BARNES |
| (15) | Samuel COX (Rangers) | | Alfred SHERWOOD |
| (1) | Thomas DOCHERTY (Preston North End) | | Roy PAUL |
| (22) | William WOODBURN (Rangers) | | Raymond DANIEL |
| (12) | Alexander FORBES (Arsenal) | | William BURGESS |
| (14) | William WADDELL (Rangers) | | William FOULKES |
| (2) | Thomas ORR (Morton) | | William MORRIS |
| (15) | Lawrence REILLY (Hibernian) | | Trevor FORD |
| (26) | William STEEL (Dundee) | | Ivor ALLCHURCH |
| (15) | William LIDDELL (Liverpool) | | Royston CLARKE |

| | Goals | |
|---|---|---|
| | 0-1 | Allchurch (89 mins) |

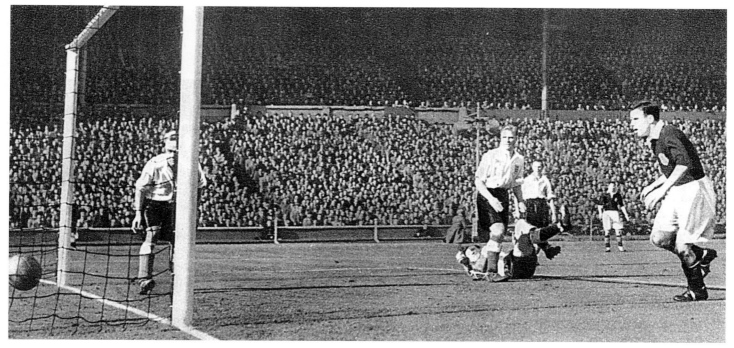

Billy Liddell (out of picture) scores Scotland's third goal in the 3-2 victory at Wembley in 1951.

Skipper George Young introduces the players to the Duke of Gloucester before the 1951 match against England at Wembley.

# 1952

| P | W | D | L | F | A |
|---|---|---|---|---|---|
| 6 | 3 | 1 | 2 | 13 | 8 |

## 220

| (Home International Championship) | Referee: Morris (Northern Ireland) |
|---|---|
| 5 April 1952 | Hampden Park, Glasgow (Att: 133,991) |

### SCOTLAND 1-2 ENGLAND      Half-time 0-2

| (3) | Robert BROWN (Rangers) | | Gilbert MERRICK |
|---|---|---|---|
| (30) | George YOUNG (Rangers) captain | | Alfred RAMSEY |
| (4) | William McNAUGHT (Raith Rovers) | | Thomas GARRETT |
| (4) | James SCOULAR (Portsmouth) | | William WRIGHT |
| (23) | William WOODBURN (Rangers) | | John FROGGATT |
| (9) | William REDPATH (Motherwell) | | James DICKINSON |
| (7) | Gordon SMITH (Hibernian) | | Thomas FINNEY |
| (5) | Robert JOHNSTONE (Hibernian) | | Ivan BROADIS |
| (16) | Lawrence REILLY (Hibernian) | | Nathaniel LOFTHOUSE |
| (1) | John McMILLAN (Airdrie) | | Stanley PEARSON |
| (16) | William LIDDELL (Liverpool) | | John ROWLEY |

|  | Goals |  |
|---|---|---|
|  | 0-1 | Pearson (9 mins) |
|  | 0-2 | Pearson (44 mins) |
| Reilly (77 mins) | 1-2 | |

## 221

| (Friendly) | Referee: Gerrard (Scotland) |
|---|---|
| 30 April 1952 | Hampden Park, Glasgow (Att: 107,765) |

### SCOTLAND 6-0 USA      Half-time 4-0

| (23) | James COWAN (Morton) | | Frank BORGHI |
|---|---|---|---|
| (31) | George YOUNG (Rangers) captain | | John O'CONNELL |
| (16) | Samuel COX (Rangers) | | Harold KEOUGH |
| (5) | James SCOULAR (Portsmouth) | | William SHEPELL |
| (24) | William WOODBURN (Rangers) | | Charles COLOMBO |
| (1) | Hugh KELLY (Blackpool) | | Walter BAHR |
| (8) | Gordon SMITH (Hibernian) | | Lloyd MONSEN |
| (2) | John McMILLAN (Airdrie) | | Ed SOUZA |
| (17) | Lawrence REILLY (Hibernian) | | Richard ROBERTS |
| (4) | Allan BROWN (Blackpool) | | John SOUZA |
| (17) | William LIDDELL (Liverpool) | | Ben McLAUGHLIN |

|  | Goals |  |
|---|---|---|
| Reilly (9 mins) | 1-0 | |
| Reilly (10 mins) | 2-0 | |
| McMillan (29 mins) | 3-0 | |
| Reilly (34 mins) | 4-0 | |
| O'Connell (60 mins o.g.) | 5-0 | |
| McMillan (89 mins) | 6-0 | |

## 222

(Friendly)
25 May 1952

Referee: Ahlner (Sweden)
Idraetsparken, Copenhagen (Att: 39,000)

### DENMARK 1-2 SCOTLAND             Half-time 0-0

| (24) | James COWAN (Morton) | Kaj JORGENSEN |
| (32) | George YOUNG (Rangers) captain | Poul PETERSEN |
| (17) | Samuel COX (Rangers) | Svend NIELSEN |
| (6) | James SCOULAR (Portsmouth) | Erik TERKELSEN |
| (1) | Andrew PATON (Motherwell) | Christen BROGGER |
| (13) | Alexander FORBES (Arsenal) | Steen BLICHER |
| (18) | Lawrence REILLY (Hibernian) | Carl HOLM |
| (3) | John McMILLAN (Airdrie) | Poul RASMUSSEN |
| (6) | William THORNTON (Rangers) | Jens TORSTENSEN |
| (5) | Allan BROWN (Blackpool) | Knud LUNDBERG |
| (18) | William LIDDELL (Liverpool) | Holger SEEBACH |

|  | Goals |  |
| Thornton (49 mins) | 1-0 | |
| | 1-1 | Rasmussen (63 mins) |
| Reilly (71 mins) | 2-1 | |

## 223

(Friendly)
30 May 1952

Referee: Van der Meer (Netherlands)
Rasunda Stadion, Stockholm (Att: 32,122)

### SWEDEN 3-1 SCOTLAND             Half-time 2-1

| (25) | James COWAN (Morton) | Karl SVENSSON |
| (33) | George YOUNG (Rangers) captain | Lennart SAMUELSSON |
| (18) | Samuel COX (Rangers) | Erik NILSSON |
| (7) | James SCOULAR (Portsmouth) | Holger HANSSON |
| (2) | Andrew PATON (Motherwell) | Bengt GUSTAVSSON |
| (14) | Alexander FORBES (Arsenal) | Gösta LINDH |
| (19) | Lawrence REILLY (Hibernian) | Sylve BENGTSSON |
| (1) | Wilson HUMPHRIES (Motherwell) | Gösta LÖFGREN |
| (7) | William THORNTON (Rangers) | Lars ERIKSSON |
| (6) | Allan BROWN (Blackpool) | Yngve BRODD |
| (19) | William LIDDELL (Liverpool) | Gösta SANDBERG |

|  | Goals |  |
| | 0-1 | Sandberg (2 mins) |
| | 0-2 | Löfgren (3 mins) |
| Liddell (6 mins) | 1-2 | |
| | 1-3 | Bengtsson (68 mins) |

Laurie Reilly in action against Sweden in Stockholm in May 1952.

## 224

(Home International Championship)
18 October 1952

Referee: Bond (England)
Ninian Park, Cardiff (Att: 60,261)

### WALES 1-2 SCOTLAND             Half-time 1-1

| (1) | George FARM (Blackpool) | William SHORTT |
| (34) | George YOUNG (Rangers) captain | Arthur LEVER |
| (19) | Samuel COX (Rangers) | Alfred SHERWOOD |
| (8) | James SCOULAR (Portsmouth) | Roy PAUL |
| (3) | Frank BRENNAN (Newcastle United) | Raymond DANIEL |
| (6) | George AITKEN (Sunderland) | William BURGESS |
| (1) | Thomas WRIGHT (Sunderland) | William FOULKES |
| (7) | Allan BROWN (Blackpool) | Ellis DAVIES |
| (20) | Lawrence REILLY (Hibernian) | Trevor FORD |
| (27) | William STEEL (Dundee) | Ivor ALLCHURCH |
| (20) | William LIDDELL (Liverpool) | Royston CLARKE |

|  | Goals |  |
| | 0-1 | Ford (23 mins) |
| Brown (32 mins) | 1-1 | |
| Liddell (69 mins) | 2-1 | |

Frank Brennan and Ivor Allchurch of Wales in action at Ninian Park in October 1952. Scotland won 2-1.

## 225

(Home International Championship)
5 November 1952

Referee: Smith (Wales)
Hampden Park, Glasgow (Att: 65,057)

### SCOTLAND 1-1 IRELAND             Half-time 0-0

| (2) | George FARM (Blackpool) | Norman UPRICHARD |
| (35) | George YOUNG (Rangers) captain | Leonard GRAHAM |
| (20) | Samuel COX (Rangers) | Alfred McMICHAEL |
| (9) | James SCOULAR (Portsmouth) | Daniel BLANCHFLOWER |
| (4) | Frank BRENNAN (Newcastle United) | William DICKSON |
| (7) | George AITKEN (Sunderland) | Frank McCOURT |
| (2) | Thomas WRIGHT (Sunderland) | William BINGHAM |
| (1) | James LOGIE (Arsenal) | Seamus D'ARCY |
| (21) | Lawrence REILLY (Hibernian) | Edward McMORRAN |
| (28) | William STEEL (Dundee) | James McILROY |
| (21) | William LIDDELL (Liverpool) | Charles TULLY |

|  | Goals |  |
| | 0-1 | D'Arcy (80 mins) |
| Reilly (90 mins) | 1-1 | |

# 1953

| P | W | D | L | F | A |
|---|---|---|---|---|---|
| 4 | 1 | 2 | 1 | 9 | 8 |

## 226
(Home International Championship)
18 April 1953

Referee: Mitchell (Northern Ireland)
Wembley Stadium, London (Att: 97,000)

### ENGLAND 2-2 SCOTLAND — Half-time 1-0

| (3) | George FARM (Blackpool) | Gilbert MERRICK |
|---|---|---|
| (36) | George YOUNG (Rangers) captain | Alfred RAMSEY |
| (21) | Samuel COX (Rangers) | Lionel SMITH |
| (2) | Thomas DOCHERTY (Preston North End) | William WRIGHT |
| (5) | Frank BRENNAN (Newcastle United) | Malcolm BARRASS |
| (1) | Douglas COWIE (Dundee) | James DICKINSON |
| (3) | Thomas WRIGHT (Sunderland) | Thomas FINNEY |
| (6) | Robert JOHNSTONE (Hibernian) | Ivan BROADIS |
| (22) | Lawrence REILLY (Hibernian) | Nathaniel LOFTHOUSE |
| (29) | William STEEL (Dundee) | Redfern FROGGATT |
| (22) | William LIDDELL (Liverpool) | John FROGGATT |

| | Goals | |
|---|---|---|
| | 0-1 | Broadis (18 mins) |
| Reilly (54 mins) | 1-1 | |
| | 1-2 | Broadis (70 mins) |
| Reilly (89 mins) | 2-2 | |

## 227
(Friendly)
6 May 1953

Referee: Ling (England)
Hampden Park, Glasgow (Att: 83,800)

### SCOTLAND 1-2 SWEDEN — Half-time 1-1

| (4) | George FARM (Blackpool) | Karl SVENSSON |
|---|---|---|
| (37) | George YOUNG (Rangers) captain | Lennart SAMUELSSON |
| (1) | John LITTLE (Rangers) | Orvar BERGMARK |
| (12) | Robert EVANS (Celtic) | Sven-Ove SVENSSON |
| (2) | Douglas COWIE (Dundee) | Bengt GUSTAVSSON |
| (3) | Thomas DOCHERTY (Preston North End) | Gösta LINDH |
| (1) | John HENDERSON (Portsmouth) | Sylve BENGTSSON |
| (7) | Robert JOHNSTONE (Hibernian) | Gösta LÖFGREN |
| (23) | Lawrence REILLY (Hibernian) | Lars ERIKSSON |
| (30) | William STEEL (Dundee) | Hans ANDERSSON-TVILLING |
| (1) | Thomas RING (Clyde) | Gösta SANDBERG |

| | Goals | |
|---|---|---|
| | 0-1 | Löfgren (33 mins) |
| Johnstone (41 mins) | 1-1 | |
| | 1-2 | Eriksson (55 mins) |

## 228
(Home International Championship/World Cup — Qualifier)
3 October 1953

Referee: Ellis (England)
Windsor Park, Belfast (Att: 58,248)

### IRELAND 1-3 SCOTLAND — Half-time 0-0

| (5) | George FARM (Blackpool) | William SMYTH |
|---|---|---|
| (38) | George YOUNG (Rangers) captain | William CUNNINGHAM |
| (22) | Samuel COX (Rangers) | Alfred McMICHAEL |
| (13) | Robert EVANS (Celtic) | Daniel BLANCHFLOWER |
| (6) | Frank BRENNAN (Newcastle United) | James McCABE |
| (3) | Douglas COWIE (Dundee) | Wilbur CUSH |
| (15) | William WADDELL (Rangers) | William BINGHAM |
| (1) | Charles FLEMING (East Fife) | James McILROY |
| (5) | John McPHAIL (Celtic) | William SIMPSON |
| (2) | James WATSON (Huddersfield Town) | Charles TULLY |
| (2) | John HENDERSON (Portsmouth) | Norman LOCKHART |

| | Goals | |
|---|---|---|
| Fleming (47 mins) | 1-0 | |
| Fleming (69 mins) | 2-0 | |
| | 2-1 | Lockhart (72 mins pen) |
| Henderson (89 mins) | 3-1 | |

## 229
(Home International Championship/World Cup — Qualifier)
4 November 1953

Referee: Mitchell (Northern Ireland)
Hampden Park, Glasgow (Att: 71,387)

### SCOTLAND 3-3 WALES — Half-time 2-0

| (6) | George FARM (Blackpool) | Ronald HOWELLS |
|---|---|---|
| (39) | George YOUNG (Rangers) captain | Walley BARNES |
| (23) | Samuel COX (Rangers) | Alfred SHERWOOD |
| (14) | Robert EVANS (Celtic) | Roy PAUL |
| (1) | William TELFER (St Mirren) | Raymond DANIEL |
| (4) | Douglas COWIE (Dundee) | William BURGESS |
| (1) | John MACKENZIE (Partick Thistle) | William FOULKES |
| (8) | Robert JOHNSTONE (Hibernian) | Ellis DAVIES |
| (24) | Lawrence REILLY (Hibernian) | John CHARLES |
| (8) | Allan BROWN (Blackpool) | Ivor ALLCHURCH |
| (23) | William LIDDELL (Liverpool) | Royston CLARKE |

| | Goals | |
|---|---|---|
| Brown (19 mins) | 1-0 | |
| Johnstone (42 mins) | 2-0 | |
| | 2-1 | Charles (49 mins) |
| Reilly (58 mins) | 3-1 | |
| | 3-2 | Allchurch (73 mins) |
| | 3-3 | Charles (88 mins) |

# 1954

| P | W | D | L | F | A |
|---|---|---|---|---|---|
| 9 | 3 | 2 | 4 | 11 | 20 |

## 230
(Home International Championship/World Cup — Qualifier)
3 April 1954

Referee: Mitchell (Northern Ireland)
Hampden Park, Glasgow (Att: 134,544)

### SCOTLAND 2-4 ENGLAND — Half-time 1-1

| (7) | George FARM (Blackpool) | Gilbert MERRICK |
|---|---|---|
| (1) | Michael HAUGHNEY (Celtic) | Ronald STANIFORTH |
| (24) | Samuel COX (Rangers) captain | Roger BYRNE |
| (15) | Robert EVANS (Celtic) | William WRIGHT |
| (7) | Frank BRENNAN (Newcastle United) | Henry CLARKE |
| (8) | George AITKEN (Sunderland) | James DICKINSON |
| (2) | John MACKENZIE (Partick Thistle) | Thomas FINNEY |
| (9) | Robert JOHNSTONE (Hibernian) | Ivan BROADIS |
| (3) | John HENDERSON (Portsmouth) | Ronald ALLEN |
| (9) | Allan BROWN (Blackpool) | John NICHOLLS |
| (1) | William ORMOND (Hibernian) | James MULLEN |

| | Goals | |
|---|---|---|
| Brown (7 mins) | 1-0 | |
| | 1-1 | Broadis (14 mins) |
| | 1-2 | Nicholls (51 mins) |
| | 1-3 | Allen (68 mins) |
| | 1-4 | Mullen (83 mins) |
| Ormond (89 mins) | 2-4 | |

## 231
(Friendly)
5 May 1954

Referee: Clough (England)
Hampden Park, Glasgow (Att: 25,897)

### SCOTLAND 1-0 NORWAY — Half-time 1-0

| (1) | Frederick MARTIN (Aberdeen) | Asbjorn HANSEN |
|---|---|---|
| (1) | William CUNNINGHAM (Preston North End) | Oddvar HANSEN |
| (1) | John AIRD (Burnley) | Harry KARLSEN |
| (4) | Thomas DOCHERTY (Preston North End) captain | Thorleif OLSEN |
| (1) | James DAVIDSON (Partick Thistle) | Tor HERNES |
| (16) | Robert EVANS (Celtic) | Arne NATLAND |
| (10) | Robert JOHNSTONE (Hibernian) | Willy FOSSLI |
| (4) | George HAMILTON (Aberdeen) | Gunnar THORESEN |
| (1) | Patrick BUCKLEY (Aberdeen) | Arne KOTTE |
| (10) | Allan BROWN (Blackpool) | Hans NORDAHL |
| (2) | William ORMOND (Hibernian) | Gunnar DYBWAD |

| | Goals | |
|---|---|---|
| Hamilton (34 mins) | 1-0 | |

## 232

(Friendly)
19 May 1954

Referee: Andersson (Sweden)
Ullevaal Stadion, Oslo (Att: 25,000)

### NORWAY 1-1 SCOTLAND — Half-time 0-0

| | | |
|---|---|---|
| (2) | Frederick MARTIN (Aberdeen) | Asbjorn HANSEN |
| (2) | William CUNNINGHAM (Preston North End) | Oddvar HANSEN |
| (2) | John AIRD (Burnley) | Harry KARLSEN |
| (5) | Thomas DOCHERTY (Preston North End) captain | Thorleif OLSEN |
| (2) | James DAVIDSON (Partick Thistle) | Thorbjorn SVENSSEN |
| (5) | Douglas COWIE (Dundee) | Tor HERNES |
| (3) | John MACKENZIE (Partick Thistle) | Ragnar HVIDSTEN |
| (5) | George HAMILTON (Aberdeen) | Gunnar THORESEN |
| (4) | John HENDERSON (Portsmouth) | Arne KOTTE |
| (11) | Allan BROWN (Blackpool) | Gunnar ARNESEN |
| (1) | Neil MOCHAN (Celtic) | Harry KURE |

Substitutions

Arne NATLAND
for Hernes 58 mins

**Goals**

| | | |
|---|---|---|
| Mackenzie (56 mins) | 1-0 | |
| | 1-1 | Kure (88 mins) |

## 233

(Friendly)
25 May 1954

Referee: Ahlner (Sweden)
Olympia Stadion, Helsinki (Att: 21,675)

### FINLAND 1-2 SCOTLAND — Half-time 0-1

| | | |
|---|---|---|
| (1) | John ANDERSON (Leicester City) | Mauno RINTANEN |
| (1) | Alexander WILSON (Portsmouth) | Ake LINDMAN |
| (3) | William CUNNINGHAM (Preston North End) captain | Lauri LEHTINEN |
| (17) | Robert EVANS (Celtic) | Ibert HENRIKSSON |
| (6) | Douglas COWIE (Dundee) | Turkka SUNDBÄCK |
| (1) | David MATHERS (Partick Thistle) | Aimo SOMMARBERG |
| (4) | John MACKENZIE (Partick Thistle) | Pertti VANHANEN |
| (11) | Robert JOHNSTONE (Hibernian) | Matti HILTUNEN |
| (12) | Allan BROWN (Blackpool) | Rainer FORSS |
| (1) | William FERNIE (Celtic) | Olavi LAHTINEN |
| (3) | William ORMOND (Hibernian) | Börje NYGARD |

Substitutions

Aarre KLINGA
for Rintanen 48 mins

**Goals**

| | | |
|---|---|---|
| Ormond (10 mins) | 1-0 | |
| Johnstone (47 mins) | 2-0 | |
| | 2-1 | Lahtinen (86 mins) |

## 234

(World Cup — Final Tournament 1st Round)
16 June 1954

Referee: Franken (Belgium)
Sportsplatz Hardturm, Zurich (Att: 25,000)

### AUSTRIA 1-0 SCOTLAND — Half-time 1-0

| | | |
|---|---|---|
| (3) | Frederick MARTIN (Aberdeen) | Kurt SCHMIED |
| (4) | William CUNNINGHAM (Preston North End) captain | Gerhard HANAPPI |
| (3) | John AIRD (Burnley) | Leopold BARSCHANDT |
| (6) | Thomas DOCHERTY (Preston North End) | Ernst OCWIRK |
| (3) | James DAVIDSON (Partick Thistle) | Ernst HAPPEL |
| (7) | Douglas COWIE (Dundee) | Karl KOLLER |
| (5) | John MACKENZIE (Partick Thistle) | Robert KÖRNER |
| (2) | William FERNIE (Celtic) | Walter SCHLEGER |
| (2) | Neil MOCHAN (Celtic) | Robert DIENST |
| (13) | Allan BROWN (Blackpool) | Erich PROBST |
| (4) | William ORMOND (Hibernian) | Alfred KÖRNER |

**Goals**

| | | |
|---|---|---|
| | 0-1 | Probst (32 mins) |

Aberdeen's Fred Martin denies Uruguay's Omar Miguez in the 1954 World Cup debacle in Basle.

## 235

(World Cup — Final Tournament 1st Round)
19 June 1954

Referee: Orlandini (Italy)
Sankt Jakob Stadion, Basle (Att: 34,000)

### URUGUAY 7-0 SCOTLAND — Half-time 2-0

| | | |
|---|---|---|
| (4) | Frederick MARTIN (Aberdeen) | Roque MÁSPOLI |
| (5) | William CUNNINGHAM (Preston North End) captain | José SANTAMARÍA |
| (4) | John AIRD (Burnley) | William MARTÍNEZ |
| (7) | Thomas DOCHERTY (Preston North End) | Víctor ANDRADE |
| (4) | James DAVIDSON (Partick Thistle) | Obdulio VARELA |
| (8) | Douglas COWIE (Dundee) | Luis CRUZ |
| (6) | John MACKENZIE (Partick Thistle) | Julio ABBADÍE |
| (3) | William FERNIE (Celtic) | Javier AMBROIS |
| (3) | Neil MOCHAN (Celtic) | Omar MÍGUEZ |
| (14) | Allan BROWN (Blackpool) | Juan SCHIAFFINO |
| (5) | William ORMOND (Hibernian) | Carlos BORGES |

**Goals**

| | | |
|---|---|---|
| 0-1 | Borges (17 mins) |
| 0-2 | Míguez (31 mins) |
| 0-3 | Borges (48 mins) |
| 0-4 | Abbadíe (55 mins) |
| 0-5 | Borges (58 mins) |
| 0-6 | Míguez (82 mins) |
| 0-7 | Abbadíe (87 mins) |

## 236

(Home International Championship)
16 October 1954

Referee: Ling (England)
Ninian Park, Cardiff (Att: 53,000)

### WALES 0-1 SCOTLAND — Half-time 0-0

| | | |
|---|---|---|
| (1) | William FRASER (Sunderland) | Alfred KELSEY |
| (40) | George YOUNG (Rangers) captain | Walley BARNES |
| (6) | William CUNNINGHAM (Preston North End) | Alfred SHERWOOD |
| (8) | Thomas DOCHERTY (Preston North End) | Roy PAUL |
| (5) | James DAVIDSON (Partick Thistle) | John CHARLES |
| (9) | Douglas COWIE (Dundee) | David BOWEN |
| (16) | William WADDELL (Rangers) | William REED |
| (1) | Henry YORSTON (Aberdeen) | Derek TAPSCOTT |
| (2) | Patrick BUCKLEY (Aberdeen) | Trevor FORD |
| (4) | William FERNIE (Celtic) | Ivor ALLCHURCH |
| (2) | Thomas RING (Clyde) | Royston CLARKE |

**Goals**

| | |
|---|---|
| Buckley (70 mins) | 1-0 |

## 237

(Home International Championship)
3 November 1954

Referee: Bond (England)
Hampden Park, Glasgow (Att: 46,200)

### SCOTLAND 2-2 NORTHERN IRELAND — Half-time 1-2

| | | |
|---|---|---|
| (2) | William FRASER (Sunderland) | Norman UPRICHARD |
| (41) | George YOUNG (Rangers) captain | Leonard GRAHAM |
| (5) | William McNAUGHT (Raith Rovers) | William CUNNINGHAM |
| (18) | Robert EVANS (Celtic) | Daniel BLANCHFLOWER |
| (6) | James DAVIDSON (Partick Thistle) | Terence McCAVANA |
| (10) | Douglas COWIE (Dundee) | Robert PEACOCK |
| (17) | William WADDELL (Rangers) | William BINGHAM |
| (12) | Robert JOHNSTONE (Hibernian) | John BLANCHFLOWER |
| (3) | Patrick BUCKLEY (Aberdeen) | William McADAMS |
| (5) | William FERNIE (Celtic) | James McILROY |
| (3) | Thomas RING (Clyde) | Peter McPARLAND |

**Goals**

| | | |
|---|---|---|
| Davidson (22 mins) | 1-0 | |
| | 1-1 | Bingham (24 mins) |
| | 1-2 | McAdams (44 mins) |
| Johnstone (74 mins) | 2-2 | |

## 238

(Friendly)
8 December 1954

Referee: Horn (Netherlands)
Hampden Park, Glasgow (Att: 113,146)

### SCOTLAND 2-4 HUNGARY — Half-time 1-3

| | | |
|---|---|---|
| (5) | Frederick MARTIN (Aberdeen) | Lajos FARAGÓ |
| (7) | William CUNNINGHAM (Preston North End) captain | Jenö BUZANSZKY |
| (1) | Harold HADDOCK (Clyde) | Gyula LÓRÁNT |
| (9) | Thomas DOCHERTY (Preston North End) | Mihály LANTOS |
| (7) | James DAVIDSON (Partick Thistle) | József BOZSIK |
| (1) | John CUMMING (Hearts) | Ferenc SZOJKA |
| (7) | John MACKENZIE (Partick Thistle) | Károly SÁNDOR |
| (13) | Robert JOHNSTONE (Hibernian) | Sándor KOCSIS |
| (25) | Lawrence REILLY (Hibernian) | Nándor HIDEGKUTI |
| (1) | James WARDHAUGH (Hearts) | Ferenc PUSKÁS |
| (4) | Thomas RING (Clyde) | Máté FENYVESI |

**Goals**

| | | |
|---|---|---|
| | 0-1 | Bozsik (20 mins) |
| | 0-2 | Hidegkuti (26 mins) |
| Ring (36 mins) | 1-2 | |
| | 1-3 | Sándor (44 mins) |
| Johnstone (46 mins) | 2-3 | |
| | 2-4 | Kocsis (90 mins) |

# 1955

| P | W | D | L | F | A |
|---|---|---|---|---|---|
| 7 | 3 | 1 | 3 | 15 | 15 |

## 239

(Home International Championship)
2 April 1955

Referee: Griffiths (Wales)
Wembley Stadium, London (Att: 96,847)

### ENGLAND 7-2 SCOTLAND — Half-time 4-1

| | | | |
|---|---|---|---|
| (6) | Frederick MARTIN (Aberdeen) | | Frederick WILLIAMS |
| (8) | William CUNNINGHAM (Preston North End) captain | | James MEADOWS |
| (2) | Harold HADDOCK (Clyde) | | Roger BYRNE |
| (10) | Thomas DOCHERTY (Preston North End) | | Kenneth ARMSTRONG |
| (8) | James DAVIDSON (Partick Thistle) | | William WRIGHT |
| (2) | John CUMMING (Hearts) | | Duncan EDWARDS |
| (8) | John MACKENZIE (Partick Thistle) | | Stanley MATTHEWS |
| (14) | Robert JOHNSTONE (Manchester City) | | Donald REVIE |
| (26) | Lawrence REILLY (Hibernian) | | Nathaniel LOFTHOUSE |
| (4) | John McMILLAN (Airdrie) | | Dennis WILSHAW |
| (5) | Thomas RING (Clyde) | | Frank BLUNSTONE |

**Goals**

| | | |
|---|---|---|
| | 0-1 | Wilshaw (1 min) |
| | 0-2 | Lofthouse (7 mins) |
| Reilly (15 mins) | 1-2 | |
| | 1-3 | Revie (25 mins) |
| | 1-4 | Lofthouse (27 mins) |
| | 1-5 | Wilshaw (70 mins) |
| | 1-6 | Wilshaw (73 mins) |
| | 1-7 | Wilshaw (80 mins) |
| Docherty (85 mins) | 2-7 | |

## 240

(Friendly)
4 May 1955

Referee: Gardeazabal (Spain)
Hampden Park, Glasgow (Att: 20,858)

### SCOTLAND 3-0 PORTUGAL — Half-time 2-0

| | | | |
|---|---|---|---|
| (1) | Thomas YOUNGER (Hibernian) | | Carlos GOMES |
| (1) | Alexander PARKER (Falkirk) | | Manuel CALDEIRA |
| (3) | Harold HADDOCK (Clyde) | | Angelo CARVALHO |
| (19) | Robert EVANS (Celtic) | | Fernando CAIADO |
| (42) | George YOUNG (Rangers) captain | | Manuel PASSOS |
| (3) | John CUMMING (Hearts) | | Emilio GRAÇA |
| (9) | Gordon SMITH (Hibernian) | | José AGUAS |
| (1) | Archibald ROBERTSON (Clyde) | | Lucas MATATEU |
| (27) | Lawrence REILLY (Hibernian) | | Mario COLUNA |
| (1) | Thomas GEMMELL (St Mirren) | | José TRAVAÇOS |
| (24) | William LIDDELL (Liverpool) | | João MARTINS |

**Goals**

| | |
|---|---|
| Gemmell (7 mins) | 1-0 |
| Liddell (36 mins) | 2-0 |
| Reilly (86 mins) | 3-0 |

## 241

(Friendly)
15 May 1955

Referee: Orlandini (Italy)
J.N.A. Stadion, Belgrade (Att: 20,000)

### YUGOSLAVIA 2-2 SCOTLAND — Half-time 2-2

| | | | |
|---|---|---|---|
| (2) | Thomas YOUNGER (Hibernian) | | Vladimir BEARA |
| (2) | Alexander PARKER (Falkirk) | | Bruno BELIN |
| (4) | Harold HADDOCK (Clyde) | | Milan ZEKOVIC |
| (20) | Robert EVANS (Celtic) | | Zlatko CAJKOVSKI |
| (43) | George YOUNG (Rangers) captain | | Suad SVRAKA |
| (4) | John CUMMING (Hearts) | | Vujadin BOSKOV |
| (10) | Gordon SMITH (Hibernian) | | Todor VESELINOVIC |
| (4) | Robert COLLINS (Celtic) | | Milos MILUTINOVIC |
| (28) | Lawrence REILLY (Hibernian) | | Bernard VUKAS |
| (2) | Thomas GEMMELL (St Mirren) | | Stjepan BOBEK |
| (25) | William LIDDELL (Liverpool) | | Branko ZEBEC |

**Substitutions**

Branko KRALJ
for Beara 68 mins

**Goals**

| | | |
|---|---|---|
| | 0-1 | Veselinovic (13 mins) |
| Reilly (30 mins) | 1-1 | |
| | 1-2 | Vukas (38 mins) |
| Smith (40 mins) | 2-2 | |

## 242

(Friendly)
19 May 1955

Referee: Bernardi (Italy)
Prater Stadion, Vienna (Att: 65,000)

### AUSTRIA 1-4 SCOTLAND — Half-time 0-2

| | | | |
|---|---|---|---|
| (3) | Thomas YOUNGER (Hibernian) | | Kurt SCHMIED |
| (3) | Alexander PARKER (Falkirk) | | Paul HALLA |
| (1) | Andrew KERR (Partick Thistle) | | Leopold BARSCHANDT |
| (11) | Thomas DOCHERTY (Preston North End) | | Gerhard HANAPPI |
| (21) | Robert EVANS (Celtic) | | Rudolf ROCKL |
| (11) | Douglas COWIE (Dundee) | | Ernst OCWIRK |
| (11) | Gordon SMITH (Hibernian) captain | | Ernst HOFBAUER |
| (5) | Robert COLLINS (Celtic) | | Theodor WAGNER |
| (29) | Lawrence REILLY (Hibernian) | | Richard BROUSEK |
| (2) | Archibald ROBERTSON (Clyde) | | Erich PROBST |
| (26) | William LIDDELL (Liverpool) | | Walter SCHLEGER |

**Substitutions**

Robert DIENST
for Brousek 42 mins

**Goals**

| | | |
|---|---|---|
| Robertson (1 min) | 1-0 | |
| Smith (44 mins) | 2-0 | |
| Liddell (70 mins) | 3-0 | |
| | 3-1 | Ocwirk (88 mins) |
| Reilly (89 mins) | 4-1 | |

## 243

(Friendly)
29 May 1955

Referee: Seipelt (Austria)
Nép Stadion, Budapest (Att: 102,000)

### HUNGARY 3-1 SCOTLAND — Half-time 0-1

| | | | |
|---|---|---|---|
| (4) | Thomas YOUNGER (Hibernian) | | Imre DANKA |
| (2) | Andrew KERR (Partick Thistle) | | Jenő BUZÁNSZKY |
| (5) | Harold HADDOCK (Clyde) | | Pál VÁRHIDI |
| (12) | Thomas DOCHERTY (Preston North End) | | Mihály LANTOS |
| (22) | Robert EVANS (Celtic) | | József BOZSIK |
| (12) | Douglas COWIE (Dundee) | | Ferenc SZOJKA |
| (12) | Gordon SMITH (Hibernian) captain | | Károly SÁNDOR |
| (6) | Robert COLLINS (Celtic) | | Nándor HIDEGKUTI |
| (30) | Lawrence REILLY (Hibernian) | | Sándor KOCSIS |
| (3) | Archibald ROBERTSON (Clyde) | | Ferenc PUSKÁS |
| (27) | William LIDDELL (Liverpool) | | Máté FENYVESI |

**Substitutions**

Péter PALOTÁS
for Sándor 44 mins

Lajos FARAGÓ
for Danka 46 mins

**Goals**

| | | |
|---|---|---|
| Smith (42 mins) | 1-0 | |
| | 1-1 | Hidegkuti (51 mins) |
| | 1-2 | Kocsis (59 mins) |
| | 1-3 | Fenyvesi (68 mins) |

## 244

(Home International Championship)
8 October 1955

Referee: Kelly (England)
Windsor Park, Belfast (Att: 48,000)

### NORTHERN IRELAND 2-1 SCOTLAND — Half-time 2-0

| | | | |
|---|---|---|---|
| (5) | Thomas YOUNGER (Hibernian) | | Norman UPRICHARD |
| (4) | Alexander PARKER (Falkirk) | | Leonard GRAHAM |
| (1) | Joseph McDONALD (Sunderland) | | William CUNNINGHAM |
| (23) | Robert EVANS (Celtic) | | Daniel BLANCHFLOWER |
| (44) | George YOUNG (Rangers) captain | | Terence McCAVANA |
| (1) | Archibald GLEN (Aberdeen) | | Robert PEACOCK |
| (13) | Gordon SMITH (Hibernian) | | William BINGHAM |
| (7) | Robert COLLINS (Celtic) | | John BLANCHFLOWER |
| (31) | Lawrence REILLY (Hibernian) | | Francis COYLE |
| (15) | Robert JOHNSTONE (Manchester City) | | James McILROY |
| (28) | William LIDDELL (Liverpool) | | Peter McPARLAND |

**Goals**

| | | |
|---|---|---|
| | 0-1 | J. Blanchflower (7 mins) |
| | 0-2 | Bingham (16 mins) |
| Reilly (62 mins) | 1-2 | |

## 245

(Home International Championship)
9 November 1955

Referee: Leafe (England)
Hampden Park, Glasgow (Att: 53,887)

### SCOTLAND 2-0 WALES — Half-time 2-0

| | | |
|---|---|---|
| (6) | Thomas YOUNGER (Hibernian) | Alfred KELSEY |
| (5) | Alexander PARKER (Falkirk) | Stuart WILLIAMS |
| (2) | Joseph McDONALD (Sunderland) | Alfred SHERWOOD |
| (24) | Robert EVANS (Celtic) | Melfyn CHARLES |
| (45) | George YOUNG (Rangers) captain | John CHARLES |
| (13) | Douglas COWIE (Dundee) | Roy PAUL |
| (14) | Gordon SMITH (Hibernian) | Derek TAPSCOTT |
| (16) | Robert JOHNSTONE (Manchester City) | Noel KINSEY |
| (32) | Lawrence REILLY (Hibernian) | Trevor FORD |
| (8) | Robert COLLINS (Celtic) | Ivor ALLCHURCH |
| (5) | John HENDERSON (Portsmouth) | Clifford JONES |

| | Goals | |
|---|---|---|
| Johnstone (14 mins) | 1-0 | |
| Johnstone (25 mins) | 2-0 | |

# 1956

| P | W | D | L | F | A |
|---|---|---|---|---|---|
| 5 | 2 | 3 | 0 | 7 | 4 |

## 246

(Home International Championship)
14 April 1956

Referee: Callaghan (Wales)
Hampden Park, Glasgow (Att: 132,817)

### SCOTLAND 1-1 ENGLAND — Half-time 0-0

| | | |
|---|---|---|
| (7) | Thomas YOUNGER (Hibernian) | Reginald MATTHEWS |
| (6) | Alexander PARKER (Falkirk) | Jeffrey HALL |
| (1) | John HEWIE (Charlton Athletic) | Roger BYRNE |
| (25) | Robert EVANS (Celtic) | James DICKINSON |
| (46) | George YOUNG (Rangers) captain | William WRIGHT |
| (2) | Archibald GLEN (Aberdeen) | Duncan EDWARDS |
| (1) | Graham LEGGAT (Aberdeen) | Thomas FINNEY |
| (17) | Robert JOHNSTONE (Manchester City) | Thomas TAYLOR |
| (33) | Lawrence REILLY (Hibernian) | Nathaniel LOFTHOUSE |
| (5) | John McMILLAN (Airdrie) | John HAYNES |
| (15) | Gordon SMITH (Hibernian) | William PERRY |

| | Goals | |
|---|---|---|
| Leggat (60 mins) | 1-0 | |
| | 1-1 | Haynes (89 mins) |

## 247

(Friendly)
2 May 1956

Referee: Bronkhurst (Netherlands)
Hampden Park, Glasgow (Att: 80,509)

### SCOTLAND 1-1 AUSTRIA — Half-time 1-1

| | | |
|---|---|---|
| (8) | Thomas YOUNGER (Hibernian) | Bruno ENGELMEIER |
| (7) | Alexander PARKER (Falkirk) | Paul HALLA |
| (2) | John HEWIE (Charlton Athletic) | Leopold BARSCHANDT |
| (26) | Robert EVANS (Celtic) | Ernst OCWIRK |
| (47) | George YOUNG (Rangers) captain | Walter KOLLMANN |
| (14) | Douglas COWIE (Dundee) | Karl KOLLER |
| (9) | John MACKENZIE (Partick Thistle) | Herbert GROHS |
| (1) | Alfred CONN (Hearts) | Theodor WAGNER |
| (34) | Lawrence REILLY (Hibernian) | Gerhard HANAPPI |
| (1) | Hugh BAIRD (Airdrie) | Alfred KÖRNER |
| (1) | Michael CULLEN (Luton Town) | Walter HAUMMER |

| | Goals | |
|---|---|---|
| Conn (12 mins) | 1-0 | |
| | 1-1 | Wagner (14 mins) |

## 248

(Home International Championship)
20 October 1956

Referee: Mann (England)
Ninian Park, Cardiff (Att: 60,000)

### WALES 2-2 SCOTLAND — Half-time 2-2

| | | |
|---|---|---|
| (9) | Thomas YOUNGER (Liverpool) | Alfred KELSEY |
| (8) | Alexander PARKER (Falkirk) | Alfred SHERWOOD |
| (3) | John HEWIE (Charlton Athletic) | Melvyn HOPKINS |
| (6) | John McCOLL (Rangers) | Alan HARRINGTON |
| (48) | George YOUNG (Rangers) captain | Raymond DANIEL |
| (15) | Douglas COWIE (Dundee) | Derrick SULLIVAN |
| (2) | Graham LEGGAT (Aberdeen) | Terence MEDWIN |
| (1) | John MUDIE (Blackpool) | John CHARLES |
| (35) | Lawrence REILLY (Hibernian) | Trevor FORD |
| (9) | Robert COLLINS (Celtic) | Ivor ALLCHURCH |
| (6) | William FERNIE (Celtic) | Clifford JONES |

| | Goals | |
|---|---|---|
| | 0-1 | Ford (7 mins) |
| Fernie (22 mins) | 1-1 | |
| | 1-2 | Medwin (32 mins) |
| Reilly (36 mins) | 2-2 | |

Alex Parker cannot reach a shot by Johnny Haynes (on right of goal-post) and England have scored an 89th-minute equaliser at Hampden in April 1956.

## 249

**(Home International Championship)**
**7 November 1956**

Referee: Leafe (England)
Hampden Park, Glasgow (Att: 62,035)

### SCOTLAND 1-0 NORTHERN IRELAND — Half-time 1-0

| | | |
|---|---|---|
| (10) | Thomas YOUNGER (Liverpool) | Harold GREGG |
| (9) | Alexander PARKER (Falkirk) | William CUNNINGHAM |
| (4) | John HEWIE (Charlton Athletic) | Alfred McMICHAEL |
| (7) | John McCOLL (Rangers) | Daniel BLANCHFLOWER |
| (49) | George YOUNG (Rangers) captain | John BLANCHFLOWER |
| (16) | Douglas COWIE (Dundee) | Thomas CASEY |
| (1) | Alexander SCOTT (Rangers) | William BINGHAM |
| (2) | John MUDIE (Blackpool) | James McILROY |
| (36) | Lawrence REILLY (Hibernian) | Bruce SHIELDS |
| (2) | James WARDHAUGH (Hearts) | Thomas DICKSON |
| (7) | William FERNIE (Celtic) | Peter McPARLAND |

| | Goals | |
|---|---|---|
| Scott (25 mins) | 1-0 | |

## 250

**(Friendly)**
**21 November 1956**

Referee: Roomer (Netherlands)
Hampden Park, Glasgow (Att: 55,521)

### SCOTLAND 2-0 YUGOSLAVIA — Half-time 1-0

| | | |
|---|---|---|
| (11) | Thomas YOUNGER (Liverpool) | Vladimir BEARA |
| (10) | Alexander PARKER (Falkirk) | Bruno BELIN |
| (5) | John HEWIE (Charlton Athletic) | Branko STANKOVIC |
| (8) | John McCOLL (Rangers) | Lazar TASIC |
| (50) | George YOUNG (Rangers) captain | Ivan HORVAT |
| (13) | Thomas DOCHERTY (Preston North End) | Vujadin BOSKOV |
| (2) | Alexander SCOTT (Rangers) | Aleksandar PETAKOVIC |
| (3) | John MUDIE (Blackpool) | Milos MILUTINOVIC |
| (37) | Lawrence REILLY (Hibernian) | Tihomir OGNJANOVIC |
| (1) | Samuel BAIRD (Rangers) | Bernard VUKAS |
| (8) | William FERNIE (Celtic) | Branko ZEBEC |

| | Goals | |
|---|---|---|
| Mudie (36 mins) | 1-0 | |
| Baird (55 mins) | 2-0 | |

# 1957

| P | W | D | L | F | A |
|---|---|---|---|---|---|
| 8 | 4 | 2 | 2 | 16 | 14 |

## 251

**(Home International Championship)**
**6 April 1957**

Referee: Roomer (Netherlands)
Wembley Stadium, London (Att: 97,520)

### ENGLAND 2-1 SCOTLAND — Half-time 0-1

| | | |
|---|---|---|
| (12) | Thomas YOUNGER (Liverpool) | Alan HODGKINSON |
| (1) | Eric CALDOW (Rangers) | Jeffrey HALL |
| (6) | John HEWIE (Charlton Athletic) | Roger BYRNE |
| (9) | John McCOLL (Rangers) | Ronald CLAYTON |
| (51) | George YOUNG (Rangers) captain | William WRIGHT |
| (14) | Thomas DOCHERTY (Preston North End) | Duncan EDWARDS |
| (10) | Robert COLLINS (Celtic) | Stanley MATTHEWS |
| (9) | William FERNIE (Celtic) | Thomas THOMPSON |
| (38) | Lawrence REILLY (Hibernian) | Thomas FINNEY |
| (4) | John MUDIE (Blackpool) | Derek KEVAN |
| (6) | Thomas RING (Clyde) | Colin GRAINGER |

| | Goals | |
|---|---|---|
| Ring (1 min) | 1-0 | |
| | 1-1 | Kevan (63 mins) |
| | 1-2 | Edwards (80 mins) |

## 252

**(World Cup — Qualifier)**
**8 May 1957**

Referee: Dusch (West Germany)
Hampden Park, Glasgow (Att: 88,890)

### SCOTLAND 4-2 SPAIN — Half-time 2-1

| | | |
|---|---|---|
| (13) | Thomas YOUNGER (Liverpool) | Antonio RAMALLETS |
| (2) | Eric CALDOW (Rangers) | Fernando OLIVELLA |
| (7) | John HEWIE (Charlton Athletic) | Marcelino CAMPANAL |
| (10) | John McCOLL (Rangers) | Jesús GARAY |
| (52) | George YOUNG (Rangers) captain | Martin VERGÉS |
| (15) | Thomas DOCHERTY (Preston North End) | José ZARRAGA |
| (16) | Gordon SMITH (Hibernian) | MIGUEL Gonzales |
| (11) | Robert COLLINS (Celtic) | Ladislao KUBALA |
| (5) | John MUDIE (Blackpool) | Alfredo DI STEFANO |
| (2) | Samuel BAIRD (Rangers) | Luís SUÁREZ |
| (7) | Thomas RING (Clyde) | Francisco GENTO |

| | Goals | |
|---|---|---|
| Mudie (22 mins) | 1-0 | |
| | 1-1 | Kubala (30 mins) |
| Hewie (41 mins pen) | 2-1 | |
| | 2-2 | Suárez (50 mins) |
| Mudie (70 mins) | 3-2 | |
| Mudie (79 mins) | 4-2 | |

## 253

**(World Cup — Qualifier)**
**19 May 1957**

Referee: Seipelt (Austria)
Sankt Jakob Stadion, Basle (Att: 48,000)

### SWITZERLAND 1-2 SCOTLAND — Half-time 1-1

| | | |
|---|---|---|
| (14) | Thomas YOUNGER (Liverpool) | Eugène PARLIER |
| (3) | Eric CALDOW (Rangers) | Willy KERNEN |
| (8) | John HEWIE (Charlton Athletic) | Harry KOCH |
| (11) | John McCOLL (Rangers) | André GROBETY |
| (53) | George YOUNG (Rangers) captain | Ivo FROSIO |
| (16) | Thomas DOCHERTY (Preston North End) | Heinz SCHNEITER |
| (17) | Gordon SMITH (Hibernian) | Charles ANTENEN |
| (12) | Robert COLLINS (Celtic) | Eugen MEIER |
| (6) | John MUDIE (Blackpool) | Roger VONLANTHEN |
| (3) | Samuel BAIRD (Rangers) | Robert BALLAMAN |
| (8) | Thomas RING (Clyde) | Fernando RIVA |

| | Goals | |
|---|---|---|
| | 0-1 | Vonlanthen (12 mins) |
| Mudie (33 mins) | 1-1 | |
| Collins (71 mins) | 2-1 | |

## 254

**(Friendly)**
**22 May 1957**

Referee: Dienst (Switzerland)
Neckar Stadion, Stuttgart (Att: 80,000)

### WEST GERMANY 1-3 SCOTLAND — Half-time 0-2

| | | |
|---|---|---|
| (15) | Thomas YOUNGER (Liverpool) | Hans TILKOWSKI |
| (4) | Eric CALDOW (Rangers) | Willi GERDAU |
| (9) | John HEWIE (Charlton Athletic) | Erich JUSKOWIAK |
| (12) | John McCOLL (Rangers) | Georg STOLLENWERK |
| (27) | Robert EVANS (Celtic) | Heinz WEWERS |
| (17) | Thomas DOCHERTY (Preston North End) captain | Horst SZYMANIAK |
| (3) | Alexander SCOTT (Rangers) | Helmut RAHN |
| (13) | Robert COLLINS (Celtic) | Willi SCHRÖDER |
| (7) | John MUDIE (Blackpool) | Alfred KELBASSA |
| (4) | Samuel BAIRD (Rangers) | Alfred SCHMIDT |
| (9) | Thomas RING (Clyde) | Gerhard SIEDL |

| | Goals | |
|---|---|---|
| Collins (20 mins) | 1-0 | |
| Mudie (33 mins) | 2-0 | |
| Collins (54 mins) | 3-0 | |
| | 3-1 | Siedl (70 mins) |

## 255

**(World Cup — Qualifier)**
**26 May 1957**

Referee: Leafe (England)
Estadio Santiago Bernabeu, Madrid (Att: 90,000)

### SPAIN 4-1 SCOTLAND — Half-time 2-0

| | | |
|---|---|---|
| (16) | Thomas YOUNGER (Liverpool) | Antonio RAMALLETS |
| (5) | Eric CALDOW (Rangers) | Juan QUINCOCES |
| (10) | John HEWIE (Charlton Athletic) | Jesús GARAY |
| (1) | David MACKAY (Hearts) | Juan SEGARRA |
| (28) | Robert EVANS (Celtic) | Martín VERGÉS |
| (18) | Thomas DOCHERTY (Preston North End) captain | Enrique GENSANA |
| (18) | Gordon SMITH (Hibernian) | Estanislao BASORA |
| (14) | Robert COLLINS (Celtic) | Ladislao KUBALA |
| (8) | John MUDIE (Blackpool) | Alfredo DI STEFANO |
| (5) | Samuel BAIRD (Rangers) | Enrique MATEOS |
| (10) | Thomas RING (Clyde) | Francisco GENTO |

| | Goals | |
|---|---|---|
| | 0-1 | Mateos (13 mins) |
| | 0-2 | Kubala (20 mins) |
| | 0-3 | Basora (57 mins) |
| Smith (79 mins) | 1-3 | |
| | 1-4 | Basora (85 mins) |

55

## 256

(Home International Championship)
5 October 1957

Referee: Callaghan (Wales)
Windsor Park, Belfast (Att: 50,000)

### NORTHERN IRELAND 1-1 SCOTLAND    Half-time 0-0

| | | |
|---|---|---|
| (17) | Thomas YOUNGER (Liverpool) | Norman UPRICHARD |
| (11) | Alexander PARKER (Falkirk) | William CUNNINGHAM |
| (6) | Eric CALDOW (Rangers) | Alfred McMICHAEL |
| (13) | John McCOLL (Rangers) | Daniel BLANCHFLOWER |
| (29) | Robert EVANS (Celtic) | John BLANCHFLOWER |
| (19) | Thomas DOCHERTY (Preston North End) captain | Robert PEACOCK |
| (3) | Graham LEGGAT (Aberdeen) | William BINGHAM |
| (15) | Robert COLLINS (Celtic) | William SIMPSON |
| (9) | John MUDIE (Blackpool) | William McADAMS |
| (6) | Samuel BAIRD (Rangers) | James McILROY |
| (11) | Thomas RING (Clyde) | Peter McPARLAND |

Goals
| | 0-1 | Simpson (47 mins) |
|---|---|---|
| Leggat (58 mins) | 1-1 | |

## 257

(World Cup — Qualifier)
6 November 1957

Referee: Leafe (England)
Hampden Park, Glasgow (Att: 58,811)

### SCOTLAND 3-2 SWITZERLAND    Half-time 1-1

| | | |
|---|---|---|
| (18) | Thomas YOUNGER (Liverpool) | Eugène PARLIER |
| (12) | Alexander PARKER (Falkirk) | Willy KERNEN |
| (7) | Eric CALDOW (Rangers) | Fritz MORF |
| (10) | William FERNIE (Celtic) | André GROBETY |
| (30) | Robert EVANS (Celtic) | Harry KOCH |
| (20) | Thomas DOCHERTY (Preston North End) captain | Heinz SCHNEITER |
| (4) | Alexander SCOTT (Rangers) | Francesco CHIESA |
| (16) | Robert COLLINS (Celtic) | Robert BALLAMAN |
| (10) | John MUDIE (Blackpool) | Eugen MEIER |
| (4) | Archibald ROBERTSON (Clyde) | Roger VONLANTHEN |
| (12) | Thomas RING (Clyde) | Fernando RIVA |

Goals
| | | |
|---|---|---|
| Robertson (29 mins) | 1-0 | |
| | 1-1 | Riva (35 mins) |
| Mudie (52 mins) | 2-1 | |
| Scott (70 mins) | 3-1 | |
| | 3-2 | Vonlanthen (80 mins) |

## 258

(Home International Championship)
13 November 1957

Referee: Clough (England)
Hampden Park, Glasgow (Att: 42,918)

### SCOTLAND 1-1 WALES    Half-time 1-0

| | | |
|---|---|---|
| (19) | Thomas YOUNGER (Liverpool) | Alfred KELSEY |
| (13) | Alexander PARKER (Falkirk) | Stuart WILLIAMS |
| (8) | Eric CALDOW (Rangers) | Melvyn HOPKINS |
| (21) | Thomas DOCHERTY (Preston North End) captain | Alan HARRINGTON |
| (31) | Robert EVANS (Celtic) | Melfyn CHARLES |
| (11) | William FERNIE (Celtic) | David BOWEN |
| (5) | Alexander SCOTT (Rangers) | Leonard ALLCHURCH |
| (17) | Robert COLLINS (Celtic) | William HARRIS |
| (1) | James GARDINER (Motherwell) | Terence MEDWIN |
| (11) | John MUDIE (Blackpool) | Royston VERNON |
| (1) | Thomas EWING (Partick Thistle) | Clifford JONES |

Goals
| | | |
|---|---|---|
| Collins (14 mins) | 1-0 | |
| | 1-1 | Medwin (76 mins) |

# 1958

| P | W | D | L | F | A |
|---|---|---|---|---|---|
| 8 | 2 | 3 | 3 | 12 | 14 |

## 259

(Home International Championship)
19 April 1958

Referee: Dusch (West Germany)
Hampden Park, Glasgow (Att: 127,874)

### SCOTLAND 0-4 ENGLAND    Half-time 0-2

| | | |
|---|---|---|
| (20) | Thomas YOUNGER (Liverpool) | Edward HOPKINSON |
| (14) | Alexander PARKER (Falkirk) | Donald HOWE |
| (6) | Harold HADDOCK (Clyde) | Ernest LANGLEY |
| (14) | John McCOLL (Rangers) | Ronald CLAYTON |
| (32) | Robert EVANS (Celtic) | William WRIGHT |
| (22) | Thomas DOCHERTY (Preston North End) captain | William SLATER |
| (1) | George HERD (Clyde) | Bryan DOUGLAS |
| (1) | James MURRAY (Hearts) | Robert CHARLTON |
| (12) | John MUDIE (Blackpool) | Derek KEVAN |
| (1) | James FORREST (Motherwell) | John HAYNES |
| (2) | Thomas EWING (Partick Thistle) | Thomas FINNEY |

Goals
| | | |
|---|---|---|
| | 0-1 | Douglas (20 mins) |
| | 0-2 | Kevan (33 mins) |
| | 0-3 | Charlton (67 mins) |
| | 0-4 | Kevan (75 mins) |

## 260

(Friendly)
7 May 1958

Referee: Clough (England)
Hampden Park, Glasgow (Att: 54,900)

### SCOTLAND 1-1 HUNGARY    Half-time 1-0

| | | |
|---|---|---|
| (21) | Thomas YOUNGER (Liverpool) captain | Gyula GROSICS |
| (9) | Eric CALDOW (Rangers) | Sándor MÁTRAI |
| (11) | John HEWIE (Charlton Athletic) | Ferenc SIPOS |
| (4) | Edward TURNBULL (Hibernian) | László SÁROSI |
| (33) | Robert EVANS (Celtic) | József BOZSIK |
| (17) | Douglas COWIE (Dundee) | Pál BERENDI |
| (4) | Graham LEGGAT (Aberdeen) | László BUDAI |
| (2) | James MURRAY (Hearts) | Ferenc MACHOS |
| (13) | John MUDIE (Blackpool) | Lajos TICHY |
| (18) | Robert COLLINS (Celtic) | Deszö BUNDZSÁK |
| (1) | James IMLACH (Nottingham Forest) | Máté FENYVESI |

Goals
| | | |
|---|---|---|
| Mudie (14 mins) | 1-0 | |
| | 1-1 | Fenyvesi (52 mins) |

## 261

(Friendly)
1 June 1958

Referee: Szranko (Hungary)
Dziesiciolecia Stadion, Warsaw (Att: 70,000)

### POLAND 1-2 SCOTLAND    Half-time 0-1

| | | |
|---|---|---|
| (22) | Thomas YOUNGER (Liverpool) captain | Edward SZYMKOWIAK |
| (10) | Eric CALDOW (Rangers) | Henryk SZCZEPANSKI |
| (12) | John HEWIE (Charlton Athletic) | Roman KORYNT |
| (5) | Edward TURNBULL (Hibernian) | Jerzy WOZNIAK |
| (34) | Robert EVANS (Celtic) | Witold MAJEWSKI |
| (18) | Douglas COWIE (Dundee) | Edmund ZIENTARA |
| (5) | Graham LEGGAT (Aberdeen) | Marian NOWARA |
| (3) | James MURRAY (Hearts) | Marian NORKOWSKI |
| (14) | John MUDIE (Blackpool) | Henryk KEMPNY |
| (19) | Robert COLLINS (Celtic) | Gerard CIESLIK |
| (2) | James IMLACH (Nottingham Forest) | Roman LENTNER |

Goals
| | | |
|---|---|---|
| Collins (21 mins) | 1-0 | |
| Collins (53 mins) | 2-0 | |
| | 2-1 | Cieslik (84 mins) |

## 262

(World Cup — Final Tournament 1st Round)
8 June 1958

Referee: Wyssling (Switzerland)
Arosvallen, Vasteras (Att: 9,591)

### YUGOSLAVIA 1-1 SCOTLAND    Half-time 1-0

| | | |
|---|---|---|
| (23) | Thomas YOUNGER (Liverpool) captain | Vladimir BEARA |
| (11) | Eric CALDOW (Rangers) | Vasilije SIJAKOVIC |
| (13) | John HEWIE (Charlton Athletic) | Tomislav CRNKOVIC |
| (6) | Edward TURNBULL (Hibernian) | Dobrosav KRSTIC |
| (35) | Robert EVANS (Celtic) | Branko ZEBEC |
| (19) | Douglas COWIE (Dundee) | Vujadin BOSKOV |
| (6) | Graham LEGGAT (Aberdeen) | Aleksandar PETAKOVIC |
| (4) | James MURRAY (Hearts) | Todor VESELINOVIC |
| (15) | John MUDIE (Blackpool) | Milos MILUTINOVIC |
| (20) | Robert COLLINS (Celtic) | Dragoslav SEKULARAC |
| (3) | James IMLACH (Nottingham Forest) | Zdravko RAJKOV |

Goals
| | | |
|---|---|---|
| | 0-1 | Petakovic (6 mins) |
| Murray (51 mins) | 1-1 | |

## 263

(World Cup — Final Tournament 1st Round)
11 June 1958

Referee: Orlandini (Italy)
Idrottsparken, Norrköping (Att: 11,665)

### PARAGUAY 3-2 SCOTLAND    Half-time 2-1

| | | |
|---|---|---|
| (24) | Thomas YOUNGER (Liverpool) captain | Samuel AGUILAR |
| (15) | Alexander PARKER (Everton) | Edelmiro ARÉVALO |
| (12) | Eric CALDOW (Rangers) | Eligio ECHAGÜE |
| (7) | Edward TURNBULL (Hibernian) | Ignacio ACHUCARO |
| (36) | Robert EVANS (Celtic) | Juan LEZCANO |
| (20) | Douglas COWIE (Dundee) | Salvador VILLALBA |
| (7) | Graham LEGGAT (Aberdeen) | Juan AGUERO |
| (21) | Robert COLLINS (Celtic) | José PARODI |
| (16) | John MUDIE (Blackpool) | Jorgelino ROMERO |
| (5) | Archibald ROBERTSON (Clyde) | Cayetano RÉ |
| (12) | William FERNIE (Celtic) | Florencio AMARILLA |

Goals
| | | |
|---|---|---|
| | 0-1 | Aguero (3 mins) |
| Mudie (23 mins) | 1-1 | |
| | 1-2 | Ré (44 mins) |
| | 1-3 | Parodi (75 mins) |
| Collins (76 mins) | 2-3 | |

Hearts' Jimmy Murray has just equalised against Yugoslavia at Vasteras in the 1958 World Cup finals in Sweden.

Full-back John Hewie clears off the line against the Yugoslavs as goalkeeper Tommy Younger looks on helplessly.

Bobby Collins and Willie Fernie are blocked by a Paraguayan defender during the 1958 World Cup match in Norrköping.

## 264

(World Cup — Final Tournament 1st Round)
15 June 1958

Referee: Brozzi (Argentina)
Eyravallen, Örebro (Att: 13,554)

### FRANCE 2-1 SCOTLAND | Half-time 2-0

| | | |
|---|---|---|
| (1) | William BROWN (Dundee) | Claude ABBES |
| (13) | Eric CALDOW (Rangers) | Raymond KAELBEL |
| (14) | John HEWIE (Charlton Athletic) | André LEROND |
| (8) | Edward TURNBULL (Hibernian) | Armand PENVERNE |
| (37) | Robert EVANS (Celtic) captain | Robert JONQUET |
| (2) | David MACKAY (Hearts) | Jean-Jacques MARCEL |
| (22) | Robert COLLINS (Celtic) | Maryan WISNIESKI |
| (5) | James MURRAY (Hearts) | Raymond KOPA |
| (17) | John MUDIE (Blackpool) | Just FONTAINE |
| (7) | Samuel BAIRD (Rangers) | Roger PIANTONI |
| (4) | James IMLACH (Nottingham Forest) | Jean VINCENT |

| | Goals | |
|---|---|---|
| | 0-1 | Kopa (22 mins) |
| | 0-2 | Fontaine (45 mins) |
| Baird (58 mins) | 1-2 | |

## 265

(Home International Championship)
18 October 1958

Referee: Leafe (England)
Ninian Park, Cardiff (Att: 59,162)

### WALES 0-3 SCOTLAND | Half-time 0-1

| | | |
|---|---|---|
| (2) | William BROWN (Dundee) | Alfred KELSEY |
| (1) | John GRANT (Hibernian) | Stuart WILLIAMS |
| (14) | Eric CALDOW (Rangers) | Melvyn HOPKINS |
| (3) | David MACKAY (Hearts) captain | Derrick SULLIVAN |
| (1) | William TONER (Kilmarnock) | Melfyn CHARLES |
| (23) | Thomas DOCHERTY (Arsenal) | David BOWEN |
| (8) | Graham LEGGAT (Fulham) | Leonard ALLCHURCH |
| (23) | Robert COLLINS (Everton) | Royston VERNON |
| (1) | David HERD (Arsenal) | Terence MEDWIN |
| (1) | Denis LAW (Huddersfield Town) | Ivor ALLCHURCH |
| (6) | John HENDERSON (Arsenal) | Phillip WOOSNAM |

| | Goals | |
|---|---|---|
| Leggat (30 mins) | 1-0 | |
| Law (70 mins) | 2-0 | |
| Collins (82 mins) | 3-0 | |

## 266

(Home International Championship)
5 November 1958

Referee: Clough (England)
Hampden Park, Glasgow (Att: 72,732)

### SCOTLAND 2-2 NORTHERN IRELAND | Half-time 0-0

| | | |
|---|---|---|
| (3) | William BROWN (Dundee) | Norman UPRICHARD |
| (2) | John GRANT (Hibernian) | Richard KEITH |
| (15) | Eric CALDOW (Rangers) | Alfred McMICHAEL |
| (4) | David MACKAY (Hearts) captain | Daniel BLANCHFLOWER |
| (2) | William TONER (Kilmarnock) | William CUNNINGHAM |
| (24) | Thomas DOCHERTY (Arsenal) | Robert PEACOCK |
| (9) | Graham LEGGAT (Fulham) | William BINGHAM |
| (24) | Robert COLLINS (Everton) | Wilbur CUSH |
| (2) | David HERD (Arsenal) | William SIMPSON |
| (2) | Denis LAW (Huddersfield Town) | James McILROY |
| (7) | John HENDERSON (Arsenal) | Peter McPARLAND |

| | Goals | |
|---|---|---|
| Herd (51 mins) | 1-0 | |
| Collins (54 mins) | 2-0 | |
| | 2-1 | Caldow (72 mins o.g.) |
| | 2-2 | McIlroy (76 mins) |

The Scotland team which beat Wales 3-0 at Ninian Park in October 1958. Back row (left to right): Jackie Henderson, Willie Toner, Willie Brown, John Grant, Eric Caldow, Tommy Docherty. Front row: Graham Leggett, Bobby Collins, Dave Mackay, Denis Law, David Herd. The game marked Matt Busby's first as the national manager and also the debut of Denis Law. Dave Mackay was the new Scotland captain.

# 1959

| P | W | D | L | F | A |
|---|---|---|---|---|---|
| 6 | 3 | 1 | 2 | 10 | 6 |

## 267
(Home International Championship)
11 April 1959

Referee: Campos (Portugal)
Wembley Stadium, London (Att: 98,329)

### ENGLAND 1-0 SCOTLAND — Half-time 0-0

| | | | |
|---|---|---|---|
| (4) | William BROWN (Dundee) | | Edward HOPKINSON |
| (1) | Duncan MACKAY (Celtic) | | Donald HOWE |
| (16) | Eric CALDOW (Rangers) | | Graham SHAW |
| (25) | Thomas DOCHERTY (Arsenal) | | Ronald CLAYTON |
| (38) | Robert EVANS (Celtic) captain | | William WRIGHT |
| (5) | David MACKAY (Tottenham Hotspur) | | Ronald FLOWERS |
| (10) | Graham LEGGAT (Fulham) | | Bryan DOUGLAS |
| (25) | Robert COLLINS (Everton) | | Peter BROADBENT |
| (3) | David HERD (Arsenal) | | Robert CHARLTON |
| (1) | John DICK (West Ham United) | | John HAYNES |
| (6) | William ORMOND (Hibernian) | | Albert HOLDEN |

Goals
0-1    Charlton (59 mins)

## 268
(Friendly)
6 May 1959

Referee: Ellis (England)
Hampden Park, Glasgow (Att: 103,415)

### SCOTLAND 3-2 WEST GERMANY — Half-time 3-2

| | | | |
|---|---|---|---|
| (8) | George FARM (Blackpool) | | Günther SAWITZKI |
| (2) | Duncan MACKAY (Celtic) | | Erich JUSKOWIAK |
| (17) | Eric CALDOW (Rangers) | | Karl-Heinz SCHNELLINGER |
| (6) | David MACKAY (Tottenham Hotspur) | | Helmut BENTHAUS |
| (39) | Robert EVANS (Celtic) captain | | Herbert ERHARDT |
| (1) | Robert McCANN (Motherwell) | | Horst SZYMANIAK |
| (11) | Graham LEGGAT (Fulham) | | Helmut RAHN |
| (1) | John WHITE (Falkirk) | | Rolf GEIGER |
| (1) | Ian ST JOHN (Motherwell) | | Uwe SEELER |
| (26) | Robert COLLINS (Everton) | | Alfred SCHMIDT |
| (1) | Andrew WEIR (Motherwell) | | Hans SCHÄFER |

Goals
White (1 min) — 1-0
Weir (6 mins) — 2-0
2-1    Seeler (14 mins)
Leggat (23 mins) — 3-1
3-2    Juskowiak (36 mins pen)

## 269
(Friendly)
27 May 1959

Referee: Campos (Portugal)
Olympisch Stadion, Amsterdam (Att: 55,000)

### NETHERLANDS 1-2 SCOTLAND — Half-time 1-0

| | | | |
|---|---|---|---|
| (9) | George FARM (Blackpool) | | Franciscus DE MUNCK |
| (3) | Duncan MACKAY (Celtic) | | Roelof WIERSMA |
| (18) | Eric CALDOW (Rangers) | | Johannes KRAAY |
| (1) | John SMITH (Celtic) | | Johannes NOTERMANS |
| (40) | Robert EVANS (Celtic) captain | | Cornelis VAN DER HART |
| (15) | John HEWIE (Charlton Athletic) | | Jean KLAASENS |
| (12) | Graham LEGGAT (Fulham) | | Pieter VAN DER KUIL |
| (27) | Robert COLLINS (Everton) | | Cornelis RIJVERS |
| (2) | John WHITE (Falkirk) | | Leopold CANJELS |
| (3) | Denis LAW (Huddersfield Town) | | Cornelis VAN DER GIJP |
| (1) | Robert AULD (Celtic) | | Coenraad MOULIJN |

Goals
0-1    Van der Gijp (19 mins)
Collins (61 mins) — 1-1
Leggat (65 mins) — 2-1

## 270
(Friendly)
3 June 1959

Referee: Zariquilgui (Spain)
Estadio José Alvalade, Lisbon (Att: 30,000)

### PORTUGAL 1-0 SCOTLAND — Half-time 1-0

| | | | |
|---|---|---|---|
| (10) | George FARM (Blackpool) | | ACÚRCIO Carrelo |
| (4) | Duncan MACKAY (Celtic) | | VIRGILIO Mendes |
| (19) | Eric CALDOW (Rangers) | | ANGELO Martins |
| (2) | John SMITH (Celtic) | | Fernando MENDES |
| (41) | Robert EVANS (Celtic) captain | | Raul FIGUEIREDO |
| (16) | John HEWIE (Charlton Athletic) | | VICENTE Lucas |
| (6) | Alexander SCOTT (Rangers) | | Carlos DUARTE |
| (28) | Robert COLLINS (Everton) | | Mario COLUNA |
| (3) | John WHITE (Falkirk) | | Lucas MATATEU |
| (4) | Denis LAW (Huddersfield Town) | | Augusto ROCHA |
| (2) | Robert AULD (Celtic) | | HERNANI Da Silva |

Goals
0-1    Matateu (25 mins)

## 271
(Home International Championship)
3 October 1959

Referee: Leafe (England)
Windsor Park, Belfast (Att: 59,000)

### NORTHERN IRELAND 0-4 SCOTLAND — Half-time 0-3

| | | | |
|---|---|---|---|
| (5) | William BROWN (Tottenham Hotspur) | | Harold GREGG |
| (20) | Eric CALDOW (Rangers) | | Richard KEITH |
| (17) | John HEWIE (Charlton Athletic) | | Alfred McMICHAEL |
| (7) | David MACKAY (Tottenham Hotspur) | | Daniel BLANCHFLOWER |
| (42) | Robert EVANS (Celtic) captain | | William CUNNINGHAM |
| (2) | Robert McCANN (Motherwell) | | Robert PEACOCK |
| (13) | Graham LEGGAT (Fulham) | | William BINGHAM |
| (4) | John WHITE (Falkirk) | | Wilbur CUSH |
| (2) | Ian ST JOHN (Motherwell) | | Derek DOUGAN |
| (5) | Denis LAW (Huddersfield Town) | | James McILROY |
| (1) | George MULHALL (Aberdeen) | | Peter McPARLAND |

Goals
Leggat (25 mins) — 1-0
Hewie (34 mins pen) — 2-0
White (41 mins) — 3-0
Mulhall (54 mins) — 4-0

## 272
(Home International Championship)
4 November 1959

Referee: Howley (England)
Hampden Park, Glasgow (Att: 55,813)

### SCOTLAND 1-1 WALES — Half-time 0-1

| | | | |
|---|---|---|---|
| (6) | William BROWN (Tottenham Hotspur) | | Alfred KELSEY |
| (21) | Eric CALDOW (Rangers) | | Stuart WILLIAMS |
| (18) | John HEWIE (Charlton Athletic) | | Melvyn HOPKINS |
| (8) | David MACKAY (Tottenham Hotspur) | | Derrick SULLIVAN |
| (43) | Robert EVANS (Celtic) captain | | John CHARLES |
| (3) | Robert McCANN (Motherwell) | | Colin BAKER |
| (14) | Graham LEGGAT (Fulham) | | Terence MEDWIN |
| (5) | John WHITE (Tottenham Hotspur) | | Phillip WOOSNAM |
| (3) | Ian ST JOHN (Motherwell) | | Graham MOORE |
| (6) | Denis LAW (Huddersfield Town) | | Ivor ALLCHURCH |
| (3) | Robert AULD (Celtic) | | Clifford JONES |

Goals
0-1    Charles (8 mins)
Leggat (46 mins) — 1-1

# 1960

| P | W | D | L | F | A |
|---|---|---|---|---|---|
| 7 | 1 | 2 | 4 | 14 | 19 |

## 273
(Home International Championship)
9 April 1960

Referee: Szranko (Hungary)
Hampden Park, Glasgow (Att: 129,783)

### SCOTLAND 1-1 ENGLAND — Half-time 1-0

| | | | |
|---|---|---|---|
| (1) | Frank HAFFEY (Celtic) | | Ronald SPRINGETT |
| (5) | Duncan MACKAY (Celtic) | | James ARMFIELD |
| (22) | Eric CALDOW (Rangers) | | Ramon WILSON |
| (5) | John CUMMING (Hearts) | | Ronald CLAYTON |
| (44) | Robert EVANS (Celtic) captain | | William SLATER |
| (4) | Robert McCANN (Motherwell) | | Ronald FLOWERS |
| (15) | Graham LEGGAT (Fulham) | | John CONNELLY |
| (1) | Alexander YOUNG (Hearts) | | Peter BROADBENT |
| (4) | Ian ST JOHN (Motherwell) | | Joseph BAKER |
| (7) | Denis LAW (Manchester City) | | Raymond PARRY |
| (2) | Andrew WEIR (Motherwell) | | Robert CHARLTON |

Goals
Leggat (16 mins) — 1-0
1-1    Charlton (50 mins pen)

## 274

(Friendly)
4 May 1960

Referee: Holland (England)
Hampden Park, Glasgow (Att: 26,643)

### SCOTLAND 2-3 POLAND | Half-time 1-2

| | | | |
|---|---|---|---|
| (7) | William BROWN (Tottenham Hotspur) | | Tomasz STEFANISZYN |
| (6) | Duncan MACKAY (Celtic) | | Henryk SZCZEPANSKI |
| (19) | John HEWIE (Charlton Athletic) | | Henryk GRZYBOWSKI |
| (9) | David MACKAY (Tottenham Hotspur) | | Fryderyk MONICA |
| (45) | Robert EVANS (Celtic) captain | | Adam MICHEL |
| (6) | John CUMMING (Hearts) | | Edmund ZIENTARA |
| (16) | Graham LEGGAT (Fulham) | | Jan KOWALSKI |
| (6) | John WHITE (Tottenham Hotspur) | | Lucjan BRYCHCZY |
| (5) | Ian ST JOHN (Motherwell) | | Stanislaw HACHOREK |
| (8) | Denis LAW (Manchester City) | | Ernest POL |
| (3) | Andrew WEIR (Motherwell) | | Krzysztof BASZKIEWICZ |

Substitutions

Edward SZYMKOWIAK
for Stefaniszyn 77 mins

| Goals | | |
|---|---|---|
| | 0-1 | Baszkiewicz (11 mins) |
| Law (23 mins) | 1-1 | |
| | 1-2 | Brychczy (29 mins) |
| St John (46 mins) | 2-2 | |
| | 2-3 | Pol (60 mins) |

## 275

(Friendly)
29 May 1960

Referee: Dusch (West Germany)
Prater Stadion, Vienna (Att: 60,000)

### AUSTRIA 4-1 SCOTLAND | Half-time 3-0

| | | | |
|---|---|---|---|
| (8) | William BROWN (Tottenham Hotspur) | | Walter ZEMAN |
| (7) | Duncan MACKAY (Celtic) | | Erich HASENKOPF |
| (23) | Eric CALDOW (Rangers) | | Franz SWOBODA |
| (10) | David MACKAY (Tottenham Hotspur) | | Walter SKOCIK |
| (46) | Robert EVANS (Chelsea) captain | | Walter GLECHNER |
| (7) | John CUMMING (Hearts) | | Karl KOLLER |
| (17) | Graham LEGGAT (Fulham) | | Rudolf FLÖGEL |
| (7) | John WHITE (Tottenham Hotspur) | | Gerhard HANAPPI |
| (6) | Ian ST JOHN (Motherwell) | | Erich HOF |
| (9) | Denis LAW (Manchester City) | | Josef HAMERL |
| (4) | Andrew WEIR (Motherwell) | | Karl SKERLAN |

Substitutions

| | |
|---|---|
| (2) | Alexander YOUNG (Hearts) |
| | for Law 12 mins |

| Goals | | |
|---|---|---|
| | 0-1 | Hanappi (26 mins) |
| | 0-2 | Hanappi (31 mins) |
| | 0-3 | Hof (44 mins) |
| | 0-4 | Hof (63 mins) |
| David Mackay (76 mins) | 1-4 | |

## 276

(Friendly)
5 June 1960

Referee: Ellis (England)
Nép Stadion, Budapest (Att: 90,000)

### HUNGARY 3-3 SCOTLAND | Half-time 1-1

| | | | |
|---|---|---|---|
| (9) | William BROWN (Tottenham Hotspur) | | Gyula GROSICS |
| (8) | Duncan MACKAY (Celtic) | | Sándor MÁTRAI |
| (24) | Eric CALDOW (Rangers) | | Ferenc SIPOS |
| (8) | John CUMMING (Hearts) | | Jenö DALNOKI |
| (47) | Robert EVANS (Chelsea) captain | | Desző BUNDZSÁK |
| (11) | David MACKAY (Tottenham Hotspur) | | Antal KOTÁSZ |
| (18) | Graham LEGGAT (Fulham) | | Károly SÁNDOR |
| (2) | George HERD (Clyde) | | János GÖRÖCS |
| (3) | Alexander YOUNG (Hearts) | | Flórián ALBERT |
| (1) | William HUNTER (Motherwell) | | Lajos TICHY |
| (5) | Andrew WEIR (Motherwell) | | Máté FENYVESI |

| Goals | | |
|---|---|---|
| | 0-1 | Sándor (19 mins) |
| Hunter (34 mins) | 1-1 | |
| Herd (62 mins) | 2-1 | |
| Young (66 mins) | 3-1 | |
| | 3-2 | Göröcs (77 mins) |
| | 3-3 | Tichy (90 mins) |

## 277

(Friendly)
8 June 1960

Referee: Steiner (Austria)
19 Mayis Stadyum, Ankara (Att: 22,500)

### TURKEY 4-2 SCOTLAND | Half-time 3-1

| | | | |
|---|---|---|---|
| (10) | William BROWN (Tottenham Hotspur) | | TURGAY Seren |
| (9) | Duncan MACKAY (Celtic) | | NACI Erdem |
| (25) | Eric CALDOW (Rangers) | | BASRI Dirimlili |
| (12) | David MACKAY (Tottenham Hotspur) | | SUAT Mamat |
| (48) | Robert EVANS (Chelsea) captain | | ERGUN Ercina |
| (9) | John CUMMING (Hearts) | | KAYA Kostepen |
| (8) | John WHITE (Tottenham Hotspur) | | LEFTER Küçükandonyadis |
| (3) | George HERD (Clyde) | | CAN Bartu |
| (4) | Alexander YOUNG (Hearts) | | METIN Oktay |
| (2) | William HUNTER (Motherwell) | | BIROL Pekel |
| (6) | Andrew WEIR (Motherwell) | | SENOL Birol |

| Goals | | |
|---|---|---|
| | 0-1 | Metin (8 mins) |
| Caldow (12 mins pen) | 1-1 | |
| | 1-2 | Lefter (32 mins) |
| | 1-3 | Lefter (35 mins) |
| | 1-4 | Senol (62 mins) |
| Young (72 mins) | 2-4 | |

## 278

(Home International Championship)
22 October 1960

Referee: Holland (England)
Ninian Park, Cardiff (Att: 55,000)

### WALES 2-0 SCOTLAND | Half-time 1-0

| | | | |
|---|---|---|---|
| (1) | Lawrence LESLIE (Airdrie) | | Alfred KELSEY |
| (10) | Duncan MACKAY (Celtic) | | Alan HARRINGTON |
| (26) | Eric CALDOW (Rangers) captain | | Graham WILLIAMS |
| (1) | James GABRIEL (Everton) | | Victor CROWE |
| (1) | John MARTIS (Motherwell) | | Melvyn NURSE |
| (13) | David MACKAY (Tottenham Hotspur) | | Colin BAKER |
| (4) | George HERD (Clyde) | | Terence MEDWIN |
| (9) | John WHITE (Tottenham Hotspur) | | Phillip WOOSNAM |
| (5) | Alexander YOUNG (Hearts) | | Kenneth LEEK |
| (3) | William HUNTER (Motherwell) | | Royston VERNON |
| (1) | David WILSON (Rangers) | | Clifford JONES |

| Goals | | |
|---|---|---|
| | 0-1 | Jones (43 mins) |
| | 0-2 | Vernon (72 mins) |

## 279

(Home International Championship)
9 November 1960

Referee: Howley (England)
Hampden Park, Glasgow (Att: 34,564)

### SCOTLAND 5-2 NORTHERN IRELAND | Half-time 2-0

| | | | |
|---|---|---|---|
| (2) | Lawrence LESLIE (Airdrie) | | Harold GREGG |
| (11) | Duncan MACKAY (Celtic) | | Richard KEITH |
| (27) | Eric CALDOW (Rangers) captain | | Alexander ELDER |
| (14) | David MACKAY (Tottenham Hotspur) | | Daniel BLANCHFLOWER |
| (1) | John PLENDERLEITH (Manchester City) | | Thomas FORDE |
| (1) | James BAXTER (Rangers) | | Robert PEACOCK |
| (5) | George HERD (Clyde) | | William BINGHAM |
| (10) | Denis LAW (Manchester City) | | Walter BRUCE |
| (6) | Alexander YOUNG (Hearts) | | William McADAMS |
| (1) | Ralph BRAND (Rangers) | | James NICHOLSON |
| (2) | David WILSON (Rangers) | | Peter McPARLAND |

| Goals | | |
|---|---|---|
| Law (8 mins) | 1-0 | |
| Caldow (43 mins pen) | 2-0 | |
| | 2-1 | Blanchflower (48 mins pen) |
| Young (78 mins) | 3-1 | |
| Brand (81 mins) | 4-1 | |
| | 4-2 | McParland (84 mins) |
| Brand (90 mins) | 5-2 | |

# 1961

| P | W | D | L | F | A |
|---|---|---|---|---|---|
| 8 | 5 | 0 | 3 | 23 | 21 |

## 280
(Home International Championship)  
15 April 1961

Referee: Lequesne (France)  
Wembley Stadium, London (Att: 97,350)

### ENGLAND 9-3 SCOTLAND      Half-time 3-0

| (2) | Frank HAFFEY (Celtic) | Ronald SPRINGETT |
|---|---|---|
| (1) | Robert SHEARER (Rangers) | James ARMFIELD |
| (28) | Eric CALDOW (Rangers) captain | Michael McNEIL |
| (15) | David MACKAY (Tottenham Hotspur) | Robert ROBSON |
| (1) | William McNEILL (Celtic) | Peter SWAN |
| (5) | Robert McCANN (Motherwell) | Ronald FLOWERS |
| (1) | John MacLEOD (Hibernian) | Bryan DOUGLAS |
| (11) | Denis LAW (Manchester City) | James GREAVES |
| (7) | Ian ST JOHN (Motherwell) | Robert SMITH |
| (1) | Patrick QUINN (Motherwell) | John HAYNES |
| (3) | David WILSON (Rangers) | Robert CHARLTON |

Goals

| | | |
|---|---|---|
| | 0-1 | Robson (8 mins) |
| | 0-2 | Greaves (20 mins) |
| | 0-3 | Greaves (29 mins) |
| Mackay (49 mins) | 1-3 | |
| Wilson (53 mins) | 2-3 | |
| | 2-4 | Douglas (55 mins) |
| | 2-5 | Smith (74 mins) |
| Quinn (75 mins) | 3-5 | |
| | 3-6 | Haynes (80 mins) |
| | 3-7 | Haynes (82 mins) |
| | 3-8 | Greaves (83 mins) |
| | 3-9 | Smith (85 mins) |

## 281
(World Cup — Qualifier)  
3 May 1961

Referee: Guigue (France)  
Hampden Park, Glasgow (Att: 46,696)

### SCOTLAND 4-1 REPUBLIC OF IRELAND      Half-time 2-0

| (3) | Lawrence LESLIE (Airdrie) | Noel DWYER |
|---|---|---|
| (2) | Robert SHEARER (Rangers) | Brendan McNALLY |
| (29) | Eric CALDOW (Rangers) captain | Noel CANTWELL |
| (1) | Patrick CRERAND (Celtic) | Anthony McEVOY |
| (2) | William McNEILL (Celtic) | Charles HURLEY |
| (2) | James BAXTER (Rangers) | Patrick SAWARD |
| (2) | John MacLEOD (Hibernian) | John GILES |
| (2) | Patrick QUINN (Motherwell) | Ambrose FOGARTY |
| (4) | David HERD (Arsenal) | Dermot CURTIS |
| (2) | Ralph BRAND (Rangers) | George CUMMINS |
| (4) | David WILSON (Rangers) | Joseph HAVERTY |

Goals

| | | |
|---|---|---|
| Brand (14 mins) | 1-0 | |
| Brand (40 mins) | 2-0 | |
| | 2-1 | Haverty (52 mins) |
| Herd (59 mins) | 3-1 | |
| Herd (85 mins) | 4-1 | |

## 282
(World Cup — Qualifier)  
7 May 1961

Referee: Grandain (Belgium)  
Dalymount Park, Dublin (Att: 45,000)

### REPUBLIC OF IRELAND 0-3 SCOTLAND      Half-time 0-2

| (4) | Lawrence LESLIE (Airdrie) | Noel DWYER |
|---|---|---|
| (3) | Robert SHEARER (Rangers) | Philip KELLY |
| (30) | Eric CALDOW (Rangers) captain | Noel CANTWELL |
| (2) | Patrick CRERAND (Celtic) | Anthony McEVOY |
| (3) | William McNEILL (Celtic) | Charles HURLEY |
| (3) | James BAXTER (Rangers) | Michael MEAGAN |
| (3) | John MacLEOD (Hibernian) | Fionan FAGAN |
| (3) | Patrick QUINN (Motherwell) | John GILES |
| (7) | Alexander YOUNG (Everton) | Peter FITZGERALD |
| (3) | Ralph BRAND (Rangers) | George CUMMINS |
| (5) | David WILSON (Rangers) | Joseph HAVERTY |

Goals

| | | |
|---|---|---|
| Young (4 mins) | 1-0 | |
| Young (16 mins) | 2-0 | |
| Brand (86 mins) | 3-0 | |

## 283
(World Cup — Qualifier)  
14 May 1961

Referee: Steiner (Austria)  
Tehelne Pole Stadion, Bratislava (Att: 50,000)

### CZECHOSLOVAKIA 4-0 SCOTLAND      Half-time 3-0

| (5) | Lawrence LESLIE (Airdrie) | Viliam SCHROJF |
|---|---|---|
| (4) | Robert SHEARER (Rangers) | Frantisek SAFRÁNEK |
| (31) | Eric CALDOW (Rangers) captain | Ján POPLUHÁR |
| (3) | Patrick CRERAND (Celtic) | Jiri TICHY |
| (4) | William McNEILL (Celtic) | Svatopluk PLUSKAL |
| (4) | James BAXTER (Rangers) | Josef MASOPUST |
| (4) | John MacLEOD (Hibernian) | Tomás POSPÍCHAL |
| (6) | John McMILLAN (Rangers) | Adolf SCHERER |
| (5) | David HERD (Arsenal) | Josef KADRABA |
| (4) | Ralph BRAND (Rangers) | Andrei KVASNÁK |
| (6) | David WILSON (Rangers) | Václav MASEK |

Goals

| | | |
|---|---|---|
| | 0-1 | Pospíchal (7 mins) |
| | 0-2 | Kvasnák (12 mins pen) |
| | 0-3 | Kadraba (44 mins) |
| | 0-4 | Pospíchal (85 mins) |

## 284
(World Cup — Qualifier)  
26 September 1961

Referee: Gulliksen (Norway)  
Hampden Park, Glasgow (Att: 51,590)

### SCOTLAND 3-2 CZECHOSLOVAKIA      Half-time 1-1

| (11) | William BROWN (Tottenham Hotspur) | Viliam SCHROJF |
|---|---|---|
| (12) | Duncan MACKAY (Celtic) | Jozef BOMBA |
| (32) | Eric CALDOW (Rangers) captain | Ján POPLUHÁR |
| (4) | Patrick CRERAND (Celtic) | Ladislav NOVAK |
| (5) | William McNEILL (Celtic) | Titus BUBERNÍK |
| (5) | James BAXTER (Rangers) | Josef MASOPUST |
| (7) | Alexander SCOTT (Rangers) | Tomás POSPÍCHAL |
| (10) | John WHITE (Tottenham Hotspur) | Adolf SCHERER |
| (8) | Ian ST JOHN (Liverpool) | Josef KADRABA |
| (12) | Denis LAW (Turin) | Andrei KVASNÁK |
| (7) | David WILSON (Rangers) | Václav MASEK |

Goals

| | | |
|---|---|---|
| | 0-1 | Kvasnák (6 mins) |
| St John (21 mins) | 1-1 | |
| | 1-2 | Scherer (51 mins) |
| Law (62 mins) | 2-2 | |
| Law (83 mins) | 3-2 | |

## 285
(Home International Championship)  
7 October 1961

Referee: Finney (England)  
Windsor Park, Belfast (Att: 41,000)

### NORTHERN IRELAND 1-6 SCOTLAND      Half-time 1-3

| (12) | William BROWN (Tottenham Hotspur) | Harold GREGG |
|---|---|---|
| (13) | Duncan MACKAY (Celtic) | James MAGILL |
| (33) | Eric CALDOW (Rangers) captain | Alexander ELDER |
| (5) | Patrick CRERAND (Celtic) | Daniel BLANCHFLOWER |
| (6) | William McNEILL (Celtic) | Terence NEILL |
| (6) | James BAXTER (Rangers) | Robert PEACOCK |
| (8) | Alexander SCOTT (Rangers) | Samuel WILSON |
| (11) | John WHITE (Tottenham Hotspur) | James McILROY |
| (9) | Ian ST JOHN (Liverpool) | Ian LAWTHER |
| (5) | Ralph BRAND (Rangers) | James HILL |
| (8) | David WILSON (Rangers) | James McLAUGHLIN |

Goals

| | | |
|---|---|---|
| Wilson (14 mins) | 1-0 | |
| | 1-1 | McLaughlin (17 mins) |
| Scott (34 mins) | 2-1 | |
| Brand (38 mins) | 3-1 | |
| Scott (53 mins) | 4-1 | |
| Brand (69 mins) | 5-1 | |
| Scott (79 mins) | 6-1 | |

**286**
(Home International Championship)
8 November 1961
Referee: Holland (England)
Hampden Park, Glasgow (Att: 74,329)

## SCOTLAND 2-0 WALES                                         Half-time 1-0

| (13) | William BROWN (Tottenham Hotspur) | Alfred KELSEY |
|---|---|---|
| (1) | Alexander HAMILTON (Dundee) | Alan HARRINGTON |
| (34) | Eric CALDOW (Rangers) captain | Stuart WILLIAMS |
| (6) | Patrick CRERAND (Celtic) | Victor CROWE |
| (1) | John URE (Dundee) | Melfyn CHARLES |
| (7) | James BAXTER (Rangers) | Colin BAKER |
| (9) | Alexander SCOTT (Rangers) | Leonard ALLCHURCH |
| (12) | John WHITE (Tottenham Hotspur) | Phillip WOOSNAM |
| (10) | Ian ST JOHN (Liverpool) | Kenneth LEEK |
| (6) | Ralph BRAND (Rangers) | Ivor ALLCHURCH |
| (9) | David WILSON (Rangers) | Clifford JONES |

Goals

St John (22 mins)   1-0
St John (50 mins)   2-0

---

**287**
(World Cup — Qualifier (Play-off))
29 November 1961
Referee: Versyp (Belgium)
Heysel Stadium, Brussels (Att: 7,000)

## CZECHOSLOVAKIA 4-2 SCOTLAND a.e.t.          Half-time 0-1; 90 mins 2-2

| (1) | Edward CONNACHAN (Dunfermline Athletic) | Viliam SCHROJF |
|---|---|---|
| (2) | Alexander HAMILTON (Dundee) | Jiri HLEDÍK |
| (35) | Eric CALDOW (Rangers) captain | Ján POPLUHAR |
| (7) | Patrick CRERAND (Celtic) | Jiri TICHY |
| (2) | John URE (Dundee) | Svatopluk PLUSKAL |
| (8) | James BAXTER (Rangers) | Josef MASOPUST |
| (7) | Ralph BRAND (Rangers) | Tomás POSPÍCHAL |
| (13) | John WHITE (Tottenham Hotspur) | Adolf SCHERER |
| (11) | Ian ST JOHN (Liverpool) | Andrei KVASNÁK |
| (13) | Denis LAW (Turin) | Rudolf KUCERA |
| (1) | Hugh ROBERTSON (Dundee) | Josef JELÍNEK |

Goals

St John (35 mins)   1-0
    1-1   Hledík (70 mins)
St John (71 mins)   2-1
    2-2   Scherer (82 mins)
    2-3   Pospíchal (95 mins)
    2-4   Kvasnák (105 mins)

---

# 1962

| P | W | D | L | F | A |
|---|---|---|---|---|---|
| 4 | 3 | 0 | 1 | 12 | 6 |

---

**288**
(Home International Championship)
14 April 1962
Referee: Horn (Netherlands)
Hampden Park, Glasgow (Att: 132,431)

## SCOTLAND 2-0 ENGLAND                                       Half-time 1-0

| (14) | William BROWN (Tottenham Hotspur) | Ronald SPRINGETT |
|---|---|---|
| (3) | Alexander HAMILTON (Dundee) | James ARMFIELD |
| (36) | Eric CALDOW (Rangers) captain | Ramon WILSON |
| (8) | Patrick CRERAND (Celtic) | Stanley ANDERSON |
| (7) | William McNEILL (Celtic) | Peter SWAN |
| (9) | James BAXTER (Rangers) | Ronald FLOWERS |
| (10) | Alexander SCOTT (Rangers) | Bryan DOUGLAS |
| (14) | John WHITE (Tottenham Hotspur) | James GREAVES |
| (12) | Ian ST JOHN (Liverpool) | Robert SMITH |
| (14) | Denis LAW (Turin) | John HAYNES |
| (10) | David WILSON (Rangers) | Robert CHARLTON |

Goals

Wilson (13 mins)   1-0
Caldow (88 mins pen)   2-0

---

**289**
(Friendly)
2 May 1962
Referee: Holland (England)
Hampden Park, Glasgow (Att: 67,181)

## SCOTLAND 2-3 URUGUAY                                        Half-time 0-2

| (2) | Edward CONNACHAN (Dunfermline Athletic) | Roberto SOSA |
|---|---|---|
| (4) | Alexander HAMILTON (Dundee) | Horacio TROCHE |
| (37) | Eric CALDOW (Rangers) captain | Ruben SORIA |
| (9) | Patrick CRERAND (Celtic) | Edgardo GONZÁLEZ |
| (8) | William McNEILL (Celtic) | Néstor GONCALVEZ |
| (10) | James BAXTER (Rangers) | Pedro CUBILLA |
| (11) | Alexander SCOTT (Rangers) | Ronald LANGÓN |
| (4) | Patrick QUINN (Motherwell) | Julio CORTÉS |
| (13) | Ian ST JOHN (Liverpool) | Vladas DOUKSAS |
| (8) | Ralph BRAND (Rangers) | José SACÍA |
| (11) | David WILSON (Rangers) | Luis CUBILLA |

Substitutions

| (1) | William RITCHIE (Rangers) for Connachan 46 mins | |
| (14) | Duncan MACKAY (Celtic) for Crerand 75 mins | |

Goals

    0-1   Sacía (37 mins)
    0-2   L. Cubilla (45 mins)
    0-3   L. Cubilla (47 mins)
Baxter (81 mins)   1-3
Brand (88 mins)   2-3

---

**290**
(Home International Championship)
20 October 1962
Referee: Dagnall (England)
Ninian Park, Cardiff (Att: 58,000)

## WALES 2-3 SCOTLAND                                          Half-time 1-1

| (15) | William BROWN (Tottenham Hotspur) | Anthony MILLINGTON |
|---|---|---|
| (5) | Alexander HAMILTON (Dundee) | Stuart WILLIAMS |
| (38) | Eric CALDOW (Rangers) captain | Melvyn HOPKINS |
| (10) | Patrick CRERAND (Celtic) | Terrence HENNESSEY |
| (3) | John URE (Dundee) | John CHARLES |
| (11) | James BAXTER (Rangers) | Malcolm LUCAS |
| (1) | William HENDERSON (Rangers) | Barrie JONES |
| (15) | John WHITE (Tottenham Hotspur) | Ivor ALLCHURCH |
| (14) | Ian ST JOHN (Liverpool) | Melfyn CHARLES |
| (15) | Denis LAW (Manchester United) | Royston VERNON |
| (12) | David WILSON (Rangers) | Clifford JONES |

Goals

Caldow (19 mins pen)   1-0
    1-1   Allchurch (40 mins)
Law (63 mins)   2-1
Henderson (79 mins)   3-1
    3-2   J. Charles (88 mins)

---

**291**
(Home International Championship)
7 November 1962
Referee: Finney (England)
Hampden Park, Glasgow (Att: 58,734)

## SCOTLAND 5-1 NORTHERN IRELAND                               Half-time 1-1

| (16) | William BROWN (Tottenham Hotspur) | Robert IRVINE |
|---|---|---|
| (6) | Alexander HAMILTON (Dundee) | James MAGILL |
| (39) | Eric CALDOW (Rangers) captain | Alexander ELDER |
| (11) | Patrick CRERAND (Celtic) | Daniel BLANCHFLOWER |
| (4) | John URE (Dundee) | Samuel HATTON |
| (12) | James BAXTER (Rangers) | James NICHOLSON |
| (2) | William HENDERSON (Rangers) | William HUMPHRIES |
| (16) | John WHITE (Tottenham Hotspur) | Samuel McMILLAN |
| (15) | Ian ST JOHN (Liverpool) | Derek DOUGAN |
| (16) | Denis LAW (Manchester United) | James McILROY |
| (2) | George MULHALL (Sunderland) | William BINGHAM |

Goals

    0-1   Bingham (8 mins)
Law (40 mins)   1-1
Law (64 mins)   2-1
Law (77 mins)   3-1
Henderson (79 mins)   4-1
Law (87 mins)   5-1

Denis Law salutes Jim Baxter after his first goal against England at Wembley in April 1963.

# 1963

| P | W | D | L | F | A |
|---|---|---|---|---|---|
| 8 | 5 | 0 | 3 | 24 | 13 |

## 292

(Home International Championship)
6 April 1963

Referee: Horn (Netherlands)
Wembley Stadium, London (Att: 98,606)

### ENGLAND 1-2 SCOTLAND · Half-time 0-2

| | | | |
|---|---|---|---|
| (17) | William BROWN (Tottenham Hotspur) | Gordon BANKS | |
| (7) | Alexander HAMILTON (Dundee) | James ARMFIELD | |
| (40) | Eric CALDOW (Rangers) captain | Gerald BYRNE | |
| (16) | David MACKAY (Tottenham Hotspur) | Robert MOORE | |
| (5) | John URE (Dundee) | Maurice NORMAN | |
| (13) | James BAXTER (Rangers) | Ronald FLOWERS | |
| (3) | William HENDERSON (Rangers) | Bryan DOUGLAS | |
| (17) | John WHITE (Tottenham Hotspur) | James GREAVES | |
| (16) | Ian ST JOHN (Liverpool) | Robert SMITH | |
| (17) | Denis LAW (Manchester United) | James MELIA | |
| (13) | David WILSON (Rangers) | Robert CHARLTON | |

| | Goals | |
|---|---|---|
| Baxter (29 mins) | 1-0 | |
| Baxter (31 mins pen) | 2-0 | |
| | 2-1 | Douglas (79 mins) |

## 293

(Friendly)
8 May 1963

Referee: Finney (England)
Hampden Park, Glasgow (Att: 94,596)

### SCOTLAND 4-1 AUSTRIA (Abandoned 79 mins) · Half-time 3-0

| | | |
|---|---|---|
| (18) | William BROWN (Tottenham Hotspur) | Gernot FRAYDL |
| (8) | Alexander HAMILTON (Dundee) | Ferdinand KOLARIK |
| (1) | David HOLT (Hearts) | Erich HASENKOPF |
| (17) | David MACKAY (Tottenham Hotspur) captain | Alfred GAGER |
| (6) | John URE (Dundee) | Walter GLECHNER |
| (14) | James BAXTER (Rangers) | Karl KOLLER |
| (4) | William HENDERSON (Rangers) | Anton LINHART |
| (1) | David GIBSON (Leicester City) | Erich HOF |
| (1) | James MILLAR (Rangers) | Horst NEMEC |
| (18) | Denis LAW (Manchester United) | Ernst FIALA |
| (14) | David WILSON (Rangers) | Friedrich RAFREIDER |

| | Goals | |
|---|---|---|
| Wilson (16 mins) | 1-0 | |
| Wilson (26 mins) | 2-0 | |
| Law (33 mins) | 3-0 | |
| Law (71 mins) | 4-0 | |
| | 4-1 | Linhart (72 mins) |

## 294

(Friendly)
4 June 1963

Referee: Oskarsson (Iceland)
Brann Stadion, Bergen (Att: 23,000)

### NORWAY 4-3 SCOTLAND · Half-time 1-2

| | | |
|---|---|---|
| (1) | Adam BLACKLAW (Burnley) | Sverre ANDERSEN |
| (9) | Alexander HAMILTON (Dundee) | Erik HAGEN |
| (2) | David HOLT (Hearts) | Edgar STAKSETH |
| (18) | David MACKAY (Tottenham Hotspur) captain | Roar JOHANSEN |
| (7) | John URE (Dundee) | Finn THORSEN |
| (15) | James BAXTER (Rangers) | Arild GULDEN |
| (5) | William HENDERSON (Rangers) | Roald JENSEN |
| (2) | David GIBSON (Leicester City) | Arne PEDERSEN |
| (17) | Ian ST JOHN (Liverpool) | John KROGH |
| (19) | Denis LAW (Manchester United) | Olav NILSEN |
| (15) | David WILSON (Rangers) | Erik JOHANSEN |

Substitutions

| | | |
|---|---|---|
| (1) | Francis McLINTOCK (Leicester City) for Mackay 78 mins | |

| | Goals | |
|---|---|---|
| | 0-1 | Nilsen (5 mins) |
| Law (14 mins) | 1-1 | |
| Law (22 mins) | 2-1 | |
| | 2-2 | E.Johansen (60 mins) |
| Law (76 mins) | 3-2 | |
| | 3-3 | Pedersen (81 mins) |
| | 3-4 | Krogh (83 mins) |

Davie Wilson and Willie Henderson parade the Lion Rampant after a famous Wembley win in April 1963.

**295**
(Friendly)
9 June 1963

## REPUBLIC OF IRELAND 1-0 SCOTLAND — Half-time 1-0

| | | |
|---|---|---|
| (1) | Thomas LAWRENCE (Liverpool) | Alan KELLY |
| (10) | Alexander HAMILTON (Dundee) | Anthony DUNNE |
| (3) | David HOLT (Hearts) | Thomas TRAYNOR |
| (2) | Francis McLINTOCK (Leicester City) | Anthony McEVOY |
| (9) | William McNEILL (Celtic) | Charles HURLEY |
| (16) | James BAXTER (Rangers) | Michael McGRATH |
| (6) | William HENDERSON (Rangers) | John GILES |
| (3) | David GIBSON (Leicester City) | Patrick TURNER |
| (2) | James MILLAR (Rangers) | Noel CANTWELL |
| (20) | Denis LAW (Manchester United) captain | Noel PEYTON |
| (16) | David WILSON (Rangers) | Joseph HAVERTY |

Substitutions

| | | |
|---|---|---|
| (18) | Ian ST JOHN (Liverpool) | Ambrose FOGARTY |
| | for Millar 44 mins | for Peyton 44 mins |

Goals
0-1    Cantwell (6 mins)

---

**296**
(Friendly)
13 June 1963

Referee: Campanati (Italy)
Estadio Santiago Bernabeu, Madrid (Att: 40,000)

## SPAIN 2-6 SCOTLAND — Half-time 2-4

| | | |
|---|---|---|
| (2) | Adam BLACKLAW (Burnley) | VICENTE Train |
| (10) | William McNEILL (Celtic) | Feliciano RIVILLA |
| (4) | David HOLT (Hearts) | José MINGORANCE |
| (3) | Francis McLINTOCK (Leicester City) | Severino REIJA |
| (8) | John URE (Dundee) | Koldo AGUIRRE |
| (17) | James BAXTER (Rangers) | Jesús GLARÍA |
| (7) | William HENDERSON (Rangers) | AMANCIO Amaro |
| (4) | David GIBSON (Leicester City) | ADELARDO Rodríguez |
| (19) | Ian ST. JOHN (Liverpool) | José VELOSO |
| (21) | Denis LAW (Manchester United) captain | Vicente GUILLOT |
| (17) | David WILSON (Rangers) | Carlos LAPETRA |

Substitutions

| | |
|---|---|
| | Ignacio ZOCO |
| | for Mingorance 32 mins |
| | Carmelo CEDRUN |
| | for Vicente 46 mins |

Goals
| | | |
|---|---|---|
| | 0-1 | Adelardo (8 mins) |
| Law (16 mins) | 1-1 | |
| Gibson (17 mins) | 2-1 | |
| McLintock (20 mins) | 3-1 | |
| Wilson (33 mins) | 4-1 | |
| | 4-2 | Veloso (43 mins) |
| Henderson (51 mins) | 5-2 | |
| St John (83 mins) | 6-2 | |

---

**297**
(Home International Championship)
12 October 1963

Referee: Taylor (England)
Windsor Park, Belfast (Att: 39,000)

## NORTHERN IRELAND 2-1 SCOTLAND — Half-time 1-0

| | | |
|---|---|---|
| (19) | William BROWN (Tottenham Hotspur) | Harold GREGG |
| (11) | Alexander HAMILTON (Dundee) | James MAGILL |
| (1) | David PROVAN (Rangers) | John PARKE |
| (12) | Patrick CRERAND (Manchester United) | Martin HARVEY |
| (9) | John URE (Arsenal) | Terence NEILL |
| (19) | David MACKAY (Tottenham Hotspur) captain | William McCULLOUGH |
| (8) | William HENDERSON (Rangers) | William BINGHAM |
| (18) | John WHITE (Tottenham Hotspur) | William HUMPHRIES |
| (20) | Ian ST JOHN (Liverpool) | Samuel WILSON |
| (5) | David GIBSON (Leicester City) | John CROSSAN |
| (3) | George MULHALL (Sunderland) | James HILL |

Goals
| | | |
|---|---|---|
| | 0-1 | Bingham (25 mins) |
| St John (49 mins) | 1-1 | |
| | 1-2 | Wilson (63 mins) |

---

**298**
(Friendly)
7 November 1963

Referee: Howley (England)
Hampden Park, Glasgow (Att: 35,416)

## SCOTLAND 6-1 NORWAY — Half-time 2-1

| | | |
|---|---|---|
| (20) | William BROWN (Tottenham Hotspur) | Sverre ANDERSEN |
| (12) | Alexander HAMILTON (Dundee) | Erik HAGEN |
| (2) | David PROVAN (Rangers) | Edgar STAKSETH |
| (20) | David MACKAY (Tottenham Hotspur) captain | Roar JOHANSEN |
| (10) | John URE (Arsenal) | Finn THORSEN |
| (18) | James BAXTER (Rangers) | Arild GULDEN |
| (12) | Alexander SCOTT (Everton) | Roald JENSEN |
| (19) | John WHITE (Tottenham Hotspur) | Arne PEDERSEN |
| (1) | Alan GILZEAN (Dundee) | Per KRISTOFFERSEN |
| (22) | Denis LAW (Manchester United) | Olav NILSEN |
| (9) | William HENDERSON (Rangers) | Erik JOHANSEN |

Substitutions

| | | |
|---|---|---|
| (2) | James GABRIEL (Everton) | Kjell KASPERSEN |
| | for Baxter 46 mins | for Andersen 78 mins |

Goals
| | | |
|---|---|---|
| | 0-1 | Kristoffersen (8 mins) |
| Law (19 mins) | 1-1 | |
| Law (44 mins) | 2-1 | |
| Law (59 mins) | 3-1 | |
| Mackay (74 mins) | 4-1 | |
| Mackay (76 mins) | 5-1 | |
| Law (82 mins) | 6-1 | |

---

**299**
(Home International Championship)
20 November 1963

Referee: Clements (England)
Hampden Park, Glasgow (Att: 56,167)

## SCOTLAND 2-1 WALES — Half-time 1-0

| | | |
|---|---|---|
| (21) | William BROWN (Tottenham Hotspur) | Gareth SPRAKE |
| (13) | Alexander HAMILTON (Dundee) | Stuart WILLIAMS |
| (1) | James KENNEDY (Celtic) | Graham WILLIAMS |
| (21) | David MACKAY (Tottenham Hotspur) captain | Terrence HENNESSEY |
| (11) | William McNEILL (Celtic) | Michael ENGLAND |
| (19) | James BAXTER (Rangers) | Melvyn NURSE |
| (10) | William HENDERSON (Rangers) | Barrie JONES |
| (20) | John WHITE (Tottenham Hotspur) | Graham MOORE |
| (2) | Alan GILZEAN (Dundee) | John CHARLES |
| (23) | Denis LAW (Manchester United) | Royston VERNON |
| (13) | Alexander SCOTT (Everton) | Clifford JONES |

Goals
| | | |
|---|---|---|
| White (44 mins) | 1-0 | |
| Law (47 mins) | 2-0 | |
| | 2-1 | B. Jones (57 mins) |

---

# 1964

| P | W | D | L | F | A |
|---|---|---|---|---|---|
| 5 | 3 | 1 | 1 | 11 | 8 |

**300**
(Home International Championship)
11 April 1964

Referee: Horn (Netherlands)
Hampden Park, Glasgow (Att: 133,245)

## SCOTLAND 1-0 ENGLAND — Half-time 0-0

| | | |
|---|---|---|
| (1) | Robert FORSYTH (Kilmarnock) | Gordon BANKS |
| (14) | Alexander HAMILTON (Dundee) | James ARMFIELD |
| (2) | James KENNEDY (Celtic) | Ramon WILSON |
| (1) | John GREIG (Rangers) | Gordon MILNE |
| (12) | William McNEILL (Celtic) captain | Maurice NORMAN |
| (20) | James BAXTER (Rangers) | Robert MOORE |
| (11) | William HENDERSON (Rangers) | Terence PAINE |
| (21) | John WHITE (Tottenham Hotspur) | Roger HUNT |
| (3) | Alan GILZEAN (Dundee) | John BYRNE |
| (24) | Denis LAW (Manchester United) | George EASTHAM |
| (18) | David WILSON (Rangers) | Robert CHARLTON |

Goals
| | |
|---|---|
| Gilzean (72 mins) | 1-0 |

## 301

(Friendly)
12 May 1964

Referee: Poulsen (Denmark)
Niedersachsen Stadion, Hanover (Att: 75,000)

**WEST GERMANY 2-2 SCOTLAND**          **Half-time 2-0**

| | | |
|---|---|---|
| (1) | James CRUICKSHANK (Hearts) | Hans TILKOWSKI |
| (15) | Alexander HAMILTON (Dundee) | Hans NOWAK |
| (3) | James KENNEDY (Celtic) | Rudolf STEINER |
| (2) | John GREIG (Rangers) | Horst SZYMANIAK |
| (13) | William McNEILL (Celtic) captain | Willi GIESEMANN |
| (21) | James BAXTER (Rangers) | Wolfgang WEBER |
| (12) | William HENDERSON (Rangers) | Reinhard LIBUDA |
| (22) | John WHITE (Tottenham Hotspur) | Alfred SCHMIDT |
| (4) | Alan GILZEAN (Dundee) | Uwe SEELER |
| (25) | Denis LAW (Manchester United) | Rolf GEIGER |
| (19) | David WILSON (Rangers) | Gerhard DORFEL |

Substitutions

| | | |
|---|---|---|
| (5) | David HOLT (Hearts) | Stefan REISCH |
| | for Hamilton 40 mins | for Schmidt 25 mins |

Goals

| | | |
|---|---|---|
| | 0-1 | Seeler (32 mins) |
| | 0-2 | Seeler (33 mins) |
| Gilzean (70 mins) | 1-2 | |
| Gilzean (84 mins) | 2-2 | |

## 302

(Home International Championship)
3 October 1964

Referee: Howley (England)
Ninian Park, Cardiff (Att: 37,093)

**WALES 3-2 SCOTLAND**          **Half-time 1-2**

| | | |
|---|---|---|
| (2) | Robert FORSYTH (Kilmarnock) | Gareth SPRAKE |
| (16) | Alexander HAMILTON (Dundee) | Stuart WILLIAMS |
| (4) | James KENNEDY (Celtic) | Graham WILLIAMS |
| (3) | John GREIG (Rangers) | Barrington HOLE |
| (1) | Ronald YEATS (Liverpool) | John CHARLES |
| (22) | James BAXTER (Rangers) | Terrence HENNESSEY |
| (1) | James JOHNSTONE (Celtic) | Clifford JONES |
| (6) | David GIBSON (Leicester City) | Kenneth LEEK |
| (1) | Stephen CHALMERS (Celtic) | Wyn DAVIES |
| (26) | Denis LAW (Manchester United) captain | Ivor ALLCHURCH |
| (1) | James ROBERTSON (Tottenham Hotspur) | Ronald REES |

Goals

| | | |
|---|---|---|
| | 0-1 | Davies (6 mins) |
| Chalmers (28 mins) | 1-1 | |
| Gibson (29 mins) | 2-1 | |
| | 2-2 | Leek (87 mins) |
| | 2-3 | Leek (89 mins) |

## 303

(World Cup — Qualifier)
21 October 1964

Referee: Hannet (Belgium)
Hampden Park, Glasgow (Att: 55,332)

**SCOTLAND 3-1 FINLAND**          **Half-time 3-0**

| | | |
|---|---|---|
| (3) | Robert FORSYTH (Kilmarnock) | Martti HALME |
| (17) | Alexander HAMILTON (Dundee) | Pertti MÄKIPÄÄ |
| (5) | James KENNEDY (Celtic) | Timo KAUTONEN |
| (4) | John GREIG (Rangers) | Stig HOLMQVIST |
| (1) | John McGRORY (Kilmarnock) | Aarno RINNE |
| (23) | James BAXTER (Rangers) | Veijo VALTONEN |
| (2) | James JOHNSTONE (Celtic) | Harri JÄRVI |
| (7) | David GIBSON (Leicester City) | Juhani PELTONEN |
| (2) | Stephen CHALMERS (Celtic) | Arto TOLSA |
| (27) | Denis LAW (Manchester United) captain | Simo SYRJÄVAARA |
| (14) | Alexander SCOTT (Everton) | Martti HYVÄRINEN |

Goals

| | | |
|---|---|---|
| Law (2 mins) | 1-0 | |
| Chalmers (38 mins) | 2-0 | |
| Gibson (42 mins) | 3-0 | |
| | 3-1 | Peltonen (70 mins) |

## 304

(Home International Championship)
25 November 1964

Referee: Powell (Wales)
Hampden Park, Glasgow (Att: 48,752)

**SCOTLAND 3-2 NORTHERN IRELAND**          **Half-time 3-2**

| | | |
|---|---|---|
| (4) | Robert FORSYTH (Kilmarnock) | Patrick JENNINGS |
| (18) | Alexander HAMILTON (Dundee) | James MAGILL |
| (6) | James KENNEDY (Celtic) | Alexander ELDER |
| (5) | John GREIG (Rangers) | Martin HARVEY |
| (2) | John McGRORY (Kilmarnock) | Terence NEILL |
| (4) | Francis McLINTOCK (Arsenal) | John PARKE |
| (1) | William WALLACE (Hearts) | George BEST |
| (28) | Denis LAW (Manchester United) | William HUMPHRIES |
| (5) | Alan GILZEAN (Dundee) | William IRVINE |
| (24) | James BAXTER (Rangers) captain | John CROSSAN |
| (20) | David WILSON (Rangers) | Robert BRAITHEWAITE |

Goals

| | | |
|---|---|---|
| | 0-1 | Best (9 mins) |
| Wilson (10 mins) | 1-1 | |
| Gilzean (17 mins) | 2-1 | |
| | 2-2 | Irvine (19 mins) |
| Wilson (31 mins) | 3-2 | |

# 1965

| P | W | D | L | F | A |
|---|---|---|---|---|---|
| 9 | 3 | 3 | 3 | 13 | 13 |

## 305

(Home International Championship)
10 April 1965

Referee: Zsolt (Hungary)
Wembley Stadium, London (Att: 98,199)

**ENGLAND 2-2 SCOTLAND**          **Half-time 2-1**

| | | |
|---|---|---|
| (22) | William BROWN (Tottenham Hotspur) | Gordon BANKS |
| (19) | Alexander HAMILTON (Dundee) | George COHEN |
| (1) | Edward McCREADIE (Chelsea) | Ramon WILSON |
| (13) | Patrick CRERAND (Manchester United) | Norbert STILES |
| (14) | William McNEILL (Celtic) captain | John CHARLTON |
| (6) | John GREIG (Rangers) | Robert MOORE |
| (13) | William HENDERSON (Rangers) | Peter THOMPSON |
| (29) | Robert COLLINS (Leeds United) | James GREAVES |
| (21) | Ian ST. JOHN (Liverpool) | Barry BRIDGES |
| (29) | Denis LAW (Manchester United) | John BYRNE |
| (21) | David WILSON (Rangers) | Robert CHARLTON |

Goals

| | | |
|---|---|---|
| | 0-1 | R.Charlton (25 mins) |
| | 0-2 | Greaves (35 mins) |
| Law (41 mins) | 1-2 | |
| St John (59 mins) | 2-2 | |

## 306

(Friendly)
8 May 1965

Referee: Howley (England)
Hampden Park, Glasgow (Att: 60,146)

**SCOTLAND 0-0 SPAIN**

| | | |
|---|---|---|
| (23) | William BROWN (Tottenham Hotspur) | José IRÍBAR |
| (20) | Alexander HAMILTON (Dundee) | Feliciano RIVILLA |
| (2) | Edward McCREADIE (Chelsea) | Fernando OLIVELLA |
| (1) | William BREMNER (Leeds United) | Severino REIJA |
| (15) | William McNEILL (Celtic) captain | Ignacio ZOCO |
| (7) | John GREIG (Rangers) | Jesús GLARÍA |
| (14) | William HENDERSON (Rangers) | José UFARTE |
| (30) | Robert COLLINS (Leeds United) | LUIS Aragonés |
| (30) | Denis LAW (Manchester United) | MARCELINO Martinez |
| (6) | Alan GILZEAN (Tottenham Hotspur) | Koldo AGUIRRE |
| (1) | John HUGHES (Celtic) | Carlos LAPETRA |

**307**

(World Cup — Qualifier)
23 May 1965

Referee: Alimov (Soviet Union)
Slaski Stadion, Chorzow (Att: 67,462)

**POLAND 1-1 SCOTLAND**                  **Half-time 0-0**

| (24) | William BROWN (Tottenham Hotspur) | Edward SZYMKOWIAK |
|---|---|---|
| (21) | Alexander HAMILTON (Dundee) | Henryk SZCZEPANSKI |
| (3) | Edward McCREADIE (Chelsea) | Jacek GMOCH |
| (8) | John GREIG (Rangers) | Stanislaw OSLIZLO |
| (16) | William McNEILL (Celtic) captain | Roman BAZAN |
| (14) | Patrick CRERAND (Manchester United) | Ryszard GRZEGORCZYK |
| (15) | William HENDERSON (Rangers) | Antoni NIEROBA |
| (31) | Robert COLLINS (Leeds United) | Jan BANAS |
| (1) | Neil MARTIN (Hibernian) | Jan LIBERDA |
| (31) | Denis LAW (Manchester United) | Ernest POL |
| (2) | John HUGHES (Celtic) | Roman LENTNER |

Goals
0-1 Lentner (50 mins)
Law (76 mins) 1-1

---

**308**

(World Cup — Qualifier)
27 May 1965

Referee: Vetter (East Germany)
Olympia Stadion, Helsinki (Att: 20,162)

**FINLAND 1-2 SCOTLAND**                  **Half-time 1-1**

| (25) | William BROWN (Tottenham Hotspur) | Lars NÄSMAN |
|---|---|---|
| (22) | Alexander HAMILTON (Dundee) | Pertti MÄKIPÄÄ |
| (4) | Edward McCREADIE (Chelsea) | Timo KAUTONEN |
| (15) | Patrick CRERAND (Manchester United) | Stig HOLMQVIST |
| (17) | William McNEILL (Celtic) captain | Aarno RINNE |
| (9) | John GREIG (Rangers) | Olli HEINONEN |
| (16) | William HENDERSON (Rangers) | Markku KUMPULAMPI |
| (32) | Denis LAW (Manchester United) | Juhani PELTONEN |
| (2) | Neil MARTIN (Hibernian) | Martti HYVÄRINEN |
| (1) | William HAMILTON (Hibernians) | Rauno RUOTSALAINEN |
| (22) | David WILSON (Rangers) | Semi NUORANEN |

Goals
0-1 Hyvarinen (5 mins)
Wilson (37 mins) 1-1
Greig (50 mins) 2-1

---

**309**

(Home International Championship)
2 October 1965

Referee: Taylor (England)
Windsor Park, Belfast (Att: 53,000)

**NORTHERN IRELAND 3-2 SCOTLAND**                  **Half-time 1-1**

| (26) | William BROWN (Tottenham Hotspur) | Patrick JENNINGS |
|---|---|---|
| (23) | Alexander HAMILTON (Dundee) | James MAGILL |
| (5) | Edward McCREADIE (Chelsea) | Alexander ELDER |
| (22) | David MACKAY (Tottenham Hotspur) | Martin HARVEY |
| (18) | William McNEILL (Celtic) captain | Terence NEILL |
| (10) | John GREIG (Rangers) | James NICHOLSON |
| (17) | William HENDERSON (Rangers) | James McILROY |
| (33) | Denis LAW (Manchester United) | John CROSSAN |
| (7) | Alan GILZEAN (Tottenham Hotspur) | William IRVINE |
| (25) | James BAXTER (Sunderland) | Derek DOUGAN |
| (3) | John HUGHES (Celtic) | George BEST |

Goals
Gilzean (17 mins) 1-0
1-1 Dougan (42 mins)
1-2 Crossan (59 mins)
Gilzean (81 mins) 2-2
2-3 Irvine (89 mins)

---

**310**

(World Cup — Qualifier)
13 October 1965

Referee: Carlsson (Sweden)
Hampden Park, Glasgow (Att: 107,580)

**SCOTLAND 1-2 POLAND**                  **Half-time 1-0**

| (27) | William BROWN (Tottenham Hotspur) | Konrad KORNEK |
|---|---|---|
| (24) | Alexander HAMILTON (Dundee) | Henryk SZCZEPANSKI |
| (6) | Edward McCREADIE (Chelsea) | Jacek GMOCH |
| (16) | Patrick CRERAND (Manchester United) | Stanislaw OSLIZLO |
| (19) | William McNEILL (Celtic) captain | Zygmunt ANCZOK |
| (11) | John GREIG (Rangers) | Antoni NIEROBA |
| (18) | William HENDERSON (Rangers) | Zygfryd SZOLTYSIK |
| (2) | William BREMNER (Leeds United) | Jerzy SADEK |
| (8) | Alan GILZEAN (Tottenham Hotspur) | Ernest POL |
| (34) | Denis LAW (Manchester United) | Jan LIBERDA |
| (1) | William JOHNSTON (Rangers) | Eugeniusz FABER |

Goals
McNEILL (14 mins) 1-0
1-1 Liberda (84 mins)
1-2 Sadek (86 mins)

---

**311**

(World Cup — Qualifier)
9 November 1965

Referee: Kreitlein (West Germany)
Hampden Park, Glasgow (Att: 100,393)

**SCOTLAND 1-0 ITALY**                  **Half-time 0-0**

| (28) | William BROWN (Tottenham Hotspur) | William NEGRI |
|---|---|---|
| (12) | John GREIG (Rangers) | Tarcisio BURGNICH |
| (3) | David PROVAN (Rangers) | Giacinto FACCHETTI |
| (1) | Robert MURDOCH (Celtic) | Aristide GUARNERI |
| (1) | Ronald McKINNON (Rangers) | Alessandro SALVADORE |
| (26) | James BAXTER (Sunderland) captain | Roberto ROSATO |
| (19) | William HENDERSON (Rangers) | Giovanni LODETTI |
| (3) | William BREMNER (Leeds United) | Alessandro MAZZOLA |
| (9) | Alan GILZEAN (Tottenham Hotspur) | Gianni RIVERA |
| (3) | Neil MARTIN (Sunderland) | Giacomo BULGARELLI |
| (4) | John HUGHES (Celtic) | Paolo BARISON |

Goals
Greig (88 mins) 1-0

---

**312**

(Home International Championship)
24 November 1965

Referee: Finney (England)
Hampden Park, Glasgow (Att: 49,888)

**SCOTLAND 4-1 WALES**                  **Half-time 3-1**

| (1) | Robert FERGUSON (Kilmarnock) | David HOLLINS |
|---|---|---|
| (13) | John GREIG (Rangers) | Peter RODRIGUES |
| (7) | Edward McCREADIE (Chelsea) | Colin GREEN |
| (2) | Robert MURDOCH (Celtic) | Terrence HENNESSEY |
| (2) | Ronald McKINNON (Rangers) | Michael ENGLAND |
| (27) | James BAXTER (Sunderland) captain | Barrington HOLE |
| (20) | William HENDERSON (Rangers) | Ronald REES |
| (1) | Charles COOKE (Dundee) | Royston VERNON |
| (1) | James FORREST (Rangers) | Wyn DAVIES |
| (10) | Alan GILZEAN (Tottenham Hotspur) | Ivor ALLCHURCH |
| (2) | William JOHNSTON (Rangers) | Gilbert REECE |

Goals
Murdoch (10 mins) 1-0
1-1 Allchurch (12 mins)
Henderson (13 mins) 2-1
Murdoch (29 mins) 3-1
Greig (86 mins) 4-1

---

**313**

(World Cup — Qualifier)
7 December 1965

Referee: Zsolt (Hungary)
Stadio San Paolo, Naples (Att: 68,873)

**ITALY 3-0 SCOTLAND**                  **Half-time 1-0**

| (3) | Adam BLACKLAW (Burnley) | Enrico ALBERTOSI |
|---|---|---|
| (4) | David PROVAN (Rangers) | Tarcisio BURGNICH |
| (8) | Edward McCREADIE (Chelsea) | Giacinto FACCHETTI |
| (3) | Robert MURDOCH (Celtic) | Roberto ROSATO |
| (3) | Ronald McKINNON (Rangers) | Alessandro SALVADORE |
| (14) | John GREIG (Rangers) captain | Giovanni LODETTI |
| (2) | James FORREST (Rangers) | Bruno MORA |
| (4) | William BREMNER (Leeds United) | Giacomo BULGARELLI |
| (2) | Ronald YEATS (Liverpool) | Alessandro MAZZOLA |
| (2) | Charles COOKE (Dundee) | Gianni RIVERA |
| (5) | John HUGHES (Celtic) | Ezio PASCUTTI |

Goals
0-1 Pascutti (38 mins)
0-2 Facchetti (74 mins)
0-3 Mora (85 mins)

# 1966

| | P | W | D | L | F | A |
|---|---|---|---|---|---|---|
| | 6 | 1 | 2 | 3 | 7 | 11 |

## 314

**(Home International Championship)**
**2 April 1966**

Referee: Faucheux (France)
Hampden Park, Glasgow (Att: 123,052)

### SCOTLAND 3-4 ENGLAND — Half-time 1-2

| | | |
|---|---|---|
| (2) | Robert FERGUSON (Kilmarnock) | Gordon BANKS |
| (15) | John GREIG (Rangers) captain | George COHEN |
| (1) | Thomas GEMMELL (Celtic) | Keith NEWTON |
| (4) | Robert MURDOCH (Celtic) | Norbert STILES |
| (4) | Ronald McKINNON (Rangers) | John CHARLTON |
| (28) | James BAXTER (Sunderland) | Robert MOORE |
| (3) | James JOHNSTONE (Celtic) | Alan BALL |
| (35) | Denis LAW (Manchester United) | Roger HUNT |
| (2) | William WALLACE (Hearts) | Robert CHARLTON |
| (5) | William BREMNER (Leeds United) | Geoffrey HURST |
| (3) | William JOHNSTON (Rangers) | John CONNELLY |

**Goals**

| | | |
|---|---|---|
| | 0-1 | Hurst (18 mins) |
| | 0-2 | Hunt (34 mins) |
| Law (42 mins) | 1-2 | |
| | 1-3 | Hunt (47 mins) |
| Johnstone (57 mins) | 2-3 | |
| | 2-4 | R.Charlton (73 mins) |
| Johnstone (82 mins) | 3-4 | |

## 315

**(Friendly)**
**11 May 1966**

Referee: Howley (England)
Hampden Park, Glasgow (Att: 16,513)

### SCOTLAND 0-3 NETHERLANDS — Half-time 0-1

| | | |
|---|---|---|
| (3) | Robert FERGUSON (Kilmarnock) | Eduard GRAAFLAND |
| (16) | John GREIG (Rangers) captain | Frederik FLINKEVLEUGEL |
| (5) | David PROVAN (Rangers) | Emil PIJS |
| (1) | Patrick STANTON (Hibernian) | Daniel SCHRIJVERS |
| (5) | Ronald McKINNON (Rangers) | Cornelis VELDHOEN |
| (1) | David SMITH (Aberdeen) | Wilhelmus DULLENS |
| (21) | William HENDERSON (Rangers) | Bernardus MULLER |
| (1) | Andrew PENMAN (Dundee) | Jesaia SWART |
| (1) | James SCOTT (Hibernian) | Wilhelmus VAN DER KUIJLEN |
| (3) | William WALLACE (Hearts) | Klaas NUNINGA |
| (4) | William JOHNSTON (Rangers) | Pieter KEIZER |

**Goals**

| | | |
|---|---|---|
| | 0-1 | Nuninga (15 mins) |
| | 0-2 | Van der Kuijlen (53 mins) |
| | 0-3 | Van der Kuijlen (84 mins) |

## 316

**(Friendly)**
**18 June 1966**

Referee: McCabe (England)
Hampden Park, Glasgow (Att: 23,321)

### SCOTLAND 0-1 PORTUGAL — Half-time 0-0

| | | |
|---|---|---|
| (4) | Robert FERGUSON (Kilmarnock) | José PEREIRA |
| (1) | William BELL (Leeds United) | Joao MORAIS |
| (9) | Edward McCREADIE (Chelsea) | Alexandre BAPTISTA |
| (17) | John GREIG (Rangers) captain | VICENTE Lucas |
| (3) | John McGRORY (Kilmarnock) | HILÁRIO Da Conceiçao |
| (6) | William BREMNER (Leeds United) | Jaime GRAÇA |
| (15) | Alexander SCOTT (Everton) | Mário COLUNA |
| (3) | Charles COOKE (Chelsea) | José AUGUSTO |
| (8) | Alexander YOUNG (Everton) | EUSÉBIO Ferreira |
| (29) | James BAXTER (Sunderland) | José TORRES |
| (1) | John SINCLAIR (Leicester City) | Antonio SIMOES |

**Substitutions**

| | | |
|---|---|---|
| (3) | Stephen CHALMERS (Celtic) | Fernando PERES |
| | for Young 46 mins | for Augusto 80 mins |

**Goals**

| | | |
|---|---|---|
| | 0-1 | Torres (72 mins) |

## 317

**(Friendly)**
**25 June 1966**

Referee: Finney (England)
Hampden Park, Glasgow (Att: 74,933)

### SCOTLAND 1-1 BRAZIL — Half-time 1-1

| | | |
|---|---|---|
| (5) | Robert FERGUSON (Kilmarnock) | GILMAR dos Santos Neves |
| (18) | John GREIG (Rangers) captain | José Maria FIDELIS |
| (2) | William BELL (Leeds United) | PAULO HENRIQUE Souza |
| (7) | William BREMNER (Leeds United) | ORLANDO Peçanha de Carvalho |
| (6) | Ronald McKINNON (Rangers) | Hideraldo Luíz BELLINI |
| (1) | John CLARK (Celtic) | José Ely de Miranda ZITO |
| (16) | Alexander SCOTT (Everton) | Jair Ventura Filho JAIRZINHO |
| (4) | Charles COOKE (Chelsea) | GÉRSON Nunes de Oliveira |
| (4) | Stephen CHALMERS (Celtic) | SERVILIO de Jesus Filho |
| (30) | James BAXTER (Sunderland) | Edson Arantes PELÉ |
| (1) | Peter CORMACK (Hibernian) | AMARILDO Tavares da Silveira |

**Substitutions**

| | | |
|---|---|---|
| | | VALTER MACHADO da Silva |
| | | for Servilio 46 mins |

**Goals**

| | | |
|---|---|---|
| Chalmers (1 min) | 1-0 | |
| | 1-1 | Servilio (16 mins) |

## 318

**(Home International Championship/European Championship — Qualifier)**
**22 October 1966**

Referee: Dagnall (England)
Ninian Park, Cardiff (Att: 33,269)

### WALES 1-1 SCOTLAND — Half-time 0-0

| | | |
|---|---|---|
| (6) | Robert FERGUSON (Kilmarnock) | Gareth SPRAKE |
| (19) | John GREIG (Rangers) captain | Peter RODRIGUES |
| (2) | Thomas GEMMELL (Celtic) | Graham WILLIAMS |
| (8) | William BREMNER (Leeds United) | Terrence HENNESSEY |
| (7) | Ronald McKINNON (Rangers) | Michael ENGLAND |
| (2) | John CLARK (Celtic) | Barrington HOLE |
| (4) | James JOHNSTONE (Celtic) | Gilbert REECE |
| (36) | Denis LAW (Manchester United) | Wyn DAVIES |
| (1) | Joseph McBRIDE (Celtic) | Ronald DAVIES |
| (31) | James BAXTER (Sunderland) | Clifford JONES |
| (22) | William HENDERSON (Rangers) | Alan JARVIS |

**Goals**

| | | |
|---|---|---|
| | 0-1 | R.Davies (76 mins) |
| Law (86 mins) | 1-1 | |

## 319

**(Home International Championship/European Championship — Qualifier)**
**16 November 1966**

Referee: Taylor (England)
Hampden Park, Glasgow (Att: 45,281)

### SCOTLAND 2-1 NORTHERN IRELAND — Half-time 2-1

| | | |
|---|---|---|
| (7) | Robert FERGUSON (Kilmarnock) | Patrick JENNINGS |
| (20) | John GREIG (Rangers) captain | John PARKE |
| (3) | Thomas GEMMELL (Celtic) | Alexander ELDER |
| (9) | William BREMNER (Leeds United) | Martin HARVEY |
| (8) | Ronald McKINNON (Rangers) | Terence NEILL |
| (3) | John CLARK (Celtic) | James NICHOLSON |
| (23) | William HENDERSON (Rangers) | Samuel WILSON |
| (5) | Robert MURDOCH (Celtic) | John CROSSAN |
| (2) | Joseph McBRIDE (Celtic) | William IRVINE |
| (5) | Stephen CHALMERS (Celtic) | Derek DOUGAN |
| (1) | Robert LENNOX (Celtic) | David CLEMENTS |

**Goals**

| | | |
|---|---|---|
| | 0-1 | Nicholson (9 mins) |
| Murdoch (14 mins) | 1-1 | |
| Lennox (35 mins) | 2-1 | |

# 1967

| P | W | D | L | F | A |
|---|---|---|---|---|---|
| 4 | 2 | 0 | 2 | 6 | 7 |

## 320

(Home International Championship/European Championship — Qualifier)

Referee: Schulenburg (West Germany)

15 April 1967      Wembley Stadium, London (Att: 99,063)

### ENGLAND 2-3 SCOTLAND      Half-time 0-1

| (1) | Ronald SIMPSON (Celtic) | Gordon BANKS |
|---|---|---|
| (4) | Thomas GEMMELL (Celtic) | George COHEN |
| (10) | Edward McCREADIE (Chelsea) | Ramon WILSON |
| (21) | John GREIG (Rangers) captain | Norbert STILES |
| (9) | Ronald McKINNON (Rangers) | John CHARLTON |
| (10) | William BREMNER (Leeds United) | Robert MOORE |
| (1) | James McCALLIOG (Sheffield Wednesday) | Alan BALL |
| (37) | Denis LAW (Manchester United) | James GREAVES |
| (4) | William WALLACE (Celtic) | Robert CHARLTON |
| (32) | James BAXTER (Sunderland) | Geoffrey HURST |
| (2) | Robert LENNOX (Celtic) | Martin PETERS |

| | Goals | |
|---|---|---|
| Law (27 mins) | 1-0 | |
| Lennox (78 mins) | 2-0 | |
| | 2-1 | J. Charlton (84 mins) |
| McCalliog (87 mins) | 3-1 | |
| | 3-2 | Hurst (88 mins) |

Ronnie Simpson (36) and Jim McCalliog (20) congratulate each other after the victory at Wembley in April 1967. They had both just made their full international debut.

## 321

(Friendly)      Referee: Van Ravens (Netherlands)

10 May 1967      Hampden Park, Glasgow (Att: 53,497)

### SCOTLAND 0-2 USSR      Half-time 0-2

| (2) | Ronald SIMPSON (Celtic) | Lev YASHIN |
|---|---|---|
| (5) | Thomas GEMMELL (Celtic) | Valentin AFONIN |
| (11) | Edward McCREADIE (Chelsea) | Albert SHESTERNEV |
| (4) | John CLARK (Celtic) | Murtaz KHURTSILAVA |
| (20) | William McNEILL (Celtic) | Vasilij DANILOV |
| (33) | James BAXTER (Sunderland) captain | Valerij VORONIN |
| (5) | James JOHNSTONE (Celtic) | Igor CHISLENKO |
| (5) | Francis McLINTOCK (Arsenal) | Iosif SABO |
| (2) | James McCALLIOG (Sheffield Wednesday) | Fëdor MEDVED |
| (38) | Denis LAW (Manchester United) | Eduard STRELTZOV |
| (3) | Robert LENNOX (Celtic) | Eduard MALOFEYEV |

| | Substitutions | |
|---|---|---|
| (5) | William WALLACE (Celtic) | |
| | for Law 46 mins | |

| | Goals | |
|---|---|---|
| | 0-1 | Gemmell (16 mins o.g.) |
| | 0-2 | Medved (41 mins) |

## 322

(Home International Championship/European Championship — Qualifier)

Referee: Finney (England)

21 October 1967      Windsor Park, Belfast (Att: 55,000)

### NORTHERN IRELAND 1-0 SCOTLAND      Half-time 0-0

| (3) | Ronald SIMPSON (Celtic) | Patrick JENNINGS |
|---|---|---|
| (6) | Thomas GEMMELL (Celtic) | William McKEAG |
| (12) | Edward McCREADIE (Chelsea) | John PARKE |
| (22) | John GREIG (Rangers) captain | Arthur STEWART |
| (10) | Ronald McKINNON (Rangers) | Terence NEILL |
| (11) | John URE (Arsenal) | David CLEMENTS |
| (6) | William WALLACE (Celtic) | William CAMPBELL |
| (6) | Robert MURDOCH (Celtic) | John CROSSAN |
| (3) | James McCALLIOG (Sheffield Wednesday) | Derek DOUGAN |
| (39) | Denis LAW (Manchester United) | James NICHOLSON |
| (1) | William MORGAN (Burnley) | George BEST |

| | Goals | |
|---|---|---|
| | 0-1 | Clements (68 mins) |

## 323

(Home International Championship/European Championship — Qualifier)

Referee: Finney (England)

22 November 1967      Hampden Park, Glasgow (Att: 57,472)

### SCOTLAND 3-2 WALES      Half-time 1-1

| (1) | Robert CLARK (Aberdeen) | Gareth SPRAKE |
|---|---|---|
| (1) | James CRAIG (Celtic) | Peter RODRIGUES |
| (13) | Edward McCREADIE (Chelsea) | Colin GREEN |
| (23) | John GREIG (Rangers) captain | Terrence HENNESSEY |
| (11) | Ronald McKINNON (Rangers) | Edward JAMES |
| (34) | James BAXTER (Sunderland) | Barrington HOLE |
| (6) | James JOHNSTONE (Celtic) | Ronald REES |
| (11) | William BREMNER (Leeds United) | Wyn DAVIES |
| (11) | Alan GILZEAN (Tottenham Hotspur) | Ronald DAVIES |
| (5) | William JOHNSTON (Rangers) | Alan DURBAN |
| (4) | Robert LENNOX (Celtic) | Clifford JONES |

| | Goals | |
|---|---|---|
| Gilzean (15 mins) | 1-0 | |
| | 1-1 | R.Davies (18 mins) |
| | 1-2 | Durban (49 mins) |
| Gilzean (65 mins) | 2-2 | |
| McKinnon (78 mins) | 3-2 | |

Scotland players pictured at their training camp at Largs before the 1968 England game. Back row (left to right): Gemmell, McKinnon, McNeil, Simpson, Greig, McCreadie. Front row: Cooke, Bremner, Gilzean, Johnston, Lennox.

# 1968

| P | W | D | L | F | A |
|---|---|---|---|---|---|
| 5 | 3 | 2 | 0 | 9 | 2 |

## 324

(Home International Championship/European Championship — Qualifier)

Referee: Van Ravens (Netherlands)

**24 February 1968** — Hampden Park, Glasgow (Att: 134,000)

### SCOTLAND 1-1 ENGLAND — Half-time 1-1

| | | | |
|---|---|---|---|
| (4) | Ronald SIMPSON (Celtic) | | Gordon BANKS |
| (7) | Thomas GEMMELL (Celtic) | | Keith NEWTON |
| (14) | Edward McCREADIE (Chelsea) | | Ramon WILSON |
| (21) | William McNEILL (Celtic) | | Alan MULLERY |
| (12) | Ronald McKINNON (Rangers) | | Brian LABONE |
| (24) | John GREIG (Rangers) captain | | Robert MOORE |
| (5) | Charles COOKE (Chelsea) | | Alan BALL |
| (12) | William BREMNER (Leeds United) | | Geoffrey HURST |
| (6) | John HUGHES (Celtic) | | Michael SUMMERBEE |
| (6) | William JOHNSTON (Rangers) | | Robert CHARLTON |
| (5) | Robert LENNOX (Celtic) | | Martin PETERS |

Goals

| | | |
|---|---|---|
| | 0-1 | Peters (20 mins) |
| Hughes (39 mins) | 1-1 | |

## 325

(Friendly)

Referee: Riegg (West Germany)

**30 May 1968** — Olympisch Stadion, Amsterdam (Att: 19,000)

### NETHERLANDS 0-0 SCOTLAND

| | | |
|---|---|---|
| (2) | Robert CLARK (Aberdeen) | Jan VAN BEVEREN |
| (1) | Douglas FRASER (West Bromwich Albion) | Pieter ROMEIJN |
| (15) | Edward McCREADIE (Chelsea) | Marinus ISRAEL |
| (1) | Robert MONCUR (Newcastle United) | Johannes EIJKENBROEK |
| (13) | Ronald McKINNON (Rangers) | Hendrik WARNAS |
| (2) | David SMITH (Rangers) | Wilhelmus JANSEN |
| (24) | William HENDERSON (Rangers) | Hendrik GROOT |
| (1) | Robert HOPE (West Bromwich Albion) | Jan KLIJNJAN |
| (1) | George McLEAN (Dundee) | Wilhelmus VAN DER KUIJLEN |
| (25) | John GREIG (Rangers) captain | Willem VAN HANEGEM |
| (6) | Charles COOKE (Chelsea) | Robert RENSENBRINK |

Substitutions

| | |
|---|---|
| (1) | James SMITH (Aberdeen) |
| | for Hope 12 mins |

## 326

(Friendly)

Referee: Carlsson (Sweden)

**16 October 1968** — Idraetsparken, Copenhagen (Att: 11,900)

### DENMARK 0-1 SCOTLAND — Half-time 0-0

| | | |
|---|---|---|
| (1) | James HERRIOT (Birmingham City) | Knud ENGEDAHL |
| (8) | Thomas GEMMELL (Celtic) | Jan LARSEN |
| (16) | Edward McCREADIE (Chelsea) | Niels YDE |
| (13) | William BREMNER (Leeds United) captain | Leif SORENSEN |
| (14) | Ronald McKINNON (Rangers) | Henning MUNK-JENSEN |
| (26) | John GREIG (Rangers) | Borge ENEMARK |
| (1) | Thomas McLEAN (Kilmarnock) | Flemming MORTENSEN |
| (4) | James McCALLIOG (Sheffield Wednesday) | Finn WIBERG |
| (1) | Colin STEIN (Rangers) | Bent JENSEN |
| (2) | Robert HOPE (West Bromwich Albion) | Ole STEFFENSEN |
| (6) | Robert LENNOX (Celtic) | Ulrik LE FEVRE |

Substitutions

| | |
|---|---|
| (2) | Peter CORMACK (Hibernian) |
| | for McCalliog 87 mins |

Goals

| | |
|---|---|
| Lennox (70 mins) | 1-0 |

## 327

**(World Cup — Qualifier)**
6 November 1968

Referee: Liedberg (Sweden)
Hampden Park, Glasgow (Att: 80,856)

### SCOTLAND 2-1 AUSTRIA — Half-time 1-1

| | | |
|---|---|---|
| (5) | Ronald SIMPSON (Celtic) | Gerald FUCHSBICHLER |
| (9) | Thomas GEMMELL (Celtic) | Walter GEBHARDT |
| (17) | Edward McCREADIE (Chelsea) | Gerhard STURMBERGER |
| (14) | William BREMNER (Leeds United) captain | Johann EIGENSTILLER |
| (15) | Ronald McKINNON (Rangers) | Peter PUMM |
| (27) | John GREIG (Rangers) | Franz HASIL |
| (7) | James JOHNSTONE (Celtic) | August STAREK |
| (7) | Charles COOKE (Chelsea) | Johann ETTMAYER |
| (7) | John HUGHES (Celtic) | Helmut MÄTZLER |
| (40) | Denis LAW (Manchester United) | Helmut SIBER |
| (7) | Robert LENNOX (Celtic) | Helmut REDL |

**Substitutions**

| | | |
|---|---|---|
| (12) | Alan GILZEAN (Tottenham Hotspur) for Law 75 mins | Helmut KÖGLBERGER for Redl 46 mins |

**Goals**

| | | |
|---|---|---|
| | 0-1 | Starek (2 mins) |
| Law (7 mins) | 1-1 | |
| Bremner (75 mins) | 2-1 | |

## 328

**(World Cup — Qualifier)**
11 December 1968

Referee: Bonnet (Malta)
G.S.P. Stadhion, Nicosia (Att: 5,895)

### CYPRUS 0-5 SCOTLAND — Half-time 0-5

| | | |
|---|---|---|
| (2) | James HERRIOT (Birmingham City) | Michalakis ALKIVIADIS |
| (2) | Douglas FRASER (West Bromwich Albion) | Panikos IAKOVOU |
| (18) | Edward McCREADIE (Chelsea) | Lakis THEODOROU |
| (15) | William BREMNER (Leeds United) captain | Michael STEFANOS |
| (16) | Ronald McKINNON (Rangers) | Kyriakos KOUREAS |
| (28) | John GREIG (Rangers) | Kostas PANAYIOTOU |
| (2) | Thomas McLEAN (Kilmarnock) | Panikos EFTHYMIADIS |
| (7) | Robert MURDOCH (Celtic) | Panikos KRYSTALLIS |
| (2) | Colin STEIN (Rangers) | Melis ASPROU |
| (13) | Alan GILZEAN (Tottenham Hotspur) | Andreas PAKKOS |
| (8) | Charles COOKE (Chelsea) | Andreas STYLIANOU |

**Substitutions**

| | | |
|---|---|---|
| (22) | William McNEILL (Celtic) for McKinnon 46 mins | Marios MARKOU for Pakkos 6 mins |
| (8) | Robert LENNOX (Celtic) for Cooke 80 mins | Yiannis XYPOLITAS for Krystallis 46 mins |

**Goals**

| | |
|---|---|
| Gilzean (3 mins) | 1-0 |
| Murdoch (23 mins) | 2-0 |
| Gilzean (30 mins) | 3-0 |
| Stein (40 mins) | 4-0 |
| Stein (43 mins) | 5-0 |

## 1969

| P | W | D | L | F | A |
|---|---|---|---|---|---|
| 8 | 2 | 3 | 3 | 19 | 15 |

## 329

**(World Cup — Qualifier)**
16 April 1969

Referee: Gardeazabal (Spain)
Hampden Park, Glasgow (Att: 95,951)

### SCOTLAND 1-1 WEST GERMANY — Half-time 0-1

| | | |
|---|---|---|
| (2) | Thomas LAWRENCE (Liverpool) | Horst WOLTER |
| (10) | Thomas GEMMELL (Celtic) | Hans-Hubert VOGTS |
| (19) | Edward McCREADIE (Chelsea) | Karl-Heinz SCHNELLINGER |
| (8) | Robert MURDOCH (Celtic) | Franz BECKENBAUER |
| (17) | Ronald McKINNON (Rangers) | Willi SCHULZ |
| (29) | John GREIG (Rangers) | Bernhard PATZKE |
| (8) | James JOHNSTONE (Celtic) | Bernhard DÖRFEL |
| (16) | William BREMNER (Leeds United) captain | Helmut HALLER |
| (41) | Denis LAW (Manchester United) | Gerhard MÜLLER |
| (14) | Alan GILZEAN (Tottenham Hotspur) | Wolfgang OVERATH |
| (9) | Robert LENNOX (Celtic) | Siegfried HELD |

**Substitutions**

| | | |
|---|---|---|
| (9) | Charles COOKE (Chelsea) for Lennox 63 mins | Josef MAIER for Wolter 46 mins |
| | | Max LORENZ for Overath 79 mins |

**Goals**

| | | |
|---|---|---|
| | 0-1 | Müller (39 mins) |
| Murdoch (88 mins) | 1-1 | |

## 330

**(Home International Championship)**
3 May 1969

Referee: Finney (England)
The Racecourse, Wrexham (Att: 18,765)

### WALES 3-5 SCOTLAND — Half-time 2-2

| | | |
|---|---|---|
| (3) | Thomas LAWRENCE (Liverpool) | Gareth SPRAKE |
| (11) | Thomas GEMMELL (Celtic) | Stephen DERRETT |
| (20) | Edward McCREADIE (Chelsea) | Colin GREEN |
| (17) | William BREMNER (Leeds United) captain | Alan DURBAN |
| (23) | William McNEILL (Celtic) | Alwyn BURTON |
| (30) | John GREIG (Rangers) | David POWELL |
| (3) | Thomas McLEAN (Kilmarnock) | Graham MOORE |
| (9) | Robert MURDOCH (Celtic) | John TOSHACK |
| (3) | Colin STEIN (Rangers) | Ronald DAVIES |
| (15) | Alan GILZEAN (Tottenham Hotspur) | Wyn DAVIES |
| (10) | Charles COOKE (Chelsea) | Barrie JONES |

**Substitutions**

| | | |
|---|---|---|
| (3) | James HERRIOT (Birmingham City) for Lawrence 46 mins | Ronald REES for Derrett 78 mins |

**Goals**

| | | |
|---|---|---|
| McNeill (12 mins) | 1-0 | |
| Stein (16 mins) | 2-0 | |
| | 2-1 | R. Davies (29 mins) |
| | 2-2 | Toshack (44 mins) |
| Gilzean (55 mins) | 3-2 | |
| | 3-3 | R.Davies (57 mins) |
| Bremner (72 mins) | 4-3 | |
| McLean (87 mins) | 5-3 | |

## 331

**(Home International Championship)**
6 May 1969

Referee: Smith (England)
Hampden Park, Glasgow (Att: 7,483)

### SCOTLAND 1-1 NORTHERN IRELAND — Half-time 0-1

| | | |
|---|---|---|
| (4) | James HERRIOT (Birmingham City) | Patrick JENNINGS |
| (12) | Thomas GEMMELL (Celtic) | David CRAIG |
| (21) | Edward McCREADIE (Chelsea) | Alexander ELDER |
| (18) | William BREMNER (Leeds United) captain | Samuel TODD |
| (31) | John GREIG (Rangers) | Terence NEILL |
| (2) | Patrick STANTON (Hibernian) | James NICHOLSON |
| (25) | William HENDERSON (Rangers) | George BEST |
| (10) | Robert MURDOCH (Celtic) | Eric McMORDIE |
| (4) | Colin STEIN (Rangers) | Derek DOUGAN |
| (42) | Denis LAW (Manchester United) | Thomas JACKSON |
| (11) | Charles COOKE (Chelsea) | David CLEMENTS |

**Substitutions**

| | |
|---|---|
| (7) | William JOHNSTON (Rangers) for Cooke 75 mins |

**Goals**

| | | |
|---|---|---|
| | 0-1 | McMordie (11 mins) |
| Stein (53 mins) | 1-1 | |

## 332

**(Home International Championship)**
10 May 1969

Referee: Helies (France)
Wembley Stadium, London (Att: 89,902)

### ENGLAND 4-1 SCOTLAND — Half-time 2-1

| | | |
|---|---|---|
| (5) | James HERRIOT (Birmingham City) | Gordon BANKS |
| (13) | Thomas GEMMELL (Celtic) | Keith NEWTON |
| (22) | Edward McCREADIE (Chelsea) | Terence COOPER |
| (11) | Robert MURDOCH (Celtic) | Alan MULLERY |
| (24) | William McNEILL (Celtic) | Brian LABONE |
| (32) | John GREIG (Rangers) | Robert MOORE |
| (26) | William HENDERSON (Rangers) | Francis LEE |
| (19) | William BREMNER (Leeds United) captain | Alan BALL |
| (5) | Colin STEIN (Rangers) | Robert CHARLTON |
| (16) | Alan GILZEAN (Tottenham Hotspur) | Geoffrey HURST |
| (1) | Edwin GRAY (Leeds United) | Martin PETERS |

**Substitutions**

| | |
|---|---|
| (7) | William WALLACE (Celtic) for Gilzean 57 mins |

**Goals**

| | | |
|---|---|---|
| | 0-1 | Peters (16 mins) |
| | 0-2 | Hurst (20 mins) |
| Stein (43 mins) | 1-2 | |
| | 1-3 | Hurst (60 mins pen) |
| | 1-4 | Peters (64 mins) |

## 333

(World Cup — Qualifier)
17 May 1969

Referee: Coates (Republic of Ireland)
Hampden Park, Glasgow (Att: 39,095)

### SCOTLAND 8-0 CYPRUS — Half-time 3-0

| | | |
|---|---|---|
| (6) | James HERRIOT (Birmingham City) | Michalakis ALKIVIADIS |
| (14) | Thomas GEMMELL (Celtic) | Ioannis ANDREOU |
| (23) | Edward McCREADIE (Chelsea) | Andreas KONSTANTINOU |
| (20) | William BREMNER (Leeds United) captain | Georgiou SOTIRAKIS |
| (25) | William McNEILL (Celtic) | Kyriakos KOUREAS |
| (33) | John GREIG (Rangers) | Michael STEFANOS |
| (27) | William HENDERSON (Rangers) | Marios MARKOU |
| (12) | Charles COOKE (Chelsea) | Panikos EFTHYMIADIS |
| (6) | Colin STEIN (Rangers) | Panikos KRYSTALLIS |
| (17) | Alan GILZEAN (Tottenham Hotspur) | Melis ASPROU |
| (2) | Edwin GRAY (Leeds United) | Andreas STYLIANOU |

Substitutions

Demos KAVAZIS
  for Konstantinou 46 mins
Paschalis FOKIS
  for Sotirakis 46 mins

| Goals | | |
|---|---|---|
| Gray (15 mins) | 1-0 | |
| McNeill (20 mins) | 2-0 | |
| Stein (28 mins) | 3-0 | |
| Stein (49 mins) | 4-0 | |
| Stein (59 mins) | 5-0 | |
| Stein (67 mins) | 6-0 | |
| Henderson (70 mins) | 7-0 | |
| Gemmell (76 mins pen) | 8-0 | |

## 334

(Friendly)
21 September 1969

Referee: Burtenshaw (England)
Dalymount Park, Dublin (Att: 27,000)

### REPUBLIC OF IRELAND 1-1 SCOTLAND — Half-time 1-1

| | | |
|---|---|---|
| (1) | Ernest McGARR (Aberdeen) | Alan KELLY |
| (34) | John GREIG (Rangers) | Seamus BRENNAN |
| (15) | Thomas GEMMELL (Celtic) | Michael MEAGAN |
| (3) | Patrick STANTON (Hibernian) | Alfred FINUCANE |
| (18) | Ronald McKINNON (Rangers) | Patrick MULLIGAN |
| (2) | Robert MONCUR (Newcastle United) | John CONWAY |
| (28) | William HENDERSON (Rangers) | Eamon ROGERS |
| (21) | William BREMNER (Leeds United) captain | John GILES |
| (7) | Colin STEIN (Rangers) | Donald GIVENS |
| (3) | Peter CORMACK (Hibernian) | Alfred HALE |
| (8) | John HUGHES (Celtic) | Ray TREACY |

Substitutions

| | |
|---|---|
| (7) | James HERRIOT (Birmingham City) |
| | for McGarr 24 mins |
| (1) | William CALLAGHAN (Dunfermline Athletic) |
| | for Gemmell 46 mins |

| Goals | | |
|---|---|---|
| Stein (8 mins) | 1-0 | |
| | 1-1 | Givens (27 mins) |

## 335

(World Cup — Qualifier)
22 October 1969

Referee: Droz (Switzerland)
Volkspark Stadion, Hamburg (Att: 72,000)

### WEST GERMANY 3-2 SCOTLAND — Half-time 1-1

| | | |
|---|---|---|
| (8) | James HERRIOT (Birmingham City) | Josef MAIER |
| (35) | John GREIG (Rangers) | Horst-Dieter HÖTTGES |
| (16) | Thomas GEMMELL (Celtic) | Hans-Hubert VOGTS |
| (22) | William BREMNER (Leeds United) captain | Franz BECKENBAUER |
| (19) | Ronald McKINNON (Rangers) | Willi SCHULZ |
| (26) | William McNEILL (Celtic) | Klaus FICHTEL |
| (9) | James JOHNSTONE (Celtic) | Reinhard LIBUDA |
| (4) | Peter CORMACK (Hibernian) | Uwe SEELER |
| (18) | Alan GILZEAN (Tottenham Hotspur) | Gerhard MÜLLER |
| (8) | Colin STEIN (Rangers) | Wolfgang OVERATH |
| (3) | Edwin GRAY (Leeds United) | Helmut HALLER |

| Goals | | |
|---|---|---|
| Johnstone (3 mins) | 1-0 | |
| | 1-1 | Fichtel (38 mins) |
| | 1-2 | Muller (60 mins) |
| Gilzean (64 mins) | 2-2 | |
| | 2-3 | Libuda (81 mins) |

## 336

(World Cup — Qualifier)
5 November 1969

Referee: Karlo (Soviet Union)
Prater Stadion, Vienna (Att: 10,091)

### AUSTRIA 2-0 SCOTLAND — Half-time 1-0

| | | |
|---|---|---|
| (2) | Ernest McGARR (Aberdeen) | Wilhelm HARREITHER |
| (36) | John GREIG (Rangers) | Helmut WALLNER |
| (1) | Francis BURNS (Manchester United) | Gerhard STURMBERGER |
| (12) | Robert MURDOCH (Celtic) | Johann SCHMIDRADNER |
| (20) | Ronald McKINNON (Rangers) | Erich FAK |
| (4) | Patrick STANTON (Hibernian) | Johann GEYER |
| (13) | Charles COOKE (Chelsea) | Norbert HOF |
| (23) | William BREMNER (Leeds United) captain | Johann ETTMAYER |
| (19) | Alan GILZEAN (Tottenham Hotspur) | Thomas PARITS |
| (1) | Hugh CURRAN (Wolverhampton Wanderers) | Robert KAISER |
| (4) | Edwin GRAY (Leeds United) | Helmut REDL |

Substitutions

| | | |
|---|---|---|
| (1) | Peter LORIMER (Leeds United) | Josef HICKERSBERGER |
| | for Curran 54 mins | for Kaiser 60 mins |
| (9) | Colin STEIN (Rangers) | |
| | for Cooke 72 mins | |

| Goals | | |
|---|---|---|
| | 0-1 | Redl (14 mins) |
| | 0-2 | Redl (53 mins) |

---

# 1970

| P | W | D | L | F | A |
|---|---|---|---|---|---|
| 4 | 2 | 2 | 0 | 2 | 0 |

## 337

(Home International Championship)
18 April 1970

Referee: Jennings (England)
Windsor Park, Belfast (Att: 31,000)

### NORTHERN IRELAND 0-1 SCOTLAND — Half-time 0-0

| | | |
|---|---|---|
| (3) | Robert CLARK (Aberdeen) | Patrick JENNINGS |
| (1) | David HAY (Celtic) | David CRAIG |
| (1) | William DICKSON (Kilmarnock) | David CLEMENTS |
| (6) | Francis McLINTOCK (Arsenal) captain | Samuel TODD |
| (21) | Ronald McKINNON (Rangers) | Terence NEILL |
| (3) | Robert MONCUR (Newcastle United) | James NICHOLSON |
| (4) | Thomas McLEAN (Kilmarnock) | William CAMPBELL |
| (1) | William CARR (Coventry City) | Samuel LUTTON |
| (1) | John O'HARE (Derby County) | Derek DOUGAN |
| (20) | Alan GILZEAN (Tottenham Hotspur) | Eric McMORDIE |
| (8) | William JOHNSTON (Rangers) | George BEST |

Substitutions

| | | |
|---|---|---|
| (10) | Colin STEIN (Rangers) | William O'KANE |
| | for Gilzean 70 mins | for Todd 46 mins |
| | | Desmond DICKSON |
| | | for Campbell 75 mins |

| Goals | | |
|---|---|---|
| O'Hare (58 mins) | 1-0 | |

## 338

(Home International Championship)
22 April 1970

Referee: Smith (England)
Hampden Park, Glasgow (Att: 30,434)

### SCOTLAND 0-0 WALES

| | | |
|---|---|---|
| (2) | James CRUICKSHANK (Hearts) | Anthony MILLINGTON |
| (2) | William CALLAGHAN (Dunfermline Athletic) | Peter RODRIGUES |
| (2) | William DICKSON (Kilmarnock) | Roderick THOMAS |
| (37) | John GREIG (Rangers) captain | Terrence HENNESSEY |
| (22) | Ronald McKINNON (Rangers) | Michael ENGLAND |
| (4) | Robert MONCUR (Newcastle United) | David POWELL |
| (5) | Thomas McLEAN (Kilmarnock) | Richard KRZYWICKI |
| (2) | David HAY (Celtic) | Alan DURBAN |
| (2) | John O'HARE (Derby County) | Ronald DAVIES |
| (11) | Colin STEIN (Rangers) | Graham MOORE |
| (2) | William CARR (Coventry City) | Ronald REES |

Substitutions

| | |
|---|---|
| (10) | Robert LENNOX (Celtic) |
| | for McLean 70 mins |

## 339

(Home International Championship)  
25 April 1970  
Referee: Schulenburg (West Germany)  
Hampden Park, Glasgow (Att: 137,438)

### SCOTLAND 0-0 ENGLAND

| | | |
|---|---|---|
| (3) | James CRUICKSHANK (Hearts) | Gordon BANKS |
| (17) | Thomas GEMMELL (Celtic) | Keith NEWTON |
| (3) | William DICKSON (Kilmarnock) | Emlyn HUGHES |
| (38) | John GREIG (Rangers) captain | Norbert STILES |
| (23) | Ronald McKINNON (Rangers) | Brian LABONE |
| (5) | Robert MONCUR (Newcastle United) | Robert MOORE |
| (10) | James JOHNSTONE (Celtic) | Peter THOMPSON |
| (3) | David HAY (Celtic) | Alan BALL |
| (12) | Colin STEIN (Rangers) | Jeffery ASTLE |
| (3) | John O'HARE (Derby County) | Geoffrey HURST |
| (3) | William CARR (Coventry City) | Martin PETERS |

Substitutions

| | | |
|---|---|---|
| (21) | Alan GILZEAN (Tottenham Hotspur) | Alan MULLERY |
| | for Moncur 82 mins | for Thompson 58 mins |

## 340

(European Championship — Qualifier)  
11 November 1970  
Referee: Linemayr (Austria)  
Hampden Park, Glasgow (Att: 24,618)

### SCOTLAND 1-0 DENMARK — Half-time 1-0

| | | |
|---|---|---|
| (4) | James CRUICKSHANK (Hearts) | Kaj POULSEN |
| (4) | David HAY (Celtic) | Torben NIELSEN |
| (39) | John GREIG (Rangers) | Poul-Henning FREDERIKSEN |
| (5) | Patrick STANTON (Hibernian) | Erik SANDVAD |
| (24) | Ronald McKINNON (Rangers) | Flemming PEDERSEN |
| (6) | Robert MONCUR (Newcastle United) captain | Jens-Jorgen HANSEN |
| (11) | James JOHNSTONE (Celtic) | Bent OUTZEN |
| (4) | William CARR (Coventry City) | Kristen NYGAARD |
| (13) | Colin STEIN (Rangers) | Morten OLSEN |
| (4) | John O'HARE (Derby County) | Keld PEDERSEN |
| (9) | William JOHNSTON (Rangers) | Benny NIELSEN |

Substitutions

| | | |
|---|---|---|
| (5) | Peter CORMACK (Nottingham Forest) | Poul-Erik THYGESEN |
| | for O'Hare 75 mins | for Olsen 46 mins |
| (1) | William JARDINE (Rangers) | |
| | for Hay 77 mins | |

Goals

| | |
|---|---|
| O'Hare (14 mins) | 1-0 |

# 1971

| P | W | D | L | F | A |
|---|---|---|---|---|---|
| 10 | 2 | 1 | 7 | 5 | 14 |

## 341

(European Championship — Qualifier)  
3 February 1971  
Referee: Sbardella (Italy)  
Stade Sclessin, Liège (Att: 13,931)

### BELGIUM 3-0 SCOTLAND — Half-time 1-0

| | | |
|---|---|---|
| (5) | James CRUICKSHANK (Hearts) | Christian PIOT |
| (5) | David HAY (Celtic) | Georges HEYLENS |
| (18) | Thomas GEMMELL (Celtic) | Nicolas DEWALQUE |
| (40) | John GREIG (Rangers) | Jean PLASKIE |
| (25) | Ronald McKINNON (Rangers) | Jean THISSEN |
| (6) | Patrick STANTON (Hibernian) | Wilfried VAN MOER |
| (7) | Robert MONCUR (Newcastle United) captain | Erwin VAN DEN DAELE |
| (1) | Archibald GEMMILL (Derby County) | Leon SEMMELING |
| (14) | Charles COOKE (Chelsea) | Henri DEPIREUX |
| (14) | Colin STEIN (Rangers) | André DENUL |
| (5) | John O'HARE (Derby County) | Paul VAN HIMST |

Substitutions

| | | |
|---|---|---|
| (1) | Anthony GREEN (Blackpool) | |
| | for Stanton 46 mins | |
| (3) | James FORREST (Aberdeen) | |
| | for Stein 46 mins | |

Goals

| | | |
|---|---|---|
| 0-1 | McKinnon (36 mins o.g.) | |
| 0-2 | Van Himst (55 mins) | |
| 0-3 | Van Himst (83 mins pen) | |

## 342

(European Championship — Qualifier)  
21 April 1971  
Referee: Kitabjian (France)  
Estadio da Luz, Lisbon (Att: 35,463)

### PORTUGAL 2-0 SCOTLAND — Half-time 1-0

| | | |
|---|---|---|
| (4) | Robert CLARK (Aberdeen) | Vitor DAMAS |
| (6) | David HAY (Celtic) | Malta DA SILVA |
| (1) | James BROGAN (Celtic) | Humberto COELHO |
| (7) | Patrick STANTON (Hibernian) | José CARLOS |
| (26) | Ronald McKINNON (Rangers) | Adolfo CALISTO |
| (8) | Robert MONCUR (Newcastle United) captain | Rui RODRIGUES |
| (29) | William HENDERSON (Rangers) | Fernando PERES |
| (1) | David ROBB (Aberdeen) | Antonio SIMOES |
| (6) | Peter CORMACK (Nottingham Forest) | Tamagnini NENÉ |
| (5) | James McCALLIOG (Wolverhampton Wanderers) | Vitor BAPTISTA |
| (22) | Alan GILZEAN (Tottenham Hotspur) | EUSÉBIO Ferreira |

Substitutions

| | | |
|---|---|---|
| (1) | Andrew JARVIE (Airdrie) | Artur JORGE |
| | for McCalliog 63 mins | for Baptista 76 mins |
| (2) | Anthony GREEN (Blackpool) | Fernando NEVES |
| | for Stanton 75 mins | for Nené 86 mins |

Goals

| | |
|---|---|
| 0-1 | Stanton (22 mins o.g.) |
| 0-2 | Eusébio (82 mins) |

## 343

(Home International Championship)  
15 May 1971  
Referee: Taylor (England)  
Ninian Park, Cardiff (Att: 19,068)

### WALES 0-0 SCOTLAND

| | | |
|---|---|---|
| (5) | Robert CLARK (Aberdeen) | Gareth SPRAKE |
| (7) | David HAY (Celtic) | Peter RODRIGUES |
| (2) | James BROGAN (Celtic) | Roderick THOMAS |
| (24) | William BREMNER (Leeds United) | Edward JAMES |
| (7) | Francis McLINTOCK (Arsenal) | John ROBERTS |
| (9) | Robert MONCUR (Newcastle United) captain | Terence YORATH |
| (2) | Peter LORIMER (Leeds United) | Leighton PHILLIPS |
| (7) | Peter CORMACK (Nottingham Forest) | Alan DURBAN |
| (5) | Edwin GRAY (Leeds United) | Gilbert REECE |
| (2) | David ROBB (Aberdeen) | John TOSHACK |
| (6) | John O'HARE (Derby County) | Ronald DAVIES |

Substitutions

| | | |
|---|---|---|
| (41) | John GREIG (Rangers) | |
| | for Bremner 72 mins | |

## 344

(Home International Championship)  
18 May 1971  
Referee: Thomas (Wales)  
Hampden Park, Glasgow (Att: 31,643)

### SCOTLAND 0-1 NORTHERN IRELAND — Half-time 0-1

| | | |
|---|---|---|
| (6) | Robert CLARK (Aberdeen) | Patrick JENNINGS |
| (8) | David HAY (Celtic) | Patrick RICE |
| (3) | James BROGAN (Celtic) | Samuel NELSON |
| (42) | John GREIG (Rangers) | William O'KANE |
| (8) | Francis McLINTOCK (Arsenal) | Allan HUNTER |
| (10) | Robert MONCUR (Newcastle United) captain | James NICHOLSON |
| (3) | Peter LORIMER (Leeds United) | Bryan HAMILTON |
| (3) | Anthony GREEN (Blackpool) | Eric McMORDIE |
| (6) | Edwin GRAY (Leeds United) | David CLEMENTS |
| (2) | Hugh CURRAN (Wolverhampton Wanderers) | George BEST |
| (7) | John O'HARE (Derby County) | Derek DOUGAN |

Substitutions

| | | |
|---|---|---|
| (2) | Andrew JARVIE (Airdrie) | David CRAIG |
| | for O'Hare 46 mins | for McMordie 67 mins |
| (1) | Francis MUNRO (Wolverhampton Wanderers) | |
| | for McLintock 71 mins | |

Goals

| | |
|---|---|
| 0-1 | Greig (14 mins o.g.) |

Bobby Moncur and Frank McLintock battle with Martin Chivers and Geoff Hurst at Wembley in May 1971.

## 345
**(Home International Championship)**
22 May 1971

Referee: Dorpmans (Netherlands)
Wembley Stadium, London (Att: 91,469)

| ENGLAND 3-1 SCOTLAND | | Half-time 3-1 |
|---|---|---|

| (7) | Robert CLARK (Aberdeen) | Gordon BANKS |
|---|---|---|
| (43) | John GREIG (Rangers) | Christopher LAWLER |
| (4) | James BROGAN (Celtic) | Terence COOPER |
| (25) | William BREMNER (Leeds United) | Roy McFARLAND |
| (9) | Francis McLINTOCK (Arsenal) | Robert MOORE |
| (11) | Robert MONCUR (Newcastle United) captain | Peter STOREY |
| (12) | James JOHNSTONE (Celtic) | Francis LEE |
| (4) | Anthony GREEN (Blackpool) | Alan BALL |
| (8) | Peter CORMACK (Nottingham Forest) | Martin PETERS |
| (3) | David ROBB (Aberdeen) | Geoffrey HURST |
| (3) | Hugh CURRAN (Wolverhampton Wanderers) | Martin CHIVERS |

**Substitutions**

| (2) | Francis MUNRO (Wolverhampton Wanderers) | Allan CLARKE |
|---|---|---|
| | for Curran 46 mins | for Lee 73 mins |
| (3) | Andrew JARVIE (Airdrie) | |
| | for Green 82 mins | |

**Goals**

| | 0-1 | Peters (9 mins) |
|---|---|---|
| Curran (11 mins) | 1-1 | |
| | 1-2 | Chivers (30 mins) |
| | 1-3 | Chivers (40 mins) |

## 346
**(European Championship — Qualifier)**
9 June 1971

Referee: Riedel (East Germany)
Idraetsparken, Copenhagen (Att: 37,682)

| DENMARK 1-0 SCOTLAND | | Half-time 1-0 |
|---|---|---|

| (8) | Robert CLARK (Aberdeen) | Erik SORENSEN |
|---|---|---|
| (3) | Francis MUNRO (Wolverhampton Wanderers) | Torben NIELSEN |
| (4) | William DICKSON (Kilmarnock) | Mogens BERG |
| (8) | Patrick STANTON (Hibernian) | Preben ARENTOFT |
| (27) | Ronald McKINNON (Rangers) | Jorgen RASMUSSEN |
| (12) | Robert MONCUR (Newcastle United) captain | Kersten BJERRE |
| (6) | Thomas McLEAN (Kilmarnock) | Finn LAUDRUP |
| (1) | Thomas FORSYTH (Motherwell) | Ole BJORNMOSE |
| (4) | James FORREST (Aberdeen) | Ulrik LE FEVRE |
| (4) | Hugh CURRAN (Wolverhampton Wanderers) | Benny NIELSEN |
| (15) | Colin STEIN (Rangers) | Jorgen KRISTENSEN |

**Substitutions**

| (4) | David ROBB (Aberdeen) | Keld PEDERSEN |
|---|---|---|
| | for Forsyth 46 mins | for B.Nielsen 46 mins |
| (1) | John SCOTT (Dundee) | Bent OUTZEN |
| | for Forrest 70 mins | for Laudrup 75 mins |

**Goals**

| | 0-1 | Laudrup (44 mins) |
|---|---|---|

## 347
**(Friendly)**
14 June 1971

Referee: Marschall (Austria)
Lenin Stadion, Moscow (Att: 20,000)

| USSR 1-0 SCOTLAND | | Half-time 1-0 |
|---|---|---|

| (9) | Robert CLARK (Aberdeen) | Yevgeni RUDAKOV |
|---|---|---|
| (1) | John BROWNLIE (Hibernian) | Iurij ISTOMIN |
| (5) | William DICKSON (Kilmarnock) | Albert SHESTERNEV |
| (4) | Francis MUNRO (Wolverhampton Wanderers) | Viktor MATVIENKO |
| (28) | Ronald McKINNON (Rangers) | Vladimir KAPLICHNI |
| (9) | Patrick STANTON (Hibernian) captain | Viktor KOLOTOV |
| (1) | Robert WATSON (Motherwell) | Anatolij KONKOV |
| (5) | David ROBB (Aberdeen) | Givi NODIJA |
| (2) | John SCOTT (Dundee) | Vladimir FEDOTOV |
| (5) | James FORREST (Aberdeen) | Vitalij SHEVCHENKO |
| (16) | Colin STEIN (Rangers) | Gennadij YEVRYUZHIKHIN |

**Substitutions**

| (5) | Hugh CURRAN (Wolverhampton Wanderers) | Vitalij KHMELNITSKI |
|---|---|---|
| | for Stein 71 mins | for Yevryuzhikin 46 mins |
| | | Nikolai DOLGOV |
| | | for Nodija 70 mins |

**Goals**

| | 0-1 | Yevryuzhikhin (24 mins) |
|---|---|---|

## 348
**(European Championship — Qualifier)**
13 October 1971

Referee: Piotrowicz (Poland)
Hampden Park, Glasgow (Att: 58,612)

| SCOTLAND 2-1 PORTUGAL | | Half-time 1-0 |
|---|---|---|

| (1) | Robert WILSON (Arsenal) | Vitor DAMAS |
|---|---|---|
| (2) | William JARDINE (Rangers) | Malta DA SILVA |
| (9) | David HAY (Celtic) | Francisco CALÓ |
| (10) | Patrick STANTON (Hibernian) | Rui RODRIGUES |
| (1) | Edmond COLQUHOUN (Sheffield United) | Adolfo CALISTO |
| (13) | James JOHNSTONE (Celtic) | Jaime GRAÇA |
| (26) | William BREMNER (Leeds United) captain | Rolando GONÇALVES |
| (1) | George GRAHAM (Arsenal) | Antonio SIMOES |
| (1) | Alexander CROPLEY (Hibernian) | Tamagnini NENÉ |
| (2) | Archibald GEMMILL (Derby County) | Vitor BAPTISTA |
| (8) | John O'HARE (Derby County) | EUSÉBIO Ferreira |

**Substitutions**

| (1) | Martin BUCHAN (Aberdeen) | Artur JORGE |
|---|---|---|
| | for Colquhoun 60 mins | for Eusébio 46 mins |
| | | Fernando PERES |
| | | for Caló 66 mins |

**Goals**

| O'Hare (23 mins) | 1-0 | |
|---|---|---|
| | 1-1 | Rodrigues (57 mins) |
| Gemmill (58 mins) | 2-1 | |

## 349
**(European Championship — Qualifier)**
10 November 1971

Referee: Boström (Sweden)
Pittodrie Park, Aberdeen (Att: 36,500)

| SCOTLAND 1-0 BELGIUM | | Half-time 1-0 |
|---|---|---|

| (10) | Robert CLARK (Aberdeen) | Christian PIOT |
|---|---|---|
| (3) | William JARDINE (Rangers) | Georges HEYLENS |
| (10) | David HAY (Celtic) | Nicolas DEWALQUE |
| (11) | Patrick STANTON (Hibernian) | André STASSART |
| (2) | Martin BUCHAN (Aberdeen) | Leon DOLMANS |
| (14) | James JOHNSTONE (Celtic) | Wilfried VAN MOER |
| (27) | William BREMNER (Leeds United) captain | Erwin VAN DEN DAELE |
| (2) | Alexander CROPLEY (Hibernian) | Wilfried PUIS |
| (7) | Edwin GRAY (Leeds United) | Leon SEMMELING |
| (1) | Stephen MURRAY (Aberdeen) | Johan DEVRINDT |
| (9) | John O'HARE (Derby County) | Paul VAN HIMST |

**Substitutions**

| (1) | Kenneth DALGLISH (Celtic) | Maurice MARTENS |
|---|---|---|
| | for Cropley 48 mins | for Van Moer 57 mins |
| (1) | John HANSEN (Partick Thistle) | Raoul LAMBERT |
| | for Johnstone 79 mins | for Puis 69 mins |

**Goals**

| O'Hare (6 mins) | 1-0 | |
|---|---|---|

## 350

(Friendly)
1 December 1971

Referee: Biwersi (West Germany)
Olympisch Stadion, Amsterdam (Att: 18,000)

### NETHERLANDS 2-1 SCOTLAND — Half-time 1-0

| | | |
|---|---|---|
| (2) | Robert WILSON (Arsenal) | Pieter SCHRIJVERS |
| (4) | William JARDINE (Rangers) | Johannes VENNEKER |
| (11) | David HAY (Celtic) | Bernardus HULSHOFF |
| (12) | Patrick STANTON (Hibernian) | Marinus ISRAËL |
| (2) | Edmond COLQUHOUN (Sheffield United) | Rudolf KROL |
| (15) | James JOHNSTONE (Celtic) | Johannes NEESKENS |
| (28) | William BREMNER (Leeds United) captain | Willem VAN HANEGEM |
| (3) | Archibald GEMMILL (Derby County) | Hendrik WERY |
| (8) | Edwin GRAY (Leeds United) | Theodorus PAHLPLATZ |
| (2) | George GRAHAM (Arsenal) | Johannes CRUIJFF |
| (2) | Kenneth DALGLISH (Celtic) | Pieter KEIZER |

Substitutions

| | | |
|---|---|---|
| (10) | John O'HARE (Derby County) | Wilhelmus JANSEN |
| | for Johnstone 56 mins | for Wery 46 mins |
| (9) | Peter CORMACK (Nottingham Forest) | Gerardus MÜHREN |
| | for Gray 84 mins | for Keizer 46 mins |

Goals

| | | |
|---|---|---|
| | 0-1 | Cruijff (5 mins) |
| Graham (58 mins) | 1-1 | |
| | 1-2 | Hulshoff (87 mins) |

---

# 1972

| P | W | D | L | F | A |
|---|---|---|---|---|---|
| 9 | 5 | 2 | 2 | 13 | 5 |

## 351

(Friendly)
26 April 1972

Referee: Partridge (England)
Hampden Park, Glasgow (Att: 21,001)

### SCOTLAND 2-0 PERU — Half-time 0-0

| | | |
|---|---|---|
| (1) | Alistair HUNTER (Kilmarnock) | Manuel URIBE |
| (2) | John BROWNLIE (Hibernian) | Rodolfo MANZO |
| (1) | William DONACHIE (Manchester City) | José VELÁSQUEZ |
| (13) | Robert MONCUR (Newcastle United) | Héctor CHUMPITAZ |
| (3) | Edmond COLQUHOUN (Sheffield United) | Antonio TRIGUEROS |
| (2) | William MORGAN (Manchester United) | Ramón MIFFLIN |
| (5) | William CARR (Coventry City) | Alfredo QUESADA |
| (1) | Richard HARTFORD (West Bromwich Albion) | Juan MUNANTE |
| (4) | Archibald GEMMILL (Derby County) | Teófilo CUBILLAS |
| (11) | John O'HARE (Derby County) | Percy ROJAS |
| (43) | Denis LAW (Manchester United) captain | Juan ORBEGOZO |

Substitutions

| | |
|---|---|
| | Hugo SOTIL |
| | for Rojas 46 mins |

Goals

| | | |
|---|---|---|
| O'Hare (47 mins) | 1-0 | |
| Law (65 mins) | 2-0 | |

## 352

(Home International Championship)
20 May 1972

Referee: Thomas (Wales)
Hampden Park, Glasgow (Att: 39,710)

### SCOTLAND 2-0 NORTHERN IRELAND — Half-time 0-0

| | | |
|---|---|---|
| (11) | Robert CLARK (Aberdeen) | Patrick JENNINGS |
| (3) | John BROWNLIE (Hibernian) | Patrick RICE |
| (2) | William DONACHIE (Manchester City) | Samuel NELSON |
| (14) | Robert MONCUR (Newcastle United) | Terence NEILL |
| (27) | William McNEILL (Celtic) | Allan HUNTER |
| (16) | James JOHNSTONE (Celtic) | David CLEMENTS |
| (29) | William BREMNER (Leeds United) captain | Daniel HEGAN |
| (3) | George GRAHAM (Arsenal) | Eric McMORDIE |
| (5) | Archibald GEMMILL (Derby County) | Thomas JACKSON |
| (12) | John O'HARE (Derby County) | William IRVINE |
| (44) | Denis LAW (Manchester United) | Derek DOUGAN |

Substitutions

| | | |
|---|---|---|
| (4) | Peter LORIMER (Leeds United) | Samuel McILROY |
| | for Johnstone 61 mins | for McMordie 68 mins |
| | | David CRAIG |
| | | for Clements 83 mins |

Goals

| | | |
|---|---|---|
| Law (86 mins) | 1-0 | |
| Lorimer (89 mins) | 2-0 | |

## 353

(Home International Championship)
24 May 1972

Referee: Lawther (Northern Ireland)
Hampden Park, Glasgow (Att: 21,332)

### SCOTLAND 1-0 WALES — Half-time 0-0

| | | |
|---|---|---|
| (12) | Robert CLARK (Aberdeen) | Gareth SPRAKE |
| (13) | Patrick STANTON (Hibernian) | Malcolm PAGE |
| (3) | Martin BUCHAN (Manchester United) | Roderick THOMAS |
| (15) | Robert MONCUR (Newcastle United) | Terrence HENNESSEY |
| (28) | William McNEILL (Celtic) | Michael ENGLAND |
| (5) | Peter LORIMER (Leeds United) | Terence YORATH |
| (30) | William BREMNER (Leeds United) captain | Alan DURBAN |
| (5) | Anthony GREEN (Newcastle United) | Wyn DAVIES |
| (6) | Archibald GEMMILL (Derby County) | Gilbert REECE |
| (13) | John O'HARE (Derby County) | Leighton PHILLIPS |
| (45) | Denis LAW (Manchester United) | Ronald DAVIES |

Substitutions

| | | |
|---|---|---|
| (2) | Richard HARTFORD (West Bromwich Albion) | Leighton JAMES |
| | for Gemmill 35 mins | for Hennessey 74 mins |
| (1) | Luigi MACARI (Celtic) | |
| | for O'Hare 56 mins | |

Goals

| | |
|---|---|
| Lorimer (72 mins) | 1-0 |

## 354

(Home International Championship)
27 May 1972

Referee: Gonella (Italy)
Hampden Park, Glasgow (Att: 119,325)

### SCOTLAND 0-1 ENGLAND — Half-time 0-1

| | | |
|---|---|---|
| (13) | Robert CLARK (Aberdeen) | Gordon BANKS |
| (4) | John BROWNLIE (Hibernian) | Paul MADELEY |
| (3) | William DONACHIE (Manchester City) | Emlyn HUGHES |
| (16) | Robert MONCUR (Newcastle United) | Roy McFARLAND |
| (29) | William McNEILL (Celtic) | Robert MOORE |
| (6) | Peter LORIMER (Leeds United) | Alan BALL |
| (31) | William BREMNER (Leeds United) captain | Norman HUNTER |
| (7) | Archibald GEMMILL (Derby County) | Peter STOREY |
| (3) | Richard HARTFORD (West Bromwich Albion) | Colin BELL |
| (2) | Luigi MACARI (Celtic) | Rodney MARSH |
| (46) | Denis LAW (Manchester United) | Martin CHIVERS |

Substitutions

| | | |
|---|---|---|
| (17) | James JOHNSTONE (Celtic) | Malcolm MACDONALD |
| | for Gemmill 49 mins | for Marsh 84 mins |
| (6) | Anthony GREEN (Newcastle United) | |
| | for Donachie 74 mins | |

Goals

| | | |
|---|---|---|
| | 0-1 | Ball (28 mins) |

## 355

(Brazilian Independence Cup 1st Round)
29 June 1972

Referee: Coerezza (Argentina)
Estadio Mineiro, Belo Horizonte (Att: 4,000)

### YUGOSLAVIA 2-2 SCOTLAND — Half-time 0-1

| | | |
|---|---|---|
| (2) | Alistair HUNTER (Kilmarnock) | Rizah MESKOVIC |
| (1) | Alexander FORSYTH (Partick Thistle) | Petar KRIVOKUCA |
| (4) | William DONACHIE (Manchester City) | Miroslav BOSKOVIC |
| (4) | Martin BUCHAN (Manchester United) | Miroslav PAVLOVIC |
| (4) | Edmond COLQUHOUN (Sheffield United) | Blagoje PAUNOVIC |
| (3) | William MORGAN (Manchester United) | Josip KATALINSKI |
| (32) | William BREMNER (Leeds United) captain | Danilo POPIVODA |
| (4) | George GRAHAM (Arsenal) | Branko OBLAK |
| (4) | Richard HARTFORD (West Bromwich Albion) | Jovan ACIMOVIC |
| (3) | Luigi MACARI (Celtic) | Dusan BAJEVIC |
| (47) | Denis LAW (Manchester United) | Dragan DZAJIC |

Substitutions

| | | |
|---|---|---|
| (2) | John HANSEN (Partick Thistle) | Slobodan SANTRAC |
| | for Forsyth 46 mins | for Boskovic 38 mins |
| (1) | James BONE (Norwich City) | Jure JERKOVIC |
| | for Law 76 mins | for Paunovic 46 mins |

Goals

| | | |
|---|---|---|
| Macari (40 mins) | 1-0 | |
| | 1-1 | Bajevic (61 mins) |
| Macari (64 mins) | 2-1 | |
| | 2-2 | Jerkovic (86 mins) |

## 356

(Brazilian Independence Cup 1st Round)  
2 July 1972

Referee: Marques (Brazil)  
Estadio Beira Rio, Porto Alegre (Att: 15,000)

**CZECHOSLOVAKIA 0-0 SCOTLAND**

| | | |
|---|---|---|
| (14) | Robert CLARK (Aberdeen) | Ivo VIKTOR |
| (2) | Alexander FORSYTH (Partick Thistle) | Karol DOBIÁS |
| (5) | William DONACHIE (Manchester City) | Ludevít ZLOCHA |
| (5) | Martin BUCHAN (Manchester United) | Vladimír HAGARA |
| (5) | Edmond COLQUHOUN (Sheffield United) | Ján PIVARNIK |
| (4) | William MORGAN (Manchester United) | Ján MEDVID |
| (33) | William BREMNER (Leeds United) captain | Ladislav KUNA |
| (5) | George GRAHAM (Arsenal) | Jaroslav POLLÁK |
| (5) | Richard HARTFORD (West Bromwich Albion) | Vladimír TERNENY |
| (4) | Luigi MACARI (Celtic) | Jozef ADAMEC |
| (48) | Denis LAW (Manchester United) | Dusan KABÁT |

Substitutions

| | | |
|---|---|---|
| (17) | Colin STEIN (Rangers) | Ján CAPKOVIC |
| | for Law 78 mins | for Kabát 60 mins |
| | | Anton HRUSECKY |
| | | for Terneny 70 mins |

## 357

(Brazilian Independence Cup 1st Round)  
5 July 1972

Referee: Klein (Israel)  
Estadio Maracana, Rio de Janeiro (Att: 130,000)

**BRAZIL 1-0 SCOTLAND** — Half-time 0-0

| | | |
|---|---|---|
| (15) | Robert CLARK (Aberdeen) | Emerson LEAO |
| (3) | Alexander FORSYTH (Partick Thistle) | José Maria Alvez ZÉ MARIA |
| (6) | William DONACHIE (Manchester City) | Hércules BRITO Ruas |
| (6) | Martin BUCHAN (Manchester United) | Galdino Gomes VANTUIR |
| (6) | Edmond COLQUHOUN (Sheffield United) | MARCO ANTÓNIO Feliciano |
| (5) | William MORGAN (Manchester United) | Tavares de Santana CLODOALDO |
| (34) | William BREMNER (Leeds United) captain | GÉRSON Nunes de Oliveira |
| (6) | George GRAHAM (Arsenal) | Roberto RIVELINO |
| (6) | Richard HARTFORD (West Bromwich Albion) | Eduardo Gonçalves TOSTAO |
| (5) | Luigi MACARI (Celtic) | Joao Leiva Campos LEIVINHA |
| (49) | Denis LAW (Manchester United) | Jair Ventura Filho JAIRZINHO |

Substitutions

| | | |
|---|---|---|
| | | José dos Santos DARIO |
| | | for Leivinha 63 mins |

Goals  
0-1 Jairzinho (80 mins)

## 358

(World Cup — Qualifier)  
18 October 1972

Referee: Bakhramov (Soviet Union)  
Idraetsparken, Copenhagen (Att: 31,200)

**DENMARK 1-4 SCOTLAND** — Half-time 1-2

| | | |
|---|---|---|
| (16) | Robert CLARK (Aberdeen) | Mogens THERKILDSEN |
| (5) | John BROWNLIE (Hibernian) | Torben NIELSEN |
| (4) | Alexander FORSYTH (Partick Thistle) | Henning MUNK-JENSEN |
| (7) | Martin BUCHAN (Manchester United) | Per RONTVED |
| (7) | Edmond COLQUHOUN (Sheffield United) | Flemming AHLBERG |
| (7) | Peter LORIMER (Leeds United) | John OLSEN |
| (35) | William BREMNER (Leeds United) captain | Jack HANSEN |
| (7) | George GRAHAM (Arsenal) | Ole BJORNMOSE |
| (6) | William MORGAN (Manchester United) | Finn LAUDRUP |
| (6) | Luigi MACARI (Celtic) | Eigil NIELSEN |
| (2) | James BONE (Norwich City) | Henning JENSEN |

Substitutions

| | | |
|---|---|---|
| (1) | Joseph HARPER (Aberdeen) | Bent JENSEN |
| | for Bone 65 mins | for Hansen 68 mins |
| (3) | Kenneth DALGLISH (Celtic) | |
| | for Macari 88 mins | |

Goals  

| | | |
|---|---|---|
| Macari (17 mins) | 1-0 | |
| Bone (19 mins) | 2-0 | |
| | 2-1 | Laudrup (28 mins) |
| Harper (80 mins) | 3-1 | |
| Morgan (83 mins) | 4-1 | |

## 359

(World Cup — Qualifier)  
15 November 1972

Referee: Corver (Netherlands)  
Hampden Park, Glasgow (Att: 47,109)

**SCOTLAND 2-0 DENMARK** — Half-time 1-0

| | | |
|---|---|---|
| (1) | David HARVEY (Leeds United) | Mogens THERKILDSEN |
| (6) | John BROWNLIE (Hibernian) | Flemming AHLBERG |
| (7) | William DONACHIE (Manchester City) | Henning MUNK-JENSEN |
| (8) | Martin BUCHAN (Manchester United) | Per RONTVED |
| (8) | Edmond COLQUHOUN (Sheffield United) | Johnny HANSEN |
| (8) | Peter LORIMER (Leeds United) | Allan MICHAELSEN |
| (36) | William BREMNER (Leeds United) captain | John OLSEN |
| (8) | George GRAHAM (Arsenal) | Kersten BJERRE |
| (7) | William MORGAN (Manchester United) | Jorgen KRISTENSEN |
| (4) | Kenneth DALGLISH (Celtic) | Bent JENSEN |
| (2) | Joseph HARPER (Aberdeen) | Ulrik LE FEVRE |

Substitutions

| | | |
|---|---|---|
| (6) | William CARR (Coventry City) | Heinz HILDEBRANDT |
| | for Dalglish 75 mins | for Therkildsen 46 mins |
| | | Finn LAUDRUP |
| | | for Kristensen 75 mins |

Goals  

| | |
|---|---|
| Dalglish (2 mins) | 1-0 |
| Lorimer (48 mins) | 2-0 |

# 1973

| P | W | D | L | F | A |
|---|---|---|---|---|---|
| 9 | 2 | 1 | 6 | 6 | 13 |

## 360

(Friendly)  
14 February 1973

Referee: Wurtz (France)  
Hampden Park, Glasgow (Att: 48,470)

**SCOTLAND 0-5 ENGLAND** — Half-time 0-3

| | | |
|---|---|---|
| (17) | Robert CLARK (Aberdeen) | Peter SHILTON |
| (5) | Alexander FORSYTH (Manchester United) | Paul MADELEY |
| (8) | William DONACHIE (Manchester City) | Emlyn HUGHES |
| (9) | Martin BUCHAN (Manchester United) | Peter STOREY |
| (9) | Edmond COLQUHOUN (Sheffield United) | Robert MOORE |
| (9) | Peter LORIMER (Leeds United) | Alan BALL |
| (37) | William BREMNER (Leeds United) captain | Colin BELL |
| (9) | George GRAHAM (Manchester United) | Michael CHANNON |
| (8) | William MORGAN (Manchester United) | Martin PETERS |
| (7) | Luigi MACARI (Manchester United) | Martin CHIVERS |
| (5) | Kenneth DALGLISH (Celtic) | Allan CLARKE |

Substitutions

| | | |
|---|---|---|
| (18) | Colin STEIN (Coventry City) | |
| | for Morgan 19 mins | |

Goals  

| | |
|---|---|
| 0-1 | Lorimer (6 mins o.g.) |
| 0-2 | Clarke (12 mins) |
| 0-3 | Channon (15 mins) |
| 0-4 | Chivers (76 mins) |
| 0-5 | Clarke (85 mins) |

## 361

(Home International Championship)  
12 May 1973

Referee: Lawther (Northern Ireland)  
The Racecourse, Wrexham (Att: 18,682)

**WALES 0-2 SCOTLAND** — Half-time 0-1

| | | |
|---|---|---|
| (1) | Peter McCLOY (Rangers) | Gareth SPRAKE |
| (1) | Daniel McGRAIN (Celtic) | Peter RODRIGUES |
| (9) | William DONACHIE (Manchester City) | Roderick THOMAS |
| (1) | James HOLTON (Manchester United) | Trevor HOCKEY |
| (1) | Derek JOHNSTONE (Rangers) | Michael ENGLAND |
| (14) | Patrick STANTON (Hibernian) captain | John ROBERTS |
| (10) | George GRAHAM (Manchester United) | John MAHONEY |
| (12) | David HAY (Celtic) | Brian EVANS |
| (9) | William MORGAN (Manchester United) | Terence YORATH |
| (6) | Kenneth DALGLISH (Celtic) | Leighton JAMES |
| (1) | Derek PARLANE (Rangers) | John TOSHACK |

Substitutions

| | | |
|---|---|---|
| (19) | Colin STEIN (Coventry City) | Wyn DAVIES |
| | for Parlane 80 mins | for Yorath 69 mins |
| (8) | Luigi MACARI (Manchester United) | Peter O'SULLIVAN |
| | for Dalglish 84 mins | for Evans 78 mins |

Goals  

| | |
|---|---|
| Graham (18 mins) | 1-0 |
| Graham (80 mins) | 2-0 |

Jim Holton and Peter Lorimer with Roy McFarland at Wembley in May 1973.

## 362

| (Home International Championship) | Referee: Burns (England) |
|---|---|
| 16 May 1973 | Hampden Park, Glasgow (Att: 39,018) |

### SCOTLAND 1-2 NORTHERN IRELAND — Half-time 0-2

| | | |
|---|---|---|
| (2) | Peter McCLOY (Rangers) | Patrick JENNINGS |
| (2) | Daniel McGRAIN (Celtic) | Patrick RICE |
| (10) | William DONACHIE (Manchester City) | David CRAIG |
| (2) | James HOLTON (Manchester United) | Terence NEILL |
| (2) | Derek JOHNSTONE (Rangers) | Allan HUNTER |
| (15) | Patrick STANTON (Hibernian) captain | David CLEMENTS |
| (11) | George GRAHAM (Manchester United) | Bryan HAMILTON |
| (13) | David HAY (Celtic) | Thomas JACKSON |
| (10) | William MORGAN (Manchester United) | Martin O'NEILL |
| (7) | Kenneth DALGLISH (Celtic) | Samuel MORGAN |
| (20) | Colin STEIN (Coventry City) | Trevor ANDERSON |

Substitutions

| | | |
|---|---|---|
| (38) | William BREMNER (Leeds United) | Samuel LUTTON |
| | for Stanton 50 mins | for Anderson 65 mins |
| (9) | Luigi MACARI (Manchester United) | |
| | for Graham 77 mins | |

Goals

| | |
|---|---|
| 0-1 | O'Neill (3 mins) |
| 0-2 | Anderson (17 mins) |
| Dalglish (89 mins) | 1-2 |

## 363

| (Home International Championship) | Referee: Tschenscher (West Germany) |
|---|---|
| 19 May 1973 | Wembley Stadium, London (Att: 95,950) |

### ENGLAND 1-0 SCOTLAND — Half-time 0-0

| | | |
|---|---|---|
| (3) | Alistair HUNTER (Celtic) | Peter SHILTON |
| (5) | William JARDINE (Rangers) | Peter STOREY |
| (3) | Daniel McGRAIN (Celtic) | Emlyn HUGHES |
| (3) | James HOLTON (Manchester United) | Roy McFARLAND |
| (3) | Derek JOHNSTONE (Rangers) | Robert MOORE |
| (10) | Peter LORIMER (Leeds United) | Alan BALL |
| (39) | William BREMNER (Leeds United) captain | Colin BELL |
| (14) | David HAY (Celtic) | Michael CHANNON |
| (11) | William MORGAN (Manchester United) | Martin PETERS |
| (10) | Luigi MACARI (Manchester United) | Martin CHIVERS |
| (8) | Kenneth DALGLISH (Celtic) | Allan CLARKE |

Substitutions

| | | |
|---|---|---|
| (1) | Joseph JORDAN (Leeds United) | |
| | for Macari 74 mins | |
| (21) | Colin STEIN (Coventry City) | |
| | for Lorimer 80 mins | |

Goals

| | |
|---|---|
| 0-1 | Peters (55 mins) |

## 364

| (Friendly) | Referee: Verbeke (France) |
|---|---|
| 22 June 1973 | Wankdorf Stadion, Berne (Att: 10,000) |

### SWITZERLAND 1-0 SCOTLAND — Half-time 0-0

| | | |
|---|---|---|
| (3) | Peter McCLOY (Rangers) | Erich BURGENER |
| (6) | William JARDINE (Rangers) | Walter MUNDSCHIN |
| (4) | Daniel McGRAIN (Celtic) | Jean-Yves VALENTINI |
| (4) | James HOLTON (Manchester United) | Peter RAMSEIER |
| (4) | Derek JOHNSTONE (Rangers) | René HASLER |
| (1) | John CONNELLY (Everton) | Karl ODERMATT |
| (40) | William BREMNER (Leeds United) captain | Jakob KUHN |
| (15) | David HAY (Celtic) | Rolf BLÄTTLER |
| (12) | William MORGAN (Manchester United) | Walter BALMER |
| (9) | Kenneth DALGLISH (Celtic) | Fernand LUISIER |
| (2) | Derek PARLANE (Rangers) | Otto DEMARMELS |

Substitutions

| | | |
|---|---|---|
| (2) | Joseph JORDAN (Leeds United) | René-Pierre QUENTIN |
| | for Connelly 46 mins | for Blättler 25 mins |
| | | Üli WEGMANN |
| | | for Ramseier 46 mins |

Goals

| | |
|---|---|
| 0-1 | Mundschin (62 mins) |

## 365

| (Friendly) | Referee: Burns (England) |
|---|---|
| 30 June 1973 | Hampden Park, Glasgow (Att: 78,181) |

### SCOTLAND 0-1 BRAZIL — Half-time 0-1

| | | |
|---|---|---|
| (4) | Peter McCLOY (Rangers) | Emerson LEAO |
| (7) | William JARDINE (Rangers) | LUÍS Edmundo PEREIRA |
| (5) | Daniel McGRAIN (Celtic) | WILSON da Silva PIAZZA |
| (5) | James HOLTON (Manchester United) | José Maria Alvez ZÉ MARIA |
| (5) | Derek JOHNSTONE (Rangers) | MARCO ANTÓNIO Feliciano |
| (16) | David HAY (Celtic) | Tavares de Santana CLODOALDO |
| (41) | William BREMNER (Leeds United) captain | PAULO CÉSAR Lima |
| (13) | William MORGAN (Manchester United) | Roberto RIVELINO |
| (10) | Kenneth DALGLISH (Celtic) | Vaz Franco VALDOMIRO |
| (3) | Joseph JORDAN (Leeds United) | Jair Ventura Filho JAIRZINHO |
| (3) | Derek PARLANE (Rangers) | José Guimaraes DIRCEU |

Substitutions

| | | |
|---|---|---|
| (12) | George GRAHAM (Manchester United) | |
| | for Dalglish 70 mins | |

Goals

| | |
|---|---|
| 0-1 | Johnstone (33 mins o.g.) |

## 366

| (World Cup - Qualifier) | Referee: Oberg (Norway) |
|---|---|
| 26 September 1973 | Hampden Park, Glasgow (Att: 100,000) |

### SCOTLAND 2-1 CZECHOSLOVAKIA — Half-time 1-1

| | | |
|---|---|---|
| (4) | Alistair HUNTER (Celtic) | Ivo VIKTOR |
| (8) | William JARDINE (Rangers) | Ján PIVARNIK |
| (6) | Daniel McGRAIN (Celtic) | Václav SAMEK |
| (17) | David HAY (Celtic) | Ludevit ZLOCHA |
| (6) | James HOLTON (Manchester United) | Jaroslav BENDL |
| (1) | Thomas HUTCHISON (Coventry City) | Premysl BICOVSKY |
| (42) | William BREMNER (Leeds United) captain | Antonin PANENKA |
| (1) | George CONNELLY (Celtic) | Ladislav KUNA |
| (14) | William MORGAN (Manchester United) | Jozef ADAMEC |
| (11) | Kenneth DALGLISH (Celtic) | Zdenek NEHODA |
| (50) | Denis LAW (Manchester City) | Pavel STRATIL |

Substitutions

| | | |
|---|---|---|
| (4) | Joseph JORDAN (Leeds United) | Karol DOBIÁS |
| | for Dalglish 63 mins | for Kuna 20 mins |
| | | Ján CAPKOVIC |
| | | for Panenka 77 mins |

Goals

| | |
|---|---|
| 0-1 | Nehoda (33 mins) |
| Holton (40 mins) | 1-1 |
| Jordan (75 mins) | 2-1 |

Billy Bremner is chaired off by his team-mates after Scotland's victory over Czechoslovakia at Hampden in September 1973 put them into the World Cup finals in West Germany.

| 367 | |
|---|---|
| **(World Cup — Qualifier)** | **Referee: Biwersi (West Germany)** |
| 17 October 1973 | Tehelne Pole Stadion, Bratislava (Att: 15,000) |

## CZECHOSLOVAKIA 1-0 SCOTLAND — Half-time 1-0

| (2) | David HARVEY (Leeds United) | Ivo VIKTOR |
|---|---|---|
| (9) | William JARDINE (Rangers) | Ján PIVARNIK |
| (7) | Daniel McGRAIN (Celtic) | Václav SAMEK |
| (2) | Thomas FORSYTH (Rangers) | Karel DVORÁK |
| (1) | John BLACKLEY (Hibernian) | Vladimir HAGARA |
| (2) | Thomas HUTCHISON (Coventry City) | Premysl BICOVSKY |
| (18) | David HAY (Celtic) captain | Jaroslav POLLÁK |
| (15) | William MORGAN (Manchester United) | Miroslav GAJDUSEK |
| (12) | Kenneth DALGLISH (Celtic) | Frantisek VESELY |
| (5) | Joseph JORDAN (Leeds United) | Zdenek NEHODA |
| (51) | Denis LAW (Manchester City) | Ján CAPKOVIC |

### Substitutions

| (1) | Donald FORD (Hearts) | Jirí KLEMENT |
|---|---|---|
| | for Law 58 mins | for Vesely 61 mins |
| | | Antonín PANENKA |
| | | for Capkovic 78 mins |

### Goals

| 0-1 | Nehoda (17 mins pen) |
|---|---|

| 368 | |
|---|---|
| **(Friendly)** | **Referee: Taylor (England)** |
| 14 November 1973 | Hampden Park, Glasgow (Att: 58,235) |

## SCOTLAND 1-1 WEST GERMANY — Half-time 1-0

| (3) | David HARVEY (Leeds United) | Wolfgang KLEFF |
|---|---|---|
| (10) | William JARDINE (Rangers) | Hans-Hubert VOGTS |
| (8) | Daniel McGRAIN (Celtic) | Horst-Dieter HÖTTGES |
| (2) | George CONNELLY (Celtic) | Franz BECKENBAUER |
| (7) | James HOLTON (Manchester United) | Wolfgang WEBER |
| (3) | Thomas HUTCHISON (Coventry City) | Ulrich HOENESS |
| (43) | William BREMNER (Leeds United) captain | Günter NETZER |
| (2) | James SMITH (Newcastle United) | Herbert WIMMER |
| (16) | William MORGAN (Manchester United) | Jürgen GRABOWSKI |
| (13) | Kenneth DALGLISH (Celtic) | Siegfried HELD |
| (52) | Denis LAW (Manchester City) | Erwin KREMERS |

### Substitutions

| (11) | Peter LORIMER (Leeds United) | Josef MAIER |
|---|---|---|
| | for Smith 81 mins | for Kleff 46 mins |
| (6) | Joseph JORDAN (Leeds United) | Josef HEYNCKES |
| | for Law 87 mins | for Kremers 46 mins |
| | | Bernhard CULLMANN |
| | | for Wimmer 75 mins |
| | | Heinz FLOHE |
| | | for Held 75 mins |

### Goals

| Holton (7 mins) | 1-0 | |
|---|---|---|
| | 1-1 | Hoeness (80 mins) |

Scotland manager Willie Ormond is chaired around the pitch after qualification for the 1974 World Cup finals.

The Scotland squad before the 1974 World Cup finals. Back row (left to right): McQueen, Stewart, Harvey, Allan, Hutchison. Middle row: Willie Ormond (manager), Schaedler, McGrain, Smith, Hay, Jardine, Jordan, Blackley, Holton, Buchan, Lorimer. Front row: Allan (trainer), Ford, Dalglish, Bremner, Law, Morgan, Johnstone, Mckenzie (trainer).

# 1974

| P | W | D | L | F | A |
|---|---|---|---|---|---|
| 11 | 5 | 2 | 4 | 15 | 9 |

## 369
(Friendly)
27 March 1974

Referee: Schiller (Austria)
Wald Stadion, Frankfurt (Att: 62,000)

### WEST GERMANY 2-1 SCOTLAND — Half-time 2-0

| | | |
|---|---|---|
| (1) | Thomson ALLAN (Dundee) | Josef MAIER |
| (11) | William JARDINE (Rangers) | Hans-Hubert VOGTS |
| (1) | Erich SCHAEDLER (Hibernian) | Paul BREITNER |
| (10) | Martin BUCHAN (Manchester United) | Georg SCHWARZENBECK |
| (1) | Kenneth BURNS (Birmingham City) | Franz BECKENBAUER |
| (4) | Thomas HUTCHISON (Coventry City) | Bernhard CULLMANN |
| (16) | Patrick STANTON (Hibernian) | Ulrich HOENESS |
| (19) | David HAY (Celtic) captain | Herbert WIMMER |
| (17) | William MORGAN (Manchester United) | Jürgen GRABOWSKI |
| (14) | Kenneth DALGLISH (Celtic) | Gerhard MÜLLER |
| (53) | Denis LAW (Manchester City) | Dieter HERZOG |

Substitutions

| | | |
|---|---|---|
| (2) | Donald FORD (Hearts) for Law 59 mins | |
| (1) | Robert ROBINSON (Dundee) for Burns 59 mins | |

Goals

| | | |
|---|---|---|
| | 0-1 | Breitner (33 mins pen) |
| | 0-2 | Grabowski (35 mins) |
| Dalglish (77 mins) | 1-2 | |

## 370
(Home International Championship)
11 May 1974

Referee: Jones (Wales)
Hampden Park, Glasgow (Att: 53,775)

### SCOTLAND 0-1 NORTHERN IRELAND — Half-time 0-1

| | | |
|---|---|---|
| (4) | David HARVEY (Leeds United) | Patrick JENNINGS |
| (12) | William JARDINE (Rangers) | Patrick RICE |
| (11) | William DONACHIE (Manchester City) | Samuel NELSON |
| (11) | Martin BUCHAN (Manchester United) | William O'KANE |
| (8) | James HOLTON (Manchester United) | Allan HUNTER |
| (5) | Thomas HUTCHISON (Coventry City) | David CLEMENTS |
| (44) | William BREMNER (Leeds United) captain | Bryan HAMILTON |
| (20) | David HAY (Celtic) | Thomas CASSIDY |
| (18) | William MORGAN (Manchester United) | Samuel MORGAN |
| (15) | Kenneth DALGLISH (Celtic) | Samuel McILROY |
| (54) | Denis LAW (Manchester City) | Christopher McGRATH |

Substitutions

| | | |
|---|---|---|
| (3) | James SMITH (Newcastle United) for Donachie 46 mins | Thomas JACKSON for Hamilton 48 mins |
| (7) | Joseph JORDAN (Leeds United) for Law 65 mins | |

Goals

| | | |
|---|---|---|
| | 0-1 | Cassidy (40 mins) |

## 371
(Home International Championship)
14 May 1974

Referee: Wright (Northern Ireland)
Hampden Park, Glasgow (Att: 41,969)

### SCOTLAND 2-0 WALES — Half-time 2-0

| | | |
|---|---|---|
| (5) | David HARVEY (Leeds United) | Gareth SPRAKE |
| (13) | William JARDINE (Rangers) | Roderick THOMAS |
| (21) | David HAY (Celtic) | Malcolm PAGE |
| (12) | Martin BUCHAN (Manchester United) | John MAHONEY |
| (9) | James HOLTON (Manchester United) | John ROBERTS |
| (18) | James JOHNSTONE (Celtic) | David ROBERTS |
| (45) | William BREMNER (Leeds United) captain | Gilbert REECE |
| (3) | Donald FORD (Hearts) | Anthony VILLARS |
| (6) | Thomas HUTCHISON (Coventry City) | Terence YORATH |
| (16) | Kenneth DALGLISH (Celtic) | Leslie CARTWRIGHT |
| (8) | Joseph JORDAN (Leeds United) | Leighton JAMES |

Substitutions

| | | |
|---|---|---|
| (4) | James SMITH (Newcastle United) for Hutchison 6 mins | David SMALLMAN for Reece 46 mins |
| (9) | Daniel McGRAIN (Celtic) for Buchan 76 mins | |

Goals

| | | |
|---|---|---|
| Dalglish (24 mins) | 1-0 | |
| Jardine (44 mins pen) | 2-0 | |

## 372
(Home International Championship)
18 May 1974

Referee: Van der Kroft (Netherlands)
Hampden Park, Glasgow (Att: 94,487)

### SCOTLAND 2-0 ENGLAND — Half-time 2-0

| | | |
|---|---|---|
| (6) | David HARVEY (Leeds United) | Peter SHILTON |
| (14) | William JARDINE (Rangers) | David NISH |
| (10) | Daniel McGRAIN (Celtic) | Michael PEJIC |
| (2) | John BLACKLEY (Hibernian) | Emlyn HUGHES |
| (10) | James HOLTON (Manchester United) | Norman HUNTER |
| (19) | James JOHNSTONE (Celtic) | Colin TODD |
| (46) | William BREMNER (Leeds United) captain | Colin BELL |
| (22) | David HAY (Celtic) | Keith WELLER |
| (12) | Peter LORIMER (Leeds United) | Martin PETERS |
| (17) | Kenneth DALGLISH (Celtic) | Michael CHANNON |
| (9) | Joseph JORDAN (Leeds United) | Frank WORTHINGTON |

Substitutions

| | |
|---|---|
| | David WATSON for Hunter 46 mins |
| | Malcolm MACDONALD for Worthington 70 mins |

Goals

| | | |
|---|---|---|
| Jordan (5 mins) | 1-0 | |
| Todd (31 mins o.g.) | 2-0 | |

## 373
(Friendly)
1 June 1974

Referee: Ohmsen (West Germany)
Klokke Stadion, Brugge (Att: 7,769)

### BELGIUM 2-1 SCOTLAND — Half-time 1-1

| | | |
|---|---|---|
| (7) | David HARVEY (Leeds United) | Christian PIOT |
| (15) | William JARDINE (Rangers) | Gilbert VAN BINST |
| (11) | Daniel McGRAIN (Celtic) | Nicolas DEWALQUE |
| (3) | John BLACKLEY (Hibernian) | Erwin VAN DEN DAELE |
| (1) | Gordon McQUEEN (Leeds United) | Maurice MARTENS |
| (20) | James JOHNSTONE (Celtic) | Wilfried VAN MOER |
| (47) | William BREMNER (Leeds United) captain | Jan VERHEYEN |
| (23) | David HAY (Celtic) | Ivo VAN HERP |
| (13) | Peter LORIMER (Leeds United) | Roger HENROTAY |
| (18) | Kenneth DALGLISH (Celtic) | Paul VAN HIMST |
| (10) | Joseph JORDAN (Leeds United) | Raoul LAMBERT |

Substitutions

| | | |
|---|---|---|
| (19) | William MORGAN (Manchester United) for Johnstone 69 mins | Jean THISSEN for Dewalque 40 mins |
| (7) | Thomas HUTCHISON (Coventry City) for Dalglish 80 mins | Julien COOLS for Henrotay 68 mins |

Goals

| | | |
|---|---|---|
| | 0-1 | Henrotay (23 mins) |
| Johnstone (41 mins) | 1-1 | |
| | 1-2 | Lambert (83 mins pen) |

## 374
(Friendly)
6 June 1974

Referee: Axelsson (Sweden)
Ullevaal Stadion, Oslo (Att: 18,432)

### NORWAY 1-2 SCOTLAND — Half-time 1-0

| | | |
|---|---|---|
| (2) | Thomson ALLAN (Dundee) | Geir KARLSEN |
| (16) | William JARDINE (Rangers) | Øystein WORMDAHL |
| (12) | Daniel McGRAIN (Celtic) | Jan BIRKELUND |
| (13) | Martin BUCHAN (Manchester United) | Tore KORDAHL |
| (11) | James HOLTON (Manchester United) | Svein GRONDALEN |
| (21) | James JOHNSTONE (Celtic) | Harald BERG |
| (48) | William BREMNER (Leeds United) captain | Tor-Egil JOHANSEN |
| (24) | David HAY (Celtic) | Svein KVIA |
| (14) | Peter LORIMER (Leeds United) | Helge SKUSETH |
| (8) | Thomas HUTCHISON (Coventry City) | Tom LUND |
| (11) | Joseph JORDAN (Leeds United) | Harry HESTAD |

Substitutions

| | | |
|---|---|---|
| (19) | Kenneth DALGLISH (Celtic) for Johnstone 70 mins | Stein THUNBERG for Berg 70 mins |

Goals

| | | |
|---|---|---|
| | 0-1 | Lund (19 mins) |
| Jordan (74 mins) | 1-1 | |
| Dalglish (86 mins) | 2-1 | |

## 375

(World Cup — Final Tournament 1st Round)

Referee: Schulenburg (West Germany)

14 June 1974

Westfalen Stadion, Dortmund (Att: 25,800)

### ZAIRE 0-2 SCOTLAND — Half-time 0-2

| | | |
|---|---|---|
| (8) | David HARVEY (Leeds United) | KAZADI Mwamba |
| (17) | William JARDINE (Rangers) | MWEPU Ilunga |
| (13) | Daniel McGRAIN (Celtic) | MUKOMBO Mwanza |
| (4) | John BLACKLEY (Hibernian) | BWANGA Tshimen |
| (12) | James HOLTON (Manchester United) | LOBILO Boba |
| (15) | Peter LORIMER (Leeds United) | KILASU Massamba |
| (49) | William BREMNER (Leeds United) captain | MAYANGA Maku |
| (25) | David HAY (Celtic) | MANA Mambwene |
| (20) | Kenneth DALGLISH (Celtic) | NDAYE Mulamba |
| (12) | Joseph JORDAN (Leeds United) | KIDUMU Mantantu |
| (55) | Denis LAW (Manchester City) | KAKOKO Etepe |

Substitutions

| | | |
|---|---|---|
| (9) | Thomas HUTCHISON (Coventry City) | KEMBO Uba |
| | for Dalglish 75 mins | for Mayanga 64 mins |
| | | KIBONGE Mafu |
| | | for Kidumu 75 mins |

Goals

| | |
|---|---|
| Lorimer (26 mins) | 1-0 |
| Jordan (33 mins) | 2-0 |

## 376

(World Cup — Final Tournament 1st Round)

Referee: Van Gemert (Netherlands)

18 June 1974

Wald Stadion, Frankfurt (Att: 60,000)

### BRAZIL 0-0 SCOTLAND

| | | |
|---|---|---|
| (9) | David HARVEY (Leeds United) | Emerson LEAO |
| (18) | William JARDINE (Rangers) | Manoel Rezende NELINHO |
| (14) | Daniel McGRAIN (Celtic) | LUÍS Edmundo PEREIRA |
| (14) | Martin BUCHAN (Manchester United) | Mario MARINHO PERES |
| (13) | James HOLTON (Manchester United) | Francisco des Chagas MARINHO |
| (16) | Peter LORIMER (Leeds United) | WILSON da Silva PIAZZA |
| (50) | William BREMNER (Leeds United) captain | Roberto RIVELINO |
| (26) | David HAY (Celtic) | PAULO CÉSAR Lima |
| (20) | William MORGAN (Manchester United) | Jair Ventura Filho JAIRZINHO |
| (21) | Kenneth DALGLISH (Celtic) | Sebastiao Miranda MIRANDINHA |
| (13) | Joseph JORDAN (Leeds United) | Joao Leiva Campos LEIVINHA |

Substitutions

| | | |
|---|---|---|
| | | Paulo César CARPEGIANI |
| | | for Leivinha 65 mins |

## 377

(World Cup — Final Tournament 1st Round)  Referee: Archundia (Mexico)

22 June 1974  Wald Stadion, Frankfurt (Att: 54,000)

### YUGOSLAVIA 1-1 SCOTLAND — Half-time 0-0

| | | |
|---|---|---|
| (10) | David HARVEY (Leeds United) | Enver MARIC |
| (19) | William JARDINE (Rangers) | Ivan BULJAN |
| (15) | Daniel McGRAIN (Celtic) | Enver HADZIABDIC |
| (15) | Martin BUCHAN (Manchester United) | Branko OBLAK |
| (14) | James HOLTON (Manchester United) | Josip KATALINSKI |
| (17) | Peter LORIMER (Leeds United) | Vladislav BOGICEVIC |
| (51) | William BREMNER (Leeds United) captain | Ilija PETKOVIC |
| (27) | David HAY (Celtic) | Jovan ACIMOVIC |
| (21) | William MORGAN (Manchester United) | Dusan BAJEVIC |
| (22) | Kenneth DALGLISH (Celtic) | Ivan SURJAK |
| (14) | Joseph JORDAN (Leeds United) | Dragan DZAJIC |

Substitutions

| | | |
|---|---|---|
| (10) | Thomas HUTCHISON (Coventry City) | Stanislav KARASI |
| | for Dalglish 65 mins | for Bajevic 72 mins |

Goals

| | | |
|---|---|---|
| | 0-1 | Karasi (83 mins) |
| Jordan (89 mins) | 1-1 | |

## 378

(Friendly)  Referee: Taylor (England)

30 October 1974  Hampden Park, Glasgow (Att: 39,445)

### SCOTLAND 3-0 EAST GERMANY — Half-time 2-0

| | | |
|---|---|---|
| (11) | David HARVEY (Leeds United) | Jürgen CROY |
| (20) | William JARDINE (Rangers) captain | Bernhard BRANSCH |
| (6) | Alexander FORSYTH (Manchester United) | Gerhard KISCHE |
| (16) | Martin BUCHAN (Manchester United) | Konrad WEISE |
| (15) | James HOLTON (Manchester United) | Siegmar WÄTZLICH |
| (22) | James JOHNSTONE (Celtic) | Lothar KURBJUWEIT |
| (1) | Graeme SOUNESS (Middlesbrough) | Reinhard HÄFNER |
| (11) | Thomas HUTCHISON (Coventry City) | Reinhard LAUCK |
| (1) | John DEANS (Celtic) | Hans-Jürgen KREISCHE |
| (23) | Kenneth DALGLISH (Celtic) | Jürgen SPARWASSER |
| (15) | Joseph JORDAN (Leeds United) | Martin HOFFMANN |

Substitutions

| | | |
|---|---|---|
| (2) | Kenneth BURNS (Birmingham City) | Manfred ZAPF |
| | for Holton 12 mins | for Bransch 38 mins |
| (6) | Derek JOHNSTONE (Rangers) | Harald IRMSCHER |
| | for Dalglish 86 mins | for Kurbjuweit 56 mins |
| | | Joachim STREICH |
| | | for Lauck 73 mins |

Goals

| | |
|---|---|
| Hutchison (34 mins pen) | 1-0 |
| Burns (36 mins) | 2-0 |
| Dalglish (75 mins) | 3-0 |

## 379

(European Championship — Qualifier)  Referee: Linemayr (Austria)

20 November 1974  Hampden Park, Glasgow (Att: 94,331)

### SCOTLAND 1-2 SPAIN — Half-time 1-1

| | | |
|---|---|---|
| (12) | David HARVEY (Leeds United) | José IRIBAR |
| (21) | William JARDINE (Rangers) | Angel CASTELLANOS |
| (7) | Alexander FORSYTH (Manchester United) | Gregorio BENITO |
| (3) | Kenneth BURNS (Birmingham City) | José CAPON |
| (2) | Gordon McQUEEN (Leeds United) | Miguel BIANQUETI |
| (23) | James JOHNSTONE (Celtic) | Enrique COSTAS |
| (52) | William BREMNER (Leeds United) captain | Roberto MARTÍNEZ |
| (2) | Graeme SOUNESS (Middlesbrough) | Angel VILLAR |
| (12) | Thomas HUTCHISON (Coventry City) | Carlos REXACH |
| (2) | John DEANS (Celtic) | Javier PLANAS |
| (16) | Joseph JORDAN (Leeds United) | Enrique CASTRO |

Substitutions

| | | |
|---|---|---|
| (24) | Kenneth DALGLISH (Celtic) | Juan SOL |
| | for Hutchison 65 mins | for Bianqueti 75 mins |
| (18) | Peter LORIMER (Leeds United) | |
| | for Deans 65 mins | |

Goals

| | | |
|---|---|---|
| Bremner (11 mins) | 1-0 | |
| | 1-1 | Castro (36 mins) |
| | 1-2 | Castro (61 mins) |

## 1975

| P | W | D | L | F | A |
|---|---|---|---|---|---|
| 10 | 4 | 5 | 1 | 15 | 12 |

## 380

(European Championship — Qualifier)  Referee: Delcourt (Belgium)

5 February 1975  Estadio Luis Casanova, Valencia (Att: 40,952)

### SPAIN 1-1 SCOTLAND — Half-time 0-1

| | | |
|---|---|---|
| (13) | David HARVEY (Leeds United) | José IRIBAR |
| (22) | William JARDINE (Rangers) | Gregorio BENITO |
| (16) | Daniel McGRAIN (Celtic) | José CAMACHO |
| (17) | Martin BUCHAN (Manchester United) | Juan SOL |
| (3) | Gordon McQUEEN (Leeds United) | Enrique COSTAS |
| (15) | Charles COOKE (Chelsea) | José CLARAMUNT |
| (4) | Kenneth BURNS (Birmingham City) | Angel VILLAR |
| (53) | William BREMNER (Leeds United) captain | Juan ASENSI |
| (13) | Thomas HUTCHISON (Coventry City) | Carlos REXACH |
| (25) | Kenneth DALGLISH (Celtic) | José GÁRATE |
| (17) | Joseph JORDAN (Leeds United) | Enrique CASTRO |

Substitutions

| | | |
|---|---|---|
| (4) | Derek PARLANE (Rangers) | Alfredo MEJIDO |
| | for Jordan 66 mins | for Gárate 66 mins |
| (1) | Paul WILSON (Celtic) | Miguel BIANQUETI |
| | for Burns 79 mins | for Costas 70 mins |

Goals

| | | |
|---|---|---|
| Jordan (2 mins) | 1-0 | |
| | 1-1 | Mejido (67 mins) |

## 381

(Friendly)
16 April 1975

Referee: Thima (Norway)
Ullevi Stadion, Gothenburg (Att: 15,574)

### SWEDEN 1-1 SCOTLAND     Half-time 1-0

| (1) | Stewart KENNEDY (Rangers) | Göran HAGBERG |
| (23) | William JARDINE (Rangers) captain | Björn ANDERSSON |
| (17) | Daniel McGRAIN (Celtic) | Kent KARLSSON |
| (5) | Francis MUNRO (Wolverhampton Wanderers) | Björn NORDQVIST |
| (1) | Colin JACKSON (Rangers) | Jörgen AUGUSTSSON |
| (2) | Robert ROBINSON (Dundee) | Eine FREDRIKSSON |
| (3) | Graeme SOUNESS (Middlesbrough) | Conny TORSTENSSON |
| (26) | Kenneth DALGLISH (Celtic) | Ralf EDSTRÖM |
| (11) | Luigi MACARI (Manchester United) | Thomas AHLSTRÖM |
| (5) | Derek PARLANE (Rangers) | Jan MATSSON |
| (1) | Edward MACDOUGALL (Norwich City) | Thomas SJÖBERG |

Substitutions

| (7) | Derek JOHNSTONE (Rangers) | Roy ANDERSSON |
| | for Macari 54 mins | for Nordqvist 46 mins |
| (1) | William HUGHES (Sunderland) | Anders LINDEROTH |
| | for Souness 54 mins | for Edström 46 mins |
| | | Thomas NORDAHL |
| | | for Ahlström 65 mins |

Goals

| | 0-1 | Sjöberg (44 mins) |
| MacDougall (86 mins) | 1-1 | |

---

## 382

(Friendly)
13 May 1975

Referee: Mathewson (England)
Hampden Park, Glasgow (Att: 34,307)

### SCOTLAND 1-0 PORTUGAL     Half-time 1-0

| (2) | Stewart KENNEDY (Rangers) | Vitor DAMAS |
| (24) | William JARDINE (Rangers) captain | ARTUR Correia |
| (18) | Daniel McGRAIN (Celtic) | Humberto COELHO |
| (18) | Martin BUCHAN (Manchester United) | Carlos ALHINHO |
| (4) | Gordon McQUEEN (Leeds United) | Antonio BARROS |
| (16) | Charles COOKE (Chelsea) | OCTÁVIO Machado |
| (1) | Bruce RIOCH (Derby County) | Samuel FRAGUITO |
| (27) | Kenneth DALGLISH (Celtic) | Antonio OLIVEIRA |
| (14) | Thomas HUTCHISON (Coventry City) | Mario MOINHOS |
| (6) | Derek PARLANE (Rangers) | Joao ALVES |
| (2) | Edward MACDOUGALL (Norwich City) | Tamagnini NENÉ |

Substitutions

| (2) | Colin JACKSON (Rangers) | Vitor PEREIRA |
| | for Buchan 27 mins | for Alves 66 mins |
| (12) | Luigi MACARI (Manchester United) | Fernando GOMES |
| | for Cooke 77 mins | for Nené 66 mins |
| (1) | Arthur DUNCAN (Hibernian) | ROMEU da Silva |
| | for Rioch 77 mins | for Moinhos 66 mins |

Goals

| Artur (43 mins o.g.) | 1-0 | |

---

## 383

(Home International Championship)
17 May 1975

Referee: Wright (Northern Ireland)
Ninian Park, Cardiff (Att: 23,509)

### WALES 2-2 SCOTLAND     Half-time 2-0

| (3) | Stewart KENNEDY (Rangers) | William DAVIES |
| (25) | William JARDINE (Rangers) captain | Roderick THOMAS |
| (19) | Daniel McGRAIN (Celtic) | Malcolm PAGE |
| (3) | Colin JACKSON (Rangers) | Terence YORATH |
| (5) | Gordon McQUEEN (Leeds United) | John ROBERTS |
| (2) | Bruce RIOCH (Derby County) | Gilbert REECE |
| (13) | Luigi MACARI (Manchester United) | John MAHONEY |
| (2) | Arthur DUNCAN (Hibernian) | Brian FLYNN |
| (28) | Kenneth DALGLISH (Celtic) | Leighton PHILLIPS |
| (7) | Derek PARLANE (Rangers) | John TOSHACK |
| (3) | Edward MACDOUGALL (Norwich City) | Leighton JAMES |

Substitutions

| (6) | Francis MUNRO (Wolverhampton Wanderers) | |
| | for Jackson 77 mins | |

Goals

| | 0-1 | Toshack (28 mins) |
| | 0-2 | Flynn (35 mins) |
| Jackson (54 mins) | 1-2 | |
| Rioch (62 mins) | 2-2 | |

---

## 384

(Home International Championship)
20 May 1975

Referee: Partridge (England)
Hampden Park, Glasgow (Att: 64,696)

### SCOTLAND 3-0 NORTHERN IRELAND     Half-time 2-0

| (4) | Stewart KENNEDY (Rangers) | Patrick JENNINGS |
| (26) | William JARDINE (Rangers) captain | Patrick RICE |
| (20) | Daniel McGRAIN (Celtic) | William O'KANE |
| (7) | Francis MUNRO (Wolverhampton Wanderers) | Christopher NICHOLL |
| (6) | Gordon McQUEEN (Leeds United) | Allan HUNTER |
| (3) | Robert ROBINSON (Dundee) | David CLEMENTS |
| (3) | Bruce RIOCH (Derby County) | Thomas FINNEY |
| (29) | Kenneth DALGLISH (Celtic) | Martin O'NEILL |
| (3) | Arthur DUNCAN (Hibernian) | Derek SPENCE |
| (8) | Derek PARLANE (Rangers) | Samuel McILROY |
| (4) | Edward MACDOUGALL (Norwich City) | Thomas JACKSON |

Substitutions

| (1) | Alfred CONN (Tottenham Hotspur) | Roland BLAIR |
| | for Robinson 76 mins | for Hunter 83 mins |
| (8) | Alexander FORSYTH (Manchester United) | Trevor ANDERSON |
| | for Jardine 89 mins | for O'Neill 87 mins |

Goals

| MacDougall (15 mins) | 1-0 | |
| Dalglish (21 mins) | 2-0 | |
| Parlane (80 mins) | 3-0 | |

---

## 385

(Home International Championship)
24 May 1975

Referee: Glockner (East Germany)
Wembley Stadium, London (Att: 98,241)

### ENGLAND 5-1 SCOTLAND     Half-time 3-1

| (5) | Stewart KENNEDY (Rangers) | Raymond CLEMENCE |
| (27) | William JARDINE (Rangers) captain | Steven WHITWORTH |
| (21) | Daniel McGRAIN (Celtic) | Colin TODD |
| (8) | Francis MUNRO (Wolverhampton Wanderers) | Kevin BEATTIE |
| (7) | Gordon McQUEEN (Leeds United) | David WATSON |
| (2) | Alfred CONN (Tottenham Hotspur) | Alan BALL |
| (4) | Bruce RIOCH (Derby County) | Colin BELL |
| (30) | Kenneth DALGLISH (Celtic) | Michael CHANNON |
| (4) | Arthur DUNCAN (Hibernian) | Kevin KEEGAN |
| (9) | Derek PARLANE (Rangers) | David JOHNSON |
| (5) | Edward MACDOUGALL (Norwich City) | Gerald FRANCIS |

Substitutions

| (15) | Thomas HUTCHISON (Coventry City) | David THOMAS |
| | for Duncan 61 mins | for Keegan 85 mins |
| (14) | Luigi MACARI (Manchester United) | |
| | for MacDougall 71 mins | |

Goals

| | 0-1 | Francis (6 mins) |
| | 0-2 | Beattie (8 mins) |
| | 0-3 | Bell (40 mins) |
| Rioch (41 mins pen) | 1-3 | |
| | 1-4 | Francis (65 mins) |
| | 1-5 | Johnson (75 mins) |

---

## 386

(European Championship — Qualifier)
1 June 1975

Referee: Gilek (Turkey)
23 August Stadionul, Bucharest (Att: 52,203)

### ROMANIA 1-1 SCOTLAND     Half-time 1-0

| (1) | James BROWN (Sheffield United) | Necula RADUCANU |
| (22) | Daniel McGRAIN (Celtic) | Florin CHERAN |
| (9) | Alexander FORSYTH (Manchester United) | Gabriel SANDU |
| (9) | Francis MUNRO (Wolverhampton Wanderers) | Alexandru SATMAREANU |
| (8) | Gordon McQUEEN (Leeds United) captain | Teodor ANGHELINI |
| (1) | William MILLER (Aberdeen) | Ioan DUMITRU |
| (5) | Bruce RIOCH (Derby County) | Cornel DINU |
| (31) | Kenneth DALGLISH (Celtic) | Nicolae DOBRIN |
| (5) | Arthur DUNCAN (Hibernian) | Zoltan CRISAN |
| (15) | Luigi MACARI (Manchester United) | Dudu GEORGESCU |
| (10) | Derek PARLANE (Rangers) | Mircea LUCESCU |

Substitutions

| (16) | Thomas HUTCHISON (Coventry City) | Ilie BALACI |
| | for Rioch 67 mins | for Georgescu 37 mins |
| (4) | Robert ROBINSON (Dundee) | Attila KUN |
| | for Macari 67 mins | for Dobrin 82 mins |

Goals

| | 0-1 | Georgescu (22 mins) |
| McQueen (89 mins) | 1-1 | |

## 387

(European Championship — Qualifier)
3 September 1975

Referee: Nyhus (Norway)
Idraetsparken, Copenhagen (Att: 40,300)

### DENMARK 0-1 SCOTLAND — Half-time 0-0

| | | |
|---|---|---|
| (14) | David HARVEY (Leeds United) | Birger JENSEN |
| (23) | Daniel McGRAIN (Celtic) | Flemming MORTENSEN |
| (10) | Alexander FORSYTH (Manchester United) | Henning MUNK-JENSEN |
| (19) | Martin BUCHAN (Manchester United) | Lars LARSEN |
| (9) | Gordon McQUEEN (Leeds United) | Niels HANSEN |
| (19) | Peter LORIMER (Leeds United) | Ove BJERG |
| (54) | William BREMNER (Leeds United) captain | Ole BJORNMOSE |
| (6) | Bruce RIOCH (Derby County) | Benny NIELSEN |
| (17) | Thomas HUTCHISON (Coventry City) | Allan SIMONSEN |
| (32) | Kenneth DALGLISH (Celtic) | Henning JENSEN |
| (3) | Joseph HARPER (Hibernian) | Ulrik LE FEVRE |

Substitutions

| | | |
|---|---|---|
| (6) | Arthur DUNCAN (Hibernian) | |
| | for Hutchison 71 mins | |

Goals

Harper (51 mins) — 1-0


## 388

(European Championship — Qualifier)
29 October 1975

Referee: Nyhus (Norway)
Hampden Park, Glasgow (Att: 48,021)

### SCOTLAND 3-1 DENMARK — Half-time 0-1

| | | |
|---|---|---|
| (15) | David HARVEY (Leeds United) | Benno LARSEN |
| (24) | Daniel McGRAIN (Celtic) | John ANDERSEN |
| (1) | Stewart HOUSTON (Manchester United) | Henning MUNK-JENSEN |
| (44) | John GREIG (Rangers) captain | Lars LARSEN |
| (4) | Colin JACKSON (Rangers) | Niels HANSEN |
| (20) | Peter LORIMER (Leeds United) | Johnny HANSEN |
| (7) | Richard HARTFORD (Manchester City) | Heino HANSEN |
| (7) | Bruce RIOCH (Derby County) | Kristen NYGAARD |
| (8) | Archibald GEMMILL (Derby County) | Niels SORENSEN |
| (33) | Kenneth DALGLISH (Celtic) | Lars BASTRUP |
| (6) | Edward MACDOUGALL (Norwich City) | Jens KOLDING |

Substitutions

| | | |
|---|---|---|
| (11) | Derek PARLANE (Rangers) | Frank NIELSEN |
| | for MacDougall 85 mins | for N. Hansen 68 mins |

Goals

| | | |
|---|---|---|
| | 0-1 | Bastrup (21 mins) |
| Dalglish (48 mins) | 1-1 | |
| Rioch (54 mins) | 2-1 | |
| MacDougall (61 mins) | 3-1 | |


## 389

(European Championship — Qualifier)
17 December 1975

Referee: Prokop (East Germany)
Hampden Park, Glasgow (Att: 11,375)

### SCOTLAND 1-1 ROMANIA — Half-time 1-0

| | | |
|---|---|---|
| (6) | James CRUICKSHANK (Hearts) | Necula RADUCANU |
| (7) | John BROWNLIE (Hibernian) | Florin CHERAN |
| (12) | William DONACHIE (Manchester City) | Gabriel SANDU |
| (20) | Martin BUCHAN (Manchester United) captain | Alexandru SATMAREANU |
| (5) | Colin JACKSON (Rangers) | Teodor ANGHELINI |
| (1) | John DOYLE (Ayr United) | Mihai ROMILA |
| (8) | Richard HARTFORD (Manchester City) | Cornel DINU |
| (8) | Bruce RIOCH (Derby County) | Ladislau BÖLÖNI |
| (9) | Archibald GEMMILL (Derby County) | Mircea LUCESCU |
| (34) | Kenneth DALGLISH (Celtic) | Dudu GEORGESCU |
| (1) | Andrew GRAY (Aston Villa) | Anghel IORDANESCU |

Substitutions

| | | |
|---|---|---|
| (21) | Peter LORIMER (Leeds United) | Zoltan CRISAN |
| | for Doyle 73 mins | for Lucescu 60 mins |
| (7) | Edward MACDOUGALL (Norwich City) | |
| | for Dalglish 73 mins | |

Goals

| | | |
|---|---|---|
| Rioch (39 mins) | 1-0 | |
| | 1-1 | Crisan (74 mins) |


# 1976

| P | W | D | L | F | A |
|---|---|---|---|---|---|
| 7 | 6 | 0 | 1 | 16 | 4 |


## 390

(Friendly)
7 April 1976

Referee: Partridge (England)
Hampden Park, Glasgow (Att: 15,531)

### SCOTLAND 1-0 SWITZERLAND — Half-time 1-0

| | | |
|---|---|---|
| (1) | Alan ROUGH (Partick Thistle) | Erich BURGENER |
| (25) | Daniel McGRAIN (Celtic) | Gilbert GUYOT |
| (1) | Francis GRAY (Leeds United) | Jörg STÖHLER |
| (3) | Thomas FORSYTH (Rangers) captain | Luciano BIZZINI |
| (5) | John BLACKLEY (Hibernian) | Pius FISCHBACH |
| (1) | Thomas CRAIG (Newcastle United) | René HASLER |
| (1) | Alexander MACDONALD (Rangers) | René BOTTERON |
| (35) | Kenneth DALGLISH (Celtic) | Peter RISI |
| (1) | William PETTIGREW (Motherwell) | Rudolf ELSENER |
| (2) | Andrew GRAY (Aston Villa) | Kurt MÜLLER |
| (8) | Derek JOHNSTONE (Rangers) | Daniel JEANDUPEUX |

Substitutions

| | | |
|---|---|---|
| (1) | Robert McKEAN (Rangers) | Claude ANDREY |
| | for Pettigrew 46 mins | for Hasler 53 mins |
| (1) | Desmond BREMNER (Hibernian) | Marc SCHNYDER |
| | for Dalglish 64 mins | for Elsener 64 mins |

Goals

Pettigrew (2 mins) — 1-0


## 391

(Home International Championship)
6 May 1976

Referee: Wright (Northern Ireland)
Hampden Park, Glasgow (Att: 35,000)

### SCOTLAND 3-1 WALES — Half-time 2-0

| | | |
|---|---|---|
| (2) | Alan ROUGH (Partick Thistle) | Brian LLOYD |
| (26) | Daniel McGRAIN (Celtic) | David JONES |
| (13) | William DONACHIE (Manchester City) | Joseph JONES |
| (4) | Thomas FORSYTH (Rangers) | David ROBERTS |
| (6) | Colin JACKSON (Rangers) | John ROBERTS |
| (10) | Archibald GEMMILL (Derby County) captain | Carl HARRIS |
| (1) | Donald MASSON (Queen's Park Rangers) | Terence YORATH |
| (9) | Bruce RIOCH (Derby County) | Arfon GRIFFITHS |
| (9) | Edwin GRAY (Leeds United) | Alan CURTIS |
| (2) | William PETTIGREW (Motherwell) | Peter O'SULLIVAN |
| (18) | Joseph JORDAN (Leeds United) | Leighton JAMES |

Substitutions

| | | |
|---|---|---|
| | | Leslie CARTWRIGHT |
| | | for Harris 46 mins |

Goals

| | | |
|---|---|---|
| Pettigrew (38 mins) | 1-0 | |
| Rioch (44 mins) | 2-0 | |
| | 2-1 | Griffiths (61 mins pen) |
| Gray (69 mins) | 3-1 | |


## 392

(Home International Championship)
8 May 1976

Referee: Reynolds (Wales)
Hampden Park, Glasgow (Att: 49,897)

### SCOTLAND 3-0 NORTHERN IRELAND — Half-time 1-0

| | | |
|---|---|---|
| (3) | Alan ROUGH (Partick Thistle) | Patrick JENNINGS |
| (27) | Daniel McGRAIN (Celtic) | Patrick RICE |
| (14) | William DONACHIE (Manchester City) | Peter SCOTT |
| (5) | Thomas FORSYTH (Rangers) | Christopher NICHOLL |
| (7) | Colin JACKSON (Rangers) | Allan HUNTER |
| (11) | Archibald GEMMILL (Derby County) captain | Thomas FINNEY |
| (2) | Donald MASSON (Queen's Park Rangers) | Bryan HAMILTON |
| (10) | Bruce RIOCH (Derby County) | Patrick SHARKEY |
| (36) | Kenneth DALGLISH (Celtic) | Thomas CASSIDY |
| (3) | William PETTIGREW (Motherwell) | Samuel McILROY |
| (19) | Joseph JORDAN (Leeds United) | Samuel MORGAN |

Substitutions

| | | |
|---|---|---|
| (9) | Richard HARTFORD (Manchester City) | David McCREERY |
| | for Rioch 56 mins | for Sharkey 61 mins |
| (9) | Derek JOHNSTONE (Rangers) | Derek SPENCE |
| | for Pettigrew 66 mins | for Morgan 85 mins |

Goals

| | | |
|---|---|---|
| Gemmill (23 mins) | 1-0 | |
| Masson (47 mins) | 2-0 | |
| Dalglish (52 mins) | 3-0 | |

**393**

(Home International Championship)
15 May 1976

Referee: Palotai (Hungary)
Hampden Park, Glasgow (Att: 85,165)

### SCOTLAND 2-1 ENGLAND — Half-time 1-1

| (4) | Alan ROUGH (Partick Thistle) | Raymond CLEMENCE |
| (28) | Daniel McGRAIN (Celtic) | Colin TODD |
| (15) | William DONACHIE (Manchester City) | Michael MILLS |
| (6) | Thomas FORSYTH (Rangers) | Philip THOMPSON |
| (8) | Colin JACKSON (Rangers) | Roy McFARLAND |
| (12) | Archibald GEMMILL (Derby County) captain | Raymond KENNEDY |
| (3) | Donald MASSON (Queen's Park Rangers) | Kevin KEEGAN |
| (11) | Bruce RIOCH (Derby County) | Gerald FRANCIS |
| (10) | Edwin GRAY (Leeds United) | Peter TAYLOR |
| (37) | Kenneth DALGLISH (Celtic) | Michael CHANNON |
| (20) | Joseph JORDAN (Leeds United) | Stuart PEARSON |

Substitutions

| (10) | Derek JOHNSTONE (Rangers) | Trevor CHERRY |
| | for Gray 79 mins | for Pearson 46 mins |
| | | Michael DOYLE |
| | | for McFarland 70 mins |

Goals

| | 0-1 | Channon (11 mins) |
| Masson (18 mins) | 1-1 | |
| Dalglish (49 mins) | 2-1 | |

---

**394**

(Friendly)
8 September 1976

Referee: Kew (England)
Hampden Park, Glasgow (Att: 16,338)

### SCOTLAND 6-0 FINLAND — Half-time 4-0

| (5) | Alan ROUGH (Partick Thistle) | Pertti ALAJA |
| (29) | Daniel McGRAIN (Celtic) | Teppo HEIKKINEN |
| (16) | William DONACHIE (Manchester City) | Erkki VIHTILÄ |
| (7) | Thomas FORSYTH (Rangers) | Ari MÄKYNEN |
| (21) | Martin BUCHAN (Manchester United) | Esko RANTA |
| (13) | Archibald GEMMILL (Derby County) captain | Pertti JANTUNEN |
| (4) | Donald MASSON (Queen's Park Rangers) | Jouko SUOMALAINEN |
| (12) | Bruce RIOCH (Derby County) | Miikka TOIVOLA |
| (11) | Edwin GRAY (Leeds United) | Olavi RISSANEN |
| (38) | Kenneth DALGLISH (Celtic) | Juha DAHLLUND |
| (3) | Andrew GRAY (Aston Villa) | Matti PAATELAINEN |

Substitutions

| (16) | David HARVEY (Leeds United) | Jyrki NIEMINEN |
| | for Rough 46 mins | for Paatelainen 39 mins |
| | | Göran ENCKELMAN |
| | | for Alaja 46 mins |
| | | Matti AHONEN |
| | | for Heikkinen 75 mins |

Goals

| Rioch (7 mins) | 1-0 |
| Masson (16 mins pen) | 2-0 |
| Dalglish (23 mins) | 3-0 |
| A. Gray (44 mins) | 4-0 |
| E. Gray (68 mins) | 5-0 |
| A. Gray (80 mins) | 6-0 |

---

**395**

(World Cup — Qualifier)
13 October 1976

Referee: Michelotti (Italy)
Sparta Stadion, Prague (Att: 38,000)

### CZECHOSLOVAKIA 2-0 SCOTLAND — Half-time 0-0

| (6) | Alan ROUGH (Partick Thistle) | Alexander VENCEL |
| (30) | Daniel McGRAIN (Celtic) | Pavel BIROS |
| (17) | William DONACHIE (Manchester City) | Jozef CAPKOVIC |
| (22) | Martin BUCHAN (Manchester United) | Anton ONDRUS |
| (10) | Gordon McQUEEN (Leeds United) | Koloman GÖGH |
| (14) | Archibald GEMMILL (Derby County) captain | Jaroslav POLLÁK |
| (5) | Donald MASSON (Queen's Park Rangers) | Karol DOBIÁS |
| (13) | Bruce RIOCH (Derby County) | Antonín PANENKA |
| (39) | Kenneth DALGLISH (Celtic) | Marián MASNY |
| (21) | Joseph JORDAN (Leeds United) | Zdenek NEHODA |
| (4) | Andrew GRAY (Aston Villa) | Ladislav PETRÁS |

Substitutions

| (5) | Kenneth BURNS (Birmingham City) | Ján KOZÁK |
| | for Dalglish 56 mins | for Gögh 13 mins |
| (10) | Richard HARTFORD (Manchester City) | Ladislav JURKEMIK |
| | for Masson 68 mins | for Capkovic 68 mins |

Goals

| | 0-1 | Panenka (46 mins) |
| | 0-2 | Petrás (48 mins) |

---

**396**

(World Cup — Qualifier)
17 November 1976

Referee: Biwersi (West Germany)
Hampden Park, Glasgow (Att: 63,233)

### SCOTLAND 1-0 WALES — Half-time 1-0

| (7) | Alan ROUGH (Partick Thistle) | William DAVIES |
| (31) | Daniel McGRAIN (Celtic) | Malcolm PAGE |
| (18) | William DONACHIE (Manchester City) | Joseph JONES |
| (6) | John BLACKLEY (Hibernian) | Leighton PHILLIPS |
| (11) | Gordon McQUEEN (Leeds United) | Ian EVANS |
| (15) | Archibald GEMMILL (Derby County) captain | Arfon GRIFFITHS |
| (6) | Kenneth BURNS (Birmingham City) | Terence YORATH |
| (14) | Bruce RIOCH (Derby County) | Brian FLYNN |
| (12) | Edwin GRAY (Leeds United) | Michael THOMAS |
| (40) | Kenneth DALGLISH (Celtic) | John TOSHACK |
| (22) | Joseph JORDAN (Leeds United) | Leighton JAMES |

Substitutions

| (11) | Richard HARTFORD (Manchester City) | Alan CURTIS |
| | for Rioch 67 mins | for James 74 mins |
| (4) | William PETTIGREW (Motherwell) | |
| | for Gray 84 mins | |

Goals

| Evans (15 mins o.g.) | 1-0 |

---

# 1977

| P | W | D | L | F | A |
|---|---|---|---|---|---|
| 10 | 6 | 2 | 2 | 18 | 9 |

**397**

(Friendly)
27 April 1977

Referee: Taylor (England)
Hampden Park, Glasgow (Att: 22,659)

### SCOTLAND 3-1 SWEDEN — Half-time 1-0

| (8) | Alan ROUGH (Partick Thistle) | Ronnie HELLSTRÖM |
| (32) | Daniel McGRAIN (Celtic) | Magnus ANDERSSON |
| (19) | William DONACHIE (Manchester City) | Björn ANDERSSON |
| (8) | Thomas FORSYTH (Rangers) | Björn NORDQVIST |
| (7) | John BLACKLEY (Hibernian) | Roy ANDERSSON |
| (1) | Ronald GLAVIN (Celtic) | Lennart LARSSON |
| (7) | Kenneth BURNS (Birmingham City) | Conny TORSTENSSON |
| (12) | Richard HARTFORD (Manchester City) | Bo BÖRJESSON |
| (10) | William JOHNSTON (West Bromwich Albion) | Sigvard JOHANSSON |
| (41) | Kenneth DALGLISH (Celtic) captain | Benny WENDT |
| (5) | William PETTIGREW (Motherwell) | Thomas SJÖBERG |

Substitutions

| (28) | William JARDINE (Rangers) | Hasse BORG |
| | for Glavin 58 mins | for Torstensson 55 mins |
| (1) | David NAREY (Dundee United) | Anders LJUNGBERG |
| | for Blackley 76 mins | for Börjesson 65 mins |
| (1) | Joseph CRAIG (Celtic) | Olle NORDIN |
| | for Burns 76 mins | for Johansson 71 mins |

Goals

| Hellström (30 mins o.g.) | 1-0 | |
| | 1-1 | Wendt (51 mins) |
| Dalglish (56 mins) | 2-1 | |
| Craig (79 mins) | 3-1 | |

Kenny Burns heads clear in the 3-1 win over Sweden at Hampden in April 1977.

## 398

(Home International Championship)
28 May 1977

Referee: Moffatt (Northern Ireland)
The Racecourse, Wrexham (Att: 14,469)

### WALES 0-0 SCOTLAND

| | | |
|---|---|---|
| (9) | Alan ROUGH (Partick Thistle) | William DAVIES |
| (33) | Daniel McGRAIN (Celtic) | Roderick THOMAS |
| (20) | William DONACHIE (Manchester City) | Joseph JONES |
| (9) | Thomas FORSYTH (Rangers) | Leighton PHILLIPS |
| (12) | Gordon McQUEEN (Leeds United) | Ian EVANS |
| (16) | Archibald GEMMILL (Derby County) | Peter SAYER |
| (6) | Donald MASSON (Queen's Park Rangers) | John MAHONEY |
| (15) | Bruce RIOCH (Everton) captain | Terence YORATH |
| (13) | Richard HARTFORD (Manchester City) | Brian FLYNN |
| (42) | Kenneth DALGLISH (Celtic) | Nicholas DEACY |
| (12) | Derek PARLANE (Rangers) | Leighton JAMES |

**Substitutions**

| | | |
|---|---|---|
| (11) | William JOHNSTON (West Bromwich Albion) | Michael THOMAS |
| | for Rioch 65 mins | for James 67 mins |
| (8) | Kenneth BURNS (Birmingham City) | |
| | for Parlane 74 mins | |

## 399

(Home International Championship)
1 June 1977

Referee: Gow (Wales)
Hampden Park, Glasgow (Att: 44,699)

### SCOTLAND 3-0 NORTHERN IRELAND — Half-time 1-0

| | | |
|---|---|---|
| (10) | Alan ROUGH (Partick Thistle) | Patrick JENNINGS |
| (34) | Daniel McGRAIN (Celtic) | James NICHOLL |
| (21) | William DONACHIE (Manchester City) | Patrick RICE |
| (10) | Thomas FORSYTH (Rangers) | Thomas JACKSON |
| (13) | Gordon McQUEEN (Leeds United) | Allan HUNTER |
| (7) | Donald MASSON (Queen's Park Rangers) | Bryan HAMILTON |
| (16) | Bruce RIOCH (Everton) captain | David McCREERY |
| (14) | Richard HARTFORD (Manchester City) | Christopher McGRATH |
| (12) | William JOHNSTON (West Bromwich Albion) | Samuel McILROY |
| (43) | Kenneth DALGLISH (Celtic) | Martin O'NEILL |
| (23) | Joseph JORDAN (Leeds United) | Trevor ANDERSON |

**Substitutions**

| | | |
|---|---|---|
| (16) | Luigi MACARI (Manchester United) | Derek SPENCE |
| | for Jordan 69 mins | for Anderson 56 mins |
| (17) | Archibald GEMMILL (Derby County) | |
| | for Johnston 86 mins | |

**Goals**

| | |
|---|---|
| Dalglish (37 mins) | 1-0 |
| McQueen (61 mins) | 2-0 |
| Dalglish (79 mins) | 3-0 |

## 400

(Home International Championship)
4 June 1977

Referee: Palotai (Hungary)
Wembley Stadium, London (Att: 98,103)

### ENGLAND 1-2 SCOTLAND — Half-time 0-1

| | | |
|---|---|---|
| (11) | Alan ROUGH (Partick Thistle) | Raymond CLEMENCE |
| (35) | Daniel McGRAIN (Celtic) | Philip NEAL |
| (22) | William DONACHIE (Manchester City) | Michael MILLS |
| (11) | Thomas FORSYTH (Rangers) | Emlyn HUGHES |
| (14) | Gordon McQUEEN (Leeds United) | David WATSON |
| (8) | Donald MASSON (Queen's Park Rangers) | Brian GREENHOFF |
| (17) | Bruce RIOCH (Everton) captain | Raymond KENNEDY |
| (15) | Richard HARTFORD (Manchester City) | Brian TALBOT |
| (13) | William JOHNSTON (West Bromwich Albion) | Michael CHANNON |
| (44) | Kenneth DALGLISH (Celtic) | Trevor FRANCIS |
| (24) | Joseph JORDAN (Leeds United) | Stuart PEARSON |

**Substitutions**

| | | |
|---|---|---|
| (17) | Luigi MACARI (Manchester United) | Trevor CHERRY |
| | for Jordan 43 mins | for Greenhoff 57 mins |
| (18) | Archibald GEMMILL (Derby County) | Dennis TUEART |
| | for Masson 83 mins | for Kennedy 67 mins |

**Goals**

| | | |
|---|---|---|
| McQueen (43 mins) | 1-0 | |
| Dalglish (61 mins) | 2-0 | |
| | 2-1 | Channon (87 mins pen) |

## 401

(Friendly)
15 June 1977

Referee: Silvagno (Chile)
Estadio Nacional, Santiago (Att: 60,000)

### CHILE 2-4 SCOTLAND — Half-time 0-3

| | | |
|---|---|---|
| (12) | Alan ROUGH (Partick Thistle) | Adolfo NEF |
| (36) | Daniel McGRAIN (Celtic) | Juan MACHUCA |
| (23) | William DONACHIE (Manchester City) | Enzo ESCOBAR |
| (23) | Martin BUCHAN (Manchester United) | Elias FIGUEROA |
| (12) | Thomas FORSYTH (Rangers) | Alberto QUINTANO |
| (9) | Donald MASSON (Queen's Park Rangers) | Waldo QUIROZ |
| (18) | Bruce RIOCH (Everton) captain | Eddio INOSTROZA |
| (16) | Richard HARTFORD (Manchester City) | Juan SOTO |
| (14) | William JOHNSTON (West Bromwich Albion) | Leonardo VÉLIZ |
| (18) | Luigi MACARI (Manchester United) | Rogelio FARÍAS |
| (45) | Kenneth DALGLISH (Celtic) | Héctor PINTO |

**Substitutions**

| | | |
|---|---|---|
| (1) | James STEWART (Kilmarnock) | Julio CRISOSTO |
| | for Rough 46 mins | for Soto 37 mins |
| (19) | Archibald GEMMILL (Derby County) | Gustavo MOSCOSO |
| | for Rioch 46 mins | for Véliz 79 mins |
| (29) | William JARDINE (Rangers) | |
| | for Hartford 80 mins | |

**Goals**

| | | |
|---|---|---|
| Dalglish (19 mins) | 1-0 | |
| Macari (30 mins) | 2-0 | |
| Hartford (37 mins) | 3-0 | |
| | 3-1 | Crisosto (49 mins) |
| Macari (57 mins) | 4-1 | |
| | 4-2 | Crisosto (72 mins) |

## 402

(Friendly)
18 June 1977

Referee: Filho (Brazil)
Estadio Boca Juniors, Buenos Aires (Att: 57,000)

### ARGENTINA 1-1 SCOTLAND — Half-time 0-0

| | | |
|---|---|---|
| (13) | Alan ROUGH (Partick Thistle) | Héctor BALEY |
| (37) | Daniel McGRAIN (Celtic) | Vicente PERNÍA |
| (24) | William DONACHIE (Manchester City) | Daniel KILLER |
| (24) | Martin BUCHAN (Manchester United) captain | Daniel PASSARELLA |
| (13) | Thomas FORSYTH (Rangers) | Jorge CARRASCOSA |
| (10) | Donald MASSON (Queen's Park Rangers) | Osvaldo ARDILES |
| (20) | Archibald GEMMILL (Derby County) | Américo GALLEGO |
| (17) | Richard HARTFORD (Manchester City) | Omar LARROSA |
| (15) | William JOHNSTON (West Bromwich Albion) | Pedro GONZÁLEZ |
| (19) | Luigi MACARI (Manchester United) | Leopoldo LUQUE |
| (46) | Kenneth DALGLISH (Celtic) | René HOUSEMAN |

**Substitutions**

| | | |
|---|---|---|
| | | Alberto TARANTINI |
| | | for González 59 mins |
| | | Victor TROSSERO |
| | | for Larrosa 70 mins |

**Goals**

| | | |
|---|---|---|
| Masson (77 mins pen) | 1-0 | |
| | 1-1 | Passarella (81 mins pen) |

## 403

(Friendly)
23 June 1977

Referee: Saltaro (Brazil)
Estadio Maracana, Rio de Janeiro (Att: 60,763)

### BRAZIL 2-0 SCOTLAND — Half-time 0-0

| | | |
|---|---|---|
| (14) | Alan ROUGH (Partick Thistle) | Emerson LEAO |
| (38) | Daniel McGRAIN (Celtic) | José Maria Alvez ZÉ MARIA |
| (25) | William DONACHIE (Manchester City) | Francisco des Chagas MARINHO |
| (25) | Martin BUCHAN (Manchester United) | LUÍS Edmundo PEREIRA |
| (14) | Thomas FORSYTH (Rangers) | Edino Nazareth Filho EDINHO |
| (11) | Donald MASSON (Queen's Park Rangers) | PAULO ISIDORO de Jesus |
| (19) | Bruce RIOCH (Everton) captain | Antonio TONINHO CEREZO |
| (21) | Archibald GEMMILL (Derby County) | Roberto RIVELINO |
| (18) | Richard HARTFORD (Manchester City) | PAULO CÉSAR Lima |
| (16) | William JOHNSTON (West Bromwich Albion) | Gilberto Alves GIL |
| (47) | Kenneth DALGLISH (Celtic) | José REINALDO de Lima |

**Substitutions**

| | | |
|---|---|---|
| (30) | William JARDINE (Rangers) | Arthur Antunes Coimbra ZICO |
| | for Johnston 61 mins | for Gil 46 mins |

**Goals**

| | | |
|---|---|---|
| | 0-1 | Zico (70 mins) |
| | 0-2 | Toninho Cerezo (75 mins) |

## 404

| | | |
|---|---|---|
| (Friendly) | | Referee: Horbas (Czechoslovakia) |
| 7 September 1977 | | Weltjugend Stadion, East Berlin (Att: 50,000) |

### EAST GERMANY 1-0 SCOTLAND — Half-time 0-0

| | | |
|---|---|
| (1) | David STEWART (Leeds United) | Jürgen CROY |
| (39) | Daniel McGRAIN (Celtic) | Hans-Jürgen DÖRNER |
| (26) | William DONACHIE (Manchester City) | Gerhard KISCHE |
| (26) | Martin BUCHAN (Manchester United) | Konrad WEISE |
| (15) | Gordon McQUEEN (Leeds United) | Gerhard WEBER |
| (12) | Donald MASSON (Queen's Park Rangers) captain | Reinhard HÄFNER |
| (19) | Richard HARTFORD (Manchester City) | Hartmut SCHADE |
| (20) | Luigi MACARI (Manchester United) | Lutz LINDEMANN |
| (17) | William JOHNSTON (West Bromwich Albion) | Gerhard HEIDLER |
| (48) | Kenneth DALGLISH (Liverpool) | Jürgen SPARWASSER |
| (25) | Joseph JORDAN (Leeds United) | Joachim STREICH |

Substitutions

| | | |
|---|---|
| (1) | Arthur GRAHAM (Leeds United) | Peter KOTTE |
| | for Johnston 59 mins | for Sparwasser 46 mins |
| (22) | Archibald GEMMILL (Derby County) | Martin HOFFMANN |
| | for Hartford 65 mins | for Streich 46 mins |

Goals

| | | |
|---|---|---|
| | 0-1 | Schade (59 mins) |

## 405

| | | |
|---|---|---|
| (World Cup — Qualifier) | | Referee: Rion (Belgium) |
| 21 September 1977 | | Hampden Park, Glasgow (Att: 85,000) |

### SCOTLAND 3-1 CZECHOSLOVAKIA — Half-time 2-0

| | | |
|---|---|
| (15) | Alan ROUGH (Partick Thistle) | Pavol MICHALÍK |
| (31) | William JARDINE (Rangers) | Miroslav PAURÍK |
| (40) | Daniel McGRAIN (Celtic) | Jozef CAPKOVIC |
| (15) | Thomas FORSYTH (Rangers) | Karel DVORÁK |
| (16) | Gordon McQUEEN (Leeds United) | Koloman GÖGH |
| (13) | Donald MASSON (Queen's Park Rangers) | Karol DOBIÁS |
| (20) | Bruce RIOCH (Everton) captain | Jaroslav POLLÁK |
| (20) | Richard HARTFORD (Manchester City) | Jozef MÓDER |
| (18) | William JOHNSTON (West Bromwich Albion) | Miroslav GAJDUSEK |
| (49) | Kenneth DALGLISH (Liverpool) | Marián MASNY |
| (26) | Joseph JORDAN (Leeds United) | Zdenek NEHODA |

Substitutions

| | | |
|---|---|
| | | Lubomír KNAPP |
| | | for Móder 46 mins |
| | | Peter GALLIS |
| | | for Dobiás 69 mins |

Goals

| | | |
|---|---|---|
| Jordan (19 mins) | 1-0 | |
| Hartford (35 mins) | 2-0 | |
| Dalglish (54 mins) | 3-0 | |
| | 3-1 | Gajdusek (80 mins) |

## 406

| | | |
|---|---|---|
| (World Cup — Qualifier) | | Referee: Wurtz (France) |
| 12 October 1977 | | Anfield Stadium, Liverpool (Att: 50,800) |

### WALES 0-2 SCOTLAND — Half-time 0-0

| | | |
|---|---|
| (16) | Alan ROUGH (Partick Thistle) | William DAVIES |
| (32) | William JARDINE (Rangers) | Roderick THOMAS |
| (27) | William DONACHIE (Manchester City) | Joseph JONES |
| (16) | Thomas FORSYTH (Rangers) | Leighton PHILLIPS |
| (17) | Gordon McQUEEN (Leeds United) | David JONES |
| (14) | Donald MASSON (Queen's Park Rangers) captain | Peter SAYER |
| (21) | Richard HARTFORD (Manchester City) | John MAHONEY |
| (21) | Luigi MACARI (Manchester United) | Terence YORATH |
| (19) | William JOHNSTON (West Bromwich Albion) | Brian FLYNN |
| (50) | Kenneth DALGLISH (Liverpool) | Michael THOMAS |
| (27) | Joseph JORDAN (Leeds United) | John TOSHACK |

Substitutions

| | | |
|---|---|
| (27) | Martin BUCHAN (Manchester United) | Nicholas DEACY |
| | for Jardine 57 mins | for Sayer 75 mins |

Goals

| | | |
|---|---|---|
| Masson (79 mins pen) | 1-0 | |
| Dalglish (87 mins) | 2-0 | |

Joe Jordan leaps high against Wales in the World Cup qualifier at Anfield in October 1977.

Don Masson opens the scoring against the Welsh on Merseyside with a controversial penalty.

# 1978

| P | W | D | L | F | A |
|---|---|---|---|---|---|
| 10 | 3 | 3 | 4 | 14 | 16 |

## 407
(Friendly)
22 February 1978

Referee: Partridge (England)
Hampden Park, Glasgow (Att: 59,524)

### SCOTLAND 2-1 BULGARIA — Half-time 1-1

| | | |
|---|---|---|
| (1) | James BLYTH (Coventry City) | Stefan STAIKOV |
| (1) | Stuart KENNEDY (Aberdeen) | Plamen NIKOLOV |
| (28) | William DONACHIE (Manchester City) | Dimitar ENCHEV |
| (2) | William MILLER (Aberdeen) | Georgi BONEV |
| (18) | Gordon McQUEEN (Manchester United) | Ivan ILIEV |
| (23) | Archibald GEMMILL (Nottingham Forest) captain | Kantcho KASHEROV |
| (4) | Graeme SOUNESS (Liverpool) | Aleksander IVANOV |
| (22) | Richard HARTFORD (Manchester City) | Georgi SLAVKOV |
| (22) | Luigi MACARI (Manchester United) | Radoslav ZDRAVKOV |
| (51) | Kenneth DALGLISH (Liverpool) | Andrei JELIAZKOV |
| (28) | Joseph JORDAN (Manchester United) | Stoicho MLADENOV |

Substitutions

| | | |
|---|---|---|
| (1) | Ian WALLACE (Coventry City) | Ivan TISHANSKI |
| | for Dalglish 65 mins | for Slavkov 68 mins |
| (11) | Derek JOHNSTONE (Rangers) | |
| | for Jordan 65 mins | |

Goals

| | | |
|---|---|---|
| | 0-1 | Mladenov (8 mins) |
| Gemmill (41 mins pen) | 1-1 | |
| Wallace (85 mins) | 2-1 | |

## 408
(Home International Championship)
13 May 1978

Referee: Gow (Wales)
Hampden Park, Glasgow (Att: 64,433)

### SCOTLAND 1-1 NORTHERN IRELAND — Half-time 1-1

| | | |
|---|---|---|
| (17) | Alan ROUGH (Partick Thistle) | James PLATT |
| (33) | William JARDINE (Rangers) | James NICHOLL |
| (28) | Martin BUCHAN (Manchester United) | Peter SCOTT |
| (17) | Thomas FORSYTH (Rangers) | Bryan HAMILTON |
| (19) | Gordon McQUEEN (Manchester United) | Christopher NICHOLL |
| (15) | Donald MASSON (Derby County) | David McCREERY |
| (21) | Bruce RIOCH (Derby County) captain | Samuel McILROY |
| (24) | Archibald GEMMILL (Nottingham Forest) | Martin O'NEILL |
| (1) | John ROBERTSON (Nottingham Forest) | Christopher McGRATH |
| (29) | Joseph JORDAN (Manchester United) | Trevor ANDERSON |
| (12) | Derek JOHNSTONE (Rangers) | Gerald ARMSTRONG |

Substitutions

| | | |
|---|---|---|
| (9) | Kenneth BURNS (Nottingham Forest) | William HAMILTON |
| | for Buchan 37 mins | for McGrath 63 mins |
| (52) | Kenneth DALGLISH (Liverpool) | Terence COCHRANE |
| | for Jordan 46 mins | for Anderson 77 mins |

Goals

| | | |
|---|---|---|
| | 0-1 | O'Neill (26 mins) |
| Johnstone (36 mins) | 1-1 | |

Derek Johnstone heads Scotland into a 12th-minute lead against Wales at Hampden in May 1978.

## 409
(Home International Championship)
17 May 1978

Referee: Wright (Northern Ireland)
Hampden Park, Glasgow (Att: 70,241)

### SCOTLAND 1-1 WALES — Half-time 1-0

| | | |
|---|---|---|
| (2) | James BLYTH (Coventry City) | William DAVIES |
| (2) | Stuart KENNEDY (Aberdeen) | Malcolm PAGE |
| (29) | William DONACHIE (Manchester City) | Joseph JONES |
| (10) | Kenneth BURNS (Nottingham Forest) | Leighton PHILLIPS |
| (20) | Gordon McQUEEN (Manchester United) | David ROBERTS |
| (25) | Archibald GEMMILL (Nottingham Forest) captain | Carl HARRIS |
| (5) | Graeme SOUNESS (Liverpool) | John MAHONEY |
| (23) | Richard HARTFORD (Manchester City) | Terence YORATH |
| (20) | William JOHNSTON (West Bromwich Albion) | Brian FLYNN |
| (53) | Kenneth DALGLISH (Liverpool) | Phillip DWYER |
| (13) | Derek JOHNSTONE (Rangers) | Alan CURTIS |

Substitutions

| | | |
|---|---|---|
| (18) | Thomas FORSYTH (Rangers) | Nicholas DEACY |
| | for McQueen 32 mins | for Page 76 mins |
| (2) | John ROBERTSON (Nottingham Forest) | |
| | for Johnston 85 mins | |

Goals

| | | |
|---|---|---|
| Johnstone (12 mins) | 1-0 | |
| | 1-1 | Donachie (89 mins o.g.) |

Joe Jordan in action against England at Hampden in May 1978.

## 410
(Home International Championship)
20 May 1978

Referee: Konrath (France)
Hampden Park, Glasgow (Att: 88,319)

### SCOTLAND 0-1 ENGLAND — Half-time 0-0

| | | |
|---|---|---|
| (18) | Alan ROUGH (Partick Thistle) | Raymond CLEMENCE |
| (3) | Stuart KENNEDY (Aberdeen) | Philip NEAL |
| (30) | William DONACHIE (Manchester City) | Michael MILLS |
| (19) | Thomas FORSYTH (Rangers) | Emlyn HUGHES |
| (11) | Kenneth BURNS (Nottingham Forest) | David WATSON |
| (16) | Donald MASSON (Derby County) | Steven COPPELL |
| (22) | Bruce RIOCH (Derby County) captain | Anthony CURRIE |
| (24) | Richard HARTFORD (Manchester City) | Raymond WILKINS |
| (21) | William JOHNSTON (West Bromwich Albion) | Peter BARNES |
| (54) | Kenneth DALGLISH (Liverpool) | Paul MARINER |
| (30) | Joseph JORDAN (Manchester United) | Trevor FRANCIS |

Substitutions

| | | |
|---|---|---|
| (6) | Graeme SOUNESS (Liverpool) | Brian GREENHOFF |
| | for Rioch 74 mins | for Hughes 73 mins |
| (26) | Archibald GEMMILL (Nottingham Forest) | Trevor BROOKING |
| | for Masson 74 mins | for Mariner 76 mins |

Goals

| | | |
|---|---|---|
| | 0-1 | Coppell (83 mins) |

Peru celebrate their third goal against the Scots in Cordoba during the 1978 World Cup finals.

## 411

(World Cup — Final Tournament 1st Round)　　Referee: Eriksson (Sweden)
3 June 1978　　Estadio Chateau Carreras, Cordoba (Att: 37,792)

### PERU 3-1 SCOTLAND　　Half-time 1-1

| | | |
|---|---|---|
| (19) | Alan ROUGH (Partick Thistle) | Ramón QUIROGA |
| (4) | Stuart KENNEDY (Aberdeen) | Jaime DUARTE |
| (29) | Martin BUCHAN (Manchester United) | Rodolfo MANZO |
| (20) | Thomas FORSYTH (Rangers) | Héctor CHUMPITÁZ |
| (12) | Kenneth BURNS (Nottingham Forest) | Toribio DÍAZ |
| (17) | Donald MASSON (Derby County) | Juan MUNANTE |
| (23) | Bruce RIOCH (Derby County) captain | José VELÁSQUEZ |
| (25) | Richard HARTFORD (Manchester City) | César CUETO |
| (22) | William JOHNSTON (West Bromwich Albion) | Juan OBLITAS |
| (55) | Kenneth DALGLISH (Liverpool) | Teófilo CUBILLAS |
| (31) | Joseph JORDAN (Manchester United) | Guillermo LA ROSA |

Substitutions

| | | |
|---|---|---|
| (23) | Luigi MACARI (Manchester United) | Hugo SOTIL |
| | for Rioch 70 mins | for La Rosa 62 mins |
| (27) | Archibald GEMMILL (Nottingham Forest) | Percy ROJAS |
| | for Masson 70 mins | for Cueto 82 mins |

Goals

| | | |
|---|---|---|
| Jordan (15 mins) | 1-0 | |
| | 1-1 | Cueto (43 mins) |
| | 1-2 | Cubillas (70 mins) |
| | 1-3 | Cubillas (76 mins) |

## 412

(World Cup — Final Tournament 1st Round)　　Referee: Ndiaye (Senegal)
7 June 1978　　Estadio Chateau Carreras, Cordoba (Att: 7,938)

### IRAN 1-1 SCOTLAND　　Half-time 0-1

| | | |
|---|---|---|
| (20) | Alan ROUGH (Partick Thistle) | Nasser HEJAZI |
| (34) | William JARDINE (Rangers) | Hassan NAZARI |
| (31) | William DONACHIE (Manchester City) | Hossein KAZERANI |
| (30) | Martin BUCHAN (Manchester United) | Nasrullah ABDOLLAHI |
| (13) | Kenneth BURNS (Nottingham Forest) | Andranik ESKANDARIAN |
| (28) | Archibald GEMMILL (Nottingham Forest) captain | Ali PARVIN |
| (26) | Richard HARTFORD (Manchester City) | Ebrahim GHASEMPOUR |
| (24) | Luigi MACARI (Manchester United) | Muhamad SADEGHI |
| (3) | John ROBERTSON (Nottingham Forest) | Iraj DANAIFAR |
| (56) | Kenneth DALGLISH (Liverpool) | Hossein FARAKI |
| (32) | Joseph JORDAN (Manchester United) | Ghafoor DJAHANI |

Substitutions

| | | |
|---|---|---|
| (21) | Thomas FORSYTH (Rangers) | Hassan ROSHAN |
| | for Buchan 57 mins | for Faraki 83 mins |
| (4) | Joseph HARPER (Aberdeen) | Hassan NAYBAGHA |
| | for Dalglish 73 mins | for Danaifar 89 mins |

Goals

| | | |
|---|---|---|
| Eskandarian (43 mins o.g.) | 1-0 | |
| | 1-1 | Danaifar (77 mins) |

## 413

(World Cup — Final Tournament 1st Round)　　Referee: Linemayr (Austria)
11 June 1978　　Estadio San Martin, Mendoza (Att: 35,130)

### NETHERLANDS 2-3 SCOTLAND　　Half-time 1-1

| | | |
|---|---|---|
| (21) | Alan ROUGH (Partick Thistle) | Jan JONGBLOED |
| (5) | Stuart KENNEDY (Aberdeen) | Willem SUURBIER |
| (32) | William DONACHIE (Manchester City) | Wilhelmus RIJSBERGEN |
| (31) | Martin BUCHAN (Manchester United) | Jan POORTVLIET |
| (22) | Thomas FORSYTH (Rangers) | Rudolf KROL |
| (29) | Archibald GEMMILL (Nottingham Forest) | Wilhelmus JANSEN |
| (24) | Bruce RIOCH (Derby County) captain | Johannes NEESKENS |
| (7) | Graeme SOUNESS (Liverpool) | Reinier VAN DE KERKHOF |
| (27) | Richard HARTFORD (Manchester City) | Robert RENSENBRINK |
| (57) | Kenneth DALGLISH (Liverpool) | Wilhelmus VAN DE KERKHOF |
| (33) | Joseph JORDAN (Manchester United) | Johannes REP |

Substitutions

| | |
|---|---|
| | Johannes BOSKAMP |
| | for Neeskens 10 mins |
| | Pieter WILDSCHUT |
| | for Rijsbergen 44 mins |

Goals

| | | |
|---|---|---|
| | 0-1 | |
| Dalglish (44 mins) | 1-1 | Rensenbrink (34 mins pen) |
| Gemmill (46 mins pen) | 2-1 | |
| Gemmill (68 mins) | 3-1 | |
| | 3-2 | Rep (71 mins) |

Kenny Dalglish beats the Dutch goalkeeper Jan Jongbloed to score Scotland's first goal at Mendoza in June 1978. The victory lit up an otherwise disappointing World Cup finals for the Scots.

The hand of God? No, it's Joe Jordan with a Maradonna-esque pose against the Dutch.

Archie Gemmill celebrates his fantastic goal against Holland.

## 414

| | |
|---|---|
| (European Championship — Qualifier) | Referee: Michelotti (Italy) |
| 20 September 1978 | Prater Stadion, Vienna (Att: 62,281) |

### AUSTRIA 3-2 SCOTLAND — Half-time 1-0

| | | |
|---|---|---|
| (22) | Alan ROUGH (Partick Thistle) | Erwin FUCHSBICHLER |
| (6) | Stuart KENNEDY (Aberdeen) | Robert SARA |
| (33) | William DONACHIE (Manchester City) | Erich OBERMAYER |
| (32) | Martin BUCHAN (Manchester United) | Heinrich STRASSER |
| (21) | Gordon McQUEEN (Manchester United) | Bruno PEZZEY |
| (30) | Archibald GEMMILL (Nottingham Forest) captain | Heribert WEBER |
| (8) | Graeme SOUNESS (Liverpool) | Kurt JARA |
| (28) | Richard HARTFORD (Manchester City) | Herbert PROHASKA |
| (58) | Kenneth DALGLISH (Liverpool) | Walter SCHACHNER |
| (34) | Joseph JORDAN (Manchester United) | Wilhelm KREUZ |
| (5) | Andrew GRAY (Aston Villa) | Johann KRANKL |

**Substitutions**

| | | |
|---|---|---|
| (2) | Arthur GRAHAM (Leeds United) | Franz OBERACHER |
| | for Jordan 61 mins | for Prohaska 87 mins |

**Goals**

| | | |
|---|---|---|
| | 0-1 | Pezzey (27 mins) |
| | 0-2 | Schachner (48 mins) |
| | 0-3 | Kreuz (64 mins) |
| McQueen (65 mins) | 1-3 | |
| Gray (77 mins) | 2-3 | |

## 415

| | |
|---|---|
| (European Championship — Qualifier) | Referee: Christov (Czechoslovakia) |
| 25 October 1978 | Hampden Park, Glasgow (Att: 65,372) |

### SCOTLAND 3-2 NORWAY — Half-time 1-1

| | | |
|---|---|---|
| (2) | James STEWART (Middlesbrough) | Tom-Rüsz JACOBSEN |
| (34) | William DONACHIE (Manchester City) | Trond PEDERSEN |
| (2) | Francis GRAY (Leeds United) | Jan BIRKELUND |
| (33) | Martin BUCHAN (Manchester United) | Svein GRONDALEN |
| (22) | Gordon McQUEEN (Manchester United) | Einar AAS |
| (31) | Archibald GEMMILL (Nottingham Forest) captain | Tore KORDAHL |
| (9) | Graeme SOUNESS (Liverpool) | Tor-Egil JOHANSEN |
| (29) | Richard HARTFORD (Manchester City) | Svein MATHISEN |
| (3) | Arthur GRAHAM (Leeds United) | Tom JACOBSEN |
| (59) | Kenneth DALGLISH (Liverpool) | Arne LARSEN-OKLAND |
| (6) | Andrew GRAY (Aston Villa) | Hallvar THORESEN |

**Substitutions**

| | |
|---|---|
| | Jan HANSEN |
| | for T. Jacobsen 37 mins |
| | Helge KARLSEN |
| | for Pedersen 86 mins |

**Goals**

| | | |
|---|---|---|
| | 0-1 | Aas (3 mins) |
| Dalglish (5 mins) | 1-1 | |
| | 1-2 | Larsen-Okland (64 mins) |
| Dalglish (82 mins) | 2-2 | |
| Gemmill (87 mins pen) | 3-2 | |

Kenny Dalglish beats Norway's goalkeeper Jacobsen in the European Championship qualifier at Hampden in October 1978.

## 416

| | |
|---|---|
| (European Championship — Qualifier) | Referee: Dolflinger (Switzerland) |
| 29 November 1978 | Estadio da Luz, Lisbon (Att: 70,000) |

### PORTUGAL 1-0 SCOTLAND — Half-time 1-0

| | | |
|---|---|---|
| (23) | Alan ROUGH (Partick Thistle) | Manuel BENTO |
| (7) | Stuart KENNEDY (Aberdeen) | ARTUR Correia |
| (3) | Francis GRAY (Leeds United) | Humberto COELHO |
| (2) | David NAREY (Dundee United) | Carlos ALHINHO |
| (23) | Gordon McQUEEN (Manchester United) | ALBERTO Fonseca |
| (34) | Martin BUCHAN (Manchester United) | Minervino PIETRA |
| (32) | Archibald GEMMILL (Nottingham Forest) captain | Antonio OLIVEIRA |
| (30) | Richard HARTFORD (Manchester City) | Joao ALVES |
| (4) | John ROBERTSON (Nottingham Forest) | José COSTA |
| (60) | Kenneth DALGLISH (Liverpool) | Tamagnini NENÉ |
| (35) | Joseph JORDAN (Manchester United) | Fernando GOMES |

**Substitutions**

| | | |
|---|---|---|
| (35) | William DONACHIE (Manchester City) | SHEU Han |
| | for Gray 65 mins | for Costa 46 mins |
| (2) | Ian WALLACE (Coventry City) | EURICO Gomes |
| | for Jordan 78 mins | for Oliveira 82 mins |

**Goals**

| | | |
|---|---|---|
| | 0-1 | Alberto (29 mins) |

# 1979

| | P | W | D | L | F | A |
|---|---|---|---|---|---|---|
| | 9 | 2 | 2 | 5 | 10 | 16 |

## 417

(Home International Championship)
19 May 1979

Referee: Partridge (England)
Ninian Park, Cardiff (Att: 20,371)

### WALES 3-0 SCOTLAND — Half-time 2-0

| (24) | Alan ROUGH (Partick Thistle) | William DAVIES |
|---|---|---|
| (1) | George BURLEY (Ipswich Town) | Byron STEVENSON |
| (4) | Francis GRAY (Leeds United) | Joseph JONES |
| (1) | Alan HANSEN (Liverpool) | Leighton PHILLIPS |
| (1) | Paul HEGARTY (Dundee United) | Phillip DWYER |
| (1) | John WARK (Ipswich Town) | Robert JAMES |
| (31) | Richard HARTFORD (Manchester City) | John MAHONEY |
| (10) | Graeme SOUNESS (Liverpool) | Terence YORATH |
| (4) | Arthur GRAHAM (Leeds United) | Brian FLYNN |
| (61) | Kenneth DALGLISH (Liverpool) captain | Alan CURTIS |
| (3) | Ian WALLACE (Coventry City) | John TOSHACK |

Substitutions

| (36) | Joseph JORDAN (Manchester United) for Wallace 55 mins | Peter NICHOLAS for Yorath 89 mins |
|---|---|---|

Goals

| 0-1 | Toshack (28 mins) |
|---|---|
| 0-2 | Toshack (35 mins) |
| 0-3 | Toshack (75 mins) |

## 418

(Home International Championship)
22 May 1979

Referee: Thomas (Wales)
Hampden Park, Glasgow (Att: 28,524)

### SCOTLAND 1-0 NORTHERN IRELAND — Half-time 0-0

| (1) | George WOOD (Everton) | Patrick JENNINGS |
|---|---|---|
| (2) | George BURLEY (Ipswich Town) | Patrick RICE |
| (5) | Francis GRAY (Leeds United) | Samuel NELSON |
| (2) | Paul HEGARTY (Dundee United) | James NICHOLL |
| (24) | Gordon McQUEEN (Manchester United) | Allan HUNTER |
| (2) | John WARK (Ipswich Town) | Victor MORELAND |
| (11) | Graeme SOUNESS (Liverpool) | Bryan HAMILTON |
| (32) | Richard HARTFORD (Manchester City) | Samuel McILROY |
| (5) | Arthur GRAHAM (Leeds United) | Thomas SLOAN |
| (62) | Kenneth DALGLISH (Liverpool) captain | Derek SPENCE |
| (37) | Joseph JORDAN (Manchester United) | Gerald ARMSTRONG |

Substitutions

| (3) | David NAREY (Dundee United) for Wark 46 mins | Peter SCOTT for Moreland 62 mins |
|---|---|---|
| (1) | Francis McGARVEY (Liverpool) for Graham 89 mins | William CASKEY for Spence 77 mins |

Goals

Graham (76 mins) — 1-0

## 419

(Home International Championship)
26 May 1979

Referee: Garrido (Portugal)
Wembley Stadium, London (Att: 100,000)

### ENGLAND 3-1 SCOTLAND — Half-time 1-1

| (2) | George WOOD (Everton) | Raymond CLEMENCE |
|---|---|---|
| (3) | George BURLEY (Ipswich Town) | Philip NEAL |
| (6) | Francis GRAY (Leeds United) | Michael MILLS |
| (3) | Paul HEGARTY (Dundee United) | Philip THOMPSON |
| (25) | Gordon McQUEEN (Manchester United) | David WATSON |
| (3) | John WARK (Ipswich Town) | Steven COPPELL |
| (6) | Graeme SOUNESS (Liverpool) | Raymond WILKINS |
| (33) | Richard HARTFORD (Manchester City) | Trevor BROOKING |
| (6) | Arthur GRAHAM (Leeds United) | Peter BARNES |
| (63) | Kenneth DALGLISH (Liverpool) captain | Kevin KEEGAN |
| (38) | Joseph JORDAN (Manchester United) | Robert LATCHFORD |

Goals

| Wark (20 mins) | 1-0 | |
|---|---|---|
| | 1-1 | Barnes (44 mins) |
| | 1-2 | Coppell (64 mins) |
| | 1-3 | Keegan (70 mins) |

## 420

(Friendly)
2 June 1979

Referee: Partridge (England)
Hampden Park, Glasgow (Att: 61,918)

### SCOTLAND 1-3 ARGENTINA — Half-time 0-1

| (25) | Alan ROUGH (Partick Thistle) | Ubaldo FILLOL |
|---|---|---|
| (4) | George BURLEY (Ipswich Town) | Jorge OLGUÍN |
| (1) | Alexander MUNRO (St Mirren) | Alberto TARANTINI |
| (2) | Alan HANSEN (Liverpool) | Hugo VILLAVERDE |
| (4) | Paul HEGARTY (Dundee United) | Daniel PASSARELLA |
| (4) | David NAREY (Dundee United) | Juan BARBAS |
| (4) | John WARK (Ipswich Town) | Américo GALLEGO |
| (34) | Richard HARTFORD (Manchester City) | Diego MARADONA |
| (7) | Arthur GRAHAM (Leeds United) | José VALENCIA |
| (64) | Kenneth DALGLISH (Liverpool) captain | René HOUSEMAN |
| (2) | Francis McGARVEY (Liverpool) | Leopoldo LUQUE |

Substitutions

| (3) | George WOOD (Everton) for Rough 46 mins | Victor TROSSERO for Villaverde 21 mins |
|---|---|---|
| (7) | Francis GRAY (Leeds United) for Hartford 70 mins | Norberto OUTES for Houseman 56 mins |

Goals

| | 0-1 | Luque (33 mins) |
|---|---|---|
| | 0-2 | Luque (60 mins) |
| | 0-3 | Maradona (70 mins) |
| Graham (85 mins) | 1-3 | |

## 421

(European Championship — Qualifier)
7 June 1979

Referee: Nielsen (Denmark)
Ullevaal Stadion, Oslo (Att: 17,269)

### NORWAY 0-4 SCOTLAND — Half-time 0-3

| (26) | Alan ROUGH (Partick Thistle) | Tom-Rüsz JACOBSEN |
|---|---|---|
| (5) | George BURLEY (Ipswich Town) | Trond PEDERSEN |
| (2) | Alexander MUNRO (St Mirren) | Helge KARLSEN |
| (14) | Kenneth BURNS (Nottingham Forest) | Svein GRONDALEN |
| (26) | Gordon McQUEEN (Manchester United) | Einar AAS |
| (8) | Arthur GRAHAM (Leeds United) | Tore KORDAHL |
| (33) | Archibald GEMMILL (Nottingham Forest) captain | Roger ALBERTSEN |
| (35) | Richard HARTFORD (Manchester City) | Stein THUNBERG |
| (5) | John ROBERTSON (Nottingham Forest) | Svein MATHISEN |
| (65) | Kenneth DALGLISH (Liverpool) | Arne LARSEN-OKLAND |
| (39) | Joseph JORDAN (Manchester United) | Hallvar THORESEN |

Substitutions

| (5) | Paul HEGARTY (Dundee United) for Burley 46 mins | Jan HANSEN for Pedersen 67 mins |
|---|---|---|
| (5) | John WARK (Ipswich Town) for Hegarty 70 mins | Torbjorn SVENDSEN for Thunberg 75 mins |

Goals

| Jordan (32 mins) | 1-0 |
|---|---|
| Dalglish (39 mins) | 2-0 |
| Robertson (43 mins) | 3-0 |
| McQueen (55 mins) | 4-0 |

## 422

(Friendly)
12 September 1979

Referee: Courtney (England)
Hampden Park, Glasgow (Att: 41,035)

### SCOTLAND 1-1 PERU — Half-time 1-0

| (27) | Alan ROUGH (Partick Thistle) | Eusébio ACASUZO |
|---|---|---|
| (35) | William JARDINE (Rangers) captain | Hugo GASTULO |
| (3) | Alexander MUNRO (St Mirren) | Jorge OLAECHEA |
| (15) | Kenneth BURNS (Nottingham Forest) | Héctor CHUMPITÁZ |
| (27) | Gordon McQUEEN (Manchester United) | Toribio DÍAZ |
| (1) | David COOPER (Rangers) | Robert MOSQUERA |
| (6) | John WARK (Ipswich Town) | José VELÁSQUEZ |
| (13) | Graeme SOUNESS (Liverpool) | César CUETO |
| (36) | Richard HARTFORD (Everton) | German LEGUÍA |
| (6) | John ROBERTSON (Nottingham Forest) | Ernesto LABARTHE |
| (66) | Kenneth DALGLISH (Liverpool) | Guillermo LA ROSA |

Substitutions

| (1) | Robert AITKEN (Celtic) for Wark 71 mins | Fredy RAVELLO for Labarthe 46 mins |
|---|---|---|
| (9) | Arthur GRAHAM (Leeds United) for Cooper 71 mins | |

Goals

| Hartford (4 mins) | 1-0 | |
|---|---|---|
| | 1-1 | Leguía (85 mins) |

## 423

(European Championship — Qualifier)
17 October 1979

Referee: Palotai (Hungary)
Hampden Park, Glasgow (Att: 67,895)

### SCOTLAND 1-1 AUSTRIA — Half-time 0-1

| | | |
|---|---|---|
| (28) | Alan ROUGH (Partick Thistle) | Friedrich KONCILIA |
| (36) | William JARDINE (Rangers) | Robert SARA |
| (4) | Alexander MUNRO (St Mirren) | Dietmar MIRNEGG |
| (16) | Kenneth BURNS (Nottingham Forest) | Roland HATTENBERGER |
| (28) | Gordon McQUEEN (Manchester United) | Bruno PEZZEY |
| (10) | Arthur GRAHAM (Leeds United) | Heribert WEBER |
| (7) | John WARK (Ipswich Town) | Kurt JARA |
| (14) | Graeme SOUNESS (Liverpool) | Herbert PROHASKA |
| (34) | Archibald GEMMILL (Birmingham City) captain | Walter SCHACHNER |
| (7) | John ROBERTSON (Nottingham Forest) | Wilhelm KREUZ |
| (67) | Kenneth DALGLISH (Liverpool) | Johann KRANKL |

Substitutions

| | | |
|---|---|---|
| (2) | David COOPER (Rangers) | Gerhard STEINKOGLER |
| | for Graham 61 mins | for Schachner 80 mins |
| | | Reinhold HINTERMAIER |
| | | for Krankl 89 mins |

Goals

| | | |
|---|---|---|
| | 0-1 | Krankl (40 mins) |
| Gemmill (75 mins) | 1-1 | |

---

## 424

(European Championship — Qualifier)
21 November 1979

Referee: Zade (Soviet Union)
Heysel Stadium, Brussels (Att: 14,289)

### BELGIUM 2-0 SCOTLAND — Half-time 1-0

| | | |
|---|---|---|
| (29) | Alan ROUGH (Partick Thistle) | Theo CUSTERS |
| (37) | William JARDINE (Rangers) captain | Eric GERETS |
| (5) | Alexander MUNRO (St Mirren) | Luc MILLECAMPS |
| (3) | Alan HANSEN (Liverpool) | Walter MEEUWS |
| (3) | William MILLER (Aberdeen) | Michel RENQUIN |
| (8) | John WARK (Ipswich Town) | Julien COOLS |
| (15) | Graeme SOUNESS (Liverpool) | Wilfried VAN MOER |
| (37) | Richard HARTFORD (Everton) | René VANDEREYCKEN |
| (8) | John ROBERTSON (Nottingham Forest) | François VAN DER ELST |
| (68) | Kenneth DALGLISH (Liverpool) | Jan CEULEMANS |
| (40) | Joseph JORDAN (Manchester United) | Eduard VOORDECKERS |

Substitutions

| | | |
|---|---|---|
| (8) | Francis GRAY (Nottingham Forest) | René VERHEYEN |
| | for Munro 61 mins | for Van Moer 66 mins |
| (1) | David PROVAN (Celtic) | |
| | for Jordan 61 mins | |

Goals

| | | |
|---|---|---|
| | 0-1 | Van der Elst (7 mins) |
| | 0-2 | Voordeckers (46 mins) |

---

## 425

(European Championship — Qualifier)
19 December 1979

Referee: Aldinger (West Germany)
Hampden Park, Glasgow (Att: 25,389)

### SCOTLAND 1-3 BELGIUM — Half-time 0-3

| | | |
|---|---|---|
| (30) | Alan ROUGH (Partick Thistle) | Theo CUSTERS |
| (38) | William JARDINE (Rangers) captain | Eric GERETS |
| (41) | Daniel McGRAIN (Celtic) | Luc MILLECAMPS |
| (17) | Kenneth BURNS (Nottingham Forest) | Walter MEEUWS |
| (29) | Gordon McQUEEN (Manchester United) | Maurice MARTENS |
| (1) | Eamonn BANNON (Dundee United) | Julien COOLS |
| (2) | Robert AITKEN (Celtic) | Wilfried VAN MOER |
| (9) | John WARK (Ipswich Town) | René VANDEREYCKEN |
| (9) | John ROBERTSON (Nottingham Forest) | François VAN DER ELST |
| (69) | Kenneth DALGLISH (Liverpool) | Jan CEULEMANS |
| (14) | Derek JOHNSTONE (Rangers) | Erwin VANDENBERGH |

Substitutions

| | | |
|---|---|---|
| (2) | David PROVAN (Celtic) | Gerard PLESSERS |
| | for Bannon 46 mins | for Van Moer 49 mins |
| | | Guy DARDENNE |
| | | for Vandenbergh 73 mins |

Goals

| | | |
|---|---|---|
| | 0-1 | Vandenbergh (18 mins) |
| | 0-2 | Van der Elst (23 mins) |
| | 0-3 | Van der Elst (29 mins) |
| Robertson (55 mins) | 1-3 | |

---

# 1980

| P | W | D | L | F | A |
|---|---|---|---|---|---|
| 8 | 3 | 1 | 4 | 7 | 8 |

## 426

(European Championship — Qualifier)
26 March 1980

Referee: Wurtz (France)
Hampden Park, Glasgow (Att: 20,233)

### SCOTLAND 4-1 PORTUGAL — Half-time 2-0

| | | |
|---|---|---|
| (31) | Alan ROUGH (Partick Thistle) | Manuel BENTO |
| (6) | George BURLEY (Ipswich Town) | Adelino TEIXEIRA |
| (42) | Daniel McGRAIN (Celtic) | Humberto COELHO |
| (4) | Alan HANSEN (Liverpool) | Carlos SIMOES |
| (1) | Alexander McLEISH (Aberdeen) | ALBERTO Fonseca |
| (5) | David NAREY (Dundee United) | Antonio FRASCO |
| (16) | Graeme SOUNESS (Liverpool) | EURICO Gomes |
| (35) | Archibald GEMMILL (Birmingham City) captain | Tamagnini NENÉ |
| (10) | John ROBERTSON (Nottingham Forest) | José COSTA |
| (70) | Kenneth DALGLISH (Liverpool) | Rui JORDAO |
| (7) | Andrew GRAY (Wolverhampton Wanderers) | Fernando GOMES |

Substitutions

| | | |
|---|---|---|
| (1) | Steven ARCHIBALD (Aberdeen) | SHEU Han |
| | for Dalglish 48 mins | for Eurico 35 mins |
| (3) | David PROVAN (Celtic) | Carlos MANUEL |
| | for Robertson 75 mins | for Frasco 77 mins |

Goals

| | | |
|---|---|---|
| Dalglish (6 mins) | 1-0 | |
| Gray (26 mins) | 2-0 | |
| Archibald (68 mins) | 3-0 | |
| | 3-1 | Gomes (74 mins) |
| Gemmill (84 mins pen) | 4-1 | |

---

## 427

(Home International Championship)
16 May 1980

Referee: Thomas (Wales)
Windsor Park, Belfast (Att: 18,000)

### NORTHERN IRELAND 1-0 SCOTLAND — Half-time 1-0

| | | |
|---|---|---|
| (1) | William THOMSON (St Mirren) | James PLATT |
| (7) | George BURLEY (Ipswich Town) | James NICHOLL |
| (43) | Daniel McGRAIN (Celtic) | Mal DONAGHY |
| (6) | David NAREY (Dundee United) | John O'NEILL |
| (2) | Alexander McLEISH (Aberdeen) | Christopher NICHOLL |
| (1) | Gordon STRACHAN (Aberdeen) | Thomas CASSIDY |
| (17) | Graeme SOUNESS (Liverpool) | Samuel McILROY |
| (36) | Archibald GEMMILL (Birmingham City) captain | Noel BROTHERSTON |
| (1) | Peter WEIR (St Mirren) | Thomas FINNEY |
| (71) | Kenneth DALGLISH (Liverpool) | William HAMILTON |
| (2) | Steven ARCHIBALD (Tottenham Hotspur) | Gerald ARMSTRONG |

Substitutions

| | | |
|---|---|---|
| (4) | David PROVAN (Celtic) | John McCLELLAND |
| | for Weir 59 mins | for Hamilton 52 mins |
| (41) | Joseph JORDAN (Manchester United) | David McCREERY |
| | for Souness 59 mins | for Cassidy 70 mins |

Goals

| | | |
|---|---|---|
| | 0-1 | Hamilton (36 mins) |

---

## 428

(Home International Championship)
21 May 1980

Referee: Wilson (Northern Ireland)
Hampden Park, Glasgow (Att: 31,359)

### SCOTLAND 1-0 WALES — Half-time 1-0

| | | |
|---|---|---|
| (32) | Alan ROUGH (Partick Thistle) | William DAVIES |
| (44) | Daniel McGRAIN (Celtic) | Paul PRICE |
| (6) | Alexander MUNRO (St Mirren) | Joseph JONES |
| (6) | Paul HEGARTY (Dundee United) | Terence YORATH |
| (3) | Alexander McLEISH (Aberdeen) | Keith PONTIN |
| (4) | William MILLER (Aberdeen) | Peter NICHOLAS |
| (2) | Gordon STRACHAN (Aberdeen) | David GILES |
| (37) | Archibald GEMMILL (Birmingham City) captain | Brian FLYNN |
| (2) | Peter WEIR (St Mirren) | Michael THOMAS |
| (72) | Kenneth DALGLISH (Liverpool) | Leighton JAMES |
| (42) | Joseph JORDAN (Manchester United) | Ian WALSH |

Substitutions

| | | |
|---|---|---|
| (3) | Robert AITKEN (Celtic) | Ian RUSH |
| | for Weir 84 mins | for Walsh 15 mins |
| | | Leighton PHILLIPS |
| | | for Pontin 46 mins |

Goals

| | | |
|---|---|---|
| Miller (26 mins) | 1-0 | |

## 429

(Home International Championship)
24 May 1980

Referee: Garrido (Portugal)
Hampden Park, Glasgow (Att: 85,000)

### SCOTLAND 0-2 ENGLAND — Half-time 0-1

| | | |
|---|---|---|
| (33) | Alan ROUGH (Partick Thistle) | Raymond CLEMENCE |
| (45) | Daniel McGRAIN (Celtic) | Trevor CHERRY |
| (7) | Alexander MUNRO (St Mirren) | Kenneth SANSOM |
| (7) | Paul HEGARTY (Dundee United) | Philip THOMPSON |
| (4) | Alexander McLEISH (Aberdeen) | David WATSON |
| (5) | William MILLER (Aberdeen) | Raymond WILKINS |
| (3) | Gordon STRACHAN (Aberdeen) | Trevor BROOKING |
| (4) | Robert AITKEN (Celtic) | Terence McDERMOTT |
| (38) | Archibald GEMMILL (Birmingham City) captain | Stephen COPPELL |
| (73) | Kenneth DALGLISH (Liverpool) | David JOHNSON |
| (43) | Joseph JORDAN (Manchester United) | Paul MARINER |

Substitutions

| | | |
|---|---|---|
| (8) | Andrew GRAY (Wolverhampton Wanderers) for Aitken 53 mins | Emlyn HUGHES for Mariner 71 mins |
| (8) | George BURLEY (Ipswich Town) for Munro 62 mins | |

Goals
0-1 Brooking (8 mins)
0-2 Coppell (75 mins)

## 430

(Friendly)
28 May 1980

Referee: Josifov (Bulgaria)
Warta Stadion, Poznan (Att: 20,000)

### POLAND 1-0 SCOTLAND — Half-time 0-0

| | | |
|---|---|---|
| (34) | Alan ROUGH (Partick Thistle) | Piotr MOWLIK |
| (9) | George BURLEY (Ipswich Town) | Marek DZIUBA |
| (46) | Daniel McGRAIN (Celtic) captain | Hieronim BARCZAK |
| (6) | William MILLER (Aberdeen) | Wladyslaw ZMUDA |
| (5) | Alexander McLEISH (Aberdeen) | Pawel JANAS |
| (7) | David NAREY (Dundee United) | Adam NAWALKA |
| (4) | Gordon STRACHAN (Aberdeen) | Andrzej PALASZ |
| (5) | Robert AITKEN (Celtic) | Kazimierz KMIECIK |
| (74) | Kenneth DALGLISH (Liverpool) | Leszek LIPKA |
| (3) | Steven ARCHIBALD (Tottenham Hotspur) | Grzegorz LATO |
| (44) | Joseph JORDAN (Manchester United) | Zbigniew BONIEK |

Substitutions

| | | |
|---|---|---|
| (1) | Alan BRAZIL (Ipswich Town) for Jordan 46 mins | Stanislaw TERLECKI for Palasz 46 mins |
| (3) | Peter WEIR (St Mirren) for Dalglish 56 mins | Wlodzimierz CIOLEK for Dziuba 69 mins |
| (1) | Alistair DAWSON (Rangers) for Burley 80 mins | |

Goals
0-1 Boniek (68 mins)

## 431

(Friendly)
31 May 1980

Referee: Baumann (Switzerland)
Nép Stadion, Budapest (Att: 6,600)

### HUNGARY 3-1 SCOTLAND — Half-time 1-0

| | | |
|---|---|---|
| (35) | Alan ROUGH (Partick Thistle) | Ferenc MÉSZÁROS |
| (47) | Daniel McGRAIN (Celtic) | Sándor PAROCZAI |
| (2) | Alistair DAWSON (Rangers) | László BÁLINT |
| (7) | William MILLER (Aberdeen) | Imre GARABA |
| (6) | Alexander McLEISH (Aberdeen) | József TÓTH |
| (8) | David NAREY (Dundee United) | József PÁSZTOR |
| (39) | Archibald GEMMILL (Birmingham City) captain | Zoltán KEREKI |
| (75) | Kenneth DALGLISH (Liverpool) | Tibor NYILASI |
| (4) | Peter WEIR (St Mirren) | Ferenc CSONGRÁDI |
| (2) | Alan BRAZIL (Ipswich Town) | László KISS |
| (4) | Steven ARCHIBALD (Tottenham Hotspur) | András TÖRÖCSIK |

Substitutions

| | | |
|---|---|---|
| (5) | Gordon STRACHAN (Aberdeen) for Brazil 46 mins | Gábor SZÁNTÓ for Paroczai 63 mins |
| | | Marton ESTERHÁZY for Kiss 68 mins |

Goals
0-1 Töröcsik (4 mins)
0-2 Töröcsik (65 mins)
Archibald (67 mins) 1-2
1-3 Kereki (69 mins)

## 432

(World Cup — Qualifier)
10 September 1980

Referee: Wohrer (Austria)
Rasunda Stadion, Stockholm (Att: 39,831)

### SWEDEN 0-1 SCOTLAND — Half-time 0-0

| | | |
|---|---|---|
| (36) | Alan ROUGH (Partick Thistle) | Ronnie HELLSTRÖM |
| (48) | Daniel McGRAIN (Celtic) | Johnny GUSTAVSSON |
| (9) | Francis GRAY (Nottingham Forest) | Hasse BORG |
| (8) | William MILLER (Aberdeen) | Per-Olof BILD |
| (7) | Alexander McLEISH (Aberdeen) | Haakan ARVIDSSON |
| (5) | Alan HANSEN (Liverpool) | Sten-Ove RAMBERG |
| (6) | Gordon STRACHAN (Aberdeen) | Ingemar ERLANDSSON |
| (40) | Archibald GEMMILL (Birmingham City) captain | Mats NORDGREN |
| (11) | John ROBERTSON (Nottingham Forest) | Billy OHLSSON |
| (76) | Kenneth DALGLISH (Liverpool) | Thomas NILSSON |
| (9) | Andrew GRAY (Wolverhampton Wanderers) | Thomas SJÖBERG |

Substitutions

| | | |
|---|---|---|
| (5) | Steven ARCHIBALD (Tottenham Hotspur) for Dalglish 80 mins | Peter NILSSON for Erlandsson 80 mins |

Goals
Strachan (72 mins) 1-0

## 433

(World Cup — Qualifier)
15 October 1980

Referee: Redelfs (West Germany)
Hampden Park, Glasgow (Att: 60,765)

### SCOTLAND 0-0 PORTUGAL

| | | |
|---|---|---|
| (37) | Alan ROUGH (Partick Thistle) | Manuel BENTO |
| (49) | Daniel McGRAIN (Celtic) | GABRIEL Mendes |
| (10) | Francis GRAY (Nottingham Forest) | Joao LARANJEIRA |
| (9) | William MILLER (Aberdeen) | Carlos SIMOES |
| (6) | Alan HANSEN (Liverpool) | Minervino PIETRA |
| (7) | Gordon STRACHAN (Aberdeen) | EURICO Gomes |
| (18) | Graeme SOUNESS (Liverpool) | Carlos MANUEL |
| (41) | Archibald GEMMILL (Birmingham City) captain | Fernando CHALANA |
| (12) | John ROBERTSON (Nottingham Forest) | José COSTA |
| (77) | Kenneth DALGLISH (Liverpool) | Rui JORDAO |
| (10) | Andrew GRAY (Wolverhampton Wanderers) | Manuel FERNANDES |

Substitutions

| | |
|---|---|
| | SHEU Han for Chalana 60 mins |
| | Tamagnini NENÉ for Jordao 60 mins |

# 1981

| P | W | D | L | F | A |
|---|---|---|---|---|---|
| 9 | 5 | 2 | 2 | 11 | 6 |

## 434

(World Cup — Qualifier)
25 February 1981

Referee: Andreco (Romania)
Ramat Gan Stadion, Tel Aviv (Att: 35,000)

### ISRAEL 0-1 SCOTLAND — Half-time 0-0

| | | |
|---|---|---|
| (38) | Alan ROUGH (Partick Thistle) | Shlomo MITZRAHI |
| (50) | Daniel McGRAIN (Celtic) | Gad MACHNES |
| (11) | Francis GRAY (Nottingham Forest) | Avi COHEN |
| (18) | Kenneth BURNS (Nottingham Forest) | Yaacov COHEN |
| (8) | Alexander McLEISH (Aberdeen) | Haim BAR |
| (10) | John WARK (Ipswich Town) | Ytszak SHUM |
| (19) | Graeme SOUNESS (Liverpool) | Yaacov EKHOIZ |
| (42) | Archibald GEMMILL (Birmingham City) captain | Moshe SINAI |
| (13) | John ROBERTSON (Nottingham Forest) | Nissim COHEN |
| (78) | Kenneth DALGLISH (Liverpool) | Beni TABAK |
| (6) | Steven ARCHIBALD (Tottenham Hotspur) | Gideon DAMTI |

Substitutions

| | |
|---|---|
| (10) | William MILLER (Aberdeen) for Wark 46 mins |
| (11) | Andrew GRAY (Wolverhampton Wanderers) for Dalglish 69 mins |

Goals
Dalglish (54 mins) 1-0

## 435

(World Cup — Qualifier)
25 March 1981

Referee: Scheurell (West Germany)
Hampden Park, Glasgow (Att: 78,444)

### SCOTLAND 1-1 NORTHERN IRELAND — Half-time 0-0

| | | |
|---|---|---|
| (39) | Alan ROUGH (Partick Thistle) | Patrick JENNINGS |
| (51) | Daniel McGRAIN (Celtic) | James NICHOLL |
| (12) | Francis GRAY (Nottingham Forest) | Samuel NELSON |
| (11) | William MILLER (Aberdeen) | John O'NEILL |
| (9) | Alexander McLEISH (Aberdeen) | Christopher NICHOLL |
| (11) | John WARK (Ipswich Town) | Terence COCHRANE |
| (19) | Kenneth BURNS (Nottingham Forest) | John McCLELLAND |
| (43) | Archibald GEMMILL (Birmingham City) captain | David McCREERY |
| (14) | John ROBERTSON (Nottingham Forest) | Samuel McILROY |
| (7) | Steven ARCHIBALD (Tottenham Hotspur) | William HAMILTON |
| (12) | Andrew GRAY (Wolverhampton Wanderers) | Gerald ARMSTRONG |

**Substitutions**

| | | |
|---|---|---|
| (38) | Richard HARTFORD (Everton) for Burns 77 mins | Derek SPENCE for Hamilton 78 mins |
| (2) | William THOMSON (St Mirren) for Rough 80 mins | |

**Goals**

| | | |
|---|---|---|
| | 0-1 | Hamilton (70 mins) |
| Wark (75 mins) | 1-1 | |

## 436

(World Cup — Qualifier)
28 April 1981

Referee: Haroldsson (Iceland)
Hampden Park, Glasgow (Att: 61,489)

### SCOTLAND 3-1 ISRAEL — Half-time 2-0

| | | |
|---|---|---|
| (40) | Alan ROUGH (Partick Thistle) | Shlomo MITZRAHI |
| (52) | Daniel McGRAIN (Celtic) captain | Gad MACHNES |
| (13) | Francis GRAY (Nottingham Forest) | Avi COHEN |
| (7) | Alan HANSEN (Liverpool) | Yaacov COHEN |
| (10) | Alexander McLEISH (Aberdeen) | Haim BAR |
| (5) | David PROVAN (Celtic) | Ytszak SHUM |
| (20) | Graeme SOUNESS (Liverpool) | Yaacov EKHOIZ |
| (39) | Richard HARTFORD (Everton) | Moshe SINAI |
| (15) | John ROBERTSON (Nottingham Forest) | Yaacov ZEITUNI |
| (8) | Steven ARCHIBALD (Tottenham Hotspur) | Beni TABAK |
| (45) | Joseph JORDAN (Manchester United) | Gideon DAMTI |

**Goals**

| | | |
|---|---|---|
| Robertson (21 mins pen) | 1-0 | |
| Robertson (30 mins pen) | 2-0 | |
| Provan (53 mins) | 3-0 | |
| | 3-1 | Sinai (58 mins) |

## 437

(Home International Championship)
16 May 1981

Referee: Donnelly (Northern Ireland)
Vetch Field, Swansea (Att: 18,985)

### WALES 2-0 SCOTLAND — Half-time 2-0

| | | |
|---|---|---|
| (41) | Alan ROUGH (Partick Thistle) | William DAVIES |
| (1) | Raymond STEWART (West Ham United) | Paul PRICE |
| (14) | Francis GRAY (Nottingham Forest) | Joseph JONES |
| (9) | David NAREY (Dundee United) | Leighton PHILLIPS |
| (30) | Gordon McQUEEN (Manchester United) | Kevin RATCLIFFE |
| (12) | William MILLER (Aberdeen) | Carl HARRIS |
| (6) | David PROVAN (Celtic) | Peter NICHOLAS |
| (20) | Kenneth BURNS (Nottingham Forest) | Brian FLYNN |
| (40) | Richard HARTFORD (Everton) captain | Michael THOMAS |
| (11) | Arthur GRAHAM (Leeds United) | Leighton JAMES |
| (46) | Joseph JORDAN (Manchester United) | Ian WALSH |

**Substitutions**

| | | |
|---|---|---|
| (53) | Daniel McGRAIN (Celtic) for Gray 46 mins | Terrence BOYLE for Jones 71 mins |
| (1) | Paul STURROCK (Dundee United) for Graham 85 mins | Jeremy CHARLES for Walsh 76 mins |

**Goals**

| | | |
|---|---|---|
| | 0-1 | Walsh (17 mins) |
| | 0-2 | Walsh (20 mins) |

## 438

(Home International Championship)
19 May 1981

Referee: Partridge (England)
Hampden Park, Glasgow (Att: 22,248)

### SCOTLAND 2-0 NORTHERN IRELAND — Half-time 1-0

| | | |
|---|---|---|
| (3) | William THOMSON (St Mirren) | Patrick JENNINGS |
| (54) | Daniel McGRAIN (Celtic) captain | James NICHOLL |
| (15) | Francis GRAY (Leeds United) | Samuel NELSON |
| (13) | William MILLER (Aberdeen) | John O'NEILL |
| (11) | Alexander McLEISH (Aberdeen) | Christopher NICHOLL |
| (2) | Raymond STEWART (West Ham United) | Terence COCHRANE |
| (1) | Thomas BURNS (Celtic) | John McCLELLAND |
| (41) | Richard HARTFORD (Everton) | Martin O'NEILL |
| (16) | John ROBERTSON (Nottingham Forest) | Samuel McILROY |
| (2) | Paul STURROCK (Dundee United) | William HAMILTON |
| (9) | Steven ARCHIBALD (Tottenham Hotspur) | Gerald ARMSTRONG |

**Substitutions**

| | | |
|---|---|---|
| | | Mal DONAGHY for Nelson 70 mins |

**Goals**

| | | |
|---|---|---|
| Stewart (5 mins) | 1-0 | |
| Archibald (49 mins) | 2-0 | |

## 439

(Home International Championship)
23 May 1981

Referee: Wurtz (France)
Wembley Stadium, London (Att: 90,000)

### ENGLAND 0-1 SCOTLAND — Half-time 0-0

| | | |
|---|---|---|
| (42) | Alan ROUGH (Partick Thistle) | Joseph CORRIGAN |
| (55) | Daniel McGRAIN (Celtic) captain | Vivian ANDERSON |
| (16) | Francis GRAY (Leeds United) | Kenneth SANSOM |
| (14) | Alexander McLEISH (Aberdeen) | Raymond WILKINS |
| (12) | Alexander McLEISH (Aberdeen) | David WATSON |
| (7) | David PROVAN (Celtic) | Stephen COPPELL |
| (3) | Raymond HARTFORD (West Ham United) | Bryan ROBSON |
| (42) | Richard HARTFORD (Everton) | Glenn HODDLE |
| (17) | John ROBERTSON (Nottingham Forest) | Graham RIX |
| (10) | Steven ARCHIBALD (Tottenham Hotspur) | Peter WITHE |
| (47) | Joseph JORDAN (Manchester United) | Anthony WOODCOCK |

**Substitutions**

| | | |
|---|---|---|
| (10) | David NAREY (Dundee United) for Hartford 27 mins | Alvin MARTIN for Watson 46 mins |
| (3) | Paul STURROCK (Dundee United) for Provan 80 mins | Trevor FRANCIS for Woodcock 46 mins |

**Goals**

| | | |
|---|---|---|
| Robertson (64 mins pen) | 1-0 | |

## 440

(World Cup — Qualifier)
9 September 1981

Referee: Daina (Switzerland)
Hampden Park, Glasgow (Att: 81,511)

### SCOTLAND 2-0 SWEDEN — Half-time 1-0

| | | |
|---|---|---|
| (43) | Alan ROUGH (Partick Thistle) | Thomas RAVELLI |
| (56) | Daniel McGRAIN (Celtic) captain | Andreas RAVELLI |
| (17) | Francis GRAY (Leeds United) | Hasse BORG |
| (8) | Alan HANSEN (Liverpool) | Stig FREDRIKSSON |
| (13) | Alexander McLEISH (Aberdeen) | Glenn HYSÉN |
| (8) | David PROVAN (Celtic) | Ingemar ERLANDSSON |
| (12) | John WARK (Ipswich Town) | Karl-Gunnar BJÖRKLUND |
| (43) | Richard HARTFORD (Everton) | Bo BÖRJESSON |
| (18) | John ROBERTSON (Nottingham Forest) | Jan SVENSSON |
| (79) | Kenneth DALGLISH (Liverpool) | Thomas LARSSON |
| (48) | Joseph JORDAN (Milan) | Thomas SJÖBERG |

**Substitutions**

| | | |
|---|---|---|
| (13) | Andrew GRAY (Wolverhampton Wanderers) for Dalglish 70 mins | Grege HALLÉN for Fredriksson 46 mins |

**Goals**

| | | |
|---|---|---|
| Jordan (20 mins) | 1-0 | |
| Robertson (83 mins pen) | 2-0 | |

## 441

(World Cup — Qualifier)
14 October 1981

Referee: Butenko (Soviet Union)
Windsor Park, Belfast (Att: 22,248)

### NORTHERN IRELAND 0-0 SCOTLAND

| | | |
|---|---|---|
| (44) | Alan ROUGH (Partick Thistle) | Patrick JENNINGS |
| (4) | Raymond STEWART (West Ham United) | James NICHOLL |
| (18) | Francis GRAY (Leeds United) | Mal DONAGHY |
| (15) | William MILLER (Aberdeen) | John O'NEILL |
| (9) | Alan HANSEN (Liverpool) | Christopher NICHOLL |
| (8) | Gordon STRACHAN (Aberdeen) | David McCREERY |
| (21) | Graeme SOUNESS (Liverpool) | Noel BROTHERSTON |
| (44) | Richard HARTFORD (Manchester City) captain | Martin O'NEILL |
| (19) | John ROBERTSON (Nottingham Forest) | Samuel McILROY |
| (80) | Kenneth DALGLISH (Liverpool) | William HAMILTON |
| (11) | Steven ARCHIBALD (Tottenham Hotspur) | Gerald ARMSTRONG |

**Substitutions**

| | | |
|---|---|---|
| (14) | Andrew GRAY (Wolverhampton Wanderers) for Strachan 76 mins | |

## 442

(World Cup — Qualifier)
18 November 1981

Referee: Corver (Netherlands)
Estadio da Luz, Lisbon (Att: 25,000)

### PORTUGAL 2-1 SCOTLAND — Half-time 1-1

| | | |
|---|---|---|
| (4) | William THOMSON (St Mirren) | Manuel BENTO |
| (5) | Raymond STEWART (West Ham United) | Adelino TEIXEIRA |
| (19) | Francis GRAY (Leeds United) | Gregorio FREIXO |
| (16) | William MILLER (Aberdeen) | Carlos SIMOES |
| (10) | Alan HANSEN (Liverpool) | Eduardo MENDES |
| (9) | David PROVAN (Celtic) | EURICO Gomes |
| (22) | Graeme SOUNESS (Liverpool) | Jaime MAGALHAES |
| (45) | Richard HARTFORD (Manchester City) captain | Antonio OLIVEIRA |
| (9) | Gordon STRACHAN (Aberdeen) | José COSTA |
| (4) | Paul STURROCK (Dundee United) | ROMEU da Silva |
| (12) | Steven ARCHIBALD (Tottenham Hotspur) | Manuel FERNANDES |

**Substitutions**

| | | |
|---|---|---|
| (8) | Stuart KENNEDY (Aberdeen) for Gray 42 mins | DIAMANTINO Miranda for Magalhaes 46 mins |
| (81) | Kenneth DALGLISH (Liverpool) for Archibald 65 mins | Antonio VELOSO for Freixo 50 mins |

**Goals**

| | | |
|---|---|---|
| Sturrock (9 mins) | 1-0 | |
| | 1-1 | Fernandes (39 mins) |
| | 1-2 | Fernandes (56 mins) |

# 1982

| P | W | D | L | F | A |
|---|---|---|---|---|---|
| 11 | 4 | 2 | 5 | 16 | 19 |

## 443
(Friendly)
24 February 1982

Referee: Thomas (Netherlands)
Estadio Luis Casanova, Valencia (Att: 30,000)

### SPAIN 3-0 SCOTLAND — Half-time 1-0

| (45) | Alan ROUGH (Partick Thistle) | | Luis ARCONADA |
|---|---|---|---|
| (57) | Daniel McGRAIN (Celtic) captain | | José CAMACHO |
| (20) | Francis GRAY (Leeds United) | | Rafael GORDILLO |
| (11) | Alan HANSEN (Liverpool) | | José ALESANCO |
| (14) | Alexander McLEISH (Aberdeen) | | Miguel TENDILLO |
| (10) | Gordon STRACHAN (Aberdeen) | | José SANCHEZ |
| (23) | Graeme SOUNESS (Liverpool) | | Miguel ALONSO |
| (46) | Richard HARTFORD (Manchester City) | | Victor MUNOZ |
| (13) | John WARK (Ipswich Town) | | Roberto LOPEZ |
| (82) | Kenneth DALGLISH (Liverpool) | | Enrique SAURA |
| (3) | Alan BRAZIL (Ipswich Town) | | Jesús SATRÚSTEGUI |

Substitutions

| (13) | Steven ARCHIBALD (Tottenham Hotspur) | | Enrique CASTRO |
|---|---|---|---|
| | for Strachan 54 mins | | for Satrústegui 46 mins |
| | | | Ricardo GALLEGO |
| | | | for Munoz 54 mins |

Goals
| | 0-1 | Munoz (26 mins) |
|---|---|---|
| | 0-2 | Castro (83 mins pen) |
| | 0-3 | Gallego (86 mins) |

## 444
(Friendly)
23 March 1982

Referee: Courtney (England)
Hampden Park, Glasgow (Att: 71,848)

### SCOTLAND 2-1 NETHERLANDS — Half-time 2-1

| (46) | Alan ROUGH (Partick Thistle) | | Johannes VAN BREUKELEN |
|---|---|---|---|
| (58) | Daniel McGRAIN (Celtic) captain | | Michaël VAN DE KORPUT |
| (21) | Francis GRAY (Leeds United) | | Ronald SPELBOS |
| (1) | Allan EVANS (Aston Villa) | | Johannes METGOD |
| (17) | William MILLER (Aberdeen) | | Rudolf KROL |
| (11) | David NAREY (Dundee United) | | Hugo HOVENKAMP |
| (1) | James BETT (Rangers) | | Johannes PETERS |
| (83) | Kenneth DALGLISH (Liverpool) | | Franklin RIJKAARD |
| (14) | John WARK (Ipswich Town) | | Arnoldus MÜHREN |
| (14) | Steven ARCHIBALD (Tottenham Hotspur) | | Simon TAHAMATA |
| (49) | Joseph JORDAN (Milan) | | Willem KIEFT |

Substitutions

| (4) | Alan BRAZIL (Ipswich Town) | |
|---|---|---|
| | for Dalglish 46 mins | |
| (2) | Thomas BURNS (Celtic) | |
| | for Archibald 46 mins | |
| (11) | Gordon STRACHAN (Aberdeen) | |
| | for Jordan 62 mins | |

Goals
| Gray (13 mins pen) | 1-0 | |
|---|---|---|
| Dalglish (21 mins) | 2-0 | |
| | 2-1 | Kieft (30 mins) |

## 445
(Home International Championship)
28 April 1982

Referee: Hunting (England)
Windsor Park, Belfast (Att: 20,000)

### NORTHERN IRELAND 1-1 SCOTLAND — Half-time 0-1

| (4) | George WOOD (Arsenal) | | James PLATT |
|---|---|---|---|
| (59) | Daniel McGRAIN (Celtic) captain | | Mal DONAGHY |
| (1) | Arthur ALBISTON (Manchester United) | | Samuel NELSON |
| (2) | Allan EVANS (Aston Villa) | | John O'NEILL |
| (15) | Alexander McLEISH (Aberdeen) | | John McCLELLAND |
| (10) | David PROVAN (Celtic) | | James CLEARY |
| (15) | John WARK (Ipswich Town) | | Felix HEALY |
| (47) | Richard HARTFORD (Manchester City) | | Martin O'NEILL |
| (20) | John ROBERTSON (Nottingham Forest) | | Samuel McILROY |
| (84) | Kenneth DALGLISH (Liverpool) | | Robert CAMPBELL |
| (5) | Alan BRAZIL (Ipswich Town) | | Noel BROTHERSTON |

Substitutions

| (12) | Alan HANSEN (Liverpool) | |
|---|---|---|
| | for McLeish 75 mins | |
| (5) | Paul STURROCK (Dundee United) | |
| | for Robertson 80 mins | |

Goals
| Wark (32 mins) | 1-0 | |
|---|---|---|
| | 1-1 | McIlroy (55 mins) |

## 446
(Home International Championship)
24 May 1982

Referee: McKnight (Northern Ireland)
Hampden Park, Glasgow (Att: 25,284)

### SCOTLAND 1-0 WALES — Half-time 1-0

| (47) | Alan ROUGH (Partick Thistle) | | William DAVIES |
|---|---|---|---|
| (6) | Raymond STEWART (West Ham United) | | Byron STEVENSON |
| (22) | Francis GRAY (Leeds United) | | Joseph JONES |
| (12) | David NAREY (Dundee United) | | Christopher MARUSTIK |
| (13) | Alan HANSEN (Liverpool) | | Nigel STEVENSON |
| (3) | Thomas BURNS (Celtic) | | Robert JAMES |
| (24) | Graeme SOUNESS (Liverpool) captain | | Peter NICHOLAS |
| (48) | Richard HARTFORD (Manchester City) | | Brian FLYNN |
| (85) | Kenneth DALGLISH (Liverpool) | | Alan CURTIS |
| (6) | Alan BRAZIL (Ipswich Town) | | Leighton JAMES |
| (50) | Joseph JORDAN (Milan) | | Ian RUSH |

Substitutions

| (10) | George BURLEY (Ipswich Town) | | Ian WALSH |
|---|---|---|---|
| | for Stewart 72 mins | | for Curtis 75 mins |
| (6) | Paul STURROCK (Dundee United) | | Michael THOMAS |
| | for Jordan 72 mins | | for Flynn 75 mins |

Goals
| Hartford (7 mins) | 1-0 |
|---|---|

## 447
(Home International Championship)
29 May 1982

Referee: Redelfs (West Germany)
Hampden Park, Glasgow (Att: 80,529)

### SCOTLAND 0-1 ENGLAND — Half-time 0-1

| (48) | Alan ROUGH (Partick Thistle) | | Peter SHILTON |
|---|---|---|---|
| (11) | George BURLEY (Ipswich Town) | | Michael MILLS |
| (60) | Daniel McGRAIN (Celtic) captain | | Kenneth SANSOM |
| (3) | Allan EVANS (Aston Villa) | | Philip THOMPSON |
| (14) | Alan HANSEN (Liverpool) | | Terence BUTCHER |
| (13) | David NAREY (Dundee United) | | Steven COPPELL |
| (25) | Graeme SOUNESS (Liverpool) | | Raymond WILKINS |
| (49) | Richard HARTFORD (Manchester City) | | Bryan ROBSON |
| (86) | Kenneth DALGLISH (Liverpool) | | Trevor BROOKING |
| (7) | Alan BRAZIL (Ipswich Town) | | Kevin KEEGAN |
| (51) | Joseph JORDAN (Milan) | | Paul MARINER |

Substitutions

| (21) | John ROBERTSON (Nottingham Forest) | | Trevor FRANCIS |
|---|---|---|---|
| | for Hartford 46 mins | | for Mariner 46 mins |
| (7) | Paul STURROCK (Dundee United) | | Terence McDERMOTT |
| | for Jordan 63 mins | | for Keegan 56 mins |

Goals
| | 0-1 | Mariner (13 mins) |
|---|---|---|

## 448
(World Cup — Final Tournament 1st Round)
15 June 1982

Referee: Socha (USA)
Estadio La Rosaleda, Malaga (Att: 20,000)

### NEW ZEALAND 2-5 SCOTLAND — Half-time 0-3

| (49) | Alan ROUGH (Partick Thistle) | | Frank VAN HATTUM |
|---|---|---|---|
| (61) | Daniel McGRAIN (Celtic) captain | | John HILL |
| (23) | Francis GRAY (Leeds United) | | Samuel MALCOLMSON |
| (4) | Allan EVANS (Aston Villa) | | Robert ALMOND |
| (15) | Alan HANSEN (Liverpool) | | Adrian ELRICK |
| (12) | Gordon STRACHAN (Aberdeen) | | Keith MACKAY |
| (26) | Graeme SOUNESS (Liverpool) | | Kenneth CRESSWELL |
| (16) | John WARK (Ipswich Town) | | Allan BOATH |
| (22) | John ROBERTSON (Nottingham Forest) | | Wynton RUFER |
| (87) | Kenneth DALGLISH (Liverpool) | | Stephen SUMNER |
| (8) | Alan BRAZIL (Ipswich Town) | | Stephen WOODDIN |

Substitutions

| (15) | Steven ARCHIBALD (Tottenham Hotspur) | | Richard HERBERT |
|---|---|---|---|
| | for Brazil 53 mins | | for Almond 66 mins |
| (14) | David NAREY (Dundee United) | | Duncan COLE |
| | for Strachan 83 mins | | for Malcolmson 77 mins |

Goals
| Dalglish (18 mins) | 1-0 | |
|---|---|---|
| Wark (29 mins) | 2-0 | |
| Wark (32 mins) | 3-0 | |
| | 3-1 | Sumner (55 mins) |
| | 3-2 | Wooddin (65 mins) |
| Robertson (73 mins) | 4-2 | |
| Archibald (80 mins) | 5-2 | |

## 449

(World Cup — Final Tournament 1st Round)     Referee: Calderon (Costa Rica)
18 June 1982     Estadio Benito Villamarin, Seville (Att: 47,379)

### BRAZIL 4-1 SCOTLAND     Half-time 1-1

| | | |
|---|---|---|
| (50) | Alan ROUGH (Partick Thistle) | WALDIR PERES Arruda |
| (15) | David NAREY (Dundee United) | José LEANDRO Souza Ferreira |
| (24) | Francis GRAY (Leeds United) | José OSCAR Bernardi |
| (18) | William MILLER (Aberdeen) | Luis Carlos LUISINHO |
| (16) | Alan HANSEN (Liverpool) | Leovegildo Lins Gama JUNIOR |
| (13) | Gordon STRACHAN (Aberdeen) | Antonio TONINHO CEREZO |
| (27) | Graeme SOUNESS (Liverpool) | Paulo Roberto FALCAO |
| (50) | Richard HARTFORD (Manchester City) | SOCRATES de Souza Vieira |
| (23) | John ROBERTSON (Nottingham Forest) | EDER Aleixo de Assis |
| (17) | John WARK (Ipswich Town) | Arthur Antunes Coimbra ZICO |
| (16) | Steven ARCHIBALD (Tottenham Hotspur) | Sergio Bernardino SERGINHO |

Substitutions

| | | |
|---|---|---|
| (88) | Kenneth DALGLISH (Liverpool) | PAULO ISIDORO de Jesus |
| | for Strachan 65 mins | for Serginho 82 mins |
| (16) | Alexander McLEISH (Aberdeen) | |
| | for Hartford 69 mins | |

Goals

| | | |
|---|---|---|
| Narey (18 mins) | 1-0 | |
| | 1-1 | Zico (33 mins) |
| | 1-2 | Oscar (48 mins) |
| | 1-3 | Eder (64 mins) |
| | 1-4 | Falcao (86 mins) |

---

## 450

(World Cup — Final Tournament 1st Round)     Referee: Rainea (Romania)
22 June 1982     Estadio La Rosaleda, Malaga (Att: 45,000)

### USSR 2-2 SCOTLAND     Half-time 0-1

| | | |
|---|---|---|
| (51) | Alan ROUGH (Partick Thistle) | Rinat DASAEV |
| (16) | David NAREY (Dundee United) | Tengiz SULAKVELIDZE |
| (25) | Francis GRAY (Leeds United) | Vladimir BESSONOV |
| (19) | William MILLER (Aberdeen) | Alexandr CHIVADZE |
| (17) | Alan HANSEN (Liverpool) | Anatolij DEMIANENKO |
| (14) | Gordon STRACHAN (Aberdeen) | Sergei BOROVSKY |
| (28) | Graeme SOUNESS (Liverpool) captain | Sergei BALTACHA |
| (18) | John WARK (Ipswich Town) | Andrei BAL |
| (24) | John ROBERTSON (Nottingham Forest) | Oleg BLOCHIN |
| (17) | Steven ARCHIBALD (Tottenham Hotspur) | Iurij GAVRILOV |
| (52) | Joseph JORDAN (Milan) | Ramaz SHENGELIA |

Substitutions

| | | |
|---|---|---|
| (62) | Daniel McGRAIN (Celtic) | Sergei ANDREEV |
| | for Strachan 71 mins | for Shengelia 89 mins |
| (9) | Alan BRAZIL (Ipswich Town) | |
| | for Jordan 71 mins | |

Goals

| | | |
|---|---|---|
| Jordan (15 mins) | 1-0 | |
| | 1-1 | Chivadze (60 mins) |
| | 1-2 | Shengelia (84 mins) |
| Souness (88 mins) | 2-2 | |

---

## 451

(European Championship — Qualifier)     Referee: Konrath (France)
13 October 1982     Hampden Park, Glasgow (Att: 40,355)

### SCOTLAND 2-0 EAST GERMANY     Half-time 0-0

| | | |
|---|---|---|
| (1) | James LEIGHTON (Aberdeen) | Bodo RUDWALEIT |
| (17) | David NAREY (Dundee United) | Ronald KREER |
| (26) | Francis GRAY (Leeds United) | Dirk STAHMANN |
| (20) | William MILLER (Aberdeen) | Norbert TRIELOFF |
| (18) | Alan HANSEN (Liverpool) | Rüdiger SCHNUPHASE |
| (15) | Gordon STRACHAN (Aberdeen) | Reinhard HÄFNER |
| (29) | Graeme SOUNESS (Liverpool) captain | Frank BAUM |
| (19) | John WARK (Ipswich Town) | Hans-Jürgen DORNER |
| (25) | John ROBERTSON (Nottingham Forest) | Hans-Uwe PILZ |
| (10) | Alan BRAZIL (Ipswich Town) | Hans-Jürgen RIEDIGER |
| (18) | Steven ARCHIBALD (Tottenham Hotspur) | Joachim STREICH |

Substitutions

| | | |
|---|---|---|
| (8) | Paul STURROCK (Dundee United) | Matthias LIEBERS |
| | for Brazil 71 mins | for Häfner 72 mins |
| | | Jürgen POMMERENKE |
| | | for Dörner 72 mins |

Goals

| | | |
|---|---|---|
| Wark (53 mins) | 1-0 | |
| Sturrock (75 mins) | 2-0 | |

---

## 452

(European Championship — Qualifier)     Referee: Christov (Czechoslovakia)
17 November 1982     Wankdorf Stadion, Berne (Att: 26,000)

### SWITZERLAND 2-0 SCOTLAND     Half-time 0-0

| | | |
|---|---|---|
| (2) | James LEIGHTON (Aberdeen) | Erich BURGENER |
| (18) | David NAREY (Dundee United) | Heinz LÜDI |
| (27) | Francis GRAY (Leeds United) | Roger WEHRLI |
| (21) | William MILLER (Aberdeen) | André EGLI |
| (19) | Alan HANSEN (Liverpool) | Alain GEIGER |
| (16) | Gordon STRACHAN (Aberdeen) | Lucien FAVRE |
| (30) | Graeme SOUNESS (Liverpool) captain | Michel DECASTEL |
| (20) | John WARK (Ipswich Town) | Heinz HERMANN |
| (26) | John ROBERTSON (Nottingham Forest) | Raimondo PONTE |
| (9) | Paul STURROCK (Dundee United) | Rudolf ELSENER |
| (11) | Alan BRAZIL (Ipswich Town) | Claudio SULSER |

Substitutions

| | | |
|---|---|---|
| (19) | Steven ARCHIBALD (Tottenham Hotspur) | Umberto BARBERIS |
| | for Sturrock 46 mins | for Decastel 61 mins |
| | | Hanspeter ZWICKER |
| | | for Elsener 85 mins |

Goals

| | | |
|---|---|---|
| | 0-1 | Sulser (49 mins) |
| | 0-2 | Egli (60 mins) |

---

## 453

(European Championship — Qualifier)     Referee: Garrido (Portugal)
15 December 1982     Heysel Stadium, Brussels (Att: 48,877)

### BELGIUM 3-2 SCOTLAND     Half-time 2-2

| | | |
|---|---|---|
| (3) | James LEIGHTON (Aberdeen) | Jean-Marie PFAFF |
| (19) | David NAREY (Dundee United) | Eric GERETS |
| (28) | Francis GRAY (Leeds United) | Jos DAERDEN |
| (20) | Alan HANSEN (Liverpool) | Walter MEEUWS |
| (17) | Alexander McLEISH (Aberdeen) | Marc BAECKE |
| (17) | Gordon STRACHAN (Aberdeen) | Guy VANDERSMISSEN |
| (31) | Graeme SOUNESS (Liverpool) captain | Ludo COECK |
| (6) | Robert AITKEN (Celtic) | Frank VERCAUTEREN |
| (2) | James BETT (Rangers) | Jan CEULEMANS |
| (89) | Kenneth DALGLISH (Liverpool) | François VAN DER ELST |
| (20) | Steven ARCHIBALD (Tottenham Hotspur) | Erwin VANDENBERGH |

Substitutions

| | | |
|---|---|---|
| (4) | Thomas BURNS (Celtic) | René VERHEYEN |
| | for Strachan 77 mins | for Vercauteren 63 mins |
| (10) | Paul STURROCK (Dundee United) | Maurice DE SCHRYVER |
| | for Bett 77 mins | for Vandenbergh 87 mins |

Goals

| | | |
|---|---|---|
| Dalglish (13 mins) | 1-0 | |
| | 1-1 | Vandenbergh (26 mins) |
| Dalglish (36 mins) | 2-1 | |
| | 2-2 | Van der Elst (39 mins) |
| | 2-3 | Van der Elst (63 mins) |

---

# 1983

| P | W | D | L | F | A |
|---|---|---|---|---|---|
| 11 | 5 | 3 | 3 | 15 | 9 |

---

## 454

(European Championship — Qualifier)     Referee: Corver (Netherlands)
30 March 1983     Hampden Park, Glasgow (Att: 36,923)

### SCOTLAND 2-2 SWITZERLAND     Half-time 0-1

| | | |
|---|---|---|
| (4) | James LEIGHTON (Aberdeen) | Erich BURGENER |
| (1) | Richard GOUGH (Dundee United) | Heinz LÜDI |
| (29) | Francis GRAY (Leeds United) | Roger WEHRLI |
| (22) | William MILLER (Aberdeen) | André EGLI |
| (21) | Alan HANSEN (Liverpool) | Alain GEIGER |
| (18) | Gordon STRACHAN (Aberdeen) | Lucien FAVRE |
| (32) | Graeme SOUNESS (Liverpool) captain | Michel DECASTEL |
| (21) | John WARK (Ipswich Town) | Heinz HERMANN |
| (5) | Peter WEIR (Aberdeen) | Raimondo PONTE |
| (90) | Kenneth DALGLISH (Liverpool) | Rudolf ELSENER |
| (1) | Charles NICHOLAS (Celtic) | Claudio SULSER |

Substitutions

| | | |
|---|---|---|
| (18) | Alexander McLEISH (Aberdeen) | Hanspeter ZWICKER |
| | for Hansen 46 mins | for Hermann 69 mins |
| | | Charles IN-ALBON |
| | | for Sulser 84 mins |

Goals

| | | |
|---|---|---|
| | 0-1 | Egli (15 mins) |
| | 0-2 | Hermann (58 mins) |
| Wark (70 mins) | 1-2 | |
| Nicholas (76 mins) | 2-2 | |

## 455

(Home International Championship)
24 May 1983

Referee: Hackett (England)
Hampden Park, Glasgow (Att: 16,238)

### SCOTLAND 0-0 NORTHERN IRELAND

| | | |
|---|---|---|
| (5) | William THOMSON (St Mirren) | Patrick JENNINGS |
| (2) | Richard GOUGH (Dundee United) | James NICHOLL |
| (3) | Alistair DAWSON (Rangers) | Mal DONAGHY |
| (20) | David NAREY (Dundee United) | John O'NEILL |
| (8) | Paul HEGARTY (Dundee United) captain | John McCLELLAND |
| (5) | Thomas BURNS (Celtic) | Gerald MULLAN |
| (1) | Neil SIMPSON (Aberdeen) | Martin O'NEILL |
| (22) | John WARK (Ipswich Town) | Samuel McILROY |
| (2) | Eamonn BANNON (Dundee United) | Ian STEWART |
| (15) | Andrew GRAY (Wolverhampton Wanderers) | William HAMILTON |
| (2) | Charles NICHOLAS (Celtic) | Gerald ARMSTRONG |

Substitutions

| | | |
|---|---|---|
| (19) | Gordon STRACHAN (Aberdeen) | Christopher NICHOLL |
| | for Simpson 65 mins | for J. O'Neill 46 mins |
| | | Noel BROTHERSTON |
| | | for Hamilton 89 mins |

## 456

(Home International Championship)
28 May 1983

Referee: Moffatt (Northern Ireland)
Ninian Park, Cardiff (Att: 14,100)

### WALES 0-2 SCOTLAND — Half-time 0-1

| | | |
|---|---|---|
| (5) | James LEIGHTON (Aberdeen) | Neville SOUTHALL |
| (3) | Richard GOUGH (Dundee United) | Neil SLATTER |
| (30) | Francis GRAY (Leeds United) | Joseph JONES |
| (21) | David NAREY (Dundee United) | Paul PRICE |
| (19) | Alexander McLEISH (Aberdeen) | Kevin RATCLIFFE |
| (20) | Gordon STRACHAN (Aberdeen) | Kenneth JACKETT |
| (23) | William MILLER (Aberdeen) | Peter NICHOLAS |
| (33) | Graeme SOUNESS (Liverpool) captain | Jeremy CHARLES |
| (3) | Eamonn BANNON (Dundee United) | Brian FLYNN |
| (16) | Andrew GRAY (Wolverhampton Wanderers) | Michael THOMAS |
| (12) | Alan BRAZIL (Tottenham Hotspur) | Gordon DAVIES |

Substitutions

| | | |
|---|---|---|
| | | Steven LOWNDES |
| | | for Flynn 57 mins |

Goals

| | |
|---|---|
| A. Gray (11 mins) | 1-0 |
| Brazil (67 mins) | 2-0 |

## 457

(Home International Championship)
1 June 1983

Referee: Fredriksson (Sweden)
Wembley Stadium, London (Att: 84,000)

### ENGLAND 2-0 SCOTLAND — Half-time 1-0

| | | |
|---|---|---|
| (6) | James LEIGHTON (Aberdeen) | Peter SHILTON |
| (4) | Richard GOUGH (Dundee United) | Philip NEAL |
| (31) | Francis GRAY (Leeds United) | Kenneth SANSOM |
| (22) | David NAREY (Dundee United) | Graham ROBERTS |
| (20) | Alexander McLEISH (Aberdeen) | Terence BUTCHER |
| (21) | Gordon STRACHAN (Aberdeen) | Samuel LEE |
| (24) | William MILLER (Aberdeen) | Bryan ROBSON |
| (34) | Graeme SOUNESS (Liverpool) captain | Glenn HODDLE |
| (4) | Eamonn BANNON (Dundee United) | Gordon COWANS |
| (17) | Andrew GRAY (Wolverhampton Wanderers) | Peter WITHE |
| (3) | Charles NICHOLAS (Celtic) | Trevor FRANCIS |

Substitutions

| | | |
|---|---|---|
| (13) | Alan BRAZIL (Tottenham Hotspur) | Gary MABBUTT |
| | for Bannon 53 mins | for Robson 25 mins |
| (23) | John WARK (Ipswich Town) | Luther BLISSETT |
| | for Nicholas 67 mins | for Withe 46 mins |

Goals

| | | |
|---|---|---|
| 0-1 | Robson (12 mins) |
| 0-2 | Cowans (52 mins) |

## 458

(Friendly)
12 June 1983

Referee: Clarke (Canada)
Empire Stadium, Vancouver (Att: 14,942)

### CANADA 0-2 SCOTLAND — Half-time 0-1

| | | |
|---|---|---|
| (6) | William THOMSON (St Mirren) | Tino LETTIERI |
| (5) | Richard GOUGH (Dundee United) | Robert LENARDUZZI |
| (4) | Alistair DAWSON (Rangers) | Robert IARUSCI |
| (23) | David NAREY (Dundee United) | Bruce WILSON |
| (21) | Alexander McLEISH (Aberdeen) | Randy RAGAN |
| (22) | Gordon STRACHAN (Aberdeen) | Ian BRIDGE |
| (25) | William MILLER (Aberdeen) captain | Peter ROE |
| (6) | Thomas BURNS (Celtic) | Gerard SWEENEY |
| (5) | Eamonn BANNON (Dundee United) | Edward McNALLY |
| (11) | Paul STURROCK (Dundee United) | Gerard GRAY |
| (4) | Charles NICHOLAS (Celtic) | Dale MITCHELL |

Substitutions

| | | |
|---|---|---|
| (1) | Mark McGHEE (Aberdeen) | John CONNOR |
| | for Nicholas 37 mins | for Roe 46 mins |
| (35) | Graeme SOUNESS (Liverpool) | Terence FELIX |
| | for Strachan 70 mins | for McNally 46 mins |

Goals

| | |
|---|---|
| Strachan (36 mins pen) | 1-0 |
| McGhee (75 mins) | 2-0 |

## 459

(Friendly)
16 June 1983

Referee: Fusco (Canada)
Commonwealth Stadium, Edmonton (Att: 12,258)

### CANADA 0-3 SCOTLAND — Half-time 0-1

| | | |
|---|---|---|
| (7) | James LEIGHTON (Aberdeen) | Tino LETTIERI |
| (6) | Richard GOUGH (Dundee United) | Robert LENARDUZZI |
| (32) | Francis GRAY (Leeds United) | Robert IARUSCI |
| (24) | David NAREY (Dundee United) | Bruce WILSON |
| (22) | Alexander McLEISH (Aberdeen) | Randy RAGAN |
| (23) | Gordon STRACHAN (Aberdeen) | Ian BRIDGE |
| (26) | William MILLER (Aberdeen) | Peter ROE |
| (36) | Graeme SOUNESS (Liverpool) captain | Gerard SWEENEY |
| (12) | Paul STURROCK (Dundee United) | Edward McNALLY |
| (2) | Mark McGHEE (Aberdeen) | Gerard GRAY |
| (5) | Charles NICHOLAS (Celtic) | Dale MITCHELL |

Substitutions

| | | |
|---|---|---|
| (7) | Robert AITKEN (Celtic) | Terence FELIX |
| | for Strachan 46 mins | for Gray 46 mins |
| (18) | Andrew GRAY (Wolverhampton Wanderers) | |
| | for McGhee 54 mins | |

Goals

| | |
|---|---|
| Nicholas (20 mins) | 1-0 |
| Gough (50 mins) | 2-0 |
| Souness (89 mins) | 3-0 |

## 460

(Friendly)
19 June 1983

Referee: Evangelista (Canada)
Varsity Stadium, Toronto (Att: 15,500)

### CANADA 0-2 SCOTLAND — Half-time 0-2

| | | |
|---|---|---|
| (8) | James LEIGHTON (Aberdeen) | Christopher TURNER |
| (7) | Richard GOUGH (Dundee United) | Terence MOORE |
| (5) | Alistair DAWSON (Rangers) | Colin MILLER |
| (25) | David NAREY (Dundee United) | Bruce WILSON |
| (23) | Alexander McLEISH (Aberdeen) | Paul LEE |
| (27) | William MILLER (Aberdeen) | Ian BRIDGE |
| (37) | Graeme SOUNESS (Liverpool) captain | Peter ROE |
| (8) | Robert AITKEN (Celtic) | John CONNOR |
| (13) | Paul STURROCK (Dundee United) | Terence FELIX |
| (19) | Andrew GRAY (Wolverhampton Wanderers) | Gerard GRAY |
| (6) | Charles NICHOLAS (Celtic) | Dale MITCHELL |

Substitutions

| | | |
|---|---|---|
| (24) | Gordon STRACHAN (Aberdeen) | Craig MARTIN |
| | for Gray 46 mins | for Lee 46 mins |
| (7) | Thomas BURNS (Celtic) | Edward McNALLY |
| | for Narey 65 mins | for Bridge 46 mins |

Goals

| | |
|---|---|
| Gray (17 mins) | 1-0 |
| Gray (32 mins) | 2-0 |

## 461

(Friendly)
21 September 1983

Referee: Richardson (England)
Hampden Park, Glasgow (Att: 20,545)

### SCOTLAND 2-0 URUGUAY — Half-time 1-0

| | | |
|---|---|---|
| (9) | James LEIGHTON (Aberdeen) | Rodolfo RODRÍGUEZ |
| (8) | Richard GOUGH (Dundee United) | Nelson GUTIÉRREZ |
| (2) | Arthur ALBISTON (Manchester United) | Eduardo ACEVEDO |
| (28) | William MILLER (Aberdeen) | Victor DIOGO |
| (24) | Alexander McLEISH (Aberdeen) | Nelson AGRESTA |
| (24) | John WARK (Ipswich Town) | Venancio RAMOS |
| (1) | Paul McSTAY (Celtic) | Washington GONZÁLEZ |
| (38) | Graeme SOUNESS (Liverpool) captain | Jorge BARRIOS |
| (27) | John ROBERTSON (Derby County) | Luis ACOSTA |
| (91) | Kenneth DALGLISH (Liverpool) | Alberto SANTELLI |
| (3) | Francis McGARVEY (Celtic) | Mario SARALEGUI |

Substitutions

| | | |
|---|---|---|
| (1) | David DODDS (Dundee United) | Néstor MONTELONGO |
| | for McGarvey 17 mins | for Ramos 70 mins |
| (2) | Neil SIMPSON (Aberdeen) | Carlos AGUILERA |
| | for McStay 77 mins | for Santelli 70 mins |

Goals

Robertson (24 mins pen)  1-0
Dodds (55 mins)  2-0

## 462

(European Championship — Qualifier)
12 October 1983

Referee: Barbaresco (Italy)
Hampden Park, Glasgow (Att: 23,475)

### SCOTLAND 1-1 BELGIUM — Half-time 0-1

| | | |
|---|---|---|
| (10) | James LEIGHTON (Aberdeen) | Jean-Marie PFAFF |
| (9) | Richard GOUGH (Dundee United) | Eric GERETS |
| (3) | Arthur ALBISTON (Manchester United) | Luc MILLECAMPS |
| (29) | William MILLER (Aberdeen) captain | Walter MEEUWS |
| (25) | Alexander McLEISH (Aberdeen) | Michel WINTACQ |
| (25) | John WARK (Ipswich Town) | Ludo COECK |
| (2) | Paul McSTAY (Celtic) | Frank VERCAUTEREN |
| (3) | James BETT (Lokeren) | Nico CLAESEN |
| (28) | John ROBERTSON (Derby County) | Jan CEULEMANS |
| (92) | Kenneth DALGLISH (Liverpool) | François VAN DER ELST |
| (7) | Charles NICHOLAS (Arsenal) | Eduard VOORDECKERS |

Substitutions

| | | |
|---|---|---|
| (4) | Francis McGARVEY (Celtic) | Michel DE WOLF |
| | for Nicholas 74 mins | for Meeuws 76 mins |
| (9) | Robert AITKEN (Celtic) | |
| | for Wark 80 mins | |

Goals

 0-1  Vercauteren (30 mins)
Nicholas (49 mins)  1-1

## 463

(European Championship — Qualifier)
16 November 1983

Referee: Wohrer (Austria)
Kurt Wabbel Stadion, Halle (Att: 18,000)

### EAST GERMANY 2-1 SCOTLAND — Half-time 2-0

| | | |
|---|---|---|
| (7) | William THOMSON (St Mirren) | Bodo RUDWALEIT |
| (10) | Richard GOUGH (Dundee United) | Ronald KREER |
| (4) | Arthur ALBISTON (Manchester United) | Dirk STAHMANN |
| (30) | William MILLER (Aberdeen) captain | Rainer TROPPA |
| (26) | Alexander McLEISH (Aberdeen) | Uwe ZÖTZSCHE |
| (25) | Gordon STRACHAN (Aberdeen) | Christian BACKS |
| (26) | John WARK (Ipswich Town) | Wolfgang STEINBACH |
| (3) | Paul McSTAY (Celtic) | Hans-Uwe PILZ |
| (6) | Eamonn BANNON (Dundee United) | Hans RICHTER |
| (93) | Kenneth DALGLISH (Liverpool) | Rainer ERNST |
| (21) | Steven ARCHIBALD (Tottenham Hotspur) | Joachim STREICH |

Substitutions

| | | |
|---|---|---|
| (5) | Francis McGARVEY (Celtic) | Jürgen RAAB |
| | for McStay 60 mins | for Ernst 87 mins |

Goals

 0-1  Kreer (33 mins)
 0-2  Streich (42 mins)
Bannon (78 mins)  1-2

## 464

(Home International Championship)
13 December 1983

Referee: Midgley (England)
Windsor Park, Belfast (Att: 12,000)

### NORTHERN IRELAND 2-0 SCOTLAND — Half-time 1-0

| | | |
|---|---|---|
| (11) | James LEIGHTON (Aberdeen) | Patrick JENNINGS |
| (11) | Richard GOUGH (Dundee United) | James NICHOLL |
| (1) | Douglas ROUGVIE (Aberdeen) | Mal DONAGHY |
| (10) | Robert AITKEN (Celtic) | John McCLELLAND |
| (27) | Alexander McLEISH (Aberdeen) | Gerald McELHINNEY |
| (26) | Gordon STRACHAN (Aberdeen) | Terence COCHRANE |
| (4) | Paul McSTAY (Celtic) | Paul RAMSEY |
| (39) | Graeme SOUNESS (Liverpool) captain | Samuel McILROY |
| (6) | Peter WEIR (Aberdeen) | Ian STEWART |
| (2) | David DODDS (Dundee United) | Norman WHITESIDE |
| (6) | Francis McGARVEY (Celtic) | William HAMILTON |

Substitutions

| | | |
|---|---|---|
| (3) | Mark McGHEE (Aberdeen) | John O'NEILL |
| | for McGarvey 60 mins | for Cochrane 86 mins |

Goals

 0-1  Whiteside (17 mins)
 0-2  McIlroy (56 mins)

## 1984

| P | W | D | L | F | A |
|---|---|---|---|---|---|
| 6 | 4 | 1 | 1 | 15 | 6 |

## 465

(Home International Championship)
28 February 1984

Referee: Poucher (Northern Ireland)
Hampden Park, Glasgow (Att: 21,542)

### SCOTLAND 2-1 WALES — Half-time 1-0

| | | |
|---|---|---|
| (12) | James LEIGHTON (Aberdeen) | Neville SOUTHALL |
| (12) | Richard GOUGH (Dundee United) | Jeffrey HOPKINS |
| (5) | Arthur ALBISTON (Manchester United) | Joseph JONES |
| (31) | William MILLER (Aberdeen) | Jeremy CHARLES |
| (28) | Alexander McLEISH (Aberdeen) | Kevin RATCLIFFE |
| (5) | Paul McSTAY (Celtic) | Robert JAMES |
| (40) | Graeme SOUNESS (Liverpool) captain | Kenneth JACKETT |
| (4) | James BETT (Lokeren) | Brian FLYNN |
| (3) | David COOPER (Rangers) | Michael THOMAS |
| (14) | Paul STURROCK (Dundee United) | Alan CURTIS |
| (7) | Francis McGARVEY (Celtic) | Ian RUSH |

Substitutions

| | | |
|---|---|---|
| (1) | Maurice JOHNSTON (Watford) | Gordon DAVIES |
| | for McGarvey 46 mins | for Rush 64 mins |
| (11) | Robert AITKEN (Celtic) | Paul PRICE |
| | for McStay 64 mins | for Curtis 84 mins |

Goals

Cooper (37 mins pen)  1-0
 1-1  James (47 mins)
Johnston (78 mins)  2-1

## 466

(Home International Championship)
26 May 1984

Referee: Casarin (Italy)
Hampden Park, Glasgow (Att: 73,064)

### SCOTLAND 1-1 ENGLAND — Half-time 1-1

| | | |
|---|---|---|
| (13) | James LEIGHTON (Aberdeen) | Peter SHILTON |
| (13) | Richard GOUGH (Dundee United) | Michael DUXBURY |
| (6) | Arthur ALBISTON (Manchester United) | Kenneth SANSOM |
| (32) | William MILLER (Aberdeen) captain | Graham ROBERTS |
| (29) | Alexander McLEISH (Aberdeen) | Terence FENWICK |
| (27) | Gordon STRACHAN (Aberdeen) | Mark CHAMBERLAIN |
| (5) | James BETT (Lokeren) | Raymond WILKINS |
| (27) | John WARK (Liverpool) | Bryan ROBSON |
| (4) | David COOPER (Rangers) | John BARNES |
| (22) | Steven ARCHIBALD (Tottenham Hotspur) | Anthony WOODCOCK |
| (4) | Mark McGHEE (Aberdeen) | Luther BLISSETT |

Substitutions

| | | |
|---|---|---|
| (6) | Paul McSTAY (Celtic) | Gary LINEKER |
| | for Strachan 62 mins | for Woodcock 72 mins |
| (2) | Maurice JOHNSTON (Watford) | Steven HUNT |
| | for McGhee 62 mins | for Chamberlain 74 mins |

Goals

McGhee (13 mins)  1-0
 1-1  Woodcock (36 mins)

## 467

(Friendly)
1 June 1984

Referee: Agnolin (Italy)
Stade Vélodrome, Marseille (Att: 24,641)

### FRANCE 2-0 SCOTLAND
Half-time 2-0

| | | | |
|---|---|---|---|
| (14) | James LEIGHTON (Aberdeen) | | Joël BATS |
| (14) | Richard GOUGH (Dundee United) | | Manuel AMOROS |
| (1) | Maurice MALPAS (Dundee United) | | Maxime BOSSIS |
| (33) | William MILLER (Aberdeen) captain | | Patrick BATTISTON |
| (30) | Alexander McLEISH (Aberdeen) | | Yvon LE ROUX |
| (28) | Gordon STRACHAN (Aberdeen) | | Luis FERNANDEZ |
| (7) | Raymond STEWART (West Ham United) | | Jean TIGANA |
| (6) | James BETT (Lokeren) | | Alain GIRESSE |
| (28) | John WARK (Liverpool) | | Michel PLATINI |
| (23) | Steven ARCHIBALD (Tottenham Hotspur) | | Bruno BELLONE |
| (3) | Maurice JOHNSTON (Watford) | | Bernard LACOMBE |

Substitutions

| | | | |
|---|---|---|---|
| (3) | Neil SIMPSON (Aberdeen) | | Daniel BRAVO |
| | for Strachan 46 mins | | for Lacombe 46 mins |
| (8) | Charles NICHOLAS (Arsenal) | | Bernard GENGHINI |
| | for Gough 67 mins | | for Fernandez 67 mins |
| | | | Didier SIX |
| | | | for Bellone 67 mins |

Goals

| | | |
|---|---|---|
| | 0-1 | Giresse (14 mins) |
| | 0-2 | Lacombe (29 mins) |

## 468

(Friendly)
12 September 1984

Referee: Hackett (England)
Hampden Park, Glasgow (Att: 18,512)

### SCOTLAND 6-1 YUGOSLAVIA
Half-time 3-1

| | | | |
|---|---|---|---|
| (15) | James LEIGHTON (Aberdeen) | | Dragan PANTELIC |
| (1) | Stephen NICOL (Liverpool) | | Branko MILJUS |
| (7) | Arthur ALBISTON (Manchester United) | | Mirsad BALJIC |
| (34) | William MILLER (Aberdeen) | | Miodrag JESIC |
| (31) | Alexander McLEISH (Aberdeen) | | Vladimir MATIJEVIC |
| (7) | James BETT (Lokeren) | | Ljubomir RADANOVIC |
| (41) | Graeme SOUNESS (Sampdoria) captain | | Edin BAHTIC |
| (29) | John WARK (Liverpool) | | Blaz SLISKOVIC |
| (5) | David COOPER (Rangers) | | Zoran BATROVIC |
| (94) | Kenneth DALGLISH (Liverpool) | | Fadilj VOKRI |
| (4) | Maurice JOHNSTON (Celtic) | | Petar GEORGIJEVSKI |

Substitutions

| | | | |
|---|---|---|---|
| (7) | Paul McSTAY (Celtic) | | Ranko STOJIC |
| | for Wark 46 mins | | for Pantelic 46 mins |
| (15) | Paul STURROCK (Dundee United) | | Darko PANCEV |
| | for Dalglish 55 mins | | for Vokri 46 mins |
| (9) | Charles NICHOLAS (Arsenal) | | Nenad GRACAN |
| | for Cooper 60 mins | | for Georgijevski 46 mins |
| | | | Davor JOZIC |
| | | | for Matijevic 65 mins |

Goals

| | | |
|---|---|---|
| | 0-1 | Vokri (10 mins) |
| Cooper (11 mins) | 1-1 | |
| Souness (18 mins) | 2-1 | |
| Dalglish (31 mins) | 3-1 | |
| Sturrock (64 mins) | 4-1 | |
| Johnston (66 mins) | 5-1 | |
| Nicholas (80 mins) | 6-1 | |

## 469

(World Cup — Qualifier)
17 October 1984

Referee: Mulder (Netherlands)
Hampden Park, Glasgow (Att: 52,829)

### SCOTLAND 3-0 ICELAND
Half-time 2-0

| | | | |
|---|---|---|---|
| (16) | James LEIGHTON (Aberdeen) | | Bjarni SIGURDSSON |
| (2) | Stephen NICOL (Liverpool) | | Thorgrimur THRAINSSON |
| (7) | Arthur ALBISTON (Manchester United) | | Árni SVEINSSON |
| (35) | William MILLER (Aberdeen) | | Magnús BERGS |
| (32) | Alexander McLEISH (Aberdeen) | | Saevar JÓNSSON |
| (6) | David COOPER (Rangers) | | Atli EDVALDSSON |
| (42) | Graeme SOUNESS (Sampdoria) captain | | Janus GUDLAUGSSON |
| (8) | Paul McSTAY (Celtic) | | Ragnar MARGEIRSSON |
| (8) | James BETT (Lokeren) | | Arnór GUDJOHNSEN |
| (95) | Kenneth DALGLISH (Liverpool) | | Pétur PÉTURSSON |
| (5) | Maurice JOHNSTON (Celtic) | | Ásgeir SIGURVINSSON |

Substitutions

| | | |
|---|---|---|
| (10) | Charles NICHOLAS (Arsenal) | |
| | for Dalglish 68 mins | |

Goals

| | | |
|---|---|---|
| McStay (22 mins) | 1-0 | |
| McStay (40 mins) | 2-0 | |
| Nicholas (70 mins) | 3-0 | |

## 470

(World Cup — Qualifier)
14 November 1984

Referee: Prokop (East Germany)
Hampden Park, Glasgow (Att: 74,299)

### SCOTLAND 3-1 SPAIN
Half-time 2-0

| | | | |
|---|---|---|---|
| (17) | James LEIGHTON (Aberdeen) | | Luis ARCONADA |
| (3) | Stephen NICOL (Liverpool) | | Santiago URQUIAGA |
| (9) | Arthur ALBISTON (Manchester United) | | José CAMACHO |
| (36) | William MILLER (Aberdeen) | | Antonio MACEDA |
| (33) | Alexander McLEISH (Aberdeen) | | Andoni GOICOECHEA |
| (7) | David COOPER (Rangers) | | Rafael GORDILLO |
| (43) | Graeme SOUNESS (Sampdoria) captain | | Victor MUNOZ |
| (9) | Paul McSTAY (Celtic) | | Ismael URTUBI |
| (9) | James BETT (Lokeren) | | Juan SENOR |
| (96) | Kenneth DALGLISH (Liverpool) | | Hipólito RINCON |
| (6) | Maurice JOHNSTON (Celtic) | | Carlos ALONSO |

Substitutions

| | | | |
|---|---|---|---|
| | | | Emilio BUTRAGUENO |
| | | | for Rincón 46 mins |
| | | | Francisco CARRASCO |
| | | | for Urtubi 80 mins |

Goals

| | | |
|---|---|---|
| Johnston (33 mins) | 1-0 | |
| Johnston (42 mins) | 2-0 | |
| | 2-1 | Goicoechea (68 mins) |
| Dalglish (75 mins) | 3-1 | |

# 1985

| P | W | D | L | F | A |
|---|---|---|---|---|---|
| 8 | 3 | 3 | 2 | 5 | 3 |

## 471

(World Cup — Qualifier)
27 February 1985

Referee: Vautrot (France)
Estadio Sánchez Pizjuán, Seville (Att: 70,410)

### SPAIN 1-0 SCOTLAND
Half-time 0-0

| | | | |
|---|---|---|---|
| (18) | James LEIGHTON (Aberdeen) | | Luis ARCONADA |
| (15) | Richard GOUGH (Dundee United) | | GERARDO Miranda |
| (10) | Arthur ALBISTON (Manchester United) | | José CAMACHO |
| (37) | William MILLER (Aberdeen) | | Antonio MACEDA |
| (34) | Alexander McLEISH (Aberdeen) | | Andoni GOICOECHEA |
| (8) | David COOPER (Rangers) | | Rafael GORDILLO |
| (44) | Graeme SOUNESS (Sampdoria) captain | | Ricardo GALLEGO |
| (10) | Paul McSTAY (Celtic) | | Roberto FERNÁNDEZ |
| (10) | James BETT (Lokeren) | | Juan SENOR |
| (24) | Steven ARCHIBALD (Barcelona) | | Fernando CLOS |
| (7) | Maurice JOHNSTON (Celtic) | | Emilio BUTRAGUENO |

Substitutions

| | | | |
|---|---|---|---|
| (29) | Gordon STRACHAN (Manchester United) | | Julio ALBERTO |
| | for McStay 76 mins | | for Gallego 80 mins |
| (11) | Charles NICHOLAS (Arsenal) | | |
| | for Archibald 84 mins | | |

Goals

| | | |
|---|---|---|
| | 0-1 | Clos (48 mins) |

## 472

(World Cup — Qualifier)
27 March 1985

Referee: Ponnet (Belgium)
Hampden Park, Glasgow (Att: 62,424)

### SCOTLAND 0-1 WALES
Half-time 0-1

| | | | |
|---|---|---|---|
| (19) | James LEIGHTON (Aberdeen) | | Neville SOUTHALL |
| (4) | Stephen NICOL (Liverpool) | | Neil SLATTER |
| (11) | Arthur ALBISTON (Manchester United) | | Joseph JONES |
| (38) | William MILLER (Aberdeen) | | David PHILLIPS |
| (35) | Alexander McLEISH (Aberdeen) | | Kevin RATCLIFFE |
| (9) | David COOPER (Rangers) | | Robert JAMES |
| (45) | Graeme SOUNESS (Sampdoria) captain | | Kenneth JACKETT |
| (11) | Paul McSTAY (Celtic) | | Peter NICHOLAS |
| (11) | James BETT (Lokeren) | | Michael THOMAS |
| (97) | Kenneth DALGLISH (Liverpool) | | Ian RUSH |
| (8) | Maurice JOHNSTON (Celtic) | | Mark HUGHES |

Substitutions

| | | |
|---|---|---|
| (22) | Alan HANSEN (Liverpool) | |
| | for Albiston 57 mins | |
| (12) | Charles NICHOLAS (Arsenal) | |
| | for McStay 75 mins | |

Goals

| | | |
|---|---|---|
| | 0-1 | Rush (37 mins) |

## 473

(Rous Cup)
25 May 1985

Referee: Vautrot (France)
Hampden Park, Glasgow (Att: 66,489)

### SCOTLAND 1-0 ENGLAND    Half-time 0-0

| | | |
|---|---|---|
| (20) | James LEIGHTON (Aberdeen) | Peter SHILTON |
| (16) | Richard GOUGH (Dundee United) | Vivian ANDERSON |
| (2) | Maurice MALPAS (Dundee United) | Kenneth SANSOM |
| (39) | William MILLER (Aberdeen) | Terence BUTCHER |
| (36) | Alexander McLEISH (Aberdeen) | Terence FENWICK |
| (30) | Gordon STRACHAN (Manchester United) | Raymond WILKINS |
| (46) | Graeme SOUNESS (Sampdoria) captain | Glenn HODDLE |
| (12) | Robert AITKEN (Celtic) | Bryan ROBSON |
| (12) | James BETT (Lokeren) | John BARNES |
| (1) | David SPEEDIE (Chelsea) | Trevor FRANCIS |
| (25) | Steven ARCHIBALD (Barcelona) | Mark HATELEY |

Substitutions

| | | |
|---|---|---|
| (1) | Murdo MacLEOD (Celtic) | Christopher WADDLE |
| | for Strachan 71 mins | for Barnes 63 mins |
| | | Gary LINEKER |
| | | for Hoddle 80 mins |

Goals

Gough (68 mins) — 1-0

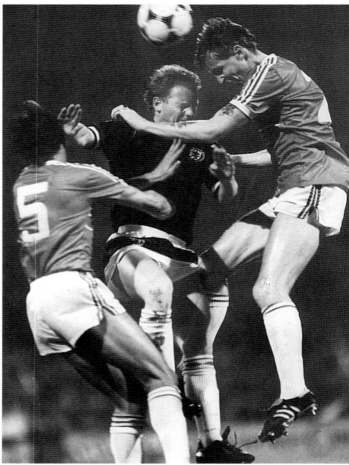

David Speedie jumps with Joey Jones and Pat Van Den Hauwe in the 1-1 World Cup qualifier at Ninian Park in September 1985.

---

## 474

(World Cup — Qualifier)
28 May 1985

Referee: Milchenko (Soviet Union)
Laugardalsvollur Stadion, Reykjavík (Att: 16,000)

### ICELAND 0-1 SCOTLAND    Half-time 0-0

| | | |
|---|---|---|
| (21) | James LEIGHTON (Aberdeen) | Eggert GUDMUNDSSON |
| (17) | Richard GOUGH (Dundee United) | Thorgrimur THRAINSSON |
| (3) | Maurice MALPAS (Dundee United) | Árni SVEINSSON |
| (40) | William MILLER (Aberdeen) | Magnús BERGS |
| (37) | Alexander McLEISH (Aberdeen) | Saevar JÓNSSON |
| (31) | Gordon STRACHAN (Manchester United) | Atli EDVALDSSON |
| (47) | Graeme SOUNESS (Sampdoria) captain | Janus GUDLAUGSSON |
| (13) | Robert AITKEN (Celtic) | Sigurdur JÓNSSON |
| (13) | James BETT (Lokeren) | Gudmundur THORBJÖRNSSON |
| (20) | Andrew GRAY (Everton) | Pétur PETURSSON |
| (1) | Graeme SHARP (Everton) | Teitur THORDARSON |

Substitutions

| | | |
|---|---|---|
| (26) | Steven ARCHIBALD (Barcelona) | Ómar TORFASON |
| | for Gray 73 mins | for Sigurdur Jónsson 25 mins |
| | | Sigurdur GRÉTARSSON |
| | | for Thordarson 57 mins |

Goals

Bett (86 mins) — 1-0

Davie Cooper's 81st-minute penalty equaliser which settled a dramatic match in Cardiff.

---

## 475

(World Cup — Qualifier)
10 September 1985

Referee: Keizer (Netherlands)
Ninian Park, Cardiff (Att: 39,500)

### WALES 1-1 SCOTLAND    Half-time 1-0

| | | |
|---|---|---|
| (22) | James LEIGHTON (Aberdeen) | Neville SOUTHALL |
| (18) | Richard GOUGH (Dundee United) | Joseph JONES |
| (4) | Maurice MALPAS (Dundee United) | Patrick VAN DEN HAUWE |
| (41) | William MILLER (Aberdeen) captain | David PHILLIPS |
| (38) | Alexander McLEISH (Aberdeen) | Kevin RATCLIFFE |
| (32) | Gordon STRACHAN (Manchester United) | Robert JAMES |
| (5) | Stephen NICOL (Liverpool) | Kenneth JACKETT |
| (14) | Robert AITKEN (Celtic) | Peter NICHOLAS |
| (14) | James BETT (Aberdeen) | Michael THOMAS |
| (2) | David SPEEDIE (Chelsea) | Ian RUSH |
| (2) | Graeme SHARP (Everton) | Mark HUGHES |

Substitutions

| | | |
|---|---|---|
| (52) | Alan ROUGH (Hibernian) | Steven LOVELL |
| | for Leighton 46 mins | for James 80 mins |
| (10) | David COOPER (Rangers) | Clayton BLACKMORE |
| | for Strachan 61 mins | for Thomas 83 mins |

Goals

| | | |
|---|---|---|
| | 0-1 | Hughes (13 mins) |
| Cooper (81 mins pen) | 1-1 | |

---

## 476

(Friendly)
16 October 1985

Referee: Worrall (England)
Hampden Park, Glasgow (Att: 41,114)

### SCOTLAND 0-0 EAST GERMANY

| | | |
|---|---|---|
| (23) | James LEIGHTON (Aberdeen) | René MÜLLER |
| (19) | Richard GOUGH (Dundee United) | Ronald KREER |
| (12) | Arthur ALBISTON (Manchester United) | Frank ROHDE |
| (42) | William MILLER (Aberdeen) | Carsten SÄNGER |
| (39) | Alexander McLEISH (Aberdeen) | Uwe ZÖTZSCHE |
| (6) | Stephen NICOL (Liverpool) | Matthias LIEBERS |
| (48) | Graeme SOUNESS (Sampdoria) captain | Hans-Uwe PILZ |
| (15) | Robert AITKEN (Celtic) | Jörg STÜBNER |
| (11) | David COOPER (Rangers) | Andreas THOM |
| (98) | Kenneth DALGLISH (Liverpool) | Rainer ERNST |
| (9) | Maurice JOHNSTON (Celtic) | Ulf KIRSTEN |

Substitutions

| | | |
|---|---|---|
| (1) | Andrew GORAM (Oldham Athletic) | Jörg WEISSFLOG |
| | for Leighton 49 mins | for Müller 46 mins |
| (3) | David SPEEDIE (Chelsea) | Andreas BIELAU |
| | for Johnston 65 mins | for Ernst 70 mins |
| (12) | Paul McSTAY (Celtic) | |
| | for Aitken 81 mins | |

## 477

(World Cup — Qualifier Play-off 1st Leg)
20 November 1985

Referee: Christov (Czechoslovakia)
Hampden Park, Glasgow (Att: 61,920)

### SCOTLAND 2-0 AUSTRALIA                Half-time 0-0

| | | |
|---|---|---|
| (24) | James LEIGHTON (Aberdeen) | Terence GREEDY |
| (7) | Stephen NICOL (Liverpool) | Alan DAVIDSON |
| (5) | Maurice MALPAS (Dundee United) | Graham JENNINGS |
| (43) | William MILLER (Aberdeen) | Charles YANKOS |
| (40) | Alexander McLEISH (Aberdeen) | David RATCLIFFE |
| (33) | Gordon STRACHAN (Manchester United) | Steven O'CONNOR |
| (49) | Graeme SOUNESS (Sampdoria) captain | Joseph WATSON |
| (16) | Robert AITKEN (Celtic) | Kenneth MURPHY |
| (12) | David COOPER (Rangers) | Oscar CRINO |
| (99) | Kenneth DALGLISH (Liverpool) | David MITCHELL |
| (1) | Francis McAVENNIE (West Ham United) | John KOSMINA |

Substitutions

| | | |
|---|---|---|
| (3) | Graeme SHARP (Everton) | James PATIKAS |
| | for Dalglish 72 mins | for Watson 65 mins |
| (15) | James BETT (Aberdeen) | Robert DUNN |
| | for Strachan 84 mins | for O'Connor 82 mins |

Goals

| | |
|---|---|
| Cooper (58 mins) | 1-0 |
| McAvennie (60 mins) | 2-0 |

Steve Nicol and Australia's Steve O'Connor and Charlie Yankos (4) in the first leg of the World Cup qualifier at Hampden in November 1985.

## 478

(World Cup — Qualifier Play-off 2nd Leg)
4 December 1985

Referee: Wright (Brazil)
Olympic Park, Melbourne (Att: 32,000)

### AUSTRALIA 0-0 SCOTLAND

| | | |
|---|---|---|
| (25) | James LEIGHTON (Aberdeen) | Terence GREEDY |
| (20) | Richard GOUGH (Dundee United) | Alan DAVIDSON |
| (6) | Maurice MALPAS (Dundee United) | Graham JENNINGS |
| (44) | William MILLER (Aberdeen) | Charles YANKOS |
| (41) | Alexander McLEISH (Aberdeen) | David RATCLIFFE |
| (17) | Robert AITKEN (Celtic) | Robert DUNN |
| (50) | Graeme SOUNESS (Sampdoria) captain | James PATIKAS |
| (13) | Paul McSTAY (Celtic) | Kenneth MURPHY |
| (13) | David COOPER (Rangers) | Oscar CRINO |
| (4) | David SPEEDIE (Chelsea) | David MITCHELL |
| (2) | Francis McAVENNIE (West Ham United) | John KOSMINA |

Substitutions

| | | |
|---|---|---|
| (4) | Graeme SHARP (Everton) | Zarko ODZAKOV |
| | for Speedie 76 mins | for Crino 68 mins |
| | | Frank FARINA |
| | | for Dunn 75 mins |

# 1986

| P | W | D | L | F | A |
|---|---|---|---|---|---|
| 10 | 3 | 4 | 3 | 9 | 5 |

## 479

(Friendly)
28 January 1986

Referee: Thomas (Netherlands)
Ramat Gan Stadium, Tel Aviv (Att: 7,000)

### ISRAEL 0-1 SCOTLAND                Half-time 0-0

| | | |
|---|---|---|
| (26) | James LEIGHTON (Aberdeen) | Avi RAN |
| (21) | Richard GOUGH (Dundee United) | Eitan AHARONI |
| (7) | Maurice MALPAS (Dundee United) | Avi COHEN |
| (26) | David NAREY (Dundee United) | Menashe SHIMINOV |
| (45) | William MILLER (Aberdeen) captain | Zion MARILI |
| (18) | Robert AITKEN (Celtic) | Rifat TURK |
| (16) | James BETT (Aberdeen) | Motti IWANIR |
| (14) | Paul McSTAY (Celtic) | Efraeem DAVIDI |
| (7) | Eamonn BANNON (Dundee United) | Uri MALMILLIAN |
| (5) | Graeme SHARP (Everton) | Zahi ARMELI |
| (13) | Charles NICHOLAS (Arsenal) | Eli OHANA |

Substitutions

| | | |
|---|---|---|
| (16) | Paul STURROCK (Dundee United) | Eli COHEN |
| | for Sharp 68 mins | for Turk 46 mins |
| | | Eyal BEGLEIBTER |
| | | for Iwanir 46 mins |
| | | Rony ROSENTHAL |
| | | for Ohana 57 mins |

Goals

| | |
|---|---|
| McStay (57 mins) | 1-0 |

## 480

(Friendly)
26 March 1986

Referee: Roth (West Germany)
Hampden Park, Glasgow (Att: 53,589)

### SCOTLAND 3-0 ROMANIA                Half-time 2-0

| | | |
|---|---|---|
| (2) | Andrew GORAM (Oldham Athletic) | Silviu LUNG |
| (22) | Richard GOUGH (Dundee United) | Mircea REDNIC |
| (8) | Maurice MALPAS (Dundee United) | Nicolae UNGUREANU |
| (27) | David NAREY (Dundee United) | Ion ANDONE |
| (46) | William MILLER (Aberdeen) | Gino IORGULESCU |
| (34) | Gordon STRACHAN (Manchester United) | Lica MOVILA |
| (19) | Robert AITKEN (Celtic) | Michael KLEIN |
| (51) | Graeme SOUNESS (Sampdoria) | Gheorghe HAGI |
| (8) | Eamonn BANNON (Dundee United) | Marcel CORAS |
| (100) | Kenneth DALGLISH (Liverpool) captain | Dorin MATEUT |
| (6) | Graeme SHARP (Everton) | Rodion CAMATARU |

Substitutions

| | | |
|---|---|---|
| (14) | Charles NICHOLAS (Arsenal) | Alexandru NICOLAE |
| | for Sharp 46 mins | for Iorgulescu 46 mins |
| (23) | Alan HANSEN (Liverpool) | Romulus GABOR |
| | for Miller 60 mins | for Coras 70 mins |
| (1) | Patrick NEVIN (Chelsea) | Nita CIREASA |
| | for Strachan 72 mins | for Andone 75 mins |

Goals

| | |
|---|---|
| Strachan (18 mins) | 1-0 |
| Gough (27 mins) | 2-0 |
| Aitken (81 mins) | 3-0 |

## 481

(Rous Cup)
23 April 1986

Referee: Vautrot (France)
Wembley Stadium, London (Att: 68,357)

### ENGLAND 2-1 SCOTLAND                Half-time 2-0

| | | |
|---|---|---|
| (53) | Alan ROUGH (Hibernian) | Peter SHILTON |
| (23) | Richard GOUGH (Dundee United) | Gary STEVENS |
| (9) | Maurice MALPAS (Dundee United) | Kenneth SANSOM |
| (47) | William MILLER (Aberdeen) | Terence BUTCHER |
| (42) | Alexander McLEISH (Aberdeen) | David WATSON |
| (8) | Stephen NICOL (Liverpool) | Stephen HODGE |
| (20) | Robert AITKEN (Celtic) | Raymond WILKINS |
| (52) | Graeme SOUNESS (Sampdoria) captain | Glenn HODDLE |
| (9) | Eamonn BANNON (Dundee United) | Christopher WADDLE |
| (5) | David SPEEDIE (Chelsea) | Trevor FRANCIS |
| (15) | Charles NICHOLAS (Arsenal) | Mark HATELEY |

Substitutions

| | | |
|---|---|---|
| (2) | Patrick NEVIN (Chelsea) | Peter REID |
| | for Nicholas 58 mins | for Wilkins 46 mins |
| | | Gary STEVENS |
| | | for Hodge 75 mins |

Goals

| | |
|---|---|
| | 0-1  Butcher (27 mins) |
| | 0-2  Hoddle (39 mins) |
| Souness (57 mins pen) | 1-2 |

The Scots before meeting West Germany in the 1986 World Cup finals in Mexico. Back row (left to right): Aitken, Leighton, Nicol, Narey, Gough, Miller. Front row: Souness, Malpas, Bannon, Strachan, Archibald.

## 482

(Friendly)                                              Referee: Kohl (Austria)
29 April 1986                    Philips Stadion, Eindhoven (Att: 14,500)

### NETHERLANDS 0-0 SCOTLAND

| | | |
|---|---|---|
| (3) | Andrew GORAM (Oldham Athletic) | Johannes VAN BREUKELEN |
| (10) | Maurice MALPAS (Dundee United) | Jan SILOOY |
| (13) | Arthur ALBISTON (Manchester United) | Adrianus VAN TIGGELEN |
| (28) | David NAREY (Dundee United) | Ronald KOEMAN |
| (43) | Alexander McLEISH (Aberdeen) | Dirk BLIND |
| (48) | William MILLER (Aberdeen) captain | Gerald VANENBURG |
| (17) | James BETT (Aberdeen) | Jan WOUTERS |
| (1) | Robert CONNOR (Dundee) | Michel VALKE |
| (14) | David COOPER (Rangers) | Johannes VAN'T SCHIP |
| (1) | Alistair McCOIST (Rangers) | Robert DE WIT |
| (17) | Paul STURROCK (Dundee United) | Johannes BOSMAN |

Substitutions

Wilbert SUVRIJN
 for Valke 72 mins

## 483

(World Cup — Final Tournament 1st Round)          Referee: Nemeth (Hungary)
4 June 1986                    Estadio Neza, Nezahualcoyotl (Att: 18,000)

### DENMARK 1-0 SCOTLAND          Half-time 0-0

| | | |
|---|---|---|
| (27) | James LEIGHTON (Aberdeen) | Trols RASMUSSEN |
| (24) | Richard GOUGH (Dundee United) | Morten OLSEN |
| (11) | Maurice MALPAS (Dundee United) | Soren LERBY |
| (49) | William MILLER (Aberdeen) | Soren BUSK |
| (44) | Alexander McLEISH (Aberdeen) | Ivan NIELSEN |
| (35) | Gordon STRACHAN (Manchester United) | Jens-Jorn BERTELSEN |
| (21) | Robert AITKEN (Celtic) | Frank ARNESEN |
| (53) | Graeme SOUNESS (Sampdoria) captain | Klaus BERGGREN |
| (9) | Stephen NICOL (Liverpool) | Jesper OLSEN |
| (18) | Paul STURROCK (Dundee United) | Preben ELKJAER-LARSEN |
| (16) | Charles NICHOLAS (Arsenal) | Michael LAUDRUP |

Substitutions

| | | |
|---|---|---|
| (3) | Francis McAVENNIE (West Ham United) | John SIVEBAEK |
| | for Sturrock 61 mins | for Arnesen 75 mins |
| (10) | Eamonn BANNON (Dundee United) | Jan MOLBY |
| | for Strachan 74 mins | for J. Olsen 80 mins |

Goals
0-1                    Elkjaer-Larsen (57 mins)

## 484

(World Cup — Final Tournament 1st Round)          Referee: Igna (Romania)
8 June 1986                    Estadio Corregidora, Queretaro (Att: 25,000)

### WEST GERMANY 2-1 SCOTLAND          Half-time 1-1

| | | |
|---|---|---|
| (28) | James LEIGHTON (Aberdeen) | Harald SCHUMACHER |
| (25) | Richard GOUGH (Dundee United) | Thomas BERTHOLD |
| (12) | Maurice MALPAS (Dundee United) | Norbert EDER |
| (29) | David NAREY (Dundee United) | Karl-Heinz FÖRSTER |
| (50) | William MILLER (Aberdeen) | Klaus AUGENTHALER |
| (36) | Gordon STRACHAN (Manchester United) | Hans-Peter BRIEGEL |
| (22) | Robert AITKEN (Celtic) | Felix MAGATH |
| (54) | Graeme SOUNESS (Sampdoria) captain | Lothar MATTHÄUS |
| (10) | Stephen NICOL (Liverpool) | Pierre LITTBARSKI |
| (11) | Eamonn BANNON (Dundee United) | Klaus ALLOFS |
| (27) | Steven ARCHIBALD (Barcelona) | Rudolf VÖLLER |

Substitutions

| | | |
|---|---|---|
| (4) | Francis McAVENNIE (West Ham United) | Ditmar JAKOBS |
| | for Nicol 59 mins | for Briegel 63 mins |
| (15) | David COOPER (Rangers) | Karl-Heinz RUMMENIGGE |
| | for Bannon 74 mins | for Littbarski 76 mins |

Goals

| | | |
|---|---|---|
| Strachan (18 mins) | 1-0 | |
| | 1-1 | Völler (22 mins) |
| | 1-2 | Allofs (49 mins) |

## 485

(World Cup — Final Tournament 1st Round)          Referee: Quiniou (France)
13 June 1986                    Estadio Neza, Nezahualcoyotl (Att: 20,000)

### URUGUAY 0-0 SCOTLAND

| | | |
|---|---|---|
| (29) | James LEIGHTON (Aberdeen) | Fernando ALVEZ |
| (26) | Richard GOUGH (Dundee United) | Nelson GUTIÉRREZ |
| (14) | Arthur ALBISTON (Manchester United) | Eduardo ACEVEDO |
| (30) | David NAREY (Dundee United) | Victor DIOGO |
| (51) | William MILLER (Aberdeen) captain | José BATISTA |
| (37) | Gordon STRACHAN (Manchester United) | Venancio RAMOS |
| (23) | Robert AITKEN (Celtic) | Jorge BARRIOS |
| (15) | Paul McSTAY (Celtic) | Alfonso PEREIRA |
| (11) | Stephen NICOL (Liverpool) | Sergio SANTÍN |
| (19) | Paul STURROCK (Dundee United) | Wilmar CABRERA |
| (7) | Graeme SHARP (Everton) | Enzo FRANCESCOLI |

Substitutions

| | | |
|---|---|---|
| (16) | David COOPER (Rangers) | Mario SARALEGUI |
| | for Nicol 70 mins | for Ramos 71 mins |
| (17) | Charles NICHOLAS (Arsenal) | Antonio ALZAMENDI |
| | for Sturrock 70 mins | for Francescoli 84 mins |

Gordon Strachan is tackled by Jorge Barrios of Uruguay during the 1986 World Cup finals in Mexico.

## 486
**(European Championship — Qualifier)**
**10 September 1986**

Referee: Fredriksson (Sweden)
Hampden Park, Glasgow (Att: 35,070)

### SCOTLAND 0-0 BULGARIA

| | | |
|---|---|---|
| (30) | James LEIGHTON (Aberdeen) | Borislav MIHAILOV |
| (27) | Richard GOUGH (Tottenham Hotspur) | Plamen NIKOLOV |
| (13) | Maurice MALPAS (Dundee United) | Petar PETROV |
| (31) | David NAREY (Dundee United) | Georgi DIMITROV |
| (52) | William MILLER (Aberdeen) captain | Nikolai ILIEV |
| (38) | Gordon STRACHAN (Manchester United) | Hristo KOLEV |
| (24) | Robert AITKEN (Celtic) | Plamen SIMEONOV |
| (16) | Paul McSTAY (Celtic) | Anyo SADKOV |
| (17) | David COOPER (Rangers) | Iliya VOINOV |
| (10) | Maurice JOHNSTON (Celtic) | Nasko SIRAKOV |
| (18) | Charles NICHOLAS (Arsenal) | Petar ALEKSANDROV |

Substitutions

| | | |
|---|---|---|
| (101) | Kenneth DALGLISH (Liverpool) | Georgi KARUSHEV |
| | for Nicholas 53 mins | for Simeonov 78 mins |
| | | Lachezar TANEV |
| | | for Aleksandrov 87 mins |

## 487
**(European Championship — Qualifier)**
**15 October 1986**

Referee: Halle (Norway)
Lansdowne Road, Dublin (Att: 48,000)

### REPUBLIC OF IRELAND 0-0 SCOTLAND

| | | |
|---|---|---|
| (31) | James LEIGHTON (Aberdeen) | Patrick BONNER |
| (28) | Richard GOUGH (Tottenham Hotspur) | David LANGAN |
| (8) | Raymond STEWART (West Ham United) | James BEGLIN |
| (32) | David NAREY (Dundee United) | Michael McCARTHY |
| (24) | Alan HANSEN (Liverpool) | Kevin MORAN |
| (39) | Gordon STRACHAN (Manchester United) | William BRADY |
| (25) | Robert AITKEN (Celtic) captain | Paul McGRATH |
| (17) | Paul McSTAY (Celtic) | Raymond HOUGHTON |
| (2) | Murdo MacLEOD (Celtic) | Kevin SHEEDY |
| (8) | Graeme SHARP (Everton) | Frank STAPLETON |
| (11) | Maurice JOHNSTON (Celtic) | John ALDRIDGE |

Substitutions

| | | |
|---|---|---|
| | | Gerard DALY |
| | | for Moran 71 mins |

## 488
**(European Championship — Qualifier)**
**12 November 1986**

Referee: Gudmundsson (Iceland)
Hampden Park, Glasgow (Att: 35,078)

### SCOTLAND 3-0 LUXEMBOURG — Half-time 2-0

| | | |
|---|---|---|
| (32) | James LEIGHTON (Aberdeen) | John VAN RIJSWICK |
| (9) | Raymond STEWART (West Ham United) | Marcel BOSSI |
| (3) | Murdo MacLEOD (Celtic) | Gianni DI PENTIMA |
| (25) | Alan HANSEN (Liverpool) | Hubert MEUNIER |
| (29) | Richard GOUGH (Tottenham Hotspur) | Laurent SCHONCKERT |
| (3) | Patrick NEVIN (Chelsea) | Guy HELLERS |
| (26) | Robert AITKEN (Celtic) captain | Carlo WEIS |
| (1) | Brian McCLAIR (Celtic) | Jean-Pierre BARBONI |
| (18) | David COOPER (Rangers) | Théo SCHOLTEN |
| (102) | Kenneth DALGLISH (Liverpool) | Théo MALGET |
| (12) | Maurice JOHNSTON (Celtic) | Robert LANGERS |

Substitutions

| | | |
|---|---|---|
| (18) | Paul McSTAY (Celtic) | Gerard JEITZ |
| | for Hansen 46 mins | for Malget 79 mins |
| (2) | Alistair McCOIST (Rangers) | Jeff SAIBENE |
| | for MacLeod 64 mins | for Scholten 89 mins |

Goals

| | |
|---|---|
| Cooper (24 mins pen) | 1-0 |
| Cooper (38 mins) | 2-0 |
| Johnston (70 mins) | 3-0 |

# 1987

| P | W | D | L | F | A |
|---|---|---|---|---|---|
| 8 | 3 | 2 | 3 | 6 | 7 |

## 489
**(European Championship — Qualifier)**
**18 February 1987**

Referee: Van Ettekoven (Netherlands)
Hampden Park, Glasgow (Att: 45,081)

### SCOTLAND 0-1 REPUBLIC OF IRELAND — Half-time 0-1

| | | |
|---|---|---|
| (33) | James LEIGHTON (Aberdeen) | Patrick BONNER |
| (10) | Raymond STEWART (West Ham United) | Paul McGRATH |
| (14) | Maurice MALPAS (Dundee United) | Ronald WHELAN |
| (26) | Alan HANSEN (Liverpool) | Michael McCARTHY |
| (30) | Richard GOUGH (Tottenham Hotspur) | Kevin MORAN |
| (4) | Patrick NEVIN (Chelsea) | William BRADY |
| (40) | Gordon STRACHAN (Manchester United) | Mark LAWRENSON |
| (27) | Robert AITKEN (Celtic) captain | Raymond HOUGHTON |
| (19) | David COOPER (Rangers) | Anthony GALVIN |
| (2) | Brian McCLAIR (Celtic) | Frank STAPLETON |
| (13) | Maurice JOHNSTON (Celtic) | John ALDRIDGE |

Substitutions

| | | |
|---|---|---|
| (19) | Paul McSTAY (Celtic) | John BYRNE |
| | for Cooper 46 mins | for Brady 60 mins |
| (3) | Alistair McCOIST (Rangers) | |
| | for Malpas 67 mins | |

Goals

| | |
|---|---|
| 0-1 | Lawrenson (8 mins) |

## 490
**(European Championship — Qualifier)**
**1 April 1987**

Referee: Vautrot (France)
Constant Van den Stock Stadian, Brussels (Att: 26,650)

### BELGIUM 4-1 SCOTLAND — Half-time 1-1

| | | |
|---|---|---|
| (34) | James LEIGHTON (Aberdeen) | Jean-Marie PFAFF |
| (31) | Richard GOUGH (Tottenham Hotspur) | Georges GRÜN |
| (15) | Maurice MALPAS (Dundee United) | Patrick VERVOORT |
| (33) | David NAREY (Dundee United) | Leo CLIJSTERS |
| (45) | Alexander McLEISH (Aberdeen) | Stéphane DEMOL |
| (1) | James McINALLY (Dundee United) | Frank VAN DER ELST |
| (20) | Paul McSTAY (Celtic) | Frank VERCAUTEREN |
| (28) | Robert AITKEN (Celtic) captain | Vincenzo SCIFO |
| (18) | James BETT (Aberdeen) | Philippe DESMET |
| (20) | Paul STURROCK (Dundee United) | Nico CLAESEN |
| (4) | Alistair McCOIST (Rangers) | Erwin VANDENBERGH |

Substitutions

| | | |
|---|---|---|
| (5) | Patrick NEVIN (Chelsea) | Leo VAN DER ELST |
| | for Bett 80 mins | for Scifo 73 mins |
| | | Guy VANDERSMISSEN |
| | | for F. Van der Elst 89 mins |

Goals

| | | |
|---|---|---|
| | 0-1 | Claesen (9 mins) |
| McStay (14 mins) | 1-1 | |
| | 1-2 | Claesen (55 mins) |
| | 1-3 | Vercauteren (74 mins) |
| | 1-4 | Claesen (86 mins) |

## 491
**(Rous Cup)**
**23 May 1987**

Referee: Pauly (West Germany)
Hampden Park, Glasgow (Att: 64,713)

### SCOTLAND 0-0 ENGLAND

| | | |
|---|---|---|
| (35) | James LEIGHTON (Aberdeen) | Christopher WOODS |
| (32) | Richard GOUGH (Tottenham Hotspur) | Gary STEVENS |
| (4) | Murdo MacLEOD (Celtic) | Stuart PEARCE |
| (53) | William MILLER (Aberdeen) | Terence BUTCHER |
| (46) | Alexander McLEISH (Aberdeen) | Mark WRIGHT |
| (21) | Paul McSTAY (Celtic) | Stephen HODGE |
| (4) | Neil SIMPSON (Aberdeen) | Glenn HODDLE |
| (29) | Robert AITKEN (Celtic) captain | Bryan ROBSON |
| (1) | Ian WILSON (Leicester City) | Christopher WADDLE |
| (3) | Brian McCLAIR (Celtic) | Peter BEARDSLEY |
| (5) | Alistair McCOIST (Rangers) | Mark HATELEY |

Substitutions

| | | |
|---|---|---|
| (19) | Charles NICHOLAS (Arsenal) | |
| | for McClair 58 mins | |

Roy Aitken and Bryan Robson exchange pennants before the game at Hampden in May 1987.

## 492

(Rous Cup)                                     Referee: Agnolin (Italy)
26 May 1987                        Hampden Park, Glasgow (Att: 41,384)

### SCOTLAND 0-2 BRAZIL                              Half-time 0-0

| | | |
|---|---|---|
| (4) | Andrew GORAM (Oldham Athletic) | CARLOS Roberto Gallo |
| (33) | Richard GOUGH (Tottenham Hotspur) | JOSIMAR Higino Pereira |
| (5) | Murdo MacLEOD (Celtic) | William DOUGLAS Menezes |
| (54) | William MILLER (Aberdeen) | RICARDO Barreta da ROCHA |
| (47) | Alexander McLEISH (Aberdeen) | Geraldo Dutra GERALDAO |
| (22) | Paul McSTAY (Celtic) | Luís Antonio Corréa MULLER |
| (2) | James McINALLY (Dundee United) | Nelson Luíz NELSINHO |
| (30) | Robert AITKEN (Celtic) captain | RAÍ Souza Oliveira |
| (2) | Ian WILSON (Leicester City) | Carlos Eduardo EDÚ |
| (20) | David COOPER (Rangers) | VALDO Candido Filho |
| (6) | Alistair McCOIST (Rangers) | Francisco Ernandi MIRANDINHA |

#### Substitutions

| | | |
|---|---|---|
| (4) | Brian McCLAIR (Celtic) | |
| | for McInally 59 mins | |

#### Goals

| | |
|---|---|
| 0-1 | Raí (51 mins) |
| 0-2 | Valdo (62 mins) |

## 493

(Friendly)                                  Referee: Keizer (Netherlands)
9 September 1987                   Hampden Park, Glasgow (Att: 21,128)

### SCOTLAND 2-0 HUNGARY                              Half-time 1-0

| | | |
|---|---|---|
| (36) | James LEIGHTON (Aberdeen) | Péter DISZTL |
| (1) | Stephen CLARKE (Chelsea) | Sándor SALLAI |
| (12) | Stephen NICOL (Liverpool) | Arpád TOMA |
| (55) | William MILLER (Aberdeen) | József CSUHAY |
| (34) | Richard GOUGH (Tottenham Hotspur) | Imre GARABA |
| (41) | Gordon STRACHAN (Manchester United) | Zoltán PÉTER |
| (23) | Paul McSTAY (Celtic) | György BOGNÁR |
| (31) | Robert AITKEN (Celtic) captain | József KELLER |
| (1) | Iain DURRANT (Rangers) | Ferenc MÉSZÁROS |
| (7) | Alistair McCOIST (Rangers) | Kálmán KOVÁCS |
| (14) | Maurice JOHNSTON (Nantes) | Gyula HAJSZÁN |

#### Substitutions

| | | |
|---|---|---|
| (1) | Eric BLACK (Metz) | Ferenc LOVÁSZ |
| | for Johnston 71 mins | for Kovács 87 mins |
| (19) | James BETT (Aberdeen) | |
| | for McStay 77 mins | |

#### Goals

| | |
|---|---|
| McCoist (34 mins) | 1-0 |
| McCoist (62 mins) | 2-0 |

## 494

(European Championship — Qualifier)         Referee: Casarin (Italy)
14 October 1987                   Hampden Park, Glasgow (Att: 20,052)

### SCOTLAND 2-0 BELGIUM                              Half-time 1-0

| | | |
|---|---|---|
| (37) | James LEIGHTON (Aberdeen) | Michel PREUD'HOMME |
| (2) | Stephen CLARKE (Chelsea) | Eric GERETS |
| (16) | Maurice MALPAS (Dundee United) | Patrick VERVOORT |
| (1) | Gary GILLESPIE (Liverpool) | Leo CLIJSTERS |
| (48) | Alexander McLEISH (Aberdeen) | Georges GRÜN |
| (24) | Paul McSTAY (Celtic) | Frank VAN DER ELST |
| (32) | Robert AITKEN (Celtic) captain | Luc BEYENS |
| (2) | Iain DURRANT (Rangers) | Frank VERCAUTEREN |
| (3) | Ian WILSON (Everton) | Jan CEULEMANS |
| (8) | Alistair McCOIST (Rangers) | Marc DEGRIJSE |
| (15) | Maurice JOHNSTON (Nantes) | Nico CLAESEN |

#### Substitutions

| | | |
|---|---|---|
| (1) | Derek WHYTE (Celtic) | Philippe DESMET |
| | for Malpas 53 mins | for Beyens 55 mins |
| (9) | Graeme SHARP (Everton) | |
| | for Johnston 72 mins | |

#### Goals

| | |
|---|---|
| McCoist (14 mins) | 1-0 |
| McStay (79 mins) | 2-0 |

## 495

(European Championship — Qualifier)         Referee: Kohl (Austria)
11 November 1987              Vasil Levski Stadion, Sofia (Att: 49,976)

### BULGARIA 0-1 SCOTLAND                              Half-time 0-0

| | | |
|---|---|---|
| (38) | James LEIGHTON (Aberdeen) | Borislav MIHAILOV |
| (3) | Stephen CLARKE (Chelsea) | Plamen NIKOLOV |
| (17) | Maurice MALPAS (Dundee United) | Krasimir BEZINSKI |
| (2) | Gary GILLESPIE (Liverpool) | Petar PETROV |
| (49) | Alexander McLEISH (Aberdeen) | Nikolai ILIEV |
| (13) | Stephen NICOL (Liverpool) | Plamen SIMEONOV |
| (25) | Paul McSTAY (Celtic) | Anyo SADKOV |
| (33) | Robert AITKEN (Celtic) captain | Hristo STOICHKOV |
| (4) | Ian WILSON (Everton) | Bozhidar ISKRENOV |
| (5) | Brian McCLAIR (Manchester United) | Nasko SIRAKOV |
| (10) | Graeme SHARP (Everton) | Petar ALEKSANDROV |

#### Substitutions

| | | |
|---|---|---|
| (1) | Gary MACKAY (Hearts) | Iliya VOINOV |
| | for McStay 57 mins | for Aleksandrov 42 mins |
| (1) | Gordon DURIE (Chelsea) | Lyuboslav PENEV |
| | for Sharp 71 mins | for Simeonov 88 mins |

#### Goals

| | |
|---|---|
| MacKay (87 mins) | 1-0 |

## 496

(European Championship — Qualifier)    Referee: Neuner (West Germany)
2 December 1987          Stade de la Frontière, Esch-sur-Alzette (Att: 1,999)

### LUXEMBOURG 0-0 SCOTLAND

| | | |
|---|---|---|
| (39) | James LEIGHTON (Aberdeen) | John VAN RIJSWICK |
| (2) | Derek WHYTE (Celtic) | Marcel BOSSI |
| (18) | Maurice MALPAS (Dundee United) | Carlo WEIS |
| (56) | William MILLER (Aberdeen) | Hubert MEUNIER |
| (50) | Alexander McLEISH (Aberdeen) captain | Pierre PETRY |
| (6) | Patrick NEVIN (Chelsea) | Jean-Paul GIRRES |
| (26) | Paul McSTAY (Celtic) | Jean-Pierre BARBONI |
| (34) | Robert AITKEN (Celtic) | Théo SCHOLTEN |
| (5) | Ian WILSON (Everton) | Jeannot REITER |
| (11) | Graeme SHARP (Everton) | Robert LANGERS |
| (16) | Maurice JOHNSTON (Nantes) | Gérard JEITZ |

#### Substitutions

| | | |
|---|---|---|
| (2) | Gary MACKAY (Hearts) | Armin KRINGS |
| | for Whyte 60 mins | for Reiter 54 mins |
| (2) | Eric BLACK (Metz) | Jeff SAIBENE |
| | for Nevin 60 mins | for Girres 87 mins |

# 1988

| | P | W | D | L | F | A |
|---|---|---|---|---|---|---|
| | 8 | 1 | 5 | 2 | 6 | 8 |

## 497

(Friendly)
17 February 1988

Referee: Nasir (Saudi Arabia)
King Fahd Stadium, Riyadh (Att: 35,000)

### SAUDI ARABIA 2-2 SCOTLAND                    Half-time 1-0

| (40) | James LEIGHTON (Aberdeen) | Abdullah AL-DIAYYE |
|---|---|---|
| (4) | Stephen CLARKE (Chelsea) | Bandar SEROUR |
| (19) | Maurice MALPAS (Dundee United) | Salah NAIMA |
| (57) | William MILLER (Aberdeen) | Ahmed JAMIL |
| (35) | Richard GOUGH (Rangers) | Mohamed ABDELJAOUAD |
| (14) | Stephen NICOL (Liverpool) | Khaled MESSAD |
| (27) | Paul McSTAY (Celtic) | Zaki SALEH |
| (35) | Robert AITKEN (Celtic) captain | Baasam ABOUDAOUD |
| (1) | John COLLINS (Hibernian) | Saad AL-DOUSSARI |
| (5) | Francis McAVENNIE (Celtic) | Youssef JAZAA |
| (17) | Maurice JOHNSTON (Nantes) | Abdullah MAJED |

Substitutions

| (1) | Henry SMITH (Hearts) | Saad MOUBARAK |
|---|---|---|
| | for Leighton 46 mins | for Al-Doussari 46 mins |
| (51) | Alexander McLEISH (Aberdeen) | Fahd HRIFI |
| | for Miller 46 mins | for Majed 84 mins |
| (1) | John COLQUHOUN (Hearts) | |
| | for Nicol 46 mins | |
| (3) | Gary MACKAY (Hearts) | |
| | for McStay 63 mins | |
| (2) | Robert CONNOR (Aberdeen) | |
| | for McAvennie 81 mins | |

| | Goals | |
|---|---|---|
| | 0-1 | Jazaa (15 mins) |
| Johnston (47 mins) | 1-1 | |
| Collins (49 mins) | 2-1 | |
| | 2-2 | Majed (71 mins) |

## 498

(Friendly)
22 March 1988

Referee: Courtney (England)
Ta'Qali Stadium, Valletta (Att: 8,000)

### MALTA 1-1 SCOTLAND                    Half-time 0-1

| (41) | James LEIGHTON (Aberdeen) | David CLUETT |
|---|---|---|
| (5) | Stephen CLARKE (Chelsea) | John BUTTIGIEG |
| (20) | Maurice MALPAS (Dundee United) | Joseph BRINCAT |
| (58) | William MILLER (Aberdeen) | Alex AZZOPARDI |
| (52) | Alexander McLEISH (Aberdeen) | Edwin CAMILLERI |
| (4) | Gary MACKAY (Hearts) | Martin SCICLUNA |
| (1) | Derek FERGUSON (Rangers) | Raymond VELLA |
| (36) | Robert AITKEN (Celtic) captain | David CARABOTT |
| (3) | Iain DURRANT (Rangers) | Charles MICALLEF |
| (12) | Graeme SHARP (Everton) | Michael DEGIORGIO |
| (9) | Alistair McCOIST (Rangers) | Carmel BUSUTTIL |

Substitutions

| (6) | Brian McCLAIR (Manchester United) | Charles SCERRI |
|---|---|---|
| | for McCoist 51 mins | for Micallef 10 mins |
| (3) | James McINALLY (Dundee United) | |
| | for MacKay 55 mins | |
| (2) | John COLQUHOUN (Hearts) | |
| | for Durrant 75 mins | |

| | Goals | |
|---|---|---|
| Sharp (21 mins) | 1-0 | |
| | 1-1 | Busuttil (53 mins) |

## 499

(Friendly)
27 April 1988

Referee: Da Silva (Portugal)
Estadio Santiago Bernabeu, Madrid (Att: 15,000)

### SPAIN 0-0 SCOTLAND

| (42) | James LEIGHTON (Aberdeen) | Andoni ZUBIZARRETA |
|---|---|---|
| (36) | Richard GOUGH (Rangers) | Pedro RENONES |
| (15) | Stephen NICOL (Liverpool) | Miguel SOLER |
| (59) | William MILLER (Aberdeen) | Victor MUNOZ |
| (53) | Alexander McLEISH (Aberdeen) | Manuel SANCHIS |
| (3) | Gary GILLESPIE (Liverpool) | Rafael GORDILLO |
| (28) | Paul McSTAY (Celtic) | Ricardo GALLEGO |
| (37) | Robert AITKEN (Celtic) captain | Miguel GONZÁLEZ |
| (4) | Iain DURRANT (Rangers) | Rafael VAZQUEZ |
| (10) | Alistair McCOIST (Rangers) | Julio SALINAS |
| (18) | Maurice JOHNSTON (Nantes) | Emilio BUTRAGUENO |

Substitutions

| (7) | Brian McCLAIR (Manchester United) | Miguel TENDILLO |
|---|---|---|
| | for McCoist 69 mins | for Gallego 46 mins |
| | | ELOY Olaya |
| | | for Salinas 78 mins |

## 500

(Rous Cup)
17 May 1988

Referee: Correia (Portugal)
Hampden Park, Glasgow (Att: 20,487)

### SCOTLAND 0-0 COLOMBIA

| (43) | James LEIGHTON (Aberdeen) | José HIGUITA |
|---|---|---|
| (37) | Richard GOUGH (Rangers) | Andrés ESCOBAR |
| (16) | Stephen NICOL (Liverpool) | Leonel ALVAREZ |
| (60) | William MILLER (Aberdeen) | Luis HERRERA |
| (54) | Alexander McLEISH (Aberdeen) | Carlos HOYOS |
| (6) | Murdo MacLEOD (Borussia Dortmund) | Luis PEREA |
| (29) | Paul McSTAY (Celtic) | Alexis GARCIA |
| (38) | Robert AITKEN (Celtic) captain | Carlos VALDERRAMA |
| (1) | Kevin GALLACHER (Dundee United) | Bernardo REDÍN |
| (11) | Alistair McCOIST (Rangers) | Arnoldo IGUARÁN |
| (19) | Maurice JOHNSTON (Nantes) | John TRELLEZ |

Substitutions

| (2) | Derek FERGUSON (Rangers) | Jaime ARANGO |
|---|---|---|
| | for McCoist 59 mins | for Trellez 78 mins |
| (1) | Andrew WALKER (Celtic) | |
| | for Gallacher 67 mins | |

In action for Scotland is Ally McCoist (far left) and Richard Gough (third from left) against Arnoldo Iguaran and Andres Escobar of Colombia in May 1988.

## 501

(Rous Cup)
21 May 1988

Referee: Quiniou (France)
Wembley Stadium, London (Att: 70,480)

### ENGLAND 1-0 SCOTLAND                    Half-time 1-0

| (44) | James LEIGHTON (Aberdeen) | Peter SHILTON |
|---|---|---|
| (38) | Richard GOUGH (Rangers) | Gary STEVENS |
| (17) | Stephen NICOL (Liverpool) | Kenneth SANSOM |
| (61) | William MILLER (Aberdeen) | Anthony ADAMS |
| (55) | Alexander McLEISH (Aberdeen) | David WATSON |
| (7) | Murdo MacLEOD (Borussia Dortmund) | Trevor STEVEN |
| (5) | Neil SIMPSON (Aberdeen) | Neil WEBB |
| (30) | Paul McSTAY (Celtic) | Bryan ROBSON |
| (39) | Robert AITKEN (Celtic) captain | John BARNES |
| (12) | Alistair McCOIST (Rangers) | Peter BEARDSLEY |
| (20) | Maurice JOHNSTON (Nantes) | Gary LINEKER |

Substitutions

| (8) | Thomas BURNS (Celtic) | Christopher WADDLE |
|---|---|---|
| | for Simpson 74 mins | for Steven 72 mins |
| (2) | Kevin GALLACHER (Dundee United) | |
| | for McCoist 77 mins | |

| | Goals | |
|---|---|---|
| | 0-1 | Beardsley (11 mins) |

## 502

(World Cup — Qualifier)
14 September 1988

Referee: Agnolin (Italy)
Ullevaal Stadion, Oslo (Att: 22,769)

### NORWAY 1-2 SCOTLAND | Half-time 1-1

| | | |
|---|---|---|
| (45) | James LEIGHTON (Manchester United) | Erik THORSTVEDT |
| (18) | Stephen NICOL (Liverpool) | Hans HENRIKSEN |
| (21) | Maurice MALPAS (Dundee United) | Anders GISKE |
| (62) | William MILLER (Aberdeen) | Rune BRATSETH |
| (56) | Alexander McLEISH (Aberdeen) | Erland JOHNSEN |
| (4) | Gary GILLESPIE (Liverpool) | Kjetil OSVOLD |
| (31) | Paul McSTAY (Celtic) | Tom SUNDBY |
| (40) | Robert AITKEN (Celtic) captain | Sverre BRANDHAUG |
| (8) | Brian McCLAIR (Manchester United) | Karl-Petter LOKEN |
| (3) | Kevin GALLACHER (Dundee United) | Goran SORLOTH |
| (21) | Maurice JOHNSTON (Nantes) | Jan-Aage FJORTOFT |

Substitutions

| | | |
|---|---|---|
| (5) | Iain DURRANT (Rangers) | Orjan BERG |
| | for Aitken 55 mins | for Sundby 2 mins |
| | | Jan-Ivar JAKOBSEN |
| | | for Berg 84 mins |

Goals

| | | |
|---|---|---|
| McStay (14 mins) | 1-0 | |
| | 1-1 | Fjortoft (44 mins) |
| Johnston (63 mins) | 2-1 | |

## 503

(World Cup — Qualifier)
19 October 1988

Referee: Trischler (West Germany)
Hampden Park, Glasgow (Att: 42,771)

### SCOTLAND 1-1 YUGOSLAVIA | Half-time 1-1

| | | |
|---|---|---|
| (5) | Andrew GORAM (Hibernian) | Tomislav IVKOVIC |
| (39) | Richard GOUGH (Rangers) | Vujadin STANOJKOVIC |
| (22) | Maurice MALPAS (Dundee United) | Predrag SPASIC |
| (63) | William MILLER (Aberdeen) captain | Srecko KATANEC |
| (57) | Alexander McLEISH (Aberdeen) | Faruk HADZIBEGIC |
| (19) | Stephen NICOL (Liverpool) | Davor JOZIC |
| (32) | Paul McSTAY (Celtic) | Ljubomir RADANOVIC |
| (41) | Robert AITKEN (Celtic) | Mehmed BAZDAREVIC |
| (20) | James BETT (Aberdeen) | Borislav CVETKOVIC |
| (9) | Brian McCLAIR (Manchester United) | Dragan STOJKOVIC |
| (22) | Maurice JOHNSTON (Nantes) | Zlatko VUJOVIC |

Substitutions

| | | |
|---|---|---|
| (13) | Alistair McCOIST (Rangers) | Dragoljub BRNOVIC |
| | for Bett 55 mins | for Spasic 83 mins |
| (6) | David SPEEDIE (Coventry City) | Refik SABANADZOVIC |
| | for Aitken 70 mins | for Cvetkovic 89 mins |

Goals

| | | |
|---|---|---|
| Johnston (19 mins) | 1-0 | |
| | 1-1 | Katanec (36 mins) |

## 504

(Friendly)
22 December 1988

Referee: Delmer (France)
Stadio Renato Curi, Perugia (Att: 25,600)

### ITALY 2-0 SCOTLAND | Half-time 0-0

| | | |
|---|---|---|
| (6) | Andrew GORAM (Hibernian) | Walter ZENGA |
| (40) | Richard GOUGH (Rangers) | Giuseppe BERGOMI |
| (23) | Maurice MALPAS (Dundee United) | Paolo MALDINI |
| (34) | David NAREY (Dundee United) | Franco BARESI |
| (58) | Alexander McLEISH (Aberdeen) | Riccardo FERRI |
| (8) | Murdo MacLEOD (Borussia Dortmund) | Massimo CRIPPA |
| (33) | Paul McSTAY (Celtic) | Nicola BERTI |
| (42) | Robert AITKEN (Celtic) captain | Giuseppe GIANNINI |
| (1) | Ian FERGUSON (Rangers) | Giancarlo MAROCCHI |
| (4) | Kevin GALLACHER (Dundee United) | Aldo SERENA |
| (23) | Maurice JOHNSTON (Nantes) | Gianluca VIALLI |

Substitutions

| | | |
|---|---|---|
| (10) | Brian McCLAIR (Manchester United) | Stefano TACCONI |
| | for McStay 56 mins | for Zenga 50 mins |
| (2) | Gordon DURIE (Chelsea) | Ciro FERRARA |
| | for Ferguson 71 mins | for Bergomi 50 mins |
| (7) | David SPEEDIE (Coventry City) | |
| | for Gough 87 mins | |

Goals

| | | |
|---|---|---|
| | 0-1 | Giannini (47 mins pen) |
| | 0-2 | Berti (70 mins) |

---

# 1989

| P | W | D | L | F | A |
|---|---|---|---|---|---|
| 8 | 4 | 1 | 3 | 11 | 12 |

## 505

(World Cup — Qualifier)
8 February 1989

Referee: Kirschen (East Germany)
Tsirion Stadhion, Limassol (Att: 25,000)

### CYPRUS 2-3 SCOTLAND | Half-time 1-1

| | | |
|---|---|---|
| (46) | James LEIGHTON (Manchester United) | Georgios PANTZIARAS |
| (41) | Richard GOUGH (Rangers) | Charalambous PITTAS |
| (24) | Maurice MALPAS (Dundee United) | Kostas MIAMILIOTIS |
| (35) | David NAREY (Dundee United) | Georgios CHRISTODOULOU |
| (59) | Alexander McLEISH (Aberdeen) | Avraam SOCRATOUS |
| (20) | Stephen NICOL (Liverpool) | Yiannakis YIANGOUDAKIS |
| (34) | Paul McSTAY (Celtic) | Christos KOLIANDRIS |
| (43) | Robert AITKEN (Celtic) captain | Pavlos SAVVA |
| (11) | Brian McCLAIR (Manchester United) | Floros NICOLAOU |
| (8) | David SPEEDIE (Coventry City) | Georgios SAVVIDES |
| (24) | Maurice JOHNSTON (Nantes) | Yiannos IOANNOU |

Substitutions

| | | |
|---|---|---|
| (2) | Ian FERGUSON (Rangers) | Kostas PETSAS |
| | for Nicol 10 mins | for Savva 39 mins |
| (1) | Alan McINALLY (Aston Villa) | Antonis ANDRELLIS |
| | for Speedie 78 mins | for Miamiliotis 77 mins |

Goals

| | | |
|---|---|---|
| Johnston (9 mins) | 1-0 | |
| | 1-1 | Koliandris (14 mins) |
| | 1-2 | Ioannou (47 mins) |
| Gough (54 mins) | 2-2 | |
| Gough (90 mins) | 3-2 | |

## 506

(World Cup — Qualifier)
8 March 1989

Referee: Stiegler (Czechoslovakia)
Hampden Park, Glasgow (Att: 65,204)

### SCOTLAND 2-0 FRANCE | Half-time 1-0

| | | |
|---|---|---|
| (47) | James LEIGHTON (Manchester United) | Joel BATS |
| (42) | Richard GOUGH (Rangers) | Manuel AMOROS |
| (25) | Maurice MALPAS (Dundee United) | Luc SONOR |
| (5) | Gary GILLESPIE (Liverpool) | Patrick BATTISTON |
| (60) | Alexander McLEISH (Aberdeen) captain | Frank SILVESTRE |
| (21) | Stephen NICOL (Liverpool) | Thierry LAUREY |
| (35) | Paul McSTAY (Celtic) | Laurent BLANC |
| (44) | Robert AITKEN (Celtic) | Frank SAUZÉE |
| (3) | Ian FERGUSON (Rangers) | Jean-Philippe DURAND |
| (14) | Alistair McCOIST (Rangers) | Daniel XUEREB |
| (25) | Maurice JOHNSTON (Nantes) | Jean-Pierre PAPIN |

Substitutions

| | | |
|---|---|---|
| (42) | Gordon STRACHAN (Leeds United) | Stéphane PAILLE |
| | for Ferguson 56 mins | for Durand 57 mins |
| (12) | Brian McCLAIR (Manchester United) | Christian PEREZ |
| | for McCoist 69 mins | for Xuereb 70 mins |

Goals

| | | |
|---|---|---|
| Johnston (28 mins) | 1-0 | |
| Johnston (52 mins) | 2-0 | |

## 507

(World Cup — Qualifier)
26 April 1989

Referee: Haraldsson (Iceland)
Hampden Park, Glasgow (Att: 50,081)

### SCOTLAND 2-1 CYPRUS | Half-time 1-0

| | | |
|---|---|---|
| (48) | James LEIGHTON (Manchester United) | Andreas CHARITOU |
| (43) | Richard GOUGH (Rangers) | Charalambous PITTAS |
| (26) | Maurice MALPAS (Dundee United) | Spiros KASTANAS |
| (1) | David McPHERSON (Hearts) | Georgios CHRISTODOULOU |
| (61) | Alexander McLEISH (Aberdeen) | Avraam SOCRATOUS |
| (7) | Patrick NEVIN (Everton) | Yiannakis YIANGOUDAKIS |
| (36) | Paul McSTAY (Celtic) | Christos KOLIANDRIS |
| (45) | Robert AITKEN (Celtic) captain | Kostas PETSAS |
| (3) | Gordon DURIE (Chelsea) | Floros NICOLAOU |
| (15) | Alistair McCOIST (Rangers) | Georgios SAVVIDES |
| (26) | Maurice JOHNSTON (Nantes) | Yiannos IOANNOU |

Substitutions

| | | |
|---|---|---|
| (9) | David SPEEDIE (Coventry City) | Antonis ANDRELLIS |
| | for Durie 59 mins | for Pittas 64 mins |
| (20) | Charles NICHOLAS (Aberdeen) | |
| | for Nevin 74 mins | |

Goals

| | | |
|---|---|---|
| Johnston (26 mins) | 1-0 | |
| | 1-1 | Nicolaou (62 mins) |
| McCoist (63 mins) | 2-1 | |

**08**

(Rous Cup)

**7 May 1989**

Referee: Vautrot (France)

Hampden Park, Glasgow (Att: 63,282)

## SCOTLAND 0-2 ENGLAND — Half-time 0-1

| 9) | James LEIGHTON (Manchester United) | Peter SHILTON |
| ) | Stewart McKIMMIE (Aberdeen) | Gary STEVENS |
| 7) | Maurice MALPAS (Dundee United) | Stuart PEARCE |
| ) | David McPHERSON (Hearts) | Terence BUTCHER |
| 2) | Alexander McLEISH (Aberdeen) | Desmond WALKER |
| ) | Patrick NEVIN (Everton) | Trevor STEVEN |
| 7) | Paul McSTAY (Celtic) | Neil WEBB |
| 6) | Robert AITKEN (Celtic) captain | Bryan ROBSON |
| ) | Robert CONNOR (Aberdeen) | Christopher WADDLE |
| 6) | Alistair McCOIST (Rangers) | John FASHANU |
| 7 | Maurice JOHNSTON (Nantes) | Anthony COTTEE |

Substitutions

| ) | Peter GRANT (Celtic) | Steven BULL |
| | for Connor 57 mins | for Fashanu 31 mins |
| | | Paul GASCOIGNE |
| | | for Cottee 75 mins |

Goals

| 0-1 | Waddle (20 mins) |
| 0-2 | Bull (80 mins) |

Scotland striker Alan McInally touches the ball past goalkeeper Roberto Rojas of Chile to score after only four minutes of the match at Hampden in May 1989.

Scotland players celebrate. McInally with Grant McLeod and McStay during their 2-0 victory against Chile.

**09**

(Rous Cup)

**0 May 1989**

Referee: Ponnet (Belgium)

Hampden Park, Glasgow (Att: 9,006)

## SCOTLAND 2-0 CHILE — Half-time 1-0

| 0) | James LEIGHTON (Manchester United) captain | Roberto ROJAS |
| ) | Stewart McKIMMIE (Aberdeen) | Oscar REYES |
| 8) | Maurice MALPAS (Dundee United) | Leonel CONTRERAS |
| ) | Gary GILLESPIE (Liverpool) | Hugo GONZÁLEZ |
| 3) | Alexander McLEISH (Aberdeen) | Jaime PIZARRO |
| ) | Peter GRANT (Celtic) | Hugo RUBIO |
| 8) | Paul McSTAY (Celtic) | Jaime VERA |
| 7) | Robert AITKEN (Celtic) | Juvenal OLMOS |
| ) | Murdo MacLEOD (Borussia Dortmund) | Alejandro HISIS |
| 0) | David SPEEDIE (Coventry City) | Juan COVARRUBIAS |
| | Alan McINALLY (Aston Villa) | Héctor PUEBLA |

Substitutions

| 8) | Maurice JOHNSTON (Nantes) | Juan LETELIER |
| | for Speedie 46 mins | for Covarrubias 46 mins |
| | Derek WHYTE (Celtic) | |
| | for Gillespie 70 mins | |

Goals

| 1-0 | McInally (4 mins) |
| 2-0 | MacLeod (52 mins) |

## 510

(World Cup — Qualifier)
6 September 1989

Referee: Van Langenhove (Netherlands)
Maksimir Stadion, Zagreb (Att: 42,500)

### YUGOSLAVIA 3-1 SCOTLAND — Half-time 0-1

| | | |
|---|---|---|
| (51) | James LEIGHTON (Manchester United) | Tomislav IVKOVIC |
| (22) | Stephen NICOL (Liverpool) | Mirsad BALJIC |
| (29) | Maurice MALPAS (Dundee United) | Predrag SPASIC |
| (64) | William MILLER (Aberdeen) | Srecko KATANEC |
| (64) | Alexander McLEISH (Aberdeen) | Faruk HADZIBEGIC |
| (7) | Gary GILLESPIE (Liverpool) | Dragoljub BRNOVIC |
| (39) | Paul McSTAY (Celtic) | Mehmed BAZDAREVIC |
| (48) | Robert AITKEN (Celtic) captain | Dragan STOJKOVIC |
| (10) | Murdo MacLEOD (Borussia Dortmund) | Safet SUSIC |
| (4) | Gordon DURIE (Chelsea) | Dragan JAKOVLJEVIC |
| (17) | Alistair McCOIST (Rangers) | Zlatko VUJOVIC |

Substitutions

| | | |
|---|---|---|
| (3) | Alan McINALLY (Bayern Munich) | Dejan SAVICEVIC |
| | for Durie 71 mins | for Jakovljevic 73 mins |

Goals

| | | |
|---|---|---|
| Durie (37 mins) | 1-0 | |
| | 1-1 | Katanec (52 mins) |
| | 1-2 | Nicol (57 mins o.g.) |
| | 1-3 | Gillespie (59 mins o.g.) |

## 511

(World Cup — Qualifier)
11 October 1989

Referee: Rothlisberger (Switzerland)
Parc des Princes, Paris (Att: 25,000)

### FRANCE 3-0 SCOTLAND — Half-time 1-0

| | | |
|---|---|---|
| (52) | James LEIGHTON (Manchester United) | Joël BATS |
| (23) | Stephen NICOL (Liverpool) | Frank SILVESTRE |
| (30) | Maurice MALPAS (Dundee United) | Eric DI MECO |
| (44) | Richard GOUGH (Rangers) | Frank SAUZÉE |
| (65) | Alexander McLEISH (Aberdeen) | Yvon LE ROUX |
| (43) | Gordon STRACHAN (Leeds United) | Jean-Philippe DURAND |
| (40) | Paul McSTAY (Celtic) | Bernard PARDO |
| (49) | Robert AITKEN (Celtic) captain | Didier DESCHAMPS |
| (11) | Murdo MacLEOD (Borussia Dortmund) | Christian PEREZ |
| (18) | Alistair McCOIST (Rangers) | Jean-Marc FERRERI |
| (29) | Maurice JOHNSTON (Rangers) | Eric CANTONA |

Substitutions

| | | |
|---|---|---|
| (4) | Alan McINALLY (Bayern Munich) | Bernard CASONI |
| | for Strachan 64 mins | for Le Roux 46 mins |
| (21) | James BETT (Aberdeen) | Daniel BRAVO |
| | for MacLeod 75 mins | for Perez 81 mins |

Goals

| | | |
|---|---|---|
| | 0-1 | Deschamps (26 mins) |
| | 0-2 | Cantona (63 mins) |
| | 0-3 | Nicol (88 mins o.g.) |

## 512

(World Cup — Qualifier)
15 November 1989

Referee: Listkiewicz (Poland)
Hampden Park, Glasgow (Att: 63,987)

### SCOTLAND 1-1 NORWAY — Half-time 1-0

| | | |
|---|---|---|
| (53) | James LEIGHTON (Manchester United) | Erik THORSTVEDT |
| (3) | David McPHERSON (Hearts) | Hugo HANSEN |
| (31) | Maurice MALPAS (Dundee United) | Terje KOJEDAL |
| (65) | William MILLER (Aberdeen) | Rune BRATSETH |
| (66) | Alexander McLEISH (Aberdeen) | Erland JOHNSEN |
| (22) | James BETT (Aberdeen) | Stig-Inge BJORNEBYE |
| (41) | Paul McSTAY (Celtic) | Tom GULBRANDSEN |
| (50) | Robert AITKEN (Celtic) captain | Per-Egil AHLSEN |
| (21) | David COOPER (Motherwell) | Bent SKAMMELSRUD |
| (19) | Alistair McCOIST (Rangers) | Goran SORLOTH |
| (30) | Maurice JOHNSTON (Rangers) | Jan-Aage FJORTOFT |

Substitutions

| | | |
|---|---|---|
| (12) | Murdo MacLEOD (Borussia Dortmund) | Lars BOHINEN |
| | for Miller 67 mins | for Skammelsrud 58 mins |
| (13) | Brian McCLAIR (Manchester United) | Jan HALVORSEN |
| | for Cooper 74 mins | for Kojedal 82 mins |

Goals

| | | |
|---|---|---|
| McCoist (44 mins) | 1-0 | |
| | 1-1 | Johnsen (89 mins) |

# 1990

| P | W | D | L | F | A |
|---|---|---|---|---|---|
| 11 | 5 | 2 | 4 | 12 | 12 |

## 513

(Friendly)
28 March 1990

Referee: Houben (Netherlands)
Hampden Park, Glasgow (Att: 51,537)

### SCOTLAND 1-0 ARGENTINA — Half-time 1-0

| | | |
|---|---|---|
| (54) | James LEIGHTON (Manchester United) | Nery PUMPIDO |
| (45) | Richard GOUGH (Rangers) | Sergio BATISTA |
| (3) | Stewart McKIMMIE (Aberdeen) | Edgardo BAUZA |
| (1) | Craig LEVEIN (Hearts) | Roberto SENSINI |
| (67) | Alexander McLEISH (Aberdeen) captain | Oscar RUGGERI |
| (23) | James BETT (Aberdeen) | Néstor FABBRI |
| (1) | Stuart McCALL (Everton) | Gabriel CALDERÓN |
| (42) | Paul McSTAY (Celtic) | José BASUALDO |
| (13) | Murdo MacLEOD (Borussia Dortmund) | Jorge BURRUCHAGA |
| (1) | Robert FLECK (Norwich City) | Jorge VALDANO |
| (5) | Alan McINALLY (Bayern Munich) | Claudio CANIGGIA |

Substitutions

| | | |
|---|---|---|
| (14) | Brian McCLAIR (Manchester United) | Abel BALBO |
| | for McInally 74 mins | for Valdano 46 mins |
| (3) | Robert AITKEN (Newcastle United) | Pedro TROGLIO |
| | for Bett 89 mins | for Burruchaga 49 mins |
| | | Pedro MONZÓN |
| | | for Ruggeri 59 mins |

Goals

| | | |
|---|---|---|
| McKimmie (32 mins) | 1-0 | |

## 514

(Friendly)
25 April 1990

Referee: Midgley (England)
Hampden Park, Glasgow (Att: 21,868)

### SCOTLAND 0-1 EAST GERMANY — Half-time 0-0

| | | |
|---|---|---|
| (7) | Andrew GORAM (Hibernian) | Perry BRAUTIGAM |
| (46) | Richard GOUGH (Rangers) | Heiko PESCHKE |
| (8) | Gary GILLESPIE (Liverpool) | Stefan BÖGER |
| (2) | Craig LEVEIN (Hearts) | Hendryk HERZOG |
| (68) | Alexander McLEISH (Aberdeen) captain | Dirk SCHUSTER |
| (14) | Murdo MacLEOD (Borussia Dortmund) | Matthias LINDNER |
| (1) | Gary McALLISTER (Leicester City) | Matthias SAMMER |
| (2) | Stuart McCALL (Everton) | Jörg STÜBNER |
| (2) | John COLLINS (Hibernian) | Thomas DOLL |
| (5) | Gordon DURIE (Chelsea) | Rainer ERNST |
| (31) | Maurice JOHNSTON (Rangers) | Ulf KIRSTEN |

Substitutions

| | | |
|---|---|---|
| (43) | Paul McSTAY (Celtic) | Stefan BÜTTNER |
| | for Gillespie 57 mins | for Stübner 85 mins |
| (20) | Alistair McCOIST (Rangers) | |
| | for Durie 68 mins | |

Goals

| | | |
|---|---|---|
| | 0-1 | Doll (73 mins pen) |

## 515

(Friendly)
16 May 1990

Referee: Pedersen (Norway)
Pittodrie Stadium, Aberdeen (Att: 23,000)

### SCOTLAND 1-3 EGYPT — Half-time 0-2

| | | |
|---|---|---|
| (1) | Bryan GUNN (Norwich City) | Ahmed SHOUBIER |
| (4) | Stewart McKIMMIE (Aberdeen) | Ibrahim HASSAN |
| (32) | Maurice MALPAS (Dundee United) | Hisham YAKIN |
| (47) | Richard GOUGH (Rangers) | Raba YASSIN |
| (69) | Alexander McLEISH (Aberdeen) captain | Hani RAMZY |
| (24) | James BETT (Aberdeen) | Ahmed EL-KAS |
| (9) | Gary GILLESPIE (Liverpool) | Magdi ABDELGHANI |
| (44) | Paul McSTAY (Celtic) | Ahmed RAMZY |
| (22) | David COOPER (Motherwell) | Ismail YOUSSEF |
| (6) | Gordon DURIE (Chelsea) | Gamal ABDELHAMID |
| (21) | Alistair McCOIST (Rangers) | Hossam HASSAN |

Substitutions

| | | |
|---|---|---|
| (3) | Stuart McCALL (Everton) | Thabet EL-BATAL |
| | for McKimmie 45 mins | for El-Kas 46 mins |
| (3) | Craig LEVEIN (Hearts) | Ala's MAYOUB |
| | for McLeish 89 mins | for Abdelghani 60 mins |

Goals

| | | |
|---|---|---|
| | 0-1 | Abdelhamid (15 mins) |
| | 0-2 | H. Hassan (28 mins) |
| McCoist (73 mins) | 1-2 | |
| | 1-3 | Youssef (83 mins) |

tewart McKimmie beats goalkeeper Nery Pumpido to score the only goal of the game against Argentina at Hampden in March 1990.

## 16

Friendly)
9 May 1990

Referee: Worrall (England)
Hampden Park, Glasgow (Att: 25,142)

### SCOTLAND 1-1 POLAND — Half-time 1-0

| | | |
|---|---|---|
| ) | Andrew GORAM (Hibernian) | Jaroslaw BAKO |
| 0) | Gary GILLESPIE (Liverpool) | Dariusz KUBICKI |
| 3) | Maurice MALPAS (Dundee United) | Dariusz WDOWCZYK |
| ) | Craig LEVEIN (Hearts) | Zbigniew KACZMAREK |
| 8) | Richard GOUGH (Rangers) | Damian LUKASIK |
| 5) | Murdo MacLEOD (Borussia Dortmund) | Waldemar PRUSIK |
| 2) | Robert AITKEN (Newcastle United) captain | Piotr CZACHOWSKI |
| ) | Stuart McCALL (Everton) | Janusz NAWROCKI |
| ) | Gary McALLISTER (Leicester City) | Jacek ZIOBER |
| 2) | Alistair McCOIST (Rangers) | Dariusz DZIEKANOWSKI |
| 2) | Maurice JOHNSTON (Rangers) | Roman KOSECKI |

Substitutions

| | | |
|---|---|---|
| ) | John COLLINS (Hibernian) | Piotr SOCZYNSKI |
| | for MacLeod 65 mins | for Lukasik 46 mins |
| ) | Alan McINALLY (Bayern Munich) | Leszek PISZ |
| | for Johnston 73 mins | for Nawrocki 70 mins |
| 5) | Paul McSTAY (Celtic) | |
| | for McAllister 83 mins | |

Goals

| | | |
|---|---|---|
| hnston (42 mins) | 1-0 | |
| | 1-1 | Gillespie (59 mins o.g.) |

## 17

Friendly)
8 May 1990

Referee: Longhi (Italy)
Ta'Qali Stadium, Valletta (Att: 3,000)

### MALTA 1-2 SCOTLAND — Half-time 1-1

| | | |
|---|---|---|
| ) | Andrew GORAM (Hibernian) | Reginald CINI |
| ) | David McPHERSON (Hearts) | Silvio VELLA |
| 4) | Maurice MALPAS (Dundee United) | David CARABOTT |
| 1) | Gary GILLESPIE (Liverpool) | John BUTTIGIEG |
| 9) | Richard GOUGH (Rangers) | Joseph GALEA |
| 5) | James BETT (Aberdeen) | Jesmond ZERAFA |
| 6) | Paul McSTAY (Celtic) | Kristian LAFERLA |
| 3) | Robert AITKEN (Newcastle United) captain | Raymond VELLA |
| ) | Stuart McCALL (Everton) | Martin GREGORY |
| ) | Alan McINALLY (Bayern Munich) | Bernard LICARI |
| 3) | Maurice JOHNSTON (Rangers) | Michael DEGIORGIO |

Substitutions

| | | |
|---|---|---|
| ) | Craig LEVEIN (Hearts) | Edwin CAMILLERI |
| | for Gillespie 40 mins | for Galea 46 mins |
| 5) | James LEIGHTON (Manchester United) | Joseph ZARB |
| | for Goram 46 mins | for Gregory 62 mins |
| ) | Gary McALLISTER (Leicester City) | Charles SCERRI |
| | for Bett 46 mins | for Licari 77 mins |
| 3) | Alistair McCOIST (Rangers) | |
| | for Johnston 69 mins | |
| ) | John COLLINS (Hibernian) | |
| | for McStay 80 mins | |

Goals

| | | |
|---|---|---|
| cInally (5 mins) | 1-0 | |
| | 1-1 | Degiorgio (43 mins) |
| cInally (81 mins) | 2-1 | |

## 518

(World Cup — Final Tournament 1st Round)
11 June 1990

Referee: Loustau (Argentina)
Stadio Luigi Ferraris, Genoa (Att: 30,867)

### COSTA RICA 1-0 SCOTLAND — Half-time 0-0

| | | |
|---|---|---|
| (56) | James LEIGHTON (Manchester United) | Luis CONEJO |
| (5) | David McPHERSON (Hearts) | German CHAVARRÍA |
| (35) | Maurice MALPAS (Dundee United) | Roger FLÓRES |
| (50) | Richard GOUGH (Rangers) | Mauricio MONTERO |
| (70) | Alexander McLEISH (Aberdeen) | José CHÁVEZ |
| (26) | James BETT (Aberdeen) | Héctor MARCHENA |
| (47) | Paul McSTAY (Celtic) | Juan CAYASSO |
| (54) | Robert AITKEN (Newcastle United) captain | Ronald GONZÁLEZ |
| (6) | Stuart McCALL (Everton) | Oscar RAMÍREZ |
| (8) | Alan McINALLY (Bayern Munich) | Roger GÓMEZ |
| (34) | Maurice JOHNSTON (Rangers) | Claudio JARA |

Substitutions

| | | |
|---|---|---|
| (5) | Stewart McKIMMIE (Aberdeen) | Hernán MEDFORD |
| | for Gough 46 mins | for Jara 85 mins |
| (24) | Alistair McCOIST (Rangers) | |
| | for Bett 74 mins | |

Goals

| | | |
|---|---|---|
| | 0-1 | Cayasso (49 mins) |

## 519

(World Cup — Final Tournament 1st Round)
16 June 1990

Referee: Maciel (Paraguay)
Stadio Luigi Ferraris, Genoa (Att: 31,823)

### SWEDEN 1-2 SCOTLAND — Half-time 0-1

| | | |
|---|---|---|
| (57) | James LEIGHTON (Manchester United) | Thomas RAVELLI |
| (6) | David McPHERSON (Hearts) | Roland NILSSON |
| (36) | Maurice MALPAS (Dundee United) | Stefan SCHWARZ |
| (6) | Craig LEVEIN (Hearts) | Peter LARSSON |
| (71) | Alexander McLEISH (Aberdeen) | Glenn HYSÉN |
| (16) | Murdo MacLEOD (Borussia Dortmund) | Anders LIMPAR |
| (55) | Robert AITKEN (Newcastle United) captain | Jonas THERN |
| (7) | Stuart McCALL (Everton) | Joakim NILSSON |
| (7) | Gordon DURIE (Chelsea) | Klas INGESSON |
| (2) | Robert FLECK (Norwich City) | Tomas BROLIN |
| (35) | Maurice JOHNSTON (Rangers) | Stefan PETTERSSON |

Substitutions

| | | |
|---|---|---|
| (48) | Paul McSTAY (Celtic) | Johnny EKSTRÖM |
| | for Durie 74 mins | for Pettersson 65 mins |
| (25) | Alistair McCOIST (Rangers) | Glenn STRÖMBERG |
| | for Fleck 84 mins | for Larsson 74 mins |

Goals

| | | |
|---|---|---|
| McCall (10 mins) | 1-0 | |
| Johnston (81 mins pen) | 2-0 | |
| | 2-1 | Strömberg (85 mins) |

## 520

(World Cup — Final Tournament 1st Round)    Referee: Kohl (Austria)
20 June 1990    Stadio Delle Alpe, Turin (Att: 62,502)

### BRAZIL 1-0 SCOTLAND    Half-time 0-0

| | | |
|---|---|---|
| (58) | James LEIGHTON (Manchester United) | Cláudio André TAFFAREL |
| (6) | Stewart McKIMMIE (Aberdeen) | Jorge de Ancrim JORGINHO |
| (37) | Maurice MALPAS (Dundee United) | Cláudio Ibrahim BRANCO |
| (7) | David McPHERSON (Hearts) | RICARDO Barreta da ROCHA |
| (72) | Alexander McLEISH (Aberdeen) | RICARDO GOMES Raymundo |
| (17) | Murdo MacLEOD (Borussia Dortmund) | MAURO Geraldo GALVAO |
| (49) | Paul McSTAY (Celtic) | Ricardo Rogério ALEMAO |
| (56) | Robert AITKEN (Newcastle United) captain | Carlos Caetano DUNGA |
| (8) | Stuart McCALL (Everton) | VALDO Candido Filho |
| (26) | Alistair McCOIST (Rangers) | ROMÁRIO de Souza Faria |
| (36) | Maurice JOHNSTON (Rangers) | Antonio de Oliveira CARECA |

Substitutions

| | | |
|---|---|---|
| (12) | Gary GILLESPIE (Liverpool) | Luís Antonio Corréa MÜLLER |
| | for MacLeod 39 mins | for Romário 64 mins |
| (3) | Robert FLECK (Norwich City) | |
| | for McCoist 77 mins | |

Goals
0-1    Müller (81 mins)

## 521

(European Championship — Qualifier)    Referee: Azpitarte (Spain)
12 September 1990    Hampden Park, Glasgow (Att: 12,801)

### SCOTLAND 2-1 ROMANIA    Half-time 1-1

| | | |
|---|---|---|
| (10) | Andrew GORAM (Hibernian) | Silviu LUNG |
| (7) | Stewart McKIMMIE (Aberdeen) | Dan PETRESCU |
| (38) | Maurice MALPAS (Dundee United) | Michael KLEIN |
| (1) | Brian IRVINE (Aberdeen) | Emil SANDOI |
| (73) | Alexander McLEISH (Aberdeen) | Gheorghe POPESCU |
| (18) | Murdo MacLEOD (Borussia Dortmund) | Dorin MATEUT |
| (50) | Paul McSTAY (Celtic) captain | Ionut LUPESCU |
| (4) | Gary McALLISTER (Leeds United) | Iosif ROTARIU |
| (4) | Robert CONNOR (Aberdeen) | Gheorghe HAGI |
| (1) | John ROBERTSON (Hearts) | Marius LACATUS |
| (27) | Alistair McCOIST (Rangers) | Rodion CAMATARU |

Substitutions

| | | |
|---|---|---|
| (1) | Thomas BOYD (Motherwell) | Florin RADUCIOIU |
| | for Connor 59 mins | for Camataru 63 mins |
| (9) | Patrick NEVIN (Everton) | Ioan SABAU |
| | for McAllister 73 mins | for Mateut 79 mins |

Goals
| | | |
|---|---|---|
| | 0-1 | Camataru (13 mins) |
| Robertson (37 mins) | 1-1 | |
| McCoist (75 mins) | 2-1 | |

## 522

(European Championship — Qualifier)    Referee: Palsi (Finland)
17 October 1990    Hampden Park, Glasgow (Att: 27,740)

### SCOTLAND 2-1 SWITZERLAND    Half-time 1-0

| | | |
|---|---|---|
| (11) | Andrew GORAM (Hibernian) | Philipp WALKER |
| (8) | Stewart McKIMMIE (Aberdeen) | Peter SCHEPULL |
| (24) | Stephen NICOL (Liverpool) | Blaise PIFFARETTI |
| (8) | David McPHERSON (Hearts) | Dominique HERR |
| (74) | Alexander McLEISH (Aberdeen) captain | André EGLI |
| (19) | Murdo MacLEOD (Hibernian) | Thomas BICKEL |
| (5) | Gary McALLISTER (Leeds United) | Heinz HERMANN |
| (9) | Stuart McCALL (Everton) | Alain SUTTER |
| (2) | Thomas BOYD (Motherwell) | Kubilay TÜRKYILMAZ |
| (2) | John ROBERTSON (Hearts) | Adrian KNUP |
| (28) | Alistair McCOIST (Rangers) | Stéphane CHAPUISAT |

Substitutions

| | | |
|---|---|---|
| (8) | Gordon DURIE (Chelsea) | Frederic CHASSOT |
| | for Boyd 68 mins | for Schepull 73 mins |
| (5) | John COLLINS (Celtic) | Beat SUTTER |
| | for McAllister 79 mins | for Piffaretti 80 mins |

Goals
| | | |
|---|---|---|
| Robertson (34 mins pen) | 1-0 | |
| McAllister (51 mins) | 2-0 | |
| | 2-1 | Knup (65 mins pen) |

## 523

(European Championship — Qualifier)    Referee: Kaupe (Austria)
14 November 1990    Vasil Levski Stadion, Sofia (Att: 42,000)

### BULGARIA 1-1 SCOTLAND    Half-time 0-1

| | | |
|---|---|---|
| (12) | Andrew GORAM (Hibernian) | Borislav MIHAILOV |
| (9) | Stewart McKIMMIE (Aberdeen) | Pavel DOCHEV |
| (39) | Maurice MALPAS (Dundee United) captain | Kalin BANKOV |
| (9) | David McPHERSON (Hearts) | Zlatko YANKOV |
| (13) | Gary GILLESPIE (Liverpool) | Dimitar MLADENOV |
| (4) | James McINALLY (Dundee United) | Kostadin YANCHEV |
| (6) | Gary McALLISTER (Leeds United) | Georgi YORDANOV |
| (15) | Brian McCLAIR (Manchester United) | Krasimir BALAKOV |
| (3) | Thomas BOYD (Motherwell) | Hristo STOICHKOV |
| (9) | Gordon DURIE (Chelsea) | Nasko SIRAKOV |
| (29) | Alistair McCOIST (Rangers) | Lyuboslav PENEV |

Substitutions

| | | |
|---|---|---|
| (10) | Patrick NEVIN (Everton) | Nikolai TODOROV |
| | for Durie 59 mins | for Yanchev 53 mins |
| | | Emil KOSTADINOV |
| | | for Balakov 75 mins |

Goals
| | | |
|---|---|---|
| McCoist (9 mins) | 1-0 | |
| | 1-1 | Todorov (70 mins) |

Italian manager Azeglio Vicini (third left) present Richard Gough (second right) and Paul McStay with pictures of themselves after achieving 50 caps for their country. Also pictured is Andy Roxburgh (right) and SFA representative William Dickie. The ceremony took place before the February 1991 game against the USSR at Ibrox.

# 1991

| P | W | D | L | F | A |
|---|---|---|---|---|---|
| 6 | 2 | 2 | 2 | 9 | 5 |

## 524

(Friendly)    Referee: Mikkelsen (Denmark)
6 February 1991    Ibrox Stadium, Glasgow (Att: 20,673)

### SCOTLAND 0-1 USSR    Half-time 0-0

| | | |
|---|---|---|
| (13) | Andrew GORAM (Hibernian) | Aleksandr UVAROV |
| (25) | Stephen NICOL (Liverpool) | Alexei CHERNISHOV |
| (40) | Maurice MALPAS (Dundee United) | Vasilij KULKOV |
| (51) | Richard GOUGH (Rangers) captain | Akhrik TSVEIBA |
| (75) | Alexander McLEISH (Aberdeen) | Sergei GORLUKOVICH |
| (44) | Gordon STRACHAN (Leeds United) | Andrei KANCHELSKIS |
| (51) | Paul McSTAY (Celtic) | Igor SHALIMOV |
| (10) | Stuart McCALL (Everton) | Sergei ALEINIKOV |
| (4) | Thomas BOYD (Motherwell) | Igor DOBROVOLSKI |
| (4) | Robert FLECK (Norwich City) | Sergei YURAN |
| (30) | Alistair McCOIST (Rangers) | Aleksandr MOSTOVOI |

Substitutions

| | | |
|---|---|---|
| (10) | David McPHERSON (Hearts) | Igor KOLIVANOV |
| | for McLeish 46 mins | for Yuran 62 mins |
| (20) | Murdo MacLEOD (Hibernian) | Dmitri KUZNETSOV |
| | for Boyd 46 mins | for Mostovoi 69 mins |
| (7) | Gary McALLISTER (Leeds United) | |
| | for McCall 69 mins | |
| (10) | Gordon DURIE (Chelsea) | |
| | for Fleck 75 mins | |

Goals
0-1    Kuznetsov (88 mins)

## 525

(European Championship — Qualifier)
27 March 1991

Referee: Fredriksson (Sweden)
Hampden Park, Glasgow (Att: 33,119)

### SCOTLAND 1-1 BULGARIA — Half-time 0-0

| | | | |
|---|---|---|---|
| (14) | Andrew GORAM (Hibernian) | | Borislav MIHAILOV |
| (11) | David McPHERSON (Hearts) | | Pavel DOCHEV |
| (41) | Maurice MALPAS (Dundee United) | | Trifon IVANOV |
| (52) | Richard GOUGH (Rangers) | | Zlatko YANKOV |
| (76) | Alexander McLEISH (Aberdeen) captain | | Nikolai ILIEV |
| (45) | Gordon STRACHAN (Leeds United) | | Ilian KIRIAKOV |
| (5) | James McINALLY (Dundee United) | | Krasimir BALAKOV |
| (52) | Paul McSTAY (Celtic) | | Nasko SIRAKOV |
| (16) | Brian McCLAIR (Manchester United) | | Georgi YORDANOV |
| (11) | Gordon DURIE (Chelsea) | | Emil KOSTADINOV |
| (31) | Alistair McCOIST (Rangers) | | Lyuboslav PENEV |

Substitutions

| | | | |
|---|---|---|---|
| (6) | John COLLINS (Celtic) | | Petar ALEKSANDROV |
| | for Strachan 80 mins | | for Sirakov 86 mins |
| (3) | John ROBERTSON (Hearts) | | Lachezar TANEV |
| | for Durie 80 mins | | for Balakov 86 mins |

Goals

| | |
|---|---|
| Collins (83 mins) | 1-0 |
| 1-1 | Kostadinov (89 mins) |

## 526

(European Championship — Qualifier)
1 May 1991

Referee: Kaimi (Albania)
Stadio di Serravalle, Serravalle (Att: 3,512)

### SAN MARINO 0-2 SCOTLAND — Half-time 0-0

| | | | |
|---|---|---|---|
| (15) | Andrew GORAM (Hibernian) | | Pierluigi BENEDETTINI |
| (10) | Stewart McKIMMIE (Aberdeen) | | Claudio CANTI |
| (42) | Maurice MALPAS (Dundee United) | | Bruno MUCCIOLI |
| (26) | Stephen NICOL (Liverpool) | | Luca GOBBI |
| (12) | David McPHERSON (Hearts) | | William GUERRA |
| (46) | Gordon STRACHAN (Leeds United) captain | | Paolo ZANOTTI |
| (8) | Gary McALLISTER (Leeds United) | | Massimo CECCOLI |
| (11) | Stuart McCALL (Everton) | | Marco MAZZA |
| (17) | Brian McCLAIR (Manchester United) | | Fabio FRANCINI |
| (5) | Kevin GALLACHER (Coventry City) | | Paolo MAZZA |
| (12) | Gordon DURIE (Chelsea) | | Valdes PASOLINI |

Substitutions

| | | | |
|---|---|---|---|
| (11) | Patrick NEVIN (Everton) | | Ivano TOCCACELI |
| | for McClair 57 mins | | for Zanotti 60 mins |
| (4) | John ROBERTSON (Hearts) | | Ivan MATTEONI |
| | for Nicol 74 mins | | for Pasolini 79 mins |

Goals

| | |
|---|---|
| Strachan (63 mins pen) | 1-0 |
| Durie (66 mins) | 2-0 |

## 527

(European Championship — Qualifier)
11 September 1991

Referee: Lanese (Italy)
Wankdorf Stadion, Berne (Att: 48,000)

### SWITZERLAND 2-2 SCOTLAND — Half-time 2-0

| | | | |
|---|---|---|---|
| (16) | Andrew GORAM (Rangers) | | Stefan HUBER |
| (11) | Stewart McKIMMIE (Aberdeen) | | Marc HOTTIGER |
| (43) | Maurice MALPAS (Dundee United) | | Christophe OHREL |
| (27) | Stephen NICOL (Liverpool) | | Dominique HERR |
| (13) | David McPHERSON (Hearts) | | Marcel HELDMANN |
| (47) | Gordon STRACHAN (Leeds United) captain | | Ciriaco SFORZA |
| (12) | Stuart McCALL (Rangers) | | Heinz HERMANN |
| (5) | Thomas BOYD (Chelsea) | | Alain SUTTER |
| (37) | Maurice JOHNSTON (Rangers) | | Kubilay TÜRKYILMAZ |
| (13) | Gordon DURIE (Tottenham Hotspur) | | Adrian KNUP |
| (32) | Alistair McCOIST (Rangers) | | Stéphane CHAPUISAT |

Substitutions

| | | | |
|---|---|---|---|
| (9) | Gary McALLISTER (Leeds United) | | Thomas BICKEL |
| | for Johnston 43 mins | | for A. Sutter 60 mins |
| (18) | Brian McCLAIR (Manchester United) | | Beat SUTTER |
| | for McKimmie 70 mins | | for Heldmann 67 mins |

Goals

| | |
|---|---|
| 0-1 | Chapuisat (29 mins) |
| 0-2 | Hermann (38 mins) |
| Durie (47 mins) | 1-2 |
| McCoist (83 mins) | 2-2 |

## 528

(European Championship — Qualifier)
16 October 1991

Referee: Schmidhuber (Germany)
Steaua Stadionul, Bucharest (Att: 30,000)

### ROMANIA 1-0 SCOTLAND — Half-time 0-0

| | | | |
|---|---|---|---|
| (17) | Andrew GORAM (Rangers) | | Silviu LUNG |
| (12) | Stewart McKIMMIE (Aberdeen) | | Dan PETRESCU |
| (44) | Maurice MALPAS (Dundee United) | | Michael KLEIN |
| (14) | David McPHERSON (Hearts) | | Emil SANDOI |
| (7) | Craig LEVEIN (Hearts) | | Gheorghe POPESCU |
| (48) | Gordon STRACHAN (Leeds United) captain | | Marius LACATUS |
| (13) | Stuart McCALL (Rangers) | | Ionut LUPESCU |
| (1) | Michael GALLOWAY (Celtic) | | Daniel TIMOFTE |
| (6) | Thomas BOYD (Chelsea) | | Dorinel MUNTEANU |
| (19) | Brian McCLAIR (Manchester United) | | Gheorghe HAGI |
| (14) | Gordon DURIE (Tottenham Hotspur) | | Florin RADUCIOIU |

Substitutions

| | | | |
|---|---|---|---|
| (6) | Kevin GALLACHER (Coventry City) | | Ion TIMOFTE |
| | for Boyd 58 mins | | for D. Timofte 62 mins |
| (57) | Robert AITKEN (St Mirren) | | Ilie DUMITRESCU |
| | for Galloway 70 mins | | for Raducioiu 75 mins |

Goals

| | |
|---|---|
| 0-1 | Hagi (73 mins pen) |

## 529

(European Championship — Qualifier)
13 November 1991

Referee: Pedersen (Norway)
Hampden Park, Glasgow (Att: 35,170)

### SCOTLAND 4-0 SAN MARINO — Half-time 3-0

| | | | |
|---|---|---|---|
| (18) | Andrew GORAM (Rangers) | | Pierluigi BENEDETTINI |
| (15) | David McPHERSON (Hearts) | | Claudio CANTI |
| (45) | Maurice MALPAS (Dundee United) | | Bruno MUCCIOLI |
| (8) | Craig LEVEIN (Hearts) | | Luca GOBBI |
| (53) | Richard GOUGH (Rangers) captain | | William GUERRA |
| (53) | Paul McSTAY (Celtic) | | Loris ZANOTTI |
| (10) | Gary McALLISTER (Leeds United) | | Marco MAZZA |
| (14) | Stuart McCALL (Rangers) | | Massimo BONINI |
| (5) | John ROBERTSON (Hearts) | | Fabio FRANCINI |
| (15) | Gordon DURIE (Tottenham Hotspur) | | Paolo MAZZA |
| (33) | Alistair McCOIST (Rangers) | | Valdes PASOLINI |

Substitutions

| | | | |
|---|---|---|---|
| (38) | Maurice JOHNSTON (Rangers) | | Marco MONTIRONI |
| | for McPherson 46 mins | | for Gobbi 46 mins |
| (7) | Kevin GALLACHER (Coventry City) | | Pierangelo MANZAROLI |
| | for Levein 60 mins | | for Pasolini 66 mins |

Goals

| | |
|---|---|
| McStay (10 mins) | 1-0 |
| Gough (31 mins) | 2-0 |
| Durie (37 mins) | 3-0 |
| McCoist (62 mins) | 4-0 |

# 1992

| P | W | D | L | F | A |
|---|---|---|---|---|---|
| 11 | 4 | 4 | 3 | 10 | 8 |

## 530

(Friendly)
19 February 1992

Referee: Worrall (England)
Hampden Park, Glasgow (Att: 13,651)

### SCOTLAND 1-0 NORTHERN IRELAND — Half-time 1-0

| | | | |
|---|---|---|---|
| (2) | Henry SMITH (Hearts) | | Thomas WRIGHT |
| (13) | Stewart McKIMMIE (Aberdeen) | | Mal DONAGHY |
| (1) | David ROBERTSON (Rangers) | | Nigel WORTHINGTON |
| (16) | David McPHERSON (Hearts) | | Gerald TAGGART |
| (54) | Richard GOUGH (Rangers) | | Alan McDONALD |
| (49) | Gordon STRACHAN (Leeds United) captain | | Kevin WILSON |
| (11) | Gary McALLISTER (Leeds United) | | Daniel WILSON |
| (20) | Brian McCLAIR (Manchester United) | | James MAGILTON |
| (46) | Maurice MALPAS (Dundee United) | | Kingsley BLACK |
| (1) | Keith WRIGHT (Hibernian) | | Michael HUGHES |
| (34) | Alistair McCOIST (Rangers) | | Colin CLARKE |

Substitutions

| | | | |
|---|---|---|---|
| (16) | Gordon DURIE (Tottenham Hotspur) | | Ian DOWIE |
| | for McKimmie 46 mins | | for Clarke 46 mins |
| (8) | Kevin GALLACHER (Coventry City) | | Michael O'NEILL |
| | for McCoist 46 mins | | for K.Wilson 81 mins |
| (7) | John COLLINS (Celtic) | | Steven MORROW |
| | for McClair 70 mins | | for Taggart 85 mins |
| (6) | John ROBERTSON (Hearts) | | |
| | for Wright 78 mins | | |

Goals

| | |
|---|---|
| McCoist (11 mins) | 1-0 |

## 531

(Friendly)
25 March 1992

Referee: Frisk (Sweden)
Hampden Park, Glasgow (Att: 9,275)

### SCOTLAND 1-1 FINLAND — Half-time 1-1

| | | |
|---|---|---|
| (19) | Andrew GORAM (Rangers) | Olavi HUTTUNEN |
| (14) | Stewart McKIMMIE (Aberdeen) | Ari HEIKKINEN |
| (47) | Maurice MALPAS (Dundee United) | Erkka PETÄJÄ |
| (7) | Thomas BOYD (Celtic) | Jari RINNE |
| (17) | David McPHERSON (Hearts) | Anders ERIKSSON |
| (50) | Gordon STRACHAN (Leeds United) captain | Kimmo TARKKIO |
| (1) | David BOWMAN (Dundee United) | Ilkka REMES |
| (54) | Paul McSTAY (Celtic) | Marko MYYRY |
| (8) | John COLLINS (Celtic) | Mika-Matti PAATELAINEN |
| (7) | John ROBERTSON (Hearts) | Jari LITMANEN |
| (17) | Gordon DURIE (Tottenham Hotspur) | Petri JÄRVINEN |

Substitutions

| | | |
|---|---|---|
| (35) | Alistair McCOIST (Rangers) | Jari VANHALA |
| | for Robertson 54 mins | for Tarkkio 69 mins |
| (12) | Gary McALLISTER (Leeds United) | Harri NYYSSÖNEN |
| | for Strachan 65 mins | for Rinne 88 mins |

Goals

| | | |
|---|---|---|
| McStay (24 mins) | 1-0 | |
| | 1-1 | Litmanen (41 mins) |

## 532

(Friendly)
17 May 1992

Referee: Escobar (Guatemala)
Mile High Stadium, Denver (Att: 24,157)

### USA 0-1 SCOTLAND — Half-time 0-1

| | | |
|---|---|---|
| (1) | Gordon MARSHALL (Celtic) | Kasey KELLER |
| (15) | Stewart McKIMMIE (Aberdeen) | Desmond ARMSTRONG |
| (48) | Maurice MALPAS (Dundee United) | John DOYLE |
| (18) | David McPHERSON (Hearts) | Fernando CLAVIJO |
| (1) | Alan McLAREN (Hearts) | Marcelo BALBOA |
| (13) | Gary McALLISTER (Leeds United) | Janusz MICHALLIK |
| (55) | Paul McSTAY (Celtic) captain | Brian QUINN |
| (15) | Stuart McCALL (Rangers) | Christopher HENDERSON |
| (12) | Patrick NEVIN (Everton) | Hugo PEREZ |
| (21) | Brian McCLAIR (Manchester United) | Dominic KINNEAR |
| (36) | Alistair McCOIST (Rangers) | Eric WYNALDA |

Substitutions

| | | |
|---|---|---|
| (1) | Duncan FERGUSON (Dundee United) | Zachary IBSEN |
| | for Nevin 50 mins | for Michallik 71 mins |
| (6) | James McINALLY (Dundee United) | |
| | for McStay 68 mins | |
| (2) | David BOWMAN (Dundee United) | |
| | for McCoist 76 mins | |
| (4) | Derek WHYTE (Celtic) | |
| | for McPherson 82 mins | |

Goals

| | |
|---|---|
| Nevin (7 mins) | 1-0 |

## 533

(Friendly)
20 May 1992

Referee: Dias (USA)
Varsity Stadium, Toronto (Att: 10,872)

### CANADA 1-3 SCOTLAND — Half-time 1-1

| | | |
|---|---|---|
| (3) | Henry SMITH (Hearts) | Craig FORREST |
| (19) | David McPHERSON (Hearts) | Frank YALLOP |
| (8) | Thomas BOYD (Celtic) | Colin MILLER |
| (55) | Richard GOUGH (Rangers) captain | Peter SARANTOPOULOS |
| (2) | Alan McLAREN (Hearts) | Randy SAMUEL |
| (14) | Gary McALLISTER (Leeds United) | John LIMNIATIS |
| (56) | Paul McSTAY (Celtic) | Nickolas DASOVIC |
| (16) | Stuart McCALL (Rangers) | Carl VALENTINE |
| (18) | Gordon DURIE (Tottenham Hotspur) | Norman ODINGA |
| (2) | Duncan FERGUSON (Dundee United) | Domenico MOBILIO |
| (37) | Alistair McCOIST (Rangers) | John CATLIFF |

Substitutions

| | | |
|---|---|---|
| (22) | Brian McCLAIR (Manchester United) | Alexander BUNBURY |
| | for Ferguson 54 mins | for Mobilio 46 mins |
| (49) | Maurice MALPAS (Dundee United) | Nicholas GILBERT |
| | for Durie 78 mins | for Limniatis 59 mins |
| (16) | Stewart McKIMMIE (Aberdeen) | Lyndon HOOPER |
| | for McCall 90 mins | for Odinga 59 mins |
| | | Geoffrey AUNGER |
| | | for Catliff 78 mins |

Goals

| | | |
|---|---|---|
| McAllister (23 mins) | 1-0 | |
| | 1-1 | Catliff (44 mins) |
| McCoist (65 mins) | 2-1 | |
| McAllister (85 mins pen) | 3-1 | |

## 534

(Friendly)
3 June 1992

Referee: Frisk (Sweden)
Ullevaal Stadion, Oslo (Att: 8,786)

### NORWAY 0-0 SCOTLAND

| | | |
|---|---|---|
| (20) | Andrew GORAM (Rangers) | Frode GRODAAS |
| (20) | David McPHERSON (Hearts) | Roger NILSEN |
| (50) | Maurice MALPAS (Dundee United) captain | Tore PEDERSEN |
| (56) | Richard GOUGH (Rangers) | Henning BERG |
| (3) | Alan McLAREN (Hearts) | Rune BRATSETH |
| (15) | Gary McALLISTER (Leeds United) | Stig-Inge BJORNEBYE |
| (57) | Paul McSTAY (Celtic) | Lars BOHINEN |
| (17) | Stuart McCALL (Rangers) | Kjetil REKDAL |
| (9) | Thomas BOYD (Celtic) | Oyvind LEONHARDSEN |
| (23) | Brian McCLAIR (Manchester United) | Tore-André DAHLUM |
| (38) | Alistair McCOIST (Rangers) | Frank STRANDLI |

Substitutions

| | | |
|---|---|---|
| (19) | Gordon DURIE (Tottenham Hotspur) | Erik MYKLAND |
| | for McClair 46 mins | for Pedersen 29 mins |
| (9) | Kevin GALLACHER (Coventry City) | Jostein FLO |
| | for McCoist 46 mins | for Dahlum 73 mins |
| (17) | Stewart McKIMMIE (Aberdeen) | Kaare INGEBRIGTSEN |
| | for Malpas 68 mins | for Bohinen 75 mins |
| (7) | James McINALLY (Dundee United) | |
| | for McAllister 78 mins | |

## 535

(European Championship — Final Tournament 1st Round)

12 June 1992

Referee: Karlsson (Sweden)
Ullevi Stadion, Gothenburg (Att: 35,720)

### NETHERLANDS 1-0 SCOTLAND — Half-time 0-0

| | | |
|---|---|---|
| (21) | Andrew GORAM (Rangers) | Johannes VAN BREUKELEN |
| (18) | Stewart McKIMMIE (Aberdeen) | Hubertus VAN AERLE |
| (51) | Maurice MALPAS (Dundee United) | Adrianus VAN TIGGELEN |
| (21) | David McPHERSON (Hearts) | Ronald KOEMAN |
| (57) | Richard GOUGH (Rangers) captain | Franklin RIJKAARD |
| (16) | Gary McALLISTER (Leeds United) | Richard WITSCHGE |
| (58) | Paul McSTAY (Celtic) | Jan WOUTERS |
| (18) | Stuart McCALL (Rangers) | Ruud GULLIT |
| (24) | Brian McCLAIR (Manchester United) | Bryan ROY |
| (20) | Gordon DURIE (Tottenham Hotspur) | Dennis BERGKAMP |
| (39) | Alistair McCOIST (Rangers) | Marco VAN BASTEN |

Substitutions

| | | |
|---|---|---|
| (10) | Kevin GALLACHER (Coventry City) | Wilhelmus JONK |
| | for McCoist 73 mins | for Wouters 54 mins |
| (3) | Duncan FERGUSON (Dundee United) | Aron WINTER |
| | for McClair 79 mins | for Bergkamp 85 mins |

Goals

| | | |
|---|---|---|
| | 0-1 | Bergkamp (77 mins) |

## 536

(European Championship — Final Tournament 1st Round)

15 June 1992

Referee: Goethals (Belgium)
Idrottsparken, Norrkoping (Att: 17,638)

### GERMANY 2-0 SCOTLAND — Half-time 1-0

| | | |
|---|---|---|
| (22) | Andrew GORAM (Rangers) | Bodo ILLGNER |
| (19) | Stewart McKIMMIE (Aberdeen) | Manfred BINZ |
| (52) | Maurice MALPAS (Dundee United) | Andreas BREHME |
| (22) | David McPHERSON (Hearts) | Jürgen KOHLER |
| (58) | Richard GOUGH (Rangers) captain | Guido BUCHWALD |
| (17) | Gary McALLISTER (Leeds United) | Stefan EFFENBERG |
| (59) | Paul McSTAY (Celtic) | Matthias SAMMER |
| (19) | Stuart McCALL (Rangers) | Thomas HÄSSLER |
| (25) | Brian McCLAIR (Manchester United) | Andreas MÖLLER |
| (21) | Gordon DURIE (Tottenham Hotspur) | Karl-Heinz RIEDLE |
| (40) | Alistair McCOIST (Rangers) | Jürgen KLINSMANN |

Substitutions

| | | |
|---|---|---|
| (13) | Patrick NEVIN (Everton) | Stefan REUTER |
| | for Durie 54 mins | for Riedle 68 mins |
| (11) | Kevin GALLACHER (Coventry City) | Michael SCHULZ |
| | for McCoist 70 mins | for Reuter 74 mins |

Goals

| | | |
|---|---|---|
| | 0-1 | Riedle (29 mins) |
| | 0-2 | Effenberg (47 mins) |

## 537

**(European Championship — Final Tournament 1st Round)**
18 June 1992

Referee: Rothlisberger (Switzerland)
Idrottsparken, Norrkoping (Att: 14,660)

### CIS 0-3 SCOTLAND | Half-time 0-2

| | | | |
|---|---|---|---|
| (23) | Andrew GORAM (Rangers) | | Dmitri KHARIN |
| (20) | Stewart McKIMMIE (Aberdeen) | | Alexei CHERNISHOV |
| (10) | Thomas BOYD (Celtic) | | Kakhaber TSKHADADZE |
| (23) | David McPHERSON (Hearts) | | Oleg KUZNETSOV |
| (59) | Richard GOUGH (Rangers) captain | | Viktor ONOPKO |
| (18) | Gary McALLISTER (Leeds United) | | Alexei MIKHAILICHENKO |
| (60) | Paul McSTAY (Celtic) | | Sergei ALEINIKOV |
| (20) | Stuart McCALL (Rangers) | | Igor DOBROVOLSKI |
| (26) | Brian McCLAIR (Manchester United) | | Andrei KANCHELSKIS |
| (12) | Kevin GALLACHER (Coventry City) | | Sergei KIRIAKOV |
| (41) | Alistair McCOIST (Rangers) | | Sergei YURAN |
| | | Substitutions | |
| (8) | James McINALLY (Dundee United) | | Dmitri KUZNETSOV |
| | for McCoist 67 mins | | for Aleinikov 46 mins |
| (14) | Patrick NEVIN (Everton) | | Igor KORNEYEV |
| | for Gallacher 78 mins | | for Kiriakov 46 mins |

| | Goals | |
|---|---|---|
| McStay (6 mins) | 1-0 | |
| McClair (16 mins) | 2-0 | |
| McAllister (83 mins pen) | 3-0 | |

## 538

**(World Cup — Qualifier)**
9 September 1992

Referee: Van der Ende (Netherlands)
Wankdorf Stadion, Berne (Att: 10,000)

### SWITZERLAND 3-1 SCOTLAND | Half-time 1-1

| | | | |
|---|---|---|---|
| (24) | Andrew GORAM (Rangers) | | Marco PASCOLO |
| (11) | Thomas BOYD (Celtic) | | Marc HOTTIGER |
| (53) | Maurice MALPAS (Dundee United) | | Yvan QUENTIN |
| (24) | David McPHERSON (Rangers) | | André EGLI |
| (60) | Richard GOUGH (Rangers) captain | | Alain GEIGER |
| (19) | Gary McALLISTER (Leeds United) | | Christophe OHREL |
| (61) | Paul McSTAY (Celtic) | | Ciriaco SFORZA |
| (21) | Stuart McCALL (Rangers) | | Alain SUTTER |
| (27) | Brian McCLAIR (Manchester United) | | Georges BREGY |
| (22) | Gordon DURIE (Tottenham Hotspur) | | Adrian KNUP |
| (42) | Alistair McCOIST (Rangers) | | Stéphane CHAPUISAT |
| | | Substitutions | |
| (6) | Iain DURRANT (Rangers) | | Beat SUTTER |
| | for McClair 57 mins | | for Knup 86 mins |
| (13) | Kevin GALLACHER (Coventry City) | | Blaise PIFFARETTI |
| | for Boyd 75 mins | | for Bregy 89 mins |

| | Goals | |
|---|---|---|
| | 0-1 | Knup (1 min) |
| McCoist (13 mins) | 1-1 | |
| | 1-2 | Knup (71 mins) |
| | 1-3 | Bregy (81 mins) |

## 539

**(World Cup — Qualifier)**
14 October 1992

Referee: Forstinger (Austria)
Ibrox Stadium, Glasgow (Att: 22,583)

### SCOTLAND 0-0 PORTUGAL

| | | | |
|---|---|---|---|
| (25) | Andrew GORAM (Rangers) | | Vítor BAÍA |
| (12) | Thomas BOYD (Celtic) | | HÉLDER Marino |
| (54) | Maurice MALPAS (Dundee United) | | Antonio VELOSO |
| (9) | Craig LEVEIN (Hearts) | | OCEANO Cruz |
| (6) | Derek WHYTE (Middlesbrough) | | Fernando COUTO |
| (20) | Gary McALLISTER (Leeds United) | | Joao PINTO |
| (62) | Paul McSTAY (Celtic) captain | | José SEMEDO |
| (22) | Stuart McCALL (Rangers) | | Antonio ANDRÉ |
| (9) | John COLLINS (Celtic) | | Vítor PANEIRA |
| (14) | Kevin GALLACHER (Coventry City) | | Paulo FUTRE |
| (43) | Alistair McCOIST (Rangers) | | DOMINGOS Oliveira |
| | | Substitutions | |
| (28) | Brian McCLAIR (Manchester United) | | Luís FIGO |
| | for Gallacher 33 mins | | for Semedo 53 mins |
| (7) | Iain DURRANT (Rangers) | | |
| | for Collins 72 mins | | |

## 540

**(World Cup — Qualifier)**
18 November 1992

Referee: Schmidhuber (Germany)
Ibrox Stadium, Glasgow (Att: 33,029)

### SCOTLAND 0-0 ITALY

| | | | |
|---|---|---|---|
| (26) | Andrew GORAM (Rangers) | | Gianluca PAGLIUCA |
| (25) | David McPHERSON (Rangers) | | Moreno MANNINI |
| (55) | Maurice MALPAS (Dundee United) | | Alberto DI CHIARA |
| (4) | Alan McLAREN (Hearts) | | Franco BARESI |
| (6) | Derek WHYTE (Middlesbrough) | | Paolo MALDINI |
| (21) | Gary McALLISTER (Leeds United) | | Alessandro BIANCHI |
| (63) | Paul McSTAY (Celtic) captain | | Demetrio ALBERTINI |
| (8) | Iain DURRANT (Rangers) | | Stefano ERANIO |
| (13) | Thomas BOYD (Celtic) | | Gianluigi LENTINI |
| (23) | Gordon DURIE (Tottenham Hotspur) | | Roberto BAGGIO |
| (44) | Alistair McCOIST (Rangers) | | Giuseppe SIGNORI |
| | | Substitutions | |
| (1) | Eoin JESS (Aberdeen) | | Alessandro COSTACURTA |
| | for Durie 71 mins | | for Di Chiara 9 mins |
| (8) | John ROBERTSON (Hearts) | | Roberto DONADONI |
| | for Durrant 86 mins | | for Signori 65 mins |

Gordon Durie (right) skips past Franco Baresi against Italy at Ibrox in November 1992.

# 1993

| P | W | D | L | F | A |
|---|---|---|---|---|---|
| 8 | 4 | 1 | 3 | 13 | 11 |

## 541

**(World Cup — Qualifier)**
17 February 1993

Referee: Koho (Finland)
Ibrox Stadium, Glasgow (Att: 35,490)

### SCOTLAND 3-0 MALTA | Half-time 1-0

| | | | |
|---|---|---|---|
| (27) | Andrew GORAM (Rangers) | | David CLUETT |
| (26) | David McPHERSON (Rangers) | | Silvio VELLA |
| (14) | Thomas BOYD (Celtic) | | Richard BUHAGIAR |
| (5) | Alan McLAREN (Hearts) | | John BUTTIGIEG |
| (77) | Alexander McLEISH (Aberdeen) captain | | Joseph GALEA |
| (15) | Patrick NEVIN (Tranmere Rovers) | | Nicholas SALIBA |
| (22) | Gary McALLISTER (Leeds United) | | Joseph BRINCAT |
| (64) | Paul McSTAY (Celtic) | | Joseph CAMILLERI |
| (10) | John COLLINS (Celtic) | | Kristian LAFERLA |
| (2) | Eoin JESS (Aberdeen) | | Stefan SULTANA |
| (45) | Alistair McCOIST (Rangers) | | Carmel BUSUTTIL |
| | | Substitutions | |
| (9) | John ROBERTSON (Hearts) | | Raymond VELLA |
| | for McPherson 64 mins | | for Sultana 74 mins |
| (4) | Ian FERGUSON (Rangers) | | Edwin CAMILLERI |
| | for McAllister 72 mins | | for Buhagiar 83 mins |

| | Goals | |
|---|---|---|
| McCoist (15 mins) | 1-0 | |
| McCoist (68 mins) | 2-0 | |
| Nevin (84 mins) | 3-0 | |

## 542

(Friendly)
24 March 1993

Referee: Schelings (Belgium)
Ibrox Stadium, Glasgow (Att: 36,400)

### SCOTLAND 0-1 GERMANY — Half-time 0-1

| | | |
|---|---|---|
| (1) | Nicholas WALKER (Hearts) | Andreas KÖPKE |
| (1) | Stephen WRIGHT (Aberdeen) | Michael ZORC |
| (15) | Thomas BOYD (Celtic) | Thomas HELMER |
| (10) | Craig LEVEIN (Hearts) captain | Jürgen KOHLER |
| (2) | Brian IRVINE (Aberdeen) | Guido BUCHWALD |
| (6) | Alan McLAREN (Hearts) | Thomas HÄSSLER |
| (9) | James McINALLY (Dundee United) | Olaf THON |
| (3) | David BOWMAN (Dundee United) | Lothar MATTHÄUS |
| (11) | John COLLINS (Celtic) | Thomas DOLL |
| (10) | John ROBERTSON (Hearts) | Karl-Heinz RIEDLE |
| (4) | Duncan FERGUSON (Dundee United) | Jürgen KLINSMANN |

Substitutions

| | | |
|---|---|---|
| (1) | Scott BOOTH (Aberdeen) | Stefan EFFENBERG |
| | for Wright 63 mins | for Doll 60 mins |
| | | Matthias SAMMER |
| | | for Matthäus 88 mins |

Goals

| | | |
|---|---|---|
| 0-1 | | Riedle (19 mins) |

## 543

(World Cup — Qualifier)
28 April 1993

Referee: Puhl (Hungary)
Estadio da Luz, Lisbon (Att: 28,000)

### PORTUGAL 5-0 SCOTLAND — Half-time 2-0

| | | |
|---|---|---|
| (28) | Andrew GORAM (Rangers) | Vítor BAÍA |
| (21) | Stewart McKIMMIE (Aberdeen) | Abel XAVIER |
| (10) | James McINALLY (Dundee United) | Jorge COSTA |
| (61) | Richard GOUGH (Rangers) captain | OCEANO Cruz |
| (27) | David McPHERSON (Rangers) | Fernando COUTO |
| (11) | Craig LEVEIN (Hearts) | José SEMEDO |
| (65) | Paul McSTAY (Celtic) | Rui COSTA |
| (23) | Stuart McCALL (Rangers) | Paulo SOUSA |
| (12) | John COLLINS (Celtic) | Rui BARROS |
| (15) | Kevin GALLACHER (Blackburn Rovers) | Paulo FUTRE |
| (46) | Alistair McCOIST (Rangers) | Jorge CADETE |

Substitutions

| | | |
|---|---|---|
| (16) | Patrick NEVIN (Tranmere Rovers) | Antonio VELOSO |
| | for Levein 59 mins | for R.Costa 53 mins |
| (9) | Iain DURRANT (Rangers) | DOMINGOS Oliveira |
| | for Collins 75 mins | for Cadete 82 mins |

Goals

| | | |
|---|---|---|
| 0-1 | | Barros (5 mins) |
| 0-2 | | Cadete (45 mins) |
| 0-3 | | Futre (67 mins) |
| 0-4 | | Barros (70 mins) |
| 0-5 | | Cadete (72 mins) |

## 544

(World Cup — Qualifier)
19 May 1993

Referee: Hollung (Norway)
Kadriorg Stadion, Tallinn (Att: 5,100)

### ESTONIA 0-3 SCOTLAND — Half-time 0-1

| | | |
|---|---|---|
| (2) | Bryan GUNN (Norwich City) | Mart POOM |
| (2) | Stephen WRIGHT (Aberdeen) | Risto KALLASTE |
| (16) | Thomas BOYD (Celtic) | Urmas KALJEND |
| (3) | Brian IRVINE (Aberdeen) | Marek LEMSALU |
| (1) | Colin HENDRY (Blackburn Rovers) | Igor PRINS |
| (66) | Paul McSTAY (Celtic) captain | Andrei BORISSOV |
| (4) | David BOWMAN (Dundee United) | Toomas KALLASTE |
| (29) | Brian McCLAIR (Manchester United) | Martin REIM |
| (13) | John COLLINS (Celtic) | Jaanus VEENSALU |
| (11) | John ROBERTSON (Hearts) | Sergei BRAGIN |
| (16) | Kevin GALLACHER (Blackburn Rovers) | Marko KRISTAL |

Substitutions

| | | |
|---|---|---|
| (2) | Scott BOOTH (Aberdeen) | Urmas HEPNER |
| | for Robertson 61 mins | for Kristal 46 mins |
| (7) | Alan McLAREN (Hearts) | Aleksander PUSTOV |
| | for Wright 80 mins | for Veensalu 76 mins |

Goals

| | | |
|---|---|---|
| Gallacher (43 mins) | 1-0 | |
| Collins (59 mins) | 2-0 | |
| Booth (73 mins) | 3-0 | |

## 545

(World Cup — Qualifier)
2 June 1993

Referee: Ouzounov (Bulgaria)
Pittodrie Stadium, Aberdeen (Att: 14,307)

### SCOTLAND 3-1 ESTONIA — Half-time 2-0

| | | |
|---|---|---|
| (3) | Bryan GUNN (Norwich City) | Mart POOM |
| (8) | Alan McLAREN (Hearts) | Risto KALLASTE |
| (17) | Thomas BOYD (Celtic) | Urmas KALJEND |
| (4) | Brian IRVINE (Aberdeen) | Marek LEMSALU |
| (2) | Colin HENDRY (Blackburn Rovers) | Igor PRINS |
| (17) | Patrick NEVIN (Tranmere Rovers) | Andrei BORISSOV |
| (67) | Paul McSTAY (Celtic) captain | Toomas KALLASTE |
| (5) | Ian FERGUSON (Rangers) | Martin REIM |
| (14) | John COLLINS (Celtic) | Indro OLUMETS |
| (30) | Brian McCLAIR (Manchester United) | Lembit RAJALA |
| (17) | Kevin GALLACHER (Blackburn Rovers) | Marko KRISTAL |

Substitutions

| | | |
|---|---|---|
| (3) | Scott BOOTH (Aberdeen) | Sergei BRAGIN |
| | for Ferguson 55 mins | for Lemsalu 46 mins |
| (22) | Stewart McKIMMIE (Aberdeen) | Jaanus VEENSALU |
| | for McLaren 71 mins | for Olumets 73 mins |

Goals

| | | |
|---|---|---|
| McClair (18 mins) | 1-0 | |
| Nevin (27 mins) | 2-0 | |
| | 2-1 | Bragin (57 mins) |
| Nevin (72 mins pen) | 3-1 | |

## 546

(World Cup — Qualifier)
8 September 1993

Referee: Quiniou (France)
Pittodrie Stadium, Aberdeen (Att: 21,500)

### SCOTLAND 1-1 SWITZERLAND — Half-time 0-0

| | | |
|---|---|---|
| (4) | Bryan GUNN (Norwich City) | Marco PASCOLO |
| (23) | Stewart McKIMMIE (Aberdeen) | Régis ROTHENBUHLER |
| (2) | David ROBERTSON (Rangers) | Yvan QUENTIN |
| (5) | Brian IRVINE (Aberdeen) | Dominique HERR |
| (12) | Craig LEVEIN (Hearts) | Alain GEIGER |
| (18) | Patrick NEVIN (Tranmere Rovers) | Christophe OHREL |
| (5) | David BOWMAN (Dundee United) | Ciriaco SFORZA |
| (23) | Gary McALLISTER (Leeds United) captain | Alain SUTTER |
| (15) | John COLLINS (Celtic) | Georges BREGY |
| (4) | Scott BOOTH (Aberdeen) | Adrian KNUP |
| (24) | Gordon DURIE (Tottenham Hotspur) | Stéphane CHAPUISAT |

Substitutions

| | | |
|---|---|---|
| (3) | Eoin JESS (Aberdeen) | Marco GRASSI |
| | for Booth 70 mins | for Rothenbühler 60 mins |
| (1) | Philip O'DONNELL (Motherwell) | Martin RUEDA |
| | for Bowman 75 mins | for Bregy 85 mins |

Goals

| | | |
|---|---|---|
| Collins (50 mins) | 1-0 | |
| | 1-1 | Bregy (69 mins pen) |

Scott Booth (left) in action for Scotland against Switzerland at Pittodrie in September 1993.

## 547

**(World Cup — Qualifier)**
**13 October 1993**

Referee: Craciunescu (Romania)
Stadio Olimpico, Rome (Att: 61,178)

### ITALY 3-1 SCOTLAND — Half-time 2-1

| | | |
|---|---|---|
| (5) | Bryan GUNN (Norwich City) | Gianluca PAGLIUCA |
| (24) | Stewart McKIMMIE (Aberdeen) | Roberto MUSSI |
| (18) | Thomas BOYD (Celtic) | Antonio BENARRIVO |
| (6) | Brian IRVINE (Aberdeen) | Franco BARESI |
| (9) | Alan McLAREN (Hearts) | Alessandro COSTACURTA |
| (6) | David BOWMAN (Dundee United) | Stefano ERANIO |
| (24) | Gary McALLISTER (Leeds United) captain | Dino BAGGIO |
| (24) | Stuart McCALL (Rangers) | Giovanni STROPPA |
| (25) | Gordon DURIE (Tottenham Hotspur) | Roberto DONADONI |
| (4) | Eoin JESS (Aberdeen) | Roberto BAGGIO |
| (18) | Kevin GALLACHER (Blackburn Rovers) | Pierluigi CASIRAGHI |

**Substitutions**

| | | |
|---|---|---|
| (10) | Iain DURRANT (Rangers) | Marco LANNA |
| | for Jess 46 mins | for Mussi 68 mins |
| (68) | Paul McSTAY (Celtic) | Gianfranco ZOLA |
| | for Bowman 70 mins | for Stroppa 89 mins |

**Goals**

| | | |
|---|---|---|
| | 0-1 | Donadoni (3 mins) |
| | 0-2 | Casiraghi (16 mins) |
| Gallacher (18 mins) | 1-2 | |
| | 1-3 | Eranio (80 mins) |

## 548

**(World Cup — Qualifier)**
**17 November 1993**

Referee: Vassilakis (Greece)
Ta'Qali Stadium, Valletta (Att: 7,000)

### MALTA 0-2 SCOTLAND — Half-time 0-1

| | | |
|---|---|---|
| (59) | James LEIGHTON (Hibernian) | David CLUETT |
| (10) | Alan McLAREN (Hearts) | Silvio VELLA |
| (1) | Robert McKINNON (Motherwell) | Richard BUHAGIAR |
| (7) | Brian IRVINE (Aberdeen) | John BUTTIGIEG |
| (3) | Colin HENDRY (Blackburn Rovers) | Joseph GALEA |
| (25) | Gary McALLISTER (Leeds United) captain | Joseph BRINCAT |
| (6) | Ian FERGUSON (Rangers) | Michael SPITERI |
| (1) | William McKINLAY (Dundee United) | Kristian LAFERLA |
| (11) | Iain DURRANT (Rangers) | Martin GREGORY |
| (19) | Patrick NEVIN (Tranmere Rovers) | Hubert SUDA |
| (19) | Kevin GALLACHER (Blackburn Rovers) | Carmel BUSUTTIL |

**Substitutions**

| | | |
|---|---|---|
| (5) | Scott BOOTH (Aberdeen) | Nicholas SALIBA |
| | for McKinlay 46 mins | for Buhagiar 46 mins |
| (19) | Thomas BOYD (Celtic) | Charles SCERRI |
| | for Durrant 74 mins | for Suda 74 mins |

**Goals**

| | | |
|---|---|---|
| McKinlay (15 mins) | 1-0 | |
| Hendry (74 mins) | 2-0 | |

# 1994

| P | W | D | L | F | A |
|---|---|---|---|---|---|
| 7 | 3 | 1 | 3 | 11 | 8 |

## 549

**(Friendly)**
**23 March 1994**

Referee: Nielsen (Denmark)
Hampden Park, Glasgow (Att: 36,809)

### SCOTLAND 0-1 NETHERLANDS — Half-time 0-1

| | | |
|---|---|---|
| (29) | Andrew GORAM (Rangers) | Eduard DE GOEIJ |
| (25) | Stewart McKIMMIE (Aberdeen) | Ulrich VAN GOBBEL |
| (3) | David ROBERTSON (Rangers) | Franciscus DE BOER |
| (11) | Alan McLAREN (Hearts) | Franklin RIJKAARD |
| (4) | Colin HENDRY (Blackburn Rovers) | Dirk BLIND |
| (13) | Craig LEVEIN (Hearts) | Gaston TAUMENT |
| (26) | Gary McALLISTER (Leeds United) captain | Wilhelmus JONK |
| (69) | Paul McSTAY (Celtic) | Robert WITSCHGE |
| (25) | Stuart McCALL (Rangers) | Bryan ROY |
| (20) | Patrick NEVIN (Tranmere Rovers) | Dennis BERGKAMP |
| (26) | Gordon DURIE (Rangers) | Johannes BOSMAN |

**Substitutions**

| | | |
|---|---|---|
| (20) | Thomas BOYD (Celtic) | Johannes GILLHAUS |
| | for Levein 46 mins | for Bosman 46 mins |
| (2) | William McKINLAY (Dundee United) | Aron WINTER |
| | for McStay 46 mins | for Bergkamp 46 mins |
| (16) | John COLLINS (Celtic) | Marc OVERMARS |
| | for Robertson 65 mins | for Taument 77 mins |
| (5) | Eoin JESS (Aberdeen) | |
| | for Nevin 67 mins | |

**Goals**

| | | |
|---|---|---|
| | 0-1 | Roy (23 mins) |

## 550

**(Friendly)**
**20 April 1994**

Referee: Albrecht (Germany)
Ernst Happel Stadion, Vienna (Att: 35,000)

### AUSTRIA 1-2 SCOTLAND — Half-time 1-1

| | | |
|---|---|---|
| (60) | James LEIGHTON (Hibernian) | Franz WOHLFAHRT |
| (26) | Stewart McKIMMIE (Aberdeen) | Christian PROSENIK |
| (21) | Thomas BOYD (Celtic) | Walter KOGLER |
| (12) | Alan McLAREN (Hearts) | Walter HOCHMAIER |
| (5) | Colin HENDRY (Blackburn Rovers) | Peter SCHÖTTEL |
| (8) | Brian IRVINE (Aberdeen) | Harald CERNY |
| (27) | Gary McALLISTER (Leeds United) captain | Michael BAUR |
| (3) | William McKINLAY (Dundee United) | Andreas HERZOG |
| (17) | John COLLINS (Celtic) | Peter STÖGER |
| (1) | John McGINLAY (Bolton Wanderers) | Adolf HÜTTER |
| (6) | Eoin JESS (Aberdeen) | Anton POLSTER |

**Substitutions**

| | | |
|---|---|---|
| (7) | Ian FERGUSON (Rangers) | Michael KONSEL |
| | for Boyd 46 mins | for Wohlfahrt 46 mins |
| (1) | Duncan SHEARER (Aberdeen) | Dietmar KUHBAUER |
| | for McGinlay 75 mins | for Stöger 46 mins |
| (21) | Patrick NEVIN (Tranmere Rovers) | Thomas WEISSENBERGER |
| | for Jess 84 mins | for Polster 62 mins |
| (26) | Stuart McCALL (Rangers) | |
| | for Collins 85 mins | |

**Goals**

| | | |
|---|---|---|
| | 0-1 | Hütter (12 mins) |
| McGinlay (35 mins) | 1-1 | |
| McKinlay (60 mins) | 2-1 | |

## 551

**(Friendly)**
**27 May 1994**

Referee: Roca (Spain)
Galgenwaard Stadion, Utrecht (Att: 22,000)

### NETHERLANDS 3-1 SCOTLAND — Half-time 1-0

| | | |
|---|---|---|
| (61) | James LEIGHTON (Hibernian) | Eduard DE GOEIJ |
| (6) | Stephen CLARKE (Chelsea) | Stanley VALCKX |
| (27) | Stewart McKIMMIE (Aberdeen) | Franciscus DE BOER |
| (9) | Brian IRVINE (Aberdeen) | Wilhelmus JONK |
| (6) | Colin HENDRY (Blackburn Rovers) | Jan WOUTERS |
| (28) | Gary McALLISTER (Leeds United) captain | Marc OVERMARS |
| (4) | William McKINLAY (Dundee United) | Robert WITSCHGE |
| (27) | Stuart McCALL (Rangers) | Ronaldus DE BOER |
| (18) | John COLLINS (Celtic) | Bryan ROY |
| (2) | John McGINLAY (Bolton Wanderers) | Aron WINTER |
| (27) | Gordon DURIE (Rangers) | Ruud GULLIT |

**Substitutions**

| | | |
|---|---|---|
| (6) | Bryan GUNN (Norwich City) | Arthur NUMAN |
| | for Leighton 46 mins | for R. De Boer 46 mins |
| (7) | Eoin JESS (Aberdeen) | Peter VAN VOSSEN |
| | for Durie 46 mins | for Gullit 46 mins |
| (8) | Ian FERGUSON (Rangers) | Gaston TAUMENT |
| | for Collins 61 mins | for Roy 71 mins |
| (2) | Duncan SHEARER (Aberdeen) | |
| | for McGinlay 76 mins | |
| (22) | Patrick NEVIN (Tranmere Rovers) | |
| | for McKinlay 88 mins | |

**Goals**

| | | |
|---|---|---|
| | 0-1 | Roy (17 mins) |
| | 0-2 | Van Vossen (61 mins) |
| | 0-3 | Irvine (71 mins o.g.) |
| Shearer (81 mins) | 1-3 | |

## 552

**(European Championship - Qualifier)**
**7 September 1994**

Referee: Wojcik (Poland)
Olympia Stadion, Helsinki (Att: 12,845)

### FINLAND 0-2 SCOTLAND — Half-time 0-1

| | | |
|---|---|---|
| (30) | Andrew GORAM (Rangers) | Petri JAKONEN |
| (28) | Stewart McKIMMIE (Aberdeen) | Janne MÄKELÄ |
| (22) | Thomas BOYD (Celtic) | Aki HYRYLÄINEN |
| (13) | Alan McLAREN (Hearts) | Markku KANERVA |
| (7) | Colin HENDRY (Blackburn Rovers) | Antti HEINOLA |
| (14) | Craig LEVEIN (Hearts) | Kim SUOMINEN |
| (29) | Gary McALLISTER (Leeds United) captain | Janne LINDBERG |
| (70) | Paul McSTAY (Celtic) | Jari RANTANEN |
| (19) | John COLLINS (Celtic) | Mika-Matti PAATELAINEN |
| (2) | Andrew WALKER (Celtic) | Jari LITMANEN |
| (3) | Duncan SHEARER (Aberdeen) | Ari HJELM |

**Substitutions**

| | | |
|---|---|---|
| (8) | Eoin JESS (Aberdeen) | Erik HOLMGREN |
| | for Walker 65 mins | for Heinola 29 mins |
| (28) | Stuart McCALL (Rangers) | Petri JÄRVINEN |
| | for Levein 78 mins | for Rantanen 41 mins |

**Goals**

| | | |
|---|---|---|
| Shearer (29 mins) | 1-0 | |
| Collins (66 mins) | 2-0 | |

**553**

(European Championship — Qualifier)    Referee: Hauge (Norway)
12 October 1994    Hampden Park, Glasgow (Att: 20,885)

### SCOTLAND 5-1 FAROE ISLANDS    Half-time 3-0

| | | |
|---|---|---|
| (31) | Andrew GORAM (Rangers) | Jens KNUDSEN |
| (29) | Stewart McKIMMIE (Aberdeen) | Jens HANSEN |
| (23) | Thomas BOYD (Celtic) | Tummas HANSEN |
| (14) | Alan McLAREN (Hearts) | Óli JOHANNESEN |
| (8) | Colin HENDRY (Blackburn Rovers) | Ossur HANSEN |
| (15) | Craig LEVEIN (Hearts) | Jan DAM |
| (23) | Patrick NEVIN (Tranmere Rovers) | Magni JARNSKOR |
| (71) | Paul McSTAY (Celtic) captain | Kurt MORKORE |
| (20) | John COLLINS (Celtic) | Henning JARNSKOR |
| (3) | John McGINLAY (Bolton Wanderers) | Todi JÓNSSON |
| (6) | Scott BOOTH (Aberdeen) | Jan MÜLLER |

Substitutions

| | | |
|---|---|---|
| (5) | William McKINLAY (Dundee United) | Djóni JOENSEN |
| | for Hendry 59 mins | for Dam 54 mins |
| (3) | Andrew WALKER (Celtic) | Janus RASMUSSEN |
| | for Booth 70 mins | for Morkore 74 mins |

Goals

| | |
|---|---|
| McGinlay (4 mins) | 1-0 |
| Booth (34 mins) | 2-0 |
| Collins (40 mins) | 3-0 |
| McKinlay (61 mins) | 4-0 |
| Collins (72 mins) | 5-0 |
| | 5-1    Müller (75 mins) |

---

**554**

(European Championship — Qualifier)    Referee: Karlsson (Sweden)
16 November 1994    Hampden Park, Glasgow (Att: 31,254)

### SCOTLAND 1-1 RUSSIA    Half-time 1-1

| | | |
|---|---|---|
| (32) | Andrew GORAM (Rangers) | Stanislav CHERCHESOV |
| (30) | Stewart McKIMMIE (Aberdeen) | Sergei GORLUKOVICH |
| (24) | Thomas BOYD (Celtic) | Vasilij KULKOV |
| (16) | Craig LEVEIN (Hearts) | Iurij NIKIFOROV |
| (15) | Alan McLAREN (Rangers) | Viktor ONOPKO |
| (30) | Gary McALLISTER (Leeds United) captain | Andrei KANCHELSKIS |
| (6) | William McKINLAY (Dundee United) | Valerij KARPIN |
| (29) | Stuart McCALL (Rangers) | Igor SHALIMOV |
| (21) | John COLLINS (Celtic) | Vladislav RADIMOV |
| (4) | John McGINLAY (Bolton Wanderers) | Andrei PIATNITSKI |
| (7) | Scott BOOTH (Aberdeen) | Dmitri RADCHENKO |

Substitutions

| | | |
|---|---|---|
| (1) | John SPENCER (Chelsea) | Omar TETRADZE |
| | for McGinlay 63 mins | for Piatnitski 71 mins |
| (24) | Patrick NEVIN (Tranmere Rovers) | |
| | for McKinlay 83 mins | |

Goals

| | |
|---|---|
| Booth (19 mins) | 1-0 |
| | 1-1    Radchenko (25 mins) |

---

**555**

(European Championship — Qualifier)    Referee: Blankenstein (Netherlands)
18 December 1994    Olympia Stadhion, Athens (Att: 20,000)

### GREECE 1-0 SCOTLAND    Half-time 1-0

| | | |
|---|---|---|
| (33) | Andrew GORAM (Rangers) | Ilias ATMATZIDIS |
| (31) | Stewart McKIMMIE (Aberdeen) | Efstratios APOSTOLAKIS |
| (25) | Thomas BOYD (Celtic) | Mihalis VLAHOS |
| (16) | Alan McLAREN (Rangers) | Theodoros ZAGORAKIS |
| (9) | Colin HENDRY (Blackburn Rovers) | Yiannis KALITZAKIS |
| (31) | Gary McALLISTER (Leeds United) captain | Mihalis KASSAPIS |
| (7) | William McKINLAY (Dundee United) | Nikolaos NIOPLIAS |
| (30) | Stuart McCALL (Rangers) | Panayotis TSALOUHIDIS |
| (22) | John COLLINS (Celtic) | Georgios TOURSOUNIDIS |
| (5) | John McGINLAY (Bolton Wanderers) | Alexandros ALEXANDRIS |
| (5) | Duncan FERGUSON (Everton) | Nikolaos MAHLAS |

Substitutions

| | | |
|---|---|---|
| (2) | John SPENCER (Chelsea) | Spiridon MARANGOS |
| | for McKinlay 46 mins | for Alexandris 72 mins |
| (62) | James LEIGHTON (Hibernian) | Theofilos KARASAVVIDIS |
| | for Goram 77 mins | for Nioplias 89 mins |

Goals

| | |
|---|---|
| | 0-1    Apostolakis (18 mins pen) |

John McGinlay and Scott Booth celebrate after the latter had opened the scoring for Scotland against Russia at Hampden in November 1994.

# 1995

| P | W | D | L | F | A |
|---|---|---|---|---|---|
| 9 | 6 | 2 | 1 | 13 | 3 |

**556**

(European Championship — Qualifier)    Referee: Strampe (Germany)
29 March 1995    Luzhniki Stadium, Moscow (Att: 30,000)

### RUSSIA 0-0 SCOTLAND

| | | |
|---|---|---|
| (63) | James LEIGHTON (Hibernian) | Dmitri KHARIN |
| (32) | Stewart McKIMMIE (Aberdeen) | Dmitri KHLESTOV |
| (26) | Thomas BOYD (Celtic) | Iurij KOVTUN |
| (17) | Alan McLAREN (Rangers) | Iurij NIKIFOROV |
| (10) | Colin HENDRY (Blackburn Rovers) | Viktor ONOPKO |
| (1) | Colin CALDERWOOD (Tottenham Hotspur) | Andrei KANCHELSKIS |
| (32) | Gary McALLISTER (Leeds United) captain | Valerij KARPIN |
| (72) | Paul McSTAY (Celtic) | Igor SHALIMOV |
| (23) | John COLLINS (Celtic) | Igor DOBROVOLSKI |
| (1) | Darren JACKSON (Hibernian) | Sergei KIRIAKOV |
| (6) | John McGINLAY (Bolton Wanderers) | Dmitri RADCHENKO |

Substitutions

| | | |
|---|---|---|
| (4) | Duncan SHEARER (Aberdeen) | Nikolai PISAREV |
| | for Jackson 77 mins | for Radchenko 57 mins |
| (8) | William McKINLAY (Dundee United) | Vladislav RADIMOV |
| | for McGinlay 83 mins | for Shalimov 69 mins |

## 557

(European Championship — Qualifier)
26 April 1995

Referee: Loizou (Cyprus)
Stadio di Serravalle, Serravalle (Att: 1,738)

### SAN MARINO 0-2 SCOTLAND — Half-time 0-1

| | | |
|---|---|---|
| (64) | James LEIGHTON (Hibernian) | Pierluigi BENEDETTINI |
| (18) | Alan McLAREN (Rangers) | Claudio CANTI |
| (27) | Thomas BOYD (Celtic) | Mirco GENNARI |
| (2) | Colin CALDERWOOD (Tottenham Hotspur) | Luca GOBBI |
| (11) | Colin HENDRY (Blackburn Rovers) | William GUERRA |
| (25) | Patrick NEVIN (Tranmere Rovers) | Marco MULARONI |
| (33) | Gary McALLISTER (Leeds United) captain | Marco MAZZA |
| (24) | John COLLINS (Celtic) | Massimo BONINI |
| (2) | Darren JACKSON (Hibernian) | Pierangelo MANZAROLI |
| (5) | Duncan SHEARER (Aberdeen) | Pierdomenico DELLA VALLE |
| (7) | John McGINLAY (Bolton Wanderers) | Nicola BACCIOCCHI |

Substitutions

| | | |
|---|---|---|
| (3) | John SPENCER (Chelsea) | Ivan MATTEONI |
| | for Shearer 67 mins | for Bonini 46 mins |
| (9) | William McKINLAY (Dundee United) | Davide GUALTIERI |
| | for Nevin 78 mins | for Mularoni 71 mins |

Goals

| | |
|---|---|
| Collins (19 mins) | 1-0 |
| Calderwood (85 mins) | 2-0 |

## 558

(Kirin Cup)
21 May 1995

Referee: Perez (Colombia)
Big Arch Stadium, Hiroshima (Att: 24,566)

### JAPAN 0-0 SCOTLAND

| | | |
|---|---|---|
| (65) | James LEIGHTON (Hibernian) captain | Kazuya MAEKAWA |
| (19) | Alan McLAREN (Rangers) | Tetsuji HASHIRATANAI |
| (2) | Robert McKINNON (Motherwell) | Aikra NARAHASHI |
| (3) | Colin CALDERWOOD (Tottenham Hotspur) | Norio OMURA |
| (1) | Brian MARTIN (Motherwell) | Masami IHARA |
| (1) | Scot GEMMILL (Nottingham Forest) | Hiroshige YANAGIMOTO |
| (1) | Paul LAMBERT (Motherwell) | Rui RAMOS |
| (10) | William McKINLAY (Dundee United) | Motohiro YAMAGUCHI |
| (1) | Craig BURLEY (Chelsea) | Hiroaki MORISHIMA |
| (3) | Darren JACKSON (Hibernian) | Kazuyoshi MIURA |
| (4) | John SPENCER (Chelsea) | Masashi NAKAYAMA |

Substitutions

| | | |
|---|---|---|
| (12) | John ROBERTSON (Hearts) | Masahiro FUKUDA |
| | for Lambert 37 mins | for Ramos 51 mins |
| (1) | Paul BERNARD (Oldham Athletic) | Tsuyoshi KITAZAWA |
| | for Gemmill 75 mins | for Morishima 81 mins |
| (7) | Derek WHYTE (Middlesbrough) | |
| | for Calderwood 79 mins | |

## 559

(Kirin Cup)
24 May 1995

Referee: Okada (Japan)
Prefectural Sports Park, Toyama (Att: 5,669)

### ECUADOR 1-2 SCOTLAND — Half-time 0-0

| | | |
|---|---|---|
| (66) | James LEIGHTON (Hibernian) captain | José CEVALLOS |
| (20) | Alan McLAREN (Rangers) | Luis CAPURRO |
| (8) | Derek WHYTE (Middlesbrough) | Raúl NORIEGA |
| (4) | Colin CALDERWOOD (Tottenham Hotspur) | Ivan HURTADO |
| (2) | Brian MARTIN (Motherwell) | Wilfrido VERDUGA |
| (2) | Scot GEMMILL (Nottingham Forest) | Juan GUAMAN |
| (2) | Paul BERNARD (Oldham Athletic) | Nixon CARCELEN |
| (11) | William McKINLAY (Dundee United) | Juan GARAY |
| (2) | Craig BURLEY (Chelsea) | Hjalmar ZAMBRANO |
| (4) | Darren JACKSON (Hibernian) | Diego HERRERA |
| (13) | John ROBERTSON (Hearts) | Eduardo HURTADO |

Substitutions

| | | |
|---|---|---|
| (1) | Steven CRAWFORD (Raith Rovers) | Agustin DELGADO |
| | for Jackson 62 mins | for Garay 46 mins |
| (2) | Paul LAMBERT (Motherwell) | José MORA |
| | for Whyte 76 mins | for Herrera 71 mins |

Goals

| | | |
|---|---|---|
| Robertson (75 mins) | 1-0 | |
| | 1-1 | I.Hurtado (79 mins pen) |
| Crawford (83 mins) | 2-1 | |

## 560

(European Championship — Qualifier)
7 June 1995

Referee: Hrinak (Slovakia)
Svangaskard Stadion, Toftir (Att: 3,881)

### FAROE ISLANDS 0-2 SCOTLAND — Half-time 0-2

| | | |
|---|---|---|
| (67) | James LEIGHTON (Hibernian) captain | Jens KNUDSEN |
| (33) | Stewart McKIMMIE (Aberdeen) | Jens HANSEN |
| (3) | Robert McKINNON (Motherwell) | Tummas HANSEN |
| (5) | Colin CALDERWOOD (Tottenham Hotspur) | Óli JOHANNESEN |
| (21) | Alan McLAREN (Rangers) | Ossur HANSEN |
| (3) | Craig BURLEY (Chelsea) | Julian JOHNSSON |
| (12) | William McKINLAY (Dundee United) | Magni JARNSKOR |
| (25) | John COLLINS (Celtic) | Janus RASMUSSEN |
| (5) | Darren JACKSON (Hibernian) | Henning JARNSKOR |
| (6) | Duncan SHEARER (Aberdeen) | Todi JÓNSSON |
| (8) | John McGINLAY (Bolton Wanderers) | Jens-Erik RASMUSSEN |

Substitutions

| | | |
|---|---|---|
| (3) | Scot GEMMILL (Nottingham Forest) | Allan JOENSEN |
| | for McGinlay 75 mins | for M. Jarnskor 55 mins |
| (14) | John ROBERTSON (Hearts) | Jan MÜLLER |
| | for Shearer 86 mins | for J.E. Rasmussen 75 mins |

Goals

| | |
|---|---|
| McKinlay (25 mins) | 1-0 |
| McGinlay (29 mins) | 2-0 |

## 561

(European Championship — Qualifier)
16 August 1995

Referee: Mikkelsen (Denmark)
Hampden Park, Glasgow (Att: 34,910)

### SCOTLAND 1-0 GREECE — Half-time 0-0

| | | |
|---|---|---|
| (68) | James LEIGHTON (Hibernian) | Ilias ATMATZIDIS |
| (34) | Stewart McKIMMIE (Aberdeen) | Efstratios APOSTOLAKIS |
| (1) | Thomas McKINLAY (Celtic) | Kyriakos KARATAIDIS |
| (6) | Colin CALDERWOOD (Tottenham Hotspur) | Nikolaos DABIZAS |
| (28) | Thomas BOYD (Celtic) | Yiannis KALITZAKIS |
| (34) | Gary McALLISTER (Leeds United) captain | Mihalis KASSAPIS |
| (4) | Craig BURLEY (Chelsea) | Theodoros ZAGORAKIS |
| (31) | Stuart McCALL (Rangers) | Panayotis TSALOUHIDIS |
| (26) | John COLLINS (Celtic) | Daniel BATISTA |
| (6) | Darren JACKSON (Hibernian) | Vassilis TSARTAS |
| (7) | Duncan SHEARER (Aberdeen) | Zisis VRIZAS |

Substitutions

| | | |
|---|---|---|
| (15) | John ROBERTSON (Hearts) | Nikolaos MAHLAS |
| | for Jackson 71 mins | for Vrizas 30 mins |
| (47) | Alistair McCOIST (Rangers) | Alexandros ALEXANDRIS |
| | for Shearer 71 mins | for Batista 51 mins |
| | | Georgios GEORGIADIS |
| | | for Zagorakis 79 mins |

Goals

| | |
|---|---|
| McCoist (72 mins) | 1-0 |

Ally McCoist celebrates after scoring for Scotland against Greece at Hampden in August 1995.

## 562

(European Championship — Qualifier)
6 September 1995

Referee: Melnichuk (Ukraine)
Hampden Park, Glasgow (Att: 35,505)

### SCOTLAND 1-0 FINLAND — Half-time 1-0

| | | |
|---|---|---|
| (69) | James LEIGHTON (Hibernian) | Kari LAUKKANEN |
| (35) | Stewart McKIMMIE (Aberdeen) | Kari RISSANEN |
| (29) | Thomas BOYD (Celtic) | Rami NIEMINEN |
| (22) | Alan McLAREN (Rangers) | Markku KANERVA |
| (7) | Colin CALDERWOOD (Tottenham Hotspur) | Erik HOLMGREN |
| (12) | Colin HENDRY (Blackburn Rovers) | Kim SUOMINEN |
| (35) | Gary McALLISTER (Leeds United) captain | Janne LINDBERG |
| (27) | John COLLINS (Celtic) | Marko MYYRY |
| (2) | Thomas McKINLAY (Celtic) | Petri JARVINEN |
| (5) | John SPENCER (Chelsea) | Jari LITMANEN |
| (8) | Scott BOOTH (Aberdeen) | Ari HJELM |

Substitutions

| | | |
|---|---|---|
| (48) | Alistair McCOIST (Rangers) for Spencer 74 mins | Tommi GRONLUND for Nieminen 62 mins |
| (7) | Darren JACKSON (Hibernian) for Booth 80 mins | |
| (13) | William McKINLAY (Dundee United) for McKimmie 88 mins | |

**Goals**

Booth (10 mins)  1-0

---

## 563

(Friendly)
11 October 1995

Referee: Diaz (Spain)
Rasunda Stadion, Stockholm (Att: 19,121)

### SWEDEN 2-0 SCOTLAND — Half-time 2-0

| | | |
|---|---|---|
| (70) | James LEIGHTON (Hibernian) | Bengt ANDERSSON |
| (36) | Stewart McKIMMIE (Aberdeen) | Mikael NILSSON |
| (30) | Thomas BOYD (Celtic) | Joachim BJÖRKLUND |
| (23) | Alan McLAREN (Rangers) | Patrik ANDERSSON |
| (8) | Colin CALDERWOOD (Tottenham Hotspur) | Teddy LUCIC |
| (13) | Colin HENDRY (Blackburn Rovers) | Stefan SCHWARZ |
| (36) | Gary McALLISTER (Leeds United) captain | Niklas ALEXANDERSSON |
| (5) | Craig BURLEY (Chelsea) | Niklas GUDMUNDSSON |
| (28) | John COLLINS (Celtic) | Jörgen PETTERSSON |
| (9) | John McGINLAY (Bolton Wanderers) | Tomas BROLIN |
| (16) | John ROBERTSON (Hearts) | Kennet ANDERSSON |

Substitutions

| | | |
|---|---|---|
| (14) | William McKINLAY (Dundee United) for Burley 46 mins | Martin PRINGLE for Gudmundsson 70 mins |
| (9) | Eoin JESS (Aberdeen) for McGinlay 46 mins | Magnus ERLINGMARK for K. Andersson 80 mins |
| (8) | Darren JACKSON (Hibernian) for McAllister 60 mins | Pontus KAAMARK for Lucic 89 mins |
| (34) | Andrew GORAM (Rangers) for Leighton 73 mins | |
| (26) | Patrick NEVIN (Tranmere Rovers) for Robertson 73 mins | |

**Goals**

| | |
|---|---|
| 0-1 | Pettersson (31 mins) |
| 0-2 | Schwarz (35 mins) |

---

## 564

(European Championship — Qualifier)
15 November 1995

Referee: Bohunek (Czech Republic)
Hampden Park, Glasgow (Att: 30,306)

### SCOTLAND 5-0 SAN MARINO — Half-time 2-0

| | | |
|---|---|---|
| (71) | James LEIGHTON (Hibernian) | Stefano MUCCIOLI |
| (24) | Alan McLAREN (Rangers) | Federico MORONI |
| (31) | Thomas BOYD (Celtic) | Mirco GENNARI |
| (9) | Colin CALDERWOOD (Tottenham Hotspur) | Mauro VALENTINI |
| (14) | Colin HENDRY (Blackburn Rovers) | William GUERRA |
| (27) | Patrick NEVIN (Tranmere Rovers) | Marco MULARONI |
| (4) | Scot GEMMILL (Nottingham Forest) | Marco MAZZA |
| (37) | Gary McALLISTER (Leeds United) captain | Fabio FRANCINI |
| (29) | John COLLINS (Celtic) | Pierangelo MANZAROLI |
| (10) | Eoin JESS (Aberdeen) | Ivan MATTEONI |
| (9) | Scott BOOTH (Aberdeen) | Nicola BACCIOCCHI |

Substitutions

| | | |
|---|---|---|
| (49) | Alistair McCOIST (Rangers) for McAllister 48 mins | Claudio CANTI for Mularoni 51 mins |
| (15) | William McKINLAY (Blackburn Rovers) for Collins 58 mins | Paolo MONTAGNA for Guerra 70 mins |
| (9) | Darren JACKSON (Hibernian) for Booth 65 mins | Pierdomenico DELLA VALLE for Mazza.81 mins |

**Goals**

| | |
|---|---|
| Jess (30 mins) | 1-0 |
| Booth (45 mins) | 2-0 |
| McCoist (49 mins) | 3-0 |
| Nevin (71 mins) | 4-0 |
| Francini (90 mins o.g.) | 5-0 |

---

# 1996

| P | W | D | L | F | A |
|---|---|---|---|---|---|
| 10 | 4 | 2 | 4 | 6 | 7 |

## 565

(Friendly)
27 March 1996

Referee: Van Dijk (Netherlands)
Hampden Park, Glasgow (Att: 20,608)

### SCOTLAND 1-0 AUSTRALIA — Half-time 0-0

| | | |
|---|---|---|
| (72) | James LEIGHTON (Hibernian) | Mark BOSNICH |
| (1) | Brian O'NEIL (Celtic) | Steven HORVAT |
| (15) | Colin HENDRY (Blackburn Rovers) | Anthony VIDMAR |
| (32) | Thomas BOYD (Celtic) | Anthony POPOVIC |
| (6) | Craig BURLEY (Chelsea) | Alexander TOBIN |
| (38) | Gary McALLISTER (Leeds United) | Stephen CORICA |
| (73) | Paul McSTAY (Celtic) | Robert SLATER |
| (16) | William McKINLAY (Blackburn Rovers) | Jason VAN BLERK |
| (30) | John COLLINS (Celtic) | Aurelio VIDMAR |
| (6) | John SPENCER (Chelsea) | Graham ARNOLD |
| (50) | Alistair McCOIST (Rangers) captain | Carl VEART |

Substitutions

| | | |
|---|---|---|
| (10) | Scott BOOTH (Aberdeen) for McStay 46 mins | Daniel TIATTO for Veart 69 mins |
| (20) | Kevin GALLACHER (Blackburn Rovers) for O'Neil 46 mins | |
| (10) | Darren JACKSON (Hibernian) for McKinlay 75 mins | |
| (28) | Patrick NEVIN (Tranmere Rovers) for McCoist 80 mins | |

**Goals**

McCoist (53 mins)  1-0

---

## 566

(Friendly)
24 April 1996

Referee: Wegereef (Netherlands)
Parken Stadion, Copenhagen (Att: 23,031)

### DENMARK 2-0 SCOTLAND — Half-time 2-0

| | | |
|---|---|---|
| (73) | James LEIGHTON (Hibernian) | Peter SCHMEICHEL |
| (37) | Stewart McKIMMIE (Aberdeen) | Thomas HELVEG |
| (33) | Thomas BOYD (Celtic) | Jens RISAGER |
| (16) | Colin HENDRY (Blackburn Rovers) | Lars OLSEN |
| (7) | Craig BURLEY (Chelsea) | Marc RIEPER |
| (39) | Gary McALLISTER (Leeds United) captain | Brian NIELSEN |
| (32) | Stuart McCALL (Rangers) | Michael SCHJONBERG |
| (31) | John COLLINS (Celtic) | Claus THOMSEN |
| (3) | Thomas McKINLAY (Celtic) | Michael LAUDRUP |
| (7) | John SPENCER (Chelsea) | Mikkel BECK |
| (21) | Kevin GALLACHER (Blackburn Rovers) | Brian LAUDRUP |

Substitutions

| | | |
|---|---|---|
| (5) | Scot GEMMILL (Nottingham Forest) for McCall 46 mins | Mogens KROGH for Schmeichel 46 mins |
| (35) | Andrew GORAM (Rangers) for Leighton 46 mins | Jacob LAURSEN for Risager 81 mins |
| (51) | Alistair McCOIST (Rangers) for Spencer 72 mins | Allan NIELSEN for M. Laudrup 85 mins |
| (11) | Darren JACKSON (Hibernian) for Gallacher 72 mins | |
| (17) | William McKINLAY (Blackburn Rovers) for Hendry 75 mins | |

**Goals**

| | |
|---|---|
| 0-1 | M.Laudrup (7 mins) |
| 0-2 | B.Laudrup (27 mins) |

---

## 567

(Friendly)
26 May 1996

Referee: Brizio (Mexico)
Willow Brook Stadium, New Britain (Att: 8,526)

### USA 2-1 SCOTLAND — Half-time 1-1

| | | |
|---|---|---|
| (74) | James LEIGHTON (Hibernian) | Jürgen SOMMER |
| (10) | Colin CALDERWOOD (Tottenham Hotspur) | Michael BURNS |
| (17) | Colin HENDRY (Blackburn Rovers) captain | Jeffrey AGOOS |
| (9) | Derek WHYTE (Middlesbrough) | Alexei LALAS |
| (8) | Craig BURLEY (Chelsea) | Thomas DOOLEY |
| (6) | Scot GEMMILL (Nottingham Forest) | John HARKES |
| (12) | Darren JACKSON (Hibernian) | Marcelo BALBOA |
| (11) | Eoin JESS (Coventry City) | Claudio REYNA |
| (34) | Thomas BOYD (Celtic) | Tabaré RAMOS |
| (11) | Scott BOOTH (Aberdeen) | Cobi JONES |
| (28) | Gordon DURIE (Rangers) | Eric WYNALDA |

Substitutions

| | | |
|---|---|---|
| (32) | John COLLINS (Celtic) for Jackson 46 mins | Jovan KIROVSKI for Dooley 53 mins |
| (40) | Gary McALLISTER (Leeds United) for Gemmill 46 mins | Brian McBRIDE for Reyna 83 mins |
| (8) | John SPENCER (Chelsea) for Durie 46 mins | |
| (33) | Stuart McCALL (Rangers) for Burley 60 mins | |
| (2) | Nicholas WALKER (Partick Thistle) for Leighton 82 mins | |

**Goals**

| | |
|---|---|
| Durie (9 mins) | 1-0 |
| | 1-1 | Wynalda (13 mins pen) |
| | 1-2 | Jones (72 mins) |

**568**

Referee: Dominguez (USA)
Orange Bowl, Miami (Att: 8,500)

### COLOMBIA 1-0 SCOTLAND — Half-time 0-0

| | | | |
|---|---|---|---|
| (36) | Andrew GORAM (Rangers) | | Farid MONDRAGON |
| (38) | Stewart McKIMMIE (Aberdeen) | | Néstor ORTÍZ |
| (35) | Thomas BOYD (Celtic) | | Antonio MORENO |
| (11) | Colin CALDERWOOD (Tottenham Hotspur) | | Francisco CASSIANI |
| (18) | Colin HENDRY (Blackburn Rovers) | | Jorge BEMUDEZ |
| (41) | Gary McALLISTER (Leeds United) captain | | Mauricio SERNA |
| (34) | Stuart McCALL (Rangers) | | Andrés ESTRADA |
| (33) | John COLLINS (Celtic) | | Edison MAFLA |
| (4) | Thomas McKINLAY (Celtic) | | Ivan VALENCIANO |
| (9) | John SPENCER (Chelsea) | | Freddy RINCÓN |
| (52) | Alistair McCOIST (Rangers) | | Adolfo VALENCIA |

Substitutions

| | | | |
|---|---|---|---|
| (9) | Craig BURLEY (Chelsea) | | Leonel ALVAREZ |
| | for Hendry 46 mins | | for Mafla 46 mins |
| (22) | Kevin GALLACHER (Blackburn Rovers) | | Victor ARISTIZABAL |
| | for McCoist 61 mins | | for Valenciano 46 mins |
| (12) | Eoin JESS (Coventry City) | | Faustino ASPRILLA |
| | for Spencer 69 mins | | for Valencia 46 mins |
| | | | Luis HERRERA |
| | | | for Ortiz 46 mins |
| | | | Alexis MENDOZA |
| | | | for Cassiani 46 mins |
| | | | Carlos VALDERRAMA |
| | | | for Estrada 46 mins |

Goals
0-1    Asprilla (82 mins)

---

**569**

(European Championship — Final Tournament 1st Round)

Referee: Sundell (Sweden)
Villa Park, Birmingham (Att: 34,363)

10 June 1996

### NETHERLANDS 0-0 SCOTLAND

| | | | |
|---|---|---|---|
| (37) | Andrew GORAM (Rangers) | | Edwin VAN DER SAR |
| (39) | Stewart McKIMMIE (Aberdeen) | | Michael REIZIGER |
| (36) | Thomas BOYD (Celtic) | | Johannes DE KOCK |
| (12) | Colin CALDERWOOD (Tottenham Hotspur) | | Winston BOGARDE |
| (19) | Colin HENDRY (Blackburn Rovers) | | Ronaldus DE BOER |
| (35) | Stuart McCALL (Rangers) | | Edgar DAVIDS |
| (42) | Gary McALLISTER (Leeds United) captain | | Clarence SEEDORF |
| (34) | John COLLINS (Celtic) | | Richard WITSCHGE |
| (23) | Kevin GALLACHER (Blackburn Rovers) | | Gaston TAUMENT |
| (12) | Scott BOOTH (Aberdeen) | | Johannes CRUIJFF |
| (29) | Gordon DURIE (Rangers) | | Dennis BERGKAMP |

Substitutions

| | | | |
|---|---|---|---|
| (10) | John SPENCER (Chelsea) | | Patrick KLUIVERT |
| | for Booth 46 mins | | for Taument 62 mins |
| (18) | William McKINLAY (Blackburn Rovers) | | Aron WINTER |
| | for Gallacher 56 mins | | for De Boer 68 mins |
| (10) | Craig BURLEY (Chelsea) | | Phillip COCU |
| | for McKimmie 85 mins | | for Witschge 78 mins |

---

**570**

(European Championship — Final Tournament 1st Round)

15 June 1996

Referee: Pairetto (Italy)
Wembley Stadium, London (Att: 76,864)

### ENGLAND 2-0 SCOTLAND — Half-time 0-0

| | | | |
|---|---|---|---|
| (38) | Andrew GORAM (Rangers) | | David SEAMAN |
| (40) | Stewart McKIMMIE (Aberdeen) | | Gary NEVILLE |
| (37) | Thomas BOYD (Celtic) | | Stuart PEARCE |
| (13) | Colin CALDERWOOD (Tottenham Hotspur) | | Gareth SOUTHGATE |
| (20) | Colin HENDRY (Blackburn Rovers) | | Anthony ADAMS |
| (36) | Stuart McCALL (Rangers) | | Darren ANDERTON |
| (43) | Gary McALLISTER (Leeds United) captain | | Paul INCE |
| (35) | John COLLINS (Celtic) | | Paul GASCOIGNE |
| (5) | Thomas McKINLAY (Celtic) | | Stephen McMANAMAN |
| (11) | John SPENCER (Chelsea) | | Edward SHERINGHAM |
| (30) | Gordon DURIE (Rangers) | | Alan SHEARER |

Substitutions

| | | | |
|---|---|---|---|
| (53) | Alistair McCOIST (Rangers) | | James REDKNAPP |
| | for Spencer 66 mins | | for Pearce 46 mins |
| (11) | Craig BURLEY (Chelsea) | | Stephen STONE |
| | for McKinlay 81 mins | | for Ince 79 mins |
| (13) | Eoin JESS (Coventry City) | | Solzeer CAMPBELL |
| | for Durie 84 mins | | for Redknapp 86 mins |

Goals
0-1    Shearer (52 mins)
0-2    Gascoigne (78 mins)

---

**571**

(European Championship — Final Tournament 1st Round)

Referee: Krondl (Czech Republic)
Villa Park, Birmingham (Att: 34,926)

18 June 1996

### SWITZERLAND 0-1 SCOTLAND — Half-time 0-1

| | | | |
|---|---|---|---|
| (39) | Andrew GORAM (Rangers) | | Marco PASCOLO |
| (12) | Craig BURLEY (Chelsea) | | Marc HOTTIGER |
| (38) | Thomas BOYD (Celtic) | | Yvan QUENTIN |
| (14) | Colin CALDERWOOD (Tottenham Hotspur) | | Stéphane HENCHOZ |
| (21) | Colin HENDRY (Blackburn Rovers) | | Ramón VEGA |
| (37) | Stuart McCALL (Rangers) | | Johann VOGEL |
| (44) | Gary McALLISTER (Leeds United) captain | | Ciriaco SFORZA |
| (36) | John COLLINS (Celtic) | | Marcel KOLLER |
| (6) | Thomas McKINLAY (Celtic) | | Christophe BONVIN |
| (31) | Gordon DURIE (Rangers) | | Kubilay TÜRKYILMAZ |
| (54) | Alistair McCOIST (Rangers) | | Stéphane CHAPUISAT |

Substitutions

| | | | |
|---|---|---|---|
| (13) | Scott BOOTH (Aberdeen) | | Raphaël WICKY |
| | for McKinlay 59 mins | | for Koller 46 mins |
| (12) | John SPENCER (Chelsea) | | Sébastien FOURNIER |
| | for McCoist 84 mins | | for Chapuisat 46 mins |
| | | | Alexandre COMISETTI |
| | | | for Quentin 81 mins |

Goals
McCoist (37 mins)    1-0

Scotland's defenders brace themselves as the Netherlands take a free-kick at Villa Park in Euro 1996.

**572**

(World Cup — Qualifier)
31 August 1996

Referee: Piraux (Belgium)
Ernst Happel Stadion, Vienna (Att: 29,500)

### AUSTRIA 0-0 SCOTLAND

| | | |
|---|---|---|
| (40) | Andrew GORAM (Rangers) | Michael KONSEL |
| (13) | Craig BURLEY (Chelsea) | Markus SCHOPP |
| (39) | Thomas BOYD (Celtic) | Peter SCHÖTTEL |
| (15) | Colin CALDERWOOD (Tottenham Hotspur) | Anton PFEFFER |
| (22) | Colin HENDRY (Blackburn Rovers) | Wolfgang FEIERSINGER |
| (38) | Stuart McCALL (Rangers) | Stefan MARASEK |
| (45) | Gary McALLISTER (Coventry City) captain | Dietmar KÜHBAUER |
| (37) | John COLLINS (Monaco) | Andreas HERZOG |
| (7) | Thomas McKINLAY (Celtic) | Andreas HERAF |
| (6) | Duncan FERGUSON (Everton) | Dieter RAMUSCH |
| (55) | Alistair McCOIST (Rangers) | Anton POLSTER |

Substitutions

| | | |
|---|---|---|
| (32) | Gordon DURIE (Rangers) | Herfried SABITZER |
| | for McCoist 69 mins | for Polster 67 mins |
| | | Andreas OGRIS |
| | | for Ramusch 76 mins |

---

**573**

(World Cup — Qualifier)
5 October 1996

Referee: Ulrich (Czech Republic)
Daugava Stadion, Riga (Att: 9,500)

### LATVIA 0-2 SCOTLAND    Half-time 0-1

| | | |
|---|---|---|
| (41) | Andrew GORAM (Rangers) | Olegs KARAVAJEVS |
| (14) | Craig BURLEY (Chelsea) | Igors TROITSKIS |
| (40) | Thomas BOYD (Celtic) | Mihails ZEMLINSKIS |
| (16) | Colin CALDERWOOD (Tottenham Hotspur) | Igors STEPANOVS |
| (10) | Derek WHYTE (Middlesbrough) | Iurijs SEVLAKOVS |
| (39) | Stuart McCALL (Rangers) | Imants BLEIDELIS |
| (46) | Gary McALLISTER (Coventry City) captain | Valerijs IVANOVS |
| (38) | John COLLINS (Monaco) | Vitalijs ASTAFJEVS |
| (8) | Thomas McKINLAY (Celtic) | Vits RIMKUS |
| (13) | Darren JACKSON (Hibernian) | Vladimirs BABICEVS |
| (13) | John SPENCER (Chelsea) | Marians PAHARS |

Substitutions

| | | |
|---|---|---|
| (3) | Paul LAMBERT (Borussia Dortmund) | Andrejs STOLCERS |
| | for McCall 46 mins | for Babicevs 46 mins |
| (1) | William DODDS (Aberdeen) | Rolands BULDERS |
| | for Spencer 59 mins | for Rimkus 79 mins |
| (1) | John McNAMARA (Celtic) | |
| | for McKinlay 80 mins | |

Goals

| | |
|---|---|
| Collins (18 mins) | 1-0 |
| Jackson (78 mins) | 2-0 |

---

**574**

(World Cup — Qualifier)
10 November 1996

Referee: Garcia (Spain)
Ibrox Stadium, Glasgow (Att: 46,738)

### SCOTLAND 1-0 SWEDEN    Half-time 1-0

| | | |
|---|---|---|
| (75) | James LEIGHTON (Hibernian) | Thomas RAVELLI |
| (2) | John McNAMARA (Celtic) | Roland NILSSON |
| (41) | Thomas BOYD (Celtic) | Gary SUNDGREN |
| (17) | Colin CALDERWOOD (Tottenham Hotspur) | Patrik ANDERSSON |
| (23) | Colin HENDRY (Blackburn Rovers) captain | Joachim BJÖRKLUND |
| (15) | Craig BURLEY (Chelsea) | Stefan SCHWARZ |
| (19) | William McKINLAY (Blackburn Rovers) | Pär ZETTERBERG |
| (39) | John COLLINS (Monaco) | Jonas THERN |
| (9) | Thomas McKINLAY (Celtic) | Niklas ALEXANDERSSON |
| (14) | Darren JACKSON (Hibernian) | Jesper BLOMQVIST |
| (10) | John McGINLAY (Bolton Wanderers) | Martin DAHLIN |

Substitutions

| | | |
|---|---|---|
| (4) | Paul LAMBERT (Borussia Dortmund) | Kennet ANDERSSON |
| | for McNamara 46 mins | for Dahlin 17 mins |
| (24) | Kevin GALLACHER (Blackburn Rovers) | Henrik LARSSON |
| | for Jackson 78 mins | for Alexandersson 69 mins |
| (56) | Alistair McCOIST (Rangers) | Andreas ANDERSSON |
| | for McGinlay 85 mins | for Zetterberg 77 mins |

Goals

| | |
|---|---|
| McGinlay (8 mins) | 1-0 |

---

# 1997

| P | W | D | L | F | A |
|---|---|---|---|---|---|
| 10 | 6 | 1 | 3 | 16 | 8 |

**575**

(World Cup — Qualifier)
11 February 1997

Referee: Radoman (Yugoslavia)
Stade Louis II, Monaco (Att: 4,000)

### ESTONIA 0-0 SCOTLAND

| | | |
|---|---|---|
| (42) | Andrew GORAM (Rangers) | Mart POOM |
| (3) | John McNAMARA (Celtic) | Urmas KIRS |
| (42) | Thomas BOYD (Celtic) | Urmas ROOBA |
| (18) | Colin CALDERWOOD (Tottenham Hotspur) | Marek LEMSALU |
| (24) | Colin HENDRY (Blackburn Rovers) | Sergei HOHLOV-SIMSON |
| (74) | Paul McSTAY (Celtic) | Viktor ALONEN |
| (47) | Gary McALLISTER (Coventry City) captain | Meelis ROOBA |
| (40) | John COLLINS (Monaco) | Martin REIM |
| (25) | Kevin GALLACHER (Blackburn Rovers) | Liivo LEETMA |
| (11) | John McGINLAY (Bolton Wanderers) | Marko KRISTAL |
| (7) | Duncan FERGUSON (Everton) | Indrek ZELINSKI |

Substitutions

| | | |
|---|---|---|
| (9) | Ian FERGUSON (Rangers) | Mati PARI |
| | for McStay 63 mins | for M. Rooba 67 mins |
| (57) | Alistair McCOIST (Rangers) | Andres OPER |
| | for McGinlay 73 mins | for Leetma 75 mins |
| (10) | Thomas McKINLAY (Celtic) | |
| | for McNamara 74 mins | |

---

**576**

(World Cup — Qualifier)
29 March 1997

Referee: Heinemann (Germany)
Rugby Park, Kilmarnock (Att: 17,996)

### SCOTLAND 2-0 ESTONIA    Half-time 1-0

| | | |
|---|---|---|
| (76) | James LEIGHTON (Hibernian) | Mart POOM |
| (16) | Craig BURLEY (Chelsea) | Urmas KIRS |
| (43) | Thomas BOYD (Celtic) | Janek MEET |
| (19) | Colin CALDERWOOD (Tottenham Hotspur) | Marek LEMSALU |
| (25) | Colin HENDRY (Blackburn Rovers) | Sergei HOHLOV-SIMSON |
| (7) | Scot GEMMILL (Nottingham Forest) | Mati PARI |
| (75) | Paul McSTAY (Celtic) | Kristen VIIKMÄE |
| (48) | Gary McALLISTER (Coventry City) captain | Martin REIM |
| (11) | Thomas McKINLAY (Celtic) | Andres OPER |
| (15) | Darren JACKSON (Hibernian) | Marko KRISTAL |
| (26) | Kevin GALLACHER (Blackburn Rovers) | Indrek ZELINSKI |

Substitutions

| | | |
|---|---|---|
| (20) | William McKINLAY (Blackburn Rovers) | Meelis ROOBA |
| | for Hendry 64 mins | for Pari 54 mins |
| (12) | John McGINLAY (Bolton Wanderers) | Liivo LEETMA |
| | for Jackson 83 mins | for Viikmäe 72 mins |
| | | Argo ARBEITER |
| | | for Zelinski 81 mins |

Goals

| | |
|---|---|
| Boyd (26 mins) | 1-0 |
| Meet (52 mins o.g.) | 2-0 |

---

**577**

(World Cup — Qualifier)
2 April 1997

Referee: Levnikov (Russia)
Celtic Park, Glasgow (Att: 43,295)

### SCOTLAND 2-0 AUSTRIA    Half-time 1-0

| | | |
|---|---|---|
| (77) | James LEIGHTON (Hibernian) | Michael KONSEL |
| (17) | Craig BURLEY (Chelsea) | Markus SCHOPP |
| (44) | Thomas BOYD (Celtic) | Peter SCHÖTTEL |
| (20) | Colin CALDERWOOD (Tottenham Hotspur) | Anton PFEFFER |
| (26) | Colin HENDRY (Blackburn Rovers) | Wolfgang FEIERSINGER |
| (49) | Gary McALLISTER (Coventry City) captain | Arnold WETL |
| (5) | Paul LAMBERT (Borussia Dortmund) | Franz AIGNER |
| (41) | John COLLINS (Monaco) | Andreas HERZOG |
| (12) | Thomas McKINLAY (Celtic) | Andreas HERAF |
| (16) | Darren JACKSON (Hibernian) | Peter STÖGER |
| (27) | Kevin GALLACHER (Blackburn Rovers) | Anton POLSTER |

Substitutions

| | | |
|---|---|---|
| (13) | John McGINLAY (Bolton Wanderers) | Walter KOGLER |
| | for Jackson 73 mins | for Schöttel 46 mins |
| (58) | Alistair McCOIST (Rangers) | Ivica VASTIC |
| | for Gallacher 86 mins | for Stöger 67 mins |
| (76) | Paul McSTAY (Celtic) | Andreas OGRIS |
| | for McAllister 88 mins | for Aigner 81 mins |

Goals

| | |
|---|---|
| Gallacher (24 mins) | 1-0 |
| Gallacher (77 mins) | 2-0 |

Craig Burley takes to the air against Austria in a World Cup qualifier at Celtic Park in April 1997.

## 578

(World Cup — Qualifier)
30 April 1997

Referee: Collina (Italy)
Ullevi Stadion, Gothenburg (Att: 40,302)

### SWEDEN 2-1 SCOTLAND — Half-time 1-0

| | | |
|---|---|---|
| (78) | James LEIGHTON (Hibernian) | Thomas RAVELLI |
| (18) | Craig BURLEY (Chelsea) | Gary SUNDGREN |
| (45) | Thomas BOYD (Celtic) | Joachim BJÖRKLUND |
| (21) | Colin CALDERWOOD (Tottenham Hotspur) | Patrik ANDERSSON |
| (27) | Colin HENDRY (Blackburn Rovers) | Pontus KAAMARK |
| (50) | Gary McALLISTER (Coventry City) captain | Stefan SCHWARZ |
| (6) | Paul LAMBERT (Borussia Dortmund) | Pär ZETTERBERG |
| (42) | John COLLINS (Monaco) | Jonas THERN |
| (13) | Thomas McKINLAY (Celtic) | Andreas ANDERSSON |
| (17) | Darren JACKSON (Hibernian) | Kennet ANDERSSON |
| (28) | Kevin GALLACHER (Blackburn Rovers) | Martin DAHLIN |

Substitutions

| | | |
|---|---|---|
| (33) | Gordon DURIE (Rangers) | Haakan MILD |
| | for Jackson 66 mins | for Schwarz 12 mins |
| (8) | Scot GEMMILL (Nottingham Forest) | |
| | for McKinlay 68 mins | |

Goals

| | | |
|---|---|---|
| | 0-1 | K. Andersson (43 mins) |
| | 0-2 | K. Andersson (63 mins) |
| Gallacher (83 mins) | 1-2 | |

## 579

(Friendly)
27 May 1997

Referee: Snoddy (Northern Ireland)
Rugby Park, Kilmarnock (Att: 8,000)

### SCOTLAND 0-1 WALES — Half-time 0-0

| | | |
|---|---|---|
| (1) | Neil SULLIVAN (Wimbledon) | Andrew MARRIOTT |
| (1) | David WEIR (Hearts) | Steven JENKINS |
| (46) | Thomas BOYD (Celtic) | Paul TROLLOPE |
| (1) | Christian DAILLY (Derby County) | Robert PAGE |
| (1) | Brian McALLISTER (Wimbledon) | Kit SYMONS |
| (9) | Scot GEMMILL (Nottingham Forest) | Robert SAVAGE |
| (51) | Gary McALLISTER (Coventry City) captain | Mark PEMBRIDGE |
| (14) | Thomas McKINLAY (Celtic) | Gary SPEED |
| (2) | William DODDS (Aberdeen) | John ROBINSON |
| (18) | Darren JACKSON (Hibernian) | John HARTSON |
| (29) | Kevin GALLACHER (Blackburn Rovers) | Dean SAUNDERS |

Substitutions

| | | |
|---|---|---|
| (14) | John SPENCER (Queen's Park Rangers) | Paul JONES |
| | for Jackson 46 mins | for Marriott 46 mins |
| (4) | John McNAMARA (Celtic) | Simon HAWORTH |
| | for Dailly 74 mins | for Hartson 71 mins |
| (79) | James LEIGHTON (Hibernian) | Marcus BROWNING |
| | for Sullivan 80 mins | for Robinson 88 mins |
| (1) | Simon DONNELLY (Celtic) | Lee JONES |
| | for Gallacher 80 mins | for Saunders 88 mins |

Goals

| | | |
|---|---|---|
| | 0-1 | Hartson (46 mins) |

## 580

(Friendly)
1 June 1997

Referee: Braschi (Italy)
Ta'Qali Stadium, Valletta (Att: 3,500)

### MALTA 2-3 SCOTLAND — Half-time 1-2

| | | |
|---|---|---|
| (80) | James LEIGHTON (Hibernian) | Mario MUSCAT |
| (19) | Craig BURLEY (Chelsea) | Lawrence ATTARD |
| (47) | Thomas BOYD (Celtic) | Jeffrey CHETCUTI |
| (2) | Christian DAILLY (Derby County) | Silvio VELLA |
| (2) | Brian McALLISTER (Wimbledon) | Darren DEBONO |
| (52) | Gary McALLISTER (Coventry City) captain | Ivan ZAMMIT |
| (1) | David HOPKIN (Crystal Palace) | Joseph BRINCAT |
| (43) | John COLLINS (Monaco) | David CARABOTT |
| (15) | Thomas McKINLAY (Celtic) | Nicholas SALIBA |
| (19) | Darren JACKSON (Hibernian) | Gilbert AGIUS |
| (30) | Kevin GALLACHER (Blackburn Rovers) | Hubert SUDA |

Substitutions

| | | |
|---|---|---|
| (2) | David WEIR (Hearts) | Stefan SULTANA |
| | for B.McAllister 46 mins | for Suda 46 mins |
| (34) | Gordon DURIE (Rangers) | Noel TURNER |
| | for Gallacher 56 mins | for Attard 53 mins |
| (10) | Scot GEMMILL (Nottingham Forest) | Stefan GIGLIO |
| | for Hopkin 56 mins | for Vella 75 mins |
| (2) | Simon DONNELLY (Celtic) | David CAMILLERI |
| | for Collins 84 mins | for Agius 75 mins |

Goals

| | | |
|---|---|---|
| Dailly (4 mins) | 1-0 | |
| | 1-1 | Suda (17 mins) |
| Jackson (44 mins) | 2-1 | |
| | 2-2 | Sultana (57 mins) |
| Jackson (81 mins) | 3-2 | |

## 581

(World Cup — Qualifier)
8 June 1997

Referee: Chakar (Turkey)
Dynamo Stadium, Minsk (Att: 14,000)

### BELARUS 0-1 SCOTLAND — Half-time 0-0

| | | |
|---|---|---|
| (81) | James LEIGHTON (Hibernian) | Andrei SATSUNKEVICH |
| (20) | Craig BURLEY (Chelsea) | Eric YAKHIMOVICH |
| (16) | Thomas McKINLAY (Celtic) | Andrei LAVRIK |
| (3) | Christian DAILLY (Derby County) | Radislav ORLOVSKY |
| (48) | Thomas BOYD (Celtic) | Sergei SHTANYUK |
| (53) | Gary McALLISTER (Coventry City) captain | Andrei KHLEBOSOLOV |
| (7) | Paul LAMBERT (Borussia Dortmund) | Miroslav ROMASHCHENKO |
| (2) | David HOPKIN (Crystal Palace) | Andrei OSTROVSKY |
| (20) | Darren JACKSON (Hibernian) | Sergei GURENKO |
| (35) | Gordon DURIE (Rangers) | Andrei DOVNAR |
| (31) | Kevin GALLACHER (Blackburn Rovers) | Sergei GERASIMETS |

Substitutions

| | | |
|---|---|---|
| (11) | Scot GEMMILL (Nottingham Forest) | Valentin BELKEVICH |
| | for Hopkin 68 mins | for Dovnar 53 mins |
| (3) | Brian McALLISTER (Wimbledon) | Vladimir MAKOVSKY |
| | for McKinlay 79 mins | for Khlebosolov 61 mins |
| (3) | William DODDS (Aberdeen) | Dmitri BALASHOV |
| | for Jackson 87 mins | for Orlovsky 66 mins |

Goals

| | | |
|---|---|---|
| G.McAllister (50 mins pen) | 1-0 | |

## 582

**(World Cup — Qualifier)**
7 September 1997

Referee: Van der Ende (Netherlands)
Pittodrie Stadium, Aberdeen (Att: 20,160)

### SCOTLAND 4-1 BELARUS — Half-time 1-0

| | | |
|---|---|---|
| (82) | James LEIGHTON (Aberdeen) | Valerij SHANTOLOSOV |
| (21) | Craig BURLEY (Celtic) | Andrei OSTROVSKY |
| (49) | Thomas BOYD (Celtic) | Andrei LAVRIK |
| (4) | Christian DAILLY (Derby County) | Vyacheslav GERASHCHENKO |
| (22) | Colin CALDERWOOD (Tottenham Hotspur) | Valentin BELKEVICH |
| (54) | Gary McALLISTER (Coventry City) captain | Alexander KULCHY |
| (8) | Paul LAMBERT (Borussia Dortmund) | Sergei GURENKO |
| (44) | John COLLINS (Monaco) | Andrei DOVNAR |
| (17) | Thomas McKINLAY (Celtic) | Vladimir ZHURAVEL |
| (36) | Gordon DURIE (Rangers) | Petr KACHURO |
| (32) | Kevin GALLACHER (Blackburn Rovers) | Sergei GERASIMETS |

Substitutions

| | | |
|---|---|---|
| (59) | Alistair McCOIST (Rangers) | Radislav ORLOVSKY |
| | for Durie 46 mins | for Gurenko 52 mins |
| (3) | David HOPKIN (Leeds United) | Oleg CHERNYAVSKY |
| | for McAllister 50 mins | for Zhuravel 65 mins |
| (4) | William DODDS (Aberdeen) | Dmitri BALASHOV |
| | for Gallacher 84 mins | for Gerasimets 77 mins |

**Goals**

| | | |
|---|---|---|
| Gallacher (5 mins) | 1-0 | |
| Hopkin (54 mins) | 2-0 | |
| Gallacher (57 mins) | 3-0 | |
| | 3-1 | Kachuro (73 mins pen) |
| Hopkin (88 mins) | 4-1 | |

## 583

**(World Cup — Qualifier)**
11 October 1997

Referee: Pillar (Hungary)
Celtic Park, Glasgow (Att: 47,613)

### SCOTLAND 2-0 LATVIA — Half-time 1-0

| | | |
|---|---|---|
| (83) | James LEIGHTON (Aberdeen) | Olegs KARAVAJEVS |
| (22) | Craig BURLEY (Celtic) | Valentins LOBANOVS |
| (50) | Thomas BOYD (Celtic) | Mihails ZEMLINSKIS |
| (23) | Colin CALDERWOOD (Tottenham Hotspur) | Igors STEPANOVS |
| (28) | Colin HENDRY (Blackburn Rovers) | Iurijs SEVLAKOVS |
| (5) | Christian DAILLY (Derby County) | Imants BLEIDELIS |
| (55) | Gary McALLISTER (Coventry City) captain | Valerijs IVANOVS |
| (9) | Paul LAMBERT (Borussia Dortmund) | Olegs BLAGONADEZDINS |
| (45) | John COLLINS (Monaco) | Aleksandrs JELISEJEVS |
| (37) | Gordon DURIE (Rangers) | Vladimirs BABICEVS |
| (33) | Kevin GALLACHER (Blackburn Rovers) | Marians PAHARS |

Substitutions

| | | |
|---|---|---|
| (18) | Thomas McKINLAY (Celtic) | Andrejs STOLCERS |
| | for Boyd 81 mins | for Blagonadezdins 61 mins |
| (3) | Simon DONNELLY (Celtic) | Vits RIMKUS |
| | for Durie 84 mins | for Jelisejevs 68 mins |
| (21) | William McKINLAY (Blackburn Rovers) | |
| | for Burley 89 mins | |

**Goals**

| | | |
|---|---|---|
| Gallacher (43 mins) | 1-0 | |
| Durie (80 mins) | 2-0 | |

## 584

**(Friendly)**
12 November 1997

Referee: Lopez (Spain)
Stade Geoffroy Guichard, Saint-Etienne (Att: 19,514)

### FRANCE 2-1 SCOTLAND — Half-time 1-1

| | | |
|---|---|---|
| (2) | Neil SULLIVAN (Wimbledon) | Fabien BARTHEZ |
| (23) | Craig BURLEY (Celtic) | Lilian THURAM |
| (51) | Thomas BOYD (Celtic) captain | Pierre LAIGLE |
| (24) | Colin CALDERWOOD (Tottenham Hotspur) | Marcel DESAILLY |
| (3) | David WEIR (Hearts) | Laurent BLANC |
| (6) | Christian DAILLY (Derby County) | Emmanuel PETIT |
| (56) | Gary McALLISTER (Coventry City) | Didier DESCHAMPS |
| (22) | William McKINLAY (Blackburn Rovers) | Zinedine ZIDANE |
| (46) | John COLLINS (Monaco) | Ibrahim BA |
| (38) | Gordon DURIE (Rangers) | Stéphane GUIVARC'H |
| (34) | Kevin GALLACHER (Blackburn Rovers) | Lilian LASLANDES |

Substitutions

| | | |
|---|---|---|
| (1) | Matthew ELLIOTT (Leicester City) | Youri DJORKAEFF |
| | for Weir 76 mins | for Laslandes 71 mins |
| (19) | Thomas McKINLAY (Celtic) | Alain BOGHOSSIAN |
| | for Boyd 80 mins | for Petit 73 mins |
| (4) | Simon DONNELLY (Celtic) | Vincent CANDELA |
| | for Gallacher 83 mins | for Laigle 80 mins |
| (4) | David HOPKIN (Leeds United) | Franck GAVA |
| | for Durie 89 mins | for Ba 80 mins |

**Goals**

| | | |
|---|---|---|
| | 0-1 | Laigle (35 mins) |
| Durie (36 mins) | 1-1 | |
| | 1-2 | Djorkaeff (78 mins pen) |

# 1998

| P | W | D | L | F | A |
|---|---|---|---|---|---|
| 10 | 2 | 5 | 3 | 10 | 13 |

## 585

**(Friendly)**
25 March 1998

Referee: Gallagher (England)
Ibrox Stadium, Glasgow (Att: 26,468)

### SCOTLAND 0-1 DENMARK — Half-time 0-1

| | | |
|---|---|---|
| (84) | James LEIGHTON (Aberdeen) | Mogens KROGH |
| (5) | John McNAMARA (Celtic) | Jacob LAURSEN |
| (52) | Thomas BOYD (Celtic) | Jan HEINTZE |
| (2) | Matthew ELLIOTT (Leicester City) | Michael SCHJONBERG |
| (29) | Colin HENDRY (Blackburn Rovers) captain | Marc RIEPER |
| (25) | Colin CALDERWOOD (Tottenham Hotspur) | Thomas HELVEG |
| (12) | Scot GEMMILL (Nottingham Forest) | Morten WIEGHORST |
| (23) | William McKINLAY (Blackburn Rovers) | Michael LAUDRUP |
| (7) | Christian DAILLY (Derby County) | Allan NIELSEN |
| (14) | Scott BOOTH (Borussia Dortmund) | Brian LAUDRUP |
| (21) | Darren JACKSON (Celtic) | Peter MOLLER |

Substitutions

| | | |
|---|---|---|
| (43) | Andrew GORAM (Rangers) | René HENRIKSEN |
| | for Leighton 46 mins | for Laursen 46 mins |
| (14) | Eoin JESS (Aberdeen) | Per FRANDSEN |
| | for Booth 46 mins | for Nielsen 62 mins |
| (4) | David WEIR (Hearts) | Martin JORGENSEN |
| | for McNamara 59 mins | for Moller 74 mins |
| (40) | Stuart McCALL (Rangers) | Bjarne GOLDBAEK |
| | for Gemmill 69 mins | for B.Laudrup 80 mins |
| (5) | Simon DONNELLY (Celtic) | |
| | for Jackson 74 mins | |

**Goals**

| | | |
|---|---|---|
| | 0-1 | B. Laudrup (37 mins) |

## 586

**(Friendly)**
22 April 1998

Referee: Van Dijk (Netherlands)
Easter Road, Edinburgh (Att: 14,315)

### SCOTLAND 1-1 FINLAND — Half-time 1-1

| | | |
|---|---|---|
| (85) | James LEIGHTON (Aberdeen) | Antti NIEMI |
| (26) | Colin CALDERWOOD (Tottenham Hotspur) | Harri YLÖNEN |
| (8) | Christian DAILLY (Derby County) | Marko TUOMELA |
| (3) | Matthew ELLIOTT (Leicester City) | Jukka KOSKINEN |
| (30) | Colin HENDRY (Blackburn Rovers) captain | Sami HYYPIÄ |
| (11) | Derek WHYTE (Aberdeen) | Juha REINI |
| (13) | Scot GEMMILL (Nottingham Forest) | Simo VALAKARI |
| (24) | William McKINLAY (Blackburn Rovers) | Sami MAHLIO |
| (47) | John COLLINS (Monaco) | Antti SUMIALA |
| (15) | Scott BOOTH (Borussia Dortmund) | Jari LITMANEN |
| (22) | Darren JACKSON (Celtic) | Jonatan JOHANSSON |

Substitutions

| | | |
|---|---|---|
| (35) | Kevin GALLACHER (Blackburn Rovers) | Joonas KOLKKA |
| | for Jackson 46 mins | for Sumiala 37 mins |
| (5) | David WEIR (Hearts) | Aarno TURPEINEN |
| | for Elliott 46 mins | for Litmanen 46 mins |
| (39) | Gordon DURIE (Rangers) | Aki RIIHILAHTI |
| | for Calderwood 71 mins | for Reini 46 mins |
| (10) | Paul LAMBERT (Celtic) | Mika-Matti PAATELAINEN |
| | for Gemmill 76 mins | for Johansson 59 mins |
| (6) | Simon DONNELLY (Celtic) | Tomi KINNUNEN |
| | for Booth 76 mins | for Tuomela 64 mins |
| (53) | Thomas BOYD (Celtic) | |
| | for Dailly 87 mins | |

**Goals**

| | | |
|---|---|---|
| | 0-1 | Johansson (10 mins) |
| Jackson (15 mins) | 1-1 | |

## 587

**(Friendly)**
23 May 1998

Referee: Hall (USA)
Giants Stadium, East Rutherford (Att: 56,404)

### COLOMBIA 2-2 SCOTLAND — Half-time 1-2

| | | |
|---|---|---|
| (3) | Neil SULLIVAN (Wimbledon) | Miguel CALERO |
| (6) | John McNAMARA (Celtic) | Ivan CORDOBA |
| (54) | Thomas BOYD (Celtic) | Mauricio SERNA |
| (27) | Colin CALDERWOOD (Tottenham Hotspur) | José SANTA |
| (31) | Colin HENDRY (Blackburn Rovers) captain | Jorge BEMUDEZ |
| (11) | Paul LAMBERT (Celtic) | Harold LOZANO |
| (24) | Craig BURLEY (Celtic) | Carlos VALDERRAMA |
| (48) | John COLLINS (Monaco) | Wilmer CABRERA |
| (9) | Christian DAILLY (Derby County) | Faustino ASPRILLA |
| (23) | Darren JACKSON (Celtic) | Freddy RINCÓN |
| (40) | Gordon DURIE (Rangers) | Adolfo VALENCIA |

Substitutions

| | | |
|---|---|---|
| (16) | Scott BOOTH (Borussia Dortmund) | |
| | for Jackson 46 mins | |
| (7) | Simon DONNELLY (Celtic) | |
| | for Durie 61 mins | |
| (25) | William McKINLAY (Blackburn Rovers) | |
| | for McNamara 71 mins | |

**Goals**

| | | |
|---|---|---|
| | 0-1 | Valderrama (22 mins pen) |
| Collins (24 mins) | 1-1 | |
| Burley (33 mins) | 2-1 | |
| | 2-2 | Rincón (79 mins) |

John Collins scores from the spot to pull Scotland level against Brazil.

588
(Friendly)
30 May 1998

Referee: Ramos (Mexico)
R.F.K. Stadium, Washington DC (Att: 46,037)

## USA 0-0 SCOTLAND

| (86) | James LEIGHTON (Aberdeen) | Kasey KELLER |
|---|---|---|
| (10) | Christian DAILLY (Derby County) | David REGIS |
| (55) | Thomas BOYD (Celtic) | Edward POPE |
| (28) | Colin CALDERWOOD (Tottenham Hotspur) | Michael BURNS |
| (32) | Colin HENDRY (Blackburn Rovers) captain | Thomas DOOLEY |
| (2) | Paul LAMBERT (Celtic) | Chad DEERING |
| (26) | William McKINLAY (Blackburn Rovers) | Ernest STEWART |
| (49) | John COLLINS (Monaco) | Tabaré RAMOS |
| (20) | Thomas McKINLAY (Celtic) | Joseph-Max MOORE |
| (24) | Darren JACKSON (Celtic) | Cobi JONES |
| (86) | Kevin GALLACHER (Blackburn Rovers) | Roy WEGERLE |

Substitutions

| (7) | John McNAMARA (Celtic) | Predrag RADOSAVLJEVIC |
|---|---|---|
| | for T. McKinlay 60 mins | for Ramos 57 mins |
| (15) | Craig BURLEY (Celtic) | Eric WYNALDA |
| | for W. McKinlay 74 mins | for Wegerle 62 mins |
| (8) | Simon DONNELLY (Celtic) | Jeffrey AGOOS |
| | for Gallacher 82 mins | for Moore 70 mins |
| | | Alexei LALAS |
| | | for Stewart 82 mins |

589
(World Cup — Final Tournament 1st Round)
10 June 1998

Referee: Garcia (Spain)
Stade de France, Saint-Denis (Att: 80,000)

## BRAZIL 2-1 SCOTLAND
**Half-time 1-1**

| (7) | James LEIGHTON (Aberdeen) | Cláudio André TAFFAREL |
|---|---|---|
| (6) | Craig BURLEY (Celtic) | Marcos Evangelista CAFÚ |
| (6) | Thomas BOYD (Celtic) | ROBERTO CARLOS da Silva |
| (9) | Colin CALDERWOOD (Tottenham Hotspur) | Raimundo Ramos JUNIOR BAIANO |
| (3) | Colin HENDRY (Blackburn Rovers) captain | Nascimento dos Santos ALDAIR |
| (3) | Paul LAMBERT (Celtic) | GIOVANNI Silva de Oliveira |
| (5) | Darren JACKSON (Celtic) | Carlos CÉSAR SAMPAIO |
| (10) | John COLLINS (Monaco) | Carlos Caetano DUNGA |
| (11) | Christian DAILLY (Derby County) | Vito Borba Ferreira RIVALDO |
| (11) | Gordon DURIE (Rangers) | José Roberto Gama BEBETO |
| (7) | Kevin GALLACHER (Blackburn Rovers) | Luís Nazario da Lima RONALDO |

Substitutions

| (7) | William McKINLAY (Blackburn Rovers) | LEONARDO de Araujo |
|---|---|---|
| | for Jackson 78 mins | for Giovanni 46 mins |
| (11) | Thomas McKINLAY (Celtic) | DENILSON de Oliveira |
| | for Dailly 85 mins | for Bebeto 70 mins |

Goals

| | 0-1 | César Sampaio (4 mins) |
|---|---|---|
| Collins (38 mins pen) | 1-1 | |
| | 1-2 | Boyd (73 mins o.g.) |

Scotland's players take to the field in kilts before the opening game of the 1998 World Cup finals, against Brazil.

Ronaldo tries to go round Jim Leighton.

## 590

(World Cup — Final Tournament 1st Round)  
16 June 1998

Referee: Vagner (Hungary)  
Parc Lescure, Bordeaux (Att: 30,236)

### NORWAY 1-1 SCOTLAND — Half-time 0-0

| | | |
|---|---|---|
| (88) | James LEIGHTON (Aberdeen) | Frode GRODAAS |
| (30) | Colin CALDERWOOD (Tottenham Hotspur) | Henning BERG |
| (12) | Christian DAILLY (Derby County) | Stig-Inge BJORNEBYE |
| (57) | Thomas BOYD (Celtic) | Dan EGGEN |
| (34) | Colin HENDRY (Blackburn Rovers) captain | Ronny JOHNSEN |
| (27) | Craig BURLEY (Celtic) | Vidar RISETH |
| (14) | Paul LAMBERT (Celtic) | Staale SOLBAKKEN |
| (51) | John COLLINS (Monaco) | Roar STRAND |
| (26) | Darren JACKSON (Celtic) | Haavard FLO |
| (42) | Gordon DURIE (Rangers) | Kjetil REKDAL |
| (38) | Kevin GALLACHER (Blackburn Rovers) | Tore-André FLO |

Substitutions

| | | |
|---|---|---|
| (6) | David WEIR (Hearts) | Jan-Ivar JAKOBSEN |
| | for Calderwood 60 mins | for H. Flo 61 mins |
| (8) | John McNAMARA (Celtic) | Egil OSTENSTAD |
| | for Jackson 62 mins | for Riseth 72 mins |
| | | Gunnar HALLE |
| | | for Berg 82 mins |

Goals

| | | |
|---|---|---|
| | 0-1 | H. Flo (46 mins) |
| Burley (66 mins) | 1-1 | |

---

## 591

(World Cup — Final Tournament 1st Round)

23 June 1998

Referee: Bujsaim (United Arab Emirates)  
Stade Geoffroy Guichard, Saint-Etienne (Att: 35,500)

### MOROCCO 3-0 SCOTLAND — Half-time 1-0

| | | |
|---|---|---|
| (89) | James LEIGHTON (Aberdeen) | Driss BENZEKRI |
| (9) | John McNAMARA (Celtic) | Abdelilah SABER |
| (58) | Thomas BOYD (Celtic) | Smahi TRIKI |
| (7) | David WEIR (Hearts) | Lahcen ABRAMI |
| (35) | Colin HENDRY (Blackburn Rovers) captain | Noureddine NAYBET |
| (28) | Craig BURLEY (Celtic) | TAHAR El-Khalej |
| (15) | Paul LAMBERT (Celtic) | Gharib AMZINE |
| (52) | John COLLINS (Monaco) | Youssef CHIPPO |
| (13) | Christian DAILLY (Derby County) | Mustapha HADJI |
| (43) | Gordon DURIE (Rangers) | Abdeljilil HADDA |
| (39) | Kevin GALLACHER (Blackburn Rovers) | Salaheddine BASSIR |

Substitutions

| | | |
|---|---|---|
| (22) | Thomas McKINLAY (Celtic) | Youssef ROSSI |
| | for McNamara 54 mins | for Saber 72 mins |
| (17) | Scott BOOTH (Borussia Dortmund) | Rachid AZZOUZI |
| | for Durie 84 mins | for Amzine 77 mins |
| | | Jamal SELLAMI |
| | | for Chippo 87 mins |

Goals

| | | |
|---|---|---|
| | 0-1 | Bassir (22 mins) |
| | 0-2 | Hadda (47 mins) |
| | 0-3 | Bassir (84 mins) |

---

## 592

(European Championship — Qualifier)  
5 September 1998

Referee: Zotta (Romania)  
Zalgiris Stadionas, Vilnius (Att: 4,000)

### LITHUANIA 0-0 SCOTLAND

| | | |
|---|---|---|
| (90) | James LEIGHTON (Aberdeen) | Gintaras STAUCÉ |
| (31) | Colin CALDERWOOD (Tottenham Hotspur) | Andrius SKERLA |
| (59) | Thomas BOYD (Celtic) | Deividas SEMBERAS |
| (4) | Matthew ELLIOTT (Leicester City) | Tomas ZVIRGZDAUSKAS |
| (36) | Colin HENDRY (Rangers) captain | Virginijus BALTUSNIKAS |
| (16) | Paul LAMBERT (Celtic) | Gediminas SUGZDA |
| (27) | Darren JACKSON (Celtic) | Raimondas ZUTAUTUS |
| (53) | John COLLINS (Everton) | Aidas PREIKSAITIS |
| (14) | Christian DAILLY (Blackburn Rovers) | Edgaras JANKAUSKAS |
| (40) | Kevin GALLACHER (Blackburn Rovers) | Grazvydas MIKULENAS |
| (60) | Alistair McCOIST (Kilmarnock) | Aurelijus SKARBALIUS |

Substitutions

| | | |
|---|---|---|
| (1) | Barry FERGUSON (Rangers) | Orestas BUITKUS |
| | for Jackson 56 mins | for Sugzda 61 mins |
| (1) | Callum DAVIDSON (Blackburn Rovers) | Vaidotas SLEKYS |
| | for Calderwood 71 mins | for Mikulenas 90 mins |
| (1) | Neil McCANN (Hearts) | |
| | for McCoist 83 mins | |

---

## 593

(European Championship — Qualifier)  
10 October 1998

Referee: Marques (Portugal)  
Tynecastle Stadium, Edinburgh (Att: 16,930)

### SCOTLAND 3-2 ESTONIA — Half-time 0-1

| | | |
|---|---|---|
| (91) | James LEIGHTON (Aberdeen) | Mart POOM |
| (32) | Colin CALDERWOOD (Tottenham Hotspur) | Urmas KIRS |
| (60) | Thomas BOYD (Celtic) | Urmas ROOBA |
| (8) | David WEIR (Hearts) | Viktor ALONEN |
| (37) | Colin HENDRY (Rangers) captain | Sergei HOHLOV-SIMSON |
| (1) | Allan JOHNSTON (Sunderland) | Sergei TEREHHOV |
| (28) | William McKINLAY (Blackburn Rovers) | Martin REIM |
| (12) | Iain DURRANT (Kilmarnock) | Marko KRISTAL |
| (2) | Callum DAVIDSON (Blackburn Rovers) | Andres OPER |
| (41) | Kevin GALLACHER (Blackburn Rovers) | Maksim SMIRNOV |
| (61) | Alistair McCOIST (Kilmarnock) | Indrek ZELINSKI |

Substitutions

| | | |
|---|---|---|
| (28) | Darren JACKSON (Celtic) | Kristen VIIKMÄE |
| | for Gallacher 18 mins | for Zelinski 88 mins |
| (9) | Simon DONNELLY (Celtic) | |
| | for Calderwood 57 mins | |
| (5) | William DODDS (Dundee United) | |
| | for McCoist 69 mins | |

Goals

| | | |
|---|---|---|
| | 0-1 | Hohlov-Simson (34 mins) |
| Dodds (70 mins) | 1-1 | |
| | 1-2 | Smirnov (75 mins) |
| Hohlov-Simson (77 mins o.g.) | 2-2 | |
| Dodds (85 mins) | 3-2 | |

---

## 594

(European Championship — Qualifier)  
14 October 1998

Referee: Kapitanis (Cyprus)  
Pittodrie Stadium, Aberdeen (Att: 18,517)

### SCOTLAND 2-1 FAROE ISLANDS — Half-time 2-0

| | | |
|---|---|---|
| (4) | Neil SULLIVAN (Wimbledon) | Jákup MIKKELSEN |
| (9) | David WEIR (Hearts) | Óli JOHANNESEN |
| (61) | Thomas BOYD (Celtic) | Jens-Kristian HANSEN |
| (5) | Matthew ELLIOTT (Leicester City) | Pól THORSTEINSSON |
| (38) | Colin HENDRY (Rangers) captain | Hans-Fródi HANSEN |
| (2) | Allan JOHNSTON (Sunderland) | Henning JARNSKOR |
| (29) | William McKINLAY (Blackburn Rovers) | Julian JOHNSON |
| (29) | Craig BURLEY (Celtic) | Sámal JOENSEN |
| (3) | Callum DAVIDSON (Blackburn Rovers) | John PETERSEN |
| (10) | Simon DONNELLY (Celtic) | Uni ARGE |
| (6) | William DODDS (Dundee United) | Todi JÓNSSON |

Substitutions

| | | |
|---|---|---|
| (13) | Iain DURRANT (Kilmarnock) | Jákup á BORG |
| | for McKinlay 46 mins | for Arge 68 mins |
| (1) | Stephen GLASS (Newcastle United) | John HANSEN |
| | for Johnston 79 mins | for Jarnskor 79 mins |

Goals

| | | |
|---|---|---|
| Burley (21 mins) | 1-0 | |
| Dodds (45 mins) | 2-0 | |
| | 2-1 | Petersen (86 mins pen) |

---

# 1999

| P | W | D | L | F | A |
|---|---|---|---|---|---|
| 10 | 5 | 2 | 3 | 12 | 9 |

## 595

(European Championship — Qualifier)  
31 March 1999

Referee: Nielsen (Denmark)  
Celtic Park, Glasgow (Att: 44,513)

### SCOTLAND 1-2 CZECH REPUBLIC — Half-time 0-2

| | | |
|---|---|---|
| (5) | Neil SULLIVAN (Wimbledon) | Pavel SRNICEK |
| (10) | David WEIR (Everton) | Tomás VOTAVA |
| (4) | Callum DAVIDSON (Blackburn Rovers) | Jiri NEMEC |
| (6) | Matthew ELLIOTT (Leicester City) | Ján SUCHOPÁREK |
| (62) | Thomas BOYD (Celtic) | Michal HORNÁK |
| (5) | David HOPKIN (Leeds United) | Martin HASEK |
| (57) | Gary McALLISTER (Coventry City) captain | Karel POBORSKY |
| (17) | Paul LAMBERT (Celtic) | Pavel NEDVED |
| (30) | Craig BURLEY (Celtic) | Patrik BERGER |
| (2) | Neil McCANN (Rangers) | Vladimir SMICER |
| (15) | Eoin JESS (Aberdeen) | Vratislav LOKVENC |

Substitutions

| | | |
|---|---|---|
| (3) | Allan JOHNSTON (Sunderland) | Pavel KUKA |
| | for Davidson 52 mins | for Lokvenc 70 mins |
| (1) | Donald HUTCHISON (Everton) | Karel RADA |
| | for McAllister 63 mins | for Poborsky 76 mins |
| | | Miroslav BARANEK |
| | | for Smicer 84 mins |

Goals

| | | |
|---|---|---|
| | 0-1 | Elliott (27 mins o.g.) |
| | 0-2 | Smicer (35 mins) |
| Jess (68 mins) | 1-2 | |

Vladamir Smicer scores the Czech Republic's second goal in the European Championship qualifier at Celtic Park in March 1999.

Eoin Jess scores Scotland's goal against the Czechs.

(Friendly)
28 April 1999

Referee: Meier (Switzerland)
Weser Stadion, Bremen (Att: 28,000)

## GERMANY 0-1 SCOTLAND                      Half-time 0-0

| | | |
|---|---|---|
| (6) | Neil SULLIVAN (Wimbledon) | Jens LEHMANN |
| (1) | David WEIR (Everton) | Christian WORNS |
| (5) | Callum DAVIDSON (Blackburn Rovers) | Jörg HEINRICH |
| (63) | Thomas BOYD (Celtic) | Lothar MATTHÄUS |
| (39) | Colin HENDRY (Rangers) captain | Jens NOWOTNY |
| (4) | Scot GEMMILL (Everton) | Thomas STRUNZ |
| (18) | Paul LAMBERT (Celtic) | Jens JEREMIES |
| (4) | Iain DURRANT (Kilmarnock) | Dietmar HAMANN |
| (1) | Allan JOHNSTON (Sunderland) | Horst HELDT |

|  |  |  |
|---|---|---|
| (2) | Donald HUTCHISON (Everton) | Oliver NEUVILLE |
| (7) | William DODDS (Dundee United) | Oliver BIERHOFF |

**Substitutions**

| | | |
|---|---|---|
| (16) | Eoin JESS (Aberdeen) | Carsten RAMELÖW |
| | for Gemmill 59 mins | for Jeremies 46 mins |
| (1) | Paul RITCHIE (Hearts) | Michael BALLACK |
| | for Hendry 66 mins | for Hamann 59 mins |
| (1) | Robert WINTERS (Aberdeen) | Ulf KIRSTEN |
| | for Durrant 71 mins | for Bierhoff 59 mins |
| (12) | Derek WHYTE (Aberdeen) | Carsten JANCKER |
| | for Davidson 77 mins | for Strunz 87 mins |
| (1) | Colin CAMERON (Hearts) | |
| | for Lambert 83 mins | |
| (2) | Brian O'NEIL (Wolfsburg) | |
| | for Johnston 86 mins | |

| | Goals |
|---|---|
| Hutchison (65 mins) | 1-0 |

## 597

(European Championship — Qualifier)
5 June 1999

Referee: Kalt (France)
Svangaskard Stadion, Toftir (Att: 1,500)

### FAROE ISLANDS 1-1 SCOTLAND — Half-time 0-1

| | | |
|---|---|---|
| (7) | Neil SULLIVAN (Wimbledon) | Jákup MIKKELSEN |
| (12) | David WEIR (Everton) | Óli JOHANNESEN |
| (64) | Thomas BOYD (Celtic) captain | Ossur HANSEN |
| (33) | Colin CALDERWOOD (Aston Villa) | Pól THORSTEINSSON |
| (7) | Matthew ELLIOTT (Leicester City) | Hans-Fródi HANSEN |
| (5) | Allan JOHNSTON (Sunderland) | Jóhannis JOENSEN |
| (19) | Paul LAMBERT (Celtic) | Julian JOHNSSON |
| (15) | Iain DURRANT (Kilmarnock) | Sámal JOENSEN |
| (6) | Callum DAVIDSON (Blackburn Rovers) | Allan MORKORE |
| (8) | William DODDS (Dundee United) | John PETERSEN |
| (42) | Kevin GALLACHER (Blackburn Rovers) | Todi JÓNSSON |

Substitutions

| | | |
|---|---|---|
| (2) | Colin CAMERON (Hearts) | Jákup á BORG |
| | for Durrant 46 mins | for J. Joensen 69 mins |
| (15) | Scot GEMMILL (Everton) | Uni ARGE |
| | for Johnston 86 mins | for Petersen 79 mins |
| (17) | Eoin JESS (Aberdeen) | John HANSEN |
| | for Gallacher 89 mins | for O. Hansen 86 mins |

Goals

| | | |
|---|---|---|
| Johnston (38 mins) | 1-0 | |
| | 1-1 | H.F. Hansen (90 mins) |

## 598

(European Championship — Qualifier)
9 June 1999

Referee: Krug (Germany)
Sparta Stadion, Prague (Att: 22,000)

### CZECH REPUBLIC 3-2 SCOTLAND — Half-time 0-1

| | | |
|---|---|---|
| (8) | Neil SULLIVAN (Wimbledon) | Pavel SRNÍCEK |
| (13) | David WEIR (Everton) | Tomás REPKA |
| (65) | Thomas BOYD (Celtic) captain | Jirí NEMEC |
| (34) | Colin CALDERWOOD (Aston Villa) | Ján SUCHOPÁREK |
| (2) | Paul RITCHIE (Hearts) | Michal HORNÁK |
| (6) | Allan JOHNSTON (Sunderland) | Martin HASEK |
| (20) | Paul LAMBERT (Celtic) | Karel POBORSKY |
| (16) | Iain DURRANT (Kilmarnock) | Pavel NEDVED |
| (7) | Callum DAVIDSON (Blackburn Rovers) | Patrik BERGER |
| (9) | William DODDS (Dundee United) | Vladimír SMICER |
| (43) | Kevin GALLACHER (Blackburn Rovers) | Vratislav LOKVENC |

Substitutions

| | | |
|---|---|---|
| (18) | Eoin JESS (Aberdeen) | Miroslav BARANEK |
| | for Durrant 70 mins | for Hasek 60 mins |
| | | Pavel KUKA |
| | | for Lokvenc 68 mins |
| | | Ján KOLLER |
| | | for Poborsky 68 mins |

Goals

| | | |
|---|---|---|
| Ritchie (30 mins) | 1-0 | |
| Johnston (62 mins) | 2-0 | |
| | 2-1 | Repka (65 mins) |
| | 2-2 | Kuka (75 mins) |
| | 2-3 | Koller (87 mins) |

## 599

(European Championship — Qualifier)
4 September 1999

Referee: Lednikov (Russia)
Kosevo Stadion, Sarajevo (Att: 26,000)

### BOSNIA 1-2 SCOTLAND — Half-time 1-2

| | | |
|---|---|---|
| (9) | Neil SULLIVAN (Wimbledon) | Mirsad DEDIC |
| (14) | David WEIR (Everton) | Omar JOLDIC |
| (6) | David HOPKIN (Leeds United) | Jasmin MUJDZA |
| (35) | Colin CALDERWOOD (Aston Villa) | Muhamed KONJIC |
| (40) | Colin HENDRY (Rangers) captain | Mirsad HIBIC |
| (31) | Craig BURLEY (Celtic) | Bakir BESIREVIC |
| (2) | Barry FERGUSON (Rangers) | Sead HALILOVIC |
| (54) | John COLLINS (Everton) | Sergej BARBAREZ |
| (3) | Neil McCANN (Rangers) | Marko TOPIC |
| (3) | Donald HUTCHISON (Everton) | Meho KODRO |
| (10) | William DODDS (Dundee United) | Elvir BOLIC |

Substitutions

| | | |
|---|---|---|
| (15) | Christian DAILLY (Blackburn Rovers) | Edin MUJCIN |
| | for Calderwood 46 mins | for Halilovic 62 mins |
| (17) | Iain DURRANT (Kilmarnock) | Enes DEMIROVIC |
| | for Ferguson 70 mins | for Mujdza 78 mins |
| (44) | Kevin GALLACHER (Blackburn Rovers) | Senad REPUH |
| | for McCann 75 mins | for Joldic 78 mins |

Goals

| | | |
|---|---|---|
| Hutchison (13 mins) | 1-0 | |
| | 1-1 | Bolic (23 mins) |
| Dodds (45 mins) | 2-1 | |

## 600

(European Championship — Qualifier)
8 September 1999

Referee: Stuchlik (Austria)
Kadriorg Stadion, Tallinn (Att: 4,500)

### ESTONIA 0-0 SCOTLAND

| | | |
|---|---|---|
| (10) | Neil SULLIVAN (Wimbledon) | Mart POOM |
| (15) | David WEIR (Everton) | Urmas KIRS |
| (8) | Callum DAVIDSON (Blackburn Rovers) | Erko SAVIAUK |
| (16) | Christian DAILLY (Blackburn Rovers) | Sergei HOHLOV-SIMSON |
| (41) | Colin HENDRY (Rangers) captain | Raio PIIROJA |
| (32) | Craig BURLEY (Celtic) | Aivar ANNISTE |
| (18) | Iain DURRANT (Kilmarnock) | Martin REIM |
| (55) | John COLLINS (Everton) | Marko KRISTAL |
| (7) | Allan JOHNSTON (Sunderland) | Andres OPER |
| (4) | Donald HUTCHISON (Everton) | Sergei TEREHHOV |
| (11) | William DODDS (Dundee United) | Ivan O'KONNEL-BRONIN |

Substitutions

| | | |
|---|---|---|
| (4) | Neil McCANN (Rangers) | Indrek ZELINSKI |
| | for Johnston 54 mins | for O'Konnel-Bronin 46 mins |
| (3) | Barry FERGUSON (Rangers) | |
| | for Durrant 66 mins | |

## 601

(European Championship — Qualifier)
5 October 1999

Referee: Sundell (Sweden)
Ibrox Stadium, Glasgow (Att: 30,000)

### SCOTLAND 1-0 BOSNIA — Half-time 1-0

| | | |
|---|---|---|
| (11) | Neil SULLIVAN (Wimbledon) | Adnan GUSO |
| (16) | David WEIR (Everton) | Sead KAPETANOVIC |
| (9) | Callum DAVIDSON (Blackburn Rovers) | Bakir BESIREVIC |
| (17) | Christian DAILLY (Blackburn Rovers) | Faruk HUJDUROVIC |
| (42) | Colin HENDRY (Rangers) captain | Mirza VARESANOVIC |
| (33) | Craig BURLEY (Celtic) | Faruk IHTIJAREVIC |
| (21) | Paul LAMBERT (Celtic) | Sergej BARBAREZ |
| (7) | David HOPKIN (Leeds United) | Nermin SABIC |
| (56) | John COLLINS (Everton) | Elvir BALJIC |
| (12) | William DODDS (Dundee United) | Edin MUJCIN |
| (45) | Kevin GALLACHER (Newcastle United) | Elvir BOLIC |

Substitutions

| | | |
|---|---|---|
| (36) | Colin CALDERWOOD (Aston Villa) | Marko TOPIC |
| | for Hendry 37 mins | for Ihtijarevic 77 mins |
| (1) | Mark BURCHILL (Celtic) | Alen AVDIC |
| | for Gallacher 78 mins | for Mujcin 84 mins |
| (1) | Gary McSWEGAN (Hearts) | |
| | for Dodds 89 mins | |

Goals

| | | |
|---|---|---|
| Collins (25 mins pen) | 1-0 | |

## 602

(European Championship — Qualifier)
9 October 1999

Referee: Bré (France)
Hampden Park, Glasgow (Att: 22,059)

### SCOTLAND 3-0 LITHUANIA — Half-time 0-0

| | | |
|---|---|---|
| (1) | Jonathan GOULD (Celtic) | Pavelas LEUS |
| (17) | David WEIR (Everton) | Andrius SKERLA |
| (10) | Callum DAVIDSON (Blackburn Rovers) | Marius SKINDERIS |
| (3) | Brian O'NEIL (Wolfsburg) | Tomas ZVIRGZDAUSKAS |
| (3) | Paul RITCHIE (Hearts) | Darius ZUTAUTAS |
| (34) | Craig BURLEY (Celtic) | Irmantas STUMBRYS |
| (22) | Paul LAMBERT (Celtic) captain | Saulias MIKALAJUNAS |
| (5) | Donald HUTCHISON (Everton) | Andrejus TERESKINAS |
| (18) | Christian DAILLY (Blackburn Rovers) | Vidas DANCENKA |
| (2) | Gary McSWEGAN (Hearts) | Grazvydas MIKULENAS |
| (2) | Mark BURCHILL (Celtic) | Tomas RAZANAUSKAS |

Substitutions

| | | |
|---|---|---|
| (3) | Colin CAMERON (Hearts) | Donatas VENCEVICIUS |
| | for Burley 46 mins | for Stumbrys 54 mins |
| (13) | William DODDS (Dundee United) | Darius MACIULEVICIUS |
| | for Burchill 78 mins | for Dancenka 54 mins |
| (46) | Kevin GALLACHER (Newcastle United) | Arturas FOMENKA |
| | for McSwegan 82 mins | for Tereskinas 65 mins |

Goals

| | | |
|---|---|---|
| Hutchison (48 mins) | 1-0 | |
| McSwegan (50 mins) | 2-0 | |
| Cameron (88 mins) | 3-0 | |

**603**

(European Championship — Qualifier Play-off 1st Leg)    Referee: Diaz (Spain)
13 November 1999    Hampden Park, Glasgow (Att: 50,132)

## SCOTLAND 0-2 ENGLAND     Half-time 0-2

| | | |
|---|---|---|
| (12) | Neil SULLIVAN (Wimbledon) | David SEAMAN |
| (18) | David WEIR (Everton) | Solzeer CAMPBELL |
| (4) | Paul RITCHIE (Hearts) | Philip NEVILLE |
| (19) | Christian DAILLY (Blackburn Rovers) | Martin KEOWN |
| (43) | Colin HENDRY (Rangers) captain | Anthony ADAMS |
| (35) | Craig BURLEY (Celtic) | David BECKHAM |
| (4) | Barry FERGUSON (Rangers) | Paul INCE |
| (6) | Donald HUTCHISON (Everton) | Paul SCHOLES |
| (57) | John COLLINS (Everton) | James REDKNAPP |
| (14) | William DODDS (Dundee United) | Michael OWEN |
| (47) | Kevin GALLACHER (Newcastle United) | Alan SHEARER |

Substitutions

| | | |
|---|---|---|
| (3) | Mark BURCHILL (Celtic) | Andrew COLE |
| | for Gallacher 82 mins | for Owen 67 mins |

Goals
0-1    Scholes (21 mins)
0-2    Scholes (42 mins)

---

**604**

(European Championship — Qualifier Play-off 2nd Leg)

Referee: Collina (Italy)
17 November 1999    Wembley Stadium, London (Att: 76,848)

## ENGLAND 0-1 SCOTLAND     Half-time 0-1

| | | |
|---|---|---|
| 13) | Neil SULLIVAN (Wimbledon) | David SEAMAN |
| 19) | David WEIR (Everton) | Solzeer CAMPBELL |
| 11) | Callum DAVIDSON (Blackburn Rovers) | Philip NEVILLE |
| 20) | Christian DAILLY (Blackburn Rovers) | Gareth SOUTHGATE |
| 14) | Colin HENDRY (Rangers) captain | Anthony ADAMS |
| 36) | Craig BURLEY (Celtic) | David BECKHAM |
| 5) | Barry FERGUSON (Rangers) | Paul INCE |
| 58) | John COLLINS (Everton) | Paul SCHOLES |
| 5) | Neil McCANN (Rangers) | James REDKNAPP |
| 7) | Donald HUTCHISON (Everton) | Michael OWEN |
| 15) | William DODDS (Dundee United) | Alan SHEARER |

Substitutions

| | | |
|---|---|---|
| 4) | Mark BURCHILL (Celtic) | Emile HESKEY |
| | for McCann 74 mins | for Owen 63 mins |
| | | Raymond PARLOUR |
| | | for Scholes 89 mins |

Goals
Hutchison (38 mins)    1-0

---

# 2000

| P | W | D | L | F | A |
|---|---|---|---|---|---|
| 7 | 3 | 2 | 2 | 6 | 6 |

**605**

(Friendly)    Referee: Pedersen (Norway)
29 March 2000    Hampden Park, Glasgow (Att: 48,157)

## SCOTLAND 0-2 FRANCE     Half-time 0-0

| | | |
|---|---|---|
| (4) | Neil SULLIVAN (Wimbledon) | Ulrich RAMÉ |
| | Paul TELFER (Coventry City) | Lilian THURAM |
| | Paul RITCHIE (Bolton Wanderers) | Bixente LIZARAZU |
| (1) | Christian DAILLY (Blackburn Rovers) | Marcel DESAILLY |
| (5) | Colin HENDRY (Coventry City) captain | Laurent BLANC |
| (2) | Callum DAVIDSON (Blackburn Rovers) | Emmanuel PETIT |
| | Barry FERGUSON (Rangers) | Youri DJORKAEFF |
| | Donald HUTCHISON (Everton) | Didier DESCHAMPS |
| | Colin CAMERON (Hearts) | Ludovic GIULY |
| (6) | William DODDS (Rangers) | Christophe DUGARRY |
| (8) | Kevin GALLACHER (Newcastle United) | Thierry HENRY |

Substitutions

| | | |
|---|---|---|
| ) | Steven PRESSLEY (Hearts) | Johan MICOUD |
| | for Ritchie 46 mins | for Giuly 46 mins |
| ) | Neil McCANN (Rangers) | Sylvain WILTORD |
| | for Cameron 46 mins | for Djorkaeff 46 mins |
| ) | Allan JOHNSTON (Sunderland) | Patrick VIEIRA |
| | for Telfer 69 mins | for Deschamps 60 mins |
| | Mark BURCHILL (Celtic) | Robert PIRES |
| | for Gallacher 80 mins | for Dugarry 72 mins |

Goals
0-1    Wiltord (53 mins)
0-2    Henry (89 mins)

Billy Dodds goes past Emmanuel Petit of France at Hampden in March 2000.

Colin Cameron in action against Didier Deschamps of France.

**606**

(Friendly)    Referee: Strampe (Germany)
26 April 2000    Gelredome, Arnhem (Att: 24,500)

## NETHERLANDS 0-0 SCOTLAND

| | | |
|---|---|---|
| (15) | Neil SULLIVAN (Wimbledon) | Edwin VAN DER SAR |
| (20) | David WEIR (Everton) | André OOIJER |
| (6) | Paul RITCHIE (Bolton Wanderers) | Arthur NUMAN |
| (22) | Christian DAILLY (Blackburn Rovers) | Franciscus DE BOER |
| (8) | Matthew ELLIOTT (Leicester City) | Bertus KONTERMAN |
| (10) | John McNAMARA (Celtic) | Marc OVERMARS |
| (23) | Paul LAMBERT (Celtic) captain | Paul BOSVELT |
| (37) | Craig BURLEY (Derby County) | Edgar DAVIDS |
| (7) | Neil McCANN (Rangers) | Roy MAKAAY |
| (9) | Donald HUTCHISON (Everton) | Dennis BERGKAMP |
| (17) | William DODDS (Rangers) | Jimmy-Floyd HASSELBAINK |

Substitutions

| | | |
|---|---|---|
| (19) | Iain DURRANT (Kilmarnock) | Boudewijn ZENDEN |
| | for Burley 46 mins | for Overmars 46 mins |
| (6) | Mark BURCHILL (Celtic) | Patrick KLUIVERT |
| | for McNamara 66 mins | for Bergkamp 46 mins |
| (4) | Brian O'NEIL (Wolfsburg) | Jeffrey TALAN |
| | for Dailly 85 mins | for Makaay 60 mins |
| | | Pierre VAN HOOIJDONK |
| | | for Hasselbaink 66 mins |

Matt Elliott looks on as his header beats Gasperoni of San Marino  but only hits the upright in the World Cup qualifier at Hampden in March 2001.

## 607

**(Friendly)**
**30 May 2000**

Referee: Pereira (Portugal)
Lansdowne Road, Dublin (Att: 30,213)

### REPUBLIC OF IRELAND 1-2 SCOTLAND — Half-time 1-2

| | | |
|---|---|---|
| (16) | Neil SULLIVAN (Wimbledon) | Alan KELLY |
| (23) | Christian DAILLY (Blackburn Rovers) | Stephen CARR |
| (1) | Gary NAYSMITH (Hearts) | Kevin KILBANE |
| (5) | Brian O'NEIL (Wolfsburg) | Philip BABB |
| (9) | Matthew ELLIOTT (Leicester City) | Gary BREEN |
| (38) | Craig BURLEY (Derby County) | Jason McATEER |
| (7) | Barry FERGUSON (Rangers) | Stephen McPHAIL |
| (24) | Paul LAMBERT (Celtic) captain | Steven FINNAN |
| (8) | Neil McCANN (Rangers) | Mark KENNEDY |
| (10) | Donald HUTCHISON (Everton) | Robert KEANE |
| (18) | William DODDS (Rangers) | Niall QUINN |

**Substitutions**

| | | |
|---|---|---|
| (49) | Kevin GALLACHER (Newcastle United) | Damien DUFF |
| | for Dodds 46 mins | for McPhail 61 mins |
| (9) | Allan JOHNSTON (Sunderland) | Terence PHELAN |
| | for Lambert 75 mins | for Kennedy 61 mins |
| (5) | Colin CAMERON (Hearts) | Richard DUNNE |
| | for Ferguson 84 mins | for Quinn 77 mins |
| (20) | Iain DURRANT (Kilmarnock) | Dominic FOLEY |
| | for Naysmith 89 mins | for Breen 77 mins |
| (2) | Steven PRESSLEY (Hearts) | |
| | for McCann 90 mins | **Goals** |
| | | 0-1 | Burley (2 mins o.g.) |
| Hutchison (15 mins) | | 1-1 |
| Ferguson (27 mins) | | 2-1 |

## 608

**(World Cup — Qualifier)**
**2 September 2000**

Referee: Schluchter (Switzerland)
Skonto Stadion, Riga (Att: 9,500)

### LATVIA 0-1 SCOTLAND — Half-time 0-0

| | | |
|---|---|---|
| (17) | Neil SULLIVAN (Tottenham Hotspur) | Aleksandrs KOLINKO |
| (21) | David WEIR (Everton) | Iurijs LAIZANS |
| (13) | Callum DAVIDSON (Leicester City) | Valentins LOBANOVS |
| (24) | Christian DAILLY (Blackburn Rovers) | Valerijs IVANOVS |
| (46) | Colin HENDRY (Coventry City) captain | Igors STEPANOVS |
| (66) | Thomas BOYD (Celtic) | Olegs BLAGONADEZDINS |
| (11) | Donald HUTCHISON (Sunderland) | Vitalijs ASTAFJEVS |
| (8) | Barry FERGUSON (Rangers) | Imants BLEIDELIS |
| (9) | Neil McCANN (Rangers) | Andrejs RUBINS |
| (10) | Matthew ELLIOTT (Leicester City) | Andrejs STOLCERS |
| (19) | William DODDS (Rangers) | Marians PAHARS |

**Substitutions**

| | | |
|---|---|---|
| (6) | Colin CAMERON (Hearts) | |
| | for Weir 46 mins | |
| (2) | Gary NAYSMITH (Hearts) | |
| | for Davidson 46 mins | |
| (1) | Gary HOLT (Kilmarnock) | |
| | for Dodds 90 mins | |
| | | **Goals** |
| McCann (88 mins) | | 1-0 |

## 609

**(World Cup — Qualifier)**
**7 October 2000**

Referee: Orrason (Iceland)
Stadio Olimpico, Serravalle (Att: 4,377)

### SAN MARINO 0-2 SCOTLAND — Half-time 0-0

| | | |
|---|---|---|
| (18) | Neil SULLIVAN (Tottenham Hotspur) | Federico GASPERONI |
| (25) | Christian DAILLY (Blackburn Rovers) | Mirco GENNARI |
| (11) | Matthew ELLIOTT (Leicester City) | Mauro MARIANI |
| (47) | Colin HENDRY (Coventry City) | Luca GOBBI |
| (11) | John McNAMARA (Celtic) | Ivan MATTEONI |
| (3) | Gary NAYSMITH (Hearts) | Simone BACCIOCCHI |
| (7) | Colin CAMERON (Hearts) | Pierangelo MANZAROLI |
| (12) | Donald HUTCHISON (Sunderland) | Ermanno ZONZINI |
| (10) | Neil McCANN (Rangers) | Bryan GASPERONI |
| (20) | William DODDS (Rangers) | Riccardo MUCCIOLI |
| (50) | Kevin GALLACHER (Newcastle United) captain | Paolo MONTAGNA |

**Substitutions**

| | | |
|---|---|---|
| (22) | David WEIR (Everton) | Marco DE LUIGI |
| | for Dailly 36 mins | for Montagna 60 mins |
| (10) | Allan JOHNSTON (Rangers) | Vittorio VALENTINI |
| | for McCann 46 mins | for Matteoni 73 mins |
| (1) | Paul DICKOV (Manchester City) | Pierdomenico DELLA VALLE |
| | for Gallacher 66 mins | for Zonzini 80 mins |
| | | **Goals** |
| Elliott (71 mins) | | 1-0 |
| Hutchison (73 mins) | | 2-0 |

## 610

**(World Cup — Qualifier)**
**11 October 2000**

Referee: Veissiere (France)
Maksimir Stadion, Zagreb (Att: 30,000)

### CROATIA 1-1 SCOTLAND — Half-time 1-1

| | | |
|---|---|---|
| (19) | Neil SULLIVAN (Tottenham Hotspur) | Zeljko PAVLOVIC |
| (23) | David WEIR (Everton) | Robert KOVAC |
| (4) | Gary NAYSMITH (Hearts) | Robert JARNI |
| (12) | Matthew ELLIOTT (Leicester City) | Igor STIMAC |
| (48) | Colin HENDRY (Coventry City) captain | Zvonimir SOLDO |
| (67) | Thomas BOYD (Celtic) | Danijel SARIC |
| (39) | Craig BURLEY (Derby County) | Robert PROSINECKI |
| (13) | Donald HUTCHISON (Sunderland) | Dario SIMIC |
| (8) | Colin CAMERON (Hearts) | Niko KOVAC |
| (11) | Allan JOHNSTON (Rangers) | Bosko BALABAN |
| (51) | Kevin GALLACHER (Newcastle United) | Alen BOKSIC |

**Substitutions**

| | | |
|---|---|---|
| (2) | Paul DICKOV (Manchester City) | Boris ZIVKOVIC |
| | for Johnston 46 mins | for Jarni 46 mins |
| (2) | Gary HOLT (Kilmarnock) | Igor BISCAN |
| | for Dickov 89 mins | for Soldo 46 mins |
| | | Davor VUGRINEC |
| | | for Boksic 75 mins |
| | | **Goals** |
| | | 0-1 | Boksic (15 mins) |
| Gallacher (24 mins) | | 1-1 |

**611**

(Friendly)
15 November 2000

Referee: Garibian (France)
Hampden Park, Glasgow (Att: 30,985)

### SCOTLAND 0-2 AUSTRALIA                Half-time 0-1

| | | |
|---|---|---|
| (2) | Jonathan GOULD (Celtic) | Mark SCHWARZER |
| (68) | Thomas BOYD (Celtic) captain | Kevin MUSCAT |
| (26) | Christian DAILLY (Blackburn Rovers) | Shaun MURPHY |
| (6) | Brian O'NEIL (Derby County) | Paul OKON |
| (24) | David WEIR (Everton) | Anthony POPOVIC |
| (40) | Craig BURLEY (Derby County) | Paul AGOSTINO |
| (9) | Barry FERGUSON (Rangers) | Stanley LAZARIDIS |
| (9) | Colin CAMERON (Hearts) | Josip SKOKO |
| (1) | Dominic MATTEO (Leeds United) | Daniel TIATTO |
| (14) | Donald HUTCHISON (Sunderland) | Brett EMERTON |
| (21) | William DODDS (Rangers) | David ZDRILIC |

Substitutions

| | | |
|---|---|---|
| (13) | Matthew ELLIOTT (Leicester City) | Mile STERJOVSKI |
| | for Weir 46 mins | for Agostino 46 mins |
| (11) | Neil McCANN (Rangers) | Jacob BURNS |
| | for Cameron 46 mins | for Tiatto 67 mins |
| (49) | Colin HENDRY (Coventry City) | Kasey WEHRMAN |
| | for O'Neil 58 mins | for Skoko 75 mins |
| (3) | Paul DICKOV (Manchester City) | Clayton ZANE |
| | for Burley 63 mins | for Zdrilic 89 mins |

Goals

| | |
|---|---|
| 0-1 | Emerton (12 mins) |
| 0-2 | Zdrilic (66 mins) |

# 2001

| P | W | D | L | F | A |
|---|---|---|---|---|---|
| 3 | 1 | 2 | 0 | 7 | 3 |

**612**

(World Cup — Qualifier)
24 March 2001

Referee: Nielsen (Denmark)
Hampden Park, Glasgow (Att: 37,480)

### SCOTLAND 2-2 BELGIUM                Half-time 2-0

| | | |
|---|---|---|
| (20) | Neil SULLIVAN (Tottenham Hotspur) | Geert DE VLIEGER |
| (25) | David WEIR (Everton) | Eric DEFLANDRE |
| (14) | Matthew ELLIOTT (Leicester City) | Didier DHEEDENE |
| (50) | Colin HENDRY (Bolton Wanderers) captain | Joos VALGAEREN |
| (69) | Thomas BOYD (Celtic) | Glen DE BOECK |
| (41) | Craig BURLEY (Derby County) | Mark HENDRIKX |
| (10) | Barry FERGUSON (Rangers) | Yves VANDERHAEGHE |
| (25) | Paul LAMBERT (Celtic) | Walter BASEGGIO |
| (2) | Dominic MATTEO (Leeds United) | Bart GOOR |
| (15) | Donald HUTCHISON (Sunderland) | Marc WILMOTS |
| (22) | William DODDS (Rangers) | Emile MPENZA |

Substitutions

| | | |
|---|---|---|
| (52) | Kevin GALLACHER (Newcastle United) | Bob PEETERS |
| | for Dodds 88 mins | for Hendrikx 46 mins |
| | | Daniel VAN BUYTEN |
| | | for Valgaeren 57 mins |
| | | Sven VERMANT |
| | | for Baseggio 79 mins |

Goals

| | | |
|---|---|---|
| Dodds (2 mins) | 1-0 | |
| Dodds (29 mins pen) | 2-0 | |
| | 2-1 | Wilmots (58 mins) |
| | 2-2 | Van Buyten (90 mins) |

**613**

(World Cup — Qualifier)
28 March 2001

Referee: Kari (Finland)
Hampden Park, Glasgow (Att: 27,313)

### SCOTLAND 4-0 SAN MARINO                Half-time 3-0

| | | |
|---|---|---|
| (21) | Neil SULLIVAN (Tottenham Hotspur) | Federico GASPERONI |
| (26) | David WEIR (Everton) | Simone DELLA BALDA |
| (15) | Matthew ELLIOTT (Leicester City) | Mauro MARANI |
| (51) | Colin HENDRY (Bolton Wanderers) captain | Luca GOBBI |
| (42) | Craig BURLEY (Derby County) | Simone BACCIOCCHI |
| (26) | Paul LAMBERT (Celtic) | Riccardo MUCCIOLI |
| (10) | Colin CAMERON (Hearts) | Ermanno ZONZINI |
| (3) | Dominic MATTEO (Leeds United) | Ivan MATTEONI |
| (12) | Allan JOHNSTON (Rangers) | Damiano VANNUCCI |
| (16) | Donald HUTCHISON (Sunderland) | Pierangelo MANZAROLI |
| (23) | William DODDS (Rangers) | Andy SELVA |

Substitutions

| | | |
|---|---|---|
| (70) | Thomas BOYD (Celtic) | Ivan BUGLI |
| | for Elliott 46 mins | for Vannucci 70 mins |
| (53) | Kevin GALLACHER (Newcastle United) | Roberto SELVA |
| | for Matteo 64 mins | for Manzaroli 81 mins |
| (6) | Scott GEMMILL (Everton) | Nicola ALBANI |
| | for Cameron 83 mins | for Della Balda 90 mins |

Goals

| | |
|---|---|
| Hendry (22 mins) | 1-0 |
| Hendry (33 mins) | 2-0 |
| Dodds (34 mins) | 3-0 |
| Cameron (65 mins) | 4-0 |

Hendry celebrates with Dominic Matteo and Colin Cameron (right) after scoring his 22nd-minute goal. 11-minutes later, he added a second in their 4-0 win against San Marino.

**614**

(Friendly)
25 April 2001

Referee: Roca (Spain)
Zawisza Stadion, Bydgoszcz (Att: 20,000)

### POLAND 1-1 SCOTLAND                Half-time 0-0

| | | |
|---|---|---|
| (22) | Neil SULLIVAN (Tottenham Hotspur) | Jerzy DUDEK |
| (27) | Christian DAILLY (West Ham United) | Tomasz KLOS |
| (71) | Thomas BOYD (Celtic) captain | Jacek ZIELINSKI |
| (1) | Barry NICHOLSON (Dunfermline Athletic) | Tomasz WALDOCH |
| (1) | Charles MILLER (Dundee United) | Michal ZEWLAKOW |
| (1) | Gavin RAE (Dundee) | Tomasz IWAN |
| (1) | John O'NEIL (Hibernian) | Tomasz HAJTO |
| (14) | Callum DAVIDSON (Leicester City) | Tomasz ZDEBEL |
| (11) | Colin CAMERON (Hearts) | Marek KOZMINSKI |
| (18) | Scott BOOTH (Twente Enschede) | Marcin ZEWLAKOW |
| (24) | William DODDS (Rangers) | Pawel KRYSZALOWICZ |

Substitutions

| | | |
|---|---|---|
| (1) | Andrew McLAREN (Kilmarnock) | Jacek KRZYNOWEK |
| | for Cameron 46 mins | for Michal Zewlakow 46 mins |
| (2) | Steven CRAWFORD (Dunfermline Athletic) | Radoslaw KALUZNY |
| | for Dodds 46 mins | for Zielinski 46 mins |
| (1) | Stephen CALDWELL (Newcastle United) | Piotr SWIERCZEWSKI |
| | for C.Miller 56 mins | for Zdebel 58 mins |
| (27) | David WEIR (Everton) | Marcin MIECIEL |
| | for Davidson 72 mins | for Marcin Zewlakow 63 mins |
| (17) | Scott GEMMILL (Everton) | Maciej ZURAWSKI |
| | for O'Neil 73 mins | for Kryszalowicz 75 mins |
| (1) | Kenneth MILLER (Rangers) | |
| | for Booth 80 mins | |

Goals

| | | |
|---|---|---|
| | 0-1 | Kaluzny (49 mins) |
| Booth (69 mins pen) | 1-1 | |

# The Players

1  ROBERT GARDNER (5/0)  — (with Queen's Park, Glasgow)
1872  v England
1873  v England
— (with Clydesdale, Glasgow)
1874  v England
1875  v England
1878  v England

2  JOSEPH TAYLOR (6/0)  — (with Queen's Park, Glasgow)
1851, Dunoon  1872  v England
1873  v England
1874  v England
1875  v England
1876  v England, Wales

3  WILLIAM KER (2/0)  — (with Queen's Park, Glasgow)
Glasgow  1872  v England
1873  v England

4  JAMES THOMSON (3/0)  — (with Queen's Park, Glasgow)
1872  v England
1873  v England
1874  v England

5  JAMES SMITH (1/0)  — (with Queen's Park, Glasgow)
1872  v England

6  WILLIAM MacKINNON (9/5)  — (with Queen's Park, Glasgow)
1872  v England
1873  v England
1874  v England
1875  v England
1876  v England (1), Wales (1)
1877  v England
1878  v England (1)
1879  v England (2)

7  JAMES WEIR (4/2)  — (with Queen's Park, Glasgow)
1853, Glasgow  1872  v England
1874  v England
1875  v England
1878  v Wales (2)

8  ROBERT LECKIE (1/0)  — (with Queen's Park, Glasgow)
1872  v England

9  DAVID WOTHERSPOON (2/0)  — (with Queen's Park, Glasgow)
1872  v England
1873  v England

10  ROBERT SMITH (2/0)  — (with Queen's Park, Glasgow)
1872  v England
1873  v England

11  ALEXANDER RHIND (1/0)  — (with Queen's Park, Glasgow)
Aberdeen  1872  v England

12  HENRY RENNY-TAILYOUR (1/1)  — (with Royal Engineers, Chatham)
9 October 1849, Mussoorie, India  1873  v England (1)

13  ARTHUR KINNAIRD (1/0)  — (with The Wanderers, London)
16 February 1847, London, England  1873  v England

14  JOHN BLACKBURN (1/0)  — (with Royal Engineers, Chatham)
30 April 1851, Edinburgh  1873  v England

15  WILLIAM GIBB (1/1)  — (with Clydesdale, Glasgow)
1873  v England (1)

16  JOHN HUNTER (4/0)  — (with Third Lanark, Glasgow)
Joppa  1874  v England
— (with Eastern, Glasgow)
1875  v England
— (with Third Lanark, Glasgow)
1876  v England
1877  v Wales

17  CHARLES CAMPBELL (13/1)  — (with Queen's Park, Glasgow)
Coupar Angus  1874  v England
1876  v Wales
1877  v England, Wales (1)
1878  v England
1879  v England
1880  v England
1881  v England
1882  v England, Wales
1884  v England
1885  v England
1886  v England

18  JOHN FERGUSON (6/5)  — (with Vale of Leven, Alexandria)
1848, Alexandria  1874  v England
1876  v England, Wales (1)
1877  v England (2), Wales
1878  v Wales (2)

19  HENRY McNEIL (10/6)  — (with Queen's Park, Glasgow)
Rhu  1874  v England
1875  v England (1)
1876  v England (1), Wales (1)
1877  v Wales
1878  v England (2)
1879  v England, Wales
1881  v England, Wales (1)

20  ANGUS McKINNON (1/1)  — (with Queen's Park, Glasgow)
1874  v England (1)

21  FREDERICK ANDERSON (1/1)  — (with Clydesdale, Glasgow)
1874  v England (1)

22  ALEXANDER KENNEDY (6/0)  — (with Eastern, Glasgow)
Dalquhairn  1875  v England
1876  v England, Wales
— (with Third Lanark, Glasgow)
1878  v England
1882  v Wales
1884  v Wales

23  ALEXANDER McLINTOCK (3/0)  — (with Vale of Leven, Alexandria)
Paisley  1875  v England
1876  v England
1880  v England

24  THOMAS HIGHET (4/1)  — (with Queen's Park, Glasgow)
1853, Ayr  1875  v England
1876  v England (1), Wales
1878  v England

25  PETER ANDREWS (1/1)  — (with Eastern, Glasgow)
1875  v England (1)

26  JOHN McPHERSON (1/0)  — (with Clydesdale, Glasgow)
1875  v England

27  ALEXANDER McGEOCH (4/0)  — (with Dumbreck, Glasgow)
1855  1876  v England, Wales
1877  v England, Wales

28  WILLIAM MILLER (1/0)  — (with Third Lanark, Glasgow)
1876  v England

29  JOHN BAIRD (3/2)  — (with Vale of Leven, Alexandria)
27 July 1856, Alexandria  1876  v England
1878  v Wales (1)
1880  v England (1)

30  ROBERT NEILL (5/0)  — (with Queen's Park, Glasgow)
1876  v Wales
1877  v England, Wales
1878  v Wales
1880  v England

| 31 | JAMES LANG (2/2) 12 March 1851, Glasgow | – | (with Clydesdale, Glasgow) 1876  v Wales (1) |
| | | – | (with Third Lanark, Glasgow) 1878  v Wales (1) |
| 32 | MOSES McNEIL (2/0) 29 October 1855, Rhu | – | (with Rangers, Glasgow) 1876  v Wales 1880  v England |
| 33 | THOMAS VALLANCE (7/0) 1856, Succoth | – | (with Rangers, Glasgow) 1877  v England, Wales 1878  v England 1879  v England, Wales 1881  v England, Wales |
| 34 | JAMES PHILLIPS (3/0) | – | (with Queen's Park, Glasgow) 1877  v England, Wales 1878  v Wales |
| 35 | JAMES RICHMOND (3/1) 22 March 1858, Glasgow | – | (with Clydesdale, Glasgow) 1877  v England (1) |
| | | – | (with Queen's Park, Glasgow) 1878  v England 1882  v Wales |
| 36 | JOHN McGREGOR (4/1) 1851, Alexandria | – | (with Vale of Leven, Alexandria) 1877  v England, Wales 1878  v England (1) 1880  v England |
| 37 | JOHN McDOUGALL (5/4) 1853 | – | (with Vale of Leven, Alexandria) 1877  v England, Wales 1878  v England (3) 1879  v England (1), Wales |
| 38 | JOHN SMITH (10/10) 12 August 1855, Mauchline | – | (with Mauchline) 1877  v England, Wales 1879  v England (1), Wales (2) |
| | | – | (with Edinburgh University) 1880  v England 1881  v England (3), Wales |
| | | – | (with Queen's Park, Glasgow) 1883  v England (2), Wales (1) 1884  v England (1) |
| 39 | ANDREW McINTYRE (2/0) 9 August 1855, Bonhill | – | (with Vale of Leven, Alexandria) 1878  v England 1882  v England |
| 40 | ROBERT PARLANE (3/0) Bonhill | – | (with Vale of Leven, Alexandria) 1878  v Wales 1879  v England, Wales |
| 41 | JAMES DUNCAN (2/0) | – | (with Alexandra Athletic, Glasgow) 1878  v Wales 1882  v Wales |
| 42 | DAVID DAVIDSON (5/1) Glasgow | – | (with Queen's Park, Glasgow) 1878  v Wales 1879  v Wales 1880  v Wales (1) 1881  v England, Wales |
| 43 | JAMES WATSON (1/1) | – | (with Rangers, Glasgow) 1878  v Wales (1) |
| 44 | PETER CAMPBELL (2/3) Rhu | – | (with Rangers, Glasgow) 1878  v Wales (2) 1879  v Wales (1) |
| 45 | WILLIAM SOMERS (3/0) | – | (with Third Lanark, Glasgow) 1879  v England, Wales |
| | | – | (with Queen's Park, Glasgow) 1880  v Wales |
| 46 | JOHN McPHERSON (8/0) | – | (with Vale of Leven, Alexandria) 1879  v England, Wales 1880  v England 1881  v Wales 1883  v England, Wales 1884  v England 1885  v Ireland |

| 47 | ROBERT PATON (2/0) Bonhill | – | (with Vale of Leven, Alexandria) 1879  v England, Wales |
| 48 | WILLIAM BEVERIDGE (3/1) 27 November 1858, Cumnock | – | (with Ayr Academy) 1879  v England, Wales |
| | | – | (with Edinburgh University) 1880  v Wales (1) |
| 49 | ARCHIBALD ROWAN (2/0) | – | (with Caledonian, Glasgow) 1880  v England |
| | | – | (with Queen's Park, Glasgow) 1882  v Wales |
| 50 | GEORGE KER (5/10) Glasgow | – | (with Queen's Park, Glasgow) 1880  v England (3) 1881  v England (2), Wales (2) 1882  v England (2), Wales (1) |
| 51 | JOHN KAY (6/5) Glasgow | – | (with Queen's Park, Glasgow) 1880  v England (1) 1882  v England (1), Wales (1) 1883  v England, Wales 1884  v Wales (2) |
| 52 | GEORGE GILLESPIE (7/0) 22 June 1859, Stirling | – | (with Rangers, Glasgow) 1880  v Wales 1881  v England, Wales 1882  v England |
| | | – | (with Queen's Park, Glasgow) 1886  v Wales |
| | | – | (with Rangers, Glasgow) 1890  v Wales |
| | | – | (with Queen's Park, Glasgow) 1891  v Ireland |
| 53 | ARCHIBALD LANG (1/0) | – | (with Dumbarton) 1880  v Wales |
| 54 | HUGH McINTYRE (1/0) 27 June 1855, Glasgow | – | (with Rangers, Glasgow) 1880  v Wales |
| 55 | JAMES DOUGLAS (1/0) 3 September 1859, Renfrew | – | (with Renfrew) 1880  v Wales |
| 56 | J. McADAM (1/1) | – | (with Third Lanark, Glasgow) 1880  v Wales (1) |
| 57 | MALCOLM FRASER (5/4) | – | (with Queen's Park, Glasgow) 1880  v Wales 1882  v England, Wales (2) 1883  v England (1), Wales (1) |
| 58 | JOSEPH LINDSAY (8/6) 13 November 1858, Dumbarton | – | (with Dumbarton) 1880  v Wales (1) 1881  v England, Wales 1884  v England, Wales (1) 1885  v England (1), Wales (3) 1886  v England |
| 59 | JOHN CAMPBELL (1/1) | – | (with South Western, Glasgow) 1880  v Wales (1) |
| 60 | ANDREW WATSON (3/0) 18 May 1857 | – | (with Queen's Park, Glasgow) 1881  v England, Wales 1882  v England |
| 61 | DAVID HILL (3/1) | – | (with Rangers, Glasgow) 1881  v England (1), Wales 1882  v Wales |
| 62 | WILLIAM McGUIRE (2/0) 24 March 1860, Beith | – | (with Beith) 1881  v England, Wales |
| 63 | PETER MILLER (3/0) | – | (with Dumbarton) 1882  v England 1883  v England, Wales |
| 64 | WILLIAM ANDERSON (6/3) Glasgow | – | (with Queen's Park, Glasgow) 1882  v England 1883  v England, Wales (1) 1884  v England 1885  v England, Wales (2) |

| | | | |
|---|---|---|---|
| 65 | WILLIAM HARROWER (3/4) | – | (with Queen's Park, Glasgow) |
| | 9 October 1861, Glasgow | | 1882 v England (1) |
| | | | 1884 v Ireland (2) |
| | | | 1886 v Wales (1) |
| 66 | ROBERT McPHERSON (1/1) | – | (with Arthurlie, Barrhead) |
| | | | 1882 v England (1) |
| 67 | ANDREW HOLM (3/0) | – | (with Queen's Park, Glasgow) |
| | 4 November 1859, Glasgow | | 1882 v Wales |
| | | | 1883 v England, Wales |
| 68 | JAMES McAULAY (9/1) | – | (with Dumbarton) |
| | 28 August 1860, Bonhill | | 1882 v Wales (1) |
| | | | 1883 v England, Wales |
| | | | 1884 v England |
| | | | 1885 v England, Wales |
| | | | 1886 v England |
| | | | 1887 v England, Wales |
| 69 | MICHAEL PATON (5/0) | – | (with Dumbarton) |
| | | | 1883 v England |
| | | – | 1884 v Wales |
| | | | 1885 v England, Wales |
| | | | 1886 v England |
| 70 | JOHN INGLIS (2/0) | – | (with Rangers, Glasgow) |
| | 1859, Glasgow | | 1883 v England, Wales |
| 71 | WILLIAM McKINNON (4/0) | – | (with Dumbarton) |
| | 6 June 1859, Bonhill | | 1883 v England, Wales |
| | | | 1884 v England, Wales |
| 72 | WALTER ARNOTT (14/0) | – | (with Queen's Park, Glasgow) |
| | 12 May 1863, Glasgow | | 1883 v Wales |
| | | | 1884 v Ireland, England |
| | | | 1885 v England, Wales |
| | | | 1886 v England |
| | | | 1887 v England, Wales |
| | | | 1888 v England |
| | | | 1889 v England |
| | | | 1890 v England |
| | | | 1891 v England |
| | | | 1892 v England |
| | | | 1893 v England |
| 73 | JOHN INGLIS (1/0) | – | (with Kilmarnock Athletic) |
| | | | 1884 v Ireland |
| 74 | JOHN FORBES (5/0) | – | (with Vale of Leven, Alexandria) |
| | 13 January 1862, Bonhill | | 1884 v Ireland, England, Wales |
| | | | 1887 v England, Wales |
| 75 | JOHN GRAHAM (1/0) | – | (with Annbank) |
| | 23 February 1857, Coylton | | 1884 v Ireland |
| 76 | WILLIAM FULTON (1/0) | – | (with Abercorn, Paisley) |
| | | | 1884 v Ireland |
| 77 | ROBERT BROWN (2/0) | – | (with Dumbarton) |
| | | | 1884 v Ireland, Wales |
| 78 | SAMUEL THOMSON (2/0) | – | (with Boswell, Lugar) |
| | 1862 | | 1884 v Ireland, Wales |
| 79 | JAMES GOSSLAND (1/2) | – | (with Rangers, Glasgow) |
| | 6 September 1860, Glasgow | | 1884 v Ireland (2) |
| 80 | JOHN GOUDIE (1/1) | – | (with Abercorn, Paisley) |
| | 5 July 1857, Paisley | | 1884 v Ireland (1) |
| 81 | J McAULAY (1/0) | – | (with Arthurlie, Barrhead) |
| | | | 1884 v Ireland |
| 82 | FRANCIS SHAW (2/1) | – | (with Pollokshields Athletic, Glasgow) |
| | 13 May 1864, Glasgow | | 1884 v England, Wales (1) |
| 83 | ROBERT CHRISTIE (1/0) | – | (with Queen's Park, Glasgow) |
| | 15 November 1865, Dunblane | | 1884 v England |
| 84 | THOMAS TURNER (1/0) | – | (with Arthurlie, Barrhead) |
| | | | 1884 v Wales |
| 85 | JAMES McINTYRE (1/0) | – | (with Rangers, Glasgow) |
| | | | 1884 v Wales |

| | | | |
|---|---|---|---|
| 86 | WILLIAM CHALMERS (1/0) | – | (with Rangers, Glasgow) |
| | | | 1885 v Ireland |
| 87 | HUGH McHARDY (1/0) | – | (with Rangers, Glasgow) |
| | | | 1885 v Ireland |
| 88 | JAMES NIVEN (1/0) | – | (with Moffat) |
| | 1862, Moffat | | 1885 v Ireland |
| 89 | ROBERT KELSO (7/0) | – | (with Renton) |
| | 2 October 1865, Cardross | | 1885 v Ireland, Wales |
| | | | 1886 v Wales |
| | | | 1887 v England, Wales |
| | | | 1888 v England |
| | | – | (with Dundee) |
| | | | 1898 v Ireland |
| 90 | ALEXANDER BARBOUR (1/1) | – | (with Renton) |
| | 7 June 1862, Dumbarton | | 1885 v Ireland (1) |
| 91 | JOHN MARSHALL (4/1) | – | (with Third Lanark, Glasgow) |
| | | | 1885 v Ireland (1) |
| | | | 1886 v Wales |
| | | | 1887 v England, Wales |
| 92 | WILLIAM TURNER (2/1) | – | (with Pollokshields Athletic, Glasgow) |
| | | | 1885 v Ireland (1) |
| | | | 1886 v Ireland |
| 93 | ALEXANDER HIGGINS (1/3) | – | (with Kilmarnock) |
| | 1865, Kilmarnock | | 1885 v Ireland (3) |
| 94 | ROBERT CALDERWOOD (3/3) | – | (with Cartvale, Busby) |
| | | | 1885 v Ireland (1), England, Wales (2) |
| 95 | W LAMONT (1/1) | – | (with Pilgrims, Glasgow) |
| | | | 1885 v Ireland (1) |
| 96 | JOHN GOW (1/0) | – | (with Queen's Park, Glasgow) |
| | 4 October 1859, Glasgow | | 1885 v England |
| 97 | ALEXANDER HAMILTON (4/0) | – | (with Queen's Park, Glasgow) |
| | 24 July 1865, Glasgow | | 1885 v England, Wales |
| | | | 1886 v England |
| | | – | 1888 v England |
| 98 | WILLIAM SELLAR (9/4) | – | (with Battlefield, Glasgow) |
| | 21 September 1866, Peterhead | | 1885 v England |
| | | | 1886 v England |
| | | | 1887 v England, Wales |
| | | | 1888 v England |
| | | – | (with Queen's Park, Glasgow) |
| | | | 1891 v England |
| | | | 1892 v England |
| | | | 1893 v Ireland (2), England (2) |
| 99 | DAVID ALLAN (3/2) | – | (with Queen's Park, Glasgow) |
| | 30 April 1863, Irvine | | 1885 v England, Wales (1) |
| | | | 1886 v Wales (1) |
| 100 | LEITCH KEIR (5/1) | – | (with Renton) |
| | 22 June 1861, Alloa | | 1885 v Wales |
| | | – | (with Dumbarton) |
| | | | 1886 v Ireland |
| | | | 1887 v England (1), Wales |
| | | | 1888 v England |
| 101 | ROBERT BROWN (1/0) | – | (with Dumbarton) |
| | 1860, Dumbarton | | 1885 v Wales |
| 102 | JAMES CONNOR (1/0) | – | (with Airdrie) |
| | 22 February 1861, Airdrie | | 1886 v Ireland |
| 103 | ANDREW THOMSON (1/0) | – | (with Arthurlie, Barrhead) |
| | Barrhead | | 1886 v Ireland |
| 104 | WILLIAM McLEOD (1/0) | – | (with Queen's Park, Glasgow) |
| | Glasgow | | 1886 v Ireland |
| 105 | JOHN CAMERON (1/0) | – | (with Rangers, Glasgow) |
| | | | 1886 v Ireland |
| 106 | ROBERT FLEMING (1/0) | – | (with Morton, Greenock) |
| | 11 March 1860, Greenock | | 1886 v Ireland |

107 JOHN LAMBIE (3/1)     – (with Queen's Park, Glasgow)
18 December 1868, Glasgow     1886 v Ireland (1)
1887 v Ireland
1888 v England

108 CHARLES HEGGIE (1/4)     – (with Rangers, Glasgow)
26 September 1862, Glasgow     1886 v Ireland (4)

109 JAMES GOURLAY (2/1)     – (with Cambuslang)
1 November 1860, Kilmaurs     1886 v Ireland (1)
1888 v Wales

110 MICHAEL DUNBAR (1/1)     – (with Cartvale, Busby)
Busby     1886 v Ireland (1)

111 JOHN MacDONALD (1/0)     – (with Edinburgh University)
24 December 1861, Inverness     1886 v England

112 GEORGE SOMERVILLE (1/1)     – (with Queen's Park, Glasgow)
1886 v England (1)

113 WOODVILLE GRAY (1/0)     – (with Pollokshields Athletic, Glasgow)
1866     1886 v England

114 RALPH AITKEN (2/1)     – (with Dumbarton)
16 February 1863, Kilbarchan     1886 v England
1888 v Ireland (1)

115 JAMES LUNDIE (1/0)     – (with Hibernian, Edinburgh)
20 April 1857, Edinburgh     1886 v Wales

116 WILLIAM SEMPLE (1/0)     – (with Cambuslang)
26 November 1861, Cambuslang     1886 v Wales

117 ANDREW JACKSON (2/0)     – (with Cambuslang)
Cambuslang     1886 v Wales
1888 v Ireland

118 ROBERT McCORMICK (1/1)     – (with Abercorn, Paisley)
1886 v Wales (1)

119 JAMES McGHEE (1/0)     – (with Hibernian, Edinburgh)
Lugar     1886 v Wales

120 JAMES McCALL (5/2)     – (with Renton)
2 March 1865, Renton     1886 v Wales (1)
1887 v England (1), Wales
1888 v England
1890 v England

121 JOHN DOIG (5/0)     – (with Arbroath)
29 October 1866, Letham     1887 v Ireland
1889 v Ireland
– (with Sunderland)
1896 v England
1899 v England
1903 v England

122 ANDREW WHITELAW (2/0)     – (with Vale of Leven, Alexandria)
19 May 1865, Jamestown     1887 v Ireland
1890 v Wales

123 ROBERT SMELLIE (6/0)     – (with Queen's Park, Glasgow)
15 October 1865, Dalziel     1887 v Ireland
1888 v Wales
1889 v England
1891 v England
1893 v Ireland, England

124 JOHN WEIR (1/0)     – (with Third Lanark, Glasgow)
1887 v Ireland

125 THOMAS McMILLAN (1/0)     – (with Dumbarton)
11 October 1866, Mauchline     1887 v Ireland

126 J HUTTON (1/0)     – (with St Bernard's, Edinburgh)
Edinburgh     1887 v Ireland

127 THOMAS JENKINSON (1/1)     – (with Heart of Midlothian, Edinburgh)
21 April 1865, Edinburgh     1887 v Ireland (1)

128 WILLIAM WATT (1/1)     – (with Queen's Park, Glasgow)
17 December 1861, Glasgow     1887 v Ireland (1)

129 JAMES LOWE (1/1)     – (with St Bernard's, Edinburgh)
1887 v Ireland (1)

130 WILLIAM JOHNSTONE (3/1)     – (with Third Lanark, Glasgow)
4 November 1864, Glasgow     1887 v Ireland (1)
1889 v Wales
1890 v England

131 JOHN AULD (3/0)     – (with Third Lanark, Glasgow)
7 January 1862, Lugar     1887 v England, Wales
1889 v Wales

132 WILLIAM ROBERTSON (2/1)     – (with Dumbarton)
1887 v England, Wales (1)

133 JAMES ALLAN (2/2)     – (with Queen's Park, Glasgow)
1887 v England (1), Wales (1)

134 JAMES WILSON (4/0)     – (with Vale of Leven, Alexandria)
Alexandria     1888 v Wales
1889 v England
1890 v England
1891 v England

135 ANDREW HANNAH (1/0)     – (with Renton)
17 September 1864, Renton     1888 v Wales

136 JAMES JOHNSTONE (1/0)     – (with Abercorn, Paisley)
1888 v Wales

137 JAMES McLAREN (3/0)     – (with Hibernian, Edinburgh)
1860, Lugar     1888 v Wales
– (with Celtic, Glasgow)
1889 v England
1890 v England

138 ALEXANDER LATTA (2/2)     – (with Dumbarton Athletic)
24 September 1867, Dumbarton     1888 v Wales (2)
1889 v England

139 WILLIAM GROVES (3/4)     – (with Hibernian, Edinburgh)
9 November 1869, Edinburgh     1888 v Wales (1)
– (with Celtic, Glasgow)
1889 v Ireland (3)
1890 v England

140 WILLIAM PAUL (3/5)     – (with Partick Thistle, Glasgow)
Glasgow     1888 v Wales (1)
1889 v Wales
1890 v Wales (4)

141 JOHN McPHERSON (9/7)     – (with Kilmarnock)
19 June 1868, Kilmarnock     1888 v Wales
– (with Cowlairs, Glasgow)
1889 v England (1)
1890 v Ireland (1), England (1)
– (with Rangers, Glasgow)
1892 v Wales (2)
1894 v England
1895 v Ireland, England
1897 v Ireland (2)

142 NEIL MUNRO (2/2)     – (with Abercorn, Paisley)
Paisley     1888 v Wales (1)
1889 v England (1)

143 JOHN LINDSAY (3/0)     – (with Renton)
1862, Renton     1888 v England
1893 v Ireland, England

144 DONALD GOW (1/0)     – (with Rangers, Glasgow)
8 February 1868, Blair-Atholl     1888 v England

145 JAMES KELLY (8/1)     – (with Renton)
15 October 1865, Renton     1888 v England
– (with Celtic, Glasgow)
1889 v England
1890 v England
1892 v England
1893 v Ireland (1), England
1894 v Wales
1896 v Ireland

146  WILLIAM BERRY (4/0)          –  (with Queen's Park, Glasgow)
     20 August 1867, Glasgow         1888  v England
                                     1889  v England
                                     1890  v England
                                     1891  v England

147  JOHN McLEOD (5/0)           –  (with Dumbarton)
     12 March 1866, Dumbarton       1888  v Ireland
                                     1889  v Wales
                                     1890  v Ireland
                                     1892  v England
                                     1893  v Wales

148  DUNCAN STEWART (1/0)        –  (with Dumbarton)
                                     1888  v Ireland

149  ARCHIBALD McCALL (1/0)      –  (with Renton)
     8 May 1867, Renton             1888  v Ireland

150  ALLAN STEWART (2/1)         –  (with Queen's Park, Glasgow)
     Kilmarnock                     1888  v Ireland (1)
                                     1889  v Wales

151  GEORGE DEWAR (2/1)          –  (with Dumbarton)
     20 July 1867, Dumbarton        1888  v Ireland (1)
                                     1889  v England

152  NEIL McCALLUM (1/1)         –  (with Renton)
     3 July 1868, Bonhill           1888  v Ireland (1)

153  JOHN GOW (1/0)              –  (with Rangers, Glasgow)
     17 April 1869, Blair Atholl    1888  v Ireland

154  WILLIAM DICKSON (1/4)       –  (with Strathmore, Dundee)
     27 August 1866, Crail          1888  v Ireland (4)

155  THOMAS BRECKENRIDGE (1/1)   –  (with Heart of Midlothian, Edinburgh)
     26 February 1865, Edinburgh    1888  v Ireland (1)

156  JAMES ADAMS (3/0)           –  (with Heart of Midlothian, Edinburgh)
     1864, Edinburgh             –  1889  v Ireland
                                     1892  v Wales
                                     1893  v Ireland

157  THOMAS McKEOWN (2/0)        –  (with Celtic, Glasgow)
     1869, Lugar                    1889  v Ireland
                                     1890  v England

158  THOMAS ROBERTSON (4/0)      –  (with Queen's Park, Glasgow)
     28 December 1864, Torrance     1889  v Ireland
                                     1890  v England
                                     1891  v Wales
                                     1892  v Ireland

159  DAVID CALDERHEAD (1/0)      –  (with Queen of the South Wanderers, Dumfries)
     19 June 1864, Hurlford         1889  v Ireland

160  JOHN BUCHANAN (1/0)         –  (with Cambuslang)
                                     1889  v Ireland

161  FRANCIS WATT (4/3)          –  (with Kilbirnie)
     16 February 1866, Beith        1889  v Ireland (2), Wales
                                     1890  v Wales
                                     1891  v England (1)

162  THOMAS McINNES (1/1)        –  (with Cowlairs, Glasgow)
     29 August 1870, Glasgow        1889  v Ireland (1)

163  R. BOYD (2/2)               –  (with Mossend Swifts, West Calder)
                                     1889  v Ireland
                                     1891  v Wales (2)

164  DAVID BLACK (1/1)           –  (with Hurlford)
     29 March 1868, Irvine          1889  v Ireland (1)

165  JAMES OSWALD (3/1)          –  (with Third Lanark, Glasgow)
     3 January 1868, Greenock       1889  v England (1)
                                 –  (with St Bernard's, Edinburgh)
                                     1895  v England
                                 –  (with Rangers, Glasgow)
                                     1897  v Wales

166  ANDREW THOMSON (1/0)        –  (with Third Lanark, Glasgow)
                                     1889  v Wales

167  JAMES RAE (2/0)             –  (with Third Lanark, Glasgow)
                                     1889  v Wales
                                     1890  v Ireland

168  ALEXANDER LOCHHEAD (1/0)    –  (with Third Lanark, Glasgow)
     12 May 1866, Johnstone         1889  v Wales

169  HENRY CAMPBELL (1/0)        –  (with Renton)
     1867, Renton                   1889  v Wales

170  JAMES HANNAH (1/0)          –  (with Third Lanark, Glasgow)
     Glasgow                        1889  v Wales

171  JOHN MURRAY (1/0)           –  (with Vale of Leven, Alexandria)
     24 April 1865, Strathblane     1890  v England

172  MATTHEW McQUEEN (2/0)       –  (with Leith Athletic, Edinburgh)
     Harthill                       1890  v Ireland
                                     1891  v Wales

173  ANDREW BROWN (2/0)          –  (with St Mirren, Paisley)
     Kilmarnock                     1890  v Wales
                                     1891  v Wales

174  HUGH WILSON (4/1)           –  (with Newmilns)
     18 March 1869, Mauchline       1890  v Wales (1)
                                 –  (with Sunderland)
                                     1897  v England
                                 –  (with Third Lanark, Glasgow)
                                     1902  v Wales
                                     1904  v Ireland

175  J. BROWN (1/0)              –  (with Cambuslang)
     Renton                         1890  v Wales

176  JAMES DUNLOP (1/0)          –  (with St Mirren, Paisley)
     1869, Paisley                  1890  v Wales

177  DANIEL BRUCE (1/0)          –  (with Vale of Leven, Alexandria)
     20 October 1870, Bonhill       1890  v Wales

178  R. HUNTER (1/0)             –  (with St Mirren, Paisley)
                                     1890  v Ireland

179  J. RUSSELL (1/0)            –  (with Cambuslang)
                                     1890  v Ireland

180  ISAAC BEGBIE (4/0)          –  (with Heart of Midlothian, Edinburgh)
     4 June 1868, Edinburgh         1890  v Ireland
                                     1891  v England
                                     1892  v Wales
                                     1894  v England

181  DAVID MITCHELL (5/0)        –  (with Rangers, Glasgow)
     29 April 1866, Kilmarnock      1890  v Ireland
                                     1892  v England
                                     1893  v Ireland, England
                                     1894  v England

182  THOMAS WYLIE (1/1)          –  (with Rangers, Glasgow)
     1872, Maybole                  1890  v Ireland (1)

183  GILBERT RANKIN (2/2)        –  (with Vale of Leven, Alexandria)
     20 March 1870, Bonhill         1890  v Ireland (2)
                                     1891  v England

184  JOHN BELL (10/5)            –  (with Dumbarton)
     6 October 1869, Dumbarton      1890  v Ireland
                                     1892  v England (1)
                                 –  (with Everton, Liverpool)
                                     1896  v England (1)
                                     1897  v England
                                     1898  v England
                                 –  (with Celtic, Glasgow)
                                     1899  v Wales, Ireland (1),
                                     England
                                     1900  v Wales (1), England (1)

185  DAVID BAIRD (3/1)           –  (with Heart of Midlothian, Edinburgh)
     1872, Dalry                    1890  v Ireland
                                     1891  v England
                                     1892  v Wales (1)

186  J McCORKINDALE (1/0)        –  (with Partick Thistle, Glasgow)
                                     1891  v Wales

187  ARCHIBALD RITCHIE (1/0)     –  (with East Stirlingshire, Falkirk)
     12 April 1872, Kirkcaldy       1891  v Wales

| | | | |
|---|---|---|---|
| 188 | JAMES HEPBURN (1/0) | – | (with Alloa Athletic) |
| | | | 1891 v Wales |
| 189 | WILLIAM GULLILAND (4/0) | – | (with Queen's Park, Glasgow) |
| | 3 February 1871, Glasgow | | 1891 v Wales |
| | | | 1892 v Ireland |
| | | | 1894 v England |
| | | | 1895 v England |
| 190 | ROBERT BUCHANAN (1/1) | – | (with Abercorn, Paisley) |
| | | | 1891 v Wales (1) |
| 191 | JAMES LOGAN (1/1) | – | (with Ayr United) |
| | 24 June 1870, Troon | | 1891 v Wales (1) |
| 192 | ALEXANDER KEILLOR (6/2) | – | (with Montrose) |
| | 20 October 1869, Dundee | | 1891 v Wales |
| | | | 1892 v Ireland (1) |
| | | – | (with Dundee) |
| | | | 1894 v Ireland |
| | | | 1895 v Wales |
| | | | 1896 v Wales (1) |
| | | | 1897 v Wales |
| 193 | DONALD SILLARS (5/0) | – | (with Queen's Park, Glasgow) |
| | 30 October 1868, Glasgow | | 1891 v Ireland |
| | | | 1892 v England |
| | | | 1893 v Wales |
| | | | 1894 v England |
| | | | 1895 v Wales |
| 194 | WILLIAM PAUL (1/0) | – | (with Dykebar, Paisley) |
| | 5 August 1868, Paisley | | 1891 v Ireland |
| 195 | T. HAMILTON (1/0) | – | (with Hurlford) |
| | | | 1891 v Ireland |
| 196 | JAMES CLELAND (1/0) | – | (with Royal Albert, Larkhall) |
| | | | 1891 v Ireland |
| 197 | JAMES CAMPBELL (2/0) | – | (with Kilmarnock) |
| | | | 1891 v Ireland |
| | | | 1892 v Wales |
| 198 | JAMES LOW (1/1) | – | (with Cambuslang) |
| | | | 1891 v Ireland (1) |
| 199 | WILLIAM BOWIE (1/0) | – | (with Linthouse, Glasgow) |
| | | | 1891 v Ireland |
| 200 | J. FRASER (1/0) | – | (with Moffat) |
| | | | 1891 v Ireland |
| 201 | ROBERT CLEMENTS (1/0) | – | (with Leith Athletic, Edinburgh) |
| | | | 1891 v Ireland |
| 202 | THOMAS WADDELL (6/1) | – | (with Queen's Park, Glasgow) |
| | 9 September 1870, Glasgow | | 1891 v Ireland (1) |
| | | | 1892 v England |
| | | | 1893 v Ireland, England |
| | | | 1895 v Ireland, England |
| 203 | JOHN McPHERSON (1/0) | – | (with Heart of Midlothian, Edinburgh) |
| | 1867, Motherwell | | 1891 v England |
| 204 | JOHN HILL (2/0) | – | (with Heart of Midlothian, Edinburgh) |
| | Plains | | 1891 v England |
| | | | 1892 v Wales |
| 205 | ANDREW BAIRD (2/0) | – | (with Queen's Park, Glasgow) |
| | 11 June 1866, Irvine | | 1892 v Ireland |
| | | | 1894 v Wales |
| 206 | GEORGE BOWMAN (1/0) | – | (with Montrose) |
| | 27 June 1872, Montrose | | 1892 v Ireland |
| 207 | JOHN DRUMMOND (14/1) | – | (with Falkirk) |
| | 13 April 1870, Alva | | 1892 v Ireland |
| | | – | (with Rangers, Glasgow) |
| | | | 1894 v Ireland |
| | | | 1895 v Ireland, England |
| | | | 1896 v Ireland, England |
| | | | 1897 v Ireland |
| | | | 1898 v England |
| | | | 1900 v England |
| | | | 1901 v England |
| | | | 1902 v Ireland, Wales (1), England |
| | | | 1903 v Ireland |

| | | | |
|---|---|---|---|
| 208 | ROBERT MARSHALL (2/0) | – | (with Rangers, Glasgow) |
| | | | 1892 v Ireland |
| | | | 1894 v Ireland |
| 209 | PETER DOWDS (1/0) | – | (with Celtic, Glasgow) |
| | 1871, Johnstone | | 1892 v Ireland |
| 210 | DAVID McPHERSON (1/0) | – | (with Kilmarnock) |
| | 22 August 1872, Kilmarnock | | 1892 v Ireland |
| 211 | JAMES ELLIS (1/1) | – | (with Mossend Swifts, West Calder) |
| | | | 1892 v Ireland (1) |
| 212 | WILLIAM LAMBIE (9/5) | – | (with Queen's Park, Glasgow) |
| | 10 January 1873, Glasgow | | 1892 v Ireland (1) |
| | | | 1893 v Wales (1) |
| | | | 1894 v England (1) |
| | | | 1895 v Ireland (1), England |
| | | | 1896 v Ireland, England (1) |
| | | | 1897 v Ireland, England |
| 213 | ROBERT DOWNIE (1/0) | – | (with Third Lanark, Glasgow) |
| | 19 March 1867, Glasgow | | 1892 v Wales |
| 214 | JAMES ORR (1/0) | – | (with Kilmarnock) |
| | 24 July 1871, Dalry | | 1892 v Wales |
| 215 | JOHN TAYLOR (4/1) | – | (with Dumbarton) |
| | 27 January 1872, Dumbarton | | 1892 v Wales |
| | | | 1893 v Wales |
| | | | 1894 v Ireland (1) |
| | | | 1895 v Ireland |
| 216 | WILLIAM THOMSON (4/1) | – | (with Dumbarton) |
| | | | 1892 v Wales (1) |
| | | | 1893 v Wales |
| | | | 1898 v Wales, Ireland |
| 217 | JAMES HAMILTON (3/3) | – | (with Queen's Park, Glasgow) |
| | Glasgow | | 1892 v Wales (2) |
| | | | 1893 v Ireland (1), England |
| 218 | DANIEL DOYLE (8/0) | – | (with Celtic, Glasgow) |
| | 16 September 1864, Paisley | | 1892 v England |
| | | | 1893 v Wales |
| | | | 1894 v England |
| | | | 1895 v Ireland, England |
| | | | 1897 v England |
| | | | 1898 v Ireland, England |
| 219 | WILLIAM TAYLOR (1/0) | – | (with Heart of Midlothian, Edinburgh) |
| | Edinburgh | | 1892 v England |
| 220 | ALEXANDER McMAHON (6/6) | – | (with Celtic, Glasgow) |
| | 1870, Selkirk | | 1892 v England |
| | | | 1893 v Ireland (1), England |
| | | | 1894 v England (1) |
| | | | 1901 v Ireland (4) |
| | | | 1902 v Wales |
| 221 | ROBERT FOYERS (2/0) | – | (with St Bernard's, Edinburgh) |
| | 22 June 1868, Hamilton | | 1893 v Wales |
| | | | 1894 v Wales |
| 222 | ANDREW McCREADIE (2/0) | – | (with Rangers, Glasgow) |
| | 19 November 1870, Girvan | | 1893 v Wales |
| | | | 1894 v England |
| 223 | DAVID STEWART (3/0) | – | (with Queen's Park, Glasgow) |
| | 1874, Glasgow | | 1893 v Wales |
| | | | 1894 v Ireland |
| | | | 1897 v Ireland |
| 224 | JOHN MADDEN (2/5) | – | (with Celtic, Glasgow) |
| | 11 June 1865, Dumbarton | | 1893 v Wales (4) |
| | | | 1895 v Wales (1) |
| 225 | JOHN BARKER (2/4) | – | (with Rangers, Glasgow) |
| | 28 June 1869, Glasgow | | 1893 v Wales (3) |
| | | | 1894 v Wales (1) |
| 226 | WILLIAM MALEY (2/0) | – | (with Celtic, Glasgow) |
| | 25 April 1868, Newry, Ireland | | 1893 v Ireland, England |

| | | |
|---|---|---|
| 227 | JOHN CAMPBELL (12/5) | – (with Celtic, Glasgow) |
| | 1871, Glasgow | 1893 v Ireland, England |
| | | 1898 v Ireland, England |
| | | 1900 v Ireland (2), England |
| | | 1901 v Ireland (2), Wales, England (1) |
| | | 1902 v Ireland, Wales |
| | | 1903 v Wales |
| 228 | DAVID CRAWFORD (3/0) | – (with St Mirren, Paisley) |
| | 9 March 1873, Paisley | 1894 v Wales, Ireland |
| | | – (with Rangers, Glasgow) |
| | | 1900 v Wales |
| 229 | JOHN JOHNSTONE (1/1) | – (with Kilmarnock) |
| | | 1894 v Wales (1) |
| 230 | EDWARD McBAIN (1/0) | – (with St Mirren, Paisley) |
| | Paisley | 1894 v Wales |
| 231 | THOMAS CHAMBERS (1/1) | – (with Heart of Midlothian, Edinburgh) |
| | | 1894 v Wales (1) |
| 232 | ANDREW STEWART (1/0) | – (with Third Lanark, Glasgow) |
| | | 1894 v Wales |
| 233 | DAVID ALEXANDER (2/1) | – (with East Stirlingshire, Falkirk) |
| | Falkirk | 1894 v Wales (1), Ireland |
| 234 | DAVIDSON BERRY (3/1) | – (with Queen's Park, Glasgow) |
| | 27 May 1875, Glasgow | 1894 v Wales |
| | | 1899 v Wales, Ireland (1) |
| 235 | FRANCIS BARRETT (2/0) | – (with Dundee) |
| | 2 August 1872, Dundee | 1894 v Ireland |
| | | 1895 v Wales |
| 236 | WILLIAM LONGAIR (1/0) | – (with Dundee) |
| | 19 July 1870, Dundee | 1894 v Ireland |
| 237 | JAMES BLESSINGTON (4/0) | – (with Celtic, Glasgow) |
| | 28 February 1874, Linlithgow | 1894 v Ireland, England |
| | | 1896 v Ireland, England |
| 238 | ROBERT SCOTT (1/0) | – (with Airdrie) |
| | 2 October 1870, Airdrie | 1894 v Ireland |
| 239 | DAVID HADDOW (1/0) | – (with Rangers, Glasgow) |
| | 12 June 1869, Dalserf | 1894 v England |
| 240 | ROBERT GLEN (3/0) | – (with Renton) |
| | 16 January 1875, Renton | 1895 v Wales |
| | | 1896 v Wales |
| | | – (with Hibernian, Edinburgh) |
| | | 1900 v Ireland |
| 241 | JAMES SIMPSON (3/0) | – (with Third Lanark, Glasgow) |
| | 2 April 1873, Ardrossan | 1895 v Wales, Ireland, England |
| 242 | WILLIAM McCOLL (1/0) | – (with Renton) |
| | Alexandria | 1895 v Wales |
| 243 | JOHN FYFE (1/0) | – (with Third Lanark, Glasgow) |
| | | 1895 v Wales |
| 244 | JOHN MURRAY (1/0) | – (with Renton) |
| | | 1895 v Wales |
| 245 | WILLIAM SAWERS (1/0) | – (with Dundee) |
| | 13 June 1871, Glasgow | 1895 v Wales |
| 246 | JOHN DIVERS (1/1) | – (with Celtic, Glasgow) |
| | 19 September 1873 | 1895 v Wales (1) |
| 247 | DANIEL McARTHUR (3/0) | – (with Celtic, Glasgow) |
| | 9 August 1867, Old Monkland | 1895 v Ireland, England |
| | | 1899 v Wales |
| 248 | DAVID RUSSELL (6/1) | – (with Heart of Midlothian, Edinburgh) |
| | 6 April 1868, Airdrie | 1895 v Ireland, England |
| | | – (with Celtic, Glasgow) |
| | | 1897 v Wales |
| | | 1898 v Ireland |
| | | 1901 v Ireland (1), Wales |
| 249 | NEIL GIBSON (14/1) | – (with Rangers, Glasgow) |
| | 23 February 1873, Larkhall | 1895 v Ireland, England |
| | | 1896 v Ireland, England |
| | | 1897 v Ireland (1), England |
| | | 1898 v England |
| | | 1899 v Wales, Ireland, England |
| | | 1900 v Ireland, England |
| | | 1901 v Wales |
| | | – (with Partick Thistle, Glasgow) |
| | | 1905 v Ireland |
| 250 | JOHN WALKER (5/3) | – (with Heart of Midlothian, Edinburgh) |
| | 31 May 1874, Coatbridge | 1895 v Ireland (2) |
| | | 1897 v Wales (1) |
| | | 1898 v Ireland |
| | | – (with Rangers, Glasgow) |
| | | 1904 v Wales, Ireland |
| 251 | ROBERT MacFARLANE (1/0) | – (with Morton, Greenock) |
| | 1875, Greenock | 1896 v Wales |
| 252 | DUNCAN McLEAN (2/0) | – (with St Bernard's, Edinburgh) |
| | 12 September 1869, Dumbarton | 1896 v Wales |
| | | 1897 v Ireland |
| 253 | JOHN GILLESPIE (1/0) | – (with Queen's Park, Glasgow) |
| | 19 January 1872, Denny | 1896 v Wales |
| 254 | ROBERT NEIL (2/2) | – (with Hibernian, Edinburgh) |
| | 1876 | 1896 v Wales (2) |
| | | – (with Rangers, Glasgow) |
| | | 1900 v Wales |
| 255 | WILLIAM BLAIR (1/0) | – (with Third Lanark, Glasgow) |
| | 11 March 1872, Greenock | 1896 v Wales |
| 256 | WILLIAM THOMSON (1/0) | – (with Dundee) |
| | Dundee | 1896 v Wales |
| 257 | DANIEL PATON (1/1) | – (with St Bernard's, Edinburgh) |
| | 1871, Bonhill | 1896 v Wales (1) |
| 258 | ROBERT McCOLL (13/13) | – (with Queen's Park, Glasgow) |
| | 13 April 1876, Glasgow | 1896 v Wales, Ireland (2) |
| | | 1897 v Ireland (1) |
| | | 1898 v Ireland (1) |
| | | 1899 v Wales (3), Ireland (3), England |
| | | 1900 v Wales, England (3) |
| | | 1901 v Wales, England |
| | | – (with Newcastle United) |
| | | 1902 v England |
| | | – (with Queen's Park, Glasgow) |
| | | 1908 v Ireland |
| 259 | ALEXANDER KING (6/1) | – (with Heart of Midlothian, Edinburgh) |
| | 27 July 1871, Dykehead | 1896 v Wales, England |
| | | – (with Celtic, Glasgow) |
| | | 1897 v Ireland (1) |
| | | 1898 v Ireland |
| | | 1899 v Wales, Ireland |
| 260 | KENNETH ANDERSON (3/0) | – (with Queen's Park, Glasgow) |
| | 23 July 1875, Glasgow | 1896 v Ireland |
| | | 1898 v Ireland, England |
| 261 | PETER MEECHAN (1/0) | – (with Celtic, Glasgow) |
| | 28 February 1872, Broxburn | 1896 v Ireland |
| 262 | GEORGE HOGG (2/0) | – (with Heart of Midlothian, Edinburgh) |
| | 2 December 1869, West Calder | 1896 v Ireland, England |
| 263 | PATRICK MURRAY (2/1) | – (with Hibernian, Edinburgh) |
| | 13 March 1874, Edinburgh | 1896 v Ireland (1) |
| | | 1897 v Wales |
| 264 | JOHN CAMERON (1/0) | – (with Queen's Park, Glasgow) |
| | 13 April 1872, Ayr | 1896 v Ireland |
| 265 | THOMAS BRANDON (1/0) | – (with Blackburn Rovers) |
| | 26 February 1869, Kilbirnie | 1896 v England |

266  JAMES COWAN (3/0)                   –   (with Aston Villa, Birmingham)
     17 October 1868, Bonhill              1896  v England
                                           1897  v England
                                           1898  v England
267  THOMAS HYSLOP (2/1)                 –   (with Stoke City)
     22 September 1874, Mauchline          1896  v England
                                       –   (with Rangers, Glasgow)
                                           1897  v England (1)
268  JOHN PATRICK (2/0)                  –   (with St Mirren, Paisley)
     10 January 1870, Kilsyth             1897  v Wales, England
269  JOHN RITCHIE (1/1)                  –   (with Queen's Park, Glasgow)
     1876                                  1897  v Wales (1)
270  DAVID GARDNER (1/0)                 –   (with Third Lanark, Glasgow)
     31 March 1873, Glasgow               1897  v Wales
271  BERNARD BRESLIN (1/0)               –   (with Hibernian, Edinburgh)
     Carfin                                1897  v Wales
272  JOHN KENNEDY (1/0)                  –   (with Hibernian, Edinburgh)
                                           1897  v Wales
273  J. McMILLAN (1/0)                   –   (with St Bernard's, Edinburgh)
                                           1897  v Wales
274  MATTHEW DICKIE (3/0)                –   (with Rangers, Glasgow)
     19 August 1873, Rhu                   1897  v Ireland
                                           1899  v Ireland
                                           1900  v Wales
275  WILLIAM BAIRD (1/0)                 –   (with St Bernard's, Edinburgh)
     1 October 1874, Edinburgh            1897  v Ireland
276  THOMAS LOW (1/0)                    –   (with Rangers, Glasgow)
     3 October 1874, Cambuslang           1897  v Ireland
277  NICOL SMITH (12/0)                  –   (with Rangers, Glasgow)
     25 December 1873, Darvel             1897  v England
                                           1898  v Wales
                                           1899  v Wales, Ireland, England
                                           1900  v Wales, Ireland, England
                                           1901  v Ireland, Wales
                                           1902  v Ireland, England
278  JAMES MILLAR (3/2)                  –   (with Rangers, Glasgow)
     2 March 1870, Annbank                1897  v England (1)
                                           1898  v Wales, England (1)
279  GEAORGE ALLAN (1/0)                 –   (with Liverpool)
     23 April 1875, Linlithgow Bridge     1897  v England
280  W. WATSON (1/0)                     –   (with Falkirk)
                                           1898  v Wales
281  MATTHEW SCOTT (1/0)                 –   (with Airdrie)
     11 July 1872, Airdrie              –   1898  v Wales
282  ALEXANDER CHRISTIE (3/1)            –   (with Queen's Park, Glasgow)
     28 September 1873, Dunblane          1898  v Wales
                                           1899  v Ireland (1), England
283  PETER CAMPBELL (1/0)                –   (with Morton, Greenock)
                                           1898  v Wales
284  JAMES GILLESPIE (1/3)               –   (with Third Lanark, Glasgow)
                                           1898  v Wales (3)
285  JAMES McKIE (1/2)                   –   (with East Stirlingshire, Falkirk)
     Arbroath                              1898  v Wales (2)
286  HUGH MORGAN (2/0)                   –   (with St Mirren, Paisley)
     20 September 1869, Longriggend       1898  v Wales
                                       –   (with Liverpool)
                                           1899  v England
287  ROBERT FINDLAY (1/0)                –   (with Kilmarnock)
     29 March 1877, Galston               1898  v Wales
288  WILLIAM STEWART (2/1)               –   (with Queen's Park, Glasgow)
     29 February 1876, Glasgow            1898  v Ireland (1)
                                           1900  v Ireland
289  THOMAS ROBERTSON (1/1)              –   (with Heart of Midlothian, Edinburgh)
                                           1898  v Ireland (1)

290  JOHN ROBERTSON (16/2)               –   (with Everton, Liverpool)
     25 February 1877, Dumbarton          1898  v England
                                       –   (with Southampton)
                                           1899  v England
                                       –   (with Rangers, Glasgow)
                                           1900  v Wales, England
                                           1901  v Ireland, Wales (1), England
                                           1902  v Ireland, Wales, England
                                           1903  v Wales, England
                                           1904  v Wales, Ireland, England
                                           1905  v Wales (1)
291  WILLIAM MAXWELL (1/0)               –   (with Stoke City)
     21  September 1876, Arbroath         1898  v England
292  ALEXANDER SMITH (20/5)              –   (with Rangers, Glasgow)
     7 November 1876, Darvel              1898  v England
                                           1900  v Wales (1), Ireland (1),
                                           England
                                           1901  v Ireland, Wales, England
                                           1902  v Ireland, Wales (3), England
                                           1903  v Wales, Ireland, England
                                           1904  v Ireland
                                           1905  v Wales
                                           1906  v Ireland, England
                                           1907  v Wales
                                           1911  v Ireland, England
293  DAVID STORRIER (3/0)                –   (with Celtic, Glasgow)
     25 October 1872, Arbroath            1899  v Wales, Ireland, England
294  HAROLD MARSHALL (2/1)               –   (with Celtic, Glasgow)
     24 November 1872, Edinburgh          1899  v Wales (1)
                                           1900  v Ireland
295  JOHN CAMPBELL (4/4)                 –   (with Rangers, Glasgow)
     1877, Glasgow                        1899  v Wales (2), Ireland (2),
                                           England
                                           1901  v Ireland
296  ROBERT HAMILTON (11/15)             –   (with Rangers, Glasgow)
     13 May 1877, Elgin                   1899  v Wales, Ireland (2),
                                           England (1)
                                           1900  v Wales (1)
                                           1901  v Ireland (4), England (1)
                                           1902  v Ireland (3), Wales
                                           1903  v England
                                           1904  v Ireland (1)
                                       –   (with Dundee)
                                           1911  v Wales (2)
297  JAMES IRONS (1/0)                   –   (with Queen's Park, Glasgow)
     30 October 1874, Scoonie             1900  v Wales
298  DAVID WILSON (1/2)                  –   (with Queen's Park, Glasgow)
                                           1900  v Wales (2)
299  HENRY RENNIE (13/0)                 –   (with Heart of Midlothian, Edinburgh)
     1 June 1873, Greenock                1900  v Ireland, England
                                       –   (with Hibernian, Edinburgh)
                                           1901  v England
                                           1902  v Ireland, Wales, England
                                           1903  v Wales, Ireland
                                           1904  v Ireland
                                           1905  v Wales
                                           1906  v Ireland
                                           1908  v Wales, Ireland
300  WILLIAM ORR (3/0)                   –   (with Celtic, Glasgow)
     20 June 1873, Shotts                 1900  v Ireland
                                           1903  v Ireland
                                           1904  v Wales

| 301 | ROBERT WALKER (29/7) | – | (with Heart of Midlothian, Edinburgh) |
|---|---|---|---|
| | 10 January 1879, Dalry | | 1900 v Ireland, England |
| | | | 1901 v Wales, England |
| | | | 1902 v Ireland (1), Wales, England |
| | | | 1903 v Wales, Ireland, England (1) |
| | | | 1904 v Wales (1), Ireland, England |
| | | | 1905 v Wales, Ireland (1), England |
| | | | 1906 v Ireland |
| | | | 1907 v Ireland (1), England |
| | | | 1908 v Wales, Ireland, England |
| | | | 1909 v Wales (1), England |
| | | | 1912 v Wales, Ireland (1), England |
| | | | 1913 v Wales, England |
| 302 | PATRICK CALLAGHAN (1/0) | – | (with Hibernian, Edinburgh) |
| | 12 August 1879, Glasgow | | 1900 v Ireland |
| 303 | ALEXANDER RAISBECK (8/0) | – | (with Liverpool) |
| | 26 December 1878, Wallacestone | | 1900 v England |
| | | | 1901 v England |
| | | | 1902 v England |
| | | | 1903 v Wales, England |
| | | | 1904 v England |
| | | | 1906 v England |
| | | | 1907 v England |
| 304 | GEORGE McWATTIE (2/0) | – | (with Queen's Park, Glasgow) |
| | 22 April 1875, Arbroath | | 1901 v Ireland, Wales |
| 305 | BERNARD BATTLES (3/0) | – | (with Celtic, Glasgow) |
| | 13 January 1875, Glasgow | | 1901 v Ireland, Wales, England |
| 306 | GEORGE ANDERSON (1/0) | – | (with Kilmarnock) |
| | 6 January 1877, Kilmarnock | | 1901 v Ireland |
| 307 | MARK BELL (1/0) | – | (with Heart of Midlothian, Edinburgh) |
| | 1881, Edinburgh | | 1901 v Wales |
| 308 | ANDREW AITKEN (14/0) | – | (with Newcastle United) |
| | 27 April 1877, Ayr | | 1901 v England |
| | | | 1902 v England |
| | | | 1903 v Wales, England |
| | | | 1904 v England |
| | | | 1905 v Wales, England |
| | | | 1906 v England |
| | | – | (with Middlesbrough) |
| | | | 1907 v Wales, England |
| | | | 1908 v England |
| | | – | (with Leicester Fosse) |
| | | | 1910 v England |
| | | | 1911 v Ireland, England |
| 309 | GEORGE KEY (1/0) | – | (with Heart of Midlothian, Edinburgh) |
| | 11 February 1882, Glasgow | | 1902 v Ireland |
| 310 | ALBERT BUICK (2/2) | – | (with Heart of Midlothian, Edinburgh) |
| | 17 January 1875, Arbroath | | 1902 v Ireland (1), Wales (1) |
| 311 | WILLIAM McCARTNEY (1/0) | – | (with Hibernian, Edinburgh) |
| | Newmilns | | 1902 v Ireland |
| 312 | HENRY ALLAN (1/0) | – | (with Heart of Midlothian, Edinburgh) |
| | 5 September 1877, Edinburgh | | 1902 v Wales |
| 313 | ROBERT TEMPLETON (11/1) | – | (with Aston Villa, Birmingham) |
| | 22 June 1879, Coylton | | 1902 v England (1) |
| | | – | (with Newcastle United) |
| | | | 1903 v Wales, England |
| | | | 1904 v England |
| | | – | (with Woolwich Arsenal, London) |
| | | | 1905 v Wales |
| | | – | (with Kilmarnock) |
| | | | 1908 v Ireland |
| | | | 1910 v Ireland, England |
| | | | 1912 v Ireland, England |
| | | | 1913 v Wales |

| 314 | RONALD ORR (2/1) | – | (with Newcastle United) |
|---|---|---|---|
| | 6 August 1880, Bartonholm | | 1902 v England (1) |
| | | | 1904 v England |
| 315 | ANDREW McCOMBIE (4/0) | – | (with Sunderland) |
| | 30 June 1876, Inverness | | 1903 v Wales, England |
| | | – | (with Newcastle United) |
| | | | 1905 v Wales, England |
| 316 | JAMES WATSON (6/0) | – | (with Sunderland) |
| | 4 October 1877, Motherwell | | 1903 v Wales, England |
| | | | 1904 v England |
| | | | 1905 v England |
| | | – | (with Middlesbrough) |
| | | | 1909 v Ireland, England |
| 317 | FINLAY SPEEDIE (3/2) | – | (with Rangers, Glasgow) |
| | 18 August 1880, Dumbarton | | 1903 v Wales (1), Ireland, England (1) |
| 318 | ARCHIBALD GRAY (1/0) | – | (with Hibernian, Edinburgh) |
| | 1883, Glasgow | | 1903 v Ireland |
| 319 | JOHN CROSS (1/0) | – | (with Third Lanark, Glasgow) |
| | | | 1903 v Ireland |
| 320 | PETER ROBERTSON (1/0) | – | (with Dundee) |
| | | | 1903 v Ireland |
| 321 | DAVID LINDSAY (1/0) | – | (with St Mirren, Paisley) |
| | | | 1903 v Ireland |
| 322 | WILLIAM PORTEOUS (1/0) | – | (with Heart of Midlothian, Edinburgh) |
| | | | 1903 v Ireland |
| 323 | LESLIE SKENE (1/0) | – | (with Queen's Park, Glasgow) |
| | 22 August 1882, Larbert | | 1904 v Wales |
| 324 | THOMAS JACKSON (6/0) | – | (with St Mirren, Paisley) |
| | 12 November 1878, Glasgow | | 1904 v Wales, Ireland, England |
| | | | 1905 v Wales |
| | | | 1907 v Wales, Ireland |
| 325 | JAMES SHARP (5/0) | – | (with Dundee) |
| | 11 October 1880, Jordanstone | | 1904 v Wales |
| | | – | (with Woolwich Arsenal, London) |
| | | | 1907 v Wales, England |
| | | | 1908 v England |
| | | – | (with Fulham, London) |
| | | | 1909 v Wales |
| 326 | THOMAS SLOAN (1/0) | – | (with Third Lanark, Glasgow) |
| | 4 October 1880, Glasgow | | 1904 v Wales |
| 327 | ALEXANDER BENNETT (11/2) | – | (with Celtic, Glasgow) |
| | 20 October 1881, Glasgow | | 1904 v Wales |
| | | | 1907 v Ireland |
| | | | 1908 v Wales (1) |
| | | – | (with Rangers, Glasgow) |
| | | | 1909 v Wales, Ireland, England |
| | | | 1910 v Wales, England |
| | | | 1911 v Wales, England |
| | | | 1913 v Ireland (1) |
| 328 | ALEXANDER MacFARLANE (5/1) | – | (with Dundee) |
| | 1878, Dundee | | 1904 v Wales |
| | | | 1906 v Wales |
| | | | 1908 v Wales |
| | | | 1909 v Ireland (1) |
| | | | 1911 v Wales |
| 329 | GEORGE WILSON (6/0) | – | (with Heart of Midlothian, Edinburgh) |
| | 1884, Lochgelly | | 1904 v Wales |
| | | | 1905 v Ireland, England |
| | | | 1906 v Wales |
| | | – | (with Everton, Liverpool) |
| | | | 1907 v England |
| | | – | (with Newcastle United) |
| | | | 1909 v England |

| 330 | JOHN CAMERON (2/0) | — | (with St Mirren, Paisley) |
| | Kirkwoodin | | 1904 v Ireland |
| | | — | (with Chelsea, London) |
| | | | 1909 v England |
| 331 | GEORGE HENDERSON (1/0) | — | (with Rangers, Glasgow) |
| | 2 May 1880, Ladhope | | 1904 v Ireland |
| 332 | CHARLES THOMSON (21/4) | — | (with Heart of Midlothian, Edinburgh) |
| | 12 June 1878, Prestonpans | | 1904 v Ireland |
| | | | 1905 v Wales, Ireland (2), England |
| | | | 1906 v Wales, Ireland |
| | | | 1907 v Wales, Ireland (1), England |
| | | | 1908 v Wales, Ireland, England |
| | | — | (with Sunderland) |
| | | | 1909 v Wales |
| | | | 1910 v England |
| | | | 1911 v Ireland |
| | | | 1912 v Wales, England |
| | | | 1913 v Wales, England |
| | | | 1914 v Ireland, England (1) |
| 333 | PETER McBRIDE (6/0) | — | (with Preston North End) |
| | 16 November 1874, Ayr | | 1904 v England |
| | | | 1906 v England |
| | | | 1907 v Wales, England |
| | | | 1908 v England |
| | | | 1909 v Wales |
| 334 | THOMAS NIBLO (1/0) | — | (with Aston Villa, Birmingham) |
| | 24 September 1877, Dunfermline | | 1904 v England |
| 335 | ALEXANDER BROWN (1/0) | — | (with Middlesbrough) |
| | 7 April 1879, Beith | | 1904 v England |
| 336 | SAMUEL KENNEDY (1/0) | — | (with Partick Thistle, Glasgow) |
| | 8 April 1881, Girvan | | 1905 v Wales |
| 337 | THOMAS FITCHIE (4/1) | — | (with Woolwich Arsenal, London) |
| | 11 December 1881, Edinburgh | | 1905 v Wales |
| | | | 1906 v Wales, Ireland (1) |
| | | — | (with Queen's Park, Glasgow) |
| | | | 1907 v Wales |
| 338 | WILLIAM HOWDEN (1/0) | — | (with Partick Thistle, Glasgow) |
| | 1874, Glasgow | | 1905 v Ireland |
| 339 | DONALD McLEOD (4/0) | — | (with Celtic, Glasgow) |
| | 28 May 1882, Laurieston | | 1905 v Ireland |
| | | | 1906 v Wales, Ireland, England |
| 340 | WILLIAM McINTOSH (1/0) | — | (with Third Lanark, Glasgow) |
| | | | 1905 v Ireland |
| 341 | JAMES HAY (11/0) | — | (with Celtic, Glasgow) |
| | 12 December 1880, Tarbolton | | 1905 v Ireland |
| | | | 1909 v Ireland |
| | | | 1910 v Wales, Ireland, England |
| | | | 1911 v Ireland, England |
| | | — | (with Newcastle United) |
| | | | 1912 v Wales, England |
| | | | 1914 v Ireland, England |
| 342 | JAMES McMENEMY (12/5) | — | (with Celtic, Glasgow) |
| | 23 August 1880, Rutherglen | | 1905 v Ireland |
| | | | 1909 v Ireland (2) |
| | | | 1910 v Wales, England (1) |
| | | | 1911 v Wales, Ireland (1), England |
| | | | 1912 v Wales |
| | | | 1914 v Wales, Ireland, England (1) |
| | | | 1920 v Ireland |
| 343 | JAMES QUINN (11/7) | — | (with Celtic, Glasgow) |
| | 8 July 1878, Croy | | 1905 v Ireland (1) |
| | | | 1906 v Wales, Ireland |
| | | | 1908 v Ireland (4), England |
| | | | 1909 v England |
| | | | 1910 v Wales, Ireland, England (1) |
| | | | 1912 v Wales (1), England |

| 344 | PETER SOMERS (4/0) | — | (with Celtic, Glasgow) |
| | 3 June 1878, Avondale | | 1905 v Ireland, England |
| | | | 1907 v Ireland |
| | | | 1909 v Wales |
| 345 | JOHN LYALL (1/0) | — | (with Sheffield Wednesday) |
| | 16 April 1881, Dundee | | 1905 v England |
| 346 | PETER McWILLIAM (8/0) | — | (with Newcastle United) |
| | 21 September 1879, Inverness | | 1905 v England |
| | | | 1906 v England |
| | | | 1907 v Wales, England |
| | | | 1909 v Wales, England |
| | | | 1910 v England |
| | | | 1911 v Wales |
| 347 | JAMES HOWIE (3/2) | — | (with Newcastle United) |
| | 19 March 1878, Galston | | 1905 v England |
| | | | 1906 v England (2) |
| | | | 1908 v England |
| 348 | ALEXANDER YOUNG (2/0) | — | (with Everton, Liverpool) |
| | 23 June 1880, Slamannan | | 1905 v England |
| | | | 1907 v Wales |
| 349 | JAMES RAESIDE (1/0) | — | (with Third Lanark, Glasgow) |
| | 1879, Glasgow | | 1906 v Wales |
| 350 | ANDREW RICHMOND (1/0) | — | (with Queen's Park, Glasgow) |
| | | | 1906 v Wales |
| 351 | ALEXANDER McNAIR (15/0) | — | (with Celtic, Glasgow) |
| | 26 December 1883, Bo'ness | | 1906 v Wales |
| | | | 1907 v Ireland |
| | | | 1908 v Wales, England |
| | | | 1909 v England |
| | | | 1910 v Wales |
| | | | 1912 v Wales, Ireland, England |
| | | | 1913 v England |
| | | | 1914 v Ireland, England |
| | | | 1920 v Wales, Ireland, England |
| 352 | JOHN MAY (5/0) | — | (with Rangers, Glasgow) |
| | 15 April 1878, Dykehead | | 1906 v Wales, Ireland |
| | | | 1908 v Ireland, England |
| | | | 1909 v Wales |
| 353 | GEORGE STEWART (4/0) | — | (with Hibernian, Edinburgh) |
| | 1883, Wishaw | | 1906 v Wales, England |
| | | — | (with Manchester City) |
| | | | 1907 v Wales, England |
| 354 | DAVID HILL (1/0) | — | (with Third Lanark, Glasgow) |
| | 16 December 1881, Saint Quivox | | 1906 v Ireland |
| 355 | JAMES YOUNG (1/0) | — | (with Celtic, Glasgow) |
| | 10 January 1882, Kilmarnock | | 1906 v Ireland |
| 356 | GLADSTONE HAMILTON (1/0) | — | (with Port Glasgow Athletic) |
| | 23 July 1879, Glasgow | | 1906 v Ireland |
| 357 | WILLIAM DUNLOP (1/0) | — | (with Liverpool) |
| | 1874, Hurlford | | 1906 v England |
| 358 | ALEXANDER MENZIES (1/0) | — | (with Heart of Midlothian, Edinburgh) |
| | 25 November 1882, Blantyre | | 1906 v England |
| 359 | GEORGE LIVINGSTON (2/0) | — | (with Manchester City) |
| | 5 May 1876, Dumbarton | | 1906 v England |
| | | — | (with Rangers, Glasgow) |
| | | | 1907 v Wales |
| 360 | WILLIAM MUIR (1/0) | — | (with Dundee) |
| | 22 September 1877, Ayr | | 1907 v Ireland |
| 361 | WILLIAM AGNEW (3/0) | — | (with Kilmarnock) |
| | 16 December 1880, Kilmarnock | | 1907 v Ireland |
| | | | 1908 v Wales, Ireland |
| 362 | WILLIAM KEY (1/0) | — | (with Queen's Park, Glasgow) |
| | Glasgow | | 1907 v Ireland |
| 363 | FRANK O'ROURKE (1/1) | — | (with Airdrie) |
| | 5 December 1878, Bargeddie | | 1907 v Ireland (1) |

| | | | |
|---|---|---|---|
| 364 | JOHN FRASER (1/0) | – | (with Dundee) |
| | 10 November 1876, Dumbarton | | 1907 v Ireland |
| 365 | ANDREW WILSON (6/2) | – | (with Sheffield Wednesday) |
| | 10 December 1880, Irvine | | 1907 v England |
| | | | 1908 v England (1) |
| | | | 1912 v England (1) |
| | | | 1913 v Wales, England |
| | | | 1914 v Ireland |
| 366 | WALTER WHITE (2/0) | – | (with Bolton Wanderers) |
| | 15 May 1882, Hurlford | | 1907 v England |
| | | | 1908 v England |
| 367 | GEORGE CHAPLIN (1/0) | – | (with Dundee) |
| | 26 September 1888, Dundee | | 1908 v Wales |
| 368 | JAMES GALT (2/1) | – | (with Rangers, Glasgow) |
| | 11 August 1885, Saltcoats | | 1908 v Wales, Ireland (1) |
| 369 | JAMES SPEIRS (1/0) | – | (with Rangers, Glasgow) |
| | 22 March 1886, Glasgow | | 1908 v Wales |
| 370 | WILLIAM LENNIE (2/1) | – | (with Aberdeen) |
| | 26 January 1882, Glasgow | | 1908 v Wales (1), Ireland |
| 371 | JAMES MITCHELL (3/0) | – | (with Kilmarnock) |
| | | | 1908 v Ireland |
| | | | 1910 v Wales, Ireland |
| 372 | THOMAS COLLINS (1/0) | – | (with Heart of Midlothian, Edinburgh) |
| | 16 April 1882, Leven | | 1909 v Wales |
| 373 | JOHN HUNTER (1/0) | – | (with Dundee) |
| | 6 April 1879, Johnstone | | 1909 v Wales |
| 374 | HAROLD PAUL (3/2) | – | (with Queen's Park, Glasgow) |
| | 31 August 1886, Gourock | | 1909 v Wales (1), Ireland (1), England |
| 375 | JAMES BROWNLIE (16/0) | – | (with Third Lanark, Glasgow) |
| | 15 May 1885, Blantyre | | 1909 v Ireland, England |
| | | | 1910 v Wales, Ireland, England |
| | | | 1911 v Wales, Ireland |
| | | | 1912 v Wales, Ireland, England |
| | | | 1913 v Wales, Ireland, England |
| | | | 1914 v Wales, Ireland, England |
| 376 | JAMES MAIN (1/0) | – | (with Hibernian, Edinburgh) |
| | 29 May 1886, West Calder | | 1909 v Ireland |
| 377 | WILLIAM WALKER (2/0) | – | (with Clyde, Glasgow) |
| | 1884, Glasgow | | 1909 v Ireland |
| | | | 1910 v Ireland |
| 378 | JAMES STARK (2/0) | – | (with Rangers, Glasgow) |
| | 1880, Glasgow | | 1909 v Ireland, England |
| 379 | ALEXANDER THOMSON (1/1) | – | (with Airdrie) |
| | Coatbridge | | 1909 v Ireland (1) |
| 380 | GEORGE LAW (3/0) | – | (with Rangers, Glasgow) |
| | 13 December 1885, Arbroath | | 1910 v Wales, Ireland, England |
| 381 | WILLIAM LONEY (2/0) | – | (with Celtic, Glasgow) |
| | 31 May 1879, Denny | | 1910 v Wales, Ireland |
| 382 | ANDREW DEVINE (1/1) | – | (with Falkirk) |
| | Lochore | | 1910 v Wales (1) |
| 383 | GEORGE ROBERTSON (4/0) | – | (with Motherwell) |
| | Stonefield | | 1910 v Wales |
| | | – | (with Sheffield Wednesday) |
| | | | 1912 v Wales |
| | | | 1913 v Ireland, England |
| 384 | GEORGE SINCLAIR (3/0) | – | (with Heart of Midlothian, Edinburgh) |
| | 25 September 1889, Edinburgh | | 1910 v Ireland |
| | | | 1912 v Wales, Ireland |
| 385 | JOHN McTAVISH (1/0) | – | (with Falkirk) |
| | 7 June 1885, Glasgow | | 1910 v Ireland |
| 386 | ALEXANDER HIGGINS (4/1) | – | (with Newcastle United) |
| | Kilmarnock | | 1910 v Ireland, England |
| | | | 1911 v Ireland, England (1) |
| 387 | DONALD COLMAN (4/0) | – | (with Aberdeen) |
| | 14 August 1878, Renton | | 1911 v Wales, Ireland, England |
| | | | 1913 v Ireland |

| | | | |
|---|---|---|---|
| 388 | JOHN WALKER (9/0) | – | (with Swindon Town) |
| | 6 November 1884, Beith | | 1911 v Wales, Ireland, England |
| | | | 1912 v Wales, Ireland, England |
| | | | 1913 v Wales, Ireland, England |
| 389 | THOMAS TAIT (1/0) | – | (with Sunderland) |
| | 13 September 1879, Carluke | | 1911 v Wales |
| 390 | WILFRID LOW (5/0) | – | (with Newcastle United) |
| | 8 December 1884, Aberdeen | | 1911 v Wales, England |
| | | | 1912 v Ireland |
| | | | 1920 v Ireland, England |
| 391 | WILLIAM REID (9/4) | – | (with Rangers, Glasgow) |
| | Glasgow | | 1911 v Wales, Ireland (1), England |
| | | | 1912 v Ireland (1) |
| | | | 1913 v Wales, Ireland (1), England |
| | | | 1914 v Ireland, England (1) |
| 392 | ANGUS DOUGLAS (1/0) | – | (with Chelsea, London) |
| | 1 January 1889, Lochmaben | | 1911 v Ireland |
| 393 | JAMES LAWRENCE (1/0) | – | (with Newcastle United) |
| | 16 February 1885, Glasgow | | 1911 v England |
| 394 | ROBERT MERCER (2/0) | – | (with Heart of Midlothian, Edinburgh) |
| | 21 September 1889, Avonbridge | | 1912 v Wales |
| | | | 1913 v Ireland |
| 395 | JAMES GORDON (10/0) | – | (with Rangers, Glasgow) |
| | 23 July 1888, Saltcoats | | 1912 v Ireland, England |
| | | | 1913 v Wales, Ireland, England |
| | | | 1914 v Ireland, England |
| | | | 1920 v Wales, Ireland, England |
| 396 | ALEXANDER BELL (1/0) | – | (with Manchester United) |
| | Cape Town, South Africa | | 1912 v Ireland |
| 397 | WALTER AITKENHEAD (1/2) | – | (with Blackburn Rovers) |
| | 21 May 1887, Glasgow | | 1912 v Ireland (2) |
| 398 | DAVID McLEAN (1/0) | – | (with Sheffield Wednesday) |
| | 13 December 1887, Forfar | | 1912 v England |
| 399 | ROBERT ORROCK (1/0) | – | (with Falkirk) |
| | 25 May 1885, Kinghorn | | 1913 v Wales |
| 400 | JAMES CAMPBELL (1/0) | – | (with Sheffield Wednesday) |
| | Edinburgh | | 1913 v Wales |
| 401 | ANDREW McATEE (1/0) | – | (with Celtic, Glasgow) |
| | 2 July 1888, Cumbernauld | | 1913 v Wales |
| 402 | THOMAS LOGAN (1/0) | – | (with Falkirk) |
| | 17 August 1888, Barrhead | | 1913 v Ireland |
| 403 | PETER NELLIES (2/0) | – | (with Heart of Midlothian, Edinburgh) |
| | 24 August 1886, Kingseat | | 1913 v Ireland |
| | | | 1914 v Wales |
| 404 | JAMES CROAL (3/0) | – | (with Falkirk) |
| | 27 July 1885, Glasgow | | 1913 v Ireland |
| | | | 1914 v Wales, England |
| 405 | DAVID WILSON (1/0) | – | (with Oldham Athletic) |
| | 14 January 1884, Irvine | | 1913 v England |
| 406 | JOSEPH DONNACHIE (3/1) | – | (with Oldham Athletic) |
| | 1885, Kilwinning | | 1913 v England |
| | | | 1914 v Ireland (1), England |
| 407 | THOMAS KELSO (1/0) | – | (with Dundee) |
| | 5 June 1882, Renton | | 1914 v Wales |
| 408 | JOSEPH DODDS (3/0) | – | (with Celtic, Glasgow) |
| | 14 July 1887, Carluke | | 1914 v Wales, Ireland, England |
| 409 | PETER PURSELL (1/0) | – | (with Queen's Park, Glasgow) |
| | 1 July 1894, Campbeltown | | 1914 v Wales |
| 410 | HAROLD ANDERSON (1/0) | – | (with Raith Rovers, Kirkcaldy) |
| | 1892, Glasgow | | 1914 v Wales |
| 411 | ALEXANDER DONALDSON (6/1) | – | (with Bolton Wanderers) |
| | 4 December 1890, Barrhead | | 1914 v Wales, Ireland, England |
| | | | 1920 v Ireland, England (1) |
| | | | 1922 v Ireland |
| 412 | JAMES REID (3/0) | – | (with Airdrie) |
| | 1 May 1890, Peebles | | 1914 v Wales |
| | | | 1920 v Wales |
| | | | 1924 v Ireland |

413 JOHN BROWNING (1/0)    – (with Celtic, Glasgow)
29 November 1888, Dumbarton    1914 v Wales

414 KENNETH CAMPBELL (8/0)    – (with Liverpool)
6 September 1892, Cambuslang    1920 v Wales, Ireland
    – (with Partick Thistle, Glasgow)
    1920 v England
    1921 v Wales, Ireland
    1922 v Wales, Ireland, England

415 DAVID THOMSON (1/0)    – (with Dundee)
1892, Dundee    1920 v Wales

416 WILLIAM CRINGAN (5/0)    – (with Celtic, Glasgow)
15 May 1890, Muirkirk    1920 v Wales
    1922 v Ireland, England
    1923 v Wales, England

417 JAMES McMULLAN (16/0)    – (with Partick Thistle, Glasgow)
26 March 1895, Denny    1920 v Wales
    1921 v Wales, Ireland, England
    1924 v Ireland, England
    1925 v England, Wales
    – (with Manchester City)
    1926 v England, Wales
    1927 v England, Wales
    1928 v England, Wales
    1929 v Ireland, England

418 JOHN CROSBIE (2/0)    – (with Ayr United)
Glenbuck    1920 v Wales
    – (with Birmingham)
    1922 v England

419 ANDREW WILSON (12/13)    – (with Dunfermline Athletic)
15 February 1896, Newmilns    1920 v Wales, Ireland (1), England (1)
    1921 v Wales (2), Ireland (1),
    England (1)
    – (with Middlesbrough)
    1922 v Wales, Ireland (2), England (1)
    1923 v Ireland (1), Wales (2), England (1)

420 THOMAS CAIRNS (8/1)    – (with Rangers, Glasgow)
30 October 1890, Merryton    1920 v Wales (1)
    1922 v England
    1923 v Wales, England
    1924 v Ireland
    1925 v Wales, Ireland, England

421 ALAN MORTON (31/5)    – (with Queen's Park, Glasgow)
24 April 1893, Glasgow    1920 v Wales, Ireland (1)
    – (with Rangers, Glasgow)
    1921 v England (1)
    1922 v Wales, England
    1923 v Ireland, Wales, England
    1924 v Wales, Ireland, England
    1925 v Wales, Ireland, England
    1927 v Ireland (2), England (1), Wales
    1928 v Ireland, England, Wales
    1929 v Ireland, England, Wales
    1930 v Ireland, England, Wales
    1931 v Ireland, England, Wales
    1932 v England, France

422 JAMES BLAIR (8/0)    – (with Sheffield Wednesday)
11 May 1888, Glenboig    1920 v Ireland, England
    – (with Cardiff City)
    1921 v England
    1922 v England
    1923 v Ireland, Wales, England
    1924 v Wales

423 JAMES BOWIE (2/0)    – (with Rangers, Glasgow)
9 July 1888, Glasgow    1920 v Ireland, England

424 ANDREW CUNNINGHAM (12/5)    – (with Rangers, Glasgow)
30 January 1891, Galston    1920 v Ireland (1)
    1921 v Wales, England (1)
    1922 v Ireland
    1923 v Wales, England (1)
    1924 v Ireland (1), England
    1926 v Ireland (1), England, Wales
    1927 v England

425 THOMAS MILLER (3/2)    – (with Liverpool)
Motherwell    1920 v England (2)
    – (with Manchester United)
    1921 v Ireland, England

426 JOHN PATERSON (1/0)    – (with Leicester City)
14 December 1896, Dundee    1920 v England

427 ALEXANDER TROUP (5/0)    – (with Dundee)
4 May 1895, Forfar    1920 v England
    1921 v Wales, Ireland
    1922 v Ireland
    – (with Everton, Liverpool)
    1926 v England

428 JOHN MARSHALL (7/0)    – (with Middlesbrough)
Saltcoats    1921 v Wales, Ireland, England
    1922 v Wales, Ireland, England
    – (with Llanelli)
    1924 v Wales

429 WILLIAM McSTAY (13/0)    – (with Celtic, Glasgow)
21 April 1894, Netherburn    1921 v Wales, Ireland
    1925 v Wales, Ireland, England, Wales
    1926 v Ireland, England, Wales
    1927 v Ireland, England, Wales
    1928 v Ireland

430 JOSEPH HARRIS (2/0)    – (with Partick Thistle, Glasgow)
19 March 1896, Glasgow    1921 v Wales, Ireland

431 CHARLES PRINGLE (1/0)    – (with St Mirren, Paisley)
18 October 1894, Barrhead    1921 v Wales

432 ALEXANDER ARCHIBALD (8/1)    – (with Rangers, Glasgow)
6 September 1897, Aberdour    1921 v Wales
    1922 v Wales (1), England
    1923 v Ireland
    1924 v Wales, England
    1931 v England
    1932 v England

433 JOSEPH CASSIDY (4/1)    – (with Celtic, Glasgow)
10 August 1896, Cadder    1921 v Wales, Ireland (1)
    1923 v Ireland
    1924 v Wales

434 JOHN GRAHAM (1/0)    – (with Arsenal, London)
11 July 1890, Hurlford    1921 v Ireland

435 ALEXANDER McNAB (2/0)    – (with Morton, Greenock)
27 December 1895, Gourock    1921 v Ireland, England

436 JOHN EWART (1/0)    – (with Bradford City)
14 February 1891, Oakbank    1921 v England

437 STEWART DAVIDSON (1/0)    – (with Middlesbrough)
1 June 1886, Aberdeen    1921 v England

438 GEORGE BREWSTER (1/0)    – (with Everton, Liverpool)
7 May 1893, Cusalmond    1921 v England

439 DONALD McKINLAY (2/0)    – (with Liverpool)
25 July 1891, Glasgow    1922 v Wales, Ireland

440 DAVID MEIKLEJOHN (15/3)    – (with Rangers, Glasgow)
12 December 1900, Glasgow    1922 v Wales
    1924 v Wales
    1925 v Wales (1), Ireland (1), England
    1927 v Wales
    1928 v Ireland
    1929 v Ireland, England
    1930 v Ireland, England
    1931 v England, Ireland, Wales
    1933 v Austria (1)

441 MICHAEL GILHOOLEY (1/0)     – (with Hull City)
26 November 1896, Edinburgh     1922 v Wales

442 WILLIAM COLLIER (1/0)     – (with Raith Rovers, Kirkcaldy)
11 December 1890, Kirkcaldy     1922 v Wales

443 JOHN WHITE (2/0)     – (with Albion Rovers, Coatbridge)
27 August 1897, Airdrie     1922 v Wales
    – (with Heart of Midlothian, Edinburgh)
    1923 v Ireland

444 FRANK WALKER (1/0)     – (with Third Lanark, Glasgow)
Paisley     1922 v Wales

445 JAMES HOGG (1/0)     – (with Ayr United)
    1922 v Ireland

446 THOMAS MUIRHEAD (8/0)     – (with Rangers, Glasgow)
31 January 1897, Cowdenbeath     1922 v Ireland
    1923 v England
    1924 v Wales
    1927 v Ireland
    1928 v Ireland, Wales
    1929 v Ireland, Wales

447 JAMES KINLOCH (1/0)     – (with Partick Thistle, Glasgow)
Glasgow     1922 v Ireland

448 JOHN GILCHRIST (1/0)     – (with Celtic, Glasgow)
30 March 1899, Glasgow     1922 v England

449 NEIL McBAIN (3/0)     – (with Manchester United)
15 November 1895, Campbeltown     1922 v England
    – (with Everton, Liverpool)
    1923 v Ireland
    1924 v Wales

450 WILLIAM HARPER (11/0)     – (with Hibernian, Edinburgh)
19 January 1897, Winchburgh     1923 v Ireland, Wales, England
    1924 v Wales, Ireland, England
    1925 v Wales, Ireland, England
    – (with Arsenal, London)
    1926 v Ireland, England

451 JOHN HUTTON (10/1)     – (with Aberdeen)
29 October 1898, Dalziel     1923 v Ireland, Wales, England
    1924 v Ireland
    1925 v Wales
    1926 v Ireland, England
    – (with Blackburn Rovers)
    1927 v Ireland, Wales (1)
    1928 v Ireland

452 DAVID STEELE (3/0)     – (with Huddersfield Town)
29 July 1894, Carluke     1923 v Ireland, Wales, England

453 DAVID MORRIS (6/1)     – (with Raith Rovers, Kirkcaldy)
21 August 1899, Edinburgh     1923 v Ireland
    1924 v Ireland (1), England
    1925 v Wales, Ireland, England

454 JOHN McNAB (1/0)     – (with Liverpool)
7 April 1894, Cleland     1923 v Wales

455 HENRY RITCHIE (2/0)     – (with Hibernian, Edinburgh)
27 October 1898, Scone     1923 v Wales
    1928 v Ireland

456 DENIS LAWSON (1/0)     – (with St Mirren, Paisley)
11 December 1897, Lennoxtown     1923 v England

457 WILLIAM RUSSELL (2/0)     – (with Airdrie)
6 December 1901, Falkirk     1924 v Wales
    1925 v England

458 JOHN McKAY (1/0)     – (with Blackburn Rovers)
1 November 1898, Glasgow     1924 v Wales

459 JAMES HAMILTON (1/0)     – (with St Mirren, Paisley)
16 June 1901, Bargeddie     1924 v Ireland

460 PETER KERR (1/0)     – (with Hibernian, Edinburgh)
20 June 1891, Prestonpans     1924 v Ireland

461 HUGH GALLACHER (20/24)     – (with Airdrie)
2 February 1903, Bellshill     1924 v Ireland
    1925 v Wales (2), Ireland (1),
    England (2), Wales
    – (with Newcastle United)
    1926 v Ireland (3), England, Wales (1)
    1927 v Ireland, England, Wales (1)
    1928 v England, Wales (3)
    1929 v Ireland (5), England, Wales (2)
    1930 v Ireland (2), France (2)
    – (with Chelsea, London)
    1934 v England
    – (with Derby County)
    1935 v England

462 JOHN SMITH (1/0)     – (with Ayr United)
Beith     1924 v England

463 PHILIP McCLOY (2/0)     – (with Ayr United)
19 April 1896, Uddingston     1924 v England
    1925 v England

464 WILLIAM CLUNAS (2/1)     – (with Sunderland)
29 April 1899, Johnstone     1924 v England
    1925 v Wales (1)

465 WILLIAM COWAN (1/1)     – (with Newcastle United)
9 August 1896, Edinburgh     1924 v England (1)

466 NEIL HARRIS (1/0)     – (with Newcastle United)
30 October 1894, Glasgow     1924 v England

467 JAMES NELSON (4/0)     – (with Cardiff City)
7 January 1901, Greenock     1925 v Wales, Ireland
    1928 v England
    1930 v France

468 ROBERT BENNIE (3/0)     – (with Airdrie)
27 March 1900, Slamannan     1925 v Wales, Ireland
    1926 v Ireland

469 ALEXANDER JACKSON (17/8)     – (with Aberdeen)
12 May 1905, Renton     1925 v Wales, Ireland, England
    – (with Huddersfield Town)
    1925 v Wales
    1926 v Ireland, England (1), Wales (2)
    1927 v Ireland, Wales
    1928 v England (3), Wales
    1929 v Ireland (2), England, Wales
    1930 v Ireland, England, France

470 JAMES DUNN (6/2)     – (with Hibernian, Edinburgh)
25 November 1900, Glasgow     1925 v Wales, Ireland (1)
    1927 v Ireland
    1928 v Ireland, England
    – (with Everton, Liverpool)
    1928 v Wales (1)

471 WILLIAM ROBB (2/0)     – (with Rangers, Glasgow)
20 March 1895, Rutherglen     1925 v Wales
    – (with Hibernian, Edinburgh)
    1927 v Wales

472 THOMAS TOWNSLEY (1/0)     – (with Falkirk)
28 April 1898, Polmont     1925 v Wales

473 JOHN DUNCAN (1/1)     – (with Leicester City)
14 February 1896, Lochgelly     1925 v Wales (1)

474 ALEXANDER JAMES (8/3)     – (with Preston North End)
14 September 1901, Mossend     1925 v Wales
    1928 v England (2)
    1929 v Ireland, England
    – (with Arsenal, London)
    1929 v Wales (1)
    1930 v Ireland, England
    1932 v Wales

475 ADAM McLEAN (4/1)     – (with Celtic, Glasgow)
27 April 1899, Glasgow     1925 v Wales (1)
    1926 v Ireland, Wales
    1927 v England

476 PETER WILSON (4/0) – (with Celtic, Glasgow)
25 November 1905, Beith 1926 v Ireland
1930 v France
1931 v Ireland
1933 v England

477 JOHN McDOUGALL (1/0) – (with Airdrie)
21 September 1901, Port Glasgow 1926 v Ireland

478 THOMAS McINALLY (2/0) – (with Celtic, Glasgow)
9 December 1900, Barrhead 1926 v Ireland, Wales

479 JAMES GIBSON (8/1) – (with Partick Thistle, Glasgow)
12 June 1901, Larkhall 1926 v England, Wales
1927 v Ireland, England
– (with Aston Villa, Birmingham)
1927 v Wales
1928 v England
1929 v Wales (1)
1930 v Ireland

480 WILLIAM SUMMERS (1/0) – (with St Mirren, Paisley)
14 July 1893, Burnbank 1926 v England

481 ALEXANDER THOMSON (3/0) – (with Celtic, Glasgow)
14 June 1901, Buckhaven 1926 v England
1932 v France, Wales

482 ALLAN McCLORY (3/0) – (with Motherwell)
11 November 1899, Armadale 1926 v Wales
1928 v Ireland
1934 v Wales

483 WILLIAM WISEMAN (2/0) – (with Queen's Park, Glasgow)
18 October 1896, Wartle 1926 v Wales
1930 v Ireland

484 ROBERT GILLESPIE (4/0) – (with Queen's Park, Glasgow)
28 April 1901, Kilsyth 1926 v Wales
1930 v Wales
1932 v France
1933 v England

485 JOHN HARKNESS (12/0) – (with Queen's Park, Glasgow)
27 September 1907, Glasgow 1927 v Ireland, England
1928 v England
– (with Heart of Midlothian, Edinburgh)
1928 v Wales
1929 v Ireland, England, Wales
1930 v England
1931 v Wales
1932 v France
1933 v Ireland, Wales

486 THOMAS CRAIG (8/1) – (with Rangers, Glasgow)
18 July 1895, Laurieston 1927 v Ireland
1928 v Ireland
1929 v Norway (1), Germany, Netherlands, Wales
1930 v Ireland, England

487 JAMES HOWIESON (1/0) – (with St Mirren, Paisley)
7 June 1900, Rutherglen 1927 v Ireland

488 ROBERT THOMSON (1/0) – (with Falkirk)
24 October 1905, Falkirk 1927 v England

489 THOMAS MORRISON (1/0) – (with St Mirren, Paisley)
Coylton 1927 v England

490 ROBERT McPHAIL (17/7) – (with Airdrie)
25 October 1905, Barrhead 1927 v England
– (with Rangers, Glasgow)
1928 v Wales
1931 v Ireland, England, Ireland (1), Wales
1932 v France, Ireland (2)
1933 v England, Ireland (1), Austria
1935 v England
1936 v Germany
1937 v England (2), Czechoslovakia (1), Wales, Ireland

491 ROBERT McKAY (1/0) – (with Newcastle United)
2 September 1900, Glasgow 1927 v Wales

492 GEORGE STEVENSON (12/4) – (with Motherwell)
4 April 1905, Kilbirnie 1927 v Wales
1928 v Ireland
1930 v Ireland (1), England, France, Wales
1931 v England (1), Ireland (1), Wales (1)
1932 v Ireland
1934 v England, Ireland

493 JAMES McGRORY (7/6) – (with Celtic, Glasgow)
26 April 1904, Glasgow 1928 v Ireland
1931 v England (1), Ireland (1), Wales (1)
1932 v Ireland (1)
1933 v England (2), Ireland

494 THOMAS LAW (2/0) – (with Chelsea, London)
1 April 1908, Glasgow 1928 v England
1930 v England

495 THOMAS BRADSHAW (1/0) – (with Bury)
7 February 1904, Bishopton 1928 v England

496 DOUGLAS GRAY (10/0) – (with Rangers, Glasgow)
4 April 1905, Alford 1928 v Wales
1929 v Ireland, Germany, Netherlands, Wales
1930 v Ireland, England, Wales
1932 v Ireland, Wales

497 DANIEL BLAIR (8/0) – (with Clyde, Glasgow)
2 February 1906, Glasgow 1928 v Wales
1929 v Ireland
1931 v England, Austria, Italy, Northern Ireland, Wales
– (with Aston Villa, Birmingham)
1932 v Wales

498 WILLIAM KING (1/0) – (with Queen's Park, Glasgow)
1900, Glasgow 1928 v Wales

499 WILLIAM CHALMERS (1/0) – (with Queen's Park, Glasgow)
5 March 1907, Glasgow 1929 v Ireland

500 JAMES CRAPNELL (9/0) – (with Airdrie)
4 June 1903, Paisley 1929 v England, Norway, Germany
1930 v France
1931 v Ireland, Switzerland
1932 v England, France, Ireland

501 JOSEPH NIBLOE (11/0) – (with Kilmarnock)
23 November 1903, Corkerhill – 1929 v England, Norway, Netherlands, Wales
1931 v Ireland, England, Austria, Italy, Switzerland
1932 v England, France

502 JOHN BUCHANAN (2/0) – (with Rangers, Glasgow)
15 March 1899, Paisley 1929 v England
1930 v England

503 ALEXANDER CHEYNE (5/4) – (with Aberdeen)
28 April 1907, Glasgow 1929 v England (1), Norway (3), Germany, Netherlands
1930 v France

504 ALEXANDER McLAREN (5/0) – (with St Johnstone, Perth)
25 December 1910, Tibbermore 1929 v Norway, Germany, Netherlands
1932 v Ireland, Wales

505 WILLIAM IMRIE (2/1) – (with St Johnstone, Perth)
4 March 1908, Methil 1929 v Norway, Germany (1)

506 ALLAN CRAIG (3/0) – (with Motherwell)
7 February 1904, Motherwell 1929 v Norway, Netherlands
1932 v England

507 JAMES NISBET (3/2) – (with Ayr United)
27 August 1904, Glenbuck 1929 v Norway (2), Germany, Netherlands

508 DAVID McCRAE (2/0) – (with St Mirren, Paisley)
23 February 1900, Bridge of Weir 1929 v Norway, Germany

509 ROBERT RANKIN (3/2) — (with St Mirren, Paisley)
7 April 1905, Paisley
1929 v Norway (1), Germany, Netherlands (1)

510 ROBERT HOWE (2/0) — (with Hamilton Academical)
3 August 1903, Dumbarton
1929 v Norway, Netherlands

511 HUGH MORTON (2/0) — (with Kilmarnock)
25 November 1902, Newmilns
1929 v Germany, Netherlands

512 JAMES FLEMING (3/3) — (with Rangers, Glasgow)
5 December 1901, Glasgow
1929 v Germany, Netherlands (1)
1930 v England (2)

513 JOHN JOHNSTONE (3/0) — (with Heart of Midlothian, Edinburgh)
17 November 1902, Stevenston
1929 v Wales
1932 v Ireland, Wales

514 ROBERT MIDDLETON (1/0) — (with Cowdenbeath)
15 January 1903, Brechin
1930 v Ireland

515 JOHN THOMSON (4/0) — (with Celtic, Glasgow)
28 January 1909, Buckhaven
1930 v France, Wales
1931 v Ireland, England

516 GEORGE WALKER (4/0) — (with St Mirren, Paisley)
24 May 1909, Musselburgh
1930 v France
1931 v Ireland, Austria, Switzerland

517 FRANK HILL (3/0) — (with Aberdeen)
21 May 1906, Forfar
1930 v France, Wales
1931 v Ireland

518 JAMES CONNOR (4/0) — (with Sunderland)
1 June 1909, Renfrew
1930 v France
1931 v Ireland
1934 v England, Ireland

519 JOHN GILMOUR (1/0) — (with Dundee)
15 June 1901, Bellshill
1930 v Wales

520 COLIN McNAB (6/0) — (with Dundee)
6 April 1902, Edinburgh
1930 v Wales
1931 v England, Austria, Italy, Switzerland
1932 v England

521 DANIEL McRORIE (1/0) — (with Morton, Greenock)
25 June 1906, Glasgow
1930 v Wales

522 GEORGE BROWN (19/0) — (with Rangers, Glasgow)
7 January 1907, Glasgow
1930 v Wales
1931 v Ireland, Wales
1932 v England
1933 v England, Austria
1934 v Wales
1935 v England, Wales
1936 v England, Germany, Ireland, Wales
1937 v England, Czechoslovakia, Wales, Czechoslovakia
1938 v England, Netherlands

523 BERNARD BATTLES (1/1) — (with Heart of Midlothian, Edinburgh)
12 October 1905, Musselburgh
1930 v Wales (1)

524 JOHN MURDOCH (1/0) — (with Motherwell)
6 February 1901, New Stevenston
1931 v Ireland

525 PETER SCARFF (1/0) — (with Celtic, Glasgow)
29 March 1908, Linwood
1931 v Ireland

526 BENJAMIN YORSTON (1/0) — (with Aberdeen)
14 October 1905, Nigg
1931 v Ireland

527 JOHN MILLER (5/0) — (with St Mirren, Paisley)
Glasgow
1931 v England, Italy, Switzerland
1932 v France
1934 v England

528 JOHN JACKSON (8/0) — (with Partick Thistle, Glasgow)
29 November 1906, Glasgow
1931 v Austria, Italy, Switzerland
1933 v England
— (with Chelsea, London)
1934 v England
1935 v England, Wales, Ireland

529 JAMES McDOUGALL (2/0) — (with Liverpool)
23 January 1904, Port Glasgow
1931 v Austria, Italy

530 ANDREW LOVE (3/1) — (with Aberdeen)
26 March 1905, Renfrew
1931 v Austria, Italy, Switzerland (1)

531 JAMES PATERSON (3/0) — (with Cowdenbeath)
1907, Stirling
1931 v Austria, Italy, Switzerland

532 JAMES EASSON (3/1) — (with Portsmouth)
3 January 1906, Brechin
1931 v Austria, Switzerland (1)
1933 v Wales

533 JAMES ROBERTSON (2/0) — (with Dundee)
Dundee
1931 v Austria, Italy

534 DANIEL LIDDLE (3/0) — (with East Fife, Methil)
17 February 1912, Bo'ness
1931 v Austria, Italy, Switzerland

535 WILLIAM BOYD (2/1) — (with Clyde, Glasgow)
27 November 1905, Cambuslang
1931 v Italy, Switzerland (1)

536 ROBERT HEPBURN (1/0) — (with Ayr United)
29 September 1903, Cambusnethan
1931 v Ireland

537 ROBERT McAULAY (2/0) — (with Rangers, Glasgow)
28 August 1904, Wishaw
1931 v Ireland, Wales

538 ALEXANDER MASSIE (18/1) — (with Heart of Midlothian, Edinburgh)
13 March 1906, Glasgow
1931 v Ireland, Wales
1932 v France, Ireland
1933 v Ireland
1934 v England, Ireland, Wales
1935 v England, Wales, Ireland
— (with Aston Villa, Birmingham)
1936 v England, Germany, Ireland, Wales
1937 v England, Austria, Wales (1)

539 JAMES CRAWFORD (5/0) — (with Queen's Park, Glasgow)
21 May 1904, Glasgow
1931 v Ireland
1932 v France, Ireland, Wales
1933 v England

540 ROBERT THOMSON (1/1) — (with Celtic, Glasgow)
12 July 1907, Johnstone
1931 v Wales (1)

541 THOMAS HAMILTON (1/0) — (with Rangers, Glasgow)
Renfrew
1932 v England

542 JAMES MARSHALL (3/0) — (with Rangers, Glasgow)
3 January 1908, Avonbridge
1932 v England
1933 v England
1934 v England

543 NEIL DEWAR (3/4) — (with Third Lanark, Glasgow)
11 November 1908, Lochgilphead
1932 v England, France (3), Wales (1)

544 CHARLES NAPIER (5/3) — (with Celtic, Glasgow)
8 October 1910, Bainsford
1932 v England
1934 v Wales (2)
1935 v England
— (with Derby County)
1936 v Ireland (1)
1937 v Austria

545 WILLIAM TELFER (2/0) — (with Motherwell)
23 March 1909, Shotts
1932 v Ireland
— 1933 v Ireland

546 JAMES KING (2/1) — (with Hamilton Academical)
16 April 1906, Craigneuk
1932 v Ireland (1)
1933 v Ireland

547 HUGH WALES (1/0) — (with Motherwell)
6 May 1910, Kilwinning
1932 v Wales

548 JOHN THOMSON (1/0) — (with Everton, Liverpool)
6 July 1906, Thornton
1932 v Wales

549 DOUGLAS DUNCAN (14/7) — (with Derby County)
14 October 1909, Aberdeen
1932 v Wales (1)
1933 v England, Wales (1), Austria
1934 v Wales (1)
1935 v England (2), Wales (1), Ireland (1)
1936 v England, Germany, Ireland, Wales
1937 v England, Wales

550  ANDREW ANDERSON (23/0)  – (with Heart of Midlothian, Edinburgh)
     21 February 1909, Airdrie     1933  v England, Ireland, Wales, Austria
                                    1934  v England, Ireland, Wales
                                    1935  v England, Wales, Ireland
                                    1936  v England, Germany, Ireland, Wales
                                    1937  v England, Austria, Wales, Northern
                                    Ireland, Czechoslovakia
                                    1938  v England, Netherlands, Wales, Hungary

551  PETER McGONAGLE (6/0)  – (with Celtic, Glasgow)
     30 April 1904, Hamilton       1933  v England, Ireland, Austria
                                    1934  v England, Ireland, Wales

552  ALEXANDER LOW (1/0)  – (with Falkirk)
     Greenhill                     1933  v Ireland

553  JAMES BOYD (1/0)  – (with Newcastle United)
     29 April 1907, Glasgow        1933  v Ireland

554  ALEXANDER VENTERS (3/0)  – (with Cowdenbeath)
     9 June 1913, Cowdenbeath      1933  v Ireland
                                  – (with Rangers, Glasgow)
                                    1936  v England
                                    1939  v England

555  DUNCAN URQUHART (1/0)  – (with Hibernian, Edinburgh)
     18 August 1908, Edinburgh     1933  v Wales

556  MATTHEW BUSBY (1/0)  – (with Manchester City)
     26 May 1909, Orbiston         1933  v Wales

557  JOHN BLAIR (1/0)  – (with Motherwell)
     1910, Glasgow                 1933  v Wales

558  JAMES McLUCKIE (1/0)  – (with Manchester City)
     2 April 1908, Stonehouse      1933  v Wales

559  FRANCIS McGURK (1/0)  – (with Birmingham)
     15 January 1909, Eddlewood    1933  v Wales

560  JOHN McMENEMY (1/0)  – (with Motherwell)
     9 February 1908, Glasgow      1933  v Wales

561  WILLIAM McFADYEN (2/2)  – (with Motherwell)
     23 June 1904, Wishaw          1933  v Wales (1), Austria (1)

562  JAMES KENNAWAY (1/0)  – (with Celtic, Glasgow)
     25 January 1905, Montreal, Canada  1933  v Austria

563  PHILIP WATSON (1/0)  – (with Blackpool)
     23 February 1907, Dykehead    1933  v Austria

564  DUNCAN OGILVIE (1/0)  – (with Motherwell)
     8 October 1911, Glasgow       1933  v Austria

565  ROBERT BRUCE (1/0)  – (with Middlesbrough)
     29 January 1906, Paisley      1933  v Austria

566  THOMAS SMITH (2/0)  – (with Kilmarnock)
     4 October 1909, Fenwick       1934  v England
                                  – (with Preston North End)
                                    1938  v England

567  WILLIAM COOK (3/0)  – (with Bolton Wanderers)
     11 March 1906, Dundee         1934  v England, Ireland, Wales

568  JAMES DAWSON (14/0)  – (with Rangers, Glasgow)
     30 October 1909, Falkirk     – 1934  v Ireland
                                    1936  v England, Germany, Ireland, Wales
                                    1937  v England, Austria, Czechoslovakia,
                                    Wales, Ireland
                                    1938  v Netherlands, Ireland, Hungary
                                    1939  v England

569  JAMES SIMPSON (14/1)  – (with Rangers, Glasgow)
     29 October 1908, Ladybank     1934  v Ireland, Wales
                                    1935  v England, Wales, Ireland
                                    1936  v England, Germany, Ireland, Wales
                                    1937  v England, Austria, Czechoslovakia (1),
                                    Wales, Ireland

570  ANDREW HERD (1/0)  – (with Heart of Midlothian, Edinburgh)
     28 June 1902, Torryburn       1934  v Ireland

571  JAMES SMITH (2/1)  – (with Rangers, Glasgow)
     24 September 1911, Airdrie    1934  v Ireland
                                    1937  v Ireland (1)

572  PATRICK GALLACHER (1/1)  – (with Sunderland)
     21 August 1909, Bridge of Weir  1934  v Ireland (1)

573  THOMAS WALKER (20/9)  – (with Heart of Midlothian, Edinburgh)
     26 May 1915, Livingston Station  1934  v Wales
                                    1935  v England, Wales, Ireland (1)
                                    1936  v England (1), Germany, Ireland,
                                    Wales (1)
                                    1937  v England, Austria, Czechoslovakia, Wales,
                                    Ireland, Czechoslovakia
                                    1938  v England (1), Netherlands (1),
                                    Ireland (1),
                                    Wales (2), Hungary (1)
                                    1939  v England

574  DAVID McCULLOCH (7/3)  – (with Heart of Midlothian, Edinburgh)
     5 October 1911, Hamilton      1934  v Wales
                                  – (with Brentford, London)
                                    1936  v England, Ireland (1), Wales
                                    1937  v Czechoslovakia (2)
                                  – (with Derby County)
                                    1938  v Wales, Hungary

575  GEORGE CUMMINGS (9/0)  – (with Partick Thistle, Glasgow)
     5 June 1913, Thornbridge      1935  v England, Wales, Ireland
                                  – (with Aston Villa, Birmingham)
                                    1936  v England, Germany
                                    1937  v Wales, Ireland, Czechoslovakia
                                    1939  v England

576  JAMES DELANEY (13/3)  – (with Celtic, Glasgow)
     3 September 1914, Cleland     1935  v Wales, Ireland
                                    1936  v Germany (2)
                                    1937  v England, Austria, Czechoslovakia,
                                    Ireland
                                    1938  v Ireland (1), Wales
                                  – (with Manchester United)
                                    1947  v England, Ireland, Wales
                                    1948  v England

577  MATTHEW ARMSTRONG (3/0)  – (with Aberdeen)
     12 November 1911, Newton Stewart  1935  v Wales, Ireland
                                    1936  v Germany

578  WILLIAM MILLS (3/0)  – (with Aberdeen)
     28 January 1915, Alexandria   1935  v Wales, Ireland
                                    1936  v Wales

579  ALEXANDER HASTINGS (2/0)  – (with Sunderland)
     17 March 1912, Falkirk        1935  v Ireland
                                    1937  v Ireland

580  JOHN CRUM (2/0)  – (with Celtic, Glasgow)
     1 January 1912, Glasgow       1936  v England
                                    1938  v Ireland

581  ROBERT ANCELL (2/0)  – (with Newcastle United)
     16 June 1911, Dumfries        1936  v Ireland, Wales

582  ALEXANDER MUNRO (3/1)  – (with Heart of Midlothian, Edinburgh)
     6 April 1912, Carriden        1936  v Ireland (1), Wales
                                  – (with Blackpool)
                                    1938  v Netherlands

583  ANDREW BEATTIE (7/0)  – (with Preston North End)
     11 August 1913, Kintore       1937  v England, Austria, Czechoslovakia
                                    1938  v England, Ireland, Wales,
                                    Hungary

584  FRANK O'DONNELL (6/2)  – (with Preston North End)
     31 August 1911, Buckhaven     1937  v England (1), Austria (1), Czechoslovakia,
                                    Wales
                                  – (with Blackpool)
                                    1938  v England, Netherlands

585  ALEXANDER McNAB (2/0)  – (with Sunderland)
     27 December 1911, Glasgow     1937  v Austria
                                  – (with West Bromwich Albion)
                                    1939  v England

586 TORRANCE GILLICK (5/3) – (with Everton, Liverpool)
19 May 1915, Airdrie
1937 v Austria, Czechoslovakia (1)
1938 v Ireland, Wales (1), Hungary (1)

587 ROBERT HOGG (1/0) – (with Celtic, Glasgow)
10 May 1914, Larkhall
1937 v Czechoslovakia

588 CHARLES THOMSON (1/0) – (with Sunderland)
11 December 1910, Glasgow
1937 v Czechoslovakia

589 ROBERT MAIN (1/0) – (with Rangers, Glasgow)
10 February 1909, Airdrie
1937 v Wales

590 DUNCAN McKENZIE (1/0) – (with Brentford, London)
10 August 1912, Glasgow
1937 v Ireland

591 ROBERT REID (2/0) – (with Brentford, London)
19 February 1911, Hamilton
1937 v Ireland
1938 v England

592 WILLIAM WAUGH (1/0) – (with Heart of Midlothian, Edinburgh)
2 February 1910, Livingston Station
1937 v Czechoslovakia

593 GEORGE ROBERTSON (1/0) – (with Kilmarnock)
Kilmarnock
1937 v Czechoslovakia

594 ROBERT JOHNSTON (1/0) – (with Sunderland)
2 June 1909, Falkirk
1937 v Czechoslovakia

595 PETER BUCHANAN (1/1) – (with Chelsea, London)
13 October 1915, Glasgow
1937 v Czechoslovakia (1)

596 ANDREW BLACK (3/3) – (with Heart of Midlothian, Edinburgh)
23 September 1917, Stirling
1937 v Czechoslovakia (1)
1938 v Netherlands (1), Hungary (1)

597 DAVID KINNEAR (1/1) – (with Rangers, Glasgow)
22 February 1917, Kirkcaldy
1937 v Czechoslovakia (1)

598 DAVID CUMMING (1/0) – (with Middlesbrough)
6 May 1910, Aberdeen
1938 v England

599 WILLIAM SHANKLY (5/0) – (with Preston North End)
2 September 1913, Glenbuck
1938 v England, Ireland, Wales, Hungary
1939 v England

600 JOHN MILNE (2/0) – (with Middlesbrough)
25 March 1911, Stirling
1938 v England
1939 v England

601 GEORGE MUTCH (1/0) – (with Preston North End)
21 September 1912, Aberdeen
1938 v England

602 JAMES CARABINE (3/0) – (with Third Lanark, Glasgow)
23 November 1911, Blantyre
1938 v Netherlands, Ireland
1939 v England

603 THOMAS McKILLOP (1/0) – (with Rangers, Glasgow)
27 October 1917, Dreghorn
1938 v Netherlands

604 JAMES DYKES (2/0) – (with Heart of Midlothian, Edinburgh)
12 October 1916, Law
1938 v Netherlands, Ireland

605 FRANCIS MURPHY (1/1) – (with Celtic, Glasgow)
6 December 1915, Clydebank
1938 v Netherlands (1)

606 GEORGE PATERSON (1/0) – (with Celtic, Glasgow)
26 September 1914, Denny
1938 v Ireland

607 JOHN DIVERS (1/0) – (with Celtic, Glasgow)
6 August 1911, Clydebank
1938 v Ireland

608 JOHN BROWN (1/0) – (with Clyde, Glasgow)
21 February 1915, Troon
1938 v Wales

609 ROBERT BAXTER (3/0) – (with Middlesbrough)
23 January 1911, Gilmerton
1938 v Wales, Hungary
1939 v England

610 ARCHIBALD MILLER (1/0) – (with Heart of Midlothian, Edinburgh)
5 September 1913, Larkhall
1938 v Wales

611 ROBERT BEATTIE (1/0) – (with Preston North End)
24 January 1916, Kilmarnock
1938 v Wales

612 JAMES SYMON (1/0) – (with Rangers, Glasgow)
9 May 1911, Errol
1938 v Hungary

613 ALEXANDER McSPADYEN (2/0) – (with Partick Thistle, Glasgow)
19 December 1914, Carfin
1938 v Hungary
1939 v England

614 JAMES DOUGALL (1/1) – (with Preston North End)
3 October 1913, Denny
1939 v England (1)

615 WILLIAM MILLER (6/0) – (with Celtic, Glasgow)
20 November 1924, Glasgow
1946 v Wales
1947 v England, Belgium, Luxembourg, Ireland, Wales

616 JAMES STEPHEN (2/0) – (with Bradford)
23 August 1922, Johnshaven
1946 v Wales
1947 v Wales

617 DAVID SHAW (8/0) – (with Hibernian, Edinburgh)
5 May 1917, Annathill
1946 v Wales, Ireland
1948 v England, Belgium, Switzerland, France, Wales, Ireland

618 HUGH BROWN (3/0) – (with Partick Thistle, Glasgow)
7 December 1921, Carmyle
1946 v Wales
1947 v Belgium, Luxembourg

619 FRANK BRENNAN (7/0) – (with Newcastle United)
23 April 1924, Annathill
1946 v Wales, Ireland
1952 v Wales, Ireland
1953 v England, Ireland
1954 v England

620 JOHN HUSBAND (1/0) – (with Partick Thistle, Glasgow)
28 May 1918, Dunfermline
1946 v Wales

621 WILLIAM WADDELL (17/6) – (with Rangers, Glasgow)
7 March 1921, Forth
1946 v Wales (1)
1948 v Wales (2), Ireland
1949 v England, France, Ireland (2)
1950 v England
1951 v England, Denmark, France, Belgium (1), Austria, Ireland, Wales
1953 v Ireland
1954 v Wales, Ireland

622 CORNELIUS DOUGALL (1/0) – (with Birmingham City)
7 November 1921, Falkirk
1946 v Wales

623 WILLIAM THORNTON (7/1) – (with Rangers, Glasgow)
3 March 1920, Winchburgh
1946 v Wales, Ireland
1947 v Ireland
1948 v England
1949 v France
1952 v Denmark (1), Sweden

624 JAMES BLAIR (1/0) – (with Blackpool)
6 January 1918, Glasgow
1946 v Wales

625 WILLIAM LIDDELL (28/6) – (with Liverpool)
10 January 1922, Dunfermline
1946 v Wales, Ireland
1947 v Ireland, Wales
1948 v England
1949 v Wales
1950 v England, Portugal, France, Wales (1), Ireland, Austria
1951 v England (1), Ireland, Wales
1952 v England, USA, Denmark, Sweden (1), Wales (1), Ireland
1953 v England, Wales
1955 v Portugal (1), Yugoslavia, Austria (1), Hungary, Ireland

626 ROBERT BROWN (3/0) – (with Rangers, Glasgow)
19 March 1923, Dunipace
1946 v Ireland
1948 v Ireland
1952 v England

627 GEORGE YOUNG (53/0) — (with Rangers, Glasgow)
27 October 1922, Grangemouth
1946 v Ireland
1947 v England, Belgium, Luxembourg, Ireland
1948 v England, Belgium, Switzerland, France, Wales, Ireland
1949 v England, France, Ireland, Wales
1950 v England, Switzerland, Portugal, France, Wales, Ireland, Austria
1951 v England, Denmark, France, Belgium, Austria, Ireland, Wales
1952 v England, USA, Denmark, Sweden, Wales, Ireland
1953 v England, Sweden, Ireland, Wales
1954 v Wales, Northern Ireland
1955 v Portugal, Yugoslavia, Northern Ireland, Wales
1956 v England, Austria, Wales, Northern Ireland, Yugoslavia
1957 v England, Spain, Switzerland

628 WILLIAM CAMPBELL (5/0) — (with Morton, Greenock)
26 July 1920, Greenock
1946 v Ireland
1948 v England, Belgium, Switzerland, France

629 HUGH LONG (1/0) — (with Clyde, Glasgow)
2 January 1923, Glasgow
1946 v Ireland

630 GORDON SMITH (18/4) — (with Hibernian, Edinburgh)
25 May 1924, Edinburgh
1946 v Ireland
1947 v England, Wales
1948 v Belgium, Switzerland, France
1952 v England, USA
1955 v Portugal, Yugoslavia (1), Austria (1), Hungary (1), Northern Ireland, Wales
1956 v England
1957 v Spain, Switzerland, Spain (1)

631 GEORGE HAMILTON (5/4) — (with Aberdeen)
7 December 1917, Irvine
1946 v Ireland
1951 v Belgium (3), Austria
1954 v Norway (1), Norway

632 JAMES DUNCANSON (1/0) — (with Rangers, Glasgow)
13 October 1919, Glasgow
1946 v Ireland

633 JOHN SHAW (4/0) — (with Rangers, Glasgow)
29 November 1912, Annathill
1947 v England, Belgium, Luxembourg, Ireland

634 ARCHIBALD MacAULEY (7/0) — (with Brentford, London)
30 July 1915, Falkirk
1947 v England
— (with Arsenal, London)
1947 v Ireland, Wales
1948 v England, Belgium, Switzerland, France

635 WILLIAM WOODBURN (24/0) — (with Rangers, Glasgow)
8 August 1919, Edinburgh
1947 v England, Belgium, Luxembourg, Ireland, Wales
1949 v England, France, Ireland, Wales
1950 v England, Portugal, France, Wales, Ireland, Austria
1951 v England, Denmark, France, Belgium, Austria, Ireland, Wales
1952 v England, USA

636 ALEXANDER FORBES (14/1) — (with Sheffield United)
21 January 1925, Dundee
1947 v England, Belgium, Luxembourg (1), Ireland, Wales
— (with Arsenal, London)
1950 v England, Portugal, France, Wales, Ireland, Austria
1951 v Wales
1952 v Denmark, Sweden

637 ANDREW McLAREN (4/3) — (with Preston North End)
24 January 1922, Larkhall
1947 v England (1), Belgium, Luxembourg (1), Wales (1)

638 WILLIAM STEEL (30/12) — (with Morton, Greenock)
1 May 1923, Denny
1947 v England, Belgium (1), Luxembourg (2)
— (with Derby County)
1947 v Ireland, Wales
1948 v England, France, Wales, Ireland
1949 v England (1), France (2), Ireland (1), Wales
1950 v England, Switzerland, Portugal, France
— (with Dundee)
1950 v Wales, Ireland (4), Austria
1951 v England, Denmark (1), France, Belgium, Austria, Wales
1952 v Wales, Ireland
1953 v England, Sweden

639 THOMAS PEARSON (2/0) — (with Newcastle United)
16 March 1913, Edinburgh
1947 v England, Belgium

640 ROBERT CAMPBELL (5/1) — (with Falkirk)
28 June 1922, Glasgow
1947 v Belgium, Luxembourg
— (with Chelsea, London)
1950 v Switzerland (1), Portugal, France

641 ROBERT FLAVELL (2/2) — (with Airdrie)
1 September 1921, Annathill
1947 v Belgium, Luxembourg (2)

642 WILLIAM MacFARLANE (1/0) — (with Heart of Midlothian, Edinburgh)
1 October 1923, Fallin
1947 v Luxembourg

643 JAMES WATSON (2/0) — (with Motherwell)
16 January 1924, Cowie
1947 v Ireland
— (with Huddersfield Town)
1953 v Ireland

644 JOHN GOVAN (6/0) — (with Hibernian, Edinburgh)
16 January 1923, Larkhall
1947 v Wales
1948 v England, Belgium, Switzerland, France, Ireland

645 IAN BLACK (1/0) — (with Southampton)
27 March 1924, Aberdeen
1948 v England

646 JAMES COMBE (3/1) — (with Hibernian, Edinburgh)
29 January 1924, Edinburgh
1948 v England, Belgium (1), Switzerland

647 JAMES COWAN (25/0) — (with Morton, Greenock)
16 June 1926, Paisley
1948 v Belgium, Switzerland, France, Wales
1949 v England, France, Ireland, Wales
1950 v England, Switzerland, Portugal, France, Wales, Ireland, Austria
1951 v England, Denmark, France, Belgium, Austria, Ireland, Wales
1952 v USA, Denmark, Sweden

648 LESLIE JOHNSTON (2/1) — (with Clyde, Glasgow)
16 August 1920, Glasgow
1948 v Belgium, Switzerland (1)

649 EDWARD TURNBULL (8/0) — (with Hibernian, Edinburgh)
12 April 1923, Falkirk
1948 v Belgium, Switzerland
1950 v Austria
1958 v Hungary, Poland, Yugoslavia, Paraguay, France

650 DAVID DUNCAN (3/1) — (with East Fife, Methil)
21 November 1921, Milton of Balgonie
1948 v Belgium (1), Switzerland, France

651 EDWARD RUTHERFORD (1/0) — (with Rangers, Glasgow)
8 February 1921, Glasgow
1948 v France

652 CHARLES COX (1/0) — (with Heart of Midlothian, Edinburgh)
19 February 1926, Glasgow
1948 v France

653 HUGH HOWIE (1/1) — (with Hibernian, Edinburgh)
14 February 1924, Glasgow
1948 v Wales (1)

| 654 | ROBERT EVANS (48/0) | – | (with Celtic, Glasgow) |
| | 16 July 1927, Glasgow | | 1948 v Wales, Ireland |
| | | | 1949 v England, France, Ireland, Wales |
| | | | 1950 v Switzerland, Portugal, Austria |
| | | | 1951 v England, Ireland |
| | | | 1953 v Sweden, Ireland, Wales |
| | | | 1954 v England, Norway, Finland, Northern Ireland |
| | | | 1955 v Portugal, Yugoslavia, Austria, Hungary, Northern Ireland, Wales |
| | | | 1956 v England, Austria |
| | | | 1957 v West Germany, Spain, Northern Ireland, Switzerland, Wales |
| | | | 1958 v England, Hungary, Poland, Yugoslavia, Paraguay, France |
| | | | 1959 v England, West Germany, Netherlands, Portugal, Northern Ireland, Wales |
| | | | 1960 v England, Poland |
| | | – | (with Chelsea, London) |
| | | | 1960 v Austria, Hungary, Turkey |
| 655 | WILLIAM REDPATH (9/0) | – | (with Motherwell) |
| | 8 August 1921, Stoneyburn | | 1948 v Wales, Ireland |
| | | | 1951 v England, Denmark, France, Belgium, Austria, Ireland |
| | | | 1952 v England |
| 656 | JAMES MASON (7/4) | – | (with Third Lanark, Glasgow) |
| | 18 June 1919, Glasgow | | 1948 v Wales, Ireland (1) |
| | | | 1949 v England (1), Ireland (1) |
| | | | 1950 v Ireland |
| | | | 1951 v Belgium (1), Austria |
| 657 | LAWRENCE REILLY (38/22) | – | (with Hibernian, Edinburgh) |
| | 28 October 1928, Edinburgh | | 1948 v Wales |
| | | | 1949 v England (1), France, Ireland (1), Wales |
| | | | 1950 v Switzerland, France, Wales (2) |
| | | | 1951 v England (1), Denmark (1), France (1), Belgium, Austria, Ireland, Wales |
| | | | 1952 v England (1), USA (3), Denmark (1), Sweden, Wales, Ireland (1) |
| | | | 1953 v England (2), Sweden, Wales (1) |
| | | | 1954 v Hungary |
| | | | 1955 v England (1), Portugal (1), Yugoslavia (1), Austria (1), Hungary, Northern Ireland (1), Wales |
| | | | 1956 v England, Austria, Wales (1), Northern Ireland, Yugoslavia |
| | | | 1957 v England |
| 658 | JOHN KELLY (2/0) | – | (with Barnsley) |
| | 21 February 1921, Paisley | | 1948 v Wales, Ireland |
| 659 | WILLIAM HOULISTON (3/2) | – | (with Queen of the South, Dumfries) |
| | 4 April 1921, Dumfries | | 1948 v Ireland (2) |
| | | | 1949 v England, France |
| 660 | SAMUEL COX (24/0) | – | (with Rangers, Glasgow) |
| | 13 April 1924, Darvel | | 1949 v England, France, Ireland, Wales |
| | | | 1950 v England, Switzerland, Portugal, France |
| | | | 1951 v England, Denmark, France, Belgium, Austria, Ireland, Wales |
| | | | 1952 v USA, Denmark, Sweden, Wales, Ireland |
| | | | 1953 v England, Ireland, Wales |
| | | | 1954 v England |
| 661 | GEORGE AITKEN (8/0) | – | (with East Fife, Methil) |
| | 28 May 1925, Lochgelly | | 1949 v England, France, Ireland, Wales |
| | | | 1950 v Switzerland |
| | | – | (with Sunderland) |
| | | | 1952 v Wales, Ireland |
| | | | 1954 v England |
| 662 | HENRY MORRIS (1/3) | – | (with East Fife, Methil) |
| | 17 December 1919, Dundee | | 1949 v Ireland (3) |

| 663 | JOHN McPHAIL (5/3) | – | (with Celtic, Glasgow) |
| | 27 December 1923, Glasgow | | 1949 v Wales (1) |
| | | | 1950 v Wales, Ireland (2), Austria |
| | | | 1953 v Ireland |
| 664 | ALEXANDER LINWOOD (1/1) | – | (with Clyde, Glasgow) |
| | 13 March 1920, Drumsmudden | | 1949 v Wales (1) |
| 665 | JOHN McCOLL (14/0) | – | (with Rangers, Glasgow) |
| | 7 June 1927, Alexandria | | 1950 v England, France, Wales, Ireland |
| | | | 1951 v Belgium |
| | | | 1956 v Wales, Northern Ireland, Yugoslavia |
| | | | 1957 v England, Spain, Switzerland, West Germany, Northern Ireland |
| | | | 1958 v England |
| 666 | WILLIAM MOIR (1/0) | – | (with Bolton Wanderers) |
| | 19 April 1922, Bucksburn | | 1950 v England |
| 667 | WILLIAM BAULD (3/2) | – | (with Heart of Midlothian, Edinburgh) |
| | 24 January 1928, Edinburgh | | 1950 v England, Switzerland (1), Portugal (1) |
| 668 | ROBERT DOUGAN (1/0) | – | (with Heart of Midlothian, Edinburgh) |
| | 3 December 1926, Glasgow | | 1950 v Switzerland |
| 669 | ALLAN BROWN (14/6) | – | (with East Fife, Methil) |
| | 12 October 1926, Kennoway | | 1950 v Switzerland (1), Portugal (1), France (1) |
| | | – | (with Blackpool) |
| | | | 1952 v USA, Denmark, Sweden, Wales (1) |
| | | | 1953 v Wales (1) |
| | | | 1954 v England (1), Norway, Norway, Finland, Austria, Uruguay |
| 670 | WILLIAM McNAUGHT (5/0) | – | (with Raith Rovers, Kirkcaldy) |
| | 7 May 1922, Dumfries | | 1950 v Wales, Ireland, Austria |
| | | | 1952 v England |
| | | | 1954 v Northern Ireland |
| 671 | ROBERT COLLINS (31/10) | – | (with Celtic, Glasgow) |
| | 16 February 1931, Glasgow | | 1950 v Wales, Ireland, Austria |
| | | | 1955 v Yugoslavia, Austria, Hungary, Northern Ireland, Wales |
| | | | 1956 v Wales |
| | | | 1957 v England, Spain, Switzerland (1), West Germany (2), Spain, Northern Ireland, Switzerland, Wales (1) |
| | | | 1958 v Hungary, Poland (2), Yugoslavia, Paraguay (1), France |
| | | – | (with Everton, Liverpool) |
| | | | 1958 v Wales (1), Northern Ireland (1) |
| | | | 1959 v England, West Germany, Netherlands (1), Portugal |
| | | – | (with Leeds United) |
| | | | 1965 v England, Spain, Poland |
| 672 | ROBERT JOHNSTONE (17/10) | – | (with Hibernian, Edinburgh) |
| | 7 September 1929, Selkirk | | 1951 v England (1), Denmark, France, Ireland (2) |
| | | | 1952 v England |
| | | | 1953 v England, Sweden (1), Wales (1) |
| | | | 1954 v England, Norway, Finland (1), Northern Ireland (1), Hungary (1) |
| | | – | (with Manchester City) |
| | | | 1955 v England, Northern Ireland, Wales (2) |
| | | | 1956 v England |
| 673 | JAMES SCOULAR (9/0) | – | (with Portsmouth) |
| | 11 January 1925, Livingston | | 1951 v Denmark, France, Austria |
| | | | 1952 v England, USA, Denmark, Sweden, Wales, Ireland |
| 674 | ROBERT MITCHELL (2/1) | – | (with Newcastle United) |
| | 16 August 1924, Glasgow | | 1951 v Denmark (1), France |
| 675 | THOMAS ORR (2/1) | – | (with Morton, Greenock) |
| | 21 April 1924, Greenock | | 1951 v Ireland (1), Wales |

676 THOMAS DOCHERTY (25/1) — (with Preston North End)
24 April 1928, Glasgow
    1951 v Wales
    1953 v England, Sweden
    1954 v Norway, Norway, Austria, Uruguay, Wales, Hungary
    1955 v England (1), Austria, Hungary
    1956 v Yugoslavia
    1957 v England, Spain, Switzerland, West Germany, Spain, Northern Ireland, Switzerland, Wales
    1958 v England
  — (with Arsenal, London)
    1958 v Wales, Northern Ireland
    1959 v England

677 JOHN McMILLAN (6/2) — (with Airdrie)
18 March 1931, Airdrie
    1952 v England, USA (2), Denmark
    1955 v England
    1956 v England
  — (with Rangers, Glasgow)
    1961 v Czechoslovakia

678 HUGH KELLY (1/0) — (with Blackpool)
23 July 1923, Valleyfield
    1952 v USA

679 ANDREW PATON (2/0) — (with Motherwell)
2 January 1923, Dreghorn
    1952 v Denmark, Sweden

680 WILSON HUMPHRIES (1/0) — (with Motherwell)
1 July 1928, Motherwell
    1952 v Sweden

681 GEORGE FARM (10/0) — (with Blackpool)
13 July 1924, Edinburgh
    1952 v Wales, Ireland
    1953 v England, Sweden, Ireland, Wales
    1954 v England
    1959 v West Germany, Netherlands, Portugal

682 THOMAS WRIGHT (3/0) — (with Sunderland)
20 January 1928, Blairhall
    1952 v Wales, Ireland
    1953 v England

683 JAMES LOGIE (1/0) — (with Arsenal, London)
23 November 1919, Edinburgh
    1952 v Ireland

684 DOUGLAS COWIE (20/0) — (with Dundee)
1 May 1926, Aberdeen
    1953 v England, Sweden, Ireland, Wales
    1954 v Norway, Finland, Austria, Uruguay, Wales, Northern Ireland
    1955 v Austria, Hungary, Wales
    1956 v Austria, Wales, Northern Ireland
    1958 v Hungary, Poland, Yugoslavia, Paraguay

685 JOHN LITTLE (1/0) — (with Rangers, Glasgow)
7 July 1930, Calgary, Canada
    1953 v Sweden

686 JOHN HENDERSON (7/1) — (with Portsmouth)
17 January 1932, Glasgow
    1953 v Sweden, Ireland (1)
    1954 v England, Norway
    1955 v Wales
  — (with Arsenal, London)
    1958 v Wales, Northern Ireland

687 THOMAS RING (12/2) — (with Clyde, Glasgow)
8 August 1930, Glasgow
    1953 v Sweden
    1954 v Wales, Northern Ireland, Hungary (1)
    1955 v England
    1957 v England (1), Spain, Switzerland, West Germany, Spain, Northern Ireland, Switzerland

688 CHARLES FLEMING (1/2) — (with East Fife, Methil)
12 July 1927, Blairhall
    1953 v Ireland (2)

689 WILLIAM TELFER (1/0) — (with St Mirren, Paisley)
26 October 1925, Larkhall
    1953 v Wales

690 JOHN MACKENZIE (9/1) - (with Partick Thistle, Glasgow)
4 September 1925, Glasgow
    1953 v Wales
    1954 v England, Norway (1), Finland, Austria, Uruguay, Hungary
    1955 v England
    1956 v Austria

691 MICHAEL HAUGHNEY (1/0) — (with Celtic, Glasgow)
10 December 1926, Paisley
    1954 v England

692 WILLIAM ORMOND (6/2) — (with Hibernian, Edinburgh)
23 February 1927, Falkirk
    1954 v England (1), Norway, Finland (1), Austria, Uruguay
    1959 v England

693 FREDERICK MARTIN (6/0) — (with Aberdeen)
13 May 1929, Carnoustie
    1954 v Norway, Norway, Austria, Uruguay, Hungary
    1955 v England

694 WILLIAM CUNNINGHAM (8/0) — (with Preston North End)
22 February 1925, Hill of Beath
    1954 v Norway, Norway, Finland, Austria, Uruguay, Wales, Hungary
    1955 v England

695 JOHN AIRD (4/0) — (with Burnley)
18 February 1926, Glencraig
    1954 v Norway, Norway, Austria, Uruguay

696 JAMES DAVIDSON (8/1) — (with Partick Thistle, Glasgow)
8 November 1925, Douglas Water
    1954 v Norway, Norway, Austria, Uruguay, Wales, Northern Ireland (1), Hungary
    1955 v England

697 PATRICK BUCKLEY (3/1) — (with Aberdeen)
31 January 1925, Edinburgh
    1954 v Norway, Wales (1), Northern Ireland

698 NEIL MOCHAN (3/0) — (with Celtic, Glasgow)
6 April 1927, Larbert
    1954 v Norway, Austria, Uruguay

699 JOHN ANDERSON (1/0) — (with Leicester City)
8 December 1929, Barrhead
    1954 v Finland

700 ALEXANDER WILSON (1/0) — (with Portsmouth)
29 October 1933, Buckie
    1954 v Finland

701 DAVID MATHERS (1/0) — (with Partick Thistle, Glasgow)
23 October 1931, Glasgow
    1954 v Finland

702 WILLIAM FERNIE (12/1) — (with Celtic, Glasgow)
22 November 1928, Kinglassie
    1954 v Finland, Austria, Uruguay, Wales, Northern Ireland
    1956 v Wales (1), Northern Ireland, Yugoslavia
    1957 v England, Switzerland, Wales
    1958 v Paraguay

703 WILLIAM FRASER (2/0) — (with Sunderland)
24 February 1929
    1954 v Wales, Northern Ireland

704 HENRY YORSTON (1/0) — (with Aberdeen)
9 June 1929, Aberdeen
    1954 v Wales

705 HAROLD HADDOCK (6/0) — (with Clyde, Glasgow)
26 July 1925, Glasgow
    1954 v Hungary
    1955 v England, Portugal, Yugoslavia, Hungary
    1958 v England

706 JOHN CUMMING (9/0) — (with Heart of Midlothian, Edinburgh)
17 March 1930, Carluke
    1954 v Hungary
    1955 v England, Portugal, Yugoslavia
    1960 v England, Poland, Austria, Hungary, Turkey

707 JAMES WARDHAUGH (2/0) — (with Heart of Midlothian, Edinburgh)
21 March 1929, Marshall Meadows
    1954 v Hungary
    1956 v Northern Ireland

708 THOMAS YOUNGER (24/0) — (with Hibernian, Edinburgh)
10 April 1930, Edinburgh
    1955 v Portugal, Yugoslavia, Austria, Hungary, Northern Ireland, Wales
    1956 v England, Austria
  — (with Liverpool)
    1956 v Wales, Northern Ireland, Yugoslavia
    1957 v England, Spain, Switzerland, West Germany, Spain, Northern Ireland, Switzerland, Wales
    1958 v England, Hungary, Poland, Yugoslavia, Paraguay

709 ALEXANDER PARKER (15/0)   – (with Falkirk)
2 August 1935, Irvine   1955 v Portugal, Yugoslavia, Austria, Northern Ireland, Wales
1956 v England, Austria, Wales, Northern Ireland, Yugoslavia
1957 v Northern Ireland, Switzerland, Wales
1958 v England
– (with Everton, Liverpool)
1958 v Paraguay

710 ARCHIBALD ROBERTSON (5/2) – (with Clyde, Glasgow)
15 September 1929, Busby   1955 v Portugal, Austria (1), Hungary
1957 v Switzerland (1)
1958 v Paraguay

711 THOMAS GEMMELL (2/1) – (with St Mirren, Paisley)
2 July 1930, Tarbolton   1955 v Portugal (1), Yugoslavia

712 ANDREW KERR (2/0) – (with Partick Thistle, Glasgow)
29 June 1931, Ayr   1955 v Austria, Hungary

713 JOSEPH McDONALD (2/0) – (with Sunderland)
10 February 1929, Blantyre   1955 v Northern Ireland, Wales

714 ARCHIBALD GLEN (2/0) – (with Aberdeen)
16 April 1929, Coalburn   1955 v Northern Ireland
1956 v England

715 JOHN HEWIE (19/2) – (with Charlton Athletic, London)
12 December 1928, Pretoria, South Africa   1956 v England, Austria, Wales, Northern Ireland, Yugoslavia
1957 v England, Spain (1), Switzerland, West Germany, Spain
1958 v Hungary, Poland, Yugoslavia, France
1959 v Netherlands, Portugal, Northern Ireland (1), Wales
1960 v Poland

716 GRAHAM LEGGAT (18/8) – (with Aberdeen)
20 June 1934, Aberdeen   1956 v England (1), Wales
1957 v Northern Ireland (1)
1958 v Hungary, Poland, Yugoslavia, Paraguay
– (with Fulham, London)
1958 v Wales (1), Northern Ireland
1959 v England, West Germany (1), Netherlands (1), Northern Ireland (1), Wales (1)
1960 v England (1), Poland, Austria, Hungary

717 ALFRED CONN (1/1) – (with Heart of Midlothian, Edinburgh)
2 October 1926, Prestonpans   1956 v Austria (1)

718 HUGH BAIRD (1/0) – (with Airdrie)
14 March 1930, Calderbank   1956 v Austria

719 MICHAEL CULLEN (1/0) – (with Luton Town)
3 July 1931, Glasgow   1956 v Austria

720 JOHN MUDIE (17/9) – (with Blackpool)
10 April 1930, Dundee   1956 v Wales, Northern Ireland, Yugoslavia (1)
1957 v England, Spain (3), Switzerland (1), West Germany (1), Spain, Northern Ireland, Switzerland (1), Wales
1958 v England, Hungary (1), Poland, Yugoslavia, Paraguay (1), France

721 ALEXANDER SCOTT (16/5) – (with Rangers, Glasgow)
22 November 1936, Falkirk   1956 v Northern Ireland (1), Yugoslavia
1957 v West Germany, Switzerland (1), Wales
1959 v Portugal
1961 v Czechoslovakia, Northern Ireland (3), Wales
1962 v England, Uruguay
– (with Everton, Liverpool)
1963 v Norway, Wales
1964 v Finland
1966 v Portugal, Brazil

722 SAMUEL BAIRD (7/2) – (with Rangers, Glasgow)
13 May 1930, Denny   1956 v Yugoslavia (1)
1957 v Spain, Switzerland, West Germany, Spain, Northern Ireland
1958 v France (1)

723 ERIC CALDOW (40/4) – (with Rangers, Glasgow)
14 May 1934, Cumnock   1957 v England, Spain, Switzerland, West Germany, Spain, Northern Ireland, Switzerland, Wales
1958 v Hungary, Poland, Yugoslavia, Paraguay, France, Wales, Northern Ireland
1959 v England, West Germany, Netherlands, Portugal, Northern Ireland, Wales
1960 v England, Austria, Hungary, Turkey (1), Wales, Northern Ireland (1)
1961 v England, Republic of Ireland, Republic of Ireland, Czechoslovakia, Czechoslovakia, Northern Ireland, Wales, Czechoslovakia
1962 v England (1), Uruguay, Wales (1), Northern Ireland
1963 v England

724 DAVID MACKAY (22/4) – (with Heart of Midlothian, Edinburgh)
14 November 1934, Edinburgh   1957 v Spain
1958 v France, Wales, Northern Ireland
– (with Tottenham Hotspur, London)
1959 v England, West Germany, Northern Ireland, Wales
1960 v Poland, Austria (1), Hungary, Turkey, Wales, Northern Ireland
1961 v England (1)
1963 v England, Austria, Norway, Northern Ireland, Norway (2), Wales
1965 v Northern Ireland

725 JAMES GARDINER (1/0) – (with Motherwell)
18 September 1928, Balbeggie   1957 v Wales

726 THOMAS EWING (2/0) – (with Partick Thistle, Glasgow)
2 May 1937, Swinhill   1957 v Wales
1958 v England

727 GEORGE HERD (5/1) – (with Clyde, Glasgow)
6 May 1936, Lanark   1958 v England
1960 v Hungary (1), Turkey, Wales, Northern Ireland

728 JAMES MURRAY (5/1) – (with Heart of Midlothian, Edinburgh)
4 February 1933, Edinburgh   1958 v England, Hungary, Poland, Yugoslavia (1), France

729 JAMES FORREST (1/0) – (with Motherwell)
31 March 1927, Bothwell   1958 v England

730 JAMES IMLACH (4/0) – (with Nottingham Forest)
6 January 1932, Lossiemouth   1958 v Hungary, Poland, Yugoslavia, France

731 WILLIAM BROWN (28/0) – (with Dundee)
8 October 1931, Arbroath   1958 v France, Wales, Northern Ireland
1959 v England
– (with Tottenham Hotspur, London)
1959 v Northern Ireland, Wales
1960 v Poland, Austria, Hungary, Turkey
1961 v Czechoslovakia, Northern Ireland, Wales
1962 v England, Wales, Northern Ireland
1963 v England, Austria, Northern Ireland, Norway, Wales
1965 v England, Spain, Poland, Finland, Northern Ireland, Poland, Italy

732 JOHN GRANT (2/0) – (with Hibernian, Edinburgh)
1931, Edinburgh   1958 v Wales, Northern Ireland

733 WILLIAM TONER (2/0) – (with Kilmarnock)
18 December 1929, Glasgow   1958 v Wales, Northern Ireland

734 DAVID HERD (5/3) – (with Arsenal, London)
15 April 1934, Hamilton   1958 v Wales, Northern Ireland (1)
1959 v England
1961 v Republic of Ireland (2), Czechoslovakia

735 DENIS LAW (55/30)  – (with Huddersfield Town)
24 February 1940, Aberdeen
  1958 v Wales (1), Northern Ireland
  1959 v Netherlands, Portugal, Northern Ireland,
  Wales
  – (with Manchester City)
  1960 v England, Poland (1), Austria,
  Northern Ireland (1)
  1961 v England
  – (with Turin)
  1961 v Czechoslovakia (2), Czechoslovakia
  1962 v England
  – (with Manchester United)
  1962 v Wales (1), Northern Ireland (4)
  1963 v England, Austria (2), Norway (3),
  Republic of Ireland, Spain (1), Norway (4), Wales (1)
  1964 v England, West Germany, Wales,
  Finland (1), Northern Ireland
  1965 v England (1), Spain, Poland (1), Finland,
  Northern Ireland, Poland
  1966 v England (1), Wales (1)
  1967 v England (1), Soviet Union, Northern Ireland
  1968 v Austria (1)
  1969 v West Germany, Northern Ireland
  1972 v Peru (1), Northern Ireland (1), Wales,
  England, Yugoslavia, Czechoslovakia, Brazil
  – (with Manchester City)
  1973 v Czechoslovakia, Czechoslovakia,
  West Germany
  1974 v West Germany, Northern Ireland, Zaire

736 DUNCAN MACKAY (14/0)  – (with Celtic, Glasgow)
14 July 1937, Glasgow
  1959 v England, West Germany, Netherlands,
  Portugal
  1960 v England, Poland, Austria, Hungary,
  Turkey, Wales, Northern Ireland
  1961 v Czechoslovakia, Northern Ireland
  1962 v Uruguay (s)

737 JOHN DICK (1/0)  – (with West Ham United, London)
19 March 1930, Glasgow
  1959 v England

738 ROBERT McCANN (5/0)  – (with Motherwell)
15 October 1932, Dundee
  1959 v West Germany, Northern Ireland, Wales
  1960 v England
  1961 v England

739 JOHN WHITE (22/3)  – (with Falkirk)
28 April 1937, Musselburgh
  1959 v West Germany (1), Netherlands, Portugal,
  Northern Ireland (1)
  – (with Tottenham Hotspur, London)
  1959 v Wales
  1960 v Poland, Austria, Turkey, Wales
  1961 v Czechoslovakia, Northern Ireland, Wales,
  Czechoslovakia
  1962 v England, Wales, Northern Ireland
  1963 v England, Northern Ireland, Norway,
  Wales (1)
  1964 v England, West Germany

740 IAN ST JOHN (21/9)  – (with Motherwell)
7 June 1938, Motherwell
  1959 v West Germany, Northern Ireland, Wales
  1960 v England, Poland (1), Austria
  1961 v England
  – (with Liverpool)
  1961 v Czechoslovakia (1), Northern Ireland,
  Wales (2), Czechoslovakia (2)
  1962 v England, Uruguay, Wales, Northern Ireland
  1963 v England, Norway, Republic of Ireland (s),
  Spain (1), Northern Ireland (1)
  1965 v England (1)

741 ANDREW WEIR (6/1)  – (with Motherwell)
1937, Paisley
  1959 v West Germany (1)
  1960 v England, Poland, Austria, Hungary, Turkey

742 JOHN SMITH (2/0)  – (with Celtic, Glasgow)
29 July 1934, Glasgow
  1959 v Netherlands, Portugal
743 ROBERT AULD (3/0)  – (with Celtic, Glasgow)
23 March 1938, Glasgow
  1959 v Netherlands, Portugal, Wales
744 GEORGE MULHALL (3/1)  – (with Aberdeen)
8 May 1936, Falkirk
  1959 v Northern Ireland (1)
  – (with Sunderland)
  1962 v Northern Ireland
  1963 v Northern Ireland

745 FRANK HAFFEY (2/0)  – (with Celtic, Glasgow)
28 November 1938, Glasgow
  1960 v England
  1961 v England

746 ALEXANDER YOUNG (8/5)  – (with Heart of Midlothian, Edinburgh)
3 March 1937, Loanhead
  1960 v England, Austria (s), Hungary (1),
  Turkey (1), Wales, Northern Ireland (1)
  – (with Everton, Liverpool)
  1961 v Republic of Ireland (2)
  1966 v Portugal

747 WILLIAM HUNTER (3/1)  – (with Motherwell)
14 February 1940, Edinburgh
  1960 v Hungary (1), Turkey, Wales
748 LAWRENCE LESLIE (5/0)  – (with Airdrie)
17 March 1935, Edinburgh
  1960 v Wales, Northern Ireland
  1961 v Republic of Ireland, Republic of Ireland,
  Czechoslovakia

749 JAMES GABRIEL (2/0)  – (with Everton, Liverpool)
10 October 1940, Dundee
  1960 v Wales
  1963 v Norway (s)

750 JOHN MARTIS (1/0)  – (with Motherwell)
30 March 1940, Motherwell
  1960 v Wales
751 DAVID WILSON (22/9)  – (with Rangers, Glasgow)
10 January 1939, Glasgow
  1960 v Wales, Northern Ireland
  1961 v England (1), Republic of Ireland,
  Republic of Ireland, Czechoslovakia,
  Czechoslovakia, Northern Ireland (1), Wales
  1962 v England (1), Uruguay, Wales
  1963 v England, Austria (2), Norway,
  Republic of Ireland, Spain (1)
  1964 v England, West Germany,
  Northern Ireland (2)
  1965 v England, Finland (1)

752 JOHN PLENDERLEITH (1/0)  – (with Manchester City)
6 October 1937, Bellshill
  1960 v Northern Ireland
753 JAMES BAXTER (34/3)  – (with Rangers, Glasgow)
29 September 1939, Hill of Beath
  1960 v Northern Ireland
  1961 v Republic of Ireland, Republic of Ireland,
  Czechoslovakia, Czechoslovakia, Northern Ireland,
  Wales, Czechoslovakia
  1962 v England, Uruguay (1), Wales,
  Northern Ireland
  1963 v England (2), Austria, Norway,
  Republic of Ireland, Spain, Norway, Wales
  1964 v England, West Germany, Wales,
  Finland, Northern Ireland
  – (with Sunderland)
  1965 v Northern Ireland, Italy, Wales
  1966 v England, Portugal, Brazil, Wales
  1967 v England, Soviet Union, Wales

754 RALPH BRAND (8/8)  – (with Rangers, Glasgow)
8 December 1936, Edinburgh
  1960 v Northern Ireland (2)
  1961 v Republic of Ireland (2),
  Republic of Ireland (1), Czechoslovakia,
  Northern Ireland (2), Wales, Czechoslovakia
  1962 v Uruguay (1)

755 ROBERT SHEARER (4/0) — (with Rangers, Glasgow)
29 December 1931, Hamilton 1961 v England, Republic of Ireland, Republic of Ireland, Czechoslovakia

756 WILLIAM McNEILL (29/3) — (with Celtic, Glasgow)
2 March 1940, Bellshill 1961 v England, Republic of Ireland, Republic of Ireland, Czechoslovakia, Czechoslovakia, Northern Ireland
1962 v England, Uruguay
1963 v Republic of Ireland, Spain, Wales
1964 v England, West Germany
1965 v England, Spain, Poland, Finland, Northern Ireland, Poland (1)
1967 v Soviet Union
1968 v England, Cyprus (s)
1969 v Wales (1), England, Cyprus (1), West Germany
1972 v Northern Ireland, Wales, England

757 JOHN MacLEOD (4/0) — (with Hibernian, Edinburgh)
23 November 1938, Edinburgh 1961 v England, Republic of Ireland, Republic of Ireland, Czechoslovakia

758 PATRICK QUINN (4/1) — (with Motherwell)
26 April 1936, Glasgow 1961 v England (1), Republic of Ireland, Republic of Ireland
1962 v Uruguay

759 PATRICK CRERAND (16/0) — (with Celtic, Glasgow)
19 February 1939, Glasgow 1961 v Republic of Ireland, Republic of Ireland, Czechoslovakia, Czechoslovakia, Northern Ireland, Wales, Czechoslovakia
1962 v England, Uruguay, Wales, Northern Ireland
— (with Manchester United)
1963 v Northern Ireland
1965 v England, Poland, Finland, Poland

760 ALEXANDER HAMILTON (24/0) — (with Dundee)
31 March 1939, Bo'ness 1961 v Wales, Czechoslovakia
1962 v England, Uruguay, Wales, Northern Ireland
1963 v England, Austria, Norway, Republic of Ireland, Northern Ireland, Norway, Wales
1964 v England, West Germany, Wales, Finland, Northern Ireland
1965 v England, Spain, Poland, Finland, Northern Ireland, Poland

761 JOHN URE (11/0) — (with Dundee)
7 December 1939, Ayr 1961 v Wales, Czechoslovakia
1962 v Wales, Northern Ireland
1963 v England, Austria, Norway, Spain
— (with Arsenal, London)
1963 v Northern Ireland, Norway
1967 v Northern Ireland

762 EDWARD CONNACHAN (2/0) — (with Dunfermline Athletic)
27 August 1935, Prestonpans 1961 v Czechoslovakia
1962 v Uruguay

763 HUGH ROBERTSON (1/0) — (with Dundee)
29 November 1939, Auchinleck 1961 v Czechoslovakia

764 WILLIAM RITCHIE (1/0) — (with Rangers, Glasgow)
11 September 1936, Newtongrange 1962 v Uruguay (s)

765 WILLIAM HENDERSON (29/5) — (with Rangers, Glasgow)
24 January 1944, Glasgow 1962 v Wales (1), Northern Ireland (1)
1963 v England, Austria, Norway, Republic of Ireland, Spain (1), Northern Ireland, Norway, Wales
1964 v England, West Germany
1965 v England, Spain, Poland, Finland, Northern Ireland, Poland, Italy, Wales (1)
1966 v Netherlands, Wales, Northern Ireland
1968 v Netherlands
1969 v Northern Ireland, England, Cyprus (1), Republic of Ireland
1971 v Portugal

766 DAVID HOLT (5/0) — (with Heart of Midlothian, Edinburgh)
3 January 1936, Glasgow 1963 v Austria, Norway, Republic of Ireland, Spain
1964 v West Germany (s)

767 DAVID GIBSON (7/3) — (with Leicester City)
23 September 1938, Kirkliston 1963 v Austria, Norway, Republic of Ireland, Spain (1), Northern Ireland
1964 v Wales (1), Finland (1)

768 JAMES MILLAR (2/0) — (with Rangers, Glasgow)
20 November 1934, Edinburgh 1963 v Austria, Republic of Ireland

769 ADAM BLACKLAW (3/0) — (with Burnley)
2 September 1937, Aberdeen 1963 v Norway, Spain
1965 v Italy

770 FRANCIS McLINTOCK (9/1) — (with Leicester City)
28 December 1939, Glasgow 1963 v Norway (s), Republic of Ireland, Spain (1)
— (with Arsenal, London)
1964 v Northern Ireland
1967 v Soviet Union
1970 v Northern Ireland
1971 v Wales, Northern Ireland, England

771 THOMAS LAWRENCE (3/0) — (with Liverpool)
14 May 1940, Dailly 1963 v Republic of Ireland
1969 v West Germany, Wales

772 DAVID PROVAN (5/0) — (with Rangers, Glasgow)
11 March 1941, Falkirk 1963 v Northern Ireland, Norway
1965 v Italy, Italy
1966 v Netherlands

773 ALAN GILZEAN (22/12) — (with Dundee)
22 October 1938, Coupar-Angus 1963 v Norway, Wales
1964 v England (1), West Germany (2), Northern Ireland (1)
— (with Tottenham Hotspur, London)
1965 v Spain, Northern Ireland (2), Poland, Italy, Wales
1967 v Wales (2)
1968 v Austria (s), Cyprus (2)
1969 v West Germany, Wales (1), England, Cyprus, West Germany (1), Austria
1970 v Northern Ireland, England (s)
1971 v Portugal

774 JAMES KENNEDY (6/0) — (with Celtic, Glasgow)
31 January 1934, Johnstone 1963 v Wales
1964 v England, West Germany, Wales, Finland, Northern Ireland

775 ROBERT FORSYTH (4/0) — (with Kilmarnock)
5 May 1939, Plean 1964 v England, Wales, Finland, Northern Ireland

776 JOHN GREIG (44/3) — (with Rangers, Glasgow)
11 September 1942, Edinburgh 1964 v England, West Germany, Wales, Finland, Northern Ireland
1965 v England, Spain, Poland, Finland (1), Northern Ireland, Poland, Italy (1), Wales (1), Italy
1966 v England, Netherlands, Portugal, Brazil, Wales, Northern Ireland
1967 v England, Northern Ireland, Wales
1968 v England, Netherlands, Denmark, Austria, Cyprus
1969 v West Germany, Wales, Northern Ireland, England, Cyprus, Republic of Ireland, West Germany, Austria
1970 v Wales, England, Denmark
1971 v Belgium, Wales (s), Northern Ireland, England
1975 v Denmark

777 JAMES CRUICKSHANK (6/0) — (with Heart of Midlothian, Edinburgh)
13 April 1941, Glasgow 1964 v West Germany
1970 v Wales, England, Denmark
1971 v Belgium
1975 v Romania

778 RONALD YEATS (2/0)
15 November 1937, Aberdeen
– (with Liverpool)
1964 v Wales
1965 v Italy

779 JAMES JOHNSTONE (23/4)
30 September 1944, Viewpark
– (with Celtic, Glasgow)
– 1964 v Wales, Finland
1966 v England (2), Wales
1967 v Soviet Union, Wales
1968 v Austria
1969 v West Germany, West Germany (1)
1970 v England, Denmark
1971 v England, Portugal, Belgium, Netherlands
1972 v Northern Ireland, England (s)
1974 v Wales, England, Belgium (1), Norway,
East Germany, Spain

780 STEPHEN CHALMERS (5/3)
26 December 1936, Glasgow
– (with Celtic, Glasgow)
1964 v Wales (1), Finland (1)
1966 v Portugal (s), Brazil (1), Northern Ireland

781 JAMES ROBERTSON (1/0)
17 December 1944, Glasgow
– (with Tottenham Hotspur, London)
1964 v Wales

782 JOHN McGRORY (3/0)
15 November 1941, Glasgow
– (with Kilmarnock)
1964 v Finland, Northern Ireland
1966 v Portugal

783 WILLIAM WALLACE (7/0)
23 June 1940, Kirkintilloch
– (with Heart of Midlothian, Edinburgh)
1964 v Northern Ireland
1966 v England, Netherlands
– (with Celtic, Glasgow)
1967 v England, Soviet Union (s), Northern Ireland
1969 v England (s)

784 EDWARD McCREADIE (23/0)
15 April 1940, Glasgow
– (with Chelsea, London)
1965 v England, Spain, Poland, Finland,
Northern Ireland, Poland, Wales, Italy
1966 v Portugal
1967 v England, Soviet Union, Northern Ireland,
Wales
1968 v England, Netherlands, Denmark,
Austria, Cyprus
1969 v West Germany, Wales, Northern Ireland,
England, Cyprus

785 WILLIAM BREMNER (54/3)
9 December 1942, Stirling
– (with Leeds United)
1965 v Spain, Poland, Italy, Italy
1966 v England, Portugal, Brazil, Wales,
Northern Ireland
1967 v England, Wales
1968 v England, Denmark, Austria (1), Cyprus
1969 v West Germany, Wales (1),
Northern Ireland, England, Cyprus,
Republic of Ireland, West Germany, Austria
1971 v Wales, England, Portugal, Belgium,
Netherlands
1972 v Northern Ireland, Wales, England,
Yugoslavia, Czechoslovakia, Brazil, Denmark,
Denmark
1973 v England, Northern Ireland (s), England,
Switzerland, Brazil, Czechoslovakia, West Germany
1974 v Northern Ireland, Wales, England, Belgium,
Norway, Zaire, Brazil, Yugoslavia, Spain (1)
1975 v Spain, Denmark

786 JOHN HUGHES (8/1)
3 April 1943, Coatbridge
– (with Celtic, Glasgow)
1965 v Spain, Poland, Northern Ireland, Italy,
Italy
1968 v England (1), Austria
1969 v Republic of Ireland

787 NEIL MARTIN (3/0)
20 October 1940, Alloa
– (with Hibernian, Edinburgh)
1965 v Poland, Finland
– (with Sunderland)
1965 v Italy

788 WILLIAM HAMILTON (1/0)
16 February 1938, Airdrie
– (with Hibernian, Edinburgh)
1965 v Finland

789 WILLIAM JOHNSTON (22/0)
19 December 1946, Glasgow
– (with Rangers, Glasgow)
1965 v Poland, Wales
1966 v England, Netherlands
1967 v Wales
1968 v England
1969 v Northern Ireland (s)
1970 v Northern Ireland, Denmark
– (with West Bromwich Albion)
1977 v Sweden, Wales (s), Northern Ireland,
England, Chile, Argentina, Brazil, East Germany,
Czechoslovakia, Wales
1978 v Wales, England, Peru

790 ROBERT MURDOCH (12/5)
17 August 1944, Bothwell
– (with Celtic, Glasgow)
1965 v Italy, Wales (2), Italy
1966 v England, Northern Ireland (1)
1967 v Northern Ireland
1968 v Cyprus (1)
1969 v West Germany (1), Wales,
Northern Ireland, England, Austria

791 RONALD McKINNON (28/1)
20 August 1940, Glasgow
– (with Rangers, Glasgow)
1965 v Italy, Wales, Italy
1966 v England, Netherlands, Brazil, Wales,
Northern Ireland
1967 v England, Northern Ireland, Wales (1)
1968 v England, Netherlands, Denmark, Austria,
Cyprus
1969 v West Germany, Republic of Ireland,
West Germany, Austria
1970 v Northern Ireland, Wales, England, Denmark
1971 v Belgium, Portugal, Denmark, Soviet Union

792 ROBERT FERGUSON (7/0)
1 March 1945, Ardrossan
– (with Kilmarnock)
1965 v Wales
1966 v England, Netherlands, Portugal, Brazil,
Wales, Northern Ireland

793 CHARLES COOKE (16/0)
14 October 1942, Saint Monance
– (with Dundee)
1965 v Wales, Italy
– (with Chelsea, London)
1966 v Portugal, Brazil
1968 v England, Netherlands, Austria, Cyprus
1969 v West Germany (s), Wales, Northern Ireland,
Cyprus, Austria
1971 v Belgium
1975 v Spain, Portugal

794 JAMES FORREST (5/0)
22 September 1944, Glasgow
– (with Rangers, Glasgow)
1965 v Wales, Italy
– (with Aberdeen)
1971 v Belgium (s), Denmark, Soviet Union

795 THOMAS GEMMELL (18/1)
16 October 1943, Glasgow
– (with Celtic, Glasgow)
1966 v England, Wales, Northern Ireland
1967 v England, Soviet Union, Northern Ireland
1968 v England, Denmark, Austria
1969 v West Germany, Wales, Northern Ireland,
England, Cyprus (1), Republic of Ireland, West Germany
1970 v England
1971 v Belgium

796 PATRICK STANTON (16/0)
13 September 1944, Edinburgh
– (with Hibernian, Edinburgh)
1966 v Netherlands
1969 v Northern Ireland, Republic of Ireland,
Austria
1970 v Denmark
1971 v Belgium, Portugal, Denmark, Soviet Union,
Portugal, Belgium, Netherlands
1972 v Wales
1973 v Wales, Northern Ireland
1974 v West Germany

797 DAVID SMITH (2/0)　　　　　　—　(with Aberdeen)
14 November 1943, Aberdeen　　　1966 v Netherlands
　　　　　　　　　　　　　　　　—　(with Rangers, Glasgow)
　　　　　　　　　　　　　　　　　1968 v Netherlands

798 ANDREW PENMAN (1/0)　　　　—　(with Dundee)
20 February 1943, Rosyth　　　　1966 v Netherlands

799 JAMES SCOTT (1/0)　　　　　　—　(with Hibernian, Edinburgh)
21 August 1940, Falkirk　　　　　1966 v Netherlands

800 WILLIAM BELL (2/0)　　　　　—　(with Leeds United)
3 September 1937, Johnstone　　1966 v Portugal, Brazil

801 JOHN SINCLAIR (1/0)　　　　　—　(with Leicester City)
21 July 1943, Culross　　　　　　1966 v Portugal

802 JOHN CLARK (4/0)　　　　　　—　(with Celtic, Glasgow)
13 March 1941, Larkhall　　　　　1966 v Brazil, Wales, Northern Ireland
　　　　　　　　　　　　　　　　　1967 v Soviet Union

803 PETER CORMACK (9/0)　　　　—　(with Hibernian, Edinburgh)
17 July 1946, Edinburgh　　　　　1966 v Brazil
　　　　　　　　　　　　　　　　　1968 v Denmark (s)
　　　　　　　　　　　　　　　　　1969 v Republic of Ireland, West Germany
　　　　　　　　　　　　　　　　—　(with Nottingham Forest)
　　　　　　　　　　　　　　　　　1970 v Denmark (s)
　　　　　　　　　　　　　　　　　1971 v Portugal, Wales, England, Netherlands (s)

804 JOSEPH McBRIDE (2/0)　　　　—　(with Celtic, Glasgow)
10 June 1938, Kilmarnock　　　　1966 v Wales, Northern Ireland

805 ROBERT LENNOX (10/3)　　　　—　(with Celtic, Glasgow)
30 August 1943, Saltcoats　　　　1966 v Northern Ireland (1)
　　　　　　　　　　　　　　　　　1967 v England (1), Soviet Union, Wales
　　　　　　　　　　　　　　　　　1968 v England, Denmark (1), Austria, Cyprus (s)
　　　　　　　　　　　　　　　　　1969 v West Germany
　　　　　　　　　　　　　　　　　1970 v Wales (s)

806 RONALD SIMPSON (5/0)　　　　—　(with Celtic, Glasgow)
11 October 1930, Glasgow　　　　1967 v England, Soviet Union, Northern Ireland
　　　　　　　　　　　　　　　　　1968 v England, Austria

807 JAMES McCALLIOG (5/1)　　　—　(with Sheffield Wednesday)
23 September 1946, Glasgow　　　1967 v England (1), Soviet Union, Northern Ireland
　　　　　　　　　　　　　　　　　1968 v Denmark
　　　　　　　　　　　　　　　　—　(with Wolverhampton Wanderers)
　　　　　　　　　　　　　　　　　1971 v Portugal

808 WILLIAM MORGAN (21/1)　　　—　(with Burnley)
2 October 1944, Glasgow　　　　　1967 v Northern Ireland
　　　　　　　　　　　　　　　　—　(with Manchester United)
　　　　　　　　　　　　　　　　　1972 v Peru, Yugoslavia, Czechoslovakia,
　　　　　　　　　　　　　　　　　Brazil, Denmark (1), Denmark
　　　　　　　　　　　　　　　　　1973 v England, Wales, Northern Ireland,
　　　　　　　　　　　　　　　　　England, Switzerland, Brazil,
　　　　　　　　　　　　　　　　　Czechoslovakia, Czechoslovakia, West Germany
　　　　　　　　　　　　　　　　　1974 v West Germany, Northern Ireland,
　　　　　　　　　　　　　　　　　Belgium (s), Brazil, Yugoslavia

809 ROBERT CLARK (17/0)　　　　—　(with Aberdeen)
26 September 1945, Glasgow　　　1967 v Wales
　　　　　　　　　　　　　　　　　1968 v Netherlands
　　　　　　　　　　　　　　　　　1970 v Northern Ireland
　　　　　　　　　　　　　　　　　1971 v Portugal, Wales, Northern Ireland,
　　　　　　　　　　　　　　　　　England, Denmark, Soviet Union, Belgium
　　　　　　　　　　　　　　　　　1972 v Northern Ireland, Wales, England,
　　　　　　　　　　　　　　　　　Czechoslovakia, Brazil, Denmark
　　　　　　　　　　　　　　　　　1973 v England

810 JAMES CRAIG (1/0)　　　　　—　(with Celtic, Glasgow)
30 April 1943, Glasgow　　　　　1967 v Wales

811 DOUGLAS FRASER (2/0)　　　—　(with West Bromwich Albion)
8 December 1941, Eaglesham　　1968 v Netherlands, Cyprus

812 ROBERT MONCUR (16/0)　　　—　(with Newcastle United)
19 January 1945, Perth　　　　　1968 v Netherlands
　　　　　　　　　　　　　　　　　1969 v Republic of Ireland
　　　　　　　　　　　　　　　　　1970 v Northern Ireland, Wales, England, Denmark
　　　　　　　　　　　　　　　　　1971 v Belgium, Portugal, Wales, Northern Ireland,
　　　　　　　　　　　　　　　　　England, Denmark
　　　　　　　　　　　　　　　　　1972 v Peru, Northern Ireland, Wales, England

813 ROBERT HOPE (2/0)　　　　　—　(with West Bromwich Albion)
28 September 1943, Bridge of Allan　1968 v Netherlands, Denmark

814 GEORGE McLEAN (1/0)　　　　—　(with Dundee)
26 May 1943, Paisley　　　　　　1968 v Netherlands

815 JAMES SMITH (4/0)　　　　　—　(with Aberdeen)
20 January 1947, Glasgow　　　　1968 v Netherlands (s)
　　　　　　　　　　　　　　　　—　(with Newcastle United)
　　　　　　　　　　　　　　　　　1973 v West Germany
　　　　　　　　　　　　　　　　　1974 v Northern Ireland (s), Wales (s)

816 JAMES HERRIOT (8/0)　　　　—　(with Birmingham City)
20 December 1939, Chapelhall　　1968 v Denmark, Cyprus
　　　　　　　　　　　　　　　　　1969 v Wales (s), Northern Ireland, England,
　　　　　　　　　　　　　　　　　Cyprus, Republic of Ireland (s), West Germany

817 THOMAS McLEAN (6/1)　　　　—　(with Kilmarnock)
2 February 1947, Ashgill　　　　1968 v Denmark, Cyprus
　　　　　　　　　　　　　　　　　1969 v Wales (1)
　　　　　　　　　　　　　　　　　1970 v Northern Ireland, Wales
　　　　　　　　　　　　　　　　　1971 v Denmark

818 COLIN STEIN (21/10)　　　　—　(with Rangers, Glasgow)
10 May 1947, Philipstoun　　　　1968 v Denmark, Cyprus (2)
　　　　　　　　　　　　　　　　　1969 v Wales (1), Northern Ireland (1),
　　　　　　　　　　　　　　　　　England (1), Cyprus (4), Republic of Ireland (1),
　　　　　　　　　　　　　　　　　West Germany, Austria (s)
　　　　　　　　　　　　　　　　　1970 v Northern Ireland (s), Wales, England,
　　　　　　　　　　　　　　　　　Denmark
　　　　　　　　　　　　　　　　　1971 v Belgium, Denmark, Soviet Union
　　　　　　　　　　　　　　　　　1972 v Czechoslovakia (s)
　　　　　　　　　　　　　　　　—　(with Coventry City)
　　　　　　　　　　　　　　　　　1973 v England (s), Wales (s), Northern Ireland,
　　　　　　　　　　　　　　　　　England (s)

819 EDWIN GRAY (12/3)　　　　　—　(with Leeds United)
17 January 1948, Glasgow　　　　1969 v England, Cyprus (1), West Germany,
　　　　　　　　　　　　　　　　　Austria
　　　　　　　　　　　　　　　　　1971 v Wales, Northern Ireland, Belgium,
　　　　　　　　　　　　　　　　　Netherlands
　　　　　　　　　　　　　　　　　1976 v Wales (1), England, Finland (1), Wales

820 ERNEST McGARR (2/0)　　　　—　(with Aberdeen)
9 March 1944, Glasgow　　　　　1969 v Republic of Ireland, Austria

821 WILLIAM CALLAGHAN (2/0)　　—　(with Dunfermline Athletic)
12 February 1943, Cowdenbeath　1969 v Republic of Ireland (s)
　　　　　　　　　　　　　　　　　1970 v Wales

822 FRANCIS BURNS (1/0)　　　　—　(with Manchester United)
17 October 1948, Glenboig　　　　1969 v Austria

823 HUGH CURRAN (5/1)　　　　　—　(with Wolverhampton Wanderers)
25 September 1943, Glasgow　　　1969 v Austria
　　　　　　　　　　　　　　　　　1971 v Northern Ireland, England (1),
　　　　　　　　　　　　　　　　　Denmark, Soviet Union (s)

824 PETER LORIMER (21/4)　　　—　(with Leeds United)
14 December 1946, Dundee　　　　1969 v Austria (s)
　　　　　　　　　　　　　　　　　1971 v Wales, Northern Ireland
　　　　　　　　　　　　　　　　　1972 v Northern Ireland (s/1), Wales (1),
　　　　　　　　　　　　　　　　　England, Denmark, Denmark (1)
　　　　　　　　　　　　　　　　　1973 v England, England, West Germany (s)
　　　　　　　　　　　　　　　　　1974 v England, Belgium, Norway, Zaire (1),
　　　　　　　　　　　　　　　　　Brazil, Yugoslavia, Spain (s)
　　　　　　　　　　　　　　　　　1975 v Denmark, Denmark, Romania (s)

825 DAVID HAY (27/0)　　　　　—　(with Celtic, Glasgow)
29 January 1948, Paisley　　　　1970 v Northern Ireland, Wales, England,
　　　　　　　　　　　　　　　　　Denmark
　　　　　　　　　　　　　　　　　1971 v Belgium, Portugal, Wales, Northern Ireland,
　　　　　　　　　　　　　　　　　Portugal, Belgium, Netherlands
　　　　　　　　　　　　　　　　　1973 v Wales, Northern Ireland, England,
　　　　　　　　　　　　　　　　　Switzerland, Brazil, Czechoslovakia, Czechoslovakia
　　　　　　　　　　　　　　　　　1974 v West Germany, Northern Ireland, Wales,
　　　　　　　　　　　　　　　　　England, Belgium, Norway, Zaire, Brazil, Yugoslavia

826   WILLIAM DICKSON (5/0)     –   (with Kilmarnock)
    8 April 1945, Larkhall         1970  v Northern Ireland, Wales, England
                         1971  v Denmark, Soviet Union

827   WILLIAM CARR (6/0)     –   (with Coventry City)
    6 January 1950, Glasgow       1970  v Northern Ireland, Wales, England, Denmark
                         1972  v Peru, Denmark (s)

828   JOHN O'HARE (13/5)     –   (with Derby County)
    24 September 1946, Renton    1970 v Northern Ireland (1), Wales, England, Denmark (1)
                         1971 v Belgium, Wales, Northern Ireland, Portugal (1), Belgium (1), Netherlands (s)
                         1972 v Peru (1), Northern Ireland, Wales

829   WILLIAM JARDINE (38/1)   –   (with Rangers, Glasgow)
    31 December 1948, Edinburgh   1970  v Denmark (s)
                         1971  v Portugal, Belgium, Netherlands
                         1973  v England, Switzerland, Brazil, Czechoslovakia, Czechoslovakia, West Germany
                         1974  v West Germany, Northern Ireland, Wales (1), England, Belgium, Norway, Zaire, Brazil, Yugoslavia, East Germany, Spain
                         1975  v Spain, Sweden, Portugal, Wales, Northern Ireland, England
                         1977  v Sweden (s), Chile (s), Brazil (s), Czechoslovakia, Wales
                         1978  v Northern Ireland, Iran
                         1979  v Peru, Austria, Belgium, Belgium

830   ARCHIBALD GEMMILL (43/8)  –   (with Derby County)
    24 March 1947, Paisley       1971  v Belgium, Portugal (1), Netherlands
                         1972  v Peru, Northern Ireland, Wales, England
                         1975  v Denmark, Romania
                         1976  v Wales, Northern Ireland (1), England, Finland, Czechoslovakia, Wales
                         1977  v Wales, Northern Ireland (s), England (s), Chile (s), Argentina, Brazil, East Germany (s)
               –   (with Nottingham Forest)
                         1978  v Bulgaria (1), Northern Ireland, Wales, England (s), Peru (s), Iran, Netherlands (2), Austria, Norway (1), Portugal
                         1979  v Norway
               –   (with Birmingham City)
                         1979  v Austria (1)
                         1980  v Portugal (1), Northern Ireland, Wales, England, Hungary, Sweden, Portugal
                         1981  v Israel, Northern Ireland

831   ANTHONY GREEN (6/0)     –   (with Blackpool)
    30 October 1946, Glasgow    1971  v Belgium (s), Portugal (s), Northern Ireland, England
                       –   (with Newcastle United)
                         1972  v Wales, England (s)

832   JAMES BROGAN (4/0)     –   (with Celtic, Glasgow)
    5 June 1944, Glasgow        1971  v Portugal, Wales, Northern Ireland, England

833   DAVID ROBB (5/0)       –   (with Aberdeen)
    15 December 1947, Broughty Ferry  1971  v Portugal, Wales, England, Denmark (s), Soviet Union

834   ANDREW JARVIE (3/0)     –   (with Airdrie)
    5 October 1948, Annathill     1971  v Portugal (s), Northern Ireland (s), England (s)

835   FRANCIS MUNRO (9/0)     –   (with Wolverhampton Wanderers)
    25 October 1947, Dundee     1971  v Northern Ireland (s), England (s), Denmark, Soviet Union
                         1975  v Sweden, Wales (s), Northern Ireland, England, Romania

836   THOMAS FORSYTH (22/0)   –   (with Motherwell)
    23 January 1949, Glasgow    1971  v Denmark
                       –   (with Rangers, Glasgow)
                         1973  v Czechoslovakia
                         1976  v Switzerland, Wales, Northern Ireland, England, Finland
                         1977  v Sweden, Wales, Northern Ireland, England, Chile, Argentina, Brazil, Czechoslovakia, Wales
                         1978  v Northern Ireland, Wales (s), England, Peru, Iran (s), Netherlands

837   JOHN SCOTT (2/0)     –   (with Dundee)
    14 January 1948, Aberdeen    1971  v Denmark (s), Soviet Union

838   JOHN BROWNLIE (7/0)     –   (with Hibernian, Edinburgh)
    11 March 1952, Caldercruix    1971  v Soviet Union
                         1972  v Peru, Northern Ireland, England, Denmark, Denmark
                         1975  v Romania

839   ROBERT WATSON (1/0)     –   (with Motherwell)
    1946, Airdrie             1971  v Soviet Union

840   ROBERT WILSON (2/0)     –   (with Arsenal, London)
    30 October 1941, Chesterfield, England  1971  v Portugal, Netherlands

841   EDMOND COLQUHOUN (9/0)  –   (with Sheffield United)
    29 March 1945, Prestonpans   1971  v Portugal, Netherlands
                         1972  v Peru, Yugoslavia, Czechoslovakia, Brazil, Denmark, Denmark
                         1973  v England

842   ALEXANDER CROPLEY (2/0)  –   (with Hibernian, Edinburgh)
    16 January 1951, Aldershot, England  1971  v Portugal, Belgium

843   GEORGE GRAHAM (12/3)   –   (with Arsenal, London)
    30 November 1944, Bargeddie   1971  v Portugal, Netherlands (1)
                         1972  v Northern Ireland, Yugoslavia, Czechoslovakia, Brazil, Denmark, Denmark
               –   (with Manchester United)
                         1973  v England, Wales (2), Northern Ireland, Brazil (s)

844   MARTIN BUCHAN (34/0)   –   (with Aberdeen)
    6 March 1949, Aberdeen      1971  v Portugal (s), Belgium
                       –   (with Manchester United)
                         1972  v Wales, Yugoslavia, Czechoslovakia, Brazil, Denmark, Denmark
                         1973  v England
                         1974  v West Germany, Northern Ireland, Wales, Norway, Brazil, Yugoslavia, East Germany
                         1975  v Spain, Portugal, Denmark, Romania
                         1976  v Finland, Czechoslovakia
                         1977  v Chile, Argentina, Brazil, East Germany, Wales (s)
                         1978  v Northern Ireland, Peru, Iran, Netherlands, Austria, Norway, Portugal

845   STEPHEN MURRAY (1/0)   –   (with Aberdeen)
    9 October 1944, Dumbarton   1971  v Belgium

846   KENNETH DALGLISH (102/30)  –   (with Celtic, Glasgow)
    4 March 1951, Glasgow      1971  v Belgium (s), Netherlands
                         1972  v Denmark (s), Denmark (1)
                         1973  v England, Wales, Northern Ireland (1), England, Switzerland, Brazil, Czechoslovakia, Czechoslovakia, West Germany
                         1974  v West Germany (1), Northern Ireland, Wales (1), England, Belgium Norway (s/1), Zaire, Brazil, Yugoslavia, East Germany (1), Spain (s)
                         1975  v Spain, Sweden, Portugal, Wales, Northern Ireland (1), England, Romania, Denmark, Denmark (1), Romania
                         1976  v Switzerland, Northern Ireland (1), England (1), Finland (1), Czechoslovakia, Wales
                         1977  v Sweden (1), Wales, Northern Ireland (2), England (1), Chile (1), Argentina, Brazil
               –   (with Liverpool)
                         1977  v East Germany, Czechoslovakia (1), Wales (1)
                         1978  v Bulgaria, Northern Ireland (s), Wales, England, Peru, Iran, Netherlands (1), Austria, Norway (2), Portugal
                         1979  v Wales, Northern Ireland, England, Argentina, Norway (1), Peru, Austria, Belgium, Belgium
                         1980  v Portugal (1), Northern Ireland, Wales, England, Poland, Hungary, Sweden, Portugal
                         1981  v Israel (1), Sweden, Northern Ireland, Portugal (s)
                         1982  v Spain, Netherlands (1), Northern Ireland, Wales, England, New Zealand (1), Brazil (s), Belgium (2)
                         1983  v Switzerland, Uruguay, Belgium, East Germany
                         1984  v Yugoslavia (1), Iceland, Spain (1)
                         1985  v Wales, East Germany, Australia
                         1986  v Romania, Bulgaria (s), Luxembourg

847 JOHN HANSEN (2/0)     – (with Partick Thistle, Glasgow)
    3 February 1950, Sauchie     1971 v Belgium (s)
    1972 v Yugoslavia (s)

848 ALISTAIR HUNTER (4/0)     – (with Kilmarnock)
    4 October 1949, Glasgow     1972 v Peru, Yugoslavia
    – (with Celtic, Glasgow)
    1973 v England, Czechoslovakia

849 WILLIAM DONACHIE (35/0)     – (with Manchester City)
    5 October 1951, Glasgow     1972 v Peru, Northern Ireland, England,
    Yugoslavia, Czechoslovakia, Brazil, Denmark
    1973 v England, Wales, Northern Ireland
    1974 v Northern Ireland
    1975 v Romania
    1976 v Wales, Northern Ireland, England,
    Finland, Czechoslovakia, Wales
    1977 v Sweden, Wales, Northern Ireland, England,
    Chile, Argentina, Brazil, East Germany, Wales
    1978 v Bulgaria, Wales, England, Iran,
    Netherlands, Austria, Norway, Portugal (s)

850 RICHARD HARTFORD (50/4)     – (with West Bromwich Albion)
    24 October 1950, Clydebank     1972 v Peru, Wales (s), England, Yugoslavia,
    Czechoslovakia, Brazil
    – (with Manchester City)
    1975 v Denmark, Romania
    1976 v Northern Ireland (s), Czechoslovakia (s),
    Wales (s)
    1977 v Sweden, Wales, Northern Ireland, England,
    Chile (1), Argentina, Brazil, East Germany,
    Czechoslovakia (1), Wales
    1978 v Bulgaria, Wales, England, Peru, Iran,
    Netherlands, Austria, Norway, Portugal
    1979 v Wales, Northern Ireland, England,
    Argentina, Norway
    – (with Everton, Liverpool)
    1979 v Peru (1), Belgium
    1981 v Northern Ireland (s), Israel, Wales,
    Northern Ireland, England, Sweden
    – (with Manchester City)
    1981 v Northern Ireland, Portugal
    1982 v Spain, Northern Ireland, Wales (1),
    England, Brazil

851 LUIGI MACARI (24/5)     – (with Celtic, Glasgow)
    7 June 1949, Edinburgh     1972 v Wales (s), England, Yugoslavia (2),
    Czechoslovakia, Brazil, Denmark (1)
    – (with Manchester United)
    1973 v England, Wales (s), Northern Ireland (s),
    England
    1975 v Sweden, Portugal (s), Wales, England (s),
    Romania
    1977 v Northern Ireland (s), England (s), Chile (2),
    Argentina, East Germany, Wales
    1978 v Bulgaria, Peru (s), Iran

852 ALEXANDER FORSYTH (10/0)     – (with Partick Thistle, Glasgow)
    5 February 1952, Swinton     1972 v Yugoslavia, Czechoslovakia, Brazil,
    Denmark
    – (with Manchester United)
    1973 v England
    1974 v East Germany, Spain
    1975 v Northern Ireland (s), Romania, Denmark

853 JAMES BONE (2/1)     – (with Norwich City)
    22 September 1949, Bridge of Allan     1972 v Yugoslavia (s), Denmark (1)

854 JOSEPH HARPER (4/2)     – (with Aberdeen)
    11 January 1948, Greenock     1972 v Denmark (s/1), Denmark
    – (with Hibernian, Edinburgh)
    1975 v Denmark (1)
    – (with Aberdeen)
    1978 v Iran (s)

855 DAVID HARVEY (16/0)     – (with Leeds United)
    7 February 1948, Leeds, England     1972 v Denmark
    1973 v Czechoslovakia, West Germany
    1974 v Northern Ireland, Wales, England, Belgium,
    Zaire, Brazil, Yugoslavia, East Germany, Spain
    1975 v Spain, Denmark, Denmark
    1976 v Finland (s)

856 PETER McCLOY (4/0)     – (with Rangers, Glasgow)
    16 November 1946, Girvan     1973 v Wales, Northern Ireland, Switzerland, Brazil

857 DANIEL McGRAIN (62/0)     – (with Celtic, Glasgow)
    1 May 1950, Glasgow     1973 v Wales, Northern Ireland, England,
    Switzerland, Brazil, Czechoslovakia,
    Czechoslovakia, West Germany
    1974 v Wales (s), England, Belgium, Norway,
    Zaire, Brazil, Yugoslavia
    1975 v Spain, Sweden, Portugal, Wales,
    Northern Ireland, England, Romania, Denmark,
    Denmark
    1976 v Switzerland, Wales, Northern Ireland,
    England, Finland, Czechoslovakia, Wales
    1977 v Sweden, Wales, Northern Ireland, England,
    Chile, Argentina, Brazil, East Germany, Czechoslovakia
    1979 v Belgium
    1980 v Portugal, Northern Ireland, Wales, England,
    Poland, Hungary, Sweden, Portugal
    1981 v Israel, Northern Ireland, Israel, Wales (s),
    Northern Ireland, England, Sweden
    1982 v Spain, Netherlands, Northern Ireland,
    England, New Zealand, Soviet Union (s)

858 JAMES HOLTON (15/2)     – (with Manchester United)
    11 April 1951, Lesmahagow     1973 v Wales, Northern Ireland, England,
    Switzerland, Brazil, Czechoslovakia (1),
    West Germany (1)
    1974 v Northern Ireland, Wales, England, Norway,
    Zaire, Brazil, Yugoslavia, East Germany

859 DEREK JOHNSTONE (14/2)     – (with Rangers, Glasgow)
    4 November 1953, Dundee     1973 v Wales, Northern Ireland, England,
    Switzerland, Brazil
    1974 v East Germany (s)
    1975 v Sweden (s)
    1976 v Switzerland, Northern Ireland (s),
    England (s)
    1978 v Bulgaria (s), Northern Ireland (1), Wales (1)
    1979 v Belgium

860 DEREK PARLANE (12/1)     – (with Rangers, Glasgow)
    5 May 1953, Helensburgh     1973 v Wales, Switzerland, Brazil
    1975 v Spain (s), Sweden, Portugal, Wales,
    Northern Ireland (1), England, Romania,
    Denmark (s)
    1977 v Wales

861 JOSEPH JORDAN (52/11)     – (with Leeds United)
    15 December 1951, Carluke     1973 v England (s), Switzerland (s), Brazil,
    Czechoslovakia (s/1), Czechoslovakia,
    West Germany (s)
    1974 v Northern Ireland (s), Wales, England (1),
    Belgium, Norway (1), Zaire (1), Brazil,
    Yugoslavia (1), East Germany, Spain
    1975 v Spain (1)
    1976 v Wales, Northern Ireland, England,
    Czechoslovakia, Wales
    1977 v Northern Ireland, England, East Germany,
    Czechoslovakia (1), Wales
    – (with Manchester United)
    1978 v Bulgaria, Northern Ireland, England,
    Peru (1), Iran, Netherlands, Austria, Portugal
    1979 v Wales (s), Northern Ireland, England,
    Norway (1), Belgium
    1980 v Northern Ireland (s), Wales, England,
    Poland
    1981 v Israel, Wales, England
    – (with Milan)
    1981 v Sweden (1)
    1982 v Netherlands, Wales, England,
    Soviet Union (1)

862 JOHN CONNELLY (1/0) – (with Everton, Liverpool)
13 June 1950, Barrhead 1973 v Switzerland

863 GEORGE CONNELLY (2/0) – (with Celtic, Glasgow)
1 March 1949 1973 v Czechoslovakia, West Germany

864 THOMAS HUTCHISON (17/1) – (with Coventry City)
22 September 1947, Cardenden 1973 v Czechoslovakia, Czechoslovakia,
West Germany
1974 v West Germany, Northern Ireland, Wales,
Belgium (s), Norway, Zaire (s), Yugoslavia (s),
East Germany (1), Spain
1975 v Spain, Portugal, England (s), Romania (s),
Denmark

865 JOHN BLACKLEY (7/0) – (with Hibernian, Edinburgh)
12 May 1948, Westquarter 1973 v Czechoslovakia
1974 v England, Belgium, Zaire
1976 v Switzerland, Wales
1977 v Sweden

866 DONALD FORD (3/0) – (with Heart of Midlothian, Edinburgh)
25 October 1944, Linlithgow 1973 v Czechoslovakia (s)
1974 v West Germany (s), Wales

867 THOMSON ALLAN (2/0) – (with Dundee)
5 October 1946, Longridge 1974 v West Germany, Norway

868 ERICH SCHAEDLER (1/0) – (with Hibernian, Edinburgh)
6 August 1949, Biggar 1974 v West Germany

869 KENNETH BURNS (20/1) – (with Birmingham City)
23 September 1953, Glasgow 1974 v West Germany, East Germany (s/1), Spain
1975 v Spain
1976 v Czechoslovakia (s), Wales
1977 v Sweden, Wales (s)
– (with Nottingham Forest)
1978 v Northern Ireland (s), Wales, England,
Peru, Iran
1979 v Norway, Peru, Austria, Belgium
1981 v Israel, Northern Ireland, Wales

870 ROBERT ROBINSON (4/0) – (with Dundee)
10 November 1950, Edinburgh 1974 v West Germany (s)
1975 v Sweden, Northern Ireland, Romania (s)

871 GORDON McQUEEN (30/5) – (with Leeds United)
26 June 1952, Kilbirnie 1974 v Belgium, Spain
1975 v Spain, Portugal, Wales, Northern Ireland,
England, Romania (1), Denmark
1976 v Czechoslovakia, Wales
1977 v Wales, Northern Ireland (1), England (1),
East Germany, Czechoslovakia, Wales
– (with Manchester United)
1978 v Bulgaria, Northern Ireland, Wales,
Austria (1), Norway, Portugal
1979 v Northern Ireland, England, Norway (1),
Peru, Austria, Belgium
1981 v Wales

872 GRAEME SOUNESS (54/4) – (with Middlesbrough)
6 May 1953, Edinburgh 1974 v East Germany, Spain
1975 v Sweden
– (with Liverpool)
1978 v Bulgaria, Wales, England (s), Netherlands,
Austria, Norway
1979 v Wales, Northern Ireland, England,
Peru, Austria, Belgium
1980 v Portugal, Northern Ireland, Portugal
1981 v Israel, Israel, Northern Ireland, Portugal
1982 v Spain, Wales, England, New Zealand, Brazil,
Soviet Union (1), East Germany, Switzerland, Belgium
1983 v Switzerland, Wales, England, Canada (s),
Canada (1), Canada, Uruguay, Northern Ireland
1984 v Wales
– (with Sampdoria, Genoa)
1984 v Yugoslavia (1), Iceland, Spain
1985 v Spain, Wales, England, Iceland,
East Germany, Australia, Australia
1986 v Romania, England (1), Denmark,
West Germany

873 JOHN DEANS (2/0) – (with Celtic, Glasgow)
30 July 1946, Linwood 1974 v East Germany, Spain

874 PAUL WILSON (1/0) – (with Celtic, Glasgow)
23 November 1950, Milngavie 1975 v Spain (s)

875 STEWART KENNEDY (5/0) – (with Rangers, Glasgow)
31 August 1949, Stirling 1975 v Sweden, Portugal, Wales, Northern Ireland,
England

876 COLIN JACKSON (8/1) – (with Rangers, Glasgow)
8 October 1946, Falkirk 1975 v Sweden, Portugal (s), Wales (1),
Denmark, Romania
1976 v Wales, Northern Ireland, England

877 EDWARD MacDOUGALL (7/3) – (with Norwich City)
8 January 1947, Inverness 1975 v Sweden (1), Portugal, Wales,
Northern Ireland (1), England, Denmark (1),
Romania (s)

878 WILLIAM HUGHES (1/0) – (with Sunderland)
30 December 1948, Coatbridge 1975 v Sweden (s)

879 BRUCE RIOCH (24/6) – (with Derby County)
6 September 1947, Aldershot, England 1975 v Portugal, Wales (1), Northern Ireland,
England (1), Romania, Denmark, Denmark (1),
Romania (1)
1976 v Wales (1), Northern Ireland, England,
Finland (1), Czechoslovakia, Wales
– (with Everton, Liverpool)
1977 v Wales, Northern Ireland, England,
Chile, Brazil, Czechoslovakia
– (with Derby County)
1978 v Northern Ireland, England, Peru,
Netherlands

880 ARTHUR DUNCAN (6/0) – (with Hibernian, Edinburgh)
5 December 1947, Falkirk 1975 v Portugal (s), Wales, Northern Ireland,
England, Romania, Denmark (s)

881 ALFRED CONN (2/0) – (with Tottenham Hotspur, London)
5 April 1952, Kirkcaldy 1975 v Northern Ireland (s), England

882 JAMES BROWN (1/0) – (with Sheffield United)
11 May 1952, Coatbridge 1975 v Romania

883 WILLIAM MILLER (65/1) – (with Aberdeen)
2 May 1955, Glasgow 1975 v Romania
1978 v Bulgaria
1979 v Belgium
1980 v Wales (1), England, Poland, Hungary,
Sweden, Portugal
1981 v Israel (s), Northern Ireland, Wales,
Northern Ireland, England,
Northern Ireland, Portugal
1982 v Netherlands, Brazil, Soviet Union,
East Germany, Switzerland
1983 v Switzerland, Wales, England, Canada,
Canada, Canada,
Uruguay, Belgium, East Germany
1984 v Wales, England, France, Yugoslavia,
Iceland, Spain
1985 v Spain, Wales, England, Iceland, Wales,
East Germany, Australia, Australia
1986 v Israel, Romania, England, Netherlands,
Denmark, West Germany, Uruguay, Bulgaria
1987 v England, Brazil, Hungary, Luxembourg
1988 v Saudi Arabia, Malta, Spain, Columbia,
England, Norway, Yugoslavia
1989 v Yugoslavia, Norway

884 STEWART HOUSTON (1/0) – (with Manchester United)
28 August 1949, Argyle 1975 v Denmark

885 JOHN DOYLE (1/0) – (with Ayr United)
11 May 1951, Uddingston 1975 v Romania

886 ANDREW GRAY (20/7)
30 November 1955, Glasgow
— (with Aston Villa, Birmingham)
1975 v Romania
1976 v Switzerland, Finland (2), Czechoslovakia
1978 v Austria (1), Norway
— (with Wolverhampton Wanderers)
1980 v Portugal (1), England (s), Sweden, Portugal
1981 v Israel (s), Northern Ireland, Sweden (s), Northern Ireland (s)
1983 v Northern Ireland, Wales (1), England, Canada (s), Canada (2)
— (with Everton, Liverpool)
1985 v Iceland

887 ALAN ROUGH (53/0)
25 November 1951, Glasgow
— (with Partick Thistle, Glasgow)
1976 v Switzerland, Wales, Northern Ireland, England, Finland, Czechoslovakia, Wales
1977 v Sweden, Wales, Northern Ireland, England, Chile, Argentina, Brazil, Czechoslovakia, Wales
1978 v Northern Ireland, England, Peru, Iran, Netherlands, Austria, Portugal
1979 v Wales, Argentina, Norway, Peru, Austria, Belgium, Belgium
1980 v Portugal, Wales, England, Poland, Hungary, Sweden, Portugal
1981 v Israel, Northern Ireland, Israel, Wales, England, Sweden, Northern Ireland
1982 v Spain, Netherlands, Wales, England, New Zealand, Brazil, Soviet Union
— (with Hibernian, Edinburgh)
1985 v Wales (s)
1986 v England

888 FRANCIS GRAY (32/1)
27 October 1954, Glasgow
— (with Leeds United)
1976 v Switzerland
1978 v Norway, Portugal
1979 v Wales, Northern Ireland, England, Argentina (s)
— (with Nottingham Forest)
1979 v Belgium (s)
1980 v Sweden, Portugal
1981 v Israel, Northern Ireland, Israel, Wales
— (with Leeds United)
1981 v Northern Ireland, England, Sweden, Northern Ireland, Portugal
1982 v Spain, Netherlands (1), Wales, New Zealand, Brazil, Soviet Union, East Germany, Switzerland, Belgium
1983 v Switzerland, Wales, England, Canada

889 THOMAS CRAIG (1/0)
21 November 1950, Glasgow
— (with Newcastle United)
1976 v Switzerland

890 WILLIAM PETTIGREW (5/2)
29 September 1953, Motherwell
— (with Motherwell)
1976 v Switzerland (1), Wales (1), Northern Ireland, Wales (s)
1977 v Sweden

891 ALEXANDER MacDONALD (1/0)
17 March 1948, Glasgow
— (with Rangers, Glasgow)
1976 v Switzerland

892 DESMOND BREMNER (1/0)
7 September 1952, Aberchirder
— (with Hibernian, Edinburgh)
1976 v Switzerland (s)

893 ROBERT McKEAN (1/0)
8 December 1952, East Kilbride
— (with Rangers, Glasgow)
1976 v Switzerland (s)

894 DONALD MASSON (17/5)
26 August 1946, Banchory
— (with Queen's Park Rangers, London)
1976 v Wales, Northern Ireland (1), England (1), Finland (1), Czechoslovakia
1977 v Wales, Northern Ireland, England, Chile, Argentina (1), Brazil, East Germany, Czechoslovakia, Wales (1)
— (with Derby County)
1978 v Northern Ireland, England, Peru

895 RONALD GLAVIN (1/0)
27 March 1951, Glasgow
— (with Celtic, Glasgow)
1977 v Sweden

896 DAVID NAREY (35/1)
12 June 1956, Dundee
— (with Dundee United)
1977 v Sweden (s)
1978 v Portugal
1979 v Northern Ireland (s), Argentina
1980 v Portugal, Northern Ireland, Poland, Hungary
1981 v Wales, England (s)
1982 v Netherlands, Wales, England, New Zealand (s), Brazil (1), Soviet Union, East Germany, Switzerland, Belgium
1983 v Northern Ireland, Wales, England, Canada, Canada, Canada
1986 v Israel, Romania, Netherlands, West Germany, Uruguay, Bulgaria, Republic of Ireland
1987 v Belgium
1988 v Italy
1989 v Cyprus

897 JOSEPH CRAIG (1/1)
14 May 1954, Bridge of Allan
— (with Celtic, Glasgow)
1977 v Sweden (s/1)

898 JAMES STEWART (2/0)
9 March 1954, Kilwinning
— (with Kilmarnock)
1977 v Chile (s)
— (with Middlesbrough)
1978 v Norway

899 DAVID STEWART (1/0)
11 March 1947, Glasgow
— (with Leeds United)
1977 v East Germany

900 ARTHUR GRAHAM (11/2)
26 October 1952, Glasgow
— (with Leeds United)
1977 v East Germany (s)
1978 v Austria (s), Norway
1979 v Wales, Northern Ireland (1), England, Argentina (1), Norway, Peru (s), Austria
1981 v Wales

901 JAMES BLYTH (2/0)
2 February 1955, Perth
— (with Coventry City)
1978 v Bulgaria, Wales

902 STUART KENNEDY (8/0)
31 May 1953, Grangemouth
— (with Aberdeen)
1978 v Bulgaria, Wales, England, Peru, Netherlands, Austria, Portugal
1981 v Portugal (s)

903 IAN WALLACE (3/1)
23 May 1956, Glasgow
— (with Coventry City)
1978 v Bulgaria (s/1), Portugal (s)
1979 v Wales

904 JOHN ROBERTSON (28/8)
20 January 1953, Uddingston
— (with Nottingham Forest)
1978 v Northern Ireland, Wales (s), Iran, Portugal
1979 v Norway (1), Peru, Austria, Belgium, Belgium (1)
1980 v Portugal, Sweden, Portugal
1981 v Israel, Northern Ireland, Israel (2), Northern Ireland, England (1), Sweden (1), Northern Ireland
1982 v Northern Ireland, England (s), New Zealand (1), Brazil, Soviet Union, East Germany, Switzerland
— (with Derby County)
1983 v Uruguay (1), Belgium

905 GEORGE BURLEY (11/0)
3 June 1956, Cumnock
— (with Ipswich Town)
1979 v Wales, Northern Ireland, England, Argentina, Norway
1980 v Portugal, Northern Ireland, England (s), Poland
1982 v Wales (s), England

**906 JOHN WARK (29/7)**
4 August 1957, Glasgow

   – (with Ipswich Town)
     1979 v Wales, Northern Ireland, England (1),
     Argentina, Norway (s), Peru, Austria, Belgium,
     Belgium
     1981 v Israel, Northern Ireland (1), Sweden
     1982 v Spain, Netherlands, Northern Ireland (1),
     New Zealand (2), Brazil, Soviet Union,
     East Germany (1), Switzerland
     1983 v Switzerland (1), Northern Ireland,
     England (s), Uruguay, Belgium, East Germany
   – (with Liverpool)
     1984 v England, France, Yugoslavia

**907 PAUL HEGARTY (8/0)**
25 July 1954, Edinburgh

   – (with Dundee United)
     1979 v Wales, Northern Ireland, England,
     Argentina, Norway (s)
     1980 v Wales, England
     1983 v Northern Ireland

**908 ALAN HANSEN (26/0)**
13 June 1955, Sauchie

   – (with Liverpool)
     1979 v Wales, Argentina, Belgium
     1980 v Portugal, Sweden, Portugal
     1981 v Israel, Sweden, Northern Ireland,
     Portugal
     1982 v Spain, Northern Ireland (s), Wales,
     England, New Zealand, Brazil, Soviet Union,
     East Germany, Switzerland, Belgium
     1983 v Switzerland
     1985 v Wales (s)
     1986 v Romania (s), Republic of Ireland,
     Luxembourg
     1987 v Republic of Ireland

**909 GEORGE WOOD (4/0)**
26 September 1952, Douglas

   – (with Everton, Liverpool)
     1979 v Northern Ireland, England, Argentina (s)
   – (with Arsenal, London)
     1982 v Northern Ireland

**910 FRANCIS McGARVEY (7/0)**
17 March 1956, Kilsyth

   – (with Liverpool)
     1979 v Northern Ireland (s), Argentina
   – (with Celtic, Glasgow)
     1983 v Uruguay, Belgium (s), East Germany (s),
     Northern Ireland
     1984 v Wales

**911 ALEXANDER MUNRO (7/0)**
24 August 1951, Uddingston

   – (with St Mirren, Paisley)
     1979 v Argentina, Norway, Peru, Austria,
     Belgium
     1980 v Wales, England

**912 DAVID COOPER (22/6)**
25 February 1956, Hamilton

   – (with Rangers, Glasgow)
     1979 v Peru, Austria (s)
     1984 v Wales (1), England, Yugoslavia (1),
     Iceland, Spain
     1985 v Spain, Wales, Wales (s/1), East Germany,
     Australia (1), Australia
     1986 v Netherlands, West Germany (s),
     Uruguay (s), Bulgaria, Luxembourg (2)
     1987 v Republic of Ireland, Brazil
   – (with Motherwell)
     1989 v Norway
     1990 v Egypt

**913 ROBERT AITKEN (57/1)**
24 November 1958, Irvine

   – (with Celtic, Glasgow)
     1979 v Peru (s), Belgium
     1980 v Wales (s), England, Poland
     1982 v Belgium
     1983 v Canada (s), Canada, Belgium (s),
     Northern Ireland
     1984 v Wales (s)
     1985 v England, Iceland, Wales, East Germany,
     Australia, Australia
     1986 v Israel, Romania (1), England, Denmark,
     West Germany, Uruguay, Bulgaria,
     Republic of Ireland, Luxembourg
     1987 v Republic of Ireland, Belgium, England,
     Brazil, Hungary, Belgium, Bulgaria, Luxembourg
     1988 v Saudi Arabia, Malta, Spain, Columbia,
     England, Norway, Yugoslavia, Italy
     1989 v Cyprus, France, Cyprus, England, Chile,
     Yugoslavia, France, Norway
   – (with Newcastle United)
     1990 v Argentina (s), Poland, Malta, Costa Rica,
     Sweden, Brazil
   – (with St Mirren, Paisley)
     1991 v Romania (s)

**914 DAVID PROVAN (10/1)**
8 May 1956, Gourock

   – (with Celtic, Glasgow)
     1979 v Belgium (s), Belgium (s)
     1980 v Portugal (s), Northern Ireland (s)
     1981 v Israel (1), Wales, England, Sweden,
     Portugal
     1982 v Northern Ireland

**915 EAMONN BANNON (11/1)**
18 April 1958, Edinburgh

   – (with Dundee United)
     1979 v Belgium
     1983 v Northern Ireland, Wales, England,
     Canada, East Germany (1)
     1986 v Israel, Romania, England, Denmark (s),
     West Germany

**916 ALEXANDER McLEISH (77/0)**
21 January 1959, Glasgow

   – (with Aberdeen)
     1980 v Portugal, Northern Ireland, Wales,
     England, Poland, Hungary, Sweden
     1981 v Israel, Northern Ireland, Israel,
     Northern Ireland, England, Sweden
     1982 v Spain, Northern Ireland, Brazil (s),
     Belgium
     1983 v Switzerland (s), Wales, England, Canada,
     Canada, Canada, Uruguay, Belgium,
     East Germany, Northern Ireland
     1984 v Wales, England, France, Yugoslavia,
     Iceland, Spain
     1985 v Spain, Wales, England, Iceland, Wales,
     East Germany, Australia, Australia
     1986 v England, Netherlands, Denmark
     1987 v Belgium, England, Brazil, Belgium,
     Bulgaria, Luxembourg
     1988 v Saudi Arabia (s), Malta, Spain,
     Columbia, England, Norway, Yugoslavia, Italy
     1989 v Cyprus, France, Cyprus, England, Chile,
     Yugoslavia, France, Norway
     1990 v Argentina, East Germany, Egypt,
     Costa Rica, Sweden, Brazil, Romania, Switzerland
     1991 v Soviet Union, Bulgaria
     1993 v Malta

**917 STEVEN ARCHIBALD (27/4)**
27 September 1956, Glasgow

   – (with Aberdeen)
     1980 v Portugal (s/1)
   – (with Tottenham Hotspur, London)
     1980 v Northern Ireland, Poland, Hungary (1),
     Sweden (s)
     1981 v Israel, Northern Ireland, Israel,
     Northern Ireland (1), England, Northern Ireland,
     Portugal
     1982 v Spain (s), Netherlands, New Zealand (s/1),
     Brazil, Soviet Union, East Germany, Switzerland (s),
     Belgium
     1983 v East Germany
     1984 v England, France
   – (with Barcelona)
     1985 v Spain, England, Iceland (s)
     1986 v West Germany

**918 WILLIAM THOMSON (7/0)**
10 February 1958, Linwood

   – (with St Mirren, Paisley)
     1980 v Northern Ireland
     1981 v Northern Ireland (s), Northern Ireland,
     Portugal
     1983 v Northern Ireland, Canada, East Germany

**919 GORDON STRACHAN (50/5)**
9 February 1957, Edinburgh

   – (with Aberdeen)
     1980 v Northern Ireland, Wales, England,
     Poland, Hungary (s), Sweden (1), Portugal
     1981 v Northern Ireland, Portugal
     1982 v Spain, Netherlands (s), New Zealand,
     Brazil, Soviet Union, East Germany, Switzerland,
     Belgium
     1983 v Switzerland, Northern Ireland (s),
     Wales, England, Canada (1), Canada, Canada (s),
     East Germany, Northern Ireland
     1984 v England, France
   – (with Manchester United)
     1985 v Spain (s), England, Iceland, Wales, Australia
     1986 v Romania (1), Denmark, West Germany (1),
     Uruguay, Bulgaria, Republic of Ireland
     1987 v Republic of Ireland, Hungary
   – (with Leeds United)
     1989 v France (s), France
     1991 v Soviet Union, Bulgaria, San Marino (1),
     Switzerland, Romania
     1992 v Northern Ireland, Finland

920 PETER WEIR (6/0)    – (with St Mirren, Paisley)
18 January 1958, Johnstone
    1980 v Northern Ireland, Wales, Poland (s), Hungary
    – (with Aberdeen)
    1983 v Switzerland, Northern Ireland

921 ALAN BRAZIL (13/1)    – (with Ipswich Town)
15 June 1959, Glasgow
    1980 v Poland (s), Hungary
    1982 v Spain, Netherlands (s), Northern Ireland, Wales, England, New Zealand, Soviet Union (s), East Germany, Switzerland
    – (with Tottenham Hotspur, London)
    1983 v Wales (1), England (s)

922 ALISTAIR DAWSON (5/0)    – (with Rangers, Glasgow)
25 February 1958, Johnstone
    1980 v Poland (s), Hungary
    1983 v Northern Ireland, Canada, Canada

923 RAYMOND STEWART (10/1)    – (with West Ham United, London)
7 September 1959, Stanley
    1981 v Wales, Northern Ireland (1), England, Northern Ireland, Portugal
    1982 v Wales
    1984 v France
    1986 v Republic of Ireland, Luxembourg
    1987 v Republic of Ireland

924 PAUL STURROCK (20/3)    – (with Dundee United)
10 October 1956, Ellon
    1981 v Wales (s), Northern Ireland, England (s), Portugal (1)
    1982 v Northern Ireland (s), Wales (s), England (s), East Germany (s/1), Switzerland, Belgium (s)
    1983 v Canada, Canada, Canada
    1984 v Wales, Yugoslavia (s/1)
    1986 v Israel (s), Netherlands, Denmark, Uruguay
    1987 v Belgium

925 THOMAS BURNS (8/0)    – (with Celtic, Glasgow)
16 December 1956, Glasgow
    1981 v Northern Ireland
    1982 v Netherlands (s), Wales, Belgium (s)
    1983 v Northern Ireland, Canada, Canada (s)
    1988 v England (s)

926 ALLAN EVANS (4/0)    – (with Aston Villa, Birmingham)
12 October 1956, Dunfermline
    1982 v Netherlands, Northern Ireland, England, New Zealand

927 JAMES BETT (26/1)    – (with Rangers, Glasgow)
25 November 1959, Hamilton
    1982 v Netherlands, Belgium
    – (with Lokeren)
    1983 v Belgium
    1984 v Wales, England, France, Yugoslavia, Iceland, Spain
    1985 v Spain, Wales, England, Iceland (1)
    – (with Aberdeen)
    1985 v Wales, Australia (s)
    1986 v Israel, Netherlands
    1987 v Belgium, Hungary (s)
    1988 v Yugoslavia
    1989 v France (s), Norway
    1990 v Argentina, Egypt, Malta, Costa Rica

928 ARTHUR ALBISTON (14/0)    – (with Manchester United)
14 July 1957, Edinburgh
    1982 v Northern Ireland
    1983 v Uruguay, Belgium, East Germany
    1984 v Wales, England, Yugoslavia, Iceland, Spain
    1985 v Spain, Wales, East Germany
    1986 v Netherlands, Uruguay

929 JAMES LEIGHTON (91/0)    – (with Aberdeen)
24 July 1958, Johnstone
    1982 v East Germany, Switzerland, Belgium
    1983 v Switzerland, Wales, England, Canada, Canada, Uruguay, Belgium, Northern Ireland
    1984 v Wales, England, France, Yugoslavia, Iceland, Spain
    1985 v Spain, Wales, England, Iceland, Wales, East Germany, Australia, Australia
    1986 v Israel, Denmark, West Germany, Uruguay, Bulgaria, Republic of Ireland, Luxembourg
    1987 v Republic of Ireland, Belgium, England, Hungary, Belgium, Bulgaria, Luxembourg
    1988 v Saudi Arabia, Malta, Spain, Columbia, England
    – (with Manchester United)
    1988 v Norway
    1989 v Cyprus, France, Cyprus, England, Chile, Yugoslavia, France, Norway
    1990 v Argentina, Malta (s), Costa Rica, Sweden, Brazil
    – (with Hibernian, Edinburgh)
    1993 v Malta
    1994 v Austria, Netherlands, Greece (s)
    1995 v Russia, San Marino, Japan, Ecuador, Faroe Islands, Greece, Finland, Sweden, San Marino
    1996 v Australia, Denmark, USA, Sweden
    1997 v Estonia, Austria, Sweden, Wales (s), Malta, Belarus
    – (with Aberdeen)
    1997 v Belarus, Latvia
    1998 v Denmark, Finland, USA, Brazil, Norway, Morocco, Lithuania, Estonia

930 RICHARD GOUGH (61/6)    – (with Dundee United)
5 April 1962, Stockholm, Sweden
    1983 v Switzerland, Northern Ireland, Wales, England, Canada, Canada (1), Canada, Uruguay, Belgium, East Germany, Northern Ireland
    1984 v Wales, England, France
    1985 v Spain, England (1), Iceland, Wales, East Germany, Australia
    1986 v Israel, Romania (1), England, Denmark, West Germany, Uruguay
    – (with Tottenham Hotspur, London)
    1986 v Bulgaria, Republic of Ireland, Luxembourg
    1987 v Republic of Ireland, Belgium, England, Brazil, Hungary
    – (with Rangers, Glasgow)
    1988 v Saudi Arabia, Spain, Columbia, England, Yugoslavia, Italy
    1989 v Cyprus (2), France, Cyprus, France
    1990 v Argentina, East Germany, Egypt, Poland, Malta, Costa Rica
    1991 v Soviet Union, Bulgaria, San Marino (1)
    1992 v Northern Ireland, Canada, Norway, Netherlands, Germany, CIS, Switzerland
    1993 v Portugal

931 CHARLES NICHOLAS (20/5)    – (with Celtic, Glasgow)
30 December 1961, Glasgow
    1983 v Switzerland (1), Northern Ireland, England, Canada, Canada (1), Canada
    – (with Arsenal, London)
    1983 v Belgium (1)
    1984 v France (s), Yugoslavia (s/1), Iceland (s/1)
    1985 v Spain (s), Wales (s)
    1986 v Israel, Romania (s), England, Denmark, Uruguay (s), Bulgaria
    1987 v England (s)
    – (with Aberdeen)
    1989 v Cyprus (s)

**932  NEIL SIMPSON (5/0)**     –     (with Aberdeen)
15 November 1961, London, England

     1983  v Northern Ireland, Uruguay (s)
     1984  v France (s)
     1987  v England
     1988  v England

**933  MARK McGHEE (4/2)**     –     (with Aberdeen)
20 May 1957, Glasgow

     1983  v Canada (s/1), Canada, Northern Ireland (s)
     1984  v England (1)

**934  PAUL McSTAY (76/9)**     –     (with Celtic, Glasgow)
22 October 1964, Hamilton

     1983  v Uruguay, Belgium, East Germany, Northern Ireland
     1984  v Wales, England (s), Yugoslavia (s), Iceland (2), Spain
     1985  v Spain, Wales, East Germany (s), Australia
     1986  v Israel (1), Uruguay, Bulgaria, Republic of Ireland, Luxembourg (s)
     1987  v Republic of Ireland (s), Belgium (1), England, Brazil, Hungary, Belgium (1), Bulgaria, Luxembourg
     1988  v Saudi Arabia, Spain, Columbia, England, Norway (1), Yugoslavia, Italy
     1989  v Cyprus, France, Cyprus, England, Chile, Yugoslavia, France, Norway
     1990  v Argentina, East Germany (s), Egypt, Poland (s), Malta, Costa Rica, Sweden (s), Brazil, Romania
     1991  v Soviet Union, Bulgaria, San Marino (1)
     1992  v Finland (1), USA, Canada, Norway, Netherlands, Germany, CIS (1), Switzerland, Portugal, Italy
     1993  v Malta, Portugal, Estonia, Estonia, Italy (s)
     1994  v Netherlands, Finland, Faroe Islands
     1995  v Russia
     1996  v Australia
     1997  v Estonia, Estonia, Austria (s)

**935  DAVID DODDS (2/1)**     –     (with Dundee United)
23 September 1958, Dundee

     1983  v Uruguay (s/1), Northern Ireland

**936  DOUGLAS ROUGVIE (1/0)**     –     (with Aberdeen)
24 May 1956, Ballingry

     1983  v Northern Ireland

**937  MAURICE JOHNSTON (38/14)**     –     (with Watford)
13 April 1963, Glasgow

     1984  v Wales (s/1), England (s), France
     –     (with Celtic, Glasgow)
     1984  v Yugoslavia (1), Iceland, Spain (2)
     1985  v Spain, Wales, East Germany
     1986  v Bulgaria, Republic of Ireland, Luxembourg (1)
     1987  v Republic of Ireland
     –     (with Nantes)
     1987  v Hungary, Belgium, Luxembourg
     1988  v Saudi Arabia (1), Spain, Columbia, England, Norway (1), Yugoslavia (1), Italy
     1989  v Cyprus (1), France (2), Cyprus (1), England, Chile (s)
     –     (with Rangers, Glasgow)
     1989  v France, Norway
     1990  v East Germany, Poland (1), Malta, Costa Rica, Sweden (1), Brazil
     1991  v Switzerland, San Marino (s)

**938  MAURICE MALPAS (55/0)**     –     (with Dundee United)
3 August 1962, Dunfermline

     1984  v France
     1985  v England, Iceland, Wales, Australia, Australia
     1986  v Israel, Romania, England, Netherlands, Denmark, West Germany, Bulgaria
     1987  v Republic of Ireland, Belgium, Belgium, Bulgaria, Luxembourg
     1988  v Saudi Arabia, Malta, Norway, Yugoslavia, Italy
     1989  v Cyprus, France, Cyprus, England, Chile, Yugoslavia, France, Norway
     1990  v Egypt, Poland, Malta, Costa Rica, Sweden, Brazil, Romania, Bulgaria
     1991  v Soviet Union, Bulgaria, San Marino, Switzerland, Romania, San Marino
     1992  v Northern Ireland, Finland, USA, Canada (s), Norway, Netherlands, Germany, Switzerland, Portugal, Italy

**939  STEPHEN NICOL (27/0)**     –     (with Liverpool)
11 December 1961, Irvine

     1984  v Yugoslavia, Iceland, Spain
     1985  v Wales, Wales, East Germany, Australia
     1986  v England, Denmark, West Germany, Uruguay
     1987  v Hungary, Bulgaria
     1988  v Saudi Arabia, Spain, Columbia, England, Norway, Yugoslavia
     1989  v Cyprus, France, Yugoslavia, France
     1990  v Switzerland
     1991  v Soviet Union, San Marino, Switzerland

**940  DAVID SPEEDIE (10/0)**     –     (with Chelsea, London)
20 February 1960, Glenrothes

     1985  v England, Wales, East Germany (s), Australia
     1986  v England
     –     (with Coventry City)
     1988  v Yugoslavia (s), Italy (s)
     1989  v Cyprus, Cyprus (s), Chile

**941  MURDO MacLEOD (20/1)**     –     (with Celtic, Glasgow)
24 September 1958, Glasgow

     1985  v England (s)
     1986  v Republic of Ireland, Luxembourg
     1987  v England, Brazil
     (with Borussia, Dortmund)
     1988  v Columbia, England, Italy
     1989  v Chile (1), Yugoslavia, France, Norway (s)
     1990  v Argentina, East Germany, Poland, Sweden, Brazil, Romania
     –     (with Hibernian, Edinburgh)
     1990  v Switzerland
     1991  v Soviet Union (s)

**942  GRAEME SHARP (12/1)**     –     (with Everton, Liverpool)
16 October 1960, Glasgow

     1985  v Iceland, Wales, Australia (s), Australia (s)
     1986  v Israel, Romania, Uruguay, Republic of Ireland
     1987  v Belgium (s), Bulgaria, Luxembourg
     1988  v Malta (1)

**943 ANDREW GORAM (43/0)**
13 April 1964, Bury, England

– (with Oldham Athletic)
1985 v East Germany (s)
1986 v Romania, Netherlands
1987 v Brazil
– (with Hibernian, Edinburgh)
1988 v Yugoslavia, Italy
1990 v East Germany, Poland, Malta, Romania, Switzerland, Bulgaria
1991 v Soviet Union, Bulgaria, San Marino
– (with Rangers, Glasgow)
1991 v Switzerland, Romania, San Marino
1992 v Finland, Norway, Netherlands, Germany, CIS, Switzerland, Portugal, Italy
1993 v Malta, Portugal
1994 v Netherlands, Finland, Faroe Islands, Russia, Greece
1995 v Sweden (s)
1996 v Denmark (s), Columbia, Netherlands, England, Switzerland, Austria, Latvia
1997 v Estonia
1998 v Denmark (s)

**944 FRANCIS McAVENNIE (5/1)**
22 November 1959, Glasgow

– (with West Ham United, London)
1985 v Australia (1), Australia
1986 v Denmark (s), West Germany (s)
– (with Celtic, Glasgow)
1988 v Saudi Arabia

**945 PATRICK NEVIN (28/5)**
6 September 1963, Glasgow

– (with Chelsea, London)
1986 v Romania (s), England (s), Luxembourg
1987 v Republic of Ireland, Belgium (s), Luxembourg
– (with Everton, Liverpool)
1989 v Cyprus, England
1990 v Romania (s), Bulgaria (s)
1991 v San Marino (s)
1992 v USA (1), Germany (s), CIS (s)
– (with Tranmere Rovers, Birkenhead)
1993 v Malta (1), Portugal (s), Estonia (2), Switzerland, Malta
1994 v Netherlands, Austria (s), Netherlands (s), Faroe Islands, Russia (s)
1995 v San Marino, Sweden (s), San Marino (1)
1996 v Australia (s)

**946 ALISTAIR McCOIST (61/19)**
24 September 1962, Bellshill

– (with Rangers, Glasgow)
1986 v Netherlands, Luxembourg (s)
1987 v Republic of Ireland (s), Belgium, England, Brazil, Hungary (2), Belgium (1)
1988 v Malta, Spain, Columbia, England, Yugoslavia (s)
1989 v France, Cyprus (1), England, Yugoslavia, France, Norway (1)
1990 v East Germany (s), Egypt (1), Poland, Malta (s), Costa Rica (s), Sweden (s), Brazil, Romania (1), Switzerland, Bulgaria (1)
1991 v Soviet Union, Bulgaria, Switzerland (1), San Marino (1)
1992 v Northern Ireland (1), Finland (s), USA, Canada (1), Norway, Netherlands, Germany, CIS, Switzerland (1), Portugal, Italy
1993 v Malta (2), Portugal
1995 v Greece (s/1), Finland (s), San Marino (s/1)
1996 v Australia (1), Denmark (s), Columbia, England (s), Switzerland (1), Austria, Sweden (s)
1997 v Estonia (s), Austria (s), Belarus (s)
– (with Kilmarnock)
1998 v Lithuania, Estonia

**947 ROBERT CONNOR (4/0)**
4 August 1960, Kilmarnock

– (with Dundee)
1986 v Netherlands
– (with Aberdeen)
1988 v Saudi Arabia (s)
1989 v England
1990 v Romania

**948 BRIAN McCLAIR (30/2)**
8 December 1963, Bellshill

– (with Celtic, Glasgow)
1986 v Luxembourg
1987 v Republic of Ireland, England, Brazil (s)
– (with Manchester United)
1987 v Bulgaria
1988 v Malta (s), Spain (s), Norway, Yugoslavia, Italy (s)
1989 v Cyprus, France (s), Norway (s)
1990 v Argentina (s), Bulgaria
1991 v Bulgaria, San Marino, Switzerland (s), Romania
1992 v Northern Ireland, USA, Canada (s), Norway, Netherlands, Germany, CIS (1), Switzerland, Portugal (s)
1993 v Estonia, Estonia (1)

**949 JAMES McINALLY (10/0)**
19 February 1964, Glasgow

– (with Dundee United)
1987 v Belgium, Brazil
1988 v Malta (s)
1990 v Bulgaria
1991 v Bulgaria
1992 v USA (s), Norway (s), CIS (s)
1993 v Germany, Portugal

**950 IAN WILSON (5/0)**
27 March 1958, Aberdeen

– (with Leicester City)
1987 v England, Brazil
– (with Everton, Liverpool)
1987 v Belgium, Bulgaria, Luxembourg

**951 STEPHEN CLARKE (6/0)**
29 August 1963, Saltcoats

– (with Chelsea, London)
1987 v Hungary, Belgium, Bulgaria
1988 v Saudi Arabia, Malta
1994 v Netherlands

**952 IAIN DURRANT (20/0)**
29 October 1966, Glasgow

– (with Rangers, Glasgow)
1987 v Hungary, Belgium
1988 v Malta, Spain, Norway (s)
1992 v Switzerland (s), Portugal (s), Italy
1993 v Portugal (s), Italy (s), Malta
– (with Kilmarnock)
1998 v Estonia, Faroe Islands (s)
1999 v Germany, Faroe Islands, Czech Republic, Bosnia (s), Estonia
2000 v Netherlands (s), Republic of Ireland (s)

**953 ERIC BLACK (2/0)**
1 October 1963, Bellshill

– (with Metz)
1987 v Hungary (s), Luxembourg (s)

**954 GARY GILLESPIE (13/0)**
5 July 1960, Stirling

– (with Liverpool)
1987 v Belgium, Bulgaria
1988 v Spain, Norway
1989 v France, Chile, Yugoslavia
1990 v East Germany, Egypt, Poland, Malta, Brazil (s), Bulgaria

**955 DEREK WHYTE (12/0)**
31 August 1968, Glasgow

– (with Celtic, Glasgow)
1987 v Belgium (s), Luxembourg
1989 v Chile (s)
1992 v USA (s)
– (with Middlesbrough)
1992 v Portugal, Italy
1995 v Japan (s), Ecuador
1996 v USA, Latvia
– (with Aberdeen)
1998 v Finland
1999 v Germany (s)

**956 GARY MACKAY (4/1)**
23 January 1964, Edinburgh

– (with Heart of Midlothian, Edinburgh)
1987 v Bulgaria (s/1), Luxembourg (s)
1988 v Saudi Arabia (s), Malta

957 GORDON DURIE (43/7)
6 December 1965, Paisley

– (with Chelsea, London)
1987 v Bulgaria (s)
1988 v Italy (s)
1989 v Cyprus, Yugoslavia (1)
1990 v East Germany, Egypt, Sweden, Switzerland (s), Bulgaria
1991 v Soviet Union (s), Bulgaria, San Marino (1)
– (with Tottenham Hotspur, London)
1991 v Switzerland (1), Romania, San Marino (1)
1992 v Northern Ireland (s), Finland, Canada, Norway (s), Netherlands, Germany, Switzerland, Italy
1993 v Switzerland, Italy
– (with Rangers, Glasgow)
1994 v Netherlands, Netherlands
1996 v USA (1), Netherlands, England, Switzerland, Austria (s)
1997 v Sweden (s), Malta (s), Belarus, Belarus, Latvia (1), France (1)
1998 v Finland (s), Columbia, Brazil, Norway, Morocco

958 JOHN COLLINS (58/12)
31 January 1968, Galashiels

– (with Hibernian, Edinburgh)
1988 v Saudi Arabia (1)
1990 v East Germany, Poland (s), Malta (s)
– (with Celtic, Glasgow)
1990 v Switzerland (s)
1991 v Bulgaria (s/1)
1992 v Northern Ireland (s), Finland, Portugal
1993 v Malta, Germany, Portugal, Estonia (1), Estonia, Switzerland (1)
1994 v Netherlands (s), Austria, Netherlands, Finland (1), Faroe Islands (2), Russia, Greece
1995 v Russia, San Marino (1), Faroe Islands, Greece, Finland, Sweden, San Marino
1996 v Australia, Denmark, USA (s), Colombia, Netherlands, England, Switzerland
– (with Monaco)
1996 v Austria, Latvia (1), Sweden
1997 v Estonia, Austria, Sweden, Malta, Belarus, Latvia, France
1998 v Finland, Columbia (1), USA, Brazil (1), Norway, Morocco
– (with Everton, Liverpool)
1998 v Lithuania
1999 v Bosnia, Estonia, Bosnia (1), England, England

959 HENRY SMITH (3/0)
10 March 1956, Lanark

– (with Heart of Midlothian, Edinburgh)
1988 v Saudi Arabia (s)
1992 v Northern Ireland, Canada

960 JOHN COLQUHOUN (2/0)
14 July 1963, Stirling

– (with Heart of Midlothian, Edinburgh)
1988 v Saudi Arabia (s), Malta (s)

961 DEREK FERGUSON (2/0)
31 July 1967, Glasgow

– (with Rangers, Glasgow)
1988 v Malta, Columbia (s).

962 KEVIN GALLACHER (53/9)
23 November 1966, Clydebank

– (with Dundee United)
1988 v Columbia, England (s), Norway, Italy
– (with Coventry City)
1991 v San Marino, Romania (s), San Marino (s)
1992 v Northern Ireland (s), Norway (s), Netherlands (s), Germany (s), CIS, Switzerland (s), Portugal
– (with Blackburn Rovers)
1993 v Portugal, Estonia (1), Estonia, Italy (1), Malta
1996 v Australia (s), Denmark, Columbia (s), Netherlands, Sweden (s)
1997 v Estonia, Estonia, Austria (2), Sweden (1), Wales, Malta, Belarus, Belarus (2), Latvia (1), France
1998 v Finland (s), USA, Brazil, Norway, Morocco, Lithuania, Estonia
1999 v Faroe Islands, Czech Republic, Bosnia (s)
– (with Newcastle United)
1999 v Bosnia, Lithuania (s), England
2000 v France, Republic of Ireland (s), San Marino, Croatia (1)
2001 v Belgium (s), San Marino (s)

963 ANDREW WALKER (3/0)
6 April 1965, Glasgow

– (with Celtic, Glasgow)
1988 v Columbia (s)
1994 v Finland, Faroe Islands (s)

964 IAN FERGUSON (9/0)
15 March 1967, Glasgow

– (with Rangers, Glasgow)
1988 v Italy
1989 v Cyprus (s), France
1993 v Malta (s), Estonia, Malta
1994 v Austria (s), Netherlands (s)
1997 v Estonia (s)

965 ALAN McINALLY (8/3)
10 February 1963, Ayr

– (with Aston Villa, Birmingham)
1989 v Cyprus (s), Chile (1)
– (with Bayern, Munich)
1989 v Yugoslavia (s), France (s)
1990 v Argentina, Poland (s), Malta (2), Costa Rica

966 DAVID McPHERSON (27/0)
28 January 1964, Paisley

– (with Heart of Midlothian, Edinburgh)
1989 v Cyprus, England, Norway
1990 v Malta, Costa Rica, Sweden, Brazil, Switzerland, Bulgaria
1991 v Soviet Union (s), Bulgaria, San Marino, Switzerland, Romania, San Marino
1992 v Northern Ireland, Finland, USA, Canada, Norway, Netherlands, Germany, CIS
– (with Rangers, Glasgow)
1992 v Switzerland, Italy
1993 v Malta, Portugal

967 STEWART McKIMMIE (40/1)
27 October 1962, Aberdeen

– (with Aberdeen)
1989 v England, Chile
1990 v Argentina (1), Egypt, Costa Rica (s), Brazil, Romania, Switzerland, Bulgaria
1991 v San Marino, Switzerland, Romania
1992 v Northern Ireland, Finland, USA, Canada (s), Norway (s), Netherlands, Germany, CIS
1993 v Portugal, Estonia (s), Switzerland, Italy
1994 v Netherlands, Austria, Netherlands, Finland, Faroe Islands, Russia, Greece
1995 v Russia, Faroe Islands, Greece, Finland, Sweden
1996 v Denmark, Columbia, Netherlands, England

968 PETER GRANT (2/0)
30 August 1965, Bellshill

– (with Celtic, Glasgow)
1989 v England (s), Chile

969 CRAIG LEVEIN (16/0)
22 October 1964, Dunfermline

– (with Heart of Midlothian, Edinburgh)
1990 v Argentina, East Germany, Egypt (s), Poland, Malta (s), Sweden
1991 v Romania, San Marino
1992 v Portugal
1993 v Germany, Portugal, Switzerland
1994 v Netherlands, Finland, Faroe Islands, Russia

970 STUART McCALL (40/1)
10 June 1964, Leeds, England

– (with Everton, Liverpool)
1990 v Argentina, East Germany, Egypt (s), Poland, Malta, Costa Rica, Sweden (1), Brazil, Switzerland
1991 v Soviet Union, San Marino
– (with Rangers, Glasgow)
1991 v Switzerland, Romania, San Marino
1992 v USA, Canada, Norway, Netherlands, Germany, CIS, Switzerland, Portugal
1993 v Portugal, Italy
1994 v Netherlands, Austria (s), Netherlands, Finland (s), Russia, Greece
1995 v Greece
1996 v Denmark, USA (s), Columbia, Netherlands, England, Switzerland, Austria, Latvia
1998 v Denmark (s)

971 ROBERT FLECK (4/0)
11 August 1965, Glasgow

– (with Norwich City)
1990 v Argentina, Sweden, Brazil (s)
1991 v Soviet Union

972  GARY McALLISTER (57/5)  —  (with Leicester City)
25 December 1964, Motherwell          1990  v East Germany, Poland, Malta (s)
                                       —  (with Leeds United)
                                          1990  v Romania, Switzerland (1), Bulgaria
                                          1991  v Soviet Union (s), San Marino,
                                          Switzerland (s), San Marino
                                          1992  v Northern Ireland, Finland (s), USA,
                                          Canada (2), Norway, Netherlands, Germany, CIS (1),
                                          Switzerland, Portugal, Italy
                                          1993  v Malta, Switzerland, Italy, Malta
                                          1994  v Netherlands, Austria, Netherlands,
                                          Finland, Russia, Greece
                                          1995  v Russia, San Marino, Greece, Finland,
                                          Sweden, San Marino
                                          1996  v Australia, Denmark, USA (s), Columbia,
                                          Netherlands, England, Switzerland
                                       —  (with Coventry City)
                                          1996  v Austria, Latvia
                                          1997  v Estonia, Estonia, Austria, Sweden, Wales,
                                          Malta, Belarus (1), Belarus, Latvia, France
                                          1999  v Czech Republic

973  BRYAN GUNN (6/0)  —  (with Norwich City)
22 December 1963, Thurso              1990  v Egypt
                                       1993  v Estonia, Estonia, Switzerland, Italy
                                       1994  v Netherlands (s)

974  BRIAN IRVINE (9/0)  —  (with Aberdeen)
24 May 1965, Bellshill                1990  v Romania
                                       1993  v Germany, Estonia, Estonia, Switzerland,
                                       Italy, Malta
                                       1994  v Austria, Netherlands

975  JOHN ROBERTSON (16/3)  —  (with Heart of Midlothian, Edinburgh)
2 October 1964, Edinburgh             1990  v Romania (1), Switzerland (1)
                                       1991  v Bulgaria (s), San Marino (s), San Marino
                                       1992  v Northern Ireland (s), Finland, Italy (s)
                                       1993  v Malta (s), Germany, Estonia
                                       1995  v Japan (s), Ecuador (1), Faroe Islands (s),
                                       Greece (s), Sweden

976  THOMAS BOYD (71/1)  —  (with Motherwell)
24 November 1965, Glasgow             1990  v Romania (s), Switzerland, Bulgaria
                                       1991  v Soviet Union
                                       —  (with Chelsea, London)
                                          1991  v Switzerland, Romania
                                       —  (with Celtic, Glasgow)
                                          1992  v Finland, Canada, Norway, CIS,
                                          Switzerland, Portugal, Italy
                                          1993  v Malta, Germany, Estonia, Estonia,
                                          Italy, Malta (s)
                                          1994  v Netherlands (s), Austria, Finland,
                                          Faroe Islands, Russia, Greece
                                          1995  v Russia, San Marino, Greece, Finland,
                                          Sweden, San Marino
                                          1996  v Australia, Denmark, USA, Columbia,
                                          Netherlands, England, Switzerland, Austria,
                                          Latvia, Sweden
                                          1997  v Estonia, Estonia (1), Austria, Sweden,
                                          Wales, Malta, Belarus, Belarus, Latvia, France
                                          1998  v Denmark, Finland (s), Columbia, USA, Brazil,
                                          Norway, Morocco, Lithuania, Estonia, Faroe Islands
                                          1999  v Czech Republic, Germany, Faroe Islands,
                                          Czech Republic
                                          2000  v Latvia, Croatia, Australia
                                          2001  v Belgium, San Marino (s), Poland

977  MICHAEL GALLOWAY (1/0)  —  (with Celtic, Glasgow)
30 May 1965, Oswestry, England        1991  v Romania
978  DAVID ROBERTSON (3/0)  —  (with Rangers, Glasgow)
17 October 1968, Aberdeen             1992  v Northern Ireland
                                       1993  v Switzerland
                                       1994  v Netherlands

979  KEITH WRIGHT (1/0)  —  (with Hibernian, Edinburgh)
17 May 1965, Edinburgh                1992  v Northern Ireland
980  DAVID BOWMAN (6/0)  —  (with Dundee United)
10 March 1964, Tunbridge Wells, England  1992  v Finland, USA (s)
                                       1993  v Germany, Estonia, Switzerland, Italy
981  GORDON MARSHALL (1/0)  —  (with Celtic, Glasgow)
19 April 1964, Edinburgh              1992  v USA
982  ALAN McLAREN (24/0)  —  (with Heart of Midlothian, Edinburgh)
4 January 1971, Edinburgh             1992  v USA, Canada, Norway, Italy
                                       1993  v Malta, Germany, Estonia (s), Estonia,
                                       Italy, Malta
                                       1994  v Netherlands, Austria, Finland., Faroe Islands
                                       —  (with Rangers, Glasgow)
                                          1994  v Russia, Greece
                                          1995  v Russia, San Marino, Japan, Ecuador,
                                          Faroe Islands, Finland, Sweden, San Marino

983  DUNCAN FERGUSON (7/0)  —  (with Dundee United)
27 December 1971, Stirling            1992  v USA (s), Canada, Netherlands (s)
                                       1993  v Germany
                                       —  (with Everton, Liverpool)
                                          1994  v Greece
                                          1996  v Austria
                                          1997  v Estonia

984  EOIN JESS (18/2)  —  (with Aberdeen)
13 December 1970, Aberdeen            1992  v Italy (s)
                                       1993  v Malta, Switzerland (s), Italy
                                       1994  v Netherlands (s), Austria, Netherlands (s),
                                       Finland (s)
                                       1995  v Sweden (s), San Marino (1)
                                       —  (with Coventry City)
                                          1996  v USA, Columbia (s), England (s)
                                       —  (with Aberdeen)
                                          1998  v Denmark (s)
                                          1999  v Czech Republic (1), Germany (s),
                                          Faroe Islands (s), Czech Republic (s)

985  NICHOLAS WALKER (2/0)  —  (with Heart of Midlothian, Edinburgh)
29 September 1962, Aberdeen           1993  v Germany
                                       —  (with Partick Thistle, Glasgow)
                                          1996  v USA (s)

986  STEPHEN WRIGHT (2/0)  —  (with Aberdeen)
27 August 1971, Bellshill             1993  v Germany, Estonia
987  SCOTT BOOTH (18/6)  —  (with Aberdeen)
16 December 1971, Aberdeen            1993  v Germany (s), Estonia (s/1), Estonia (s),
                                       Switzerland, Malta (s)
                                       1994  v Faroe Islands (1), Russia (1)
                                       1995  v Finland (1), San Marino (1)
                                       1996  v Australia (s), Denmark, Netherlands,
                                       Switzerland (s)
                                       —  (with Borussia, Dortmund)
                                          1998  v Denmark, Finland, Columbia (s), Morocco (s)
                                       —  (with Twente, Enschede)
                                          2001  v Poland (1)

988  COLIN HENDRY (51/3)  —  (with Blackburn Rovers)
7 December 1965, Keith                1993  v Estonia, Estonia, Malta (1)
                                       1994  v Netherlands, Austria, Netherlands,
                                       Finland, Faroe Islands, Greece
                                       1995  v Russia, San Marino, Finland, Sweden,
                                       San Marino
                                       1996  v Australia, Denmark, USA, Columbia,
                                       Netherlands, England, Switzerland, Austria, Sweden
                                       1997  v Estonia, Estonia, Austria, Sweden, Latvia
                                       1998  v Denmark, Finland, Columbia, USA,
                                       Brazil, Norway, Morocco
                                       —  (with Rangers, Glasgow)
                                          1998  v Lithuania, Estonia, Faroe Islands
                                          1999  v Germany, Bosnia, Estonia, Bosnia,
                                          England, England
                                       —  (with Coventry City)
                                          2000  v France, Latvia, San Marino, Croatia,
                                          Australia (s)
                                       —  (with Bolton Wanderers)
                                          2001  v Belgium, San Marino (2)

989  PHILIP O'DONNELL (1/0)
      25 March 1972, Bellshill
                                    –  (with Motherwell)
                                       1993  v Switzerland (s)
990  ROBERT McKINNON (3/0)
      31 July 1966, Glasgow
                                    –  (with Motherwell)
                                       1993  v Malta
                                       1995  v Japan, Faroe Islands
991  WILLIAM McKINLAY (29/4)
      22 April 1969, Glasgow
                                    –  (with Dundee United)
                                       1993  v Malta (1)
                                       1994  v Netherlands (s), Austria (1), Netherlands,
                                       Faroe Islands (s/1), Russia, Greece
                                       1995  v Russia (s), San Marino (s), Japan, Ecuador,
                                       Faroe Islands (1), Finland (s), Sweden (s)
                                    –  (with Blackburn Rovers)
                                       1995  v San Marino (s)
                                       1996  v Australia, Denmark (s), Netherlands (s),
                                       Sweden
                                       1997  v Estonia (s), Latvia (s), France
                                       1998  v Denmark, Finland, Columbia (s), USA,
                                       Brazil (s), Estonia, Faroe Islands

992  JOHN McGINLAY (13/4)
      8 April 1964, Inverness
                                    –  (with Bolton Wanderers)
                                       1994  v Austria (1), Netherlands, Faroe Islands (1),
                                       Russia, Greece
                                       1995  v Russia, San Marino, Faroe Islands (1),
                                       Sweden
                                       1996  v Sweden (1)
                                       1997  v Estonia, Estonia (s), Austria (s)

993  DUNCAN SHEARER (7/2)
      28 August 1962, Fort William
                                    –  (with Aberdeen)
                                       1994  v Austria (s), Netherlands (s/1), Finland (1)
                                       1995  v Russia (s), San Marino, Faroe Islands,
                                       Greece

994  JOHN SPENCER (14/0)
      11 September 1970, Glasgow
                                    –  (with Chelsea, London)
                                       1994  v Russia (s), Greece (s)
                                       1995  v San Marino (s), Japan, Finland
                                       1996  v Australia, Denmark, USA (s), Columbia,
                                       Netherlands (s), England, Switzerland (s), Latvia
                                    –  (with Queen's Park Rangers, London)
                                       1997  v Wales (s)

995  COLIN CALDERWOOD (36/1)
      20 January 1965, Stranraer
                                    –  (with Tottenham Hotspur, London)
                                       1995  v Russia, San Marino (1), Japan, Ecuador,
                                       Faroe Islands, Greece, Finland, Sweden, San Marino
                                       1996  v USA, Columbia, Netherlands, England,
                                       Switzerland, Austria, Latvia, Sweden
                                       1997  v Estonia, Estonia, Austria, Sweden,
                                       Belarus, Latvia, France
                                       1998  v Denmark, Finland, Columbia, USA,
                                       Brazil, Norway, Lithuania, Estonia
                                    –  (with Aston Villa, Birmingham)
                                       1999  v Faroe Islands, Czech Republic, Bosnia,
                                       Bosnia (s)

996  DARREN JACKSON (28/4)
      25 July 1966, Edinburgh
                                    –  (with Hibernian, Edinburgh)
                                       1995  v Russia, San Marino, Japan, Ecuador,
                                       Faroe Islands, Greece, Finland (s), Sweden (s),
                                       San Marino (s)
                                       1996  v Australia (s), Denmark (s), USA,
                                       Latvia (1), Sweden
                                       1997  v Estonia, Austria, Sweden, Wales,
                                       Malta (2), Belarus
                                    –  (with Celtic, Glasgow)
                                       1998  v Denmark, Finland (1), Columbia, USA,
                                       Brazil, Norway, Lithuania, Estonia (s)

997  BRIAN MARTIN (2/0)
      24 February 1963, Bellshill
                                    –  (with Motherwell)
                                       1995  v Japan, Ecuador

998  PAUL LAMBERT (26/0)
      7 August 1969, Glasgow
                                    –  (with Motherwell)
                                       1995  v Japan, Ecuador (s)
                                    –  (with Borussia, Dortmund)
                                       1996  v Latvia (s), Sweden (s)
                                       1997  v Austria, Sweden, Belarus, Belarus,
                                       Latvia
                                    –  (with Celtic, Glasgow)
                                       1998  v Finland (s), Columbia, USA, Brazil,
                                       Norway, Morocco, Lithuania
                                       1999  v Czech Republic, Germany, Faroe Islands,
                                       Czech Republic, Bosnia, Lithuania
                                       2000  v Netherlands, Republic of Ireland
                                       2001  v Belgium, San Marino

999  SCOT GEMMILL (17/0)
      2 January 1971, Paisley
                                    –  (with Nottingham Forest)
                                       1995  v Japan, Ecuador, Faroe Islands (s),
                                       San Marino
                                       1996  v Denmark (s), USA
                                       1997  v Estonia, Sweden (s), Wales, Malta (s),
                                       Belarus (s)
                                       1998  v Denmark, Finland
                                    –  (with Everton, Liverpool)
                                       1999  v Germany, Faroe Islands (s)
                                       2001  v San Marino (s), Poland (s)

1000 CRAIG BURLEY (42/3)
      24 September 1971, Ayr
                                    –  (with Chelsea, London)
                                       1995  v Japan, Ecuador, Faroe Islands, Greece,
                                       Sweden
                                       1996  v Australia, Denmark, USA, Columbia (s),
                                       Netherlands (s), England (s), Switzerland,
                                       Austria, Latvia, Sweden
                                       1997  v Estonia, Austria, Sweden, Malta, Belarus
                                    –  (with Celtic, Glasgow)
                                       1997  v Belarus, Latvia, France
                                       1998  v Colombia (1), USA (s), Brazil, Norway (1),
                                       Morocco, Faroe Islands (1)
                                       1999  v Czech Republic, Bosnia, Estonia,
                                       Bosnia, Lithuania, England, England
                                    –  (with Derby County)
                                       2000  v Netherlands, Republic of Ireland,
                                       Croatia, Australia
                                       2001  v Belgium, San Marino

1001 PAUL BERNARD (2/0)
      30 December 1972, Edinburgh
                                    –  (with Oldham Athletic)
                                       1995  v Japan (s), Ecuador
1002 STEVEN CRAWFORD (2/1)
      9 January 1974, Dunfermline
                                    –  (with Raith Rovers, Kirkcaldy)
                                       1995  v Ecuador (s/1)
                                    –  (with Dunfermline Athletic)
                                       2001  v Poland (s)

1003 THOMAS McKINLAY (22/0)
      3 December 1964, Glasgow
                                    –  (with Celtic, Glasgow)
                                       1995  v Greece, Finland
                                       1996  v Denmark, Columbia, England,
                                       Switzerland, Austria, Latvia, Sweden
                                       1997  v Estonia (s), Estonia, Austria, Sweden,
                                       Wales, Malta, Belarus, Belarus, Latvia (s), France (s)
                                       1998  v USA, Brazil (s), Morocco (s)

1004 BRIAN O'NEIL (6/0)
      6 September 1972, Paisley
                                    –  (with Celtic, Glasgow)
                                       1996  v Australia
                                    –  (with Wolfsburg)
                                       1999  v Germany (s), Lithuania
                                       2000  v Netherlands (s), Republic of Ireland
                                    –  (with Derby County)
                                       2000  v Australia

1005 WILLIAM DODDS (24/7)   –  (with Aberdeen)
5 February 1969, New Cumnock
– (with Aberdeen)
1996  v Latvia (s)
1997  v Wales, Belarus (s), Belarus (s)
– (with Dundee United)
1998  v Estonia (s/2), Faroe Islands (1)
1999  v Germany, Faroe Islands, Czech Republic, Bosnia (1), Estonia, Bosnia, Lithuania (s), England, England
– (with Rangers, Glasgow)
2000  v France, Netherlands, Republic of Ireland, Latvia, San Marino, Australia
2001  v Belgium (2), San Marino (1), Poland

1006 JOHN McNAMARA (11/0)
24 October 1973, Glasgow
– (with Celtic, Glasgow)
1996  v Latvia (s), Sweden
1997  v Estonia, Wales (s)
1998  v Denmark, Columbia, USA (s), Norway (s), Morocco
2000  v Netherlands, San Marino

1007 NEIL SULLIVAN (22/0)
24 February 1970, Sutton, England
– (with Wimbledon, London)
1997  v Wales, France
1998  v Columbia, Faroe Islands
1999  v Czech Republic, Germany, Faroe Islands, Czech Republic, Bosnia, Estonia, Bosnia, England, England
2000  v France, Netherlands, Republic of Ireland
– (with Tottenham Hotspur, London)
2000  v Latvia, San Marino, Croatia
2001  v Belgium, San Marino, Poland

1008 DAVID WEIR (27/0)
10 May 1970, Falkirk
– (with Heart of Midlothian, Edinburgh)
1997  v Wales, Malta (s), France
1998  v Denmark (s), Finland (s), Norway (s), Morocco, Estonia, Faroe Islands
– (with Everton, Liverpool)
1999  v Czech Republic, Germany, Faroe Islands, Czech Republic, Bosnia, Estonia, Bosnia, Lithuania, England, England
2000  v Netherlands, Latvia, San Marino (s), Croatia, Australia
2001  v Belgium, San Marino, Poland (s)

1009 CHRISTIAN DAILLY (27/1)
23 October 1973, Dundee
– (with Derby County)
1997  v Wales, Malta (1), Belarus, Belarus, Latvia, France
1998  v Denmark, Finland, Columbia, USA, Brazil, Norway, Morocco
– (with Blackburn Rovers)
1998  v Lithuania
1999  v Bosnia (s), Estonia, Bosnia, Lithuania, England, England
2000  v France, Netherlands, Republic of Ireland, Latvia, San Marino, Australia
– (with West Ham United, London)
2001  v Poland

1010 BRIAN McALLISTER (3/0)
30 October 1970, Glasgow
– (with Wimbledon, London)
1997  v Wales, Malta, Belarus (s)

1011 SIMON DONNELLY (10/0)
1 December 1974, Glasgow
– (with Celtic, Glasgow)
1997  v Wales (s), Malta (s), Latvia (s), France (s)
1998  v Denmark (s), Finland (s), Columbia (s), USA (s), Estonia (s), Faroe Islands

1012 DAVID HOPKIN (7/2)
21 August 1970, Greenock
– (with Crystal Palace, London)
1997  v Malta, Belarus
– (with Leeds United)
1997  v Belarus (s/2), France (s)
1999  v Czech Republic, Bosnia, Bosnia

1013 MATTHEW ELLIOTT (15/1)
1 November 1968, Roehampton, England
– (with Leicester City)
1997  v France (s)
1998  v Denmark, Finland, Lithuania, Faroe Islands
1999  v Czech Republic, Faroe Islands
2000  v Netherlands, Republic of Ireland, Latvia, San Marino (1), Croatia, Australia (s)
2001  v Belgium, San Marino

1014 BARRY FERGUSON (10/1)
2 February 1978, Glasgow
– (with Rangers, Glasgow)
1998  v Lithuania (s)
1999  v Bosnia, Estonia (s), England, England
2000  v France, Republic of Ireland (1), Latvia, Australia
2001  v Belgium

1015 CALLUM DAVIDSON (14/0)
25 June 1976, Stirling
– (with Blackburn Rovers)
1998  v Lithuania (s), Estonia, Faroe Islands
1999  v Czech Republic, Germany, Faroe Islands, Czech Republic, Estonia, Bosnia, Lithuania, England
2000  v France
– (with Leicester City)
2000  v Latvia
2001  v Poland

1016 NEIL McCANN (11/1)
11 August 1974, Greenock
– (with Heart of Midlothian, Edinburgh)
1998  v Lithuania (s)
– (with Rangers, Glasgow)
1999  v Czech Republic, Bosnia, Estonia (s), England
2000  v France (s), Netherlands, Republic of Ireland, Latvia (1), San Marino, Australia (s)

1017 ALLAN JOHNSTON (12/2)
14 December 1973, Glasgow
– (with Sunderland)
1998  v Estonia, Faroe Islands
1999  v Czech Republic (s), Germany, Faroe Islands (1), Czech Republic (1), Estonia
2000  v France (s), Republic of Ireland (s)
– (with Rangers, Glasgow)
2000  v San Marino (s), Croatia
2001  v San Marino

1018 STEPHEN GLASS (1/0)
25 May 1976, Dundee
– (with Newcastle United)
1998  v Faroe Islands (s)

1019 DONALD HUTCHISON (16/6)
9 May 1971, Gateshead, England
– (with Everton, Liverpool)
1999  v Czech Republic (s), Germany (1), Bosnia (1), Estonia, Lithuania (1), England, England (1)
2000  v France, Netherlands, Republic of Ireland (1)
– (with Sunderland)
2000  v Latvia, San Marino (1), Croatia, Australia
2001  v Belgium, San Marino

1020 PAUL RITCHIE (6/1)
21 August 1975, Kirkcaldy
– (with Heart of Midlothian, Edinburgh)
1999  v Germany (s), Czech Republic (1), Lithuania, England
– (with Bolton Wanderers)
2000  v France, Netherlands

1021 ROBERT WINTERS (1/0)
4 November 1974, East Kilbride
– (with Aberdeen)
1999  v Germany (s)

1022 COLIN CAMERON (11/2)
23 October 1972, Kirkcaldy
– (with Heart of Midlothian, Edinburgh)
1999  v Germany (s), Faroe Islands (s), Lithuania (s/1)
2000  v France, Republic of Ireland (s), Latvia (s), San Marino, Croatia, Australia
2001  v San Marino (1), Poland

1023 MARK BURCHILL (6/0)
18 August 1980, Broxburn
– (with Celtic, Glasgow)
1999  v Bosnia (s), Lithuania, England (s), England (s)
2000  v France (s), Netherlands (s)

1024 GARY McSWEGAN (2/1)
24 September 1970, Glasgow
– (with Heart of Midlothian, Edinburgh)
1999  v Bosnia (s), Lithuania (1)

1025 JONATHAN GOULD (2/0)
18 July 1968, London, England
– (with Celtic, Glasgow)
1999  v Lithuania
2000  v Australia

1026 PAUL TELFER (1/0)
21 October 1971, Edinburgh
– (with Coventry City)
2000  v France

1027 STEVEN PRESSLEY (2/0)      —   (with Heart of Midlothian, Edinburgh)
11 October 1973, Elgin      2000   v France (s), Republic of Ireland (s)

1028 GARY NAYSMITH (4/0)      —   (with Heart of Midlothian, Edinburgh)
16 November 1978, Edinburgh      2000   v Republic of Ireland, Latvia (s),
San Marino, Croatia

1029 GARY HOLT (2/0)      —   (with Kilmarnock)
9 March 1973, Irvine      2000   v Latvia (s), Croatia (s)

1030 PAUL DICKOV (3/0)      —   (with Manchester City)
1 November 1972, Glasgow      2000   v San Marino (s), Croatia (s), Australia (s)

1031 DOMINIC MATTEO (3/0)      —   (with Leeds United)
24 April 1974, Dumfries      2000   v Australia
2001   v Belgium, San Marino

1032 BARRY NICHOLSON (1/0)      —   (with Dunfermline Athletic)
24 August 1978, Dumfries      2001   v Poland

1033 CHARLES MILLER (1/0)      —   (with Dundee United)
18 March 1976, Glasgow      2001   v Poland

1034 GAVIN RAE (1/0)      —   (with Dundee)
28 November 1977, Aberdeen      2001   v Poland

1035 JOHN O'NEIL (1/0)      —   (with Hibernian, Edinburgh)
6 July 1971, Bellshill      2001   v Poland

1036 ANDREW McLAREN (1/0)      —   (with Kilmarnock)
5 June 1973, Glasgow      2001   v Poland (s)

1037 STEPHEN CALDWELL (1/0)      —   (with Newcastle United)
12 September 1980, Stirling      2001   v Poland (s)

1038 KENNETH MILLER (1/0)      —   (with Rangers, Glasgow)
23 December 1979, Edinburgh      2001   v Poland (s)

# All-Time Lists

## Opponents

| | | P | W | D | L | F | A |
|---|---|---|---|---|---|---|---|
| 1 | ARGENTINA | 3 | 1 | 1 | 1 | 3 | 4 |
| 2 | AUSTRALIA | 4 | 2 | 1 | 1 | 3 | 2 |
| 3 | AUSTRIA | 17 | 5 | 5 | 7 | 22 | 29 |
| 4 | BELARUS | 2 | 2 | 0 | 0 | 5 | 1 |
| 5 | BELGIUM | 13 | 4 | 2 | 7 | 19 | 22 |
| 6 | BOSNIA | 2 | 2 | 0 | 0 | 3 | 1 |
| 7 | BRAZIL | 9 | 0 | 2 | 7 | 3 | 14 |
| 8 | BULGARIA | 5 | 2 | 3 | 0 | 5 | 3 |
| 9 | CANADA | 4 | 4 | 0 | 0 | 10 | 1 |
| 10 | CHILE | 2 | 2 | 0 | 0 | 6 | 2 |
| 11 | COLOMBIA | 3 | 0 | 2 | 1 | 2 | 3 |
| 12 | COSTA RICA | 1 | 0 | 0 | 1 | 0 | 1 |
| 13 | CROATIA | 1 | 0 | 1 | 0 | 1 | 1 |
| 14 | CYPRUS | 4 | 4 | 0 | 0 | 18 | 3 |
| 15 | CZECHOSLOVAKIA | 10 | 5 | 1 | 4 | 18 | 16 |
| 16 | CZECH REPUBLIC | 2 | 0 | 0 | 2 | 3 | 5 |
| 17 | DENMARK | 12 | 8 | 0 | 4 | 17 | 9 |
| 18 | ECUADOR | 1 | 1 | 0 | 0 | 2 | 1 |
| 19 | EGYPT | 1 | 0 | 0 | 1 | 1 | 3 |
| 20 | ENGLAND | 110 | 41 | 24 | 45 | 169 | 192 |
| 21 | ESTONIA | 6 | 4 | 2 | 0 | 11 | 3 |
| 22 | FAROE ISLANDS | 4 | 3 | 1 | 0 | 10 | 3 |
| 23 | FINLAND | 8 | 6 | 2 | 0 | 18 | 5 |
| 24 | FRANCE | 12 | 6 | 0 | 6 | 13 | 15 |
| 25 | GERMANY (EAST) | 6 | 2 | 1 | 3 | 6 | 4 |
| 26 | GERMANY (WEST) | 13 | 4 | 4 | 5 | 18 | 18 |
| 27 | GREECE | 2 | 1 | 0 | 1 | 1 | 1 |
| 28 | HUNGARY | 7 | 2 | 2 | 3 | 13 | 15 |
| 29 | ICELAND | 2 | 2 | 0 | 0 | 4 | 0 |
| 30 | IRAN | 1 | 0 | 1 | 0 | 1 | 1 |
| 31 | IRELAND (NORTHERN) | 92 | 61 | 16 | 15 | 254 | 81 |
| 32 | IRELAND (REPUBLIC OF) | 7 | 3 | 2 | 2 | 10 | 5 |
| 33 | ISRAEL | 3 | 3 | 0 | 0 | 5 | 1 |
| 34 | ITALY | 6 | 1 | 1 | 4 | 2 | 11 |
| 35 | JAPAN | 1 | 0 | 1 | 0 | 0 | 0 |
| 36 | LATVIA | 3 | 3 | 0 | 0 | 5 | 0 |
| 37 | LITHUANIA | 2 | 1 | 1 | 0 | 3 | 0 |
| 38 | LUXEMBOURG | 3 | 2 | 1 | 0 | 9 | 0 |
| 39 | MALTA | 5 | 4 | 1 | 0 | 11 | 4 |
| 40 | MOROCCO | 1 | 0 | 0 | 1 | 0 | 3 |
| 41 | NETHERLANDS | 14 | 5 | 4 | 5 | 14 | 15 |
| 42 | NEW ZEALAND | 1 | 1 | 0 | 0 | 5 | 2 |
| 43 | NORWAY | 12 | 7 | 4 | 1 | 31 | 15 |
| 44 | PARAGUAY | 1 | 0 | 0 | 1 | 2 | 3 |
| 45 | PERU | 3 | 1 | 1 | 1 | 4 | 4 |
| 46 | POLAND | 7 | 1 | 3 | 3 | 8 | 10 |
| 47 | PORTUGAL | 13 | 4 | 3 | 6 | 13 | 16 |
| 48 | ROMANIA | 5 | 2 | 2 | 1 | 7 | 4 |
| 49 | RUSSIA | 2 | 0 | 2 | 0 | 1 | 1 |
| 50 | SAN MARINO | 6 | 6 | 0 | 0 | 19 | 0 |
| 51 | SAUDI ARABIA | 1 | 0 | 1 | 0 | 2 | 2 |
| 52 | SPAIN | 10 | 3 | 3 | 4 | 16 | 16 |
| 53 | SWEDEN | 10 | 5 | 1 | 4 | 13 | 12 |
| 54 | SWITZERLAND | 14 | 7 | 3 | 4 | 22 | 20 |
| 55 | TURKEY | 1 | 0 | 0 | 1 | 2 | 4 |
| 56 | URUGUAY | 4 | 1 | 1 | 2 | 4 | 10 |
| 57 | USA | 4 | 2 | 1 | 1 | 8 | 2 |
| 58 | USSR/CIS | 5 | 1 | 1 | 3 | 5 | 6 |
| 59 | WALES | 102 | 60 | 23 | 19 | 238 | 112 |
| 60 | YUGOSLAVIA | 8 | 2 | 5 | 1 | 16 | 11 |
| 61 | ZAIRE | 1 | 1 | 0 | 0 | 2 | 0 |
| | TOTAL | 614 | 300 | 136 | 178 | 1136 | 748 |

## Home Matches – Cities

| | | P | W | D | L | F | A |
|---|---|---|---|---|---|---|---|
| 1 | GLASGOW | 251 | 147 | 53 | 51 | 513 | 232 |
| 2 | EDINBURGH | 10 | 7 | 1 | 2 | 26 | 16 |
| 3 | ABERDEEN | 10 | 7 | 2 | 1 | 23 | 13 |
| 4 | KILMARNOCK | 4 | 3 | 0 | 1 | 8 | 3 |
| 5 | DUNDEE | 4 | 2 | 1 | 1 | 8 | 4 |
| 6 | PAISLEY | 2 | 2 | 0 | 0 | 7 | 0 |
| 7 | MOTHERWELL | 1 | 1 | 0 | 0 | 5 | 2 |
| 8 | GREENOCK | 1 | 1 | 0 | 0 | 5 | 1 |

## Home Matches – Venues

| | | P | W | D | L | F | A |
|---|---|---|---|---|---|---|---|
| 1 | HAMPDEN PARK, (GLASGOW) | 190 | 105 | 45 | 40 | 337 | 177 |
| 2 | CELTIC PARK, (GLASGOW) | 23 | 16 | 2 | 5 | 65 | 20 |
| 3 | IBROX PARK/STADIUM, (GLASGOW) | 19 | 12 | 3 | 4 | 43 | 13 |
| 4 | FIRST HAMPDEN PARK, (GLASGOW) | 11 | 9 | 1 | 1 | 53 | 18 |
| 5 | PITTODRIE PARK/STADIUM, (ABERDEEN) | 10 | 7 | 2 | 1 | 23 | 13 |
| 6 | TYNECASTLE PARK/STADIUM, (EDINBURGH) | 8 | 6 | 0 | 2 | 20 | 14 |
| 7 | WEST OF SCOTLAND CRICKET GROUND, (GLASGOW) | 4 | 3 | 1 | 0 | 9 | 1 |
| 8 | RUGBY PARK, (KILMARNOCK) | 4 | 3 | 0 | 1 | 8 | 3 |
| 9 | DENS PARK, (DUNDEE) | 3 | 1 | 1 | 1 | 4 | 4 |
| 10 | CATHKIN PARK, (GLASGOW) | 2 | 2 | 0 | 0 | 5 | 1 |
| 11 | EASTER ROAD, (EDINBURGH) | 2 | 1 | 1 | 0 | 6 | 2 |
| 12 | UNDERWOOD PARK, (PAISLEY) | 1 | 1 | 0 | 0 | 5 | 0 |
| 13 | SECOND HAMPDEN PARK, (GLASGOW) | 1 | 0 | 1 | 0 | 1 | 1 |
| 14 | CAROLINA PORT, (DUNDEE) | 1 | 1 | 0 | 0 | 4 | 0 |
| 15 | FIR PARK, (MOTHERWELL) | 1 | 1 | 0 | 0 | 5 | 2 |
| 16 | CAPPIELOW PARK, (GREENOCK) | 1 | 1 | 0 | 0 | 5 | 1 |
| 17 | LOVE STREET, (PAISLEY) | 1 | 1 | 0 | 0 | 2 | 0 |
| 18 | FIRHILL PARK, (GLASGOW) | 1 | 0 | 0 | 1 | 0 | 1 |
| | TOTAL | 283 | 170 | 57 | 56 | 595 | 271 |

# Away Matches — Cities

| | | P | W | D | L | F | A |
|---|---|---|---|---|---|---|---|
| 1 | LONDON (ENGLAND) | 43 | 13 | 8 | 22 | 68 | 96 |
| 2 | BELFAST (IRELAND) | 39 | 24 | 6 | 9 | 106 | 40 |
| 3 | WREXHAM (WALES) | 24 | 12 | 7 | 5 | 63 | 29 |
| 4 | CARDIFF (WALES) | 24 | 10 | 8 | 6 | 40 | 32 |
| 5 | DUBLIN (IRELAND) | 9 | 5 | 3 | 1 | 15 | 5 |
| 6 | VIENNA (AUSTRIA) | 9 | 2 | 2 | 5 | 10 | 21 |
| 7 | BRUSSELS (BELGIUM) | 6 | 1 | 0 | 5 | 11 | 15 |
| 8 | LISBON (PORTUGAL) | 6 | 0 | 1 | 5 | 3 | 13 |
| 9 | COPENHAGEN (DENMARK) | 6 | 4 | 0 | 2 | 8 | 5 |
| 10 | BIRMINGHAM (ENGLAND) | 5 | 2 | 2 | 1 | 5 | 4 |
| 11 | AMSTERDAM (NETHERLANDS) | 5 | 3 | 1 | 1 | 8 | 4 |
| 12 | PARIS (FRANCE) | 5 | 3 | 0 | 2 | 6 | 7 |
| 13 | BERNE (SWITZERLAND) | 5 | 0 | 1 | 4 | 4 | 10 |
| 14 | OSLO (NORWAY) | 5 | 3 | 2 | 0 | 9 | 3 |
| 15 | VALLETTA (MALTA) | 4 | 3 | 1 | 0 | 8 | 4 |
| 16 | SHEFFIELD (ENGLAND) | 3 | 2 | 0 | 1 | 9 | 8 |
| 17 | LIVERPOOL (ENGLAND) | 3 | 1 | 1 | 1 | 3 | 4 |
| 18 | PRAGUE (CZECH REPUBLIC) | 3 | 1 | 0 | 2 | 5 | 6 |
| 19 | STOCKHOLM (SWEDEN) | 3 | 1 | 0 | 2 | 2 | 5 |
| 20 | HELSINKI (FINLAND) | 3 | 3 | 0 | 0 | 6 | 2 |
| 21 | BUDAPEST (HUNGARY) | 3 | 0 | 1 | 2 | 5 | 9 |
| 22 | MADRID (SPAIN) | 3 | 1 | 1 | 1 | 7 | 6 |
| 23 | NORRKÖPING (SWEDEN) | 3 | 1 | 0 | 2 | 5 | 5 |
| 24 | FRANKFURT (GERMANY) | 3 | 0 | 2 | 1 | 2 | 3 |
| 25 | GOTHENBURG (SWEDEN) | 3 | 0 | 1 | 2 | 2 | 4 |
| 26 | SERRAVALLE (SAN MARINO) | 3 | 3 | 0 | 0 | 6 | 0 |
| 27 | BLACKBURN (ENGLAND) | 2 | 1 | 0 | 1 | 4 | 4 |
| 28 | BERGEN (NORWAY) | 2 | 1 | 0 | 1 | 10 | 7 |
| 29 | BERLIN (GERMANY) | 2 | 0 | 1 | 1 | 1 | 2 |
| 30 | ROME (ITALY) | 2 | 0 | 0 | 2 | 1 | 6 |
| 31 | BASLE (SWITZERLAND) | 2 | 1 | 0 | 1 | 2 | 8 |
| 32 | BRATISLAVA (SLOVAKIA) | 2 | 0 | 0 | 2 | 0 | 5 |
| 33 | MOSCOW (RUSSIA) | 2 | 0 | 1 | 1 | 0 | 1 |
| 34 | RIO DE JANEIRO (BRAZIL) | 2 | 0 | 0 | 2 | 0 | 3 |
| 35 | VALENCIA (SPAIN) | 2 | 0 | 1 | 1 | 1 | 4 |
| 36 | BUCHAREST (ROMANIA) | 2 | 0 | 1 | 1 | 1 | 2 |
| 37 | CORDOBA (ARGENTINA) | 2 | 0 | 1 | 1 | 2 | 4 |
| 38 | TEL AVIV (ISRAEL) | 2 | 2 | 0 | 0 | 2 | 0 |
| 39 | MALAGA (SPAIN) | 2 | 1 | 1 | 0 | 7 | 4 |
| 40 | SEVILLE (SPAIN) | 2 | 0 | 0 | 2 | 1 | 5 |
| 41 | TORONTO (CANADA) | 2 | 2 | 0 | 0 | 5 | 1 |
| 42 | NEZAHUALCOYOTL (MEXICO) | 2 | 0 | 1 | 1 | 0 | 1 |
| 43 | SOFIA (BULGARIA) | 2 | 1 | 1 | 0 | 2 | 1 |
| 44 | ZAGREB (CROATIA) | 2 | 0 | 1 | 1 | 2 | 4 |
| 45 | GENOA (ITALY) | 2 | 1 | 0 | 1 | 2 | 2 |
| 46 | TALLINN (ESTONIA) | 2 | 1 | 1 | 0 | 3 | 0 |
| 47 | TOFTIR (FAROE ISLANDS) | 2 | 1 | 1 | 0 | 3 | 1 |
| 48 | RIGA (LATVIA) | 2 | 2 | 0 | 0 | 3 | 0 |
| 49 | SAINT-ETIENNE (FRANCE) | 2 | 0 | 0 | 2 | 1 | 5 |
| 50 | NEWCASTLE (ENGLAND) | 1 | 0 | 1 | 0 | 1 | 1 |
| 51 | MANCHESTER (ENGLAND) | 1 | 1 | 0 | 0 | 1 | 0 |
| 52 | GENEVA (SWITZERLAND) | 1 | 1 | 0 | 0 | 3 | 2 |
| 53 | LUXEMBOURG-VILLE (LUXEMBOURG) | 1 | 1 | 0 | 0 | 6 | 0 |
| 54 | ZURICH (SWITZERLAND) | 1 | 0 | 0 | 1 | 0 | 1 |
| 55 | BELGRADE (YUGOSLAVIA) | 1 | 0 | 1 | 0 | 2 | 2 |
| 56 | STUTTGART (GERMANY) | 1 | 1 | 0 | 0 | 3 | 1 |
| 57 | WARSAW (POLAND) | 1 | 1 | 0 | 0 | 2 | 1 |
| 58 | VÄSTERAS (SWEDEN) | 1 | 0 | 1 | 0 | 1 | 1 |
| 59 | OREBRÖ (SWEDEN) | 1 | 0 | 0 | 1 | 1 | 2 |
| 60 | ANKARA (TURKEY) | 1 | 0 | 0 | 1 | 2 | 4 |
| 61 | HANOVER (GERMANY) | 1 | 0 | 1 | 0 | 2 | 2 |
| 62 | CHORZÓW (POLAND) | 1 | 0 | 1 | 0 | 1 | 1 |
| 63 | NAPLES (ITALY) | 1 | 0 | 0 | 1 | 0 | 3 |
| 64 | NICOSIA (CYPRUS) | 1 | 1 | 0 | 0 | 5 | 0 |
| 65 | HAMBURG (GERMANY) | 1 | 0 | 0 | 1 | 2 | 3 |
| 66 | LIÈGE (BELGIUM) | 1 | 0 | 0 | 1 | 0 | 3 |
| 67 | BELO HORIZONTE (BRAZIL) | 1 | 0 | 1 | 0 | 2 | 2 |
| 68 | PORTO ALEGRE (BRAZIL) | 1 | 0 | 1 | 0 | 0 | 0 |
| 69 | BRUGGE (BELGIUM) | 1 | 0 | 0 | 1 | 1 | 2 |
| 70 | DORTMUND (GERMANY) | 1 | 1 | 0 | 0 | 2 | 0 |
| 71 | SANTIAGO (CHILE) | 1 | 1 | 0 | 0 | 4 | 2 |
| 72 | BUENOS AIRES (ARGENTINA) | 1 | 0 | 1 | 0 | 1 | 1 |
| 73 | MENDOZA (ARGENTINA) | 1 | 1 | 0 | 0 | 3 | 2 |
| 74 | POZNAN (POLAND) | 1 | 0 | 0 | 1 | 0 | 1 |
| 75 | SWANSEA (WALES) | 1 | 0 | 0 | 1 | 0 | 2 |
| 76 | VANCOUVER (CANADA) | 1 | 1 | 0 | 0 | 2 | 0 |
| 77 | EDMONTON (CANADA) | 1 | 1 | 0 | 0 | 3 | 0 |
| 78 | HALLE (GERMANY) | 1 | 0 | 0 | 1 | 1 | 2 |
| 79 | MARSEILLE (FRANCE) | 1 | 0 | 0 | 1 | 0 | 2 |
| 80 | REYKJAVÍK (ICELAND) | 1 | 1 | 0 | 0 | 1 | 0 |
| 81 | MELBOURNE (AUSTRALIA) | 1 | 0 | 1 | 0 | 0 | 0 |
| 82 | EINDHOVEN (NETHERLANDS) | 1 | 0 | 1 | 0 | 0 | 0 |
| 83 | QUERETARO (MEXICO) | 1 | 0 | 0 | 1 | 1 | 2 |
| 84 | ESCH-SUR-ALZETTE (LUXEMBOURG) | 1 | 0 | 1 | 0 | 0 | 0 |
| 85 | RIYADH (SAUDI ARABIA) | 1 | 0 | 1 | 0 | 2 | 2 |
| 86 | PERUGIA (ITALY) | 1 | 0 | 1 | 0 | 2 | 2 |
| 87 | LIMASSOL (CYPRUS) | 1 | 1 | 0 | 0 | 3 | 2 |
| 88 | TURIN (ITALY) | 1 | 0 | 0 | 1 | 0 | 1 |
| 89 | DENVER (USA) | 1 | 1 | 0 | 0 | 1 | 0 |
| 90 | UTRECHT (NETHERLANDS) | 1 | 0 | 0 | 1 | 1 | 3 |
| 91 | ATHENS (GREECE) | 1 | 0 | 0 | 1 | 0 | 1, |
| 92 | HIROSHIMA (JAPAN) | 1 | 0 | 1 | 0 | 0 | 0 |
| 93 | TOYAMA (JAPAN) | 1 | 1 | 0 | 0 | 2 | 1 |
| 94 | NEW BRITAIN (USA) | 1 | 0 | 0 | 1 | 1 | 2 |
| 95 | MIAMI (USA) | 1 | 0 | 0 | 1 | 0 | 1 |
| 96 | MONACO (MONACO) | 1 | 0 | 1 | 0 | 0 | 0 |
| 97 | MINSK (BELARUS) | 1 | 1 | 0 | 0 | 1 | 0 |
| 98 | EAST RUTHERFORD (USA) | 1 | 0 | 1 | 0 | 2 | 2 |
| 99 | WASHINGTON DC (USA) | 1 | 0 | 1 | 0 | 0 | 0 |
| 100 | SAINT-DENIS (FRANCE) | 1 | 0 | 0 | 1 | 1 | 2 |
| 101 | BORDEAUX (FRANCE) | 1 | 0 | 1 | 0 | 1 | 1 |
| 102 | VILNIUS (LITHUANIA) | 1 | 0 | 1 | 0 | 0 | 0 |
| 103 | BREMEN (GERMANY) | 1 | 1 | 0 | 0 | 1 | 0 |
| 104 | SARAJEVO (BOSNIA) | 1 | 1 | 0 | 0 | 2 | 1 |
| 105 | ARNHEM (NETHERLANDS) | 1 | 0 | 0 | 0 | 0 | 0 |
| 106 | BYDGOSZCZ (POLAND) | 1 | 0 | 1 | 0 | 1 | 1 |
| | TOTAL | 331 | 130 | 79 | 122 | 541 | 477 |

# Match Types

| | | P | W | D | L | F | A |
|---|---|---|---|---|---|---|---|
| 1 | HOME INTERNATIONAL CHAMPIONSHIP | 267 | 141 | 57 | 69 | 574 | 342 |
| 2 | FRIENDLY | 163 | 77 | 33 | 53 | 302 | 206 |
| 3 | WORLD CUP QUALIFIER | 84 | 47 | 17 | 20 | 150 | 91 |
| 4 | EURO CHAMPIONSHIP QUALIFIER | 70 | 32 | 19 | 19 | 101 | 71 |
| 5 | WORLD CUP FINAL TOURNAMENT | 23 | 4 | 7 | 12 | 25 | 41 |
| 6 | ROUS CUP | 8 | 2 | 2 | 4 | 4 | 7 |
| 7 | EUROPEAN CHAMPIONSHIP FINAL TOURNAMENT | 6 | 2 | 1 | 3 | 4 | 5 |
| 8 | BRAZILIAN INDEPENDENCE TOURNAMENT | 3 | 0 | 2 | 1 | 2 | 3 |
| 9 | KIRIN CUP | 2 | 1 | 1 | 0 | 2 | 1 |

## Managers

| | | P | W | D | L | F | A |
|---|---|---|---|---|---|---|---|
| 1 | ANDREW BEATTIE | 6 | 2 | 1 | 3 | 6 | 14 |
| | (3 April 1954-19 June 1954) | | | | | | |
| 2 | MATTHEW BUSBY | 2 | 1 | 1 | 0 | 5 | 2 |
| | (18 October 1958-5 November 1958) | | | | | | |
| 3 | ANDREW BEATTIE | 11 | 3 | 3 | 5 | 19 | 21 |
| | (11 April 1959-8 June 1960) | | | | | | |
| 4 | JOHN McCOLL | 27 | 16 | 3 | 8 | 72 | 50 |
| | (15 April 1961-8 May 1965) | | | | | | |
| 5 | JOHN STEIN | 7 | 3 | 1 | 3 | 11 | 11 |
| | (23 May 1965-7 December 1965) | | | | | | |
| 6 | JOHN PRENTICE | 4 | 0 | 1 | 3 | 4 | 9 |
| | (2 April 1966-25 June 1966) | | | | | | |
| 7 | MALCOLM MACDONALD | 2 | 1 | 1 | 0 | 3 | 2 |
| | (22 October 1966-16 November 1966) | | | | | | |
| 8 | ROBERT BROWN | 28 | 9 | 8 | 11 | 37 | 35 |
| | (15 April 1967-14 June 1971) | | | | | | |
| 9 | THOMAS DOCHERTY | 12 | 7 | 2 | 3 | 17 | 8 |
| | (13 October 1971-15 November 1972) | | | | | | |
| 10 | WILLIAM ORMOND | 38 | 18 | 8 | 12 | 55 | 39 |
| | (14 February 1973-27 April 1977) | | | | | | |
| 11 | ALISTAIR MacLEOD | 17 | 7 | 5 | 5 | 26 | 21 |
| | (28 May 1977-20 September 1978) | | | | | | |
| 12 | JOHN STEIN | 61 | 26 | 12 | 23 | 80 | 70 |
| | (25 October 1978-10 September 1985) | | | | | | |
| 13 | ALEXANDER FERGUSON | 10 | 3 | 4 | 3 | 8 | 5 |
| | (16 October 1985-13 June 1986) | | | | | | |
| 14 | ANDREW ROXBURGH | 61 | 23 | 19 | 19 | 67 | 60 |
| | (10 September 1986-8 September 1993) | | | | | | |
| 15 | CRAIG BROWN | 68 | 31 | 17 | 20 | 84 | 60 |
| | (13 October 1993-) | | | | | | |

## Goalscoring Feats

| PLAYER | DATE | OPPONENTS | GOALS |
|---|---|---|---|
| Hugh GALLACHER | 23 February 1929 | NORTHERN IRELAND | 5 |
| Charles HEGGIE | 20 March 1886 | IRELAND | 4 |
| William DICKSON | 24 March 1888 | IRELAND | 4 |
| William PAUL | 22 March 1890 | WALES | 4 |
| John MADDEN | 18 March 1893 | WALES | 4 |
| Alexander McMAHON | 23 February 1901 | IRELAND | 4 |
| Robert HAMILTON | 23 February 1901 | IRELAND | 4 |
| James QUINN | 14 March 1908 | IRELAND | 4 |
| William STEEL | 1 November 1950 | NORTHERN IRELAND | 4 |
| Denis LAW | 7 November 1962 | NORTHERN IRELAND | 4 |
| Denis LAW | 7 November 1963 | NORWAY | 4 |
| Colin STEIN | 17 May 1969 | CYPRUS | 4 |
| John McDOUGALL | 2 March 1878 | ENGLAND | 3 |
| George KER | 13 March 1880 | ENGLAND | 3 |
| John SMITH | 12 March 1881 | ENGLAND | 3 |
| Alexander HIGGINS | 14 March 1885 | IRELAND | 3 |
| Joseph LINDSAY | 23 March 1885 | WALES | 3 |
| William GROVES | 9 March 1889 | IRELAND | 3 |
| John BARKER | 18 March 1893 | WALES | 3 |
| James GILLESPIE | 19 March 1898 | WALES | 3 |
| Robert McCOLL | 18 March 1899 | WALES | 3 |
| Robert McCOLL | 25 March 1899 | IRELAND | 3 |
| Robert McCOLL | 7 April 1900 | ENGLAND | 3 |
| Robert HAMILTON | 1 March 1902 | IRELAND | 3 |
| Alexander SMITH | 15 March 1902 | WALES | 3 |

| PLAYER | DATE | OPPONENTS | GOALS |
|---|---|---|---|
| Hugh GALLACHER | 27 February 1926 | NORTHERN IRELAND | 3 |
| Alexander JACKSON | 31 March 1928 | ENGLAND | 3 |
| Hugh GALLACHER | 27 October 1928 | WALES | 3 |
| Alexander CHEYNE | 26 May 1929 | NORWAY | 3 |
| Neil DEWAR | 8 May 1932 | FRANCE | 3 |
| Henry MORRIS | 1 October 1949 | NORTHERN IRELAND | 3 |
| George HAMILTON | 20 May 1951 | BELGIUM | 3 |
| Lawrence REILLY | 30 April 1952 | USA | 3 |
| John MUDIE | 8 May 1957 | SPAIN | 3 |
| Alexander SCOTT | 7 October 1961 | NORTHERN IRELAND | 3 |
| Denis LAW | 4 June 1963 | NORWAY | 3 |

## Fastest Goals

| PLAYER | DATE | OPPONENTS | GOAL MINUTE |
|---|---|---|---|
| William THOMSON | 26 March 1892 | WALES | 1 |
| William LAMBIE | 30 March 1895 | IRELAND | 1 |
| Robert McCOLL | 7 April 1900 | ENGLAND | 1 |
| Andrew BLACK | 8 December 1937 | CZECHOSLOVAKIA | 1 |
| Archibald ROBERTSON | 19 May 1955 | AUSTRIA | 1 |
| Thomas RING | 6 April 1957 | ENGLAND | 1 |
| John WHITE | 6 May 1959 | WEST GERMANY | 1 |
| Stephen CHALMERS | 25 June 1966 | BRAZIL | 1 |
| John BELL | 3 February 1900 | WALES | 2 |
| Robert CROMPTON (O.G.) | 6 April 1907 | ENGLAND | 2 |
| Charles THOMSON | 4 April 1914 | ENGLAND | 2 |
| Henry MORRIS | 1 October 1949 | NORTHERN IRELAND | 2 |
| Denis LAW | 21 October 1964 | FINLAND | 2 |
| Kenneth DALGLISH | 15 November 1972 | DENMARK | 2 |
| Joseph JORDAN | 5 February 1975 | SPAIN | 2 |
| William PETTIGREW | 7 April 1976 | SWITZERLAND | 2 |
| William DODDS | 24 March 2001 | BELGIUM | 2 |
| Robert TEMPLETON | 3 May 1902 | ENGLAND | 3 |
| James QUINN | 14 March 1908 | IRELAND | 3 |
| Alexander JACKSON | 31 March 1928 | ENGLAND | 3 |
| Hugh GALLACHER | 23 February 1929 | NORTHERN IRELAND | 3 |
| James KING | 17 September 1932 | NORTHERN IRELAND | 3 |
| Alan GILZEAN | 11 December 1968 | CYPRUS | 3 |
| James JOHNSTONE | 22 October 1969 | WEST GERMANY | 3 |
| Peter CAMPBELL | 23 March 1878 | WALES | 4 |
| John MADDEN | 18 March 1893 | WALES | 4 |
| David MEIKLEJOHN | 28 February 1925 | IRELAND | 4 |
| James McGRORY | 1 April 1933 | ENGLAND | 4 |
| Alexander YOUNG | 7 May 1961 | REP. OF IRELAND | 4 |
| Richard HARTFORD | 12 September 1979 | PERU | 4 |
| Alan McINALLY | 30 May 1989 | CHILE | 4 |
| John McGINLAY | 12 October 1994 | FAROE ISLANDS | 4 |
| Christian DAILLY | 1 June 1997 | MALTA | 4 |

## Red Cards

| | PLAYER | OPPONENTS | DATE |
|---|---|---|---|
| 1 | William STEEL | AUSTRIA | 27 May 1951 |
| 2 | Robert AULD | NETHERLANDS | 27 May 1959 |
| 3 | Patrick CRERAND | CZECHOSLOVAKIA | 14 May 1961 |
| 4 | Thomas GEMMELL | WEST GERMANY | 22 October 1969 |
| 5 | Peter LORIMER | DENMARK | 15 November 1972 |
| 6 | Andrew GRAY | CZECHOSLOVAKIA | 13 October 1976 |
| 7 | William JOHNSTON | ARGENTINA | 18 June 1977 |
| 8 | Joseph JORDAN | WALES | 16 May 1981 |
| 9 | Richard GOUGH | SWITZERLAND | 9 September 1992 |
| 10 | John SPENCER | JAPAN | 21 May 1995 |
| 11 | Craig BURLEY | MOROCCO | 23 June 1998 |
| 12 | Matthew ELLIOTT | FAROE ISLANDS | 5 June 1999 |

# Own-Goals

| | PLAYER | COUNTRY | DATE |
|---|---|---|---|
| 1 | William EVANS | WALES | 5 March 1877 |
| 2 | William BELL | WALES | 14 March 1881 |
| 3 | John MORGAN | WALES | 14 March 1881 |
| 4 | Robert WILSON | IRELAND | 24 March 1888 |
| 5 | Samuel TORRANS | IRELAND | 25 March 1893 |
| 6 | Samuel TORRANS | IRELAND | 31 March 1894 |
| 7 | Robert CROMPTON | ENGLAND | 6 April 1907 |
| 8 | John O'CONNELL | USA | 30 April 1952 |
| 9 | Colin TODD | ENGLAND | 18 May 1974 |
| 10 | ARTUR Correia | PORTUGAL | 13 May 1975 |
| 11 | Ian EVANS | WALES | 17 November 1976 |
| 12 | Ronnie HELLSTROM | SWEDEN | 27 April 1977 |
| 13 | Andranik ESKANDARIAN | IRAN | 7 June 1978 |
| 14 | Fabio FRANCINI | SAN MARINO | 15 November 1995 |
| 15 | Janek MEET | ESTONIA | 29 March 1997 |
| 16 | Sergei HOHLOV–SIMSON | ESTONIA | 10 October 1998 |

# Penalties Scored

| | PLAYER | OPPONENTS | DATE |
|---|---|---|---|
| 1 | John RITCHIE | WALES | 20 March 1897 |
| 2 | Charles THOMSON | IRELAND | 18 March 1905 |
| 3 | Charles THOMSON | IRELAND | 18 March 1905 |
| 4 | Charles THOMSON | IRELAND | 16 March 1907 |
| 5 | Andrew WILSON | IRELAND | 26 February 1921 |
| 6 | John HUTTON | WALES | 29 October 1927 |
| 7 | Robert RANKIN | NETHERLANDS | 4 June 1929 |
| 8 | Thomas WALKER | ENGLAND | 4 April 1936 |
| 9 | Thomas WALKER | HUNGARY | 7 December 1938 |
| 10 | William WADDELL | WALES | 19 October 1946 |
| 11 | William WADDELL | NORTHERN IRELAND | 1 October 1949 |
| 12 | John HEWIE | SPAIN | 8 May 1957 |
| 13 | John HEWIE | NORTHERN IRELAND | 3 October 1959 |
| 14 | Eric CALDOW | TURKEY | 8 June 1960 |
| 15 | Eric CALDOW | NORTHERN IRELAND | 9 November 1960 |
| 16 | Eric CALDOW | ENGLAND | 14 April 1962 |
| 17 | Eric CALDOW | WALES | 20 October 1962 |
| 18 | James BAXTER | ENGLAND | 6 April 1963 |
| 19 | Thomas GEMMELL | CYPRUS | 17 May 1969 |
| 20 | William JARDINE | WALES | 14 May 1974 |
| 21 | Thomas HUTCHISON | EAST GERMANY | 30 October 1974 |
| 22 | Bruce RIOCH | ENGLAND | 24 May 1975 |
| 23 | Donald MASSON | FINLAND | 8 September 1976 |
| 24 | Donald MASSON | ARGENTINA | 18 June 1977 |
| 25 | Donald MASSON | WALES | 12 October 1977 |
| 26 | Archibald GEMMILL | BULGARIA | 22 February 1978 |
| 27 | Archibald GEMMILL | NETHERLANDS | 11 June 1978 |
| 28 | Archibald GEMMILL | NORWAY | 25 October 1978 |
| 29 | Archibald GEMMILL | PORTUGAL | 26 March 1980 |
| 30 | John ROBERTSON | ISRAEL | 28 April 1981 |
| 31 | John ROBERTSON | ISRAEL | 28 April 1981 |
| 32 | John ROBERTSON | ENGLAND | 23 May 1981 |
| 33 | John ROBERTSON | SWEDEN | 9 September 1981 |
| 34 | Francis GRAY | NETHERLANDS | 23 March 1982 |
| 35 | Gordon STRACHAN | CANADA | 12 June 1983 |
| 36 | John ROBERTSON | URUGUAY | 21 September 1983 |
| 37 | David COOPER | WALES | 28 February 1984 |
| 38 | David COOPER | WALES | 10 September 1985 |
| 39 | Graeme SOUNESS | ENGLAND | 23 April 1986 |
| 40 | David COOPER | LUXEMBOURG | 12 November 1986 |
| 41 | Maurice JOHNSTON | SWEDEN | 16 June 1990 |
| 42 | John ROBERTSON | SWITZERLAND | 17 October 1990 |
| 43 | Gordon STRACHAN | SAN MARINO | 1 May 1991 |
| 44 | Gary McALLISTER | CANADA | 20 May 1992 |
| 45 | Gary McALLISTER | CIS | 18 June 1992 |
| 46 | Patrick NEVIN | ESTONIA | 2 June 1993 |
| 47 | Gary McALLISTER | BELARUS | 8 June 1997 |
| 48 | John COLLINS | BRAZIL | 10 June 1998 |
| 49 | John COLLINS | BOSNIA | 5 October 1999 |
| 50 | William DODDS | BELGIUM | 24 March 2001 |
| 51 | Scott BOOTH | POLAND | 25 April 2001 |

# Captains

| | PLAYER | MATCHES | | PLAYER | MATCHES |
|---|---|---|---|---|---|
| 1 | George YOUNG | 48 | | Robert NEILL | 2 |
| 2 | William BREMNER | 39 | | David DAVIDSON | 2 |
| 3 | Gary McALLISTER | 32 | | Andrew HOLM | 2 |
| 4 | Graeme SOUNESS | 27 | | Michael PATON | 2 |
| | Robert AITKEN | 27 | | John LAMBIE | 2 |
| 6 | Archibald GEMMILL | 23 | | James McAULAY | 2 |
| | Colin HENDRY | 23 | | Robert SMELLIE | 2 |
| 8 | Eric CALDOW | 15 | | George GILLESPIE | 2 |
| | John GREIG | 15 | | Donald SILLARS | 2 |
| 10 | Charles THOMSON | 13 | | Nicol SMITH | 2 |
| | James SIMPSON | 13 | | Robert HAMILTON | 2 |
| 12 | Robert EVANS | 12 | | Andrew AITKEN | 2 |
| 13 | William MILLER | 11 | | James STARK | 2 |
| 14 | Bruce RIOCH | 10 | | John MARSHALL | 2 |
| | Daniel McGRAIN | 10 | | Thomas MUIRHEAD | 2 |
| 16 | Charles CAMPBELL | 9 | | Alexander MASSIE | 2 |
| | William JARDINE | 9 | | George BROWN | 2 |
| 18 | Thomas DOCHERTY | 8 | | Gordon SMITH | 2 |
| | William McNEILL | 8 | | David HAY | 2 |
| | Alexander McLEISH | 8 | | Martin BUCHAN | 2 |
| | Richard GOUGH | 8 | | Donald MASSON | 2 |
| 22 | David MACKAY | 7 | | Maurice MALPAS | 2 |
| | Robert MONCUR | 7 | 78 | James THOMSON | 1 |
| | Paul McSTAY | 7 | | John McDOUGALL | 1 |
| 25 | James McMULLAN | 6 | | Archibald ROWAN | 1 |
| | David MEIKLEJOHN | 6 | | John McPHERSON | 1 |
| | Kenneth DALGLISH | 6 | | William SEMPLE | 1 |
| 28 | John ROBERTSON | 5 | | Donald GOW | 1 |
| | Alexander McNAIR | 5 | | Duncan STEWART | 1 |
| | William McSTAY | 5 | | Andrew THOMSON | 1 |
| | William CUNNINGHAM | 5 | | John McLEOD | 1 |
| | Denis LAW | 5 | | James McLAREN | 1 |
| | Gordon STRACHAN | 5 | | John HILL | 1 |
| | Thomas BOYD | 5 | | William SELLAR | 1 |
| 35 | James KELLY | 4 | | Robert MARSHALL | 1 |
| | John DRUMMOND | 4 | | Daniel DOYLE | 1 |
| | Alexander RAISBECK | 4 | | James OSWALD | 1 |
| | James CRAPNELL | 4 | | John GILLESPIE | 1 |
| | Andrew ANDERSON | 4 | | John RITCHIE | 1 |
| | John SHAW | 4 | | William LAMBIE | 1 |
| | Thomas YOUNGER | 4 | | Matthew SCOTT | 1 |
| | James BAXTER | 4 | | Robert KELSO | 1 |
| | James LEIGHTON | 4 | | James COWAN | 1 |
| 44 | Walter ARNOTT | 3 | | David STORRIER | 1 |
| | Thomas ROBERTSON | 3 | | Harold MARSHALL | 1 |
| | James HAY | 3 | | Albert BUICK | 1 |
| | William CRINGAN | 3 | | John CAMPBELL | 1 |
| | James BLAIR | 3 | | James SHARP | 1 |
| | David MORRIS | 3 | | Thomas JACKSON | 1 |
| | Thomas CRAIG | 3 | | Neil GIBSON | 1 |
| | Robert GILLESPIE | 3 | | Peter McWILLIAM | 1 |
| | Patrick STANTON | 3 | | Donald COLMAN | 1 |
| | Richard HARTFORD | 3 | | Peter NELLIES | 1 |
| | Paul LAMBERT | 3 | | James GORDON | 1 |
| 55 | Robert GARDNER | 2 | | Kenneth CAMPBELL | 1 |
| | Joseph TAYLOR | 2 | | Andrew WILSON | 1 |

| PLAYER | MATCHES | | PLAYER | MATCHES |
|---|---|---|---|---|
| Andrew CUNNINGHAM | 1 | | David SHAW | 1 |
| John HUTTON | 1 | | William WOODBURN | 1 |
| Thomas TOWNSLEY | 1 | | Samuel COX | 1 |
| Alan MORTON | 1 | | Francis McLINTOCK | 1 |
| Daniel BLAIR | 1 | | Gordon McQUEEN | 1 |
| James McDOUGALL | 1 | | Thomas FORSYTH | 1 |
| John JOHNSTONE | 1 | | Paul HEGARTY | 1 |
| Peter McGONAGLE | 1 | | Craig LEVEIN | 1 |
| James CARABINE | 1 | | Alistair McCOIST | 1 |
| James DOUGALL | 1 | 132 | Kevin GALLACHER | 1 |
| James STEPHEN | 1 | | | |

# Club Representation

In Individual Matches

| CLUB | DATE | OPPONENTS | NUMBER OF PLAYERS SELECTED |
|---|---|---|---|
| Queen's Park, Glasgow | 30 November 1872 | ENGLAND | 11 |
| Queen's Park, Glasgow | 8 March 1873 | ENGLAND | 7 |
| Queen's Park, Glasgow | 7 March 1874 | ENGLAND | 7 |
| Queen's Park, Glasgow | 11 March 1882 | ENGLAND | 7 |
| Queen's Park, Glasgow | 25 March 1882 | WALES | 7 |
| Rangers, Glasgow | 3 February 1900 | WALES | 7 |
| Queen's Park, Glasgow | 25 March 1876 | WALES | 6 |
| Queen's Park, Glasgow | 12 March 1883 | WALES | 6 |
| Queen's Park, Glasgow | 21 March 1885 | ENGLAND | 6 |
| Third Lanark, Glasgow | 15 April 1889 | WALES | 6 |
| Rangers, Glasgow | 5 April 1930 | ENGLAND | 6 |
| Rangers, Glasgow | 14 May 1961 | CZECHOSLOVAKIA | 6 |
| Celtic, Glasgow | 16 November 1966 | NORTHERN IRELAND | 6 |
| Celtic, Glasgow | 10 May 1967 | USSR | 6 |

(Note: The above list is taken from starting line-ups only.)

# Individual Club Representation

Scottish Clubs (69)

### 1    ABERCORN FC, PAISLEY

| | Player | Period | Caps | Goals |
|---|---|---|---|---|
| 1 | Neil MUNRO | 1888-1889 | 2 | 2 |
| 2 | William FULTON | 1884 | 1 | 0 |
| 3 | John GOUDIE | 1884 | 1 | 1 |
| 4 | Robert McCORMICK | 1886 | 1 | 1 |
| 5 | James JOHNSTONE | 1888 | 1 | 0 |
| 6 | Robert BUCHANAN | 1891 | 1 | 1 |
| | TOTAL | 1884-1891 | 7 | 5 |

### 2    ABERDEEN FC

| | Player | Period | Caps | Goals |
|---|---|---|---|---|
| 1 | Alexander McLEISH | 1980-1993 | 77 | 0 |
| 2 | William MILLER | 1975-1989 | 65 | 1 |
| 3 | James LEIGHTON | 1982-1998 | 54 | 0 |
| 4 | Stewart McKIMMIE | 1989-1996 | 40 | 1 |
| 5 | Gordon STRACHAN | 1980-1984 | 28 | 2 |
| 6 | Robert CLARK | 1967-1973 | 17 | 0 |
| 7 | Eoin JESS | 1992-1999 | 15 | 2 |
| 8 | James BETT | 1985-1990 | 13 | 0 |
| 9 | Scott BOOTH | 1993-1996 | 13 | 5 |
| 10 | Brian IRVINE | 1990-1994 | 9 | 0 |
| 11 | Stuart KENNEDY | 1978-1981 | 8 | 0 |
| 12 | John HUTTON | 1923-1926 | 7 | 0 |
| 13 | Graham LEGGAT | 1956-1958 | 7 | 2 |
| 14 | Duncan SHEARER | 1994-1995 | 7 | 2 |
| 15 | Frederick MARTIN | 1954-1955 | 6 | 0 |
| 16 | Alexander CHEYNE | 1929-1930 | 5 | 4 |
| 17 | George HAMILTON | 1946-1954 | 5 | 4 |
| 18 | David ROBB | 1971 | 5 | 0 |
| 19 | Neil SIMPSON | 1983-1988 | 5 | 0 |
| 20 | Donald COLMAN | 1911-1913 | 4 | 0 |
| 21 | Mark McGHEE | 1983-1984 | 4 | 2 |
| 22 | William DODDS | 1996-1997 | 4 | 0 |
| 23 | Alexander JACKSON | 1925 | 3 | 0 |
| 24 | Frank HILL | 1930-1931 | 3 | 0 |
| 25 | Andrew LOVE | 1931 | 3 | 1 |
| 26 | Matthew ARMSTRONG | 1935-1936 | 3 | 0 |
| 27 | William MILLS | 1935-1936 | 3 | 0 |
| 28 | Patrick BUCKLEY | 1954 | 3 | 1 |
| 29 | James FORREST | 1971 | 3 | 0 |
| 30 | Joseph HARPER | 1972-1978 | 3 | 1 |
| 31 | Robert CONNOR | 1988-1990 | 3 | 0 |
| 32 | William LENNIE | 1908 | 2 | 1 |
| 33 | Archibald GLEN | 1955-1956 | 2 | 0 |
| 34 | Ernest McGARR | 1969 | 2 | 0 |
| 35 | Martin BUCHAN | 1971 | 2 | 0 |
| 36 | Peter WEIR | 1983 | 2 | 0 |
| 37 | Stephen WRIGHT | 1993 | 2 | 0 |
| 38 | Derek WHYTE | 1998-1999 | 2 | 0 |
| 39 | Benjamin YORSTON | 1931 | 1 | 0 |
| 40 | Henry YORSTON | 1954 | 1 | 0 |
| 41 | George MULHALL | 1959 | 1 | 1 |
| 42 | David SMITH | 1966 | 1 | 0 |
| 43 | James SMITH | 1968 | 1 | 0 |
| 44 | Stephen MURRAY | 1971 | 1 | 0 |
| 45 | Steven ARCHIBALD | 1980 | 1 | 1 |
| 46 | Douglas ROUGVIE | 1983 | 1 | 0 |
| 47 | Charles NICHOLAS | 1989 | 1 | 0 |
| 48 | Robert WINTERS | 1999 | 1 | 0 |
| | TOTAL | 1908-1999 | 440 | 31 |

### 3    AIRDRIE FC

| | Player | Period | Caps | Goals |
|---|---|---|---|---|
| 1 | James CRAPNELL | 1929-1932 | 9 | 0 |
| 2 | Hugh GALLACHER | 1924-1925 | 5 | 5 |
| 3 | John McMILLAN | 1952-1956 | 5 | 2 |
| 4 | Lawrence LESLIE | 1960-1961 | 5 | 0 |
| 5 | James REID | 1914-1924 | 3 | 0 |
| 6 | Robert BENNIE | 1925-1926 | 3 | 0 |
| 7 | Andrew JARVIE | 1971 | 3 | 0 |
| 8 | William RUSSELL | 1924-1925 | 2 | 0 |
| 9 | Robert FLAVELL | 1947 | 2 | 2 |
| 10 | James CONNOR | 1886 | 1 | 0 |
| 11 | Robert SCOTT | 1894 | 1 | 0 |
| 12 | Matthew SCOTT | 1898 | 1 | 0 |
| 13 | Frank O'ROURKE | 1907 | 1 | 1 |
| 14 | Alexander THOMSON | 1909 | 1 | 1 |
| 15 | John McDOUGALL | 1926 | 1 | 0 |
| 16 | Robert McPHAIL | 1927 | 1 | 0 |
| 17 | Hugh BAIRD | 1956 | 1 | 0 |
| | TOTAL | 1886-1971 | 45 | 11 |

### 4    ALBION ROVERS FC, COATBRIDGE

| | Player | Period | Caps | Goals |
|---|---|---|---|---|
| 1 | John WHITE | 1922 | 1 | 0 |
| | TOTAL | 1922 | 1 | 0 |

### 5    ALEXANDRA ATHLETIC FC, GLASGOW

| | Player | Period | Caps | Goals |
|---|---|---|---|---|
| 1 | James DUNCAN | 1878-1882 | 2 | 0 |
| | TOTAL | 1878-1882 | 2 | 0 |

## 6 ALLOA ATHLETIC FC

| | Player | Period | Caps | Goals |
|---|---|---|---|---|
| 1 | James HEPBURN | 1891 | 1 | 0 |
| | TOTAL | 1891 | 1 | 0 |

## 7 ANNBANK FC

| | Player | Period | Caps | Goals |
|---|---|---|---|---|
| 1 | John GRAHAM | 1884 | 1 | 0 |
| | TOTAL | 1884 | 1 | 0 |

## 8 ARBROATH FC

| | Player | Period | Caps | Goals |
|---|---|---|---|---|
| 1 | John DOIG | 1887-1889 | 2 | 0 |
| | TOTAL | 1887-1889 | 2 | 0 |

## 9 ARTHURLIE FC, BARRHEAD

| | Player | Period | Caps | Goals |
|---|---|---|---|---|
| 1 | Robert McPHERSON | 1882 | 1 | 1 |
| 2 | J. McAULAY | 1884 | 1 | 0 |
| 3 | Thomas TURNER | 1884 | 1 | 0 |
| 4 | Andrew THOMSON | 1886 | 1 | 0 |
| | TOTAL | 1882-1886 | 4 | 1 |

## 10 AYR ACADEMY FC

| | Player | Period | Caps | Goals |
|---|---|---|---|---|
| 1 | William BEVERIDGE | 1879 | 2 | 0 |
| | TOTAL | 1879 | 2 | 0 |

## 11 AYR UNITED FC

| | Player | Period | Caps | Goals |
|---|---|---|---|---|
| 1 | James NISBET | 1929 | 3 | 2 |
| 2 | Philip McCLOY | 1924-1925 | 2 | 0 |
| 3 | James LOGAN | 1891 | 1 | 1 |
| 4 | John CROSBIE | 1920 | 1 | 0 |
| 5 | James HOGG | 1922 | 1 | 0 |
| 6 | John SMITH | 1924 | 1 | 0 |
| 7 | Robert HEPBURN | 1931 | 1 | 0 |
| 8 | John DOYLE | 1975 | 1 | 0 |
| | TOTAL | 1891-1975 | 11 | 3 |

## 12 BATTLEFIELD FC, GLASGOW

| | Player | Period | Caps | Goals |
|---|---|---|---|---|
| 1 | William SELLAR | 1885-1888 | 5 | 0 |
| | TOTAL | 1885-1888 | 5 | 0 |

## 13 BEITH FC

| | Player | Period | Caps | Goals |
|---|---|---|---|---|
| 1 | William McGUIRE | 1881 | 2 | 0 |
| | TOTAL | 1881 | 2 | 0 |

## 14 BOSWELL FC, LUGAR

| | Player | Period | Caps | Goals |
|---|---|---|---|---|
| 1 | Samuel THOMSON | 1884 | 2 | 0 |
| | TOTAL | 1884 | 2 | 0 |

## 15 CALEDONIAN FC, GLASGOW

| | Player | Period | Caps | Goals |
|---|---|---|---|---|
| 1 | Archibald ROWAN | 1880 | 1 | 0 |
| | TOTAL | 1880 | 1 | 0 |

## 16 CAMBUSLANG FC

| | Player | Period | Caps | Goals |
|---|---|---|---|---|
| 1 | James GOURLAY | 1886-1888 | 2 | 1 |
| 2 | Andrew JACKSON | 1886-1888 | 2 | 0 |
| 3 | William SEMPLE | 1886 | 1 | 0 |
| 4 | John BUCHANAN | 1889 | 1 | 0 |
| 5 | J. BROWN | 1890 | 1 | 0 |
| 6 | J. RUSSELL | 1890 | 1 | 0 |
| 7 | James LOW | 1891 | 1 | 1 |
| | TOTAL | 1886-1891 | 9 | 2 |

## 17 CARTVALE FC, BUSBY

| | Player | Period | Caps | Goals |
|---|---|---|---|---|
| 1 | Robert CALDERWOOD | 1885 | 3 | 3 |
| 2 | Michael DUNBAR | 1886 | 1 | 1 |
| | TOTAL | 1885-1886 | 4 | 4 |

## 18 CELTIC FC, GLASGOW

| | Player | Period | Caps | Goals |
|---|---|---|---|---|
| 1 | Paul McSTAY | 1983-1997 | 76 | 9 |
| 2 | Thomas BOYD | 1992-2001 | 65 | 1 |
| 3 | Daniel McGRAIN | 1973-1982 | 62 | 0 |
| 4 | Robert AITKEN | 1979-1989 | 50 | 1 |
| 5 | Kenneth DALGLISH | 1971-1977 | 47 | 16 |
| 6 | Robert EVANS | 1948-1960 | 45 | 0 |
| 7 | John COLLINS | 1990-1996 | 32 | 7 |
| 8 | William McNEILL | 1961-1972 | 29 | 3 |
| 9 | David HAY | 1970-1974 | 27 | 0 |
| 10 | James JOHNSTONE | 1964-1974 | 23 | 4 |
| 11 | Robert COLLINS | 1950-1958 | 22 | 7 |
| 12 | Thomas McKINLAY | 1995-1998 | 22 | 0 |
| 13 | Thomas GEMMELL | 1966-1971 | 18 | 1 |
| 14 | Paul LAMBERT | 1998-2001 | 17 | 0 |
| 15 | Craig BURLEY | 1997-1999 | 16 | 3 |
| 16 | Alexander McNAIR | 1906-1920 | 15 | 0 |
| 17 | Duncan MACKAY | 1959-1962 | 14 | 0 |
| 18 | William McSTAY | 1921-1928 | 13 | 0 |
| 19 | John CAMPBELL | 1893-1903 | 12 | 5 |
| 20 | James McMENEMY | 1905-1920 | 12 | 5 |
| 21 | William FERNIE | 1954-1958 | 12 | 1 |
| 22 | Robert MURDOCH | 1965-1969 | 12 | 5 |
| 23 | James QUINN | 1905-1912 | 11 | 7 |
| 24 | Patrick CRERAND | 1961-1962 | 11 | 0 |
| 25 | John McNAMARA | 1996-2000 | 11 | 0 |
| 26 | Robert LENNOX | 1966-1970 | 10 | 3 |
| 27 | David PROVAN | 1979-1982 | 10 | 1 |
| 28 | Maurice JOHNSTON | 1984-1987 | 10 | 4 |
| 29 | Simon DONNELLY | 1997-1998 | 10 | 0 |
| 30 | James DELANEY | 1935-1938 | 9 | 3 |
| 31 | Daniel DOYLE | 1892-1898 | 8 | 0 |
| 32 | John HUGHES | 1965-1969 | 8 | 1 |
| 33 | Thomas BURNS | 1981-1988 | 8 | 0 |
| 34 | Darren JACKSON | 1998 | 8 | 1 |
| 35 | James KELLY | 1889-1896 | 7 | 1 |
| 36 | James HAY | 1905-1911 | 7 | 0 |
| 37 | James McGRORY | 1928-1933 | 7 | 6 |
| 38 | Alexander McMAHON | 1892-1902 | 6 | 6 |
| 39 | Peter McGONAGLE | 1933-1934 | 6 | 0 |
| 40 | William MILLER | 1946-1947 | 6 | 0 |
| 41 | James KENNEDY | 1963-1964 | 6 | 0 |
| 42 | Luigi MACARI | 1972 | 6 | 3 |
| 43 | Charles NICHOLAS | 1983 | 6 | 2 |
| 44 | Mark BURCHILL | 1999-2000 | 6 | 0 |
| 45 | John BELL | 1899-1900 | 5 | 3 |
| 46 | William CRINGAN | 1920-1923 | 5 | 0 |
| 47 | John McPHAIL | 1949-1953 | 5 | 3 |
| 48 | Stephen CHALMERS | 1964-1966 | 5 | 3 |
| 49 | Ronald SIMPSON | 1967-1968 | 5 | 0 |
| 50 | Francis McGARVEY | 1983-1984 | 5 | 0 |
| 51 | Murdo MacLEOD | 1985-1987 | 5 | 0 |
| 52 | James BLESSINGTON | 1894-1896 | 4 | 0 |
| 53 | David RUSSELL | 1897-1901 | 4 | 1 |
| 54 | Alexander KING | 1897-1899 | 4 | 1 |

| 55 | Donald McLEOD | 1905-1906 | 4 | 0 |
|---|---|---|---|---|
| 56 | Peter SOMERS | 1905-1909 | 4 | 0 |
| 57 | Joseph CASSIDY | 1921-1924 | 4 | 1 |
| 58 | Adam McLEAN | 1925-1927 | 4 | 1 |
| 59 | Peter WILSON | 1926-1933 | 4 | 0 |
| 60 | John THOMSON | 1930-1931 | 4 | 0 |
| 61 | John CLARK | 1966-1967 | 4 | 0 |
| 62 | William WALLACE | 1967-1969 | 4 | 0 |
| 63 | James BROGAN | 1971 | 4 | 0 |
| 64 | Brian McCLAIR | 1986-1987 | 4 | 0 |
| 65 | Derek WHYTE | 1987-1992 | 4 | 0 |
| 66 | Daniel McARTHUR | 1895-1899 | 3 | 0 |
| 67 | David STORRIER | 1899 | 3 | 0 |
| 68 | William ORR | 1900-1904 | 3 | 0 |
| 69 | Bernard BATTLES | 1901 | 3 | 0 |
| 70 | Alexander BENNETT | 1904-1908 | 3 | 1 |
| 71 | Joseph DODDS | 1914 | 3 | 0 |
| 72 | Alexander THOMSON | 1926-1932 | 3 | 0 |
| 73 | Charles NAPIER | 1932-1935 | 3 | 2 |
| 74 | Neil MOCHAN | 1954 | 3 | 0 |
| 75 | Robert AULD | 1959 | 3 | 0 |
| 76 | Andrew WALKER | 1988-1994 | 3 | 0 |
| 77 | Thomas McKEOWN | 1889-1890 | 2 | 0 |
| 78 | William GROVES | 1889-1890 | 2 | 3 |
| 79 | James McLAREN | 1889-1890 | 2 | 0 |
| 80 | John MADDEN | 1893-1895 | 2 | 5 |
| 81 | William MALEY | 1893 | 2 | 0 |
| 82 | Harold MARSHALL | 1899-1900 | 2 | 1 |
| 83 | William LONEY | 1910 | 2 | 0 |
| 84 | Thomas McINALLY | 1926 | 2 | 0 |
| 85 | John CRUM | 1936-1938 | 2 | 0 |
| 86 | John SMITH | 1959 | 2 | 0 |
| 87 | Frank HAFFEY | 1960-1961 | 2 | 0 |
| 88 | Joseph McBRIDE | 1966 | 2 | 0 |
| 89 | Alistair HUNTER | 1973 | 2 | 0 |
| 90 | George CONNELLY | 1973 | 2 | 0 |
| 91 | John DEANS | 1974 | 2 | 0 |
| 92 | Peter GRANT | 1989 | 2 | 0 |
| 93 | Jonathan GOULD | 1999-2000 | 2 | 0 |
| 94 | Peter DOWDS | 1892 | 1 | 0 |
| 95 | John DIVERS | 1895 | 1 | 1 |
| 96 | Peter MEECHAN | 1896 | 1 | 0 |
| 97 | James YOUNG | 1906 | 1 | 0 |
| 98 | Andrew McATEE | 1913 | 1 | 0 |
| 99 | John BROWNING | 1914 | 1 | 0 |
| 100 | John GILCHRIST | 1922 | 1 | 0 |
| 101 | Peter SCARFF | 1931 | 1 | 0 |
| 102 | Robert THOMSON | 1931 | 1 | 1 |
| 103 | James KENNAWAY | 1933 | 1 | 0 |
| 104 | Robert HOGG | 1937 | 1 | 0 |
| 105 | Francis MURPHY | 1938 | 1 | 1 |
| 106 | George PATERSON | 1938 | 1 | 0 |
| 107 | John DIVERS | 1938 | 1 | 0 |
| 108 | Michael HAUGHNEY | 1954 | 1 | 0 |
| 109 | James CRAIG | 1967 | 1 | 0 |
| 110 | Paul WILSON | 1975 | 1 | 0 |
| 111 | Ronald GLAVIN | 1977 | 1 | 0 |
| 112 | Joseph CRAIG | 1977 | 1 | 1 |
| 113 | Francis McAVENNIE | 1988 | 1 | 0 |
| 114 | Michael GALLOWAY | 1991 | 1 | 0 |
| 115 | Gordon MARSHALL | 1992 | 1 | 0 |
| 116 | Brian O'NEIL | 1996 | 1 | 0 |
| | TOTAL | 1889-2001 | 999 | 135 |

## 19 CLYDE FC, GLASGOW

| | Player | Period | Caps | Goals |
|---|---|---|---|---|
| 1 | Thomas RING | 1953-1957 | 12 | 2 |
| 2 | Daniel BLAIR | 1928-1931 | 7 | 0 |
| 3 | Harold HADDOCK | 1954-1958 | 6 | 0 |
| 4 | Archibald ROBERTSON | 1955-1958 | 5 | 2 |
| 5 | George HERD | 1958-1960 | 5 | 1 |
| 6 | William WALKER | 1909-1910 | 2 | 0 |
| 7 | William BOYD | 1931 | 2 | 1 |
| 8 | Leslie JOHNSTON | 1948 | 2 | 1 |
| 9 | John BROWN | 1938 | 1 | 0 |
| 10 | Hugh LONG | 1946 | 1 | 0 |
| 11 | Alexander LINWOOD | 1949 | 1 | 1 |
| | TOTAL | 1909-1960 | 44 | 8 |

## 20 CLYDESDALE FC, GLASGOW

| | Player | Period | Caps | Goals |
|---|---|---|---|---|
| 1 | Robert GARDNER | 1874-1878 | 3 | 0 |
| 2 | William GIBB | 1873 | 1 | 1 |
| 3 | Frederick ANDERSON | 1874 | 1 | 1 |
| 4 | John McPHERSON | 1875 | 1 | 0 |
| 5 | James LANG | 1876 | 1 | 1 |
| 6 | James RICHMOND | 1877 | 1 | 1 |
| | TOTAL | 1873-1878 | 8 | 4 |

## 21 COWDENBEATH FC

| | Player | Period | Caps | Goals |
|---|---|---|---|---|
| 1 | James PATERSON | 1931 | 3 | 0 |
| 2 | Robert MIDDLETON | 1930 | 1 | 0 |
| 3 | Alexander VENTERS | 1933 | 1 | 0 |
| | TOTAL | 1930-1933 | 5 | 0 |

## 22 COWLAIRS FC, GLASGOW

| | Player | Period | Caps | Goals |
|---|---|---|---|---|
| 1 | John McPHERSON | 1889-1890 | 3 | 3 |
| 2 | Thomas McINNES | 1889 | 1 | 1 |
| | TOTAL | 1889-1890 | 4 | 4 |

## 23 DUMBARTON FC

| | Player | Period | Caps | Goals |
|---|---|---|---|---|
| 1 | James McAULAY | 1882-1887 | 9 | 1 |
| 2 | Joseph LINDSAY | 1880-1886 | 8 | 6 |
| 3 | Michael PATON | 1883-1886 | 5 | 0 |
| 4 | John McLEOD | 1888-1893 | 5 | 0 |
| 5 | William McKINNON | 1883-1884 | 4 | 0 |
| 6 | Leitch KEIR | 1886-1888 | 4 | 1 |
| 7 | William THOMSON | 1892-1898 | 4 | 1 |
| 8 | Peter MILLER | 1882-1883 | 3 | 0 |
| 9 | John TAYLOR | 1892-1894 | 3 | 1 |
| 10 | Robert BROWN | 1884 | 2 | 0 |
| 11 | Ralph AITKEN | 1886-1888 | 2 | 1 |
| 12 | William ROBERTSON | 1887 | 2 | 1 |
| 13 | George DEWAR | 1888-1889 | 2 | 1 |
| 14 | John BELL | 1890-1892 | 2 | 1 |
| 15 | Archibald LANG | 1880 | 1 | 0 |
| 16 | Robert BROWN | 1885 | 1 | 0 |
| 17 | Thomas McMILLAN | 1887 | 1 | 0 |
| 18 | Duncan STEWART | 1888 | 1 | 0 |
| | TOTAL | 1880-1898 | 59 | 14 |

## 24 DUMBARTON ATHLETIC FC

| | Player | Period | Caps | Goals |
|---|---|---|---|---|
| 1 | Alexander LATTA | 1888-1889 | 2 | 2 |
| | TOTAL | 1888-1889 | 2 | 2 |

## 25 DUMBRECK FC, GLASGOW

| | Player | Period | Caps | Goals |
|---|---|---|---|---|
| 1 | Alexander McGEOCH | 1876-1877 | 4 | 0 |
| | TOTAL | 1876-1877 | 4 | 0 |

## 26 DUNDEE FC

| | Player | Period | Caps | Goals |
|---|---|---|---|---|
| 1 | Alexander HAMILTON | 1961-1965 | 24 | 0 |
| 2 | Douglas COWIE | 1953-1958 | 20 | 0 |
| 3 | William STEEL | 1950-1953 | 13 | 5 |
| 4 | John URE | 1961-1963 | 8 | 0 |
| 5 | Colin McNAB | 1930-1932 | 6 | 0 |
| 6 | Alexander MacFARLANE | 1904-1911 | 5 | 1 |
| 7 | Alan GILZEAN | 1963-1964 | 5 | 4 |
| 8 | Alexander KEILLOR | 1894-1897 | 4 | 1 |
| 9 | Alexander TROUP | 1920-1922 | 4 | 0 |
| 10 | William BROWN | 1958-1959 | 4 | 0 |
| 11 | Robert ROBINSON | 1974-1975 | 4 | 0 |
| 12 | Francis BARRETT | 1894-1895 | 2 | 0 |
| 13 | James ROBERTSON | 1931 | 2 | 0 |
| 14 | Charles COOKE | 1965 | 2 | 0 |
| 15 | John SCOTT | 1971 | 2 | 0 |
| 16 | Thomson ALLAN | 1974 | 2 | 0 |
| 17 | William LONGAIR | 1894 | 1 | 0 |
| 18 | William SAWERS | 1895 | 1 | 0 |
| 19 | William THOMSON | 1896 | 1 | 0 |
| 20 | Robert KELSO | 1898 | 1 | 0 |
| 21 | Peter ROBERTSON | 1903 | 1 | 0 |
| 22 | James SHARP | 1904 | 1 | 0 |
| 23 | William MUIR | 1907 | 1 | 0 |
| 24 | John FRASER | 1907 | 1 | 0 |
| 25 | George CHAPLIN | 1908 | 1 | 0 |
| 26 | John HUNTER | 1909 | 1 | 0 |
| 27 | Robert HAMILTON | 1911 | 1 | 2 |
| 28 | Thomas KELSO | 1914 | 1 | 0 |
| 29 | David THOMSON | 1920 | 1 | 0 |
| 30 | John GILMOUR | 1930 | 1 | 0 |
| 31 | Hugh ROBERTSON | 1961 | 1 | 0 |
| 32 | Andrew PENMAN | 1966 | 1 | 0 |
| 33 | George McLEAN | 1968 | 1 | 0 |
| 34 | Robert CONNOR | 1986 | 1 | 0 |
| 35 | Gavin RAE | 2001 | 1 | 0 |
| | TOTAL | 1894-2001 | 126 | 13 |

## 27 DUNDEE UNITED FC

| | Player | Period | Caps | Goals |
|---|---|---|---|---|
| 1 | Maurice MALPAS | 1984-1992 | 55 | 0 |
| 2 | David NAREY | 1977-1989 | 35 | 1 |
| 3 | Richard GOUGH | 1983-1986 | 26 | 3 |
| 4 | Paul STURROCK | 1981-1987 | 20 | 3 |
| 5 | William McKINLAY | 1993-1995 | 14 | 4 |
| 6 | Eamonn BANNON | 1979-1986 | 11 | 1 |
| 7 | William DODDS | 1998-1999 | 11 | 4 |
| 8 | James McINALLY | 1987-1993 | 10 | 0 |
| 9 | Paul HEGARTY | 1979-1983 | 8 | 0 |
| 10 | David BOWMAN | 1992-1993 | 6 | 0 |
| 11 | Kevin GALLACHER | 1988 | 4 | 0 |
| 12 | Duncan FERGUSON | 1992-1993 | 4 | 0 |
| 13 | David DODDS | 1983 | 2 | 1 |
| 14 | Charles MILLER | 2001 | 1 | 0 |
| | TOTAL | 1977-2001 | 207 | 17 |

## 28 DUNFERMLINE ATHLETIC FC

| | Player | Period | Caps | Goals |
|---|---|---|---|---|
| 1 | Andrew WILSON | 1920-1921 | 6 | 6 |
| 2 | Edward CONNACHAN | 1961-1962 | 2 | 0 |
| 3 | William CALLAGHAN | 1969-1970 | 2 | 0 |
| 4 | Barry NICHOLSON | 2001 | 1 | 0 |
| 5 | Steven CRAWFORD | 2001 | 1 | 0 |
| | TOTAL | 1920-2001 | 12 | 6 |

## 29 DYKEBAR FC, PAISLEY

| | Player | Period | Caps | Goals |
|---|---|---|---|---|
| 1 | William PAUL | 1891 | 1 | 0 |
| | TOTAL | 1891 | 1 | 0 |

## 30 EASTERN FC, GLASGOW

| | Player | Period | Caps | Goals |
|---|---|---|---|---|
| 1 | Alexander KENNEDY | 1875-1876 | 3 | 0 |
| 2 | John HUNTER | 1875 | 1 | 0 |
| 3 | Peter ANDREWS | 1875 | 1 | 1 |
| | TOTAL | 1875-1876 | 5 | 1 |

## 31 EAST FIFE FC, METHIL

| | Player | Period | Caps | Goals |
|---|---|---|---|---|
| 1 | George AITKEN | 1949-1950 | 5 | 0 |
| 2 | Daniel LIDDLE | 1931 | 3 | 0 |
| 3 | David DUNCAN | 1948 | 3 | 1 |
| 4 | Allan BROWN | 1950 | 3 | 3 |
| 5 | Henry MORRIS | 1949 | 1 | 3 |
| 6 | Charles FLEMING | 1953 | 1 | 2 |
| | TOTAL | 1931-1953 | 16 | 9 |

## 32 EAST STIRLINGSHIRE FC, FALKIRK

| | Player | Period | Caps | Goals |
|---|---|---|---|---|
| 1 | David ALEXANDER | 1894 | 2 | 1 |
| 2 | Archibald RITCHIE | 1891 | 1 | 0 |
| 3 | James McKIE | 1898 | 1 | 2 |
| | TOTAL | 1891-1898 | 4 | 3 |

## 33 EDINBURGH UNIVERSITY FC

| | Player | Period | Caps | Goals |
|---|---|---|---|---|
| 1 | John SMITH | 1880-1881 | 3 | 3 |
| 2 | William BEVERIDGE | 1880 | 1 | 1 |
| 3 | John MACDONALD | 1886 | 1 | 0 |
| | TOTAL | 1880-1886 | 5 | 4 |

## 34 FALKIRK FC

| | Player | Period | Caps | Goals |
|---|---|---|---|---|
| 1 | Alexander PARKER | 1955-1958 | 14 | 0 |
| 2 | John WHITE | 1959 | 4 | 2 |
| 3 | James CROAL | 1913-1914 | 3 | 0 |
| 4 | Robert CAMPBELL | 1947 | 2 | 0 |
| 5 | John DRUMMOND | 1892 | 1 | 0 |
| 6 | W. WATSON | 1898 | 1 | 0 |
| 7 | Andrew DEVINE | 1910 | 1 | 1 |
| 8 | John McTAVISH | 1910 | 1 | 0 |
| 9 | Robert ORROCK | 1913 | 1 | 0 |
| 10 | Thomas LOGAN | 1913 | 1 | 0 |
| 11 | Thomas TOWNSLEY | 1925 | 1 | 0 |
| 12 | Robert THOMSON | 1927 | 1 | 0 |
| 13 | Alexander LOW | 1933 | 1 | 0 |
| | TOTAL | 1892-1959 | 32 | 3 |

## 35 HAMILTON ACADEMICAL FC

| | Player | Period | Caps | Goals |
|---|---|---|---|---|
| 1 | Robert HOWE | 1929 | 2 | 0 |
| 2 | James KING | 1932-1933 | 2 | 1 |
| | TOTAL | 1929-1933 | 4 | 1 |

## 36 HEART OF MIDLOTHIAN FC, EDINBURGH

| | Player | Period | Caps | Goals |
|---|---|---|---|---|
| 1 | Robert WALKER | 1900-1913 | 29 | 7 |
| 2 | Andrew ANDERSON | 1933-1938 | 23 | 0 |
| 3 | David McPHERSON | 1989-1992 | 23 | 0 |
| 4 | Thomas WALKER | 1934-1939 | 20 | 9 |
| 5 | Craig LEVEIN | 1990-1994 | 16 | 0 |
| 6 | John ROBERTSON | 1990-1995 | 16 | 3 |

| # | Player | Period | Caps | Goals |
|---|---|---|---|---|
| 7 | Alan MCLAREN | 1992-1994 | 14 | 0 |
| 8 | Charles THOMSON | 1904-1908 | 12 | 3 |
| 9 | Alexander MASSIE | 1931-1935 | 11 | 0 |
| 10 | Colin CAMERON | 1999-2001 | 11 | 2 |
| 11 | John HARKNESS | 1928-1933 | 9 | 0 |
| 12 | John CUMMING | 1954-1960 | 9 | 0 |
| 13 | David WEIR | 1997-1998 | 9 | 0 |
| 14 | Alexander YOUNG | 1960 | 6 | 3 |
| 15 | James CRUICKSHANK | 1964-1975 | 6 | 0 |
| 16 | James MURRAY | 1958 | 5 | 1 |
| 17 | David HOLT | 1963-1964 | 5 | 0 |
| 18 | Isaac BEGBIE | 1890-1894 | 4 | 0 |
| 19 | George WILSON | 1904-1906 | 4 | 0 |
| 20 | David MACKAY | 1957-1958 | 4 | 0 |
| 21 | Gary MACKAY | 1987-1988 | 4 | 1 |
| 22 | Paul RITCHIE | 1999 | 4 | 1 |
| 23 | Gary NAYSMITH | 2000 | 4 | 0 |
| 24 | James ADAMS | 1889-1893 | 3 | 0 |
| 25 | David BAIRD | 1890-1892 | 3 | 1 |
| 26 | John WALKER | 1895-1898 | 3 | 3 |
| 27 | George SINCLAIR | 1910-1912 | 3 | 0 |
| 28 | John JOHNSTONE | 1929-1932 | 3 | 0 |
| 29 | Andrew BLACK | 1937-1938 | 3 | 3 |
| 30 | William BAULD | 1950 | 3 | 2 |
| 31 | William WALLACE | 1964-1966 | 3 | 0 |
| 32 | Donald FORD | 1973-1974 | 3 | 0 |
| 33 | Henry SMITH | 1988-1992 | 3 | 0 |
| 34 | John HILL | 1891-1892 | 2 | 0 |
| 35 | David RUSSELL | 1895 | 2 | 0 |
| 36 | Alexander KING | 1896 | 2 | 0 |
| 37 | George HOGG | 1896 | 2 | 0 |
| 38 | Henry RENNIE | 1900 | 2 | 0 |
| 39 | Albert BUICK | 1902 | 2 | 2 |
| 40 | Robert MERCER | 1912-1913 | 2 | 0 |
| 41 | Peter NELLIES | 1913-1914 | 2 | 0 |
| 42 | Alexander MUNRO | 1936 | 2 | 1 |
| 43 | James DYKES | 1938 | 2 | 0 |
| 44 | James WARDHAUGH | 1954-1956 | 2 | 0 |
| 45 | John COLQUHOUN | 1988 | 2 | 0 |
| 46 | Gary McSWEGAN | 1999 | 2 | 1 |
| 47 | Steven PRESSLEY | 2000 | 2 | 0 |
| 48 | Thomas JENKINSON | 1887 | 1 | 1 |
| 49 | Thomas BRECKENRIDGE | 1888 | 1 | 1 |
| 50 | John McPHERSON | 1891 | 1 | 0 |
| 51 | William TAYLOR | 1892 | 1 | 0 |
| 52 | Thomas CHAMBERS | 1894 | 1 | 1 |
| 53 | Thomas ROBERTSON | 1898 | 1 | 1 |
| 54 | Mark BELL | 1901 | 1 | 0 |
| 55 | George KEY | 1902 | 1 | 0 |
| 56 | Henry ALLAN | 1902 | 1 | 0 |
| 57 | William PORTEOUS | 1903 | 1 | 0 |
| 58 | Alexander MENZIES | 1906 | 1 | 0 |
| 59 | Thomas COLLINS | 1909 | 1 | 0 |
| 60 | John WHITE | 1923 | 1 | 0 |
| 61 | Bernard BATTLES | 1930 | 1 | 1 |
| 62 | Andrew HERD | 1934 | 1 | 0 |
| 63 | David McCULLOCH | 1934 | 1 | 0 |
| 64 | William WAUGH | 1937 | 1 | 0 |
| 65 | Archibald MILLER | 1938 | 1 | 0 |
| 66 | William MacFARLANE | 1947 | 1 | 0 |
| 67 | Charles COX | 1948 | 1 | 0 |
| 68 | Robert DOUGAN | 1950 | 1 | 0 |
| 69 | Alfred CONN | 1956 | 1 | 1 |
| 70 | Nicholas WALKER | 1993 | 1 | 0 |
| 71 | Neil McCANN | 1998 | 1 | 0 |
| | TOTAL | 1887-2001 | 330 | 49 |

## 37  HIBERNIAN FC, EDINBURGH

| # | Player | Period | Caps | Goals |
|---|---|---|---|---|
| 1 | Lawrence REILLY | 1948-1957 | 38 | 22 |
| 2 | James LEIGHTON | 1993-1997 | 23 | 0 |
| 3 | Darren JACKSON | 1995-1997 | 20 | 3 |
| 4 | Gordon SMITH | 1946-1957 | 18 | 4 |
| 5 | Patrick STANTON | 1966-1974 | 16 | 0 |
| 6 | Robert JOHNSTONE | 1951-1954 | 13 | 8 |
| 7 | Henry RENNIE | 1901-1908 | 11 | 0 |
| 8 | Andrew GORAM | 1988-1991 | 11 | 0 |
| 9 | William HARPER | 1923-1925 | 9 | 0 |
| 10 | David SHAW | 1946-1948 | 8 | 0 |
| 11 | Edward TURNBULL | 1948-1958 | 8 | 0 |
| 12 | Thomas YOUNGER | 1955-1956 | 8 | 0 |
| 13 | John BROWNLIE | 1971-1975 | 7 | 0 |
| 14 | John BLACKLEY | 1973-1977 | 7 | 0 |
| 15 | John GOVAN | 1947-1948 | 6 | 0 |
| 16 | William ORMOND | 1954-1959 | 6 | 2 |
| 17 | Arthur DUNCAN | 1975 | 6 | 0 |
| 18 | James DUNN | 1925-1928 | 5 | 1 |
| 19 | John MacLEOD | 1961 | 4 | 0 |
| 20 | Peter CORMACK | 1966-1969 | 4 | 0 |
| 21 | John COLLINS | 1988-1990 | 4 | 1 |
| 22 | James COMBE | 1948 | 3 | 1 |
| 23 | Patrick MURRAY | 1896-1897 | 2 | 1 |
| 24 | George STEWART | 1906 | 2 | 0 |
| 25 | Henry RITCHIE | 1923-1928 | 2 | 0 |
| 26 | John GRANT | 1958 | 2 | 0 |
| 27 | Neil MARTIN | 1965 | 2 | 0 |
| 28 | Alexander CROPLEY | 1971 | 2 | 0 |
| 29 | Alan ROUGH | 1985-1986 | 2 | 0 |
| 30 | Murdo MACLEOD | 1990-1991 | 2 | 0 |
| 31 | James LUNDIE | 1886 | 1 | 0 |
| 32 | James McGHEE | 1886 | 1 | 0 |
| 33 | James McLAREN | 1888 | 1 | 0 |
| 34 | William GROVES | 1888 | 1 | 1 |
| 35 | Robert NEIL | 1896 | 1 | 2 |
| 36 | Bernard BRESLIN | 1897 | 1 | 0 |
| 37 | John KENNEDY | 1897 | 1 | 0 |
| 38 | Robert GLEN | 1900 | 1 | 0 |
| 39 | Patrick CALLAGHAN | 1900 | 1 | 0 |
| 40 | William McCARTNEY | 1902 | 1 | 0 |
| 41 | Archibald GRAY | 1903 | 1 | 0 |
| 42 | James MAIN | 1909 | 1 | 0 |
| 43 | Peter KERR | 1924 | 1 | 0 |
| 44 | William ROBB | 1927 | 1 | 0 |
| 45 | Duncan URQUHART | 1933 | 1 | 0 |
| 46 | Hugh HOWIE | 1948 | 1 | 1 |
| 47 | William HAMILTON | 1965 | 1 | 0 |
| 48 | James SCOTT | 1966 | 1 | 0 |
| 49 | Erich SCHAEDLER | 1974 | 1 | 0 |
| 50 | Joseph HARPER | 1975 | 1 | 1 |
| 51 | Desmond BREMNER | 1976 | 1 | 0 |
| 52 | Keith WRIGHT | 1992 | 1 | 0 |
| 53 | John O'NEIL | 2001 | 1 | 0 |
| | TOTAL | 1886-2001 | 274 | 48 |

## 38  HURLFORD FC

| # | Player | Period | Caps | Goals |
|---|---|---|---|---|
| 1 | David BLACK | 1889 | 1 | 1 |
| 2 | T. HAMILTON | 1891 | 1 | 0 |
| | TOTAL | 1889-1891 | 2 | 1 |

## 39  KILBIRNIE FC

| # | Player | Period | Caps | Goals |
|---|---|---|---|---|
| 1 | Francis WATT | 1889-1891 | 4 | 3 |
| | TOTAL | 1889-1891 | 4 | 3 |

## 40 KILMARNOCK FC

| | Player | Period | Caps | Goals |
|---|---|---|---|---|
| 1 | Joseph NIBLOE | 1929-1932 | 11 | 0 |
| 2 | Iain DURRANT | 1998-2000 | 9 | 0 |
| 3 | Robert FERGUSON | 1965-1966 | 7 | 0 |
| 4 | Robert TEMPLETON | 1908-1913 | 6 | 0 |
| 5 | Thomas McLEAN | 1968-1971 | 6 | 1 |
| 6 | William DICKSON | 1970-1971 | 5 | 0 |
| 7 | Robert FORSYTH | 1964 | 4 | 0 |
| 8 | William AGNEW | 1907-1908 | 3 | 0 |
| 9 | James MITCHELL | 1908-1910 | 3 | 0 |
| 10 | John McGRORY | 1964-1966 | 3 | 0 |
| 11 | James CAMPBELL | 1891-1892 | 2 | 0 |
| 12 | Hugh MORTON | 1929 | 2 | 0 |
| 13 | William TONER | 1958 | 2 | 0 |
| 14 | Alistair HUNTER | 1972 | 2 | 0 |
| 15 | Alistair McCOIST | 1998 | 2 | 0 |
| 16 | Gary HOLT | 2000 | 2 | 0 |
| 17 | Alexander HIGGINS | 1885 | 1 | 3 |
| 18 | John McPHERSON | 1888 | 1 | 0 |
| 19 | David McPHERSON | 1892 | 1 | 0 |
| 20 | James ORR | 1892 | 1 | 0 |
| 21 | John JOHNSTONE | 1894 | 1 | 1 |
| 22 | Robert FINDLAY | 1898 | 1 | 0 |
| 23 | George ANDERSON | 1901 | 1 | 0 |
| 24 | Thomas SMITH | 1934 | 1 | 0 |
| 25 | George ROBERTSON | 1937 | 1 | 0 |
| 26 | James STEWART | 1977 | 1 | 0 |
| 27 | Andrew McLAREN | 2001 | 1 | 0 |
| | TOTAL | 1885-2001 | 80 | 5 |

## 41 KILMARNOCK ATHLETIC FC

| | Player | Period | Caps | Goals |
|---|---|---|---|---|
| 1 | John INGLIS | 1884 | 1 | 0 |
| | TOTAL | 1884 | 1 | 0 |

## 42 LEITH ATHLETIC FC, EDINBURGH

| | Player | Period | Caps | Goals |
|---|---|---|---|---|
| 1 | Matthew McQUEEN | 1890-1891 | 2 | 0 |
| 2 | Robert CLEMENTS | 1891 | 1 | 0 |
| | TOTAL | 1890-1891 | 3 | 0 |

## 43 LINTHOUSE FC, GLASGOW

| | Player | Period | Caps | Goals |
|---|---|---|---|---|
| 1 | William BOWIE | 1891 | 1 | 0 |
| | TOTAL | 1891 | 1 | 0 |

## 44 MAUCHLINE FC

| | Player | Period | Caps | Goals |
|---|---|---|---|---|
| 1 | John SMITH | 1877-1879 | 4 | 3 |
| | TOTAL | 1877-1879 | 4 | 3 |

## 45 MOFFAT FC

| | Player | Period | Caps | Goals |
|---|---|---|---|---|
| 1 | James NIVEN | 1885 | 1 | 0 |
| 2 | J. FRASER | 1891 | 1 | 0 |
| | TOTAL | 1885-1891 | 2 | 0 |

## 46 MONTROSE FC

| | Player | Period | Caps | Goals |
|---|---|---|---|---|
| 1 | Alexander KEILLOR | 1891-1892 | 2 | 1 |
| 2 | George BOWMAN | 1892 | 1 | 0 |
| | TOTAL | 1891-1892 | 3 | 1 |

## 47 MORTON FC, GREENOCK

| | Player | Period | Caps | Goals |
|---|---|---|---|---|
| 1 | James COWAN | 1948-1952 | 25 | 0 |
| 2 | William CAMPBELL | 1946-1948 | 5 | 0 |
| 3 | William STEEL | 1947 | 3 | 3 |
| 4 | Alexander McNAB | 1921 | 2 | 0 |
| 5 | Thomas ORR | 1951 | 2 | 1 |
| 6 | Robert FLEMING | 1886 | 1 | 0 |
| 7 | Robert MacFARLANE | 1896 | 1 | 0 |
| 8 | Peter CAMPBELL | 1898 | 1 | 0 |
| 9 | Daniel McRORIE | 1930 | 1 | 0 |
| | TOTAL | 1886-1952 | 41 | 4 |

## 48 MOSSEND SWIFTS FC, WEST CALDER

| | Player | Period | Caps | Goals |
|---|---|---|---|---|
| 1 | R. BOYD | 1889-1891 | 2 | 2 |
| 2 | James ELLIS | 1892 | 1 | 1 |
| | TOTAL | 1889-1892 | 3 | 3 |

## 49 MOTHERWELL FC

| | Player | Period | Caps | Goals |
|---|---|---|---|---|
| 1 | George STEVENSON | 1927-1934 | 12 | 4 |
| 2 | William REDPATH | 1948-1952 | 9 | 0 |
| 3 | Ian ST JOHN | 1959-1961 | 7 | 1 |
| 4 | Andrew WEIR | 1959-1960 | 6 | 1 |
| 5 | Robert McCANN | 1959-1961 | 5 | 0 |
| 6 | William PETTIGREW | 1976-1977 | 5 | 2 |
| 7 | Patrick QUINN | 1961-1962 | 4 | 1 |
| 8 | Thomas BOYD | 1990-1991 | 4 | 0 |
| 9 | Allan McCLORY | 1926-1934 | 3 | 0 |
| 10 | Allan CRAIG | 1929-1932 | 3 | 0 |
| 11 | William HUNTER | 1960 | 3 | 1 |
| 12 | Robert McKINNON | 1993-1995 | 3 | 0 |
| 13 | William TELFER | 1932-1933 | 2 | 0 |
| 14 | William MCFADYEN | 1933 | 2 | 2 |
| 15 | Andrew PATON | 1952 | 2 | 0 |
| 16 | David COOPER | 1989-1990 | 2 | 0 |
| 17 | Brian MARTIN | 1995 | 2 | 0 |
| 18 | Paul LAMBERT | 1995 | 2 | 0 |
| 19 | George ROBERTSON | 1910 | 1 | 0 |
| 20 | John MURDOCH | 1931 | 1 | 0 |
| 21 | Hugh WALES | 1932 | 1 | 0 |
| 22 | John BLAIR | 1933 | 1 | 0 |
| 23 | John McMENEMY | 1933 | 1 | 0 |
| 24 | Duncan OGILVIE | 1933 | 1 | 0 |
| 25 | James WATSON | 1947 | 1 | 0 |
| 26 | Wilson HUMPHRIES | 1952 | 1 | 0 |
| 27 | James GARDINER | 1957 | 1 | 0 |
| 28 | James FORREST | 1958 | 1 | 0 |
| 29 | John MARTIS | 1960 | 1 | 0 |
| 30 | Thomas FORSYTH | 1971 | 1 | 0 |
| 31 | Robert WATSON | 1971 | 1 | 0 |
| 32 | Philip O'DONNELL | 1993 | 1 | 0 |
| | TOTAL | 1910-1995 | 90 | 12 |

## 50 NEWMILNS FC

| | Player | Period | Caps | Goals |
|---|---|---|---|---|
| 1 | Hugh WILSON | 1890 | 1 | 1 |
| | TOTAL | 1890 | 1 | 1 |

## 51 PARTICK THISTLE FC, GLASGOW

| | Player | Period | Caps | Goals |
|---|---|---|---|---|
| 1 | Alan ROUGH | 1976-1982 | 51 | 0 |
| 2 | John MACKENZIE | 1953-1956 | 9 | 1 |
| 3 | James McMULLAN | 1920-1925 | 8 | 0 |
| 4 | James DAVIDSON | 1954-1955 | 8 | 1 |
| 5 | Kenneth CAMPBELL | 1920-1922 | 6 | 0 |
| 6 | James GIBSON | 1926-1927 | 4 | 0 |
| 7 | John JACKSON | 1931-1933 | 4 | 0 |
| 8 | Alexander FORSYTH | 1972 | 4 | 0 |

| 9 | William PAUL | 1888-1890 | 3 | 5 |
| 10 | George CUMMINGS | 1935 | 3 | 0 |
| 11 | Hugh BROWN | 1946-1947 | 3 | 0 |
| 12 | Joseph HARRIS | 1921 | 2 | 0 |
| 13 | Alexander McSPADYEN | 1938-1939 | 2 | 0 |
| 14 | Andrew KERR | 1955 | 2 | 0 |
| 15 | Thomas EWING | 1957-1958 | 2 | 0 |
| 16 | John HANSEN | 1971-1972 | 2 | 0 |
| 17 | J. McCORKINDALE | 1891 | 1 | 0 |
| 18 | Samuel KENNEDY | 1905 | 1 | 0 |
| 19 | Neil GIBSON | 1905 | 1 | 0 |
| 20 | William HOWDEN | 1905 | 1 | 0 |
| 21 | James KINLOCH | 1922 | 1 | 0 |
| 22 | John HUSBAND | 1946 | 1 | 0 |
| 23 | David MATHERS | 1954 | 1 | 0 |
| 24 | Nicholas WALKER | 1996 | 1 | 0 |
| | TOTAL | 1888-1996 | 121 | 7 |

## 52 PILGRIMS FC, GLASGOW

| | Player | Period | Caps | Goals |
|---|---|---|---|---|
| 1 | W. LAMONT | 1885 | 1 | 1 |
| | TOTAL | 1885 | 1 | 1 |

## 53 POLLOKSHIELDS ATHLETIC FC, GLASGOW

| | Player | Period | Caps | Goals |
|---|---|---|---|---|
| 1 | Francis SHAW | 1884 | 2 | 1 |
| 2 | William TURNER | 1885-1886 | 2 | 1 |
| 3 | Woodville GRAY | 1886 | 1 | 0 |
| | TOTAL | 1884-1886 | 5 | 2 |

## 54 PORT GLASGOW ATHLETIC FC

| | Player | Period | Caps | Goals |
|---|---|---|---|---|
| 1 | Gladstone HAMILTON | 1906 | 1 | 0 |
| | TOTAL | 1906 | 1 | 0 |

## 55 QUEEN OF THE SOUTH FC, DUMFRIES

| | Player | Period | Caps | Goals |
|---|---|---|---|---|
| 1 | William HOULISTON | 1948-1949 | 3 | 2 |
| | TOTAL | 1948-1949 | 3 | 2 |

## 56 QUEEN OF THE SOUTH WANDERERS FC, DUMFRIES

| | Player | Period | Caps | Goals |
|---|---|---|---|---|
| 1 | David CALDERHEAD | 1889 | 1 | 0 |
| | TOTAL | 1889 | 1 | 0 |

## 57 QUEEN'S PARK FC, GLASGOW

| | Player | Period | Caps | Goals |
|---|---|---|---|---|
| 1 | Walter ARNOTT | 1883-1893 | 14 | 0 |
| 2 | Charles CAMPBELL | 1874-1886 | 13 | 1 |
| 3 | Robert McCOLL | 1896-1908 | 12 | 13 |
| 4 | Henry McNEIL | 1874-1881 | 10 | 6 |
| 5 | William MacKINNON | 1872-1879 | 9 | 5 |
| 6 | William LAMBIE | 1892-1897 | 9 | 5 |
| 7 | Joseph TAYLOR | 1872-1876 | 6 | 0 |
| 8 | John KAY | 1880-1884 | 6 | 5 |
| 9 | William ANDERSON | 1882-1885 | 6 | 3 |
| 10 | Robert SMELLIE | 1887-1893 | 6 | 0 |
| 11 | Thomas WADDELL | 1891-1895 | 6 | 1 |
| 12 | Robert NEILL | 1876-1880 | 5 | 0 |
| 13 | David DAVIDSON | 1878-1881 | 5 | 1 |
| 14 | George KER | 1880-1882 | 5 | 10 |
| 15 | Malcolm FRASER | 1880-1883 | 5 | 4 |
| 16 | Donald SILLARS | 1891-1895 | 5 | 0 |
| 17 | James CRAWFORD | 1931-1933 | 5 | 0 |
| 18 | James WEIR | 1872-1878 | 4 | 2 |
| 19 | Thomas HIGHET | 1875-1878 | 4 | 1 |
| 20 | Alexander HAMILTON | 1885-1888 | 4 | 0 |

| 21 | William BERRY | 1888-1891 | 4 | 0 |
| 22 | Thomas ROBERTSON | 1889-1892 | 4 | 0 |
| 23 | William GULLILAND | 1891-1895 | 4 | 0 |
| 24 | William SELLAR | 1891-1893 | 4 | 4 |
| 25 | Robert GILLESPIE | 1926-1933 | 4 | 0 |
| 26 | James THOMSON | 1872-1874 | 3 | 0 |
| 27 | James PHILLIPS | 1877-1878 | 3 | 0 |
| 28 | Andrew WATSON | 1881-1882 | 3 | 0 |
| 29 | William HARROWER | 1882-1886 | 3 | 4 |
| 30 | Andrew HOLM | 1882-1883 | 3 | 0 |
| 31 | John SMITH | 1883-1884 | 3 | 4 |
| 32 | David ALLAN | 1885-1886 | 3 | 2 |
| 33 | John LAMBIE | 1886-1888 | 3 | 1 |
| 34 | James HAMILTON | 1892-1893 | 3 | 3 |
| 35 | David STEWART | 1893-1897 | 3 | 0 |
| 36 | Davidson BERRY | 1894-1899 | 3 | 1 |
| 37 | Kenneth ANDERSON | 1896-1898 | 3 | 0 |
| 38 | Alexander CHRISTIE | 1898-1899 | 3 | 1 |
| 39 | Harold PAUL | 1909 | 3 | 2 |
| 40 | John HARKNESS | 1927-1928 | 3 | 0 |
| 41 | Robert GARDNER | 1872-1873 | 2 | 0 |
| 42 | William KER | 1872-1873 | 2 | 0 |
| 43 | Robert SMITH | 1872-1873 | 2 | 0 |
| 44 | David WOTHERSPOON | 1872-1873 | 2 | 0 |
| 45 | James RICHMOND | 1878-1882 | 2 | 0 |
| 46 | George GILLESPIE | 1886-1891 | 2 | 0 |
| 47 | James ALLAN | 1887 | 2 | 2 |
| 48 | Allan STEWART | 1888-1889 | 2 | 1 |
| 49 | Andrew BAIRD | 1892-1894 | 2 | 0 |
| 50 | William STEWART | 1898-1900 | 2 | 1 |
| 51 | George MCWATTIE | 1901 | 2 | 0 |
| 52 | Alan MORTON | 1920 | 2 | 1 |
| 53 | William WISEMAN | 1926-1930 | 2 | 0 |
| 54 | James SMITH | 1872 | 1 | 0 |
| 55 | Robert LECKIE | 1872 | 1 | 0 |
| 56 | Alexander RHIND | 1872 | 1 | 0 |
| 57 | Angus MCKINNON | 1874 | 1 | 1 |
| 58 | William SOMERS | 1880 | 1 | 0 |
| 59 | Archibald ROWAN | 1882 | 1 | 0 |
| 60 | Robert CHRISTIE | 1884 | 1 | 0 |
| 61 | John GOW | 1885 | 1 | 0 |
| 62 | William McLEOD | 1886 | 1 | 0 |
| 63 | George SOMERVILLE | 1886 | 1 | 1 |
| 64 | William WATT | 1887 | 1 | 1 |
| 65 | John GILLESPIE | 1896 | 1 | 0 |
| 66 | John CAMERON | 1896 | 1 | 0 |
| 67 | John RITCHIE | 1897 | 1 | 1 |
| 68 | James IRONS | 1900 | 1 | 0 |
| 69 | David WILSON | 1900 | 1 | 2 |
| 70 | Leslie SKENE | 1904 | 1 | 0 |
| 71 | Andrew RICHMOND | 1906 | 1 | 0 |
| 72 | Thomas FITCHIE | 1907 | 1 | 0 |
| 73 | William KEY | 1907 | 1 | 0 |
| 74 | Peter PURSELL | 1914 | 1 | 0 |
| 75 | William KING | 1928 | 1 | 0 |
| 76 | William CHALMERS | 1929 | 1 | 0 |
| | TOTAL | 1872-1933 | 252 | 90 |

## 58 RAITH ROVERS FC, KIRKCALDY

| | Player | Period | Caps | Goals |
|---|---|---|---|---|
| 1 | David MORRIS | 1923-1925 | 6 | 1 |
| 2 | William McNAUGHT | 1950-1954 | 5 | 0 |
| 3 | Harold ANDERSON | 1914 | 1 | 0 |
| 4 | William COLLIER | 1922 | 1 | 0 |
| 5 | Steven CRAWFORD | 1995 | 1 | 1 |
| | TOTAL | 1914-1995 | 14 | 2 |

## 59 RANGERS FC, GLASGOW

| # | Player | Period | Caps | Goals |
|---|--------|--------|------|-------|
| 1 | Alistair McCOIST | 1986-1997 | 59 | 19 |
| 2 | George YOUNG | 1946-1957 | 53 | 0 |
| 3 | John GREIG | 1964-1975 | 44 | 3 |
| 4 | Eric CALDOW | 1957-1963 | 40 | 4 |
| 5 | William JARDINE | 1970-1979 | 38 | 1 |
| 6 | Alan MORTON | 1921-1932 | 29 | 4 |
| 7 | William HENDERSON | 1962-1971 | 29 | 5 |
| 8 | Stuart McCALL | 1991-1998 | 29 | 0 |
| 9 | Ronald McKINNON | 1965-1971 | 28 | 1 |
| 10 | Andrew GORAM | 1991-1998 | 28 | 0 |
| 11 | Richard GOUGH | 1988-1993 | 27 | 3 |
| 12 | William WOODBURN | 1947-1952 | 24 | 0 |
| 13 | Samuel COX | 1949-1954 | 24 | 0 |
| 14 | James BAXTER | 1960-1964 | 24 | 3 |
| 15 | David WILSON | 1960-1965 | 22 | 9 |
| 16 | Thomas FORSYTH | 1973-1978 | 21 | 0 |
| 17 | Alexander SMITH | 1898-1911 | 20 | 5 |
| 18 | David COOPER | 1979-1987 | 20 | 6 |
| 19 | George BROWN | 1930-1938 | 19 | 0 |
| 20 | Gordon DURIE | 1994-1998 | 18 | 3 |
| 21 | William WADDELL | 1946-1954 | 17 | 6 |
| 22 | Colin STEIN | 1968-1972 | 17 | 10 |
| 23 | Robert McPHAIL | 1928-1937 | 16 | 7 |
| 24 | David MEIKLEJOHN | 1922-1933 | 15 | 3 |
| 25 | John ROBERTSON | 1900-1905 | 14 | 2 |
| 26 | James DAWSON | 1934-1939 | 14 | 0 |
| 27 | James SIMPSON | 1934-1937 | 14 | 1 |
| 28 | John McCOLL | 1950-1958 | 14 | 0 |
| 29 | Derek JOHNSTONE | 1973-1979 | 14 | 2 |
| 30 | John DRUMMOND | 1894-1903 | 13 | 1 |
| 31 | Neil GIBSON | 1895-1901 | 13 | 1 |
| 32 | Nicol SMITH | 1897-1902 | 12 | 0 |
| 33 | Andrew CUNNINGHAM | 1920-1927 | 12 | 5 |
| 34 | Derek PARLANE | 1973-1977 | 12 | 1 |
| 35 | Alexander SCOTT | 1956-1962 | 11 | 5 |
| 36 | Iain DURRANT | 1987-1993 | 11 | 0 |
| 37 | Robert HAMILTON | 1899-1904 | 10 | 13 |
| 38 | James GORDON | 1912-1920 | 10 | 0 |
| 39 | Douglas GRAY | 1928-1932 | 10 | 0 |
| 40 | Maurice JOHNSTON | 1989-1991 | 10 | 2 |
| 41 | Alan McLAREN | 1994-1995 | 10 | 0 |
| 42 | Neil McCANN | 1999-2000 | 10 | 1 |
| 43 | Barry FERGUSON | 1998-2001 | 10 | 1 |
| 44 | William REID | 1911-1914 | 9 | 4 |
| 45 | William JOHNSTON | 1965-1970 | 9 | 0 |
| 46 | Ian FERGUSON | 1988-1997 | 9 | 0 |
| 47 | Colin HENDRY | 1998-1999 | 9 | 0 |
| 48 | William DODDS | 2000-2001 | 9 | 3 |
| 49 | Alexander BENNETT | 1909-1913 | 8 | 1 |
| 50 | Thomas CAIRNS | 1920-1925 | 8 | 1 |
| 51 | Alexander ARCHIBALD | 1921-1932 | 8 | 1 |
| 52 | Thomas MUIRHEAD | 1922-1929 | 8 | 0 |
| 53 | Thomas CRAIG | 1927-1930 | 8 | 1 |
| 54 | Ralph BRAND | 1960-1962 | 8 | 8 |
| 55 | Colin JACKSON | 1975-1976 | 8 | 1 |
| 56 | Thomas VALLANCE | 1877-1881 | 7 | 0 |
| 57 | William THORNTON | 1946-1952 | 7 | 1 |
| 58 | Samuel BAIRD | 1956-1958 | 7 | 2 |
| 59 | George GILLESPIE | 1880-1890 | 5 | 0 |
| 60 | David MITCHELL | 1890-1894 | 5 | 0 |
| 61 | John McPHERSON | 1892-1897 | 5 | 4 |
| 62 | John MAY | 1906-1909 | 5 | 0 |
| 63 | David PROVAN | 1963-1966 | 5 | 0 |
| 64 | Stewart KENNEDY | 1975 | 5 | 0 |
| 65 | Alistair DAWSON | 1980-1983 | 5 | 0 |
| 66 | John CAMPBELL | 1899-1901 | 4 | 4 |
| 67 | John SHAW | 1947 | 4 | 0 |
| 68 | Robert SHEARER | 1961 | 4 | 0 |
| 69 | Peter McCLOY | 1973 | 4 | 0 |
| 70 | David McPHERSON | 1992-1993 | 4 | 0 |
| 71 | David HILL | 1881-1882 | 3 | 1 |
| 72 | Matthew DICKIE | 1897-1900 | 3 | 0 |
| 73 | James MILLAR | 1897-1898 | 3 | 2 |
| 74 | Finlay SPEEDIE | 1903 | 3 | 2 |
| 75 | George LAW | 1910 | 3 | 0 |
| 76 | James FLEMING | 1929-1930 | 3 | 3 |
| 77 | James MARSHALL | 1932-1934 | 3 | 0 |
| 78 | Robert BROWN | 1946-1952 | 3 | 0 |
| 79 | David ROBERTSON | 1992-1994 | 3 | 0 |
| 80 | Allan JOHNSTON | 2000-2001 | 3 | 0 |
| 81 | Moses McNEIL | 1876-1880 | 2 | 0 |
| 82 | Peter CAMPBELL | 1878-1879 | 2 | 3 |
| 83 | John INGLIS | 1883 | 2 | 0 |
| 84 | Robert MARSHALL | 1892-1894 | 2 | 0 |
| 85 | Andrew McCREADIE | 1893-1894 | 2 | 0 |
| 86 | John BARKER | 1893-1894 | 2 | 4 |
| 87 | John WALKER | 1904 | 2 | 0 |
| 88 | James GALT | 1908 | 2 | 1 |
| 89 | James STARK | 1909 | 2 | 0 |
| 90 | James BOWIE | 1920 | 2 | 0 |
| 91 | John BUCHANAN | 1929-1930 | 2 | 0 |
| 92 | Robert McAULAY | 1931 | 2 | 0 |
| 93 | James SMITH | 1934-1937 | 2 | 1 |
| 94 | Alexander VENTERS | 1936-1939 | 2 | 0 |
| 95 | James MILLAR | 1963 | 2 | 0 |
| 96 | James FORREST | 1965 | 2 | 0 |
| 97 | James BETT | 1982 | 2 | 0 |
| 98 | Derek FERGUSON | 1988 | 2 | 0 |
| 99 | James WATSON | 1878 | 1 | 1 |
| 100 | Hugh McINTYRE | 1880 | 1 | 0 |
| 101 | James GOSSLAND | 1884 | 1 | 2 |
| 102 | James McINTYRE | 1884 | 1 | 0 |
| 103 | William CHALMERS | 1885 | 1 | 0 |
| 104 | Hugh McHARDY | 1885 | 1 | 0 |
| 105 | John CAMERON | 1886 | 1 | 0 |
| 106 | Charles HEGGIE | 1886 | 1 | 4 |
| 107 | Donald GOW | 1888 | 1 | 0 |
| 108 | John GOW | 1888 | 1 | 0 |
| 109 | Thomas WYLIE | 1890 | 1 | 1 |
| 110 | David HADDOW | 1894 | 1 | 0 |
| 111 | James OSWALD | 1897 | 1 | 0 |
| 112 | Thomas LOW | 1897 | 1 | 0 |
| 113 | Thomas HYSLOP | 1897 | 1 | 1 |
| 114 | David CRAWFORD | 1900 | 1 | 0 |
| 115 | Robert NEIL | 1900 | 1 | 0 |
| 116 | George HENDERSON | 1904 | 1 | 0 |
| 117 | George LIVINGSTON | 1907 | 1 | 0 |
| 118 | James SPEIRS | 1908 | 1 | 0 |
| 119 | William ROBB | 1925 | 1 | 0 |
| 120 | Thomas HAMILTON | 1932 | 1 | 0 |
| 121 | Robert MAIN | 1937 | 1 | 0 |
| 122 | David KINNEAR | 1937 | 1 | 1 |
| 123 | Thomas McKILLOP | 1938 | 1 | 0 |
| 124 | James SYMON | 1938 | 1 | 0 |
| 125 | James DUNCANSON | 1946 | 1 | 0 |
| 126 | Edward RUTHERFORD | 1948 | 1 | 0 |
| 127 | John LITTLE | 1953 | 1 | 0 |
| 128 | John McMILLAN | 1961 | 1 | 0 |
| 129 | William RITCHIE | 1962 | 1 | 0 |
| 130 | David SMITH | 1968 | 1 | 0 |
| 131 | Alexander MACDONALD | 1976 | 1 | 0 |
| 132 | Robert McKEAN | 1976 | 1 | 0 |
| 133 | Kenneth MILLER | 2001 | 1 | 0 |
| | TOTAL | 1876-2001 | 1162 | 185 |

## 60 RENFREW FC

| | Player | Period | Caps | Goals |
|---|---|---|---|---|
| 1 | James DOUGLAS | 1880 | 1 | 0 |
| | TOTAL | 1880 | 1 | 0 |

## 61 RENTON FC

| | Player | Period | Caps | Goals |
|---|---|---|---|---|
| 1 | Robert KELSO | 1885-1888 | 6 | 0 |
| 2 | James McCALL | 1886-1890 | 5 | 2 |
| 3 | John LINDSAY | 1888-1893 | 3 | 0 |
| 4 | Robert GLEN | 1895-1896 | 2 | 0 |
| 5 | Alexander BARBOUR | 1885 | 1 | 1 |
| 6 | Leitch KEIR | 1885 | 1 | 0 |
| 7 | Andrew HANNAH | 1888 | 1 | 0 |
| 8 | James KELLY | 1888 | 1 | 0 |
| 9 | Archibald McCALL | 1888 | 1 | 0 |
| 10 | Neil McCALLUM | 1888 | 1 | 1 |
| 11 | Henry CAMPBELL | 1889 | 1 | 0 |
| 12 | William McCOLL | 1895 | 1 | 0 |
| 13 | John MURRAY | 1895 | 1 | 0 |
| | TOTAL | 1885-1896 | 25 | 4 |

## 62 ROYAL ALBERT FC, LARKHALL

| | Player | Period | Caps | Goals |
|---|---|---|---|---|
| 1 | James CLELAND | 1891 | 1 | 0 |
| | TOTAL | 1891 | 1 | 0 |

## 63 ST BERNARD'S FC, EDINBURGH

| | Player | Period | Caps | Goals |
|---|---|---|---|---|
| 1 | Robert FOYERS | 1893-1894 | 2 | 0 |
| 2 | Duncan McLEAN | 1896-1897 | 2 | 0 |
| 3 | J. HUTTON | 1887 | 1 | 0 |
| 4 | James LOWE | 1887 | 1 | 1 |
| 5 | James OSWALD | 1895 | 1 | 0 |
| 6 | Daniel PATON | 1896 | 1 | 1 |
| 7 | J. MCMILLAN | 1897 | 1 | 0 |
| 8 | William BAIRD | 1897 | 1 | 0 |
| | TOTAL | 1887-1897 | 10 | 2 |

## 64 ST JOHNSTONE FC, PERTH

| | Player | Period | Caps | Goals |
|---|---|---|---|---|
| 1 | Alexander McLAREN | 1929-1932 | 5 | 0 |
| 2 | William IMRIE | 1929 | 2 | 1 |
| | TOTAL | 1929-1932 | 7 | 1 |

## 65 ST MIRREN FC, PAISLEY

| | Player | Period | Caps | Goals |
|---|---|---|---|---|
| 1 | Alexander MUNRO | 1979-1980 | 7 | 0 |
| 2 | William THOMSON | 1980-1983 | 7 | 0 |
| 3 | Thomas JACKSON | 1904-1907 | 6 | 0 |
| 4 | John MILLER | 1931-1934 | 5 | 0 |
| 5 | George WALKER | 1930-1931 | 4 | 0 |
| 6 | Peter WEIR | 1980 | 4 | 0 |
| 7 | Robert RANKIN | 1929 | 3 | 2 |
| 8 | Andrew BROWN | 1890-1891 | 2 | 0 |
| 9 | David CRAWFORD | 1894 | 2 | 0 |
| 10 | John PATRICK | 1897 | 2 | 0 |
| 11 | David McCRAE | 1929 | 2 | 0 |
| 12 | Thomas GEMMELL | 1955 | 2 | 1 |
| 13 | James DUNLOP | 1890 | 1 | 0 |
| 14 | R. HUNTER | 1890 | 1 | 0 |
| 15 | Edward McBAIN | 1894 | 1 | 0 |
| 16 | John TAYLOR | 1895 | 1 | 0 |
| 17 | Hugh MORGAN | 1898 | 1 | 0 |
| 18 | David LINDSAY | 1903 | 1 | 0 |
| 19 | John CAMERON | 1904 | 1 | 0 |
| 20 | Charles PRINGLE | 1921 | 1 | 0 |
| 21 | Denis LAWSON | 1923 | 1 | 0 |
| 22 | James HAMILTON | 1924 | 1 | 0 |
| 23 | William SUMMERS | 1926 | 1 | 0 |
| 24 | James HOWIESON | 1927 | 1 | 0 |
| 25 | Thomas MORRISON | 1927 | 1 | 0 |
| 26 | William TELFER | 1953 | 1 | 0 |
| 27 | Robert AITKEN | 1991 | 1 | 0 |
| | TOTAL | 1890-1991 | 61 | 3 |

## 66 SOUTH WESTERN FC, GLASGOW

| | Player | Period | Caps | Goals |
|---|---|---|---|---|
| 1 | John CAMPBELL | 1880 | 1 | 1 |
| | TOTAL | 1880 | 1 | 1 |

## 67 STRATHMORE FC, DUNDEE

| | Player | Period | Caps | Goals |
|---|---|---|---|---|
| 1 | William DICKSON | 1888 | 1 | 4 |
| | TOTAL | 1888 | 1 | 4 |

## 68 THIRD LANARK FC, GLASGOW

| | Player | Period | Caps | Goals |
|---|---|---|---|---|
| 1 | James BROWNLIE | 1909-1914 | 16 | 0 |
| 2 | James MASON | 1948-1951 | 7 | 4 |
| 3 | John MARSHALL | 1885-1887 | 4 | 1 |
| 4 | John HUNTER | 1874-1877 | 3 | 0 |
| 5 | Alexander KENNEDY | 1878-1884 | 3 | 0 |
| 6 | William JOHNSTONE | 1887-1890 | 3 | 1 |
| 7 | John AULD | 1887-1889 | 3 | 0 |
| 8 | James SIMPSON | 1895 | 3 | 0 |
| 9 | Neil DEWAR | 1932 | 3 | 4 |
| 10 | James CARABINE | 1938-1939 | 3 | 0 |
| 11 | William SOMERS | 1879 | 2 | 0 |
| 12 | James RAE | 1889-1890 | 2 | 0 |
| 13 | Hugh WILSON | 1902-1904 | 2 | 0 |
| 14 | William MILLER | 1876 | 1 | 0 |
| 15 | James LANG | 1878 | 1 | 1 |
| 16 | J. McADAM | 1880 | 1 | 1 |
| 17 | John WEIR | 1887 | 1 | 0 |
| 18 | James OSWALD | 1889 | 1 | 1 |
| 19 | Andrew THOMSON | 1889 | 1 | 0 |
| 20 | Alexander LOCHHEAD | 1889 | 1 | 0 |
| 21 | James HANNAH | 1889 | 1 | 0 |
| 22 | Robert DOWNIE | 1892 | 1 | 0 |
| 23 | Andrew STEWART | 1894 | 1 | 0 |
| 24 | John FYFE | 1895 | 1 | 0 |
| 25 | William BLAIR | 1896 | 1 | 0 |
| 26 | David GARDNER | 1897 | 1 | 0 |
| 27 | James GILLESPIE | 1898 | 1 | 3 |
| 28 | John CROSS | 1903 | 1 | 0 |
| 29 | Thomas SLOAN | 1904 | 1 | 0 |
| 30 | William McINTOSH | 1905 | 1 | 0 |
| 31 | James RAESIDE | 1906 | 1 | 0 |
| 32 | David HILL | 1906 | 1 | 0 |
| 33 | Frank WALKER | 1922 | 1 | 0 |
| | TOTAL | 1874-1951 | 74 | 16 |

## 69 VALE OF LEVEN FC, ALEXANDRIA

| | Player | Period | Caps | Goals |
|---|---|---|---|---|
| 1 | John McPHERSON | 1879-1885 | 8 | 0 |
| 2 | John FERGUSON | 1874-1878 | 6 | 5 |
| 3 | John McDOUGALL | 1877-1879 | 5 | 4 |
| 4 | John FORBES | 1884-1887 | 5 | 0 |
| 5 | John McGREGOR | 1877-1880 | 4 | 1 |
| 6 | James WILSON | 1888-1891 | 4 | 0 |
| 7 | Alexander McLINTOCK | 1875-1880 | 3 | 0 |
| 8 | John BAIRD | 1876-1880 | 3 | 2 |
| 9 | Robert PARLANE | 1878-1879 | 3 | 0 |

| 10 | Andrew McINTYRE | 1878-1882 | 2 | 0 |
| 11 | Robert PATON | 1879 | 2 | 0 |
| 12 | Andrew WHITELAW | 1887-1890 | 2 | 0 |
| 13 | Gilbert RANKIN | 1890-1891 | 2 | 2 |
| 14 | John MURRAY | 1890 | 1 | 0 |
| 15 | Daniel BRUCE | 1890 | 1 | 0 |
| | TOTAL | 1874-1891 | 51 | 14 |

## English Clubs (50)

### 1 ASTON VILLA FC, BIRMINGHAM

| | Player | Period | Caps | Goals |
|---|---|---|---|---|
| 1 | Alexander MASSIE | 1936-1937 | 7 | 1 |
| 2 | George CUMMINGS | 1936-1939 | 6 | 0 |
| 3 | Andrew GRAY | 1975-1978 | 6 | 3 |
| 4 | James GIBSON | 1927-1930 | 4 | 1 |
| 5 | Allan EVANS | 1982 | 4 | 0 |
| 6 | Colin CALDERWOOD | 1999 | 4 | 0 |
| 7 | James COWAN | 1896-1898 | 3 | 0 |
| 8 | Alan McINALLY | 1989 | 2 | 1 |
| 9 | Robert TEMPLETON | 1902 | 1 | 1 |
| 10 | Thomas NIBLO | 1904 | 1 | 0 |
| 11 | Daniel BLAIR | 1932 | 1 | 0 |
| | TOTAL | 1896-1999 | 39 | 7 |

### 2 BARNSLEY FC

| | Player | Period | Caps | Goals |
|---|---|---|---|---|
| 1 | John KELLY | 1948 | 2 | 0 |
| | TOTAL | 1948 | 2 | 0 |

### 3 BIRMINGHAM/BIRMINGHAM CITY FC

| | Player | Period | Caps | Goals |
|---|---|---|---|---|
| 1 | Archibald GEMMILL | 1979-1981 | 10 | 2 |
| 2 | James HERRIOT | 1968-1969 | 8 | 0 |
| 3 | Kenneth BURNS | 1974-1977 | 8 | 1 |
| 4 | John CROSBIE | 1922 | 1 | 0 |
| 5 | Francis McGURK | 1933 | 1 | 0 |
| 6 | Cornelius DOUGALL | 1946 | 1 | 0 |
| | TOTAL | 1922-1981 | 29 | 3 |

### 4 BLACKBURN ROVERS FC

| | Player | Period | Caps | Goals |
|---|---|---|---|---|
| 1 | Colin HENDRY | 1993-1998 | 35 | 1 |
| 2 | Kevin GALLACHER | 1993-1999 | 30 | 8 |
| 3 | William McKINLAY | 1995-1998 | 15 | 0 |
| 4 | Christian DAILLY | 1998-2000 | 13 | 0 |
| 5 | Callum DAVIDSON | 1998-2000 | 12 | 0 |
| 6 | John HUTTON | 1927-1928 | 3 | 1 |
| 7 | Thomas BRANDON | 1896 | 1 | 0 |
| 8 | Walter AITKENHEAD | 1912 | 1 | 2 |
| 9 | John McKAY | 1924 | 1 | 0 |
| | TOTAL | 1896-2000 | 111 | 12 |

### 5 BLACKPOOL FC

| | Player | Period | Caps | Goals |
|---|---|---|---|---|
| 1 | John MUDIE | 1956-1958 | 17 | 9 |
| 2 | Allan BROWN | 1952-1954 | 11 | 3 |
| 3 | George FARM | 1952-1959 | 10 | 0 |
| 4 | Anthony GREEN | 1971 | 4 | 0 |
| 5 | Frank O'DONNELL | 1938 | 2 | 0 |
| 6 | Philip WATSON | 1933 | 1 | 0 |
| 7 | Alexander MUNRO | 1938 | 1 | 0 |
| 8 | James BLAIR | 1946 | 1 | 0 |
| 9 | Hugh KELLY | 1952 | 1 | 0 |
| | TOTAL | 1933-1971 | 48 | 12 |

### 6 BOLTON WANDERERS FC

| | Player | Period | Caps | Goals |
|---|---|---|---|---|
| 1 | John McGINLAY | 1994-1997 | 13 | 4 |
| 2 | Alexander DONALDSON | 1914-1922 | 6 | 1 |
| 3 | William COOK | 1934 | 3 | 0 |
| 4 | Walter WHITE | 1907-1908 | 2 | 0 |
| 5 | Paul RITCHIE | 2000 | 2 | 0 |
| 6 | Colin HENDRY | 2001 | 2 | 2 |
| 7 | William MOIR | 1950 | 1 | 0 |
| | TOTAL | 1907-2001 | 29 | 7 |

### 7 BRADFORD CITY FC

| | Player | Period | Caps | Goals |
|---|---|---|---|---|
| 1 | James STEPHEN | 1946-1947 | 2 | 0 |
| 2 | John EWART | 1921 | 1 | 0 |
| | TOTAL | 1921-1947 | 3 | 0 |

### 8 BRENTFORD FC, LONDON

| | Player | Period | Caps | Goals |
|---|---|---|---|---|
| 1 | David McCULLOCH | 1936-1937 | 4 | 3 |
| 2 | Robert REID | 1937-1938 | 2 | 0 |
| 3 | Duncan McKENZIE | 1937 | 1 | 0 |
| 4 | Archibald MACAULEY | 1947 | 1 | 0 |
| | TOTAL | 1936-1947 | 8 | 3 |

### 9 BURNLEY FC

| | Player | Period | Caps | Goals |
|---|---|---|---|---|
| 1 | John AIRD | 1954 | 4 | 0 |
| 2 | Adam BLACKLAW | 1963-1965 | 3 | 0 |
| 3 | William MORGAN | 1967 | 1 | 0 |
| | TOTAL | 1954-1967 | 8 | 0 |

### 10 BURY FC

| | Player | Period | Caps | Goals |
|---|---|---|---|---|
| 1 | Thomas BRADSHAW | 1928 | 1 | 0 |
| | TOTAL | 1928 | 1 | 0 |

### 11 CHARLTON ATHLETIC FC, LONDON

| | Player | Period | Caps | Goals |
|---|---|---|---|---|
| 1 | John HEWIE | 1956-1960 | 19 | 2 |
| | TOTAL | 1956-1960 | 19 | 2 |

### 12 CHELSEA FC, LONDON

| | Player | Period | Caps | Goals |
|---|---|---|---|---|
| 1 | Edward McCREADIE | 1965-1969 | 23 | 0 |
| 2 | Craig BURLEY | 1995-1997 | 20 | 0 |
| 3 | Charles COOKE | 1966-1975 | 14 | 0 |
| 4 | John SPENCER | 1994-1996 | 13 | 0 |
| 5 | Gordon DURIE | 1987-1991 | 12 | 2 |
| 6 | Patrick NEVIN | 1986-1987 | 6 | 0 |
| 7 | Stephen CLARKE | 1987-1994 | 6 | 0 |
| 8 | David SPEEDIE | 1985-1986 | 5 | 0 |
| 9 | John JACKSON | 1934-1935 | 4 | 0 |
| 10 | Robert CAMPBELL | 1950 | 3 | 1 |
| 11 | Robert EVANS | 1960 | 3 | 0 |
| 12 | Thomas LAW | 1928-1930 | 2 | 0 |
| 13 | Thomas BOYD | 1991 | 2 | 0 |
| 14 | John CAMERON | 1909 | 1 | 0 |
| 15 | Angus DOUGLAS | 1911 | 1 | 0 |
| 16 | Hugh GALLACHER | 1934 | 1 | 0 |
| 17 | Peter BUCHANAN | 1937 | 1 | 1 |
| | TOTAL | 1909-1997 | 117 | 4 |

### 13 COVENTRY CITY FC

| | Player | Period | Caps | Goals |
|---|---|---|---|---|
| 1 | Thomas HUTCHISON | 1973-1975 | 17 | 1 |
| 2 | Gary McALLISTER | 1996-1999 | 13 | 1 |

| | | | | |
|---|---|---|---|---|
| 3 | Kevin GALLACHER | 1991-1992 | 10 | 0 |
| 4 | William CARR | 1970-1972 | 6 | 0 |
| 5 | David SPEEDIE | 1988-1989 | 5 | 0 |
| 6 | Colin HENDRY | 2000 | 5 | 0 |
| 7 | Colin STEIN | 1973 | 4 | 0 |
| 8 | Ian WALLACE | 1978-1979 | 3 | 1 |
| 9 | Eoin JESS | 1996 | 3 | 0 |
| 10 | James BLYTH | 1978 | 2 | 0 |
| 11 | Paul TELFER | 2000 | 1 | 0 |
| | TOTAL | 1970-2000 | 69 | 3 |

## 14  CRYSTAL PALACE FC, LONDON

| | Player | Period | Caps | Goals |
|---|---|---|---|---|
| 1 | David HOPKIN | 1997 | 2 | 0 |
| | TOTAL | 1997 | 2 | 0 |

## 15  DERBY COUNTY FC

| | Player | Period | Caps | Goals |
|---|---|---|---|---|
| 1 | Archibald GEMMILL | 1971-1977 | 22 | 2 |
| 2 | Bruce RIOCH | 1975-1978 | 18 | 6 |
| 3 | Douglas DUNCAN | 1932-1937 | 14 | 7 |
| 4 | William STEEL | 1947-1950 | 14 | 4 |
| 5 | John O'HARE | 1970-1972 | 13 | 5 |
| 6 | Christian DAILLY | 1997-1998 | 13 | 1 |
| 7 | Craig BURLEY | 2000-2001 | 6 | 0 |
| 8 | Donald MASSON | 1978 | 3 | 0 |
| 9 | Charles NAPIER | 1936-1937 | 2 | 1 |
| 10 | David McCULLOCH | 1938 | 2 | 0 |
| 11 | John ROBERTSON | 1983 | 2 | 1 |
| 12 | Hugh GALLACHER | 1935 | 1 | 0 |
| 13 | Brian O'NEIL | 2000 | 1 | 0 |
| | TOTAL | 1932-2001 | 111 | 27 |

## 16  EVERTON FC, LIVERPOOL

| | Player | Period | Caps | Goals |
|---|---|---|---|---|
| 1 | David WEIR | 1999-2001 | 18 | 0 |
| 2 | Graeme SHARP | 1985-1988 | 12 | 1 |
| 3 | Stuart McCALL | 1990-1991 | 11 | 1 |
| 4 | Donald HUTCHISON | 1999-2000 | 10 | 1 |
| 5 | Richard HARTFORD | 1979-1981 | 8 | 1 |
| 6 | Patrick NEVIN | 1989-1992 | 8 | 1 |
| 7 | Robert COLLINS | 1958-1959 | 6 | 3 |
| 8 | Bruce RIOCH | 1977 | 6 | 0 |
| 9 | John COLLINS | 1998-1999 | 6 | 1 |
| 10 | Torrance GILLICK | 1937-1938 | 5 | 3 |
| 11 | Alexander SCOTT | 1963-1966 | 5 | 0 |
| 12 | Scot GEMMILL | 1999-2001 | 4 | 0 |
| 13 | John BELL | 1896-1898 | 3 | 1 |
| 14 | George WOOD | 1979 | 3 | 0 |
| 15 | Ian WILSON | 1987 | 3 | 0 |
| 16 | Duncan FERGUSON | 1994-1997 | 3 | 0 |
| 17 | Alexander YOUNG | 1905-1907 | 2 | 0 |
| 18 | Neil McBAIN | 1923-1924 | 2 | 0 |
| 19 | James GABRIEL | 1960-1963 | 2 | 0 |
| 20 | Alexander YOUNG | 1961-1966 | 2 | 2 |
| 21 | John ROBERTSON | 1898 | 1 | 0 |
| 22 | George WILSON | 1907 | 1 | 0 |
| 23 | George BREWSTER | 1921 | 1 | 0 |
| 24 | Alexander TROUP | 1926 | 1 | 0 |
| 25 | James DUNN | 1928 | 1 | 1 |
| 26 | John THOMSON | 1932 | 1 | 0 |
| 27 | Alexander PARKER | 1958 | 1 | 0 |
| 28 | John CONNELLY | 1973 | 1 | 0 |
| 29 | Andrew GRAY | 1985 | 1 | 0 |
| | TOTAL | 1896-2001 | 128 | 20 |

## 17  FULHAM FC, LONDON

| | Player | Period | Caps | Goals |
|---|---|---|---|---|
| 1 | Graham LEGGAT | 1958-1960 | 11 | 6 |
| 2 | James SHARP | 1909 | 1 | 0 |
| | TOTAL | 1909-1960 | 12 | 6 |

## 18  HUDDERSFIELD TOWN FC

| | Player | Period | Caps | Goals |
|---|---|---|---|---|
| 1 | Alexander JACKSON | 1925-1930 | 14 | 8 |
| 2 | Denis LAW | 1958-1959 | 6 | 1 |
| 3 | David STEELE | 1923 | 3 | 0 |
| 4 | James WATSON | 1953 | 1 | 0 |
| | TOTAL | 1923-1959 | 24 | 9 |

## 19  HULL CITY FC

| | Player | Period | Caps | Goals |
|---|---|---|---|---|
| 1 | Michael GILHOOLEY | 1922 | 1 | 0 |
| | TOTAL | 1922 | 1 | 0 |

## 20  IPSWICH TOWN FC

| | Player | Period | Caps | Goals |
|---|---|---|---|---|
| 1 | John WARK | 1979-1983 | 26 | 7 |
| 2 | George BURLEY | 1979-1982 | 11 | 0 |
| 3 | Alan BRAZIL | 1980-1982 | 11 | 0 |
| | TOTAL | 1979-1983 | 48 | 7 |

## 21  LEEDS UNITED FC

| | Player | Period | Caps | Goals |
|---|---|---|---|---|
| 1 | William BREMNER | 1965-1975 | 54 | 3 |
| 2 | Gary McALLISTER | 1990-1996 | 41 | 4 |
| 3 | Joseph JORDAN | 1973-1977 | 27 | 7 |
| 4 | Francis GRAY | 1976-1983 | 25 | 1 |
| 5 | Peter LORIMER | 1969-1975 | 21 | 4 |
| 6 | Gordon McQUEEN | 1974-1977 | 17 | 3 |
| 7 | David HARVEY | 1972-1976 | 16 | 0 |
| 8 | Edwin GRAY | 1969-1976 | 12 | 3 |
| 9 | Arthur GRAHAM | 1977-1981 | 11 | 2 |
| 10 | Gordon STRACHAN | 1989-1992 | 9 | 1 |
| 11 | David HOPKIN | 1997-1999 | 5 | 2 |
| 12 | Robert COLLINS | 1965 | 3 | 0 |
| 13 | Dominic MATTEO | 2000-2001 | 3 | 0 |
| 14 | William BELL | 1966 | 2 | 0 |
| 15 | David STEWART | 1977 | 1 | 0 |
| | TOTAL | 1965-2001 | 247 | 30 |

## 22  LEICESTER FOSSE/LEICESTER CITY FC

| | Player | Period | Caps | Goals |
|---|---|---|---|---|
| 1 | Matthew ELLIOTT | 1997-2001 | 15 | 1 |
| 2 | David GIBSON | 1963-1964 | 7 | 3 |
| 3 | Andrew AITKEN | 1910-1911 | 3 | 0 |
| 4 | Francis McLINTOCK | 1963 | 3 | 1 |
| 5 | Gary McALLISTER | 1990 | 3 | 0 |
| 6 | Ian WILSON | 1987 | 2 | 0 |
| 7 | Callum DAVIDSON | 2000-2001 | 2 | 0 |
| 8 | John PATERSON | 1920 | 1 | 0 |
| 9 | John DUNCAN | 1925 | 1 | 1 |
| 10 | John ANDERSON | 1954 | 1 | 0 |
| 11 | John SINCLAIR | 1966 | 1 | 0 |
| | TOTAL | 1910-2001 | 39 | 6 |

## 23  LIVERPOOL FC

| | Player | Period | Caps | Goals |
|---|---|---|---|---|
| 1 | Kenneth DALGLISH | 1977-1986 | 55 | 14 |
| 2 | Graeme SOUNESS | 1978-1984 | 37 | 2 |
| 3 | William LIDDELL | 1946-1955 | 28 | 6 |
| 4 | Stephen NICOL | 1984-1991 | 27 | 0 |
| 5 | Alan HANSEN | 1979-1987 | 26 | 0 |

| 6 | Thomas YOUNGER | 1956-1958 | 16 | 0 |
|---|---|---|---|---|
| 7 | Ian ST JOHN | 1961-1965 | 14 | 8 |
| 8 | Gary GILLESPIE | 1987-1990 | 13 | 0 |
| 9 | Alexander RAISBECK | 1900-1907 | 8 | 0 |
| 10 | Thomas LAWRENCE | 1963-1969 | 3 | 0 |
| 11 | John WARK | 1984 | 3 | 0 |
| 12 | Kenneth CAMPBELL | 1920 | 2 | 0 |
| 13 | Donald McKINLAY | 1922 | 2 | 0 |
| 14 | James McDOUGALL | 1931 | 2 | 0 |
| 15 | Ronald YEATS | 1964-1965 | 2 | 0 |
| 16 | Francis McGARVEY | 1979 | 2 | 0 |
| 17 | George ALLAN | 1897 | 1 | 0 |
| 18 | Hugh MORGAN | 1899 | 1 | 0 |
| 19 | William DUNLOP | 1906 | 1 | 0 |
| 20 | Thomas MILLER | 1920 | 1 | 2 |
| 21 | John McNAB | 1923 | 1 | 0 |
| | TOTAL | 1897-1991 | 245 | 32 |

## 24 LUTON TOWN FC

| | Player | Period | Caps | Goals |
|---|---|---|---|---|
| 1 | Michael CULLEN | 1956 | 1 | 0 |
| | TOTAL | 1956 | 1 | 0 |

## 25 MANCHESTER CITY FC

| | Player | Period | Caps | Goals |
|---|---|---|---|---|
| 1 | Richard HARTFORD | 1975-1982 | 36 | 3 |
| 2 | William DONACHIE | 1972-1978 | 35 | 0 |
| 3 | Denis LAW | 1960-1974 | 11 | 2 |
| 4 | James McMULLAN | 1926-1929 | 8 | 0 |
| 5 | Robert JOHNSTONE | 1955-1956 | 4 | 2 |
| 6 | Paul DICKOV | 2000 | 3 | 0 |
| 7 | George STEWART | 1907 | 2 | 0 |
| 8 | George LIVINGSTON | 1906 | 1 | 0 |
| 9 | Matthew BUSBY | 1933 | 1 | 0 |
| 10 | James McLUCKIE | 1933 | 1 | 0 |
| 11 | John PLENDERLEITH | 1960 | 1 | 0 |
| | TOTAL | 1906-2000 | 103 | 7 |

## 26 MANCHESTER UNITED FC

| | Player | Period | Caps | Goals |
|---|---|---|---|---|
| 1 | Denis LAW | 1962-1972 | 35 | 25 |
| 2 | Martin BUCHAN | 1972-1978 | 32 | 0 |
| 3 | Brian McCLAIR | 1987-1993 | 26 | 2 |
| 4 | William MORGAN | 1972-1974 | 20 | 1 |
| 5 | Joseph JORDAN | 1978-1981 | 20 | 2 |
| 6 | Luigi MACARI | 1973-1978 | 18 | 2 |
| 7 | James HOLTON | 1973-1974 | 15 | 2 |
| 8 | Arthur ALBISTON | 1982-1986 | 14 | 0 |
| 9 | James LEIGHTON | 1988-1990 | 14 | 0 |
| 10 | Gordon McQUEEN | 1978-1981 | 13 | 2 |
| 11 | Gordon STRACHAN | 1985-1987 | 13 | 2 |
| 12 | Alexander FORSYTH | 1973-1975 | 6 | 0 |
| 13 | Patrick CRERAND | 1963-1965 | 5 | 0 |
| 14 | James DELANEY | 1947-1948 | 4 | 0 |
| 15 | George GRAHAM | 1973 | 4 | 2 |
| 16 | Thomas MILLER | 1921 | 2 | 0 |
| 17 | Alexander BELL | 1912 | 1 | 0 |
| 18 | Neil McBAIN | 1922 | 1 | 0 |
| 19 | Francis BURNS | 1969 | 1 | 0 |
| 20 | Stewart HOUSTON | 1975 | 1 | 0 |
| | TOTAL | 1912-1993 | 245 | 40 |

## 27 MIDDLESBROUGH FC

| | Player | Period | Caps | Goals |
|---|---|---|---|---|
| 1 | John MARSHALL | 1921-1922 | 6 | 0 |
| 2 | Andrew WILSON | 1922-1923 | 6 | 7 |
| 3 | Derek WHYTE | 1992-1996 | 6 | 0 |

| 4 | Andrew AITKEN | 1907-1908 | 3 | 0 |
|---|---|---|---|---|
| 5 | Robert BAXTER | 1938-1939 | 3 | 0 |
| 6 | Graeme SOUNESS | 1974-1975 | 3 | 0 |
| 7 | James WATSON | 1909 | 2 | 0 |
| 8 | John MILNE | 1938-1939 | 2 | 0 |
| 9 | Alexander BROWN | 1904 | 1 | 0 |
| 10 | Stewart DAVIDSON | 1921 | 1 | 0 |
| 11 | Robert BRUCE | 1933 | 1 | 0 |
| 12 | David CUMMING | 1938 | 1 | 0 |
| 13 | James STEWART | 1978 | 1 | 0 |
| | TOTAL | 1904-1996 | 36 | 7 |

## 28 NEWCASTLE UNITED FC

| | Player | Period | Caps | Goals |
|---|---|---|---|---|
| 1 | Robert MONCUR | 1968-1972 | 16 | 0 |
| 2 | Hugh GALLACHER | 1926-1930 | 13 | 19 |
| 3 | Kevin GALLACHER | 1999-2001 | 9 | 1 |
| 4 | Andrew AITKEN | 1901-1906 | 8 | 0 |
| 5 | Peter McWILLIAM | 1905-1911 | 8 | 0 |
| 6 | Frank BRENNAN | 1946-1954 | 7 | 0 |
| 7 | Robert AITKEN | 1990 | 6 | 0 |
| 8 | Wilfrid LOW | 1911-1920 | 5 | 0 |
| 9 | Alexander HIGGINS | 1910-1911 | 4 | 1 |
| 10 | James HAY | 1912-1914 | 4 | 0 |
| 11 | Robert TEMPLETON | 1903-1904 | 3 | 0 |
| 12 | James HOWIE | 1905-1908 | 3 | 2 |
| 13 | James SMITH | 1973-1974 | 3 | 0 |
| 14 | Ronald ORR | 1902-1904 | 2 | 1 |
| 15 | Andrew McCOMBIE | 1905 | 2 | 0 |
| 16 | Robert ANCELL | 1936 | 2 | 0 |
| 17 | Thomas PEARSON | 1947 | 2 | 0 |
| 18 | Robert MITCHELL | 1951 | 2 | 1 |
| 19 | Anthony GREEN | 1972 | 2 | 0 |
| 20 | Robert McCOLL | 1902 | 1 | 0 |
| 21 | George WILSON | 1909 | 1 | 0 |
| 22 | James LAWRENCE | 1911 | 1 | 0 |
| 23 | William COWAN | 1924 | 1 | 1 |
| 24 | Neil HARRIS | 1924 | 1 | 0 |
| 25 | Robert McKAY | 1927 | 1 | 0 |
| 26 | James BOYD | 1933 | 1 | 0 |
| 27 | Thomas CRAIG | 1976 | 1 | 0 |
| 28 | Stephen GLASS | 1998 | 1 | 0 |
| 29 | Stephen CALDWELL | 2001 | 1 | 0 |
| | TOTAL | 1901-2001 | 111 | 26 |

## 29 NORWICH CITY FC

| | Player | Period | Caps | Goals |
|---|---|---|---|---|
| 1 | Edward MacDOUGALL | 1975 | 7 | 3 |
| 2 | Bryan GUNN | 1990-1994 | 6 | 0 |
| 3 | Robert FLECK | 1990-1991 | 4 | 0 |
| 4 | James BONE | 1972 | 2 | 1 |
| | TOTAL | 1972-1994 | 19 | 4 |

## 30 NOTTINGHAM FOREST FC

| | Player | Period | Caps | Goals |
|---|---|---|---|---|
| 1 | John ROBERTSON | 1978-1982 | 26 | 7 |
| 2 | Scot GEMMILL | 1995-1998 | 13 | 0 |
| 3 | Kenneth BURNS | 1978-1981 | 12 | 0 |
| 4 | Archibald GEMMILL | 1978-1979 | 11 | 4 |
| 5 | Francis GRAY | 1979-1981 | 7 | 0 |
| 6 | Peter CORMACK | 1970-1971 | 5 | 0 |
| 7 | James IMLACH | 1958 | 4 | 0 |
| | TOTAL | 1958-1998 | 78 | 11 |

## 31 OLDHAM ATHLETIC FC

| | Player | Period | Caps | Goals |
|---|---|---|---|---|
| 1 | Andrew GORAM | 1985-1987 | 4 | 0 |
| 2 | Joseph DONNACHIE | 1913-1914 | 3 | 1 |
| 3 | Paul BERNARD | 1995 | 2 | 0 |
| 4 | David WILSON | 1913 | 1 | 0 |
| | TOTAL | 1913-1995 | 10 | 1 |

## 32 PORTSMOUTH FC

| | Player | Period | Caps | Goals |
|---|---|---|---|---|
| 1 | James SCOULAR | 1951-1952 | 9 | 0 |
| 2 | John HENDERSON | 1953-1955 | 5 | 1 |
| 3 | James EASSON | 1931-1933 | 3 | 1 |
| 4 | Alexander WILSON | 1954 | 1 | 0 |
| | TOTAL | 1931-1955 | 18 | 2 |

## 33 PRESTON NORTH END FC

| | Player | Period | Caps | Goals |
|---|---|---|---|---|
| 1 | Thomas DOCHERTY | 1951-1958 | 22 | 1 |
| 2 | William CUNNINGHAM | 1954-1955 | 8 | 0 |
| 3 | Andrew BEATTIE | 1937-1938 | 7 | 0 |
| 4 | Peter McBRIDE | 1904-1909 | 6 | 0 |
| 5 | William SHANKLY | 1938-1939 | 5 | 0 |
| 6 | Alexander JAMES | 1925-1929 | 4 | 2 |
| 7 | Frank O'DONNELL | 1937 | 4 | 2 |
| 8 | Andrew McLAREN | 1947 | 4 | 3 |
| 9 | Thomas SMITH | 1938 | 1 | 0 |
| 10 | George MUTCH | 1938 | 1 | 0 |
| 11 | Robert BEATTIE | 1938 | 1 | 0 |
| 12 | James DOUGALL | 1939 | 1 | 1 |
| | TOTAL | 1904-1958 | 64 | 9 |

## 34 QUEEN'S PARK RANGERS FC, LONDON

| | Player | Period | Caps | Goals |
|---|---|---|---|---|
| 1 | Donald MASSON | 1976-1977 | 14 | 5 |
| 2 | John SPENCER | 1997 | 1 | 0 |
| | TOTAL | 1976-1997 | 15 | 5 |

## 35 ROYAL ENGINEERS FC, CHATHAM

| | Player | Period | Caps | Goals |
|---|---|---|---|---|
| 1 | Henry RENNY-TAILYOUR | 1873 | 1 | 1 |
| 2 | John BLACKBURN | 1873 | 1 | 0 |
| | TOTAL | 1873 | 2 | 1 |

## 36 SHEFFIELD UNITED FC

| | Player | Period | Caps | Goals |
|---|---|---|---|---|
| 1 | Edmond COLQUHOUN | 1971-1973 | 9 | 0 |
| 2 | Alexander FORBES | 1947 | 5 | 1 |
| 3 | James BROWN | 1975 | 1 | 0 |
| | TOTAL | 1947-1975 | 15 | 1 |

## 37 SHEFFIELD WEDNESDAY FC

| | Player | Period | Caps | Goals |
|---|---|---|---|---|
| 1 | Andrew WILSON | 1907-1914 | 6 | 2 |
| 2 | James McCALLIOG | 1967-1968 | 4 | 1 |
| 3 | George ROBERTSON | 1912-1913 | 3 | 0 |
| 4 | James BLAIR | 1920 | 2 | 0 |
| 5 | John LYALL | 1905 | 1 | 0 |
| 6 | David McLEAN | 1912 | 1 | 0 |
| 7 | James CAMPBELL | 1913 | 1 | 0 |
| | TOTAL | 1905-1968 | 18 | 3 |

## 38 SOUTHAMPTON FC

| | Player | Period | Caps | Goals |
|---|---|---|---|---|
| 1 | John ROBERTSON | 1899 | 1 | 0 |
| 2 | Ian BLACK | 1948 | 1 | 0 |
| | TOTAL | 1899-1948 | 2 | 0 |

## 39 STOKE CITY FC

| | Player | Period | Caps | Goals |
|---|---|---|---|---|
| 1 | Thomas HYSLOP | 1896 | 1 | 0 |
| 2 | William MAXWELL | 1898 | 1 | 0 |
| | TOTAL | 1896-1898 | 2 | 0 |

## 40 SUNDERLAND FC

| | Player | Period | Caps | Goals |
|---|---|---|---|---|
| 1 | James BAXTER | 1965-1967 | 10 | 0 |
| 2 | Charles THOMSON | 1909-1914 | 9 | 1 |
| 3 | Allan JOHNSTON | 1998-2000 | 9 | 2 |
| 4 | Donald HUTCHISON | 2000-2001 | 6 | 1 |
| 5 | James WATSON | 1903-1905 | 4 | 0 |
| 6 | James CONNOR | 1930-1934 | 4 | 0 |
| 7 | John DOIG | 1896-1903 | 3 | 0 |
| 8 | George AITKEN | 1952-1954 | 3 | 0 |
| 9 | Thomas WRIGHT | 1952-1953 | 3 | 0 |
| 10 | Andrew McCOMBIE | 1903 | 2 | 0 |
| 11 | William CLUNAS | 1924-1925 | 2 | 1 |
| 12 | Alexander HASTINGS | 1935-1937 | 2 | 0 |
| 13 | William FRASER | 1954 | 2 | 0 |
| 14 | Joseph McDONALD | 1955 | 2 | 0 |
| 15 | George MULHALL | 1962-1963 | 2 | 0 |
| 16 | Hugh WILSON | 1897 | 1 | 0 |
| 17 | Thomas TAIT | 1911 | 1 | 0 |
| 18 | Patrick GALLACHER | 1934 | 1 | 1 |
| 19 | Alexander McNAB | 1937 | 1 | 0 |
| 20 | Charles THOMSON | 1937 | 1 | 0 |
| 21 | Robert JOHNSTON | 1937 | 1 | 0 |
| 22 | Neil MARTIN | 1965 | 1 | 0 |
| 23 | William HUGHES | 1975 | 1 | 0 |
| | TOTAL | 1896-2001 | 71 | 6 |

## 41 SWINDON TOWN FC

| | Player | Period | Caps | Goals |
|---|---|---|---|---|
| 1 | John WALKER | 1911-1913 | 9 | 0 |
| | TOTAL | 1911-1913 | 9 | 0 |

## 42 THE WANDERERS FC, LONDON

| | Player | Period | Caps | Goals |
|---|---|---|---|---|
| 1 | Arthur KINNAIRD | 1873 | 1 | 0 |
| | TOTAL | 1873 | 1 | 0 |

## 43 TOTTENHAM HOTSPUR FC, LONDON

| | Player | Period | Caps | Goals |
|---|---|---|---|---|
| 1 | Colin CALDERWOOD | 1995-1998 | 32 | 1 |
| 2 | William BROWN | 1959-1965 | 24 | 0 |
| 3 | Steven ARCHIBALD | 1980-1984 | 22 | 3 |
| 4 | David MACKAY | 1959-1965 | 18 | 4 |
| 5 | John WHITE | 1959-1964 | 18 | 1 |
| 6 | Alan GILZEAN | 1965-1971 | 17 | 8 |
| 7 | Gordon DURIE | 1991-1993 | 13 | 2 |
| 8 | Richard GOUGH | 1986-1987 | 8 | 0 |
| 9 | Neil SULLIVAN | 2000-2001 | 6 | 0 |
| 10 | Alfred CONN | 1975 | 2 | 0 |
| 11 | Alan BRAZIL | 1983 | 2 | 1 |
| 12 | James ROBERTSON | 1964 | 1 | 0 |
| | TOTAL | 1959-2001 | 163 | 20 |

## 44 TRANMERE ROVERS FC, BIRKENHEAD

| | Player | Period | Caps | Goals |
|---|---|---|---|---|
| 1 | Patrick NEVIN | 1993-1996 | 14 | 4 |
| | TOTAL | 1993-1996 | 14 | 4 |

## 45 WATFORD FC

| | Player | Period | Caps | Goals |
|---|---|---|---|---|
| 1 | Maurice JOHNSTON | 1984 | 3 | 1 |
| | TOTAL | 1984 | 3 | 1 |

## 46 WEST BROMWICH ALBION FC

| | Player | Period | Caps | Goals |
|---|---|---|---|---|
| 1 | William JOHNSTON | 1977-1978 | 13 | 0 |
| 2 | Richard HARTFORD | 1972 | 6 | 0 |

| 3 | Douglas FRASER | 1968 | 2 | 0 |
| 4 | Robert HOPE | 1968 | 2 | 0 |
| 5 | Alexander McNAB | 1939 | 1 | 0 |
| | TOTAL | 1939-1978 | 24 | 0 |

## 47 WEST HAM UNITED FC, LONDON

| | Player | Period | Caps | Goals |
|---|---|---|---|---|
| 1 | Raymond STEWART | 1981-1987 | 10 | 1 |
| 2 | Francis McAVENNIE | 1985-1986 | 4 | 1 |
| 3 | John DICK | 1959 | 1 | 0 |
| 4 | Christian DAILLY | 2001 | 1 | 0 |
| | TOTAL | 1959-2001 | 16 | 2 |

## 48 WIMBLEDON FC, LONDON

| | Player | Period | Caps | Goals |
|---|---|---|---|---|
| 1 | Neil SULLIVAN | 1997-2000 | 16 | 0 |
| 2 | Brian McALLISTER | 1997 | 3 | 0 |
| | TOTAL | 1997-2000 | 19 | 0 |

## 49 WOLVERHAMPTON WANDERERS FC

| | Player | Period | Caps | Goals |
|---|---|---|---|---|
| 1 | Andrew GRAY | 1980-1983 | 13 | 4 |
| 2 | Francis MUNRO | 1971-1975 | 9 | 0 |
| 3 | Hugh CURRAN | 1969-1971 | 5 | 1 |
| 4 | James McCALLIOG | 1971 | 1 | 0 |
| | TOTAL | 1969-1983 | 28 | 5 |

## 50 WOOLWICH ARSENAL/ARSENAL FC, LONDON

| | Player | Period | Caps | Goals |
|---|---|---|---|---|
| 1 | Charles NICHOLAS | 1983-1987 | 13 | 3 |
| 2 | Alexander FORBES | 1950-1952 | 9 | 0 |
| 3 | George GRAHAM | 1971-1972 | 8 | 1 |
| 4 | Archibald MACAULEY | 1947-1948 | 6 | 0 |
| 5 | Francis McLINTOCK | 1964-1971 | 6 | 0 |
| 6 | David HERD | 1958-1961 | 5 | 3 |
| 7 | Alexander JAMES | 1929-1932 | 4 | 1 |
| 8 | Thomas FITCHIE | 1905-1906 | 3 | 1 |
| 9 | James SHARP | 1907-1908 | 3 | 0 |
| 10 | Thomas DOCHERTY | 1958-1959 | 3 | 0 |
| 11 | John URE | 1963-1967 | 3 | 0 |
| 12 | William HARPER | 1926 | 2 | 0 |
| 13 | John HENDERSON | 1958 | 2 | 0 |
| 14 | Robert WILSON | 1971 | 2 | 0 |
| 15 | Robert TEMPLETON | 1905 | 1 | 0 |
| 16 | John GRAHAM | 1921 | 1 | 0 |
| 17 | James LOGIE | 1952 | 1 | 0 |
| 18 | George WOOD | 1982 | 1 | 0 |
| | TOTAL | 1905-1987 | 73 | 9 |

## French Clubs (3)

### 1 FC METZ

| | Player | Period | Caps | Goals |
|---|---|---|---|---|
| 1 | Eric BLACK | 1987 | 2 | 0 |
| | TOTAL | 1987 | 2 | 0 |

### 2 AS MONACO

| | Player | Period | Caps | Goals |
|---|---|---|---|---|
| 1 | John COLLINS | 1996-1998 | 16 | 3 |
| | TOTAL | 1996-1998 | 16 | 3 |

### 3 FC NANTES

| | Player | Period | Caps | Goals |
|---|---|---|---|---|
| 1 | Maurice JOHNSTON | 1987-1989 | 15 | 7 |
| | TOTAL | 1987-1989 | 15 | 7 |

## German Clubs (3)

### 1 FC BAYERN, MUNICH

| | Player | Period | Caps | Goals |
|---|---|---|---|---|
| 1 | Alan MCINALLY | 1989-1990 | 6 | 2 |
| | TOTAL | 1989-1990 | 6 | 2 |

### 2 BV BORUSSIA, DORTMUND

| | Player | Period | Caps | Goals |
|---|---|---|---|---|
| 1 | Murdo MACLEOD | 1988-1990 | 13 | 1 |
| 2 | Paul LAMBERT | 1996-1997 | 7 | 0 |
| 3 | Scott BOOTH | 1998 | 4 | 0 |
| | TOTAL | 1988-1998 | 24 | 1 |

### 3 VFL WOLFSBURG

| | Player | Period | Caps | Goals |
|---|---|---|---|---|
| 1 | Brian O'NEIL | 1999-2000 | 4 | 0 |
| | TOTAL | 1999-2000 | 4 | 0 |

## Italian Clubs (3)

### 1 AC MILAN

| | Player | Period | Caps | Goals |
|---|---|---|---|---|
| 1 | Joseph JORDAN | 1981-1982 | 5 | 2 |
| | TOTAL | 1981-1982 | 5 | 2 |

### 2 UC SAMPDORIA, GENOA

| | Player | Period | Caps | Goals |
|---|---|---|---|---|
| 1 | Graeme SOUNESS | 1984-1986 | 14 | 2 |
| | TOTAL | 1984-1986 | 14 | 2 |

### 3 TURIN

| | Player | Period | Caps | Goals |
|---|---|---|---|---|
| 1 | Denis LAW | 1961-1962 | 3 | 2 |
| | TOTAL | 1961-1962 | 3 | 2 |

## Welsh Clubs (2)

### 1 CARDIFF CITY FC

| | Player | Period | Caps | Goals |
|---|---|---|---|---|
| 1 | James BLAIR | 1921-1924 | 6 | 0 |
| 2 | James NELSON | 1925-1930 | 4 | 0 |
| | TOTAL | 1921-1930 | 10 | 0 |

### 2 LLANELLI FC

| | Player | Period | Caps | Goals |
|---|---|---|---|---|
| 1 | John MARSHALL | 1924 | 1 | 0 |
| | TOTAL | 1924 | 1 | 0 |

## Belgian Clubs (1)

### 1 SC LOKEREN

| | Player | Period | Caps | Goals |
|---|---|---|---|---|
| 1 | James BETT | 1983-1985 | 11 | 1 |
| | TOTAL | 1983-1985 | 11 | 1 |

## Spanish Clubs (1)

### 1 FC BARCELONA

| | Player | Period | Caps | Goals |
|---|---|---|---|---|
| 1 | Steven ARCHIBALD | 1985-1986 | 4 | 0 |
| | TOTAL | 1985-1986 | 4 | 0 |

## Dutch Clubs (1)

### 1 FC TWENTE, ENSCHEDE

| | Player | Period | Caps | Goals |
|---|---|---|---|---|
| 1 | Scott BOOTH | 2001 | 1 | 1 |
| | TOTAL | 2001 | 1 | 1 |

# Appearances

| | Player | Period | Apps |
|---|---|---|---|
| 1 | Kenneth DALGLISH | 1971-1986 | 102 |
| 2 | James LEIGHTON | 1982-1998 | 91 |
| 3 | Alexander McLEISH | 1980-1993 | 77 |
| 4 | Paul McSTAY | 1983-1997 | 76 |
| 5 | Thomas BOYD | 1990-2001 | 71 |
| 6 | William MILLER | 1975-1989 | 65 |
| 7 | Daniel MCGRAIN | 1973-1982 | 62 |
| 8 | Richard GOUGH | 1983-1993 | 61 |
| | Alistair McCOIST | 1986-1998 | 61 |
| 10 | John COLLINS | 1988-1999 | 58 |
| 11 | Robert AITKEN | 1979-1991 | 57 |
| | Gary McALLISTER | 1990-1999 | 57 |
| 13 | Denis LAW | 1958-1974 | 55 |
| | Maurice MALPAS | 1984-1992 | 55 |
| 15 | William BREMNER | 1965-1975 | 54 |
| | Graeme SOUNESS | 1974-1986 | 54 |
| 17 | George YOUNG | 1946-1957 | 53 |
| | Alan ROUGH | 1976-1986 | 53 |
| | Kevin GALLACHER | 1988-2001 | 53 |
| 20 | Joseph JORDAN | 1973-1982 | 52 |
| 21 | Colin HENDRY | 1993-2001 | 51 |
| 22 | Richard HARTFORD | 1972-1982 | 50 |
| | Gordon STRACHAN | 1980-1992 | 50 |
| 24 | Robert EVANS | 1948-1960 | 48 |
| 25 | John GREIG | 1964-1975 | 44 |
| 26 | Archibald GEMMILL | 1971-1981 | 43 |
| | Andrew GORAM | 1985-1998 | 43 |
| | Gordon DURIE | 1987-1998 | 43 |
| 29 | Craig BURLEY | 1995-2001 | 42 |
| 30 | Eric CALDOW | 1957-1963 | 40 |
| | Stewart McKIMMIE | 1989-1996 | 40 |
| | Stuart McCALL | 1990-1998 | 40 |
| 33 | Lawrence REILLY | 1948-1957 | 38 |
| | William JARDINE | 1970-1979 | 38 |
| | Maurice JOHNSTON | 1984-1991 | 38 |
| 36 | Colin CALDERWOOD | 1995-1999 | 36 |
| 37 | William DONACHIE | 1972-1978 | 35 |
| | David NAREY | 1977-1989 | 35 |
| 39 | James BAXTER | 1960-1967 | 34 |
| | Martin BUCHAN | 1971-1978 | 34 |
| 41 | Francis GRAY | 1976-1983 | 32 |
| 42 | Alan MORTON | 1920-1932 | 31 |
| | Robert COLLINS | 1950-1965 | 31 |
| 44 | William STEEL | 1947-1953 | 30 |
| | Gordon McQUEEN | 1974-1981 | 30 |
| | Brian McCLAIR | 1986-1993 | 30 |
| 47 | Robert WALKER | 1900-1913 | 29 |
| | William McNEILL | 1961-1972 | 29 |
| | William HENDERSON | 1962-1971 | 29 |
| | John WARK | 1979-1984 | 29 |
| | William McKINLAY | 1993-1998 | 29 |
| 52 | William LIDDELL | 1946-1955 | 28 |
| | William BROWN | 1958-1965 | 28 |
| | Ronald McKINNON | 1965-1971 | 28 |
| | John ROBERTSON | 1978-1983 | 28 |
| | Patrick NEVIN | 1986-1996 | 28 |
| | Darren JACKSON | 1995-1998 | 28 |
| 58 | David HAY | 1970-1974 | 27 |
| | Steven ARCHIBALD | 1980-1986 | 27 |
| | Stephen NICOL | 1984-1991 | 27 |
| | David McPHERSON | 1989-1993 | 27 |
| | Christian DAILLY | 1997-2001 | 27 |
| | David WEIR | 1997-2001 | 27 |
| 64 | Alan HANSEN | 1979-1987 | 26 |
| | James BETT | 1982-1990 | 26 |
| | Paul LAMBERT | 1995-2001 | 26 |
| 67 | James COWAN | 1948-1952 | 25 |
| | Thomas DOCHERTY | 1951-1959 | 25 |
| 69 | William WOODBURN | 1947-1952 | 24 |
| | Samuel COX | 1949-1954 | 24 |
| | Thomas YOUNGER | 1955-1958 | 24 |
| | Alexander HAMILTON | 1961-1965 | 24 |
| | Luigi MACARI | 1972-1978 | 24 |
| | Bruce RIOCH | 1975-1978 | 24 |
| | Alan McLAREN | 1992-1995 | 24 |
| | William DODDS | 1996-2001 | 24 |
| 77 | Andrew ANDERSON | 1933-1938 | 23 |
| | James JOHNSTONE | 1964-1974 | 23 |
| | Edward McCREADIE | 1965-1969 | 23 |
| 80 | David MACKAY | 1957-1965 | 22 |
| | John WHITE | 1959-1964 | 22 |
| | David WILSON | 1960-1965 | 22 |
| | Alan GILZEAN | 1963-1971 | 22 |
| | William JOHNSTON | 1965-1978 | 22 |
| | Thomas FORSYTH | 1971-1978 | 22 |
| | David COOPER | 1979-1990 | 22 |
| | Thomas McKINLAY | 1995-1998 | 22 |
| | Neil SULLIVAN | 1997-2001 | 22 |
| 89 | Charles THOMSON | 1904-1914 | 21 |
| | Ian ST JOHN | 1959-1965 | 21 |
| | William MORGAN | 1967-1974 | 21 |
| | Colin STEIN | 1968-1973 | 21 |
| | Peter LORIMER | 1969-1975 | 21 |
| 94 | Alexander SMITH | 1898-1911 | 20 |
| | Hugh GALLACHER | 1924-1935 | 20 |
| | Thomas WALKER | 1934-1939 | 20 |
| | Douglas COWIE | 1953-1958 | 20 |
| | Kenneth BURNS | 1974-1981 | 20 |
| | Andrew GRAY | 1975-1985 | 20 |
| | Paul STURROCK | 1981-1987 | 20 |
| | Charles NICHOLAS | 1983-1989 | 20 |
| | Murdo MacLEOD | 1985-1991 | 20 |
| | Iain DURRANT | 1987-2000 | 20 |
| 104 | George BROWN | 1930-1938 | 19 |
| | John HEWIE | 1956-1960 | 19 |
| 106 | Alexander MASSIE | 1931-1937 | 18 |
| | Gordon SMITH | 1946-1957 | 18 |
| | Graham LEGGAT | 1956-1960 | 18 |
| | Thomas GEMMELL | 1966-1971 | 18 |
| | Eoin JESS | 1992-1999 | 18 |
| | Scott BOOTH | 1993-2001 | 18 |
| 112 | Alexander JACKSON | 1925-1930 | 17 |
| | Robert McPHAIL | 1927-1937 | 17 |
| | William WADDELL | 1946-1954 | 17 |
| | Robert JOHNSTONE | 1951-1956 | 17 |
| | John MUDIE | 1956-1958 | 17 |
| | Robert CLARK | 1967-1973 | 17 |
| | Thomas HUTCHISON | 1973-1975 | 17 |
| | Donald MASSON | 1976-1978 | 17 |
| | Scot GEMMILL | 1995-2001 | 17 |
| 121 | John ROBERTSON | 1898-1905 | 16 |
| | James BROWNLIE | 1909-1914 | 16 |
| | James McMULLAN | 1920-1929 | 16 |
| | Alexander SCOTT | 1956-1966 | 16 |
| | Patrick CRERAND | 1961-1965 | 16 |
| | Charles COOKE | 1965-1975 | 16 |
| | Patrick STANTON | 1966-1974 | 16 |
| | Robert MONCUR | 1968-1972 | 16 |
| | David HARVEY | 1972-1976 | 16 |
| | Craig LEVEIN | 1990-1994 | 16 |
| | John ROBERTSON | 1990-1995 | 16 |
| | Donald HUTCHISON | 1999-2001 | 16 |
| 133 | Alexander McNAIR | 1906-1920 | 15 |
| | David MEIKLEJOHN | 1922-1933 | 15 |
| | Alexander PARKER | 1955-1958 | 15 |
| | James HOLTON | 1973-1974 | 15 |
| | Matthew ELLIOTT | 1997-2001 | 15 |
| 138 | Walter ARNOTT | 1883-1893 | 14 |
| | John DRUMMOND | 1892-1903 | 14 |
| | Neil GIBSON | 1895-1905 | 14 |
| | Andrew AITKEN | 1901-1911 | 14 |
| | Douglas DUNCAN | 1932-1937 | 14 |
| | James DAWSON | 1934-1939 | 14 |
| | James SIMPSON | 1934-1937 | 14 |
| | Alexander FORBES | 1947-1952 | 14 |
| | Allan BROWN | 1950-1954 | 14 |
| | John McCOLL | 1950-1958 | 14 |
| | Duncan MACKAY | 1959-1962 | 14 |
| | Derek JOHNSTONE | 1973-1979 | 14 |
| | Arthur ALBISTON | 1982-1986 | 14 |
| | John SPENCER | 1994-1997 | 14 |
| | Callum DAVIDSON | 1998-2001 | 14 |
| 152 | Charles CAMPBELL | 1874-1886 | 13 |
| | Robert McCOLL | 1896-1908 | 13 |
| | Henry RENNIE | 1900-1908 | 13 |
| | William McSTAY | 1921-1928 | 13 |
| | James DELANEY | 1935-1948 | 13 |
| | John O'HARE | 1970-1972 | 13 |
| | Alan BRAZIL | 1980-1983 | 13 |
| | Gary GILLESPIE | 1987-1990 | 13 |
| | John McGINLAY | 1994-1997 | 13 |
| 162 | John CAMPBELL | 1893-1903 | 12 |
| | Nicol SMITH | 1897-1902 | 12 |
| | James McMENEMY | 1905-1920 | 12 |
| | Andrew CUNNINGHAM | 1920-1927 | 12 |
| | Andrew WILSON | 1920-1923 | 12 |
| | John HARKNESS | 1927-1933 | 12 |
| | George STEVENSON | 1927-1934 | 12 |
| | Thomas RING | 1953-1957 | 12 |
| | William FERNIE | 1954-1958 | 12 |
| | Robert MURDOCH | 1965-1969 | 12 |
| | Edwin GRAY | 1969-1976 | 12 |
| | George GRAHAM | 1971-1973 | 12 |
| | Derek PARLANE | 1973-1977 | 12 |
| | Graeme SHARP | 1985-1988 | 12 |
| | Derek WHYTE | 1987-1999 | 12 |
| | Allan JOHNSTON | 1998-2001 | 12 |
| 178 | Robert HAMILTON | 1899-1911 | 11 |
| | Robert TEMPLETON | 1902-1913 | 11 |
| | Alexander BENNETT | 1904-1913 | 11 |
| | James HAY | 1905-1914 | 11 |
| | James QUINN | 1905-1912 | 11 |
| | William HARPER | 1923-1926 | 11 |
| | Joseph NIBLOE | 1929-1932 | 11 |
| | John URE | 1961-1967 | 11 |
| | Arthur GRAHAM | 1977-1981 | 11 |
| | Eamonn BANNON | 1979-1986 | 11 |
| | George BURLEY | 1979-1982 | 11 |
| | John McNAMARA | 1996-2000 | 11 |
| | Neil McCANN | 1998-2000 | 11 |
| | Colin CAMERON | 1999-2001 | 11 |
| 192 | Henry McNEIL | 1874-1881 | 10 |
| | John SMITH | 1877-1884 | 10 |
| | John BELL | 1890-1900 | 10 |
| | James GORDON | 1912-1920 | 10 |
| | John HUTTON | 1923-1928 | 10 |

| Player | Period | Apps |
|---|---|---|
| Douglas GRAY | 1928-1932 | 10 |
| George FARM | 1952-1959 | 10 |
| Robert LENNOX | 1966-1970 | 10 |
| Alexander FORSYTH | 1972-1975 | 10 |
| David PROVAN | 1979-1982 | 10 |
| Raymond STEWART | 1981-1987 | 10 |
| David SPEEDIE | 1985-1989 | 10 |
| James McINALLY | 1987-1993 | 10 |
| Simon DONNELLY | 1997-1998 | 10 |
| Barry FERGUSON | 1998-2001 | 10 |
| 207 William MacKINNON | 1872-1879 | 9 |
| James McAULAY | 1882-1887 | 9 |
| William SELLAR | 1885-1893 | 9 |
| John McPHERSON | 1888-1897 | 9 |
| William LAMBIE | 1892-1897 | 9 |
| William REID | 1911-1914 | 9 |
| John WALKER | 1911-1913 | 9 |
| James CRAPNELL | 1929-1932 | 9 |
| George CUMMINGS | 1935-1939 | 9 |
| William REDPATH | 1948-1952 | 9 |
| James SCOULAR | 1951-1952 | 9 |
| John MACKENZIE | 1953-1956 | 9 |
| John CUMMING | 1954-1960 | 9 |
| Francis McLINTOCK | 1963-1971 | 9 |
| Peter CORMACK | 1966-1971 | 9 |
| Edmond COLQUHOUN | 1971-1973 | 9 |
| Francis MUNRO | 1971-1975 | 9 |
| Ian FERGUSON | 1988-1997 | 9 |
| Brian IRVINE | 1990-1994 | 9 |
| 226 John McPHERSON | 1879-1885 | 8 |
| Joseph LINDSAY | 1880-1886 | 8 |
| James KELLY | 1888-1896 | 8 |
| Daniel DOYLE | 1892-1898 | 8 |
| Alexander RAISBECK | 1900-1907 | 8 |
| Peter McWILLIAM | 1905-1911 | 8 |
| James BLAIR | 1920-1924 | 8 |
| Thomas CAIRNS | 1920-1925 | 8 |
| Kenneth CAMPBELL | 1920-1922 | 8 |
| Alexander ARCHIBALD | 1921-1932 | 8 |
| Thomas MUIRHEAD | 1922-1929 | 8 |
| Alexander JAMES | 1925-1932 | 8 |
| James GIBSON | 1926-1930 | 8 |
| Thomas CRAIG | 1927-1930 | 8 |
| Daniel BLAIR | 1928-1932 | 8 |
| John JACKSON | 1931-1935 | 8 |
| David SHAW | 1946-1948 | 8 |
| Edward TURNBULL | 1948-1958 | 8 |
| George AITKEN | 1949-1954 | 8 |
| William CUNNINGHAM | 1954-1955 | 8 |
| James DAVIDSON | 1954-1955 | 8 |
| Ralph BRAND | 1960-1962 | 8 |
| Alexander YOUNG | 1960-1966 | 8 |
| John HUGHES | 1965-1969 | 8 |
| James HERRIOT | 1968-1969 | 8 |
| Colin JACKSON | 1975-1976 | 8 |
| Stuart KENNEDY | 1978-1981 | 8 |
| Paul HEGARTY | 1979-1983 | 8 |
| Thomas BURNS | 1981-1988 | 8 |
| Alan McINALLY | 1989-1990 | 8 |
| 256 Thomas VALLANCE | 1877-1881 | 7 |
| George GILLESPIE | 1880-1891 | 7 |
| Robert KELSO | 1885-1898 | 7 |
| John MARSHALL | 1921-1924 | 7 |
| James McGRORY | 1928-1933 | 7 |
| David McCULLOCH | 1934-1938 | 7 |
| Andrew BEATTIE | 1937-1938 | 7 |

| Player | Period | Apps |
|---|---|---|
| Frank BRENNAN | 1946-1954 | 7 |
| William THORNTON | 1946-1952 | 7 |
| Archibald MacAULEY | 1947-1948 | 7 |
| James MASON | 1948-1951 | 7 |
| John HENDERSON | 1953-1958 | 7 |
| Samuel BAIRD | 1956-1958 | 7 |
| David GIBSON | 1963-1964 | 7 |
| William WALLACE | 1964-1969 | 7 |
| Robert FERGUSON | 1965-1966 | 7 |
| John BROWNLIE | 1971-1975 | 7 |
| John BLACKLEY | 1973-1977 | 7 |
| Edward MacDOUGALL | 1975 | 7 |
| Francis McGARVEY | 1979-1984 | 7 |
| Alexander MUNRO | 1979-1980 | 7 |
| William THOMSON | 1980-1983 | 7 |
| Duncan FERGUSON | 1992-1997 | 7 |
| Duncan SHEARER | 1994-1995 | 7 |
| David HOPKIN | 1997-1999 | 7 |
| 281 Joseph TAYLOR | 1872-1876 | 6 |
| John FERGUSON | 1874-1878 | 6 |
| Alexander KENNEDY | 1875-1884 | 6 |
| John KAY | 1880-1884 | 6 |
| William ANDERSON | 1882-1885 | 6 |
| Robert SMELLIE | 1887-1893 | 6 |
| Alexander KEILLOR | 1891-1897 | 6 |
| Thomas WADDELL | 1891-1895 | 6 |
| Alexander McMAHON | 1892-1902 | 6 |
| David RUSSELL | 1895-1901 | 6 |
| Alexander KING | 1896-1899 | 6 |
| James WATSON | 1903-1909 | 6 |
| Thomas JACKSON | 1904-1907 | 6 |
| Peter McBRIDE | 1904-1909 | 6 |
| George WILSON | 1904-1909 | 6 |
| Andrew WILSON | 1907-1914 | 6 |
| Alexander DONALDSON | 1914-1922 | 6 |
| David MORRIS | 1923-1925 | 6 |
| James DUNN | 1925-1928 | 6 |
| Colin McNAB | 1930-1932 | 6 |
| Peter McGONAGLE | 1933-1934 | 6 |
| Frank O'DONNELL | 1937-1938 | 6 |
| William MILLER | 1946-1947 | 6 |
| John GOVAN | 1947-1948 | 6 |
| John McMILLAN | 1952-1961 | 6 |
| Harold HADDOCK | 1954-1958 | 6 |
| Frederick MARTIN | 1954-1955 | 6 |
| William ORMOND | 1954-1959 | 6 |
| Andrew WEIR | 1959-1960 | 6 |
| James KENNEDY | 1963-1964 | 6 |
| James CRUICKSHANK | 1964-1975 | 6 |
| Thomas McLEAN | 1968-1971 | 6 |
| William CARR | 1970-1972 | 6 |
| Anthony GREEN | 1971-1972 | 6 |
| Arthur DUNCAN | 1975 | 6 |
| Peter WEIR | 1980-1983 | 6 |
| Stephen CLARKE | 1987-1994 | 6 |
| Bryan GUNN | 1990-1994 | 6 |
| David BOWMAN | 1992-1993 | 6 |
| Brian O'NEIL | 1996-2000 | 6 |
| Mark BURCHILL | 1999-2000 | 6 |
| Paul RITCHIE | 1999-2000 | 6 |
| 323 Robert GARDNER | 1872-1878 | 5 |
| Robert NEILL | 1876-1880 | 5 |
| John McDOUGALL | 1877-1879 | 5 |
| David DAVIDSON | 1878-1881 | 5 |
| Malcolm FRASER | 1880-1883 | 5 |
| George KER | 1880-1882 | 5 |

| Player | Period | Apps |
|---|---|---|
| Michael PATON | 1883-1886 | 5 |
| John FORBES | 1884-1887 | 5 |
| Leitch KEIR | 1885-1888 | 5 |
| James McCALL | 1886-1890 | 5 |
| John DOIG | 1887-1903 | 5 |
| John McLEOD | 1888-1893 | 5 |
| David MITCHELL | 1890-1894 | 5 |
| Donald SILLARS | 1891-1895 | 5 |
| John WALKER | 1895-1904 | 5 |
| Alexander MacFARLANE | 1904-1911 | 5 |
| James SHARP | 1904-1909 | 5 |
| John MAY | 1906-1909 | 5 |
| Wilfrid LOW | 1911-1920 | 5 |
| William CRINGAN | 1920-1923 | 5 |
| Alexander TROUP | 1920-1926 | 5 |
| Alexander CHEYNE | 1929-1930 | 5 |
| Alexander McLAREN | 1929-1932 | 5 |
| James CRAWFORD | 1931-1933 | 5 |
| John MILLER | 1931-1934 | 5 |
| Charles NAPIER | 1932-1937 | 5 |
| Torrance GILLICK | 1937-1938 | 5 |
| William SHANKLY | 1938-1939 | 5 |
| William CAMPBELL | 1946-1948 | 5 |
| George HAMILTON | 1946-1954 | 5 |
| Robert CAMPBELL | 1947-1950 | 5 |
| John McPHAIL | 1949-1953 | 5 |
| William McNAUGHT | 1950-1954 | 5 |
| Archibald ROBERTSON | 1955-1958 | 5 |
| David HERD | 1958-1961 | 5 |
| George HERD | 1958-1960 | 5 |
| James MURRAY | 1958 | 5 |
| Robert McCANN | 1959-1961 | 5 |
| Lawrence LESLIE | 1960-1961 | 5 |
| David HOLT | 1963-1964 | 5 |
| David PROVAN | 1963-1966 | 5 |
| Stephen CHALMERS | 1964-1966 | 5 |
| James FORREST | 1965-1971 | 5 |
| James McCALLIOG | 1967-1971 | 5 |
| Ronald SIMPSON | 1967-1968 | 5 |
| Hugh CURRAN | 1969-1971 | 5 |
| William DICKSON | 1970-1971 | 5 |
| David ROBB | 1971 | 5 |
| Stewart KENNEDY | 1975 | 5 |
| William PETTIGREW | 1976-1977 | 5 |
| Alistair DAWSON | 1980-1983 | 5 |
| Neil SIMPSON | 1983-1988 | 5 |
| Francis McAVENNIE | 1985-1988 | 5 |
| Ian WILSON | 1987 | 5 |
| 377 James WEIR | 1872-1878 | 4 |
| John HUNTER | 1874-1877 | 4 |
| Thomas HIGHET | 1875-1878 | 4 |
| Alexander McGEOCH | 1876-1877 | 4 |
| John McGREGOR | 1877-1880 | 4 |
| William McKINNON | 1883-1884 | 4 |
| Alexander HAMILTON | 1885-1888 | 4 |
| John MARSHALL | 1885-1887 | 4 |
| William BERRY | 1888-1891 | 4 |
| James WILSON | 1888-1891 | 4 |
| Thomas ROBERTSON | 1889-1892 | 4 |
| Francis WATT | 1889-1891 | 4 |
| Isaac BEGBIE | 1890-1894 | 4 |
| Hugh WILSON | 1890-1904 | 4 |
| William GULLILAND | 1891-1895 | 4 |
| John TAYLOR | 1892-1895 | 4 |
| William THOMSON | 1892-1898 | 4 |
| James BLESSINGTON | 1894-1896 | 4 |

| Player | Period | Apps | Player | Period | Apps | Player | Period | Apps |
|---|---|---|---|---|---|---|---|---|
| John CAMPBELL | 1899-1901 | 4 | Davidson BERRY | 1894-1899 | 3 | Andrew JARVIE | 1971 | 3 |
| Andrew McCOMBIE | 1903-1905 | 4 | David CRAWFORD | 1894-1900 | 3 | Donald FORD | 1973-1974 | 3 |
| Thomas FITCHIE | 1905-1907 | 4 | Robert GLEN | 1895-1900 | 3 | Ian WALLACE | 1978-1979 | 3 |
| Donald MCLEOD | 1905-1906 | 4 | Daniel McARTHUR | 1895-1899 | 3 | Henry SMITH | 1988-1992 | 3 |
| Peter SOMERS | 1905-1909 | 4 | James SIMPSON | 1895 | 3 | Andrew WALKER | 1988-1994 | 3 |
| George STEWART | 1906-1907 | 4 | Kenneth ANDERSON | 1896-1898 | 3 | David ROBERTSON | 1992-1994 | 3 |
| Alexander HIGGINS | 1910-1911 | 4 | James COWAN | 1896-1898 | 3 | Robert McKINNON | 1993-1995 | 3 |
| George ROBERTSON | 1910-1913 | 4 | Matthew DICKIE | 1897-1900 | 3 | Brian McALLISTER | 1997 | 3 |
| Donald COLMAN | 1911-1913 | 4 | James MILLAR | 1897-1898 | 3 | Paul DICKOV | 2000 | 3 |
| Joseph CASSIDY | 1921-1924 | 4 | Alexander CHRISTIE | 1898-1899 | 3 | Dominic MATTEO | 2001 | 3 |
| Adam MCLEAN | 1925-1927 | 4 | David STORRIER | 1899 | 3 | 537  William KER | 1872-1873 | 2 |
| James NELSON | 1925-1930 | 4 | William ORR | 1900-1904 | 3 | Robert SMITH | 1872-1873 | 2 |
| Robert GILLESPIE | 1926-1933 | 4 | Bernard BATTLES | 1901 | 3 | David WOTHERSPOON | 1872-1873 | 2 |
| Peter WILSON | 1926-1933 | 4 | Finlay SPEEDIE | 1903 | 3 | James LANG | 1876-1878 | 2 |
| James CONNOR | 1930-1934 | 4 | James HOWIE | 1905-1908 | 3 | Moses McNEIL | 1876-1880 | 2 |
| John THOMSON | 1930-1931 | 4 | William AGNEW | 1907-1908 | 3 | Peter CAMPBELL | 1878-1879 | 2 |
| George WALKER | 1930-1931 | 4 | James MITCHELL | 1908-1910 | 3 | James DUNCAN | 1878-1882 | 2 |
| Andrew McLAREN | 1947 | 4 | Harold PAUL | 1909 | 3 | Andrew McINTYRE | 1878-1882 | 2 |
| John SHAW | 1947 | 4 | George LAW | 1910 | 3 | Robert PATON | 1879 | 2 |
| John AIRD | 1954 | 4 | George SINCLAIR | 1910-1912 | 3 | Archibald ROWAN | 1880-1882 | 2 |
| James IMLACH | 1958 | 4 | James CROAL | 1913-1914 | 3 | William McGUIRE | 1881 | 2 |
| John MACLEOD | 1961 | 4 | Joseph DONNACHIE | 1913-1914 | 3 | John INGLIS | 1883 | 2 |
| Patrick QUINN | 1961-1962 | 4 | Joseph DODDS | 1914 | 3 | Robert BROWN | 1884 | 2 |
| Robert SHEARER | 1961 | 4 | James REID | 1914-1924 | 3 | Francis SHAW | 1884 | 2 |
| Robert FORSYTH | 1964 | 4 | Thomas MILLER | 1920-1921 | 3 | Samuel THOMSON | 1884 | 2 |
| John CLARK | 1966-1967 | 4 | Neil McBAIN | 1922-1924 | 3 | William TURNER | 1885-1886 | 2 |
| James SMITH | 1968-1974 | 4 | David STEELE | 1923 | 3 | Ralph AITKEN | 1886-1888 | 2 |
| James BROGAN | 1971 | 4 | Robert BENNIE | 1925-1926 | 3 | James GOURLAY | 1886-1888 | 2 |
| Joseph HARPER | 1972-1978 | 4 | Allan McCLORY | 1926-1934 | 3 | Andrew JACKSON | 1886-1888 | 2 |
| Alistair HUNTER | 1972-1973 | 4 | Alexander THOMSON | 1926-1932 | 3 | James ALLAN | 1887 | 2 |
| Peter McCLOY | 1973 | 4 | Allan CRAIG | 1929-1932 | 3 | William ROBERTSON | 1887 | 2 |
| Robert ROBINSON | 1974-1975 | 4 | James FLEMING | 1929-1930 | 3 | Andrew WHITELAW | 1887-1890 | 2 |
| George WOOD | 1979-1982 | 4 | John JOHNSTONE | 1929-1932 | 3 | George DEWAR | 1888-1889 | 2 |
| Allan EVANS | 1982 | 4 | James NISBET | 1929 | 3 | Alexander LATTA | 1888-1889 | 2 |
| Mark McGHEE | 1983-1984 | 4 | Robert RANKIN | 1929 | 3 | Neil MUNRO | 1888-1889 | 2 |
| Robert CONNOR | 1986-1990 | 4 | Frank HILL | 1930-1931 | 3 | Allan STEWART | 1888-1889 | 2 |
| Gary MACKAY | 1987-1988 | 4 | James EASSON | 1931-1933 | 3 | R. BOYD | 1889-1891 | 2 |
| Robert FLECK | 1990-1991 | 4 | Daniel LIDDLE | 1931 | 3 | Thomas McKEOWN | 1889-1890 | 2 |
| Gary NAYSMITH | 2000 | 4 | Andrew LOVE | 1931 | 3 | James RAE | 1889-1890 | 2 |
| 434  James THOMSON | 1872-1874 | 3 | James PATERSON | 1931 | 3 | Andrew BROWN | 1890-1891 | 2 |
| Alexander McLINTOCK | 1875-1880 | 3 | Neil DEWAR | 1932 | 3 | Matthew McQUEEN | 1890-1891 | 2 |
| John BAIRD | 1876-1880 | 3 | James MARSHALL | 1932-1934 | 3 | Gilbert RANKIN | 1890-1891 | 2 |
| James PHILLIPS | 1877-1878 | 3 | Alexander VENTERS | 1933-1939 | 3 | James CAMPBELL | 1891-1892 | 2 |
| James RICHMOND | 1877-1882 | 3 | William COOK | 1934 | 3 | John HILL | 1891-1892 | 2 |
| Robert PARLANE | 1878-1879 | 3 | Matthew ARMSTRONG | 1935-1936 | 3 | Andrew BAIRD | 1892-1894 | 2 |
| William BEVERIDGE | 1879-1880 | 3 | William MILLS | 1935-1936 | 3 | Robert MARSHALL | 1892-1894 | 2 |
| William SOMERS | 1879-1880 | 3 | Alexander MUNRO | 1936-1938 | 3 | John BARKER | 1893-1894 | 2 |
| David HILL | 1881-1882 | 3 | Andrew BLACK | 1937-1938 | 3 | Robert FOYERS | 1893-1894 | 2 |
| Andrew WATSON | 1881-1882 | 3 | Robert BAXTER | 1938-1939 | 3 | Andrew McCREADIE | 1893-1894 | 2 |
| William HARROWER | 1882-1886 | 3 | James CARABINE | 1938-1939 | 3 | John MADDEN | 1893-1895 | 2 |
| Andrew HOLM | 1882-1883 | 3 | Hugh BROWN | 1946-1947 | 3 | William MALEY | 1893 | 2 |
| Peter MILLER | 1882-1883 | 3 | Robert BROWN | 1946-1952 | 3 | David ALEXANDER | 1894 | 2 |
| David ALLAN | 1885-1886 | 3 | James COMBE | 1948 | 3 | Francis BARRETT | 1894-1895 | 2 |
| Robert CALDERWOOD | 1885 | 3 | David DUNCAN | 1948 | 3 | George HOGG | 1896 | 2 |
| John LAMBIE | 1886-1888 | 3 | William HOULISTON | 1948-1949 | 3 | Thomas HYSLOP | 1896-1897 | 2 |
| John AULD | 1887-1889 | 3 | William BAULD | 1950 | 3 | Duncan MCLEAN | 1896-1897 | 2 |
| William JOHNSTONE | 1887-1890 | 3 | Thomas WRIGHT | 1952-1953 | 3 | Patrick MURRAY | 1896-1897 | 2 |
| William GROVES | 1888-1890 | 3 | Patrick BUCKLEY | 1954 | 3 | Robert NEIL | 1896-1900 | 2 |
| John LINDSAY | 1888-1893 | 3 | Neil MOCHAN | 1954 | 3 | John PATRICK | 1897 | 2 |
| James McLAREN | 1888-1890 | 3 | Robert AULD | 1959 | 3 | Hugh MORGAN | 1898-1899 | 2 |
| William PAUL | 1888-1890 | 3 | George MULHALL | 1959-1963 | 3 | William STEWART | 1898-1900 | 2 |
| James ADAMS | 1889-1893 | 3 | William HUNTER | 1960 | 3 | Harold MARSHALL | 1899-1900 | 2 |
| James OSWALD | 1889-1897 | 3 | Adam BLACKLAW | 1963-1965 | 3 | George McWATTIE | 1901 | 2 |
| David BAIRD | 1890-1892 | 3 | Thomas LAWRENCE | 1963-1969 | 3 | Albert BUICK | 1902 | 2 |
| James HAMILTON | 1892-1893 | 3 | John McGRORY | 1964-1966 | 3 | Ronald ORR | 1902-1904 | 2 |
| David STEWART | 1893-1897 | 3 | Neil MARTIN | 1965 | 3 | John CAMERON | 1904-1909 | 2 |

| Player | Period | Apps |
| --- | --- | --- |
| Alexander YOUNG | 1905-1907 | 2 |
| George LIVINGSTON | 1906-1907 | 2 |
| Walter WHITE | 1907-1908 | 2 |
| James GALT | 1908 | 2 |
| William LENNIE | 1908 | 2 |
| James STARK | 1909 | 2 |
| William WALKER | 1909-1910 | 2 |
| William LONEY | 1910 | 2 |
| Robert MERCER | 1912-1913 | 2 |
| Peter NELLIES | 1913-1914 | 2 |
| James BOWIE | 1920 | 2 |
| John CROSBIE | 1920-1922 | 2 |
| Joseph HARRIS | 1921 | 2 |
| Alexander McNAB | 1921 | 2 |
| Donald McKINLAY | 1922 | 2 |
| John WHITE | 1922-1923 | 2 |
| Henry RITCHIE | 1923-1928 | 2 |
| William CLUNAS | 1924-1925 | 2 |
| Philip McCLOY | 1924-1925 | 2 |
| William RUSSELL | 1924-1925 | 2 |
| William ROBB | 1925-1927 | 2 |
| Thomas McINALLY | 1926 | 2 |
| William WISEMAN | 1926-1930 | 2 |
| Thomas LAW | 1928-1930 | 2 |
| John BUCHANAN | 1929-1930 | 2 |
| Robert HOWE | 1929 | 2 |
| William IMRIE | 1929 | 2 |
| David McCRAE | 1929 | 2 |
| Hugh MORTON | 1929 | 2 |
| William BOYD | 1931 | 2 |
| Robert McAULAY | 1931 | 2 |
| James McDOUGALL | 1931 | 2 |
| James ROBERTSON | 1931 | 2 |
| James KING | 1932-1933 | 2 |
| William TELFER | 1932-1933 | 2 |
| William McFADYEN | 1933 | 2 |
| James SMITH | 1934-1937 | 2 |
| Thomas SMITH | 1934-1938 | 2 |
| Alexander HASTINGS | 1935-1937 | 2 |
| Robert ANCELL | 1936 | 2 |
| John CRUM | 1936-1938 | 2 |
| Alexander McNAB | 1937-1939 | 2 |
| Robert REID | 1937-1938 | 2 |
| James DYKES | 1938 | 2 |
| Alexander McSPADYEN | 1938-1939 | 2 |
| John MILNE | 1938-1939 | 2 |
| James STEPHEN | 1946-1947 | 2 |
| Robert FLAVELL | 1947 | 2 |
| Thomas PEARSON | 1947 | 2 |
| James WATSON | 1947-1953 | 2 |
| Leslie JOHNSTON | 1948 | 2 |
| John KELLY | 1948 | 2 |
| Robert MITCHELL | 1951 | 2 |
| Thomas ORR | 1951 | 2 |
| Andrew PATON | 1952 | 2 |
| William FRASER | 1954 | 2 |
| James WARDHAUGH | 1954-1956 | 2 |
| Thomas GEMMELL | 1955 | 2 |
| Archibald GLEN | 1955-1956 | 2 |
| Andrew KERR | 1955 | 2 |
| Joseph McDONALD | 1955 | 2 |
| Thomas EWING | 1957-1958 | 2 |
| John GRANT | 1958 | 2 |
| William TONER | 1958 | 2 |
| John SMITH | 1959 | 2 |
| James GABRIEL | 1960-1963 | 2 |
| Frank HAFFEY | 1960-1961 | 2 |
| Edward CONNACHAN | 1961-1962 | 2 |
| James MILLAR | 1963 | 2 |
| Ronald YEATS | 1964-1965 | 2 |
| William BELL | 1966 | 2 |
| Joseph McBRIDE | 1966 | 2 |
| David SMITH | 1966-1968 | 2 |
| Douglas FRASER | 1968 | 2 |
| Robert HOPE | 1968 | 2 |
| William CALLAGHAN | 1969-1970 | 2 |
| Ernest McGARR | 1969 | 2 |
| Alexander CROPLEY | 1971 | 2 |
| John HANSEN | 1971-1972 | 2 |
| John SCOTT | 1971 | 2 |
| Robert WILSON | 1971 | 2 |
| James BONE | 1972 | 2 |
| George CONNELLY | 1973 | 2 |
| Thomson ALLAN | 1974 | 2 |
| John DEANS | 1974 | 2 |
| Alfred CONN | 1975 | 2 |
| James STEWART | 1977-1978 | 2 |
| James BLYTH | 1978 | 2 |
| David DODDS | 1983 | 2 |
| Eric BLACK | 1987 | 2 |
| John COLQUHOUN | 1988 | 2 |
| Derek FERGUSON | 1988 | 2 |
| Peter GRANT | 1989 | 2 |
| Nicholas WALKER | 1993-1996 | 2 |
| Stephen WRIGHT | 1993 | 2 |
| Paul BERNARD | 1995 | 2 |
| Brian MARTIN | 1995 | 2 |
| Jonathan GOULD | 1999-2000 | 2 |
| Gary McSWEGAN | 1999 | 2 |
| Gary HOLT | 2000 | 2 |
| Steven PRESSLEY | 2000 | 2 |
| Steven CRAWFORD | 1995-2001 | 2 |
| 695 Robert LECKIE | 1872 | 1 |
| James SMITH | 1872 | 1 |
| Alexander RHIND | 1872 | 1 |
| John BLACKBURN | 1873 | 1 |
| William GIBB | 1873 | 1 |
| Arthur KINNAIRD | 1873 | 1 |
| Henry RENNY-TAILYOUR | 1873 | 1 |
| Frederick ANDERSON | 1874 | 1 |
| Angus McKINNON | 1874 | 1 |
| Peter ANDREWS | 1875 | 1 |
| John McPHERSON | 1875 | 1 |
| William MILLER | 1876 | 1 |
| James WATSON | 1878 | 1 |
| John CAMPBELL | 1880 | 1 |
| James DOUGLAS | 1880 | 1 |
| Archibald LANG | 1880 | 1 |
| J. McADAM | 1880 | 1 |
| Hugh McINTYRE | 1880 | 1 |
| Robert McPHERSON | 1882 | 1 |
| Robert CHRISTIE | 1884 | 1 |
| William FULTON | 1884 | 1 |
| James GOSSLAND | 1884 | 1 |
| John GOUDIE | 1884 | 1 |
| John GRAHAM | 1884 | 1 |
| John INGLIS | 1884 | 1 |
| J. McAULAY | 1884 | 1 |
| James McINTYRE | 1884 | 1 |
| Thomas TURNER | 1884 | 1 |
| Alexander BARBOUR | 1885 | 1 |
| Robert BROWN | 1885 | 1 |
| William CHALMERS | 1885 | 1 |
| John GOW | 1885 | 1 |
| Alexander HIGGINS | 1885 | 1 |
| W. LAMONT | 1885 | 1 |
| Hugh McHARDY | 1885 | 1 |
| James NIVEN | 1885 | 1 |
| John CAMERON | 1886 | 1 |
| James CONNOR | 1886 | 1 |
| Michael DUNBAR | 1886 | 1 |
| Robert FLEMING | 1886 | 1 |
| Woodville GRAY | 1886 | 1 |
| Charles HEGGIE | 1886 | 1 |
| James LUNDIE | 1886 | 1 |
| Robert McCORMICK | 1886 | 1 |
| John MACDONALD | 1886 | 1 |
| James McGHEE | 1886 | 1 |
| William McLEOD | 1886 | 1 |
| William SEMPLE | 1886 | 1 |
| George SOMERVILLE | 1886 | 1 |
| Andrew THOMSON | 1886 | 1 |
| J. HUTTON | 1887 | 1 |
| Thomas JENKINSON | 1887 | 1 |
| James LOWE | 1887 | 1 |
| Thomas McMILLAN | 1887 | 1 |
| William WATT | 1887 | 1 |
| John WEIR | 1887 | 1 |
| Thomas BRECKENRIDGE | 1888 | 1 |
| William DICKSON | 1888 | 1 |
| Donald GOW | 1888 | 1 |
| John GOW | 1888 | 1 |
| Andrew HANNAH | 1888 | 1 |
| James JOHNSTONE | 1888 | 1 |
| Neil McCALLUM | 1888 | 1 |
| Archibald McCALL | 1888 | 1 |
| Duncan STEWART | 1888 | 1 |
| David BLACK | 1889 | 1 |
| John BUCHANAN | 1889 | 1 |
| David CALDERHEAD | 1889 | 1 |
| Henry CAMPBELL | 1889 | 1 |
| James HANNAH | 1889 | 1 |
| Alexander LOCHHEAD | 1889 | 1 |
| Thomas McINNES | 1889 | 1 |
| Andrew THOMSON | 1889 | 1 |
| J. BROWN | 1890 | 1 |
| Daniel BRUCE | 1890 | 1 |
| James DUNLOP | 1890 | 1 |
| R. HUNTER | 1890 | 1 |
| John MURRAY | 1890 | 1 |
| J. RUSSELL | 1890 | 1 |
| Thomas WYLIE | 1890 | 1 |
| William BOWIE | 1891 | 1 |
| Robert BUCHANAN | 1891 | 1 |
| James CLELAND | 1891 | 1 |
| Robert CLEMENTS | 1891 | 1 |
| J. FRASER | 1891 | 1 |
| T. HAMILTON | 1891 | 1 |
| James HEPBURN | 1891 | 1 |
| James LOGAN | 1891 | 1 |
| James LOW | 1891 | 1 |
| J. McCORKINDALE | 1891 | 1 |
| John McPHERSON | 1891 | 1 |
| William PAUL | 1891 | 1 |
| Archibald RITCHIE | 1891 | 1 |
| George BOWMAN | 1892 | 1 |
| Peter DOWDS | 1892 | 1 |
| Robert DOWNIE | 1892 | 1 |
| James ELLIS | 1892 | 1 |
| David McPHERSON | 1892 | 1 |
| James ORR | 1892 | 1 |

| Player | Period | Apps | Player | Period | Apps | Player | Period | Apps |
|---|---|---|---|---|---|---|---|---|
| William TAYLOR | 1892 | 1 | John FRASER | 1907 | 1 | Robert THOMSON | 1931 | 1 |
| Thomas CHAMBERS | 1894 | 1 | William KEY | 1907 | 1 | Benjamin YORSTON | 1931 | 1 |
| David HADDOW | 1894 | 1 | William MUIR | 1907 | 1 | Thomas HAMILTON | 1932 | 1 |
| John JOHNSTONE | 1894 | 1 | Frank O'ROURKE | 1907 | 1 | John THOMSON | 1932 | 1 |
| William LONGAIR | 1894 | 1 | George CHAPLIN | 1908 | 1 | Hugh WALES | 1932 | 1 |
| Edward McBAIN | 1894 | 1 | James SPEIRS | 1908 | 1 | John BLAIR | 1933 | 1 |
| Robert SCOTT | 1894 | 1 | Thomas COLLINS | 1909 | 1 | James BOYD | 1933 | 1 |
| Andrew STEWART | 1894 | 1 | John HUNTER | 1909 | 1 | Robert BRUCE | 1933 | 1 |
| John DIVERS | 1895 | 1 | James MAIN | 1909 | 1 | Matthew BUSBY | 1933 | 1 |
| John FYFE | 1895 | 1 | Alexander THOMSON | 1909 | 1 | James KENNAWAY | 1933 | 1 |
| William McCOLL | 1895 | 1 | Andrew DEVINE | 1910 | 1 | Alexander LOW | 1933 | 1 |
| John MURRAY | 1895 | 1 | John McTAVISH | 1910 | 1 | Francis McGURK | 1933 | 1 |
| William SAWERS | 1895 | 1 | Angus DOUGLAS | 1911 | 1 | James McLUCKIE | 1933 | 1 |
| William BLAIR | 1896 | 1 | James LAWRENCE | 1911 | 1 | John McMENEMY | 1933 | 1 |
| Thomas BRANDON | 1896 | 1 | Thomas TAIT | 1911 | 1 | Duncan OGILVIE | 1933 | 1 |
| John CAMERON | 1896 | 1 | Walter AITKENHEAD | 1912 | 1 | Duncan URQUHART | 1933 | 1 |
| John GILLESPIE | 1896 | 1 | Alexander BELL | 1912 | 1 | Philip WATSON | 1933 | 1 |
| Robert MacFARLANE | 1896 | 1 | David McLEAN | 1912 | 1 | Patrick GALLACHER | 1934 | 1 |
| Peter MEECHAN | 1896 | 1 | James CAMPBELL | 1913 | 1 | Andrew HERD | 1934 | 1 |
| Daniel PATON | 1896 | 1 | Thomas LOGAN | 1913 | 1 | Peter BUCHANAN | 1937 | 1 |
| William THOMSON | 1896 | 1 | Andrew McATEE | 1913 | 1 | Robert HOGG | 1937 | 1 |
| George ALLAN | 1897 | 1 | Robert ORROCK | 1913 | 1 | Robert JOHNSTON | 1937 | 1 |
| William BAIRD | 1897 | 1 | David WILSON | 1913 | 1 | David KINNEAR | 1937 | 1 |
| Bernard BRESLIN | 1897 | 1 | Harold ANDERSON | 1914 | 1 | Duncan McKENZIE | 1937 | 1 |
| David GARDNER | 1897 | 1 | John BROWNING | 1914 | 1 | Robert MAIN | 1937 | 1 |
| John KENNEDY | 1897 | 1 | Thomas KELSO | 1914 | 1 | George ROBERTSON | 1937 | 1 |
| Thomas LOW | 1897 | 1 | Peter PURSELL | 1914 | 1 | Charles THOMSON | 1937 | 1 |
| J. MCMILLAN | 1897 | 1 | John PATERSON | 1920 | 1 | William WAUGH | 1937 | 1 |
| John RITCHIE | 1897 | 1 | David THOMSON | 1920 | 1 | Robert BEATTIE | 1938 | 1 |
| Peter CAMPBELL | 1898 | 1 | George BREWSTER | 1921 | 1 | John BROWN | 1938 | 1 |
| Robert FINDLAY | 1898 | 1 | Stewart DAVIDSON | 1921 | 1 | David CUMMING | 1938 | 1 |
| James GILLESPIE | 1898 | 1 | John EWART | 1921 | 1 | John DIVERS | 1938 | 1 |
| James McKIE | 1898 | 1 | John GRAHAM | 1921 | 1 | Thomas McKILLOP | 1938 | 1 |
| William MAXWELL | 1898 | 1 | Charles PRINGLE | 1921 | 1 | Archibald MILLER | 1938 | 1 |
| Thomas ROBERTSON | 1898 | 1 | William COLLIER | 1922 | 1 | Francis MURPHY | 1938 | 1 |
| Matthew SCOTT | 1898 | 1 | John GILCHRIST | 1922 | 1 | George MUTCH | 1938 | 1 |
| W. WATSON | 1898 | 1 | Michael GILHOOLEY | 1922 | 1 | George PATERSON | 1938 | 1 |
| Patrick CALLAGHAN | 1900 | 1 | James HOGG | 1922 | 1 | James SYMON | 1938 | 1 |
| James IRONS | 1900 | 1 | James KINLOCH | 1922 | 1 | James DOUGALL | 1939 | 1 |
| David WILSON | 1900 | 1 | Frank WALKER | 1922 | 1 | James BLAIR | 1946 | 1 |
| George ANDERSON | 1901 | 1 | Denis LAWSON | 1923 | 1 | Cornelius DOUGALL | 1946 | 1 |
| Mark BELL | 1901 | 1 | John MCNAB | 1923 | 1 | James DUNCANSON | 1946 | 1 |
| Henry ALLAN | 1902 | 1 | William COWAN | 1924 | 1 | John HUSBAND | 1946 | 1 |
| George KEY | 1902 | 1 | James HAMILTON | 1924 | 1 | Hugh LONG | 1946 | 1 |
| William McCARTNEY | 1902 | 1 | Neil HARRIS | 1924 | 1 | William MacFARLANE | 1947 | 1 |
| John CROSS | 1903 | 1 | Peter KERR | 1924 | 1 | Ian BLACK | 1948 | 1 |
| Archibald GRAY | 1903 | 1 | John McKAY | 1924 | 1 | Charles COX | 1948 | 1 |
| David LINDSAY | 1903 | 1 | John SMITH | 1924 | 1 | Hugh HOWIE | 1948 | 1 |
| William PORTEOUS | 1903 | 1 | John DUNCAN | 1925 | 1 | Edward RUTHERFORD | 1948 | 1 |
| Peter ROBERTSON | 1903 | 1 | Thomas TOWNSLEY | 1925 | 1 | Alexander LINWOOD | 1949 | 1 |
| Alexander BROWN | 1904 | 1 | John McDOUGALL | 1926 | 1 | Henry MORRIS | 1949 | 1 |
| George HENDERSON | 1904 | 1 | William SUMMERS | 1926 | 1 | Robert DOUGAN | 1950 | 1 |
| Thomas NIBLO | 1904 | 1 | James HOWIESON | 1927 | 1 | William MOIR | 1950 | 1 |
| Leslie SKENE | 1904 | 1 | Robert McKAY | 1927 | 1 | Wilson HUMPHRIES | 1952 | 1 |
| Thomas SLOAN | 1904 | 1 | Thomas MORRISON | 1927 | 1 | Hugh KELLY | 1952 | 1 |
| William HOWDEN | 1905 | 1 | Robert THOMSON | 1927 | 1 | James LOGIE | 1952 | 1 |
| Samuel KENNEDY | 1905 | 1 | Thomas BRADSHAW | 1928 | 1 | Charles FLEMING | 1953 | 1 |
| John LYALL | 1905 | 1 | William KING | 1928 | 1 | John LITTLE | 1953 | 1 |
| William MCINTOSH | 1905 | 1 | William CHALMERS | 1929 | 1 | William TELFER | 1953 | 1 |
| William DUNLOP | 1906 | 1 | Bernard BATTLES | 1930 | 1 | John ANDERSON | 1954 | 1 |
| Gladstone HAMILTON | 1906 | 1 | John GILMOUR | 1930 | 1 | Michael HAUGHNEY | 1954 | 1 |
| David HILL | 1906 | 1 | Daniel McRORIE | 1930 | 1 | David MATHERS | 1954 | 1 |
| Alexander MENZIES | 1906 | 1 | Robert MIDDLETON | 1930 | 1 | Alexander WILSON | 1954 | 1 |
| James RAESIDE | 1906 | 1 | Robert HEPBURN | 1931 | 1 | Henry YORSTON | 1954 | 1 |
| Andrew RICHMOND | 1906 | 1 | John MURDOCH | 1931 | 1 | Hugh BAIRD | 1956 | 1 |
| James YOUNG | 1906 | 1 | Peter SCARFF | 1931 | 1 | Alfred CONN | 1956 | 1 |

| | Player | Period | Apps |
|---|---|---|---|
| | Michael CULLEN | 1956 | 1 |
| | James GARDINER | 1957 | 1 |
| | James FORREST | 1958 | 1 |
| | John DICK | 1959 | 1 |
| | John MARTIS | 1960 | 1 |
| | John PLENDERLEITH | 1960 | 1 |
| | Hugh ROBERTSON | 1961 | 1 |
| | William RITCHIE | 1962 | 1 |
| | James ROBERTSON | 1964 | 1 |
| | William HAMILTON | 1965 | 1 |
| | Andrew PENMAN | 1966 | 1 |
| | James SCOTT | 1966 | 1 |
| | John SINCLAIR | 1966 | 1 |
| | James CRAIG | 1967 | 1 |
| | George McLEAN | 1968 | 1 |
| | Francis BURNS | 1969 | 1 |
| | Stephen MURRAY | 1971 | 1 |
| | Robert WATSON | 1971 | 1 |
| | John CONNELLY | 1973 | 1 |
| | Erich SCHAEDLER | 1974 | 1 |
| | James BROWN | 1975 | 1 |
| | John DOYLE | 1975 | 1 |
| | Stewart HOUSTON | 1975 | 1 |
| | William HUGHES | 1975 | 1 |
| | Paul WILSON | 1975 | 1 |
| | Desmond BREMNER | 1976 | 1 |
| | Thomas CRAIG | 1976 | 1 |
| | Alexander MACDONALD | 1976 | 1 |
| | Robert McKEAN | 1976 | 1 |
| | Joseph CRAIG | 1977 | 1 |
| | Ronald GLAVIN | 1977 | 1 |
| | David STEWART | 1977 | 1 |
| | Douglas ROUGVIE | 1983 | 1 |
| | Michael GALLOWAY | 1991 | 1 |
| | Gordon MARSHALL | 1992 | 1 |
| | Keith WRIGHT | 1992 | 1 |
| | Philip O'DONNELL | 1993 | 1 |
| | Stephen GLASS | 1998 | 1 |
| | Robert WINTERS | 1999 | 1 |
| | Paul TELFER | 2000 | 1 |
| | Stephen CALDWELL | 2001 | 1 |
| | Andrew McCLAREN | 2001 | 1 |
| | Charles MILLER | 2001 | 1 |
| | Kenneth MILLER | 2001 | 1 |
| | Barry NICHOLSON | 2001 | 1 |
| | John O'NEIL | 2001 | 1 |
| 1038 | Gavin RAE | 2001 | 1 |

# Goalscorers

| | Player | Period | Goals |
|---|---|---|---|
| 1 | Denis LAW | 1958-1974 | 30 |
| | Kenneth DALGLISH | 1971-1986 | 30 |
| 3 | Hugh GALLACHER | 1924-1935 | 24 |
| 4 | Lawrence REILLY | 1948-1957 | 22 |
| 5 | Alistair McCOIST | 1986-1998 | 19 |
| 6 | Robert HAMILTON | 1899-1911 | 15 |
| 7 | Maurice JOHNSTON | 1984-1991 | 14 |
| 8 | Robert McCOLL | 1896-1908 | 13 |
| | Andrew WILSON | 1920-1923 | 13 |
| 10 | William STEEL | 1947-1953 | 12 |
| | Alan GILZEAN | 1963-1971 | 12 |
| | John COLLINS | 1988-1999 | 12 |
| 13 | Joseph JORDAN | 1973-1982 | 11 |
| 14 | John SMITH | 1877-1884 | 10 |
| | George KER | 1880-1882 | 10 |

| | Player | Period | Goals |
|---|---|---|---|
| | Robert JOHNSTONE | 1951-1956 | 10 |
| | Robert COLLINS | 1950-1965 | 10 |
| | Colin STEIN | 1968-1973 | 10 |
| 19 | Thomas WALKER | 1934-1939 | 9 |
| | John MUDIE | 1956-1958 | 9 |
| | Ian ST JOHN | 1959-1965 | 9 |
| | David WILSON | 1960-1965 | 9 |
| | Paul McSTAY | 1983-1997 | 9 |
| | Kevin GALLACHER | 1988-2001 | 9 |
| 25 | Alexander JACKSON | 1925-1930 | 8 |
| | Graham LEGGAT | 1956-1960 | 8 |
| | Ralph BRAND | 1960-1962 | 8 |
| | Archibald GEMMILL | 1971-1981 | 8 |
| | John ROBERTSON | 1978-1983 | 8 |
| 30 | John McPHERSON | 1888-1897 | 7 |
| | Robert WALKER | 1900-1913 | 7 |
| | James QUINN | 1905-1912 | 7 |
| | Robert McPHAIL | 1927-1937 | 7 |
| | Douglas DUNCAN | 1932-1937 | 7 |
| | Andrew GRAY | 1975-1985 | 7 |
| | John WARK | 1979-1984 | 7 |
| | Gordon DURIE | 1987-1998 | 7 |
| | William DODDS | 1996-2001 | 7 |
| 39 | Henry McNEIL | 1874-1881 | 6 |
| | Joseph LINDSAY | 1880-1886 | 6 |
| | Alexander McMAHON | 1892-1902 | 6 |
| | James McGRORY | 1928-1933 | 6 |
| | William WADDELL | 1946-1954 | 6 |
| | Allan BROWN | 1950-1954 | 6 |
| | William LIDDELL | 1946-1955 | 6 |
| | Bruce RIOCH | 1975-1978 | 6 |
| | Richard GOUGH | 1983-1993 | 6 |
| | David COOPER | 1979-1990 | 6 |
| | Scott BOOTH | 1993-2001 | 6 |
| | Donald HUTCHISON | 1999-2001 | 6 |
| 51 | William MacKINNON | 1872-1879 | 5 |
| | John FERGUSON | 1874-1878 | 5 |
| | John KAY | 1880-1884 | 5 |
| | William PAUL | 1888-1890 | 5 |
| | William LAMBIE | 1892-1897 | 5 |
| | John BELL | 1890-1900 | 5 |
| | John MADDEN | 1893-1895 | 5 |
| | Alexander SMITH | 1898-1911 | 5 |
| | John CAMPBELL | 1893-1903 | 5 |
| | James McMENEMY | 1905-1920 | 5 |
| | Alan MORTON | 1920-1932 | 5 |
| | Andrew CUNNINGHAM | 1920-1927 | 5 |
| | Alexander SCOTT | 1956-1966 | 5 |
| | Alexander YOUNG | 1960-1966 | 5 |
| | William HENDERSON | 1962-1971 | 5 |
| | Robert MURDOCH | 1965-1969 | 5 |
| | John O'HARE | 1970-1972 | 5 |
| | Luigi MACARI | 1972-1978 | 5 |
| | Gordon McQUEEN | 1974-1981 | 5 |
| | Donald MASSON | 1976-1978 | 5 |
| | Gordon STRACHAN | 1980-1992 | 5 |
| | Charles NICHOLAS | 1983-1989 | 5 |
| | Gary McALLISTER | 1990-1999 | 5 |
| | Patrick NEVIN | 1986-1996 | 5 |
| 75 | John McDOUGALL | 1877-1879 | 4 |
| | William HARROWER | 1882-1886 | 4 |
| | Malcolm FRASER | 1880-1883 | 4 |
| | Charles HEGGIE | 1886 | 4 |
| | William GROVES | 1888-1890 | 4 |
| | William DICKSON | 1888 | 4 |
| | John BARKER | 1893-1894 | 4 |

| | Player | Period | Goals |
|---|---|---|---|
| | William SELLAR | 1885-1893 | 4 |
| | John CAMPBELL | 1899-1901 | 4 |
| | Charles THOMSON | 1904-1914 | 4 |
| | William REID | 1911-1914 | 4 |
| | Alexander CHEYNE | 1929-1930 | 4 |
| | George STEVENSON | 1927-1934 | 4 |
| | Neil DEWAR | 1932 | 4 |
| | James MASON | 1948-1951 | 4 |
| | George HAMILTON | 1946-1954 | 4 |
| | Gordon SMITH | 1946-1957 | 4 |
| | David MACKAY | 1957-1965 | 4 |
| | Eric CALDOW | 1957-1963 | 4 |
| | James JOHNSTONE | 1964-1974 | 4 |
| | Peter LORIMER | 1969-1975 | 4 |
| | Richard HARTFORD | 1972-1982 | 4 |
| | Steven ARCHIBALD | 1980-1986 | 4 |
| | Graeme SOUNESS | 1974-1986 | 4 |
| | William McKINLAY | 1993-1998 | 4 |
| | John McGINLAY | 1994-1997 | 4 |
| | Darren JACKSON | 1995-1998 | 4 |
| 102 | Peter CAMPBELL | 1878-1879 | 3 |
| | William ANDERSON | 1882-1885 | 3 |
| | Robert CALDERWOOD | 1885 | 3 |
| | Alexander HIGGINS | 1885 | 3 |
| | Francis WATT | 1889-1891 | 3 |
| | James HAMILTON | 1892-1893 | 3 |
| | John WALKER | 1895-1904 | 3 |
| | James GILLESPIE | 1898 | 3 |
| | David MEIKLEJOHN | 1922-1933 | 3 |
| | Alexander JAMES | 1925-1932 | 3 |
| | James FLEMING | 1929-1930 | 3 |
| | Charles NAPIER | 1932-1937 | 3 |
| | James DELANEY | 1935-1948 | 3 |
| | David McCULLOCH | 1934-1938 | 3 |
| | Torrance GILLICK | 1937-1938 | 3 |
| | Andrew BLACK | 1937-1938 | 3 |
| | Andrew McLAREN | 1947 | 3 |
| | Henry MORRIS | 1949 | 3 |
| | John McPHAIL | 1949-1953 | 3 |
| | David HERD | 1958-1961 | 3 |
| | John WHITE | 1959-1964 | 3 |
| | James BAXTER | 1960-1967 | 3 |
| | David GIBSON | 1963-1964 | 3 |
| | Stephen CHALMERS | 1964-1966 | 3 |
| | John GREIG | 1964-1975 | 3 |
| | William McNEILL | 1961-1972 | 3 |
| | Robert LENNOX | 1966-1970 | 3 |
| | William BREMNER | 1965-1975 | 3 |
| | Edwin GRAY | 1969-1976 | 3 |
| | George GRAHAM | 1971-1973 | 3 |
| | Edward MacDOUGALL | 1975 | 3 |
| | Paul STURROCK | 1981-1987 | 3 |
| | Alan McINALLY | 1989-1990 | 3 |
| | John ROBERTSON | 1990-1995 | 3 |
| | Craig BURLEY | 1995-2001 | 3 |
| | Colin HENDRY | 1993-2001 | 3 |
| 138 | James LANG | 1876-1878 | 2 |
| | James WEIR | 1872-1878 | 2 |
| | John BAIRD | 1876-1880 | 2 |
| | James GOSSLAND | 1884 | 2 |
| | David ALLAN | 1885-1886 | 2 |
| | James McCALL | 1886-1890 | 2 |
| | James ALLAN | 1887 | 2 |
| | Neil MUNRO | 1888-1889 | 2 |
| | Alexander LATTA | 1888-1889 | 2 |
| | Gilbert RANKIN | 1890-1891 | 2 |

| Player | Period | Goals | Player | Period | Goals | Player | Period | Goals |
|---|---|---|---|---|---|---|---|---|
| R. BOYD | 1889-1891 | 2 | Michael DUNBAR | 1886 | 1 | John HUTTON | 1923-1928 | 1 |
| Alexander KEILLOR | 1891-1897 | 2 | James GOURLAY | 1886-1888 | 1 | Thomas CRAIG | 1927-1930 | 1 |
| Robert NEIL | 1896-1900 | 2 | George SOMERVILLE | 1886 | 1 | William IMRIE | 1929 | 1 |
| James MILLAR | 1897-1898 | 2 | Robert McCORMICK | 1886 | 1 | James GIBSON | 1926-1930 | 1 |
| James McKIE | 1898 | 2 | William WATT | 1887 | 1 | Bernard BATTLES | 1930 | 1 |
| David WILSON | 1900 | 2 | Thomas JENKINSON | 1887 | 1 | James EASSON | 1931-1933 | 1 |
| John ROBERTSON | 1898-1905 | 2 | William JOHNSTONE | 1887-1890 | 1 | William BOYD | 1931 | 1 |
| Albert BUICK | 1902 | 2 | James LOWE | 1887 | 1 | Andrew LOVE | 1931 | 1 |
| Finlay SPEEDIE | 1903 | 2 | Leitch KEIR | 1885-1888 | 1 | Robert THOMSON | 1931 | 1 |
| James HOWIE | 1905-1908 | 2 | William ROBERTSON | 1887 | 1 | James KING | 1932-1933 | 1 |
| Alexander BENNETT | 1904-1913 | 2 | George DEWAR | 1888-1889 | 1 | Patrick GALLACHER | 1934 | 1 |
| Andrew WILSON | 1907-1914 | 2 | Thomas BRECKENRIDGE | 1888 | 1 | Alexander MUNRO | 1936-1938 | 1 |
| Harold PAUL | 1909 | 2 | Ralph AITKEN | 1886-1888 | 1 | James SIMPSON | 1934-1937 | 1 |
| Walter AITKENHEAD | 1912 | 2 | Neil McCALLUM | 1888 | 1 | Alexander MASSIE | 1931-1937 | 1 |
| Thomas MILLER | 1920-1921 | 2 | Allan STEWART | 1888-1889 | 1 | James SMITH | 1934-1937 | 1 |
| James DUNN | 1925-1928 | 2 | David BLACK | 1889 | 1 | Peter BUCHANAN | 1937 | 1 |
| James NISBET | 1929 | 2 | Thomas McINNES | 1889 | 1 | David KINNEAR | 1937 | 1 |
| Robert RANKIN | 1929 | 2 | James OSWALD | 1889-1897 | 1 | Francis MURPHY | 1938 | 1 |
| William McFADYEN | 1933 | 2 | Hugh WILSON | 1890-1904 | 1 | James DOUGALL | 1939 | 1 |
| Frank O'DONNELL | 1937-1938 | 2 | Thomas WYLIE | 1890 | 1 | Alexander FORBES | 1947-1952 | 1 |
| Robert FLAVELL | 1947 | 2 | James LOGAN | 1891 | 1 | James COMBE | 1948 | 1 |
| William HOULISTON | 1948-1949 | 2 | Robert BUCHANAN | 1891 | 1 | David DUNCAN | 1948 | 1 |
| William BAULD | 1950 | 2 | James LOW | 1891 | 1 | Leslie JOHNSTON | 1948 | 1 |
| John McMILLAN | 1952-1961 | 2 | Thomas WADDELL | 1891-1895 | 1 | Hugh HOWIE | 1948 | 1 |
| Charles FLEMING | 1953 | 2 | James ELLIS | 1892 | 1 | Alexander LINWOOD | 1949 | 1 |
| William ORMOND | 1954-1959 | 2 | William THOMSON | 1892 | 1 | Robert CAMPBELL | 1947-1950 | 1 |
| Thomas RING | 1953-1957 | 2 | David BAIRD | 1890-1892 | 1 | Robert MITCHELL | 1951 | 1 |
| Archibald ROBERTSON | 1955-1958 | 2 | James KELLY | 1888-1896 | 1 | Thomas ORR | 1951 | 1 |
| Samuel BAIRD | 1956-1958 | 2 | Davidson BERRY | 1894-1899 | 1 | William THORNTON | 1946-1952 | 1 |
| John HEWIE | 1956-1960 | 2 | Thomas CHAMBERS | 1894 | 1 | John HENDERSON | 1953-1958 | 1 |
| Joseph HARPER | 1972-1978 | 2 | David ALEXANDER | 1894 | 1 | John MACKENZIE | 1953-1956 | 1 |
| James HOLTON | 1973-1974 | 2 | John JOHNSTONE | 1894 | 1 | Patrick BUCKLEY | 1954 | 1 |
| William PETTIGREW | 1976-1977 | 2 | John TAYLOR | 1892-1895 | 1 | James DAVIDSON | 1954-1955 | 1 |
| Derek JOHNSTONE | 1973-1979 | 2 | John DIVERS | 1895 | 1 | Thomas DOCHERTY | 1951-1959 | 1 |
| Arthur GRAHAM | 1977-1981 | 2 | Daniel PATON | 1896 | 1 | Thomas GEMMELL | 1955 | 1 |
| Mark McGHEE | 1983-1984 | 2 | Patrick MURRAY | 1896-1897 | 1 | Alfred CONN | 1956 | 1 |
| Brian McCLAIR | 1986-1993 | 2 | John RITCHIE | 1897 | 1 | William FERNIE | 1954-1958 | 1 |
| Duncan SHEARER | 1994-1995 | 2 | Neil GIBSON | 1895-1905 | 1 | James MURRAY | 1958 | 1 |
| Eoin JESS | 1992-1999 | 2 | Alexander KING | 1896-1899 | 1 | Andrew WEIR | 1959-1960 | 1 |
| David HOPKIN | 1997-1999 | 2 | Thomas HYSLOP | 1896-1897 | 1 | George MULHALL | 1959-1963 | 1 |
| Allan JOHNSTON | 1998-2001 | 2 | Thomas ROBERTSON | 1898 | 1 | William HUNTER | 1960 | 1 |
| Colin CAMERON | 1999-2001 | 2 | William STEWART | 1898-1900 | 1 | George HERD | 1958-1960 | 1 |
| 190 Henry RENNY-TAILYOUR | 1873 | 1 | Harold MARSHALL | 1899-1900 | 1 | Patrick QUINN | 1961-1962 | 1 |
| William GIBB | 1873 | 1 | Alexander CHRISTIE | 1898-1899 | 1 | Francis McLINTOCK | 1963-1971 | 1 |
| Frederick ANDERSON | 1874 | 1 | David RUSSELL | 1895-1901 | 1 | James McCALLIOG | 1967-1971 | 1 |
| Angus McKINNON | 1874 | 1 | John DRUMMOND | 1892-1903 | 1 | Ronald McKINNON | 1965-1971 | 1 |
| Peter ANDREWS | 1875 | 1 | Robert TEMPLETON | 1902-1913 | 1 | John HUGHES | 1965-1969 | 1 |
| Thomas HIGHET | 1875-1878 | 1 | Ronald ORR | 1902-1904 | 1 | Thomas McLEAN | 1968-1971 | 1 |
| James RICHMOND | 1877-1882 | 1 | Thomas FITCHIE | 1905-1907 | 1 | Thomas GEMMELL | 1966-1971 | 1 |
| Charles CAMPBELL | 1874-1886 | 1 | Frank O'ROURKE | 1907 | 1 | Hugh CURRAN | 1969-1971 | 1 |
| John McGREGOR | 1877-1880 | 1 | William LENNIE | 1908 | 1 | James BONE | 1972 | 1 |
| James WATSON | 1878 | 1 | James GALT | 1908 | 1 | William MORGAN | 1967-1974 | 1 |
| David DAVIDSON | 1878-1881 | 1 | Alexander MacFARLANE | 1904-1911 | 1 | William JARDINE | 1970-1979 | 1 |
| William BEVERIDGE | 1879-1880 | 1 | Alexander THOMSON | 1909 | 1 | Thomas HUTCHISON | 1973-1975 | 1 |
| J. McADAM | 1880 | 1 | Andrew DEVINE | 1910 | 1 | Kenneth BURNS | 1974-1981 | 1 |
| John CAMPBELL | 1880 | 1 | Alexander HIGGINS | 1910-1911 | 1 | Colin JACKSON | 1975-1976 | 1 |
| David HILL | 1881-1882 | 1 | Joseph DONNACHIE | 1913-1914 | 1 | Derek PARLANE | 1973-1977 | 1 |
| Robert McPHERSON | 1882 | 1 | Thomas CAIRNS | 1920-1925 | 1 | Joseph CRAIG | 1977 | 1 |
| James McAULAY | 1882-1887 | 1 | Alexander DONALDSON | 1914-1922 | 1 | Ian WALLACE | 1978-1979 | 1 |
| John GOUDIE | 1884 | 1 | Joseph CASSIDY | 1921-1924 | 1 | William MILLER | 1975-1989 | 1 |
| Francis SHAW | 1884 | 1 | Alexander ARCHIBALD | 1921-1932 | 1 | David PROVAN | 1979-1982 | 1 |
| W. LAMONT | 1885 | 1 | David MORRIS | 1923-1925 | 1 | Raymond STEWART | 1981-1987 | 1 |
| William TURNER | 1885-1886 | 1 | William COWAN | 1924 | 1 | Francis GRAY | 1976-1983 | 1 |
| John MARSHALL | 1885-1887 | 1 | John DUNCAN | 1925 | 1 | David NAREY | 1977-1989 | 1 |
| Alexander BARBOUR | 1885 | 1 | Adam McLEAN | 1925-1927 | 1 | Alan BRAZIL | 1980-1983 | 1 |
| John LAMBIE | 1886-1888 | 1 | William CLUNAS | 1924-1925 | 1 | David DODDS | 1983 | 1 |

| Player | Period | Goals |
|---|---|---|
| Eamonn BANNON | 1979-1986 | 1 |
| James BETT | 1982-1990 | 1 |
| Francis McAVENNIE | 1985-1988 | 1 |
| Robert AITKEN | 1979-1991 | 1 |
| Gary MACKAY | 1987-1988 | 1 |
| Graeme SHARP | 1985-1988 | 1 |
| Murdo MacLEOD | 1985-1991 | 1 |
| Stewart McKIMMIE | 1989-1996 | 1 |
| Stuart McCALL | 1990-1998 | 1 |
| Colin CALDERWOOD | 1995-1999 | 1 |
| Steven CRAWFORD | 1995-2001 | 1 |
| Thomas BOYD | 1990-2001 | 1 |
| Christian DAILLY | 1997-2001 | 1 |
| Paul RITCHIE | 1999-2000 | 1 |
| Gary McSWEGAN | 1999 | 1 |
| Barry FERGUSON | 1998-2001 | 1 |
| Neil McCANN | 1998-2000 | 1 |
| 363 Matthew ELLIOTT | 1997-2001 | 1 |

# The Record Holders
## Appearances

| Player | Period | Appearances |
|---|---|---|
| Robert GARDNER (1) | 30 November 1872–8 March 1873 | 1 |
| Robert GARDNER (2) | 8 March 1873–7 March 1874 | 2 |
| Robert GARDNER (3) | 7 March 1874–6 March 1875 | 3 |
| Robert GARDNER (4) | 6 March 1875–4 March 1876 | 4 |
| Joseph TAYLOR (5) | 4 March 1876–3 March 1877 | 5-6 |
| William MacKINNON | 3 March 1877–14 March 1881 | 7-9 |
| Henry McNEIL | 14 March 1881–15 March 1884 | 10 |
| Charles CAMPBELL | 15 March 1884–1 April 1893 | 11-13 |
| Walter ARNOTT (6) | 1 April 1893–9 April 1904 | 14 |
| John ROBERTSON | 9 April 1904–17 March 1906 | 15-16 |
| Robert WALKER | 17 March 1906–4 March 1907 | 17 |
| Alexander SMITH | 4 March 1907–6 April 1907 | 18 |
| Robert WALKER | 6 April 1907–9 April 1932 | 19-29 |
| Alan MORTON | 9 April 1932–25 May 1952 | 30-31 |
| George YOUNG | 25 May 1952–11 May 1974 | 32-53 |
| Denis LAW | 11 May 1974–7 June 1978 | 54-55 |
| Kenneth DALGLISH * | 7 June 1978– | 56-102 |

### Notes

(1) The record was jointly held by Joseph Taylor, William Ker, James Thomson, James Smith, William MacKinnon, James Weir, Robert Leckie, David Wotherspoon, Robert Smith and Alexander Rhind.

(2) The record was jointly held by Joseph Taylor, William Ker, James Thomson, Robert Smith, William MacKinnon and David Wotherspoon.

(3) The record was jointly held by Joseph Taylor, James Thomson and William MacKinnon.

(4) The record was jointly held by Joseph Taylor and William MacKinnon.

(5) The record was jointly held by William MacKinnon.

(6) The record was jointly held by John Drummond from 21 March 1903.

(*) Current record holder.

# The Record Holders
## Goalscorers

| Player | Period | Goals |
|---|---|---|
| Henry RENNY-TAILYOUR (1) | 8 March 1873–4 March 1876 | 1 |
| Henry McNEIL (2) | 4 March 1876–2 March 1878 | 2-3 |
| Henry McNEIL (3) | 2 March 1878–12 March 1881 | 4-5 |
| John SMITH | 12 March 1881–14 March 1881 | 6 |
| George KER (4) | 14 March 1881–7 April 1900 | 7-10 |
| Robert McCOLL | 7 April 1900–6 March 1911 | 11-13 |
| Robert HAMILTON | 6 March 1911–23 February 1929 | 14-15 |
| Hugh GALLACHER | 23 February 1929–2 April 1966 | 16-24 |
| Denis LAW (5) * | 2 April 1966– | 25-30 |

## Notes

(1) The record was jointly held by William Gibb from 8 March 1873, Frederick Anderson and Angus McKinnon from 7 March 1874, Henry McNeil and Peter Andrews from 6 March 1875.

(2) The record was jointly held by John Ferguson from 3 March 1877.

(3) The record was jointly held by John Ferguson from 23 March 1878 and William MacKinnon from 5 April 1879.

(4) The record was jointly held by John Smith from 15 March 1884.

(5) The record has been jointly held by Kenneth Dalglish since 14 November 1984.

(*) Current record holder.

# Other Records

## Largest Win

| | | | | |
|---|---|---|---|---|
| Home | – 11-0 | 23 February 1901 | v | Ireland in Glasgow |
| Away | – 10-2 | 24 March 1888 | v | Ireland in Belfast |
| | 8-0 | 18 March 1893 | v | Wales in Wrexham |

## Largest Defeat

| | | | | |
|---|---|---|---|---|
| Home | – 0-5 | 17 March 1888 | v | England in Glasgow |
| | 0-5 | 14 February 1973 | v | England in Glasgow |
| Away | – 0-7 | 19 June 1954 | v | Uruguay in Basle |

## Highest Attendance

| | | | | |
|---|---|---|---|---|
| Home | – 149,547 | 17 April 1937 | v | England in Glasgow |
| Away | – 130,000 | 5 July 1972 | v | Brazil in Rio de Janeiro |

## Lowest Attendance

| | | | | |
|---|---|---|---|---|
| Home | – 600 | 26 March 1892 | v | Wales in Edinburgh |
| Away | – 1,000 | 26 March 1904 | v | Ireland in Dublin |

## Longest Run Without a Defeat

| | | | |
|---|---|---|---|
| Overall | – 22 | (20 wins, 2 draws) | 7 April 1879– 10 March 1888 |
| Home | – 23 | (19 wins, 4 draws) | 7 April 1906– 30 October 1926 |
| Away | – 16 | (14 wins, 2 draws) | 7 April 1879– 21 March 1891 |

## Longest Run Without a Win

| | | | |
|---|---|---|---|
| Overall | – 9 | (4 defeats, 5 draws) | 12 November 1997– 5 September 1998 |
| Home | – 4 | (3 defeats, 1 draw) | 15 April 1939– 10 April 1948 |
| | 4 | (2 defeats, 2 draws) | 5 November 1952– 3 April 1954 |
| | 4 | (1 defeat, 3 draws) | 13 November 1957– 5 November 1958 |
| | 4 | (3 defeats, 1 draw) | 2 April 1966– 25 June 1966 |
| | 4 | (2 defeats, 2 draws) | 2 June 1979– 19 December 1979 |
| | 4 | (3 defeats, 1 draw) | 13 November 1999– 24 March 2001 |
| Away | – 10 | (7 defeats, 3 draws) | 3 February 1971– 5 July 1972 |

## Longest Time Without Conceding a Goal

| | | | | |
|---|---|---|---|---|
| Team | – 746 minutes | – From 43rd min v Wales | 14 February 1925 | |
| | | To 69th min v England | 2 April 1927 | |
| Goalkeeper – 469 minutes | – From 86th min v Belgium | 1 April 1987 | | |
| (James LEIGHTON) | To 15th min v Saudi Arabia | 17 February 1988 | | |

## Longest Time Without Scoring a Goal

| | | | | |
|---|---|---|---|---|
| Team | – 447 minutes | – From 14th min v Denmark | 11 November 1970 | |
| | | To 11th min v England | 22 May 1971 | |

## Most Consecutive Appearances

Kenneth DALGLISH 43 8 May 1976–25 February 1981

## Most Consecutive Goalscoring

| | | |
|---|---|---|
| Robert HAMILTON | 6 | 25 March 1899–1 March 1902 |
| Colin STEIN | 6 | 11 December 1968–21 September 1969 |

## Youngest Debutant

John LAMBIE  17 years, 92 days  Born:  18 December 1868

Debut:  20 March 1886

## Oldest Debutant

Ronald SIMPSON  36 years, 186 days  Born:  11 October 1930

Debut:  15 April 1967

## Honours

World Cup Final Tournament — 1954, 1958, 1974, 1978, 1982, 1986, 1990, 1998

European Championship Final Tournament — 1992, 1996

Home International Championship — 1884, 1885, 1887, 1889, 1894, 1896, 1897, 1900, 1902,
(Winners) — 1910, 1921, 1922, 1923, 1925, 1926, 1929, 1936, 1949,
1951, 1962, 1963, 1967, 1976, 1977

Rous Cup (Winners) — 1985

# Milestone Goalscorers

| | | | |
|---|---|---|---|
| 1st | Henry RENNY-TAILYOUR | 8 March 1873 | v England |
| 100th | David ALLAN | 23 March 1885 | v Wales |
| 200th | Samuel TORRANS (og) | 31 March 1894 | v Ireland |
| 300th | Thomas FITCHIE | 17 March 1906 | v Ireland |
| 400th | Hugh GALLACHER | 27 October 1928 | v Wales |
| 500th | Torrance GILLICK | 7 December 1938 | v Hungary |
| 600th | Thomas DOCHERTY | 2 April 1955 | v England |
| 700th | Eric CALDOW | 20 October 1962 | v Wales |
| 800th | John O'HARE | 13 October 1971 | v Portugal |
| 900th | Archibald GEMMILL | 25 October 1978 | v Norway |
| 1,000th | Maurice JOHNSTON | 19 October 1988 | v Yugoslavia |
| 1,100th | Gordon DURIE | 11 October 1997 | v Latvia |